T0319836

Portfolio
Construction
and Analytics

The Frank J. Fabozzi Series

Fixed Income Securities, Second Edition by Frank J. Fabozzi

Focus on Value: A Corporate and Investor Guide to Wealth Creation by James L. Grant and James A. Abate

Handbook of Global Fixed Income Calculations by Dragomir Krgin

Managing a Corporate Bond Portfolio by Leland E. Crabbe and Frank J. Fabozzi

Real Options and Option-Embedded Securities by William T. Moore

Capital Budgeting: Theory and Practice by Pamela P. Peterson and Frank J. Fabozzi

The Exchange-Traded Funds Manual by Gary L. Gastineau

Professional Perspectives on Fixed Income Portfolio Management, Volume 3 edited by Frank J. Fabozzi

Investing in Emerging Fixed Income Markets edited by Frank J. Fabozzi and Efstathia Pilarinu

Handbook of Alternative Assets by Mark J. P. Anson

The Global Money Markets by Frank J. Fabozzi, Steven V. Mann, and Moorad Choudhry

The Handbook of Financial Instruments edited by Frank J. Fabozzi

Interest Rate, Term Structure, and Valuation Modeling edited by Frank J. Fabozzi

Investment Performance Measurement by Bruce J. Feibel

The Handbook of Equity Style Management edited by T. Daniel Coggin and Frank J. Fabozzi

The Theory and Practice of Investment Management edited by Frank J. Fabozzi and Harry M. Markowitz

Foundations of Economic Value Added, Second Edition by James L. Grant

Financial Management and Analysis, Second Edition by Frank J. Fabozzi and Pamela P. Peterson

Measuring and Controlling Interest Rate and Credit Risk, Second Edition by Frank J. Fabozzi, Steven V. Mann, and Moorad Choudhry

Professional Perspectives on Fixed Income Portfolio Management, Volume 4 edited by Frank J. Fabozzi

The Handbook of European Fixed Income Securities edited by Frank J. Fabozzi and Moorad Choudhry

The Handbook of European Structured Financial Products edited by Frank J. Fabozzi and Moorad Choudhry

The Mathematics of Financial Modeling and Investment Management by Sergio M. Focardi and Frank J. Fabozzi

Short Selling: Strategies, Risks, and Rewards edited by Frank J. Fabozzi

The Real Estate Investment Handbook by G. Timothy Haight and Daniel Singer

Market Neutral Strategies edited by Bruce I. Jacobs and Kenneth N. Levy

Securities Finance: Securities Lending and Repurchase Agreements edited by Frank J. Fabozzi and Steven V. Mann

Fat-Tailed and Skewed Asset Return Distributions by Svetlozar T. Rachev, Christian Menn, and Frank J. Fabozzi

Financial Modeling of the Equity Market: From CAPM to Cointegration by Frank J. Fabozzi, Sergio M. Focardi, and Petter N. Kolm

Advanced Bond Portfolio Management: Best Practices in Modeling and Strategies edited by Frank J. Fabozzi, Lionel Martellini, and Philippe Priaulet

Analysis of Financial Statements, Second Edition by Pamela P. Peterson and Frank J. Fabozzi

Collateralized Debt Obligations: Structures and Analysis, Second Edition by Douglas J. Lucas, Laurie S. Goodman, and Frank J. Fabozzi

Handbook of Alternative Assets, Second Edition by Mark J. P. Anson

Introduction to Structured Finance by Frank J. Fabozzi, Henry A. Davis, and Moorad Choudhry

Financial Econometrics by Svetlozar T. Rachev, Stefan Mittnik, Frank J. Fabozzi, Sergio M. Focardi, and Teo Jasic

Developments in Collateralized Debt Obligations: New Products and Insights by Douglas J. Lucas, Laurie S. Goodman, Frank J. Fabozzi, and Rebecca J. Manning

Robust Portfolio Optimization and Management by Frank J. Fabozzi, Peter N. Kolm, Dessislava A. Pachamanova, and Sergio M. Focardi

Advanced Stochastic Models, Risk Assessment, and Portfolio Optimizations by Svetlozar T. Rachev, Stogan V. Stoyanov, and Frank J. Fabozzi

How to Select Investment Managers and Evaluate Performance by G. Timothy Haight, Stephen O. Morrell, and Glenn E. Ross

Bayesian Methods in Finance by Svetlozar T. Rachev, John S. J. Hsu, Biliana S. Bagasheva, and Frank J. Fabozzi

Simulation and Optimization in Finance: Modeling with MATLAB, @RISK, or VBA + Website by Dessislava A. Pachamanova and Frank J. Fabozzi

The Handbook of Municipal Bonds edited by Sylvan G. Feldstein and Frank J. Fabozzi

Subprime Mortgage Credit Derivatives by Laurie S. Goodman, Shumin Li, Douglas J. Lucas, Thomas A Zimmerman, and Frank J. Fabozzi

Introduction to Securitization by Frank J. Fabozzi and Vinod Kothari

Structured Products and Related Credit Derivatives edited by Brian P. Lancaster, Glenn M. Schultz, and Frank J. Fabozzi

Handbook of Finance: Volume I: Financial Markets and Instruments edited by Frank J. Fabozzi

Handbook of Finance: Volume II: Financial Management and Asset Management edited by Frank J. Fabozzi

Handbook of Finance: Volume III: Valuation, Financial Modeling, and Quantitative Tools edited by Frank J. Fabozzi

Finance: Capital Markets, Financial Management, and Investment Management by Frank J. Fabozzi and Pamela Peterson-Drake

Active Private Equity Real Estate Strategy edited by David J. Lynn

Foundations and Applications of the Time Value of Money by Pamela Peterson-Drake and Frank J. Fabozzi

Leveraged Finance: Concepts, Methods, and Trading of High-Yield Bonds, Loans, and Derivatives by Stephen Antczak, Douglas Lucas, and Frank J. Fabozzi

Modern Financial Systems: Theory and Applications by Edwin Neave

Institutional Investment Management: Equity and Bond Portfolio Strategies and Applications by Frank J. Fabozzi

Robust Equity Portfolio Management + Website by Woo Chang Kim, Jang Ho Kim, and Frank J. Fabozzi

Portfolio Construction and Analytics

DESSISLAVA A. PACHAMANOVA
FRANK J. FABOZZI

WILEY

Published by John Wiley & Sons, Inc., Hoboken, New Jersey.
Published simultaneously in Canada.

For general information on our other products and services or for technical support, please contact our Customer Care Department within the United States at (800) 762-2974, outside the United States at (317) 572-3993 or fax (317) 572-4002.

Wiley publishes in a variety of print and electronic formats and by print-on-demand. Some material included with standard print versions of this book may not be included in e-books or in print-on-demand. If this book refers to media such as a CD or DVD that is not included in the version you purchased, you may download this material at http://booksupport.wiley.com. For more information about Wiley products, visit www.wiley.com.

Library of Congress Cataloging-in-Publication Data:

Names: Fabozzi, Frank J., author. | Pachamanova, Dessislava A., author.
Title: Portfolio construction and analytics / Frank J. Fabozzi, Dessislava Pachamanova.
Description: Hoboken, New Jersey : John Wiley & Sons, Inc., [2016] | Series:
    Frank J. Fabozzi series | Includes bibliographical references and index.
Identifiers: LCCN 2015040278 (print) | LCCN 2016003023 (ebook) | ISBN 9781118445594
    (hardback) | ISBN 9781119238140 (ePub) | ISBN 9781119238164 (Adobe PDF)
Subjects: LCSH: Portfolio management. | BISAC: BUSINESS & ECONOMICS / Finance.
Classification: LCC HG4529.5 .F33456 2016 (print) | LCC HG4529.5 (ebook) |
    DDC 332.6—dc23
LC record available at http://lccn.loc.gov/2015040278

Cover Design: Wiley
Cover Image: © kentoh/Shutterstock

Printed in the United States of America

10 9 8 7 6 5 4 3 2 1

Contents

Preface   **xix**

About the Authors   **xxv**

Acknowledgments   **xxvii**

CHAPTER 1
Introduction to Portfolio Management and Analytics   **1**
1.1   Asset Classes and the Asset Allocation Decision   1
1.2   The Portfolio Management Process   4
     1.2.1   Setting the Investment Objectives   4
     1.2.2   Developing and Implementing a Portfolio Strategy   6
     1.2.3   Monitoring the Portfolio   8
     1.2.4   Adjusting the Portfolio   9
1.3   Traditional versus Quantitative Asset Management   9
1.4   Overview of Portfolio Analytics   10
     1.4.1   Market Analytics   12
     1.4.2   Financial Screening   15
     1.4.3   Asset Allocation Models   16
     1.4.4   Strategy Testing and Evaluating Portfolio
           Performance   17
     1.4.5   Systems for Portfolio Analytics   20
1.5   Outline of Topics Covered in the Book   22

PART ONE
Statistical Models of Risk and Uncertainty

CHAPTER 2
Random Variables, Probability Distributions, and Important
Statistical Concepts   **31**
2.1   What Is a Probability Distribution?   31
2.2   The Bernoulli Probability Distribution and Probability
     Mass Functions   32

2.3   The Binomial Probability Distribution and Discrete
      Distributions   34
2.4   The Normal Distribution and Probability Density
      Functions   38
2.5   The Concept of Cumulative Probability   41
2.6   Describing Distributions   44
      2.6.1   Measures of Central Tendency   44
      2.6.2   Measures of Risk   47
      2.6.3   Skew   54
      2.6.4   Kurtosis   55
2.7   Dependence between Two Random Variables: Covariance
      and Correlation   55
2.8   Sums of Random Variables   57
2.9   Joint Probability Distributions and Conditional
      Probability   61
2.10 Copulas   64
2.11 From Probability Theory to Statistical Measurement:
      Probability Distributions and Sampling   66
      2.11.1 Central Limit Theorem   70
      2.11.2 Confidence Intervals   71
      2.11.3 Bootstrapping   72
      2.11.4 Hypothesis Testing   73

CHAPTER 3
Important Probability Distributions   **77**
3.1   Examples of Probability Distributions   79
      3.1.1   Notation Used in Describing Continuous
              Probability Distributions   79
      3.1.2   Discrete and Continuous Uniform Distributions   80
      3.1.3   Student's t Distribution   82
      3.1.4   Lognormal Distribution   83
      3.1.5   Poisson Distribution   85
      3.1.6   Exponential Distribution   87
      3.1.7   Chi-Square Distribution   88
      3.1.8   Gamma Distribution   90
      3.1.9   Beta Distribution   90
3.2   Modeling Financial Return Distributions   91
      3.2.1   Elliptical Distributions   92
      3.2.2   Stable Paretian Distributions   94
      3.2.3   Generalized Lambda Distribution   96

3.3 Modeling Tails of Financial Return Distributions 98
    3.3.1 Generalized Extreme Value Distribution 98
    3.3.2 Generalized Pareto Distribution 99
    3.3.3 Extreme Value Models 101

CHAPTER 4
Statistical Estimation Models **106**
4.1 Commonly Used Return Estimation Models 106
4.2 Regression Analysis 108
    4.2.1 A Simple Regression Example 109
    4.2.2 Regression Applications in the Investment
         Management Process 114
4.3 Factor Analysis 116
4.4 Principal Components Analysis 118
4.5 Autoregressive Conditional Heteroscedastic Models 125

PART TWO
Simulation and Optimization Modeling

CHAPTER 5
Simulation Modeling **133**
5.1 Monte Carlo Simulation: A Simple Example 133
    5.1.1 Selecting Probability Distributions for the Inputs 135
    5.1.2 Interpreting Monte Carlo Simulation Output 137
5.2 Why Use Simulation? 140
    5.2.1 Multiple Input Variables and Compounding
         Distributions 141
    5.2.2 Incorporating Correlations 142
    5.2.3 Evaluating Decisions 144
5.3 How Many Scenarios? 147
5.4 Random Number Generation 149

CHAPTER 6
Optimization Modeling **151**
6.1 Optimization Formulations 152
    6.1.1 Minimization versus Maximization 154
    6.1.2 Local versus Global Optima 155
    6.1.3 Multiple Objectives 156

6.2   Important Types of Optimization Problems   157
       6.2.1   Convex Programming   157
       6.2.2   Linear Programming   158
       6.2.3   Quadratic Programming   159
       6.2.4   Second-Order Cone Programming   160
       6.2.5   Integer and Mixed Integer Programming   161
6.3   A Simple Optimization Problem Formulation Example:
       Portfolio Allocation   161
6.4   Optimization Algorithms   166
6.5   Optimization Software   168
6.6   A Software Implementation Example   170
       6.6.1   Optimization with Excel Solver   171
       6.6.2   Solution to the Portfolio Allocation Example   175

CHAPTER 7
Optimization under Uncertainty   **180**
7.1   Dynamic Programming   181
7.2   Stochastic Programming   183
       7.2.1   Multistage Models   184
       7.2.2   Mean-Risk Stochastic Models   189
       7.2.3   Chance-Constrained Models   191
7.3   Robust Optimization   194

PART THREE

Portfolio Theory

CHAPTER 8
Asset Diversification   **203**
8.1   The Case for Diversification   204
8.2   The Classical Mean-Variance Optimization Framework   208
8.3   Efficient Frontiers   212
8.4   Alternative Formulations of the Classical Mean-Variance
       Optimization Problem   215
       8.4.1   Expected Return Formulation   215
       8.4.2   Risk Aversion Formulation   215
8.5   The Capital Market Line   216
8.6   Expected Utility Theory   220
       8.6.1   Quadratic Utility Function   221
       8.6.2   Linear Utility Function   223
       8.6.3   Exponential Utility Function   224

8.6.4   Power Utility Function   224
8.6.5   Logarithmic Utility Function   224
8.7   Diversification Redefined   226

CHAPTER 9
Factor Models   **232**
9.1   Factor Models in the Financial Economics Literature   233
9.2   Mean-Variance Optimization with Factor Models   236
9.3   Factor Selection in Practice   239
9.4   Factor Models for Alpha Construction   243
9.5   Factor Models for Risk Estimation   245
        9.5.1   Macroeconomic Factor Models   245
        9.5.2   Fundamental Factor Models   246
        9.5.3   Statistical Factor Models   248
        9.5.4   Hybrid Factor Models   250
        9.5.5   Selecting the "Right" Factor Model   250
9.6   Data Management and Quality Issues   251
        9.6.1   Data Alignment   252
        9.6.2   Survival Bias   253
        9.6.3   Look-Ahead Bias   253
        9.6.4   Data Snooping   254
9.7   Risk Decomposition, Risk Attribution, and Performance
      Attribution   254
9.8   Factor Investing   256

CHAPTER 10
Benchmarks and the Use of Tracking Error in Portfolio Construction   **260**
10.1   Tracking Error versus Alpha: Calculation and
       Interpretation   261
10.2   Forward-Looking versus Backward-Looking Tracking
       Error   264
10.3   Tracking Error and Information Ratio   265
10.4   Predicted Tracking Error Calculation   265
        10.4.1   Variance-Covariance Method for Tracking Error
                 Calculation   266
        10.4.2   Tracking Error Calculation Based on a
                 Multifactor Model   266
10.5   Benchmarks and Indexes   268
        10.5.1   Market Indexes   268
        10.5.2   Noncapitalization Weighted Indexes   270
10.6   Smart Beta Investing   272

PART FOUR

Equity Portfolio Management

CHAPTER 11
Advances in Quantitative Equity Portfolio Management   281
11.1	Portfolio Constraints Commonly Used in Practice	282
	11.1.1 Long-Only (No-Short-Selling) Constraints	283
	11.1.2 Holding Constraints	283
	11.1.3 Turnover Constraints	284
	11.1.4 Factor Constraints	284
	11.1.5 Cardinality Constraints	286
	11.1.6 Minimum Holding and Transaction Size Constraints	287
	11.1.7 Round Lot Constraints	288
	11.1.8 Tracking Error Constraints	290
	11.1.9 Soft Constraints	291
	11.1.10 Misalignment Caused by Constraints	291
11.2	Portfolio Optimization with Tail Risk Measures	291
	11.2.1 Portfolio Value-at-Risk Optimization	292
	11.2.2 Portfolio Conditional Value-at-Risk Optimization	294
11.3	Incorporating Transaction Costs	297
	11.3.1 Linear Transaction Costs	299
	11.3.2 Piecewise-Linear Transaction Costs	300
	11.3.3 Quadratic Transaction Costs	302
	11.3.4 Fixed Transaction Costs	302
	11.3.5 Market Impact Costs	303
11.4	Multiaccount Optimization	304
11.5	Incorporating Taxes	308
11.6	Robust Parameter Estimation	312
11.7	Portfolio Resampling	314
11.8	Robust Portfolio Optimization	317

CHAPTER 12
Factor-Based Equity Portfolio Construction and Performance Evaluation   325
12.1	Equity Factors Used in Practice	325
	12.1.1 Fundamental Factors	326
	12.1.2 Macroeconomic Factors	327
	12.1.3 Technical Factors	327
	12.1.4 Additional Factors	327

12.2	Stock Screens	328
12.3	Portfolio Selection	331
	12.3.1 Ad-Hoc Portfolio Selection	331
	12.3.2 Stratification	332
	12.3.3 Factor Exposure Targeting	333
12.4	Risk Decomposition	334
12.5	Stress Testing	343
12.6	Portfolio Performance Evaluation	346
12.7	Risk Forecasts and Simulation	350

PART FIVE

Fixed Income Portfolio Management

CHAPTER 13

Fundamentals of Fixed Income Portfolio Management **361**

13.1	Fixed Income Instruments and Major Sectors of the Bond Market	361
	13.1.1 Treasury Securities	362
	13.1.2 Federal Agency Securities	363
	13.1.3 Corporate Bonds	363
	13.1.4 Municipal Bonds	364
	13.1.5 Structured Products	364
13.2	Features of Fixed Income Securities	365
	13.2.1 Term to Maturity and Maturity	365
	13.2.2 Par Value	366
	13.2.3 Coupon Rate	366
	13.2.4 Bond Valuation and Yield	367
	13.2.5 Provisions for Paying Off Bonds	368
	13.2.6 Bondholder Option Provisions	370
13.3	Major Risks Associated with Investing in Bonds	371
	13.3.1 Interest Rate Risk	371
	13.3.2 Call and Prepayment Risk	372
	13.3.3 Credit Risk	373
	13.3.4 Liquidity Risk	374
13.4	Fixed Income Analytics	375
	13.4.1 Measuring Interest Rate Risk	375
	13.4.2 Measuring Spread Risk	383
	13.4.3 Measuring Credit Risk	384
	13.4.4 Estimating Fixed Income Portfolio Risk Using Simulation	384

13.5   The Spectrum of Fixed Income Portfolio Strategies   386
         13.5.1 Pure Bond Indexing Strategy   387
         13.5.2 Enhanced Indexing/Primary Factor Matching   388
         13.5.3 Enhanced Indexing/Minor Factor Mismatches   389
         13.5.4 Active Management/Larger Factor Mismatches   389
         13.5.5 Active Management/Full-Blown Active   390
         13.5.6 Smart Beta Strategies for Fixed Income Portfolios   390
13.6   Value-Added Fixed Income Strategies   391
         13.6.1 Interest Rate Expectations Strategies   391
         13.6.2 Yield Curve Strategies   392
         13.6.3 Inter- and Intra-sector Allocation Strategies   393
         13.6.4 Individual Security Selection Strategies   394

CHAPTER 14
Factor-Based Fixed Income Portfolio Construction and Evaluation   398
14.1   Fixed Income Factors Used in Practice   398
         14.1.1 Term Structure Factors   399
         14.1.2 Credit Spread Factors   400
         14.1.3 Currency Factors   401
         14.1.4 Emerging Market Factors   401
         14.1.5 Volatility Factors   402
         14.1.6 Prepayment Factors   402
14.2   Portfolio Selection   402
         14.2.1 Stratification Approach   403
         14.2.2 Optimization Approach   405
         14.2.3 Portfolio Rebalancing   408
14.3   Risk Decomposition   410

CHAPTER 15
Constructing Liability-Driven Portfolios   420
15.1   Risks Associated with Liabilities   421
         15.1.1 Interest Rate Risk   421
         15.1.2 Inflation Risk   422
         15.1.3 Longevity Risk   423
15.2   Liability-Driven Strategies of Life Insurance Companies   423
         15.2.1 Immunization   424
         15.2.2 Advanced Optimization Approaches   435
         15.2.3 Constructing Replicating Portfolios   437

15.3 Liability-Driven Strategies of Defined Benefit
Pension Funds   438
  15.3.1 High-Grade Bond Portfolio Solution   439
  15.3.2 Including Other Assets   442
  15.3.3 Advanced Modeling Strategies   443

PART SIX

Derivatives and Their Application to Portfolio Management

CHAPTER 16
Basics of Financial Derivatives   **449**
16.1 Overview of the Use of Derivatives in Portfolio
Management   449
16.2 Forward and Futures Contracts   451
  16.2.1 Risk and Return of Forward/Futures Position   453
  16.2.2 Leveraging Aspect of Futures   453
  16.2.3 Pricing of Futures and Forward Contracts   454
16.3 Options   459
  16.3.1 Risk and Return Characteristics of Options   460
  16.3.2 Option Pricing Models   470
16.4 Swaps   485
  16.4.1 Interest Rate Swaps   485
  16.4.2 Equity Swaps   486
  16.4.3 Credit Default Swaps   487

CHAPTER 17
Using Derivatives in Equity Portfolio Management   **490**
17.1 Stock Index Futures and Portfolio Management
Applications   490
  17.1.1 Basic Features of Stock Index Futures   490
  17.1.2 Theoretical Price of a Stock Index Futures
    Contract   491
  17.1.3 Portfolio Management Strategies with Stock
    Index Futures   494
17.2 Equity Options and Portfolio Management
Applications   504
  17.2.1 Types of Equity Options   504
  17.2.2 Equity Portfolio Management Strategies
    with Options   506
17.3 Equity Swaps   511

CHAPTER 18
Using Derivatives in Fixed Income Portfolio Management   **515**
18.1 Controlling Interest Rate Risk Using Treasury Futures   515
    18.1.1 Strategies for Controlling Interest Rate Risk with
           Treasury Futures   518
    18.1.2 Pricing of Treasury Futures   520
18.2 Controlling Interest Rate Risk Using Treasury
     Futures Options   521
    18.2.1 Strategies for Controlling Interest Rate Risk Using
           Treasury Futures Options   524
    18.2.2 Pricing Models for Treasury Futures Options   526
18.3 Controlling Interest Rate Risk Using Interest Rate Swaps   527
    18.3.1 Strategies for Controlling Interest Rate Risk Using
           Interest Rate Swaps   528
    18.3.2 Pricing of Interest Rate Swaps   530
18.4 Controlling Credit Risk with Credit Default Swaps   532
    18.4.1 Strategies for Controlling Credit Risk with Credit
           Default Swaps   534
    18.4.2 General Principles for Valuing a Single-Name
           Credit Default Swap   535

Appendix: Basic Linear Algebra Concepts   **541**

References   **549**

Index   **563**

Preface

"**A**nalytics" and "Big Data" have become buzzwords in many industries, and have dominated the news over the past few years. In finance, analytics and big data have been around for a long time, even if they were described with different terms. As J.R. Lowry, chief operating officer of State Street Global Exchange, stated in a 2014 interview published in the *MIT Sloan Management Review*, "In general, data and analytics have pervaded our business for many, many years, but it wasn't something that we were focused on in any kind of coherent way."

The need to focus on investment analytics in a coherent way has never been greater. In the aftermath of the 2007–2009 financial crisis, there has been a tremendous amount of regulatory change. Like most industries, the financial industry is trying to cope with the challenges of managing big data and the risks associated with using models. Many asset management firms face increasing pressure to address important questions such as

- How to measure, visualize, and manage risks better?
- How to find new sources of return?
- How to manage trading activity effectively?
- How to keep costs down?

The solution of banking giant State Street Corporation was to launch a new business, State Street Global Exchange (SSGX), which applies "a wrapper of information, insights and analytics around the investment process," and provides a "more purposeful approach to data and analytics across the company."[1] SSGX is a center that has pulled in software capabilities and analytics groups focused on risk, as well as electronic trading platforms focused on foreign exchange, fixed income, and derivatives trading.

Portfolio and risk analytics platforms are offered by investment product providers such as Barclays (the POINT Advanced Analytics Platform)[2] and BlackRock (the Aladdin Platform)[3] with a similar goal of combining sophisticated risk analytics with comprehensive portfolio management, trading

---

[1] Ferguson (2014).
[2] See https://ecommerce.barcap.com/point/point.dxml.
[3] See https://www.blackrock.com/aladdin/offerings/aladdin-overview.

and operations tools. Longtime portfolio software vendors (Axioma, IBM Algorithmics, MSCI Barra, and Northfield Information Services) and data providers (Bloomberg, FactSet, Thomson Reuters) are adding both advanced analytics tools and the ability to link to various data sources. New partnerships are being formed—for example, financial data provider Thomson Reuters joined forces with Palantir Technologies, a leading Silicon Valley big data technology company, to create QA Studio, a solution for quantitative research that combines powerful analytics and intuitive visualizations to help with the generation of investment ideas.[4] The development of free open source software such as the statistical modeling environment R[5] and the open source programming environment Python[6] with libraries for financial applications has greatly improved accessibility to analytical tools and has reduced the costs of implementing portfolio analytics solutions.

In this book, we often refer to the traditional asset management company model, in which the focus is on the selection of star portfolio managers in charge of different portions of a firm's funds under management. However, new technologies have been disrupting the investment industry as a whole. The bundling of asset management practice and software platform offerings is a recent phenomenon, as is the democratization of access to financial data[7] and trading opportunities.[8] The popularity of automated investment services companies, also called robo advisors,[9] has been increasing. New-generation asset management companies include Quantopian,[10] which provides an analytics and trading platform and crowdsources investment ideas from contributors from all over the world, with the goal of rewarding top performers and applying tested strategies to asset management instead of hiring and managing individual portfolio managers. The core of Quantopian's strategy involves providing useful market and stock fundamentals data, as well as a tool for backtesting, zipline, which has been made open source (free) to help create and support a community of contributors.

Nobody can tell what the future of the portfolio management industry will look like but it certainly seems inevitable that data and analytics will play a major role in it.

---

[4]See http://alphanow.thomsonreuters.com/solutions/qa-studio/.
[5]See https://www.r-project.org/.
[6]See https://www.python.org/.
[7]See https://www.quandl.com/. Quandl offers free financial data.
[8]See https://www.interactivebrokers.com/.
[9]Examples of robo advisors include Betterment, WealthFront, WiseBanyan, Personal Capital, Motif Investing, FutureAdvisor, and Bloom.
[10]See https://www.quantopian.com/.

CENTRAL THEMES

Portfolio Construction and Analytics attempts to look at the analytics process at investment firms from multiple perspectives: the data management side, the modeling side, and the software resources side. It reviews many widely used approaches to portfolio analytics and discusses new trends in metrics, modeling approaches, and portfolio analytics system design. The theoretical underpinnings of some of the modeling approaches are provided for context; however, our goal is to emphasize how such models are used in practice.

The book contains 18 chapters in six parts. Part One, Statistical Models of Risk and Uncertainty, contains the fundamental statistical modeling concepts necessary to understand the modeling and measurement of portfolio risk. Part Two, Simulation and Optimization Modeling, explains two important modeling techniques for constructing portfolios with desired characteristics and evaluating their risk and performance—simulation and optimization. Part Three, Portfolio Theory, introduces the classical quantitative portfolio risk optimization approach and new tools for optimizing portfolios, both in terms of total risk and in terms of risk relative to a selected benchmark. Parts Four and Five, Equity Portfolio Management and Fixed Income Portfolio Management, focus on specific factors and strategies used in equity and fixed income portfolio management, respectively. Part Six describes the basics of financial derivative instruments and how financial derivatives can be used for portfolio construction and risk management.

The material is presented at a high level but with practical real-world examples created with R and Microsoft Excel or provided by established portfolio software vendors, and should be accessible to a broad audience. We believe that practitioners and analysts who would like to get an overview of tools for portfolio analytics will find these themes—along with the examples of applications and instructions for implementation—useful. At the same time, we address the topics in this book in a rigorous way, and provide references to the original works, so the book should be of interest to academics, students, and researchers who need an updated and integrated view of portfolio construction and analytics.

SOFTWARE

We were wary of using a specific software package and turning this book into a software tutorial because the popularity of different tools changes quickly. The examples in this book were created with Microsoft Excel and R, as well as portfolio risk management software by Barclays Capital and FactSet. We assume basic familiarity with spreadsheets and Microsoft Excel. Because of the wide variability of online resources and tutorials for Microsoft Excel and the open source software package R, we do not provide tutorials with the book;[11] however, we try to provide hints for the implementation of the examples with R and point to the libraries that have the analytics capabilities needed to implement the examples.[12]

TEACHING

Portfolio Construction and Analytics covers finance and applied analytical techniques topics. It can be used as a textbook for upper-level undergraduate or lower-level graduate (such as MBA or master's) courses with emphasis on modeling, such as applied investments, financial analytics, or the decision sciences. The book can be used also as a supplement in a special topics course in quantitative methods or finance, as a reference for student projects, or as a self-study aid by students.

The book assumes that the reader has only very basic background in finance or quantitative methods, such as understanding of the time value of money, knowledge of basic calculus, and comfort with numbers and metrics. Most analytical concepts necessary for understanding the notation or applications are introduced and explained in footnotes or in specified references. This makes the book suitable for readers with a wide range of backgrounds.

Every chapter follows the same outline. The concepts are introduced in the main body of the chapter, and illustrations are provided. Instructions for implementation of the examples are provided in footnotes. There is a summary that contains the most important discussion points at the end of each chapter.

A typical course may start with the material in Chapters 1 through 6. It can then cover Chapters 8 through 14, which discuss equity and fixed income portfolio construction strategies. Chapters 7 and 15 contain special topics that would be of interest in more quantitatively oriented courses and more advanced finance courses, respectively, or can be assigned for student projects. Depending on the amount of time an instructor has, Chapters 16

---

[11] A simple online search of "primer in R" will bring up a number of websites with helpful introductions to the software.

[12] When it comes to equity portfolio management, a free learning resource is provided by the Quantopian trading platform (https://www.quantopian.com), where readers can create an account, view examples of the software implementation of popular investment strategies and risk metrics calculation (with Python), and modify them to test new strategies with real data.

through 18 would be good to include in a course on investment management, as they discuss the fundamentals of portfolio risk management with financial derivative instruments.

DISCLOSURE

Frank J. Fabozzi is a member of two board fund complexes where Black-Rock Inc. is the manager of the funds. Mention of BlackRock's analytics or products in this book should not be construed as any form of endorsement.

About the Authors

Dessislava A. Pachamanova is professor of analytics and computational finance and Zwerling Family Endowed Research Scholar at Babson College. Her research spans multiple areas, including portfolio risk management, simulation, high-performance and robust optimization, predictive analytics, and financial engineering. She has published dozens of articles in operations research, finance, engineering, marketing and management journals, numerous book chapters, as well as two Wiley titles: *Robust Portfolio Optimization and Management* (2007) and *Simulation and Optimization in Finance: Modeling with MATLAB, @RISK, or VBA* (2010), both part of the Frank J. Fabozzi Series in Finance. Dessislava's academic research is supplemented by consulting and previous work in the financial industry, including projects with quantitative strategy groups at WestLB and Goldman Sachs. She holds an AB in mathematics from Princeton University and a PhD from the Sloan School of Management at MIT.

Frank J. Fabozzi is professor of finance at EDHEC Business School and a senior scientific adviser at EDHEC-Risk Institute. Since 1984 he has served as editor of the *Journal of Portfolio Management*. A CFA and CPA holder, Fabozzi is a trustee for both the BlackRock closed-end fund complex and the equity-liquidity fund complex. He is the CFA Institute's 2007 recipient of the C. Stewart Sheppard Award and the CFA Institute's 2015 recipient of the James R. Vertin Award. Fabozzi was inducted into the Fixed Income Analysts Society Hall of Fame in November 2002. He has served on the faculty of Yale, MIT, and Princeton. The author and editor of numerous books in asset management, he earned a BA and MA in economics from The City College of New York and a doctorate in economics from the Graduate Center of the City University of New York.

Acknowledgments

In writing a book that covers a wide range of topics in finance and draws on tools in statistics, simulation, and optimization, we were fortunate to have received valuable help from a number of individuals.

We are very grateful to Andrew Geer, Ed Reis, Rick Barrett, and Bill McCoy of FactSet for creating the equity portfolio risk management example in Chapter 12. In addition, we thank Ed Reis for generating the exhibits for the example and for his careful proofreading of Chapter 12.

Special thanks are due also to Anthony Lazanas and Cenk Ural of Barclays for preparing the fixed income portfolio risk management example in Chapter 14. The real-world examples are a true asset to the book.

We are indebted to Andrew Aziz of IBM Algorithmics and Robert Bry of IBM for sharing materials about the IBM Algorithmics enterprise risk management software and for spending time discussing with us the specifics of systems for quantitative portfolio risk management and the role of cloud-based computing in making such systems more efficient and affordable.

We thank Professor Alper Atamturk of the University of California at Berkeley and Bloomberg, Matt Nuffort (formerly of Amazon), Jack Cahill, manager of the Cutler Center for Investments and Finance at Babson College, Hugh Crowther of Crowther Investment, and Delaney Granizo-Mackenzie, Jess Stauth, David Edwards, Seong Lee, Scott Sanderson, and John Fawcett of Quantopian for helpful discussions.

We also thank the R and Python developer communities, bloggers and contributors to online forums, who have made such tremendous resources for analytics available to the world free of charge, and whose advice and willingness to share code helped with the creation of some of the examples and illustrations in the book.

We appreciate the patience and understanding of Evan Burton and Meg Freeborn of Wiley as we worked through changes in the timeline for the book submission and several iterations of the table of contents.

This book would not have been possible without the support of our families—Christian, Anna, and Coleman (D.A.P.) and Donna, Karly,

Patricia, and Francesco (F.J.F.). We thank them for allowing us to spend precious time away from them so that we could complete this book, and for serving as a reminder that there is so much more to life.

Dessislava A. Pachamanova
Frank J. Fabozzi

CHAPTER 1

Introduction to Portfolio Management and Analytics

Portfolio management is the process of managing money. Other terms commonly used to describe this process are *investment management*, *asset management*, and *money management*. Accordingly, the individual who manages a portfolio of investment vehicles is referred to as a *portfolio manager*, *investment manager*, *asset manager*, or *money manager*. We use these terms interchangeably throughout this book.

In discussing portfolio management, reference is made to the "investor." The investor is the entity that will receive the benefits from the investment of proceeds that results from managing of the portfolio. Typically, an investor does not make portfolio management decisions. Rather, the investor delegates that responsibility to professional portfolio managers. Professional portfolio managers rely to varying degrees on portfolio analytics for identifying investment opportunities, keeping portfolios aligned with investment objectives, and monitoring portfolio risk and performance.

In this book we review widely used approaches to portfolio analytics and discuss new trends in metrics, modeling approaches, and portfolio analytics system design. This chapter provides an introduction to the portfolio management process. We begin with an overview of asset classes. We then describe the main areas of portfolio management where analytics are used, review trends in systems for portfolio analytics, and explain how the themes in this introduction chapter map to the content of the chapters to follow.

1.1 ASSET CLASSES AND THE ASSET ALLOCATION DECISION

An important decision in portfolio management is the allocation of funds among asset classes. This is referred to as the *asset allocation decision*.

The funds are then managed within the asset classes.[1] In most developed countries, the four major asset classes are (1) common stocks, (2) bonds, (3) cash equivalents, and (4) real estate. How do market participants define an asset class? There are several ways to do so. The first is in terms of the investment attributes that the members of an asset class have in common. These investment characteristics include (1) the major economic factors that influence the value of the asset class and, as a result, correlate highly with the returns of each member included in the asset class; (2) similar risk and return characteristics; and (3) a common legal or regulatory structure. Based on this way of defining an asset class, the correlation between the returns of different asset classes should be low.

The four major asset classes above can be extended to create other asset classes. From the perspective of a U.S. investor, for example, the four major asset classes can be expanded by separating foreign securities from U.S. securities: (1) U.S. common stocks, (2) non-U.S. (or foreign) common stocks, (3) U.S. bonds, (4) non-U.S. bonds, (5) cash equivalents, and (6) real estate. Common stock and bonds are commonly further partitioned into sectors, loosely referred to by some practitioners as asset classes. For U.S. common stocks (also referred to as *U.S. equities*), the following are classified as sectors: market capitalization stocks and value/growth stocks.

A company's market capitalization (or simply market cap) is the total market value of its common stock outstanding. For example, suppose that a corporation has 600 million shares of common stock outstanding and each share has a market value of $100. Then the market capitalization of this company is $60 billion (600 million shares times $100 per share). The convention in the market for classifying companies based on market capital is as follows: mega-cap stocks (greater than $200 billion), large-cap stocks ($10 billion to $200 billion), mid-cap stocks ($1 billion to $10 billion), small-cap stocks ($300 million to $1 billion), micro-cap stocks ($50 million to $300 million), and nano-cap stocks (less than $50 million).

A publicly traded company's market cap is easy to determine given the market price per share and the number of shares outstanding are known. How are "value" and "growth" stocks defined? These definitions are based on the investment style pursued by portfolio managers for stock selection. Specifically, a growth stock manager seeks to perform better than the broad market by buying companies with high-earnings-growth expectations. It is notable that the growth manager terminology emanates from the

---

[1]Although managing funds within asset classes is the dominant way of approaching the investment decision, more recently there has been a trend toward investing in factors rather than asset classes (see, for example, Hogan, Hodges, Potts, and Ransenberg [2015]). We discuss these trends in more detail in Chapters 9 and 10.

term "growth company." There is no analog for the value manager—as in "value company." Accordingly to value managers, two characteristics of value companies are that they trade at a low multiple relative to earnings and that they trade at a low price relative to their book value.

For U.S. bonds, also referred to as *fixed income securities*, the following are classified as sectors: (1) U.S. government bonds, (2) corporate bonds, (3) U.S. municipal bonds (i.e., state and local bonds), (4) residential mortgage-backed securities, (5) commercial mortgage-backed securities, and (6) asset-backed securities. In turn, several of these sectors are further segmented by the credit rating of the issuer assigned by commercial firms referred to as credit rating agencies. For example, for corporate bonds, investment-grade (i.e., high credit quality) corporate bonds and noninvestment-grade corporate bonds (i.e., speculative quality) are treated as two sectors.

For non-U.S. stocks and bonds, the following are classified as sectors: (1) developed market foreign stocks, (2) developed market foreign bonds, (3) emerging market foreign stocks, and (4) emerging market foreign bonds. The characteristics that market participants use to describe emerging markets is that the countries in this group:

- Have economies that are in transition but have started implementing political, economic, and financial market reforms in order to participate in the global capital market.
- May expose investors to significant price volatility attributable to political risk and the unstable value of their currency.
- Have a short period over which their financial markets have operated.

Loucks, Penicook, and Schillhorn (2008, 340) describe what is meant by an emerging market as follows:

> *Emerging market issuers rely on international investors for capital. Emerging markets cannot finance their fiscal deficits domestically because domestic capital markets are poorly developed and local investors are unable or unwilling to lend to the government. Although emerging market issuers differ greatly in terms of credit risk, dependence on foreign capital is the most basic characteristic of the asset class.*

With the exception of real estate, all of the asset classes we identified earlier are referred to as *traditional asset classes*. Real estate and all other asset classes that are not in the list are referred to as *nontraditional asset classes* or *alternative asset classes*. The latter include also hedge funds, private equity, and commodities.

1.2 THE PORTFOLIO MANAGEMENT PROCESS

Regardless of the asset class being managed, the portfolio management process follows the same integrated activities. These activities can be defined as follows:[2]

1. The investor's objectives, preferences, and constraints are identified and specified to develop explicit investment policies.
2. Strategies are developed and implemented through the choice of optimal combinations of assets in the marketplace.
3. Portfolio performance evaluation is performed; market conditions, relative asset values, and the investor's circumstances are monitored.
4. Portfolio adjustments are made as appropriate to reflect significant changes in any or all of the relevant variables.

In this book we focus on the second activity of the portfolio management process, developing and implementing a portfolio strategy. Our emphasis is on analytics-based portfolio management.

1.2.1 Setting the Investment Objectives

Setting investment objectives starts with a thorough analysis of the investor's investment objectives. Investors can be classified as individual investors and institutional investors. Within each of these broad classifications is a wide range of investment objectives.

The objectives of an individual investor may be to accumulate funds to purchase a home or other major acquisition, to have sufficient funds to be able to retire at a specified age, or to accumulate funds to pay for college tuition for children. An individual investor may engage the services of a financial advisor/consultant in establishing investment objectives.

The investment objectives of institutional investors fall into one of the following two broad categories: nonliability-driven objectives and liability-driven objectives. Those institutional investors that fall into the first category can manage their assets without regard to satisfying any liabilities. An example of an institutional investor that is not driven by liabilities is a regulated investment company. The second category includes institutional investors that must meet contractually specified liabilities. A liability is a cash outlay that must be made at a specific future date in

---

[2]This categorization of the portfolio management process is described in Chapter 1 in Maginn and Tuttle (1990).

order to satisfy the contractual terms of an obligation. An institutional investor is concerned with both the amount and timing of liabilities, because its assets must produce the cash flow to meet any payments it has promised to make in a timely way.

Two examples of institutional investors that face liabilities are life insurance companies and defined benefit plans. Life insurance companies have a wide range of products. Some provide for pure life insurance protection while others offer investment-oriented life insurance products. One product that is investment-oriented is a guaranteed investment contract (GIC) whereby the life insurance company guarantees an interest rate over a predetermined time period on the funds given it to by a policyholder. When managing funds for a GIC account, the investment objective of the portfolio manager is to earn a return greater than the rate guaranteed.

In the case of pension funds, there are two types of pension plans offered by sponsors. The sponsor can be a corporation, a state government, or a local government. The two types of pension plans that can be sponsored are a defined contribution or a defined benefit plan. For defined contribution plans, the sponsor need only provide a specified amount for an employee to invest and the employee is then responsible for investing those funds. The plan sponsor has no further obligation. In the case of a defined benefit plan, the plan sponsor has agreed to make specified payments to the employee after retirement. Thus, the plan sponsor has created a liability against itself and in managing the assets of the pension plan, the portfolio manager must earn a return adequate to meet those future pension liabilities.[3]

Regardless of the type of investment objective, a benchmark is typically established to evaluate the performance of the portfolio manager. The determination of the benchmark to be used is made by the client in consultation with the portfolio manager and/or the client's consultant. As we explain in more detail in Chapter 10, a benchmark can be either a market index or a customized index.

---

[3]Institutional investors may have accounts that have both nonliability-driven objectives and liability-driven objectives. For example, a life insurance company may have a GIC account (which as explained above is a liability-driven objective product) and a variable annuity account. With a variable annuity account, an investor makes either a single payment or a series of payments to the life insurance company and in turn the life insurance company (1) invests the payments received and (2) makes payments to the investor at some future date. The payments that the life insurance company makes will depend on the performance of the insurance company's asset manager. Although the life insurance company has a liability, the insurance company does not guarantee any specific dollar payment.

1.2.2   Developing and Implementing a Portfolio Strategy

Typically, an investment policy is developed by the investor in conjunction with a consultant. Given the investment policy, investment guidelines are established for individual managers hired by the investor. The portfolio allocation among different asset classes is usually decided in advance, and then each portfolio manager is hired to manage a specific asset class, or a subset of an asset class. In this book, we discuss the actual implementation of portfolio strategies for two specific asset classes—equities and fixed income securities.

The implementation of the portfolio strategy can be divided into the following tasks:

- Selecting the type of investment strategy.
- Formulating the inputs for portfolio construction.
- Constructing the portfolio.

We explain each task next.

1.2.2.1   Selecting the Type of Investment Strategy   Portfolio strategies can be classified as either *active* (*alpha*) or *passive* (*beta*) strategies. Between these extremes of passive and active strategies, there are strategies that have elements of both. For example, the core of a portfolio may be passively managed with the balance actively managed.

A *passive portfolio strategy* involves minimal expectational input, and instead relies on diversification to match the performance of some benchmark. In effect, a passive strategy assumes that the marketplace will efficiently reflect all available information in the price paid for securities and it is difficult to earn a return in excess of the benchmark without being exposed to more risk than the benchmark and after taking into account higher management fees and transaction costs. Passive portfolio strategies are also referred to as *indexing* since the typical benchmark is some market index. The strategies are also referred to as *beta strategies* because for historical reasons the term *beta* refers to the risk a well-diversified portfolio (such as an indexed portfolio) faces relative to a market index.

An *active portfolio strategy* uses available information and forecasting techniques to seek a better performance than a portfolio that is simply diversified broadly. These strategies are often referred to as *alpha strategies* because for historical reasons the term *alpha* refers to the return realized in excess of the return offered by the market. Essential to all active strategies are expectations about the factors that have been found to influence the performance of an asset class. For example, with active common stock strategies this may include forecasts of future earnings, dividends, or price/ earnings ratios. With bond portfolios that are actively managed, expectations may involve forecasts of future interest rates and sector spreads. Active portfolio strategies involving foreign securities may require forecasts of local interest rates and exchange rates.

A useful way of thinking about active versus passive management is in terms of the following three activities performed by the manager: (1) portfolio construction (deciding on the securities to buy and sell), (2) trading of securities, and (3) portfolio monitoring. Generally, active managers devote the majority of their time to portfolio construction. In contrast, passive managers devote less time to this activity.

Given the choice among passive and active portfolio strategies, what factors should a client consider in selecting a strategy? Three factors that should be considered are (1) the investor's view of how "price efficient" the market is, (2) the investor's risk tolerance, and (3) the nature of the investor's liabilities. *Marketplace price efficiency* refers to the difficulty a portfolio manager faces in earning a greater return than passive portfolio management after adjusting for the risk associated with a strategy and the transaction costs associated with implementing that strategy. There is a considerable literature in finance dealing with the issue of market efficiency. Given the existence of active portfolio managers and the flow of funds to those managers, clients obviously are not convinced that markets are sufficiently price efficient to warrant pursuing an indexing strategy.

1.2.2.2 Formulating the Inputs for Portfolio Construction

Formulating the inputs for portfolio construction in an active portfolio strategy involves forecasting the inputs that are expected to impact the performance of a security and the portfolio as a whole. For example, often of interest are the factors that determine the expected returns of the assets in the portfolio and the covariance structure of the portfolio. Some of these inputs are extrapolated from past market data; others reflect the market's "expectations" that are priced into observed security prices in the market today.[4] In the end, quantitatively generated forecasts are combined with the manager's subjective evaluation to form the inputs to the portfolio allocation framework.

1.2.2.3 Constructing the Portfolio

Given the manager's forecasts and the market-derived information, the manager identifies attractive securities, and

---

[4]We discuss such asset pricing models in Chapter 9.

assembles the portfolio. The exact portfolio allocation may be based on solving an optimization problem as explained in Chapters 8, 10, 11, and 14, but the ultimate decision is made after careful human evaluation of the portfolio strategy.

In constructing the portfolio, there may be constraints that an investor may impose. For example, an investor may impose a constraint that is a concentration limit (i.e., maximum exposure) to a particular issuer or a particular market sector. When the objective is to outperform a benchmark, there may be a restriction imposed by the investor with respect to the degree to which the portfolio manager hired may deviate from some key characteristics of the benchmark. For example, there are portfolio risk measures that are used to quantify different types of risk that we describe in later chapters. These portfolio risk measures provide an estimate of the exposure of a portfolio to changes in key factors that affect the portfolio's performance. Typically, an investor will not set a specific value for the level of risk exposure. Instead, an investor may impose a maximum on the level of the risk exposure or a permissible range for the risk measure relative to the benchmark.

In addition to constraints that must be considered in constructing a portfolio, an investor may request that the portfolio manager take into consideration taxes. Tax considerations are important for most investors but certain institutional investors such as pension funds, endowments, and foundations are exempt from federal income taxation. Consequently, the asset classes in which they invest will not necessarily be those that are tax-advantaged investments.

1.2.3 Monitoring the Portfolio

Once the portfolio has been constructed, it must be monitored. Monitoring involves two activities. The first is to assess whether there have been changes in the market that might suggest that any of the key inputs used in constructing the portfolio may not be realized. The second task is to monitor the performance of the portfolio.

Portfolio performance is monitored in two phases. The first phase is *performance measurement*, which involves the calculation of the return realized by the portfolio manager over a specified time interval (the *evaluation period*). The second phase is *performance evaluation*, which determines whether the manager has added value, and how the portfolio manager achieved the observed return. The decomposition of the performance results to explain why those results were achieved is called *return attribution analysis*. A detailed example of performance evaluation is described in Chapter 12.

1.2.4 Adjusting the Portfolio

Portfolio management is an ongoing process, and portfolio strategies are in fact performed in a multiperiod context. Portfolio selection strategies are designed to take advantage of market conditions, but those conditions exist temporarily, and as the conditions change, the portfolio manager must perform *portfolio rebalancing*. In doing so, the portfolio manager typically takes the following steps.

By monitoring developments in the capital market, the portfolio manager determines whether to revise the inputs used in the portfolio construction process. Based on the new inputs, the portfolio manager constructs a new portfolio. In constructing a new portfolio, the costs of trading are often evaluated against the benefits of rebalancing.

Specifically, a portfolio manager who wants to adjust the portfolio can do so by changing the risk exposure of each security in the portfolio. When doing so, the portfolio manager must consider the adverse implication of rebalancing the portfolio exposures resulting from the incurrence of transactions costs associated with purchasing and selling securities. Moreover, adjusting a portfolio's risk can have adverse tax consequences. A transactionally efficient vehicle for controlling portfolio risk is to use financial derivatives. These instruments, which include futures, forwards, swaps, and options, are discussed in Chapters 16 through 18, where we also show how they can be used to control a portfolio's risk. The notion that financial derivatives can be used to control portfolio risk may seem contrary to stories in the popular press about how some investors who have used derivatives have incurred major financial losses. It suffices to say at this juncture of our discussion of portfolio management that although financial derivatives can be used for speculative purposes, prudent portfolio management utilizes these instruments to modify a portfolio's risk exposure.

1.3 TRADITIONAL VERSUS QUANTITATIVE ASSET MANAGEMENT

There are two general approaches to portfolio management: traditional and quantitative. Both approaches seek to find the best securities to include in a portfolio in order to construct an efficient portfolio. Our focus in this book is on quantitative portfolio management and we provide the essential portfolio analytics needed to implement the activities of portfolio management described in this chapter.

Let's briefly look at how in general the traditional and quantitative approaches to portfolio management differ. Recall that inputs in constructing a portfolio are the expected return and risk of the securities under consideration. Given the generated inputs for each security and other attributes that a portfolio manager uses to select potential candidate securities, how that information is used differentiates traditional and quantitative portfolio managers. To illustrate, suppose that a portfolio manager is considering 3,000 securities as potential candidates for creating a portfolio. The first step is screening the 3,000 securities to select potential investments. With the traditional approach, the 3,000 securities would be screened by using certain criteria that are provided by the portfolio manager. Once the 3,000 securities are whittled down to a reasonable number of securities, say, N (which is much less than 3,000), security analysts who are part of the portfolio management team will perform an in-depth analysis of each security, looking at the fundamental characteristics of the security and the security issuer. The determination of N is constrained by the size of the portfolio management team. At the end of this process, the candidate list will be less than N. With quantitative portfolio management, the 3,000 securities would be screened based on quantitative criteria that the portfolio manager believes are drivers of returns to create acceptable securities but the number of candidate securities, N, will be far larger than the candidate list created by the traditional approach. The reason is that the criteria used in the quantitative approach will create a list that is not necessarily further investigated by the portfolio management team. The candidate list will be used as the *trade universe* from which to construct the portfolio.

The next step under both approaches is the selection of the securities from the candidate list, less than N in the traditional approach and N in the quantitative approach. That is, this step involves the selection of the securities and the amount that should be allocated to each. In the traditional approach, this is often done in a somewhat arbitrary manner by the portfolio manager. The portfolio constructed from the candidate list of securities will be structured to obtain the desired risk exposure and potential return. With the quantitative approach, the portfolio is typically created from the N securities using the optimization models described in this book. Doing so will allow for the creation of a portfolio with risk and return attributes based on various risk metrics that we describe in this book.

1.4 OVERVIEW OF PORTFOLIO ANALYTICS[5]

The term *analytics* in the context of investments refers to all the ways in which investments are screened, modeled, tracked, and evaluated. Investment analytics can include:

1. *Market analytics*: analysis of real-time market data, prices, financials, earnings estimates, market research reports.

---

[5]Based on Pachamanova and Fabozzi (2014).

2. *Financial screening*: selection of investments of interest based on pre-specified financial and nonfinancial criteria.
3. *Quantitative modeling*: asset allocation and trading models.
4. *Financial analytics*: performance evaluation, characteristics and attribution, risk measurement, asset allocation or asset-liability management.

Qualitative and quantitative asset managers rely on quantitative investment models to a different extent. Different modeling tools are used by managers employing active versus passive investment styles. However, utilizing some fundamental level of portfolio analytics is critical for identifying investment opportunities, keeping portfolios aligned with investment objectives, and monitoring portfolio risk and performance. Analytics-based portfolio management enables investment managers to filter information quickly, take advantage of statistical arbitrage opportunities, and smoothen out inefficiencies such as transaction costs incurred during trading and tax consequences of investment decisions.

In this section we review standard paradigms for portfolio analytics and survey recent developments. We also explain the quantitative methodology behind the techniques and the software implementation so that readers can catch a glimpse of the process from beginning to end. To introduce the subject, in this chapter we walk the reader through the analytics methods during the steps of the investment process outlined earlier: (1) market analytics, (2) securities screening, (3) asset allocation and trade timing analytics, and (4) investment strategy testing and performance evaluation. Portfolio analytics is an iterative process, and investment managers often go back and forth between these steps rather than following them in a strict sequence. In Section 1.5, we explain how these topics are addressed in the book.

Before we begin, it is helpful to outline how a typical system for quantitative investment management is structured. A possible structure is outlined in Exhibit 1.1. The fundamental piece of the system is *data*— data can be sourced from external sources, from a data vendor such as Thomson Reuters, FactSet, S&P Capital IQ, or Bloomberg, or from proprietary research. Most generally, there are two types of financial data structures: time series and cross-sectional data. *Time series data* contain records of the values of prices, factors, and market variables over time. *Cross-sectional data* are information collected about multiple factors and companies at a single point in time (so that the data provide a *cross-section* of the companies of interest). Sometimes, data are stored in *panels*: panels contain cross-sectional data collected at different points in time. The cross-sectional data stored in panels may be different at the different points in time—for example, the collection of companies may be different.

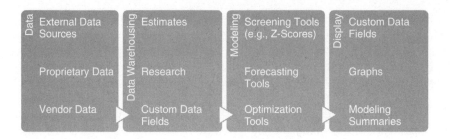

Exhibit 1.1   A typical system for quantitative investment management.

The data then typically get processed through a *data warehousing tool,* which could contain estimates, research, and custom data fields calculated from the original data. Data warehousing is also where the data cleanup and organization occur. On top of the data warehousing tool sit tools that enable *modeling* based on the data, such as statistical and optimization modeling tools. Finally, the results of the analysis are summarized and displayed to aid the investment manager's decision making. The last two stages— modeling and visualization—are often employed in an iterative process of evaluating trends, determining strategies, backtesting, and assessing portfolio performance.

We discuss systems for portfolio analytics later in this chapter, including not only well-established vendors of portfolio management analytics tools but also general principles of building custom systems using cloud-based resources and open-source modeling software such as R.

1.4.1 Market Analytics

A large percentage of investment performance is contributed by trends in the overall market. A successful investment manager constantly analyzes market trends and thinks about ways to capitalize on new market information. Market analysis can be as straightforward as thinking through the implications of news, new market reports, and changes in political or economic conditions. Simple, but effective ways to follow market trends include considering time series plots of important market indices over time, or how market indices and industries move against each other. The latter trends can be analyzed by looking at *relative strength*—the ratio of one sector returns over another sector returns, or the ratio of the returns of one sector over particular indices.

An interesting composite view of the relative strength of multiple stocks or sectors as well as the momentum that exists in the market is provided by Relative Rotation Graphs (RRGs).[6] Such graphs enable visualization of the movement of a selected industry relative to the benchmark across a prespecified time period such as 12 weeks. RRGs are now a part of the Bloomberg analytics suite. Because most investment managers measure their performance against a benchmark, knowing which groups of securities are trending toward outperforming or underperforming the portfolio manager's benchmark is valuable information. RRGs summarize multiple time series in such a way that the momentum and relative performance of sectors against the benchmark can all be displayed in one graph. On the horizontal axis of RRGs is the proprietary JdK RS-Ratio. It is a normalized metric of the relative strength of multiple sectors and indices against each other. On the vertical axis is a metric of the momentum of the stock or industry. The concept of momentum has to do with the belief that if the stock or industry had a positive return in the previous time period, it is more likely to have a positive return in the next time period. Depending on the value of their metrics, sectors can be in the "leading" (top right), "weakening" (bottom right), "lagging" (bottom left) or "improving" (top left) quadrant of the scatter plot. The expected movement of sectors in the graph over time is clockwise—an industry becomes "hot," prices rise as investors swarm to invest in it, which decreases relative performance and eventually the industry's relative worth decreases again.[7] An investment strategy based on the expected behavior in an RRG would invest when an industry is in the upper left quadrant, and sell when the industry is in the lower right quadrant.[8]

Marketing analytics can be as complex as *technical analysis*, which uses statistical and econometric techniques to evaluate market activity, and decides whether to buy a security or increase holdings in an industry based on trends in prices and trading volume. Technicians look for patterns in the time series of the data related to securities in the market. Momentum, briefly explained earlier, is one such pattern identified by technical analysis. Technicians believe that, eventually, prices will adjust to their proper levels, but that in the meantime there are opportunities to make profits.

Making above-average returns in the market is not easy, and should be virtually impossible if one believes a group of theories known collectively as the *Efficient Market Theory*. In its weak form, the Efficient Market Theory

---

[6]www.relativerotationgraphs.com/.
[7]If the prespecified time periods are small in length, the movement of a particular industry may not follow the expected trend. Weekly observations often provide a stable enough view.
[8]Good illustrations are available from http://allstarcharts.com/relative-rotation-graph-explained/ and www.scribd.com/doc/119943614/Relative-Rotation-Graph.

claims that current security prices reflect all the information available in previous security prices, so one should not expect technical analysis to lead to increased profits. In its semi-strong form, the Efficient Market Theory claims that security prices reflect all *publicly* available information in the market, so models based on publicly available data should not be helpful for picking out "winners." Finally, the strong form of the Efficient Market Theory claims that security prices reflect all publicly or privately held information in the market, so inside information should not be helpful in picking out stocks.

While multiple studies have disproved the strong form of the Efficient Market Theory, there is sufficient evidence that the market is at least *very* efficient. Still, one of the reasons the market is so efficient may be that investors are exploiting mispricing to bring market prices to their equilibrium levels. The past decade has witnessed the spread of *algorithmic trading* (also called *algo trading, automated trading, smart order trading, program trading,* and *rules-based trading*), which has taken technical analysis to the next level. Algorithmic trading is the use of electronic platforms to execute trading orders in an automated fashion according to a set of rules that could take into consideration market impact of the trade, execution risk analytics, cost-aware portfolio construction, and the use of market microstructure effects (Fabozzi, Focardi, and Kolm 2010). A special type of algorithmic trading is high-frequency trading, which involves rapid trading so that investment positions are held only for seconds or milliseconds.

More recently, technicians have added text analytics and social media analytics to their toolbox. Mining for the presence of words or phrases that have an impact on prices or the volatility in the stock market can discover opportunities to realize short-term gains. Social media data sources include Twitter, Facebook, YouTube, and Instagram, and involve huge, unstructured data that cannot be handled with spreadsheets and require new tools to process. A variety of data-crawling tools such as IBM Info-Sphere, SAP NetBase, and Supermetrics Data Grabber have made sorting through such data more manageable. Database Management Systems (DBMS) such as Oracle and Microsoft SQL Server can be used to store and organize the information, and analytics tools such as R (a free open-source language for statistical computing and data mining), IBM SPSS Modeler, IBM Cognos, RapidMiner, SAS, and SAP Predictive Analytics can be used to mine for interesting patterns. Several instances of automated trading based on reactions to tweets garnered attention recently. For example, it was believed that a "bot" was able to take advantage of information about Intel's planned acquisition of Altera, a company that makes digital circuits, on Friday, March 27, 2015. Within a second of the headlines on the possible deal appearing on Dow Jones Newswires, and before Altera's shares were halted, somebody purchased $110,530 worth of cheap Altera options to realize a $2.4 million profit by the time humans digested the news.[9]

With the exception of momentum or autocorrelation, tests of technical rules do not confirm a clear advantage of particular strategies. Technical trading also is not exactly comparable to portfolio management because it tries to identify profit-maximizing strategies over the short term while most portfolio strategies are supposed to work for months or years. In contrast to technicians, portfolio managers try to identify factors that are drivers of performance over a longer term. The next section reviews analytical approaches for doing so.[10]

1.4.2 Financial Screening

The *screening* of investments typically relies on the identification of important factors that influence investment performance. Such factors may be fundamental, macroeconomic, statistical, technical, analyst views, and social responsibility. Once factors and industries of interest have been identified, specific securities can be selected as candidates for inclusion in the portfolio. A variety of screening methods are used by portfolio managers, including some that rely on simple statistical metrics of a particular security's desirability relative to other securities. Advanced quantitative methods for portfolio construction include using *factor models* built based on multivariate statistical techniques. In addition to helping in the screening process, factor models provide important inputs, such as expected returns, covariances, and possible scenarios for returns, that are then used in asset allocation, portfolio rebalancing, and risk attribution models. Factor model construction from a technical point of view is covered in Chapter 9. Chapters 12 and 14 contain examples of using factor models for equity and fixed income portfolio construction and risk decomposition.

---

[9]The full story is available from www.slate.com/articles/business/moneybox/2015/ 04/bot_makes_2_4_million_reading_twitter_meet_the_guy_it_cost_a_fortune.html.
[10]The distinction between long-term and short-term is sometimes ambiguous. For example, Northfield Information Services, a vendor of portfolio risk management software, recently incorporated a tool for scoring news about companies into its portfolio risk models. Two vendors of such tools are Alexandria Investment Research and Thomson Reuters. Portfolio risk model vendors have typically targeted longer term investors but in this case, the risk scoring is based on data mining algorithms applied to recent data from news sources found to be significant for prediction.

1.4.3 Asset Allocation Models

When investors research securities, they can separate attractive from unattractive investments. An important part of the investment decision, however, is how much to invest in securities deemed attractive. This decision reduces to finding the "best" weights of the different securities in the portfolio. Some portfolio managers use *ad hoc* methods for determining portfolio weights, while some rely on structured risk-return analysis methods that require employing advanced modeling techniques such as optimization.

1.4.3.1 Ad Hoc Methods for Portfolio Allocation There is a variety of ad hoc and computational methods that investment managers use for portfolio allocation in practice. Simple ways to invest include selecting interesting securities and then investing in them equally. Some researchers (see, for example, DeMiguel et al., 2009) have found after substantial computational tests that in the case of equity portfolios, such a seemingly naïve strategy may actually have merit. Other ad hoc methods imitate the calculation of well-known market indices. For example, some equity portfolio managers may weigh the stocks in their portfolios by their market capitalization, which is how the S&P 500 Index is calculated. This method is referred to as *value weighting*. To obtain the market capitalization for a company, the number of shares outstanding is multiplied by the current market price per share. The market capitalizations of all companies under consideration are added up, and the weight of each company's stock in the portfolio is determined as the ratio of the company's market capitalization and the total market capitalization. Other equity investment schemes imitate the *price-weighting* method favored by indices like the Dow Jones Index. The same number of shares is bought from each stock, so that the weight of the stocks in the portfolio is proportional to their price in the market.

1.4.3.2 Asset Allocation as an Optimization Problem More complex analytical weighting methods of securities in the portfolio are based on using optimization algorithms. Such algorithms enable portfolio managers to sort quickly through a vast possible set of investment decisions that often involve conflicting tradeoffs between goals and limited resources or constraints imposed by clients. As we explain in Chapters 6 and 7, optimization problems generally consist of three parts:

1. A list of decision variables that state the quantities under the manager's control (in the investment management context, these are typically the portfolio weights).
2. An objective function, which states in mathematical terms the goal of the optimization, and expresses it in terms of the decision variables.

3. A set of constraints that represents the requirements and limitations faced by the investment manager.

To implement the optimization, a manager can use directly optimization solvers such as IBM ILOG's CPLEX, or portfolio optimization software provided by vendors such as Bloomberg, Northfield, MSCI Barra, and Axioma. The optimization formulation must be in a form that the software understands.

Before specifying the optimization problem for the software, the manager needs to specify the trade universe, that is, the set of securities that are under consideration for investment. For an active manager, the trade universe may be a set of stocks that were selected based on fundamental research (in the case of equity portfolio management) or credit quality (in the case of fixed income portfolio management), or the securities in a particular industry. For a passive portfolio manager, the trade universe may be the securities in a benchmark index such as the Russell 3000 Index or the Barclays Capital U.S. Aggregate Bond Index.

The optimization software then determines the optimal weights of the securities in the portfolio (when used for portfolio construction), or the optimal trades to accomplish specific targets (when used for portfolio rebalancing).

Many investors take a single-period view of investing, in the sense that the goal of the portfolio allocation procedure is to invest optimally over a single predetermined period of time, such as one month. Even though some investment companies, especially institutional investors, have a long investment horizon, they often treat that horizon as a sequence of shorter period horizons. Risk budgets are often stated over a time period of a year, and return performance is monitored quarterly or monthly.

1.4.4 Strategy Testing and Evaluating Portfolio Performance

Strategy testing and continuous evaluation of portfolio risk and performance are very important elements of a disciplined investment management process. This section discusses issues in backtesting and reviews metrics for portfolio performance evaluation. We should mention that the data quality plays a critical role for the validity of portfolio performance evaluation. We spend more time on data quality issues when we discuss predictive model estimation in Chapter 9 but we provide a few important considerations in this chapter.

1.4.4.1 Strategy Testing The first step in evaluating an investment strategy is to test it on historical data—a process referred to as *backtesting*.

Before running the test, the investment manager needs to make a decision on the time period over which the strategy is to be tested, the rebalancing frequency, and how to assess the results of the backtest. The available data are usually split into *in-sample* (test) data and *out-of-sample* (validation) data. The manager tests a number of models on the in-sample data and when a satisfactory model is found, the manager uses the out-of-sample data to check whether the model performs well. It is tempting to find different interesting models based on the in-sample data, and then pick one from among them that performs the best on the out-of-sample data. However, this procedure may have serious issues.[11] To follow a statistically sound methodology, once a model has been picked based on the in-sample data, if it fails on the out-of-sample data, it should be discarded, and the process should not be repeated again with the same data set.

In statistics, this problem is referred to as the *multiple testing problem*, and can be explained as follows (American Statistical Association 1999, guideline #8):

> *Running multiple tests on the same dataset at the same stage of an analysis increases the chance of obtaining at least one invalid result. Selecting the one "significant" result from a multiplicity of parallel tests poses a grave risk of an incorrect conclusion. Failure to disclose the full extent of tests and their results in such a case would be highly misleading.*

Multiple testing combined with partial reporting (that is, reporting of only favorable results) results in *selection bias*. A similarly concerning issue is *backtest overfitting*, which results from selecting a strategy that appears to fit well a realized configuration of security returns but, because such configurations are random in nature, rarely has a chance of repeating itself in the future and can hence lead to very suboptimal investments. Multiple testing problems and backtest overfitting have become hot research topics in statistics in recent years.[12]

1.4.4.2 Evaluating Performance   Proper understanding of whether recorded performance was a result of skill or luck is critical for maintaining performance going forward. Popular metrics of portfolio performance are listed below. In this book, we review a number of statistical concepts and methods

---

[11] For a discussion of the issues, see Bailey and Lopez de Prado (2014) and Chincarini and Kim (2006).

[12] See Bailey and Lopez de Prado (2014) for a list of references and specific applications to portfolio management.

used for their estimation, including the concepts of variability (standard deviation, quantiles) and model building (in particular, regression). The chapters in which we review the metrics of portfolio performance in more detail are listed in parentheses after the definition of each metric in the list below.

- *Portfolio end-of-year return:* This provides a quick view of the end result of the investment policies. (Chapter 12)
- *Variability of the portfolio returns over the year:* A popular metric of variability is the standard deviation. The higher the standard deviation of returns over the year, the riskier the investment strategy. However, standard deviation is only valid as a measure of risk when returns are symmetrically distributed. Sometimes, portfolio managers use a one-sided risk measure such as semi-standard deviation, value-at-risk (VaR), or conditional value-at-risk (CVaR) to assess the portfolio downside risk. (Chapters 2, 12, 14)
- *Tracking error:* Tracking error focuses on the difference between the portfolio returns and the returns of a benchmark. This difference is referred to as the *active return*. Portfolio performance measurement is concerned with evaluating ex-post (as opposed to ex-ante) tracking error, which is calculated as the standard deviation of active returns, and is reported on an annualized basis. (Chapters 10, 12, 14)
- *CAPM beta (β):* The investment manager may assess the risk of the portfolio against the market by running a regression with the realized returns on the portfolio as the explanatory variable and the realized returns on the market as the response variable. The CAPM beta (β) is the regression coefficient in front of the explanatory variable, and reflects the risk of the portfolio in relation to the market. (Chapters 4, 9, 12)
- *Alpha:* Alpha is the average difference between the portfolio returns and the returns of a benchmark over a prespecified time period. Alpha is used to measure the value of the investment manager. A positive alpha means that the portfolio manager outperformed the benchmark; a negative alpha means that the portfolio manager underperformed the benchmark.
- *Information ratio:* The information ratio (IR) is the ratio of the excess return or alpha the manager produced and the tracking error incurred relative to the benchmark. The IR is computed by dividing the portfolio returns in excess of the benchmark return (the alpha) by the volatility (standard deviation) of the excess portfolio return (the tracking error). (Chapter 10)
- *Sharpe ratio:* The Sharpe ratio measures the portfolio excess return per unit of risk, where the excess return is measured as the difference

between the portfolio return and the risk-free return (typically, the average return on the one-month or three-month U.S. Treasury bill), and the risk is measured as the standard deviation of the portfolio returns over the time period analyzed. The Sharpe ratio is only useful as a relative metric of performance, but in general, a higher Sharpe ratio is better. (Chapter 8)

- *Maximum drawdown:* The maximum drawdown is measured from a time series of portfolio values. It is reported as a percentage, and is the largest peak-to-trough decline of the portfolio value (as a percentage of the largest peak) before a new peak is achieved. For example, suppose that a portfolio reaches \$20 million, then drops to \$17 million, then climbs to \$18 million, then drops to \$15 million, and then reaches a new peak of \$23 million. In this case, the maximum drawdown is (\$20,000,000 − \$15,000,000)/\$20,000,000 = 25%.
- *Calmar ratio:* The Calmar ratio is the ratio of the portfolio return to the maximum drawdown over a prespecified time period. The lower the Calmar ratio, the worse the portfolio performance over that time period.[13]

As we explained in Section 1.2.3, an important part of portfolio performance measurement is *performance attribution*: breaking down the portfolio return in a way that allows for identifying the individual causes that led to the realized portfolio performance. Multifactor models (explained in Chapter 9) are often used to evaluate exposure to different factors and to monitor performance.

1.4.5 Systems for Portfolio Analytics

As explained at the beginning of this chapter, systems for portfolio analytics typically have four components: data sources, data warehousing, modeling, and visualization. Banks and investment companies structure their systems differently. Data, for example, may be purchased from data providers such as Bloomberg L.P., Thomson Reuters, FactSet Research Systems, or S&P's Capital IQ. Data warehousing may be done in-house or by companies like IBM Algorithmics, Bloomberg, or Xignate. Data modeling and visualization tools can be implemented in-house or purchased from specialized portfolio management software providers like IBM Algorithmics, MSCI

---

[13] Other Sharpe-like (reward/risk) ratios that substitute drawdown for standard deviation are used as well, such as the Sterling ratio, which uses average drawdown over a given time period instead of maximum drawdown.

Barra, Northfield Information Services, Bloomberg, Axioma, and FactSet Research Systems, among others. More general computing and modeling environments such as MATLAB have also been deployed enterprise-wide.

There have been two major trends in the design of systems for portfolio analytics. The first trend is that portfolio analytics tools are being integrated with data feeds, making the different components of the system compatible and easier to manage for the end customer. Recognizing this trend, companies like Bloomberg and FactSet Research Systems, which had traditionally been providers for real-time news coverage, data feeds, and single security analytics, have added portfolio analytics tools to their suites of buy-side trading systems. Specialized portfolio analytics software providers such as MSCI Barra, IBM Algorithmics, and Northfield Financial Services are also addressing the integration of analytics tools and data feeds, providing services to help customers integrate their data with the modeling tools provided by the companies.

The second trend is that the availability of cheap computing infrastructure through cloud-based resources provided by companies like Amazon, Google, IBM, and Microsoft as well as free open-source modeling tools like the statistical language environment R and the programming language Python have empowered more asset management firms to build such systems in-house. The availability of cloud-based resources has meant that such investment houses do not need to maintain expensive IT solutions in-house, but have access to computing power on as-needed basis for nominal fees. The availability of open-source customizable software for statistical analysis and optimization has also meant that investment management companies have cheap flexible solutions to implementing portfolio rebalancing and trading routines that they consider important even if such solutions are not the industry norm and are not prebuilt by portfolio analytics vendors.

Some companies have moved in to fill intermediary roles. For example, companies such as Xignite that provide financial market data on demand fill the gap between the data layer and the modeling layer. Xignite itself uses the Amazon cloud for delivery of real-time financial information with minimal waste of computing and network resources. Vichara Technologies, a company that specializes in providing technology solutions to institutional capital market participants, uses the cloud to help banks, dealers, portfolio managers, issuers, and technology firms to develop platforms for trading decision support, portfolio management, risk management, securitization, data management and analysis, trading operations, and e-finance. These systems are used to manage multibillion-dollar positions and all aspects of risks.

Large companies that can otherwise provide complete portfolio analytics solutions also take advantage of cloud-based resources. As an example, IBM Algorithmics offers its clients a componentized framework for assessing portfolio risk that generates scenarios for various factors, uses a list of products provided by their clients, and estimates the risk in a particular client's portfolio based on the combination of the factors in the product list provided by the client. The scenario generation, or simulation piece can be done remotely at IBM instead of the client site using the IBM SmartCloud. This allows for computationally intensive pieces of the risk analysis to be run overnight, using scalable technology. Cloud-based solutions have been offered by Algorithmics since 2006–2007, and IBM's purchase of Algorithmics has made the integration of IBM SmartCloud and Algo portfolio risk management tools smoother and easier.

1.5   OUTLINE OF TOPICS COVERED IN THE BOOK

This book is organized as follows. Part One (Chapters 2–4) lays the statistical foundation for a variety of concepts used in portfolio allocation and risk measurement and decomposition. Part Two (Chapters 5–7) provides background on important modeling techniques such as simulation (used for risk estimation) and optimization (used in portfolio allocation algorithms). Part Three (Chapters 8–10) introduces the classical underpinnings of Modern Portfolio Theory as well as recent developments in portfolio allocation schemes. Parts Four (Chapters 11–12) and Five (Chapters 13–15) provide an overview and practical examples of equity portfolio construction and fixed income portfolio construction, respectively. Part Six (Chapters 16–18) describes the use of financial derivatives for portfolio risk management and return enhancement strategies. Appendix A contains basic linear algebra concepts necessary to understand some of the statistical and optimization formulations in the book. Analytical concepts and techniques are weaved throughout the book.

Many examples are constructed using Microsoft Excel and the open-source modeling language R. There are a variety of online resources for learning both. The R community is very active, and the website www.r-project.org is a wonderful resource for both beginners and advanced users of the software. We attempt to provide enough references to software functions and libraries that can help the reader reconstruct the examples in the book.

We begin by outlining statistical concepts that are critical for representation of risk and return in Chapter 2. We explain the concept of probability distribution, probability mass (density) function and cumulative probability distribution, as well as metrics for summarizing a probability distribution's central tendency (mean, median, mode), variability (variance, standard deviation, coefficient of variation, percentiles), skew (how asymmetric it is), and kurtosis (how "fat" its tails are). We introduce two important risk measures for portfolio management, value-at-risk and conditional value-at-risk, show how they relate to statistical measures of variability, and explain how they are estimated from data. In the remainder of the chapter, we discuss modeling dependency (correlation, covariance, copula functions), sums of random variables, and concepts from statistical inference such as hypothesis testing (necessary for understanding the concepts in the asset price forecasting and risk estimation chapters), bootstrapping, and confidence intervals.

Chapter 3 reviews observed characteristics of financial return data and introduces important probability distributions that are used for modeling financial returns for the purpose of portfolio risk measurement. We discuss the families of elliptic, stable Paretian and generalized lambda distributions, as well as the families of generalized extreme value distributions and generalized Pareto distributions. The latter two families are used in the context of modeling extreme portfolio risk, also referred to as "risk in the tail."[14]

Chapter 4 takes a different approach to representing observed characteristics of financial return data: it introduces several statistical estimation models that help explain these characteristics by identifying factors that contribute to financial performance and, in some cases, incorporating dynamics in these factors. Regression, factor models, principal component analysis, and ARCH/GARCH models are explained on an intuitive level with examples.

Chapter 5 moves the discussion from statistical modeling to simulation modeling. It illustrates the main idea behind simulation with an extensive example that also demonstrates how the statistical concepts from the preceding chapters aid the construction of simulation models, the interpretation of simulation output, and the decision making of a risk manager when there is uncertainty.

Chapter 6 provides a practical introduction to optimization, a technique with many applications that in the context of portfolio construction is used for determining optimal portfolio allocation and rebalancing strategies. We elaborate on the concept of "difficult" versus "easy" optimization problems and describe intuitively how optimization algorithms work. An illustration of a simple portfolio allocation problem that can be handled with optimization is provided, and its implementation with spreadsheet optimization software (Excel Solver) is outlined.

---

[14]Most undergraduate students and MBA students take a general course in statistics; however, the coverage in such courses is for business students in general. Our motivation for covering the topics in this chapter is that we have observed a need to cover the special statistical properties that have been identified for return distributions of importance in financial modeling in particular.

Classical optimization methods treat the inputs to optimization problems as deterministic and accurate. In reality, however, these inputs are estimated through error-prone statistical procedures or based on subjective evaluation, resulting in estimates with significant estimation errors. Chapter 7 provides a taxonomy of methods for optimization when the input parameters are uncertain. We review the main ideas behind dynamic programming, stochastic programming, and robust optimization, and illustrate the techniques with examples.

Chapter 8 uses the concept of optimization to introduce the mean-variance portfolio optimization framework, which was the first practical analytical framework for portfolio allocation. The mean-variance portfolio model quantified the idea of risk and presented an argument for diversification (that is, distributing the risk) of investments, which is widely accepted in the investment industry. We present an alternative framework for optimization decision making in investments—expected utility maximization—and also discuss recent work in redefining the concept of diversification.

Chapter 9 explains factor models—statistical models that link asset returns to the returns of underlying factors—that were originally suggested as a way to improve the computational properties of the mean-variance optimization framework described in Chapter 8, and now provide the basis for portfolio risk decomposition schemes and new investment strategies. We discuss practical aspects of the construction and selection of factor models in industry, as well as issues with the data used for the estimation of the models.

Chapter 10 builds on concepts from Chapter 8 to introduce portfolio management relative to a benchmark and a range of analytical concepts that come with it, including risk measurement relative to a benchmark and benchmark construction. Concepts from Chapter 9 are used to explain how benchmark construction can be enhanced by taking into consideration factors, and the reader is introduced to a range of what is popularly known as "smart beta" investment strategies.

Chapter 11 reviews recent advances in quantitative equity portfolio management, including common constraints in portfolio optimization and the use of two important risk measures (value-at-risk and conditional value-at-risk) as an objective. We also show how the classical framework for equity portfolio optimization can be extended to include transaction costs and taxes, optimization of trades across multiple client accounts, and robust statistical, simulation, and optimization techniques to minimize the effect of estimation errors in the inputs to portfolio optimization routines.

Chapter 12 continues the discussion of the use of analytics for equity portfolio management from Chapter 11 but focuses specifically on the application of factor models. It lists several important groups of equity factors, shows how to incorporate such factors in stock screens, and provides a detailed example of portfolio risk decomposition, stress testing, performance evaluation, and risk forecasting with simulation.

Chapter 13 introduces fundamental concepts and terminology for fixed income portfolio management in practice. We review the sectors of the bond market, basics of fixed income analytics (yield, duration, convexity) and major sources of risk for bond investors, concluding with a description of the spectrum of bond portfolio strategies.

Chapter 14 integrates the concepts from Chapter 13 in a real-world example of fixed income portfolio construction and risk decomposition using factor models. It also discusses the most common factors used in fixed income portfolio management, and outlines analytical approaches to fixed income portfolio construction and rebalancing.

Chapter 15 focuses on the management of funds to satisfy contractual liabilities. We describe the spectrum of liability-driven investment strategies and discuss strategies used by two major types of institutional investors: life insurance companies and defined benefit pension plans. We provide explicit examples of the use of statistical, simulation, and optimization techniques in the context of asset-liability management.

No discussion of portfolio construction is complete without mentioning derivatives—financial instruments portfolio managers can use for risk management, cost management, and return enhancement purposes. The last three chapters of the book are dedicated to this topic. While the analytics of derivative instruments can be very complex, we keep the discussion at a practical, intuitive level, and wherever appropriate mention how the advanced statistical and modeling techniques from Parts One and Two of the book can be applied for the estimation of risk metrics and important ratios related to the use of derivatives in portfolio construction and management.

Chapter 16 is an introduction to the topic of financial derivatives. It lists the three main classes of financial derivative contracts (futures and forwards, options, and swaps), describes their risk/return characteristics, and outlines approaches for finding the fair prices of such contracts, including the basic model for pricing a futures contract, the Black-Scholes formula for European options, and binomial trees.

Chapters 17 and 18 focus on the applications of derivatives in equity and fixed income portfolio management, respectively. We describe the types of derivatives used for different purposes in each application, and demonstrate some of the difficulties of implementing strategies involving derivatives.

Summary

- In most developed countries, the four major asset classes are (1) common stocks, (2) bonds, (3) cash equivalents, and (4) real estate.
- The asset allocation decision is how to allocate assets among asset classes.
- A company's market capitalization (or simply market cap) is the total market value of its common stock outstanding.
- The two principal characteristics of what are referred to as "value" companies are that they trade at a low multiple relative to earnings and that they trade at a low price relative to their book value.
- U.S. fixed income securities are classified into the following sectors: (1) U.S. government bonds, (2) corporate bonds, (3) U.S. municipal bonds (i.e., state and local bonds), (4) residential mortgage-backed securities, (5) commercial mortgage-backed securities, and (6) asset-backed securities.
- The portfolio management process includes the following activities: (1) the investor's objectives, preferences, and constraints are identified and specified to develop explicit investment policies; (2) strategies are developed and implemented through the choice of optimal combinations of assets in the marketplace; (3) market conditions, relative asset values, and the investor's circumstances are monitored; and (4) portfolio adjustments are made as appropriate to reflect significant changes in any or all of the relevant variables.
- Investment objectives of institutional investors fall into one of the following two broad categories: nonliability-driven objectives and liability-driven objectives.
- A liability is a cash outlay that must be made at a specific future date in order to satisfy the contractual terms of an obligation.
- An active portfolio strategy uses available information and forecasting techniques to seek a superior performance. These strategies are often referred to as alpha strategies, where for historical reasons the term "alpha" refers to the return realized in excess of the return offered by the market.
- A passive portfolio strategy relies on diversification to match the performance of some benchmark. Passive portfolio strategies are also referred to as "indexing" since the benchmark is typically some market index. These strategies are also referred to as "beta strategies" where for historical reasons the term *beta* refers to the risk a well-diversified portfolio (such as an indexed portfolio) faces relative to a market index.
- The decomposition of the performance results to explain why those results were achieved is called return attribution analysis.

- Portfolio rebalancing is the adjustment in portfolio holdings at predetermined intervals or when market conditions change.
- Traditional and quantitative portfolio managers can be differentiated by how they use information to select potential candidate securities.
- Portfolio analytics is applied to several aspects of the portfolio management process: (1) market analytics (analysis of real-time market data, prices, financials, earnings estimates, market research reports); (2) financial screening: selection of investments of interest based on pre-specified financial and nonfinancial criteria; (3) quantitative modeling: asset allocation and trading models; and (4) financial analytics: performance evaluation, characteristics and attribution, risk measurement, asset allocation/asset-liability analysis.
- Systems for portfolio analytics typically have four components: (1) data sources, (2) data warehousing, (3) modeling, and (4) visualization.
- Market analytics is aided by visualizations that help identify momentum in the movement of securities or sectors. A variety of new tools such as text analytics exist for capturing market information as soon as it becomes available so that investors can take advantage of it quickly.
- In the process of financial screening of investments, portfolio managers often take advantage of data on company fundamentals and statistical methods for ranking companies and forecasting returns.
- Asset allocation models and portfolio rebalancing schemes sometimes rely on the application of optimization tools.
- In evaluating an investment strategy on historical data—a process referred to as backtesting—a portfolio manager needs to be aware of backtest overfitting and selection bias issues.
- Commonly used metrics of portfolio performance include portfolio return, variability of the portfolio return, tracking error, CAPM beta, alpha, Sharpe ratio, information ratio, maximum drawdown, and Calmar ratio.

Statistical Models of Risk and Uncertainty

Random Variables, Probability Distributions, and Important Statistical Concepts

To understand the risk and expected return associated with an individual asset or a portfolio, one needs a way to model uncertainty. Mathematically, information about uncertainty can be summarized with probability distributions. Expected return and risk are measures describing features of these probability distributions.

This chapter reviews the concepts of random variables, discrete and continuous probability distributions, distribution summary measures, and a law in statistics called the Central Limit Theorem. An important part of the chapter is the introduction of the concept of risk measures. Some of the most widely used risk measures in portfolio management such as standard deviation, value-at-risk, and conditional value-at-risk are explained.

2.1 WHAT IS A PROBABILITY DISTRIBUTION?

A natural way to think of uncertainty is in terms of *scenarios*. Scenarios represent possible events that could happen. For example, the value of a stock you own but are contemplating selling may go up (one scenario) or down (another scenario) one year from now. To these scenarios, you could assign *probabilities*, which reflect your estimate of the likelihood that the scenarios will occur. For example, you estimate that the probability that the stock's value will go up is 0.30 (30%), and the probability that it will go down is 0.70 (70%).

The information contained in the scenarios and the probabilities can be summarized in probability distributions. Basically, probability distributions are listings of the possible uncertain values and their probabilities. This information is often presented in graphs—we will see examples later in this chapter. We will also see that in order to analyze and summarize insights from probability distributions, it is better to have numbers (not categories) on the horizontal axis of the graph, popularly referred to as the "*x*-axis." Thus, it is not a good idea to create a probability distribution for which the random event mentioned in the previous paragraph—that the stock's value will go up or down—is plotted, because "up" and "down" are not numerical quantities.

In order to create a probability distribution, we need to assign numerical values to the uncertain outcomes. Let us think of the outcome "up" as a 1, and of the outcome "down" as a 0. Such *mapping* of events to numerical values is called a *random variable*. The term "random variable" is actually a misnomer, because random variables are neither random nor variables. They are numerical representations, or, equivalently, function assignments, of the outcomes of uncertain events to numbers. Probability distributions are plots of distributions of random variables, and do not necessarily map one-to-one to a list of outcomes.

Note, by the way, that the two probabilities of the two scenarios for the movement of the value of the stock add up to 1 (100%). This is because we assume that only one of the two events can happen (so, for example, the stock's value cannot stay the same), which means that the two scenarios exhaust the possible states of the world, and thus should add up to 100%. This is a general feature of probability distributions—the probabilities of all the values of the random variable in the probability distribution must add up to 1, or 100%. We should not specify a probability distribution in which they do not add up to 1. For example, if we wanted to add a third scenario—say, that the value of the stock stays the same—then we would need to reassign probabilities to the three scenarios in such a way that the total sum of the probabilities remains 1.

2.2 THE BERNOULLI PROBABILITY DISTRIBUTION AND PROBABILITY MASS FUNCTIONS

Exhibit 2.1 shows the probability distribution we described in the previous section when there are two scenarios. It is in fact a special kind of distribution, and has a name because it is used so often—the Bernoulli distribution. The random variable that follows this distribution (the random variable takes values 0 and 1) is called the *Bernoulli random variable*. Let us denote this random variable $\tilde{X}$. Notice that a tilde sign "~" is placed over the X. We will use the tilde sign to denote uncertainty and randomness.

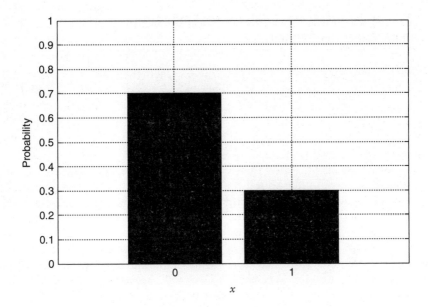

Exhibit 2.1 Bernoulli distribution with $p = 0.3$.

We can describe one possible Bernoulli distribution as

$$P(\widetilde{X} = 0) = 0.70$$
$$P(\widetilde{X} = 1) = 0.30$$

We read a mathematical statement of this kind as "the probability that the random variable $\widetilde{X}$ takes a value of 0 is 0.70 or 70%." This listing of values of the random variable and the associated probabilities is called the *probability mass function* (PMF). It only exists for random variables that take *discrete* (countably many) values, that is, that have discrete probability distributions. More generally, given a probability p, the PMF for a Bernoulli distribution is

$$p(\widetilde{X} = x) = \begin{cases} 1 - p, & x = 0 \\ p, & x = 1 \end{cases}$$

We used x inside the parentheses to signal that this is the *realization* of the random variable $\widetilde{X}$, not the random variable $\widetilde{X}$ itself (which is a function); x is a specific value $\widetilde{X}$ takes.

Exhibit 2.1 corresponds to the probability listing above as follows: there is a bar at each of the values the random variable can take (0 and 1) and the height of the bar equals the probability that the specific value for the random variable occurs. The heights of all bars in the graph add up to 1.

2.3   THE BINOMIAL PROBABILITY DISTRIBUTION AND DISCRETE DISTRIBUTIONS

Now suppose that you would like to model whether the value of the stock will be up or down in three years. Every year, it can go up with probability 0.30, and down with probability 0.70. Let the specific realizations of this Bernoulli random variable for each of the three years be X_1, X_2, and X_3.[1] We can visualize the movement of the stock value from the tree drawn in Exhibit 2.2. For example, when $X_1 = 1$, $X_2 = 1$, and $X_3 = 1$, the movement in all three years is "up" and the stock's value will be at its highest.

Since you would like to sell the stock for as much money as you can, let us call the event of the value of the stock going up in any particular year

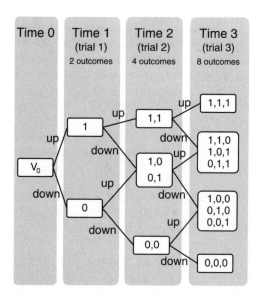

Exhibit 2.2   Movement of stock's value over three years. "1" = "success" (stock's value goes up). "0" = "failure" (stock's value goes down). Note: At the end of three years, we can have three successes in a row, two successes out of three, one success out of three, or no successes. The (0,1) combinations in the tree show the order of the successes or the failures up to that point in time.

---

[1]The notation X_i, a capital letter corresponding to the name of the random variable, followed by an index, is standard statistics notation to denote the ith observation in a sample of observations drawn from the distribution of the random variable $\tilde{X}$.

a "success." Assume that the success in one year is independent of the success in another year, and let us count the number of successes out of the three possible times. This is going to be an uncertain quantity. The probability distribution of the number of successes in a prefixed number of trials is called the *binomial* distribution. In our example, the number of trials is three, because in each of the three years there is a chance that the trial will be a "success" (the stock's value will go up) or a "failure" (the stock's value will go down). Note that the Bernoulli distribution is in fact a special case of the binomial distribution, in which the number of trials is 1. The binomial distribution is very important and widely used in a variety of applications—from statistical analysis of polling results to modeling prices of financial securities and evaluating the economic prospects of a capital budgeting project.

To be mathematically specific, the binomial distribution can be used when the following four conditions are satisfied:

1. The number of trials is fixed in advance.
2. There can be only two outcomes (success and failure).
3. Success in each trial is independent of the result of the previous trial.
4. The probability of success remains the same from trial to trial.

Perhaps the easiest way to envision whether applying the binomial distribution is appropriate is to think of whether the situation under evaluation is equivalent to a sequence of coin flips with the same coin, in which we are interested in the probability that we get a given number (x) of tails in n flips.

Suppose we would like to plot the binomial distribution of the random variable describing the price movements of the stock over the next three years. What would be the values on the x-axis? The values for the random variable can be 0, 1, 2, or 3—the number of successes can be either 0 (the stock's value went down every year), 1 (the stock's value went up in one of the three years but went down in the remaining two), and so on. We will denote the random variable by $\tilde{X}$, but note that this is not the same random variable as the random variable in Section 2.2. In order to create the listing of probabilities, we compute:

$P(\tilde{X} = 0) = (0.70) \cdot (0.70) \cdot (0.70) = 0.343 = 34.3\%$

$P(\tilde{X} = 1) = (0.30) \cdot (0.70) \cdot (0.70) + (0.70) \cdot (0.30) \cdot (0.70) + (0.70) \cdot (0.70)$

$\qquad \cdot (0.30) = .441 = 44.1\%$

$P(\tilde{X} = 2) = (0.30) \cdot (0.30) \cdot (0.70) + (0.70) \cdot (0.30) \cdot (0.30) + (0.30)$

$\qquad \cdot (0.70) \cdot (0.30) = .189 = 18.9\%$

$P(\tilde{X} = 3) = (0.30) \cdot (0.30) \cdot (0.30) = 0.027 = 2.7\%$

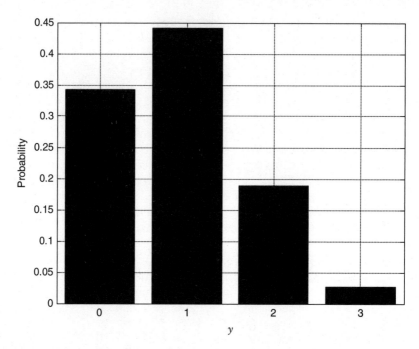

Exhibit 2.3 Binomial distribution with $n = 3$ trials and $p = 0.30$ probability of success.

Therefore, the distribution can be represented as the graph in Exhibit 2.3.

To clarify why the probabilities were computed in the way illustrated above, note that there is only one way to have three successes in three trials ($\widetilde{X} = 3$): when every trial is a success. The probability of this event is the product of the probabilities that each of the three trials is a success. (The multiplication of probabilities to obtain the total probability is permitted because the trials are assumed to be independent.) However, there are three ways to have one success in three trials: the success can be in the first, second, or third trial. To account for these different combinations, we can use the following well-known formula from the branch of mathematics called *combinatorics* (sometimes referred to as the "science of counting"):

$$\frac{n!}{x!(n - x)!}$$

The formula above computes the number of ways in which one can select x out of n objects. The symbol "$n!$" (pronounced "n factorial") stands for the expression $1 \cdot 2 \cdot \ldots \cdot n$. The exact formula for computing the probability of obtaining x successes in n trials when the probability of success is p (in our example, $p = 0.30$) is

$$P(\widetilde{X} = x) = \frac{n!}{x!(n-x)!}p^x(1-p)^{n-x}, \quad x = 0, \ldots, n$$

This is the PMF of the binomial distribution, and is the formula software packages use to compute the binomial distribution probabilities. Note that depending on the magnitude of the probability of success, the binomial distribution can be shaped differently. Exhibit 2.4 illustrates the binomial distribution for three different values of the probability of success.

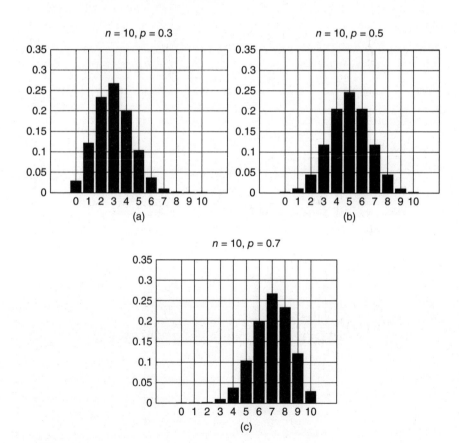

Exhibit 2.4 Shape of binomial distributions with the same number of trials and different values for the probability of success p: (a) $p = 0.3$; (b) $p = 0.5$; (c) $p = 0.7$.

2.4 THE NORMAL DISTRIBUTION AND PROBABILITY DENSITY FUNCTIONS

The binomial distribution is a *discrete* probability distribution because the values the random variable can take are countable (0, 1, 2, etc.). Let us see what happens if we try to model the movements of the stock in 100 years. Exhibit 2.5 shows the binomial distribution for probability of success $p = 0.30$ and number of trials $n = 3, 20,$ and 100.

Note that the binomial distribution begins to look symmetric as the number of trials increases. Also, the range of values begins to look like a *continuum*. When the random variable takes values on a range, as opposed to discrete points, the random variable is called *continuous*, and its probability distribution is called *continuous* as well. Continuous distributions are defined by their *probability density functions* (PDFs)—basically, functions

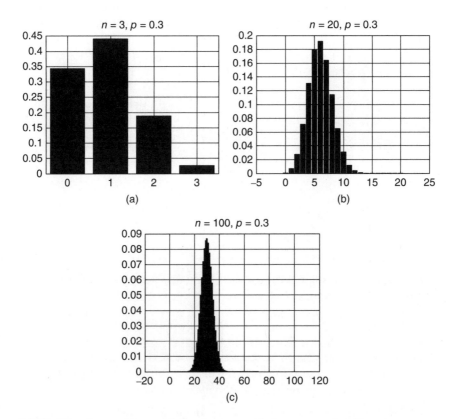

Exhibit 2.5 Shape of binomial distributions with the same probability of success $p = 0.3$ and an increasing number of trials n: (a) $n = 3$; (b) $n = 20$; (c) $n = 100$.

that describe the shape of the curve on the graph. They are often denoted by the standard mathematical notation for functions, $f(x)$, where x represents the possible values the random variable can take.

It appears logical to think of the value of $f(x)$ as the probability that the random variable will take the value x, analogously to the way we defined the PMF $p(x)$. This is, however, incorrect. In fact, the value of $f(x)$ may be greater than 1, which a probability cannot be. Instead, we need to think about probabilities for continuous distributions in terms of *areas* under a curve that describes the probability distribution. Intuitively, the reason continuous distributions are associated with areas under the PDF $f(x)$ is that a continuum represents an infinite number of values that the random variable can take. If we try to assign a bar whose height equals a nonzero probability to each value the random variable can take, as we did in the case of the binomial distribution, the total sum of all bars (and, hence the total probability for that distribution) will be infinity. However, the total probability, added up over all possible values for the random variable, cannot be more than 1.

Consequently, a better way to think of the probability of each particular value of the random variable is as infinitely small (virtually, 0), but then realize that when many, many of these values are added together, they have a significant probability mass. This is the concept of *integration* in calculus. The area under a given curve can be computed by adding up an infinite number of tiny areas above intervals of length dx on the x-axis. The probability that a continuous random variable takes values between two constants a and b can be expressed as the integral

$$\int_a^b f(x)\ dx$$

and the total probability (the area under the entire curve) should be 1:

$$\int_{-\infty}^{\infty} f(x)\ dx = 1$$

It turns out that the binomial distribution approaches a very important continuous distribution, called the *normal* distribution, as the number of trials becomes large. The normal distribution is bell-shaped, and is entirely defined by two parameters: its mean μ and standard deviation σ, which means that if we know them, we can draw the shape of the distribution. (We will introduce the concepts of mean and standard deviation shortly. For now, just think of μ and σ as inputs to the formula for the normal distribution PDF.) This is because the normal PDF is given by the formula

$$f(x) = \frac{1}{\sigma\sqrt{2\pi}} e^{-\frac{(x-\mu)^2}{2\sigma^2}}$$

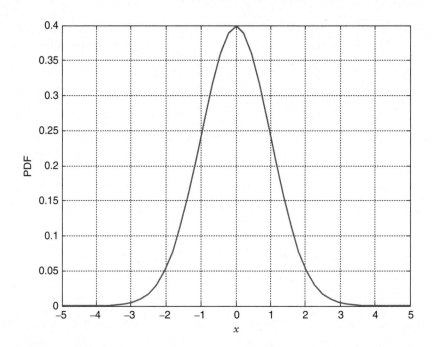

Exhibit 2.6   Standard normal distribution.

(In this formula, π is the mathematical constant *pi*, which has value 3.14159 . . . .)

The standard normal distribution has $\mu = 0$ and $\sigma = 1$ (see Exhibit 2.6). You may also encounter the notation $f(x|\mu, \sigma)$, that is,

$$f(x|\mu, \sigma) = \frac{1}{\sigma \sqrt{2\pi}} e^{-\frac{(x-\mu)^2}{2\sigma^2}}$$

The symbol "|" stands for "conditional on" or "given." In other words, given specific values for μ or σ, the PDF for the normal distribution is given by the above formula. The symbol "|" will be useful in other circumstances as well, such as stating the PDF of a random variable conditional on the realization of another random variable. For example, the probability distribution of asset returns in one time period may depend on ("be conditional on") the realization of asset returns in the previous time period. We will provide a more formal definition of conditioning in Section 2.9.

A unique property of normal probability distributions is that a normal random variable $\tilde{X}$ from a normal distribution with any values for μ and

σ becomes a standard normal random variable $\widetilde{Z}$ (that is, it follows the standard normal distribution in Exhibit 2.6) if the following transformation is made:

$$\widetilde{Z} = \frac{\widetilde{X} - \mu}{\sigma}$$

For any particular value x of $\widetilde{X}$,

$$z = \frac{x - \mu}{\sigma}$$

is the *z-score* of x. The z-score measures how many standard deviations (σ) the value x is from the mean μ. We will see applications of z-scores in the context of stock screens in Chapter 12.

The normal distribution appears surprisingly often in nature and was studied in detail well before its prominent use in finance. Modern-day random process modeling in finance has borrowed a lot of findings from natural sciences such as physics and biology. For example, a classical assumption in modeling asset returns is that the changes in asset prices over small periods of time are normally distributed (despite the fact that the empirical evidence from real-world markets does not support the position that changes in asset returns follow a normal distribution).

The binomial and the normal distributions are famous representatives of the two classes of probability distributions: discrete and continuous. However, there are numerous other useful probability distributions that appear in practice. Empirical return distributions can take a variety of shapes. We review additional probability distributions useful for modeling financial returns for risk management purposes in Chapter 3. Next, let us introduce a few important concepts for describing probability distributions and measuring risk.

2.5   THE CONCEPT OF CUMULATIVE PROBABILITY

Cumulative probability is the probability that a random variable takes a value that is less than or equal to a given value. Cumulative probability is an important concept, and is available as a function from a number of software packages, including Excel and R. The *cumulative distribution function* (CDF) can be thought of as a listing of the cumulative probabilities up to every possible value the random variable can take. Examples of CDFs for a continuous and a discrete distribution are shown in Exhibit 2.7. The CDFs always start at 0 and end at 1, but the shape of the curve on the graph is determined by the PDF or PMF of the underlying random variable. (The CDF for

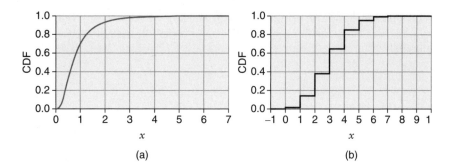

Exhibit 2.7 The CDF of (a) a continuous random variable (lognormal), and (b) a discrete random variable (binomial with 10 trials and probability of success 0.30). Note: The values on the horizontal axis are the values the random variable takes.

a discrete random variable has a characteristic staircase-like shape—"step function" in mathematical jargon.)

To show how one would compute the cumulative probability for a discrete distribution, let us consider the binomial distribution example from Section 2.3, which is also the CDF plotted in Exhibit 2.7(b).

Suppose that the probability of success is 0.30, and we would like to compute the probability that the number of successes in 10 trials will be at most 6. Intuitively, we are trying to estimate the total height of the first 6 bars in Exhibit 2.4(a). We can write this expression as

$$P(\widetilde{X} \leq 6) = P(\widetilde{X} = 0) + \ldots + P(\widetilde{X} = 6)$$

$$= \frac{10!}{0!(10 - 0)!}0.30^0(1 - 0.30)^{10-0} + \ldots$$

$$+ \frac{10!}{6!(10 - 6)!}0.30^6(1 - 0.30)^{10-6}$$

$$= \sum_{k=0}^{6} \frac{10!}{k!(10 - k)!}0.30^k(1 - 0.30)^{10-k}$$

where we have used the classical symbol $\sum$ to denote "sum."

To construct the entire CDF, we would perform the same calculation for all possible values of $\widetilde{X}$, that is, compute $P(\widetilde{X} \leq 0)$, $P(\widetilde{X} \leq 1)$, ..., $P(\widetilde{X} \leq 10)$. We would then plot $\widetilde{X}$ on the x-axis, and the corresponding $P(\widetilde{X} \leq x)$ on the vertical axis (by convention referred to as the y-axis).

For continuous distributions, we would replace the sum by an integral, and find the area under the PDF that is less than or equal to a given constant.

For example, if $f(x)$ is the PDF of a continuous probability distribution (such as the normal distribution and other distributions such as t, chi-square, and exponential distributions that we describe later), then the CDF (usually denoted by $F(x)$) can be computed as

$$F(x) = P(\widetilde{X} \leq x) = \int_{-\infty}^{x} f(x)\ dx$$

Further, the probability that a random variable takes values between two constants a and b can be linked to the CDF as follows:

$$P(a \leq \widetilde{X} \leq b) = \int_{a}^{b} f(x)\ dx = F(b) - F(a)$$

To illustrate this, let us look at the picture in Exhibit 2.8. Suppose we would like to compute the probability that the random variable takes a value between 20 and 60 (which is the area under the PDF between 20 and 60, and is 45.7% according to the picture). To compute that probability, we can equivalently compute the cumulative probability (the area) up to 20 (which is 39.9% according to the picture) and subtract it from the cumulative probability (the area) up to 60 (which is 100% $-$ 14.4% = 85.6%). We obtain $F(60) - F(20) = 85.6\% - 39.9\% = 45.7\%$, which is the same number.

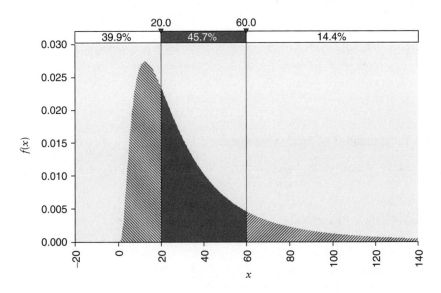

Exhibit 2.8 Calculation of the probability that the random variable falls between 20 and 60 as a difference of cumulative probabilities up to 20 and 60.

Using the same idea, we can calculate the probability that a normal random variable takes values within a particular range. All normal distributions have the property that approximately 68% of their probability mass falls within one standard deviation from the mean, approximately 95% of their probability mass falls within two standard deviations from the mean, and approximately 99% of their probability mass falls within three standard deviations from the mean.

2.6 DESCRIBING DISTRIBUTIONS

A probability distribution can be used to represent the possible future values of an asset. But what does the picture of this probability distribution tell us, and how can we convey the most important insights to others? This section introduces mathematical terminology for describing probability distributions. Specifically, the graph of a probability distribution gives us information about

- Where the most likely or most representative outcomes are (central tendency).
- Whether we can be optimistic or pessimistic about the future (skew).
- What the risk is (spread and tails of the distribution).

Finance practitioners are also often concerned with how "fat" the tails of the distribution are—which tells us how likely it is that "extreme" events, that is, events that are very far from the "representative" outcomes in the middle of the distribution, will occur. We discuss a measure of this distribution characteristic (*kurtosis*) in Section 2.6.4.

2.6.1 Measures of Central Tendency

Measures of central tendency include

- Mean
- Median
- Mode

The mean is by far the most commonly utilized measure in financial applications for theoretical reasons, despite the fact that it has some serious drawbacks, most notably sensitivity to extreme values. We discuss the mean in the most detail, and review briefly the other two measures.

2.6.1.1 **Mean**   On an intuitive level, the *mean* (also called the "expected value" or the "average") is the weighted average of all possible outcomes in the distribution, where the weights equal the probabilities that these values are taken. This is easier to imagine in the case of discrete distributions than in the case of continuous distributions, but the main idea is the same.

In mathematical jargon, the mean is called the *first moment* of a probability distribution.[2] It is denoted as $E[\widetilde{X}]$ (for "expected value of the random variable $\widetilde{X}$").

In the case of a discrete distribution,

$$E[\widetilde{X}] = \sum_{\text{All values } x \text{ of the random variable}} x \cdot P(\widetilde{X} = x)$$

---

[2] A complete review of probability theory is beyond the scope of this book, but the concept of moments of probability distributions is often mentioned in quantitative finance, so let us explain briefly what a moment-generating function (MGF) is. The kth moment of a random variable is defined as

$$m_k(\widetilde{X}) = E[\widetilde{X}^k] = \begin{cases} \sum_{\text{All values } x \text{ of the random variable}} x^k \cdot P(\widetilde{X} = x) \\ \int_{-\infty}^{\infty} x^k \cdot f(x) \ dx \end{cases}$$

For many useful cases (albeit not for all, because for some distributions some moments may not exist), knowing these moments allows us to identify uniquely the actual probability distribution. The MGF lets us generate these moments. It is defined as

$$M_t(\widetilde{X}) = E[e^{t\widetilde{X}}] = \begin{cases} \sum_{\text{All values } x \text{ of the random variable}} e^{tx} \cdot P(\widetilde{X} = x) \\ \int_{-\infty}^{\infty} e^{tx} \cdot f(x) \ dx \end{cases}$$

By setting the value of the parameter t to different values (i.e., 1, 2, 3), we can recover the first, second, and third moment. While this construction looks rather awkward, it is very useful for proving theoretical results such as "The sum of two independent normal random variables is also a normal random variable." (The sum of two random variables does not necessarily have the same distribution as the random variables in the general case.) This is done by computing the MGF of the sum of two normal variables, and then checking if the resulting MGF is of the same type as the MGF of a normal random variable, which is computationally more convenient than computing the actual probability distribution of the sum of two random variables.

In the case of a continuous distribution,

$$E[\widetilde{X}] = \int_{-\infty}^{\infty} x \cdot f(x) \; dx$$

For example, the mean of the Bernoulli distribution in Section 2.2 is

$$0 \cdot 0.70 + 1 \cdot 0.30 = 0.30$$

The mean of a normal distribution can be computed as

$$E[\widetilde{X}] = \int_{-\infty}^{\infty} x \cdot \frac{1}{\sigma\sqrt{2\pi}} e^{-\frac{(x-\mu)^2}{2\sigma^2}} \; dx$$

In the case of the normal distribution, of course, this calculation is redundant, since the parameter μ in the expression inside the integral is actually the mean. However, the mean is not a parameter in the PDF formulas for most probability distributions, and this is the calculation that would be used to compute it.

Note that the mean is not always the "middle point" of the range of the distribution. It is sensitive to outliers (values for the random variable that are very far from the majority of values). One outlier can shift the mean significantly. Note also that the mean may not be one of the possible values of the probability distribution, as the Bernoulli example above illustrated. (The mean for the Bernoulli distribution was 0.30, which is not 0 or 1, the possible values of the random variable.) The mean is merely the "center of gravity" of the probability distribution, and it may not be appropriate to use it as a representative value for the distribution under all circumstances.

2.6.1.2 Median The *median* is a more robust measure of the "middle" of the distribution. It is the value on the x-axis so that 50% of the distribution lies on each side of it. Because the median does not take into consideration where the values on each side of it lie (as opposed to the mean, which considers the actual values and their probabilities of occurrence), the median is not as influenced by the presence of outliers or extreme values as the mean.

2.6.1.3 Mode The *mode* of a distribution is the most likely outcome. One can think of it as the value at which the PDF/PMF of the distribution is at its highest. For example, in Exhibit 2.4, the mode of the first binomial distribution is 3, the mode of the second distribution is 5, and the mode of the third distribution is 7.

You may hear about "unimodal," "bimodal," and, in general, "multimodal" distributions. These terms simply refer to how many modes or "peaks" the distribution has. Almost all theoretical distributions used in financial modeling are unimodal, as their properties are easier to model mathematically. The distributions we have introduced so far, for example, are unimodal, because they have a single mode. Of course, real-world data do not always follow neat mathematical rules, and may present investors with distributions that have more than one mode.

2.6.2   Measures of Risk

Quantitative portfolio risk management often relies on statistical measures related to the spread or the tails of the distribution of portfolio returns. Such measures include variance and standard deviation (spread), coefficient of variation (risk relative to mean), and percentiles of the distribution (tails). Value-at-risk and conditional value-at-risk are the financial terms used to describe two popular risk measures based on the percentiles of the distribution of portfolio returns. Below we explain the statistical measures and their corresponding portfolio risk measures in more detail.

2.6.2.1   Variance and Standard Deviation   When thinking of risk, one usually thinks of how far the actual realization of an uncertain variable will fall from what one expects. Therefore, a natural way to define a measure of uncertainty is as the average *spread* or *dispersion* of a distribution. Two measures that describe the spread of the distribution are *variance* and *standard deviation*. The two are strongly related: the standard deviation is the square root of the variance, and we usually need to compute the variance before computing the standard deviation. Exhibit 2.9 illustrates the relationship between variance/standard deviation and the spread of the distribution. Suppose we are considering investing in two assets, A and B. The probability distribution for B has a wider spread and higher variance/standard deviation than probability distribution A, so B could be considered riskier than A.

Mathematically, the variance of a random variable is related to the *second moment* of a probability distribution, and is computed as follows:

$$\text{Var}(\widetilde{X}) = \sum_{\substack{\text{All values } x \text{ of the random variable}}} (x - \mu)^2 \cdot \text{P}(\widetilde{X} = x)$$

$$\text{(for discrete distributions)}$$

$$\text{Var}(\widetilde{X}) = \int_{-\infty}^{\infty} (x - \mu)^2 \cdot f(x) \ dx \text{ (for continuous distributions)}$$

In the equations above, μ denotes the mean of the distribution.

In words, the variance is the sum of the squared deviations of all values in the probability distribution from the mean (used as a measure for the

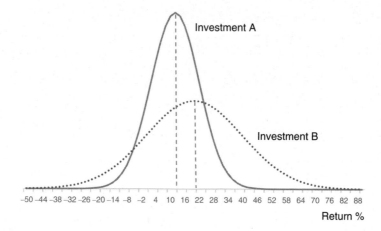

Exhibit 2.9 Comparison of two probability distributions in terms of risk and central tendency.

center) of the distribution. The reason why squared deviations are used is so that deviations to the left of the mean do not cancel deviations to the right of the mean when added together.[3] Otherwise, a distribution that has many observations far from the center and, therefore, has a large "spread," may end up with the same variance as a distribution with values very close to the mean and a small spread. In fact, a distribution that has a very wide spread may end up with a variance of 0 if all large positive deviations from the mean have corresponding large negative deviations. This would make variance useless as a measure of spread.

Sometimes, a more convenient (and equivalent) way of expressing the variance is through the equation

$$\text{Var}(\widetilde{X}) = E[\widetilde{X}^2] - (E[\widetilde{X}])^2$$

$$= \sum_{\text{All values } x} x^2 \cdot P(\widetilde{X} = x) - \left(\sum_{\text{All values } x} x \cdot P(\widetilde{X} = x) \right)^2$$

(in the discrete case)

$$= \int_{-\infty}^{\infty} x^2 \cdot f(x) \, dx - \left(\int_{-\infty}^{\infty} x \cdot f(x) \, dx \right)^2 \text{(in the continuous case)}$$

These expressions link the variance explicitly to the first and the second moments of the distribution.

---

[3]Recall that squaring a number always results in a nonnegative number, so the sum of squared terms is nonnegative.

The variance of a distribution measures the spread in square units of the random variable, and the number is difficult to interpret. The *standard deviation* is widely used instead. The standard deviation takes the square root of the variance ($\sigma_X = \sqrt{\mathrm{Var}(\widetilde{X})}$), and presents a measure of the average deviation of the values in the distribution from the mean that has the same units as the random variable, hence making it easier to interpret. In finance, standard deviation is often used interchangeably with the term "volatility."

Standard deviation and variance were popularized as portfolio risk measures by the seminal work of Markowitz (1952), who suggested that investors are concerned with the trade-off between the portfolio expected return and the portfolio risk as defined by the portfolio variance. There are issues with using standard deviation and variance as portfolio risk measures, and Markowitz himself acknowledged some of their shortcomings. For example, standard deviation and variance treat upside and downside equally, and are only appropriate to use when asset returns follow symmetric (elliptical) distributions, which is not the case in practice. However, standard deviation and variance continue to be widely used in portfolio management, especially in the context of tracking error minimization, and a number of other important concepts in finance rely implicitly on some kind of a normality or distributional symmetry assumption.

2.6.2.2 Coefficient of Variation Let us consider again the picture in Exhibit 2.9. We mentioned that the probability distribution for A has a smaller standard deviation than the probability distribution for B, but notice also that the mean of the distribution for A is lower than the mean for the distribution for B. If you had to invest in one of them, which one would you choose? This is a situation in which one may want to measure spread (the "risk" of the distribution) relative to the mean (the "representative" value of the distribution). This is the concept behind *coefficient of variation* (CV), which is reported as a percentage, and is mathematically expressed as

$$CV = \frac{\sigma}{\mu} \times 100$$

where μ is the mean and σ is the standard deviation of the distribution. The CV calculates a unit-free ratio that can be used to compare random variables. If the CV for investment A is 80% and the CV for investment B is 50%, we may decide that investment A is "riskier" than B relative to the average return we can expect, even though investment A has a smaller standard deviation.

CV represents the trade-off between expectation and risk from a statistical point of view. In finance, the inverse ratio is often used. (In other words, instead of the amount of risk per unit of expected reward, one looks at the expected reward per unit of risk.) The financial measure was popularized by the work of Sharpe (see, for example, Sharpe 1994). The Sharpe ratio is discussed in the context of portfolio optimization in Chapter 8. The main idea behind using both the statistical and the financial measures, however, is the same.

2.6.2.3 Range The *range* of a random variable is the difference between the maximum and the minimum value a random variable can take. It is sometimes used as a measure of "riskiness"; however, be on alert that it is not applicable in many situations. For example, some important probability distributions, such as the normal distribution, have an infinite range, as the random variables can take values from negative infinity to positive infinity.

2.6.2.4 Percentiles Another useful term for describing probability distributions is the *percentile*. The α-percentile of a distribution is the number on the horizontal axis so that a percentage α of the total probability lies to the left of that number. Probability distributions can be compared by their percentiles: for example, if the 5th percentile of the distribution for investment B in Exhibit 2.9 is less than the 5th percentile of the distribution for investment A, we may argue that investment B is riskier than investment A because it will result in a lower outcome than investment A with 5% probability. Two popular portfolio tail risk measures, value-at-risk and conditional value-at-risk, are directly linked to the concept of percentile of the distribution of future portfolio returns. Their presence in portfolio risk management is important enough that it is worth spending some time understanding how they evolved and how they are interpreted.

2.6.2.5 Value-at-Risk Value-at-risk (VaR) is related to the statistical measure percentile. VaR measures the predicted maximum portfolio *dollar loss* at a specified probability level over a certain time horizon. Commonly used probability levels include 0.95 and 0.99, and the corresponding VaR is referred to as 95% VaR and 99% VaR (in other words, the probability is stated as a percentage). Typical time horizons include 1 day and 10 days. The portfolio loss is defined as the difference between the initial value of the portfolio at the current time t, V_t, and the future value of the portfolio at time $t + 1$, V_{t+1}.[4]

VaR can be used to measure dollar losses for individual assets, trading positions, and portfolios, which makes it convenient for reporting firm-wide risk. JP Morgan was one of the early leaders in developing a firm-wide

---

[4]Note that the difference $V_t - V_{t+1}$ is a positive number if there is a loss, and a negative number if there is a profit.

integrated risk management system, and is responsible for popularizing VaR as a risk measure in the 1990s. Industry legend has it that JP Morgan's integrated risk management system was started when Dennis Weatherstone, the then-chairman of JP Morgan, asked his staff to give him a daily one-page report describing the firm-wide risk over the next 24 hours, taking into consideration the bank's entire trading portfolio. The "4:15" report, as the report became widely known because it was delivered at the close of trading every day, used VaR to estimate the maximum loss with a given probability over the next trading day. The fact that VaR was quoted as a dollar amount, rather than a percentage, or a probability, made it convenient for reporting results to management, and eliminated the need to explain complex mathematics.

Among banks, the consensus to use the maximum likely loss as a way to look at risk was established formally in 1996, when the Basel Committee on Banking Supervision of the Bank for International Settlements (BIS) proposed several amendments to the original 1988 Basel Accord for minimal capital requirements for banks of its member countries. While the original accord covered only credit risk, the new proposal that took effect in 1998 also covered market risk, including organization-wide commodities exposures (measured by the 10-day 95% VaR).

Mathematically, VaR at a probability level $100(1 - \epsilon)\%$ is defined as the value γ such that the probability that the negative of the portfolio return will exceed γ is not more than some small number ϵ:

$$\text{VaR}_{(1-\epsilon)} \; (\tilde{r}) = \min \; \{\gamma \mid P(-\tilde{r} > \gamma) \leq \epsilon\}$$

In the expression above, $\tilde{r}$ denotes the random variable representing the portfolio return, and $-\tilde{r}$ is associated with the portfolio loss. For example, when $\epsilon = 0.05$, then $(1 - \epsilon) = 0.95$, $100(1 - \epsilon)\% = 95\%$, and we are interested in the 95% VaR, which is the level of the portfolio losses that will not be exceeded with probability of more than 5%. Asset managers sometimes use a modified version of VaR, which measures the loss relative to a benchmark. The formula for VaR above still stands, but $\tilde{r}$ is the *excess return* relative to the benchmark, that is, the difference between the return on the portfolio and the return on the benchmark.

To report the $100(1 - \epsilon)\%$ VaR as a dollar amount of losses, one can roughly approximate its value with the product of the negative of the ϵth% return and the initial value of the portfolio. Alternatively, one can compute the $100(1 - \epsilon)\%$ VaR directly from the profit/loss (P/L) distribution for the portfolio, which is already reported in dollars. Exhibit 2.10 shows how in the case of the P/L distribution one looks at the left tail of the distribution to estimate VaR, whereas in the case of the loss/profit (L/P) distribution (for which performance is recorded as losses), one looks at the right tail of the distribution.

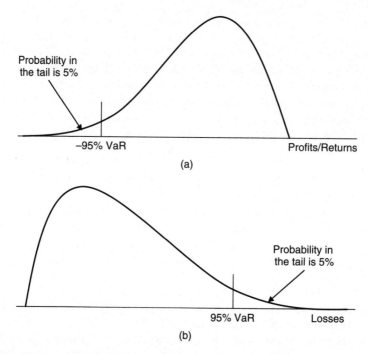

Exhibit 2.10 (a) 95% VaR computed from P/L data; (b) 95% VaR computed from L/P data.

Software vendors often provide several values for VaR. One is based on the assumption that the portfolio returns will follow a normal distribution, and is typically abbreviated "Normal VaR." It calculates VaR as a multiple of the number of standard deviations of the possible distribution of portfolio returns. (This is easy to do because the percentiles of the normal distribution can be represented through an expression that involves the mean and the standard deviation of the distribution.) In particular,

$$\text{Normal VaR}_{(1-\epsilon)} = (-\mu_r + q_{(1-\epsilon)} \cdot \sigma_r) \cdot V_t$$

where μ_r is the expected return, σ_r is the standard deviation of the return, V_t is the current portfolio value, and $q_{(1-\epsilon)}$ is the $100(1-\epsilon)$th percentile of a standard normal distribution.[5]

---

[5]Most spreadsheet and statistical software packages contain a function for computing $q_{(1-\epsilon)}$. In Excel, it is computed with the formula NORMSINV$(1-\epsilon)$. (So, for example, $q_{0.95}$ corresponding to the 95th percentile is computed as

Normal-distribution-based VaR suffers from a number of problems but many financial institutions use it, not understanding (or choosing to ignore) its drawbacks. As a measure of tail risk, VaR should enable financial institutions to evaluate risk in unusual situations that cannot be represented by normal distributions for returns. Thus, it is not satisfactory to measure tail risk as a multiple of the standard deviation, as the normal approximation to the VaR does.

"Simulated VaR" is calculated based on generating a number of representative scenarios, calculating the portfolio return in each of these scenarios, and using the ϵth% return as an estimate of the VaR. If S scenarios are generated for possible portfolio losses (by simulation or using historical data), the Simulated VaR is obtained by sorting the portfolio loss scenarios data in an increasing order, and selecting the scenario with index $(S - \lfloor \epsilon \cdot S \rfloor + 1)$ in the sorted data array.

VaR suffers from some unique disadvantages as a risk measure. First, VaR does not tell a portfolio manager how much could be lost if a low-probability tail event occurs. Thus, using VaR as the "threshold" for approving an investment strategy can leave investors exposed to extreme losses. Second, VaR's reporting of the loss at a certain percentile of the distribution without consideration for the size of the losses in the tail of the distribution encourages portfolio managers and traders to take more low-probability, high-impact bets. Such risks do not show up in the VaR estimates, but can have a devastating effect on the portfolio and a financial institution and, in fact, can destabilize the entire financial system, as the financial system collapse in the fall of 2008 demonstrated. There are issues also with the theoretical foundations of using VaR as a risk measure.[6] Conditional value-at-risk, the risk measure described next, addresses some of these issues.

2.6.2.6 Conditional Value-at-Risk Conditional value-at-risk (CVaR) measures the average portfolio loss that happens with at most ϵ probability, that is, the average loss in the tail. Although CVaR is a tail-based risk measure like VaR, unlike VaR, it provides information about the magnitude of the loss that can be expected if an event in the tail of the distribution happens. The formal definition of the $100(1 - \epsilon)\%$ CVaR is

$$\text{CVaR}_{(1-\epsilon)}\ (\tilde{r}) = E\left[-\tilde{r} \mid -\tilde{r} \geq \text{VaR}_{(1-\epsilon)}\ (\tilde{r})\right]$$

The $100(1 - \epsilon)\%$ CVaR is always greater than or equal to the $100(1 - \epsilon)\%$ VaR.

NORMSINV(0.95), which is 1.6445.) In R, $q_{(1-\epsilon)}$ can be computed with a similar command: qnorm$(1 - \epsilon)$.

[6]See Chapter 8 in Pachamanova and Fabozzi (2010) for more details.

Like VaR, CVaR is reported as a dollar amount. When scenarios are generated for possible future portfolio losses, CVaR is calculated by sorting the portfolio loss data in increasing order and calculating the average of the largest $\epsilon\%$ of losses.

Similarly to the case of VaR, software vendors often provide several values for CVaR. The "Normal CVaR" is again calculated as a multiple of the standard deviation of portfolio returns assuming that portfolio returns will follow a normal distribution, whereas "Simulated CVaR" is calculated as the average loss in the appropriate number of the highest-loss generated scenarios. The Normal CVaR is computed as follows:

$$\text{CVaR}_{(1-\epsilon)} = \left(-\mu_r + \frac{\varphi\left(q_{(1-\epsilon)}\right)}{\epsilon} \cdot \sigma_r \right) \cdot V_t$$

where the number $q_{(1-\epsilon)}$ is the $100(1-\epsilon)$th percentile of a standard normal distribution, as before, and we use $\varphi\left(q_{(1-\epsilon)}\right)$ to denote the value of the normal probability density at the point $q_{(1-\epsilon)}$.[7]

2.6.3 Skew

Distributions can be symmetric or asymmetric (skewed), depending on whether the "tails" at the two ends of the distribution are the same or different. Whether distributions are further classified as *left-skewed (negatively skewed)* or *right-skewed (positively skewed)* depends on where the mean is relative to the median. Symmetric distributions have the same mean and median, whereas left-skewed distributions have a longer left tail (which implies that the mean is to the left of the median, as it has been skewed by extreme values). There are several rather involved definitions that are used to represent skew mathematically, and it is beyond the scope of the book to present them here. The important thing to note is that all of the formulas for skew use the *third moment* of a probability distribution, and agree on the intuitive definition of skew above: that left skew means longer left tail, whereas right skew means longer right tail. The normal distribution, which is symmetric, has a skew of zero.

---

[7]The value of $\varphi\left(q_{(1-\epsilon)}\right)$ can be found with the command $\text{NORMDIST}\left(q_{(1-\epsilon)}, 0, 1, 0\right)$ in Excel, or $\text{dnorm}\left(q_{(1-\epsilon)}\right)$ in R. For example, let $\epsilon = 0.05$. Therefore, $1 - \epsilon = 0.95$ and $q_{(1-\epsilon)} = \text{norminv}(0.95) = 1.6448$. The value of $\varphi\left(q_{(1-\epsilon)}\right)$ is then 0.1031 (computed as $\text{normdist}(1.6448, 0, 1, 0)$ in Excel or $\text{dnorm}(1.6448)$ in R).

2.6.4   Kurtosis

In finance, one is often interested in the behavior in the "tails" of a distribution. If the tails are "fat," this means that extreme observations are more likely to happen, and the mean, or expected value, is less useful for describing typical outcomes. *Kurtosis* measures the "fatness" of the tails of a distribution. The normal distribution, which is used as the standard for comparison, has a kurtosis of 3. A kurtosis of more than 3 (in general, high value for kurtosis) means that the probability distribution has fatter tails and a sharper peak than the normal distribution, whereas a low value for kurtosis means that the tails are "leaner" than the tails of the normal distribution.[8] The mathematical formula for kurtosis, just as the formula for skew, is rather involved, but the important thing to note is that kurtosis is related to the *fourth moment* of a probability distribution.

As we discuss in Chapter 3, financial returns tend to have greater kurtosis than the normal distribution. They are often described as "leptokurtic," that is, their distribution exhibits a sharper peak and fatter tails than the normal distribution. Relatively small changes in returns are thus not observed as often as they would be in a normal distribution, and extreme deviations from the mean happen more frequently than one would expect with the normal distribution.

2.7   DEPENDENCE BETWEEN TWO RANDOM VARIABLES: COVARIANCE AND CORRELATION

So far, we have shown how one can describe a single random variable. In finance, we often need to worry about the relationships between two or more variables. For example, in the context of investments, if the return for investment A in Exhibit 2.9 goes up on average, does the return for investment B go up as well? If we can measure these kinds of relationships, we can, for example, protect ourselves against extreme situations in which all of our investments crash simultaneously.

---

[8]Some software and simulation software packages report *excess kurtosis*, rather than kurtosis, as default. The excess kurtosis is computed as the value for kurtosis minus 3 (the kurtosis of the normal distribution), so that the normal distribution has reported kurtosis of 0. Make sure that you check the help file for the software package you are using before you interpret the value for kurtosis in statistical output.

Two commonly used measures of codependence between random variables are covariance (often denoted by Cov) and correlation (often denoted by the Greek letter ρ (rho)). The two are strongly related.

The idea behind covariance is to measure simultaneous deviations from the means for two random variables, $\widetilde{X}$ and $\widetilde{Y}$. If $\widetilde{X}$ takes a value above its mean μ_X, does $\widetilde{Y}$ take a value above its mean μ_Y as well? If it does, then we would like to increase our measure of covariation to reflect a higher degree of codependence. If the two random variables move in opposite directions (i.e., when one of them takes a value above its mean, the other one takes a value below its mean), then we would like to subtract from our measure of covariation. Mathematically, this idea is expressed as

$$\mathrm{Cov}(\widetilde{X}, \widetilde{Y}) = E\left[(\widetilde{X} - \mu_X)(\widetilde{Y} - \mu_Y)\right]$$

Recall that "E" stands for "expectation," or "average." Thus, the covariance measures whether the two random variables move together on average. If the covariance is 0, the two variables are independent.

The concept of covariance appears very often in modern portfolio theory, and we come back to it in Chapter 8. However, sometimes it is more convenient to use a normalized form of the expression for covariance—the *correlation coefficient*. The problem with covariance is that its units are products of the original units of the two random variables, so the value for covariance is difficult to interpret. The correlation coefficient divides the covariance by the product of the standard deviations of the two random variables:

$$\rho = \mathrm{Corr}(\widetilde{X}, \widetilde{Y}) = \frac{\mathrm{Cov}(\widetilde{X}, \widetilde{Y})}{\sigma_X \sigma_Y}$$

The result is a value that is always between −1 and 1. If the correlation between two random variables is close to 1, they are strongly positively correlated; that is, if one of them takes a value above its mean, the other one is very likely to take a value above its mean as well. If the correlation is close to −1, they are strongly negatively correlated; that is, if one of them takes a value above its mean, the other one is very likely to take a value below its mean. If the correlation is 0, then the two variables are independent— meaning knowing whether one of them is above or below its mean value does not tell you anything about where the value of the other variable may be.

An important point is that covariance and correlation exist only for pairs of random variables. They are not computed for more than two variables at a time. Thus, if the situation calls for analysis of dependence between more than two random variables, the covariances or correlations are reported in a table (referred to as a *covariance matrix* or *correlation matrix*, respectively). If there are N variables to analyze, the covariance and the correlation tables each have N rows and N columns. The entry in the ith row and jth column is the covariance/correlation of the ith variable and the jth variable. The values in the diagonal of these matrices (i.e., the entries in the ith row and ith column) are equal to the variance of the ith variable (in the case of the covariance matrix) and 1 (in the case of the correlation matrix). See the Appendix for a brief introduction to matrix arrays. We discuss covariance and correlation matrices in more detail in Chapter 8.

When dealing with financial data, we often need to be concerned also with *autocorrelation*. Autocorrelation exists when the realizations of a random process over time (such as the movement of a stock price) depend on the history of the process, that is, when a random variable (such as a security's return) in one time period is correlated with itself (the security's return) during previous time periods.

It is worth noting that while covariance and correlation are useful measures of dependence, and are widely used in financial applications, they do not paint a complete picture of how random variables are codependent, and can sometimes be misleading. This is particularly true in cases in which two variables are nonlinearly related.[9] Consider two random variables, $\widetilde{X}$ and $\widetilde{Y}$, where $\widetilde{X}$ follows a continuous uniform distribution on the interval $[0,20]$, and $\widetilde{Y} = e^{\widetilde{X}}$. One hundred observations from the probability distribution of $\widetilde{X}$ are drawn, the corresponding values for $\widetilde{Y}$ are computed, and the points are plotted in Exhibit 2.11. Note that $\widetilde{X}$ and $\widetilde{Y}$ are perfectly dependent—knowing the value of $\widetilde{X}$, we can predict the exact value for $\widetilde{Y}$. However, when we compute the correlation coefficient between $\widetilde{X}$ and $\widetilde{Y}$, we get a value of about 0.5. A correlation of 0.5 shows relatively strong positive dependence, but is not 1, that is, it does not reflect the fact that $\widetilde{X}$ and $\widetilde{Y}$ are actually perfectly dependent. The correlation coefficient would measure the dependence correctly, however, if $\widetilde{X}$ and $\widetilde{Y}$ had a linear relationship, that is, if $\widetilde{Y}$ were a linear function of $\widetilde{X}$ of the kind $a\widetilde{X} + b$ for some constants a and b.

2.8 SUMS OF RANDOM VARIABLES

As we mentioned in Section 2.7, we often need to consider more than one uncertainty at a time, and thus we need tools to deal with sums of random variables, for example, the behavior of a portfolio. Summarizing the joint

---

[9]In other words, when pairs of realizations are plotted in a scatterplot, the points cannot be fitted well by a straight line.

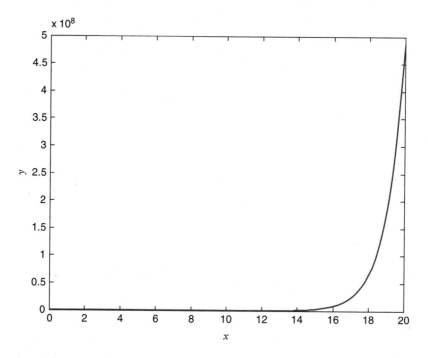

Exhibit 2.11   A connected graph of the realizations of $\widetilde{X}$ versus the realizations of $\widetilde{Y} = e^{\widetilde{X}}$.

probability distributions for sums of two or more random variables is not as easy as summing the two distributions. In this section, we review a few important facts about analyzing sums of random variables.

Suppose the return on investment A in Exhibit 2.9 is the random variable $\widetilde{X}$, and the return on investment B is the random variable $\widetilde{Y}$. Let $E[\widetilde{X}]$ and $E[\widetilde{Y}]$ be the expected returns of the two investments, and σ_X and σ_Y be their standard deviations. Suppose now that we invest 0.40 (40%) of our funds in A, and 0.60 (60%) of our funds in B. Therefore, the return on the portfolio is $0.40 \cdot \widetilde{X} + 0.60 \cdot \widetilde{Y}$. What is the expected return on the portfolio, and what is the portfolio's standard deviation?

First, we need to ask what the expected values of $0.40 \cdot \widetilde{X}$ and $0.60 \cdot \widetilde{Y}$ are. Note that even though 0.40 and 0.60 are numbers (constants), the products $0.40 \cdot \widetilde{X}$ and $0.60 \cdot \widetilde{Y}$ are random variables because they depend on the random variables $\widetilde{X}$ and $\widetilde{Y}$.

It turns out that for any random variable $\widetilde{X}$,

$$E[a \cdot \widetilde{X}] = a \cdot E[\widetilde{X}]$$

if *a* is a constant, that is, the expected (mean) value of a constant times the random variable is simply the constant times the expected value of the random variable.

Furthermore, it is always true that the expectation of the sum of two random variables is equal to the sum of the expectations:

$$E[\tilde{X} + \tilde{Y}] = E[\tilde{X}] + E[\tilde{Y}]$$

Therefore

$$E[a \cdot \tilde{X} + b \cdot \tilde{Y}] = a \cdot E[\tilde{X}] + b \cdot E[\tilde{Y}]$$

This allows us to compute the expected value of the portfolio:

$$E[0.40 \cdot \tilde{X} + 0.60 \cdot \tilde{Y}] = 0.40 \cdot E[\tilde{X}] + 0.60 \cdot E[\tilde{Y}]$$

What about the risk of the portfolio? Most people would be tempted to extend the reasoning above to portfolio variance and standard deviation as well. However, variance and standard deviation are not nearly as "convenient" as the expectation operator. It turns out that

$$\text{Var}[a \cdot \tilde{X}] = a^2 \cdot \text{Var}[\tilde{X}]$$

$$\text{Var}(\tilde{X} + \tilde{Y}) = \text{Var}(\tilde{X}) + \text{Var}(\tilde{Y}) + 2 \cdot \text{Covar}(\tilde{X}, \tilde{Y}), \text{ and}$$

$$\text{Var}(a \cdot \tilde{X} + b \cdot \tilde{Y}) = a^2 \cdot \text{Var}(\tilde{X}) + b^2 \cdot \text{Var}(\tilde{Y}) + 2 \cdot a \cdot b \cdot \text{Covar}(\tilde{X}, \tilde{Y})$$

There are no "nice" formulas for the standard deviation of a sum of random variables. We need to compute the variance of the sum (as we did above) and take the square root of the resulting expression to compute the standard deviation.[10]

There are two things to note. First, the constants *a* and *b* are squared once they are taken out of the expression inside the parentheses for the variance. Second, there is an additional term in the sum of the variances,

---

[10]Note that this also eliminates the possibility that the standard deviation of the sum of two random variables is the sum of the standard deviations of the two variables. This is never true if the two random variables have different variances. For example, if the two variables are independent (and the covariance is 0), we get

$$\sigma_{a \cdot \tilde{X} + b \cdot \tilde{Y}} = \sqrt{\text{Var}(a \cdot \tilde{X} + b \cdot \tilde{Y})} = \sqrt{a^2 \cdot \text{Var}(\tilde{X}) + b^2 \cdot \text{Var}(\tilde{Y})}$$

$$\neq a \cdot \sqrt{\text{Var}(\tilde{X})} + b \cdot \sqrt{\text{Var}(\tilde{Y})} = a \cdot \sigma_{\tilde{X}} + b \cdot \sigma_{\tilde{Y}}$$

which involves the covariance of the two random variables. Why does this hold at an intuitive level? We provide some examples of this effect in Chapter 8, but the main idea is that if the random variables move in opposite directions of each other on average (this means that their covariance is negative), the variance of their sum (i.e., the variance of the portfolio) is reduced. We are more likely to get extreme values for the combination of investments if they move in the same direction, that is, if they are strongly positively correlated. This was one of the great insights that came out of Harry Markowitz's theory on optimal portfolio construction, which won him the 1990 Nobel Prize in Economic Science. It led to the proliferation of *diversification* as a strategy in managing assets.

So far, we reviewed what happens to the mean and the variance of a sum of two random variables. What about the actual probability distribution of a random variable that equals the sum of two random variables, for example, $\tilde{Z} = \tilde{X} + \tilde{Y}$?

Computing the distribution of $\tilde{Z}$ is not as easy as adding up the PMFs or PDFs of $\tilde{X}$ and $\tilde{Y}$. If it was, the total sum of probabilities for the distribution of $\tilde{Z}$ would be more than 1. Moreover, the distribution of the sum of the two random variables may look nothing like the distributions of the individual variables. For example, Exhibit 2.12 illustrates the distribution of the sum of two uniform random variables on [0,1].[11] The resulting distribution is a triangular distribution. Intuitively, this makes sense. For example, the mean values for both uniform distributions are in the middle—at 0.5. So, it appears logical that most of the mass for the sum of the probability distributions would be in the middle, too—at the sum of the expected values, $0.5 + 0.5 = 1$. Also, the range for the new variable $\tilde{Z}$ should be [0,2]. This is because the ranges for $\tilde{X}$ and $\tilde{Y}$ are both [0,1], so the minimum value for their sum is $0 + 0 = 0$, and the maximum value for their sum is $1 + 1 = 2$.

Unfortunately, most sums of probability distributions are not as easy to visualize. The actual formula for computing the distribution of the sum of two random variables involves nontrivial integration, and is referred to as *convolution*. Let $f_X(x)$, $f_Y(y)$, and $f_Z(z)$ be the PDFs of the random variables $\tilde{X}$, $\tilde{Y}$, and $\tilde{Z}$ at points x, y, and z, respectively. Then the PDF for the sum $\tilde{Z}$ is

$$f_Z(z) = \int_{-\infty}^{\infty} f_Y(z - x) f_X(x) \; dx$$

As we learn more about simulation techniques in Chapter 5, the advantages of using simulation to evaluate such complex integrals in the context of evaluating the risk of portfolio return distributions will become evident.

---

[11]We provide a formal introduction to this probability distribution in Chapter 3.

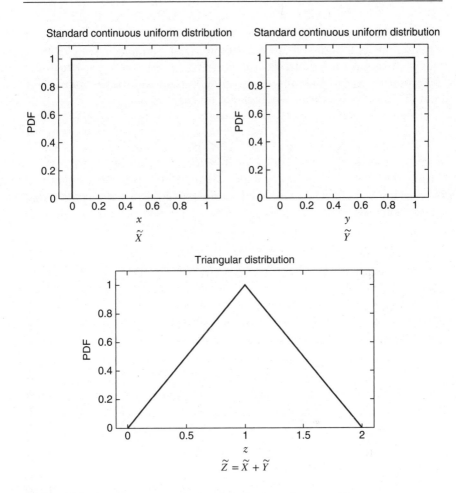

Exhibit 2.12   Sum (convolution) of two uniform random variables.

2.9   JOINT PROBABILITY DISTRIBUTIONS AND CONDITIONAL PROBABILITY

Section 2.8 reviewed important facts about sums of random variables. In this section, we introduce the concepts of joint probability distribution and conditional probability, which are also useful in situations in which we are dealing with more than one random variable.

Joint probability is the probability that two random variables take a pair of values at the same time. The joint PMF of two discrete random variables $\widetilde{X}$ and $\widetilde{Y}$ is denoted $p(\widetilde{X}, \widetilde{Y})$ or $p(\widetilde{X} = x, \widetilde{Y} = y)$. The joint PDF of two continuous random variables $\widetilde{X}$ and $\widetilde{Y}$ is denoted $f(\widetilde{X}, \widetilde{Y})$. When $\widetilde{X}$ and $\widetilde{Y}$ both follow a specific probability distribution, their *joint probability distribution* is referred to as a "multivariate" distribution. For example, if $\widetilde{X}$ and $\widetilde{Y}$ both follow normal distributions, their joint distribution is called a *multivariate normal distribution*. If $\widetilde{X}$ and $\widetilde{Y}$ both follow binomial distributions, their joint distribution is called a *multinomial distribution*.

When two random variables are dependent, then knowing something about the realization of one of them should give us information about the likely realizations of the other one. (If it did not, then the two variables would be independent by definition.) In Section 2.4, we briefly introduced the notation "|", which means "conditional on." The *conditional probability* that a random variable $\widetilde{X}$ will take a value x given that a random variable $\widetilde{Y}$ has taken value y is

$$P(\widetilde{X} = x | \widetilde{Y} = y) = \frac{P(\widetilde{X} = x \text{ and } \widetilde{Y} = y)}{P(\widetilde{Y} = y)}$$

Intuitively, the fact that $\widetilde{Y}$ has taken the value y eliminates some of the possible outcomes for $\widetilde{X}$, and the revised probability that $\widetilde{X}$ will take a value x is computed as a percentage of all those instances in which $\widetilde{X} = x$ given $\widetilde{Y} = y$.

The *conditional PDF* of a continuous random variable $\widetilde{X}$ given $\widetilde{Y}$ is

$$f_{\widetilde{X}|\widetilde{Y}}(x|y) = \frac{f_{\widetilde{X},\widetilde{Y}}(x, y)}{f_{\widetilde{Y}}(y)}$$

This concept and notation extend to the summary measures for probability distributions as well. The *conditional expectation* of the random variable $\widetilde{X}$ given that $\widetilde{Y}$ has taken value y is simply the weighted average for the values of $\widetilde{X}$ that are possible given the realization y of $\widetilde{Y}$. The conditional expectation is denoted $E[\widetilde{X}|\widetilde{Y} = y]$, and the notation carries over to variance, covariance, and so on. The following facts hold:

1. $E[\widetilde{X}] = E_Y[E_X[\widetilde{X}|\widetilde{Y}]]$
2. $\text{Var}(\widetilde{X}) = E_X[\text{Var}(\widetilde{X}|\widetilde{Y})] + \text{Var}(E_X[\widetilde{X}|\widetilde{Y}])$
3. $\text{Cov}(\widetilde{X}, \widetilde{Z}) = E_Y[\text{Cov}(\widetilde{X}, \widetilde{Z})|\widetilde{Y}] + \text{Cov}(E_X[\widetilde{X}|\widetilde{Y}], E_Z[\widetilde{Z}|\widetilde{Y}])$

For example, the first statement says that if we compute the mean of the possible values of a random variable $\widetilde{X}$ when a specific realization of a random variable $\widetilde{Y}$ has occurred and then compute the sum (integral) of the means of the possible value of $\widetilde{X}$ for all possible realizations of $\widetilde{Y}$ (weighted by the probability of obtaining these realizations for $\widetilde{Y}$), we should obtain the actual mean of $\widetilde{X}$.

Having defined the concepts of joint probability distribution and conditional probability, we can now introduce the concept of *marginal probability distribution*. Knowing the joint distribution of two random variables $\widetilde{X}$ and $\widetilde{Y}$, one can compute the *marginal distribution* for each individual random variable by averaging over the values of the other. On an intuitive level, the marginal probability distribution of $\widetilde{X}$ is the probability distribution of $\widetilde{X}$ if $\widetilde{Y}$ was not known.

For discrete random variables, the formula for the marginal probability can be written as

$$P(\widetilde{X} = x) = \sum_y P(\widetilde{X} = x, \widetilde{Y} = y) = \sum_y P(\widetilde{X} = x | \widetilde{Y} = y) \cdot P(\widetilde{Y} = y)$$

For continuous variables, the formula is

$$f(x) = \int_y f(x, y) dy = \int_y f(x|y) \cdot f(y) dy$$

Exhibit 2.13 contains an illustration of the joint (scatterplot) and marginal (histograms along the horizontal and vertical axes) distributions for two normal random variables, $\widetilde{X}$ with mean 100 and standard deviation 30 and $\widetilde{Y}$ with mean 50 and standard deviation 10.

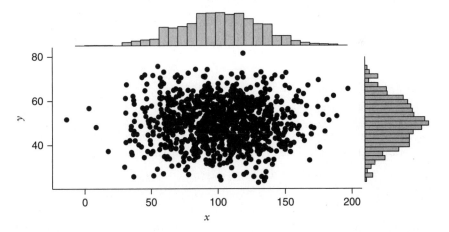

Exhibit 2.13 Joint (scatterplot) and marginal (histograms) distributions obtained from 1,000 realizations of normal random variable $\widetilde{X}$ with mean 100 and standard deviation 30 and normal variable $\widetilde{Y}$ with mean 50 and standard deviation 10.

2.10   COPULAS

In Section 2.7, we introduced two measures of dependence of random variables: covariance and correlation. We mentioned that they are only useful as measures of linear dependence. Copulas allow for incorporating more general dependencies between random variables. Moreover, they are very useful from a modeling perspective because they allow for separating the modeling of the dependence structure from the modeling of the marginal distributions of the individual random variables. In finance, copulas are widely used in asset allocation, default risk modeling, credit scoring, derivative pricing, and risk management.[12] When working with data, one can always calculate the empirical copula of a data set and plot it. Such plots are useful because they may reveal asymmetric or nonlinear patterns that cannot be captured with correlation coefficients.

The word "copula" comes from Latin for a "link" or a "bond," and was first used by Sklar (1959), who proved that a collection of marginal probability distributions can be "linked" together via a copula function to form a multivariate probability distribution.

The main result in Sklar (1959) states that any multivariate cumulative[13] probability distribution function F for n random variables $\widetilde{X}_1, \ldots, \widetilde{X}_n$ can be represented with the help of a copula function C in the following form:

$$
\begin{aligned}
F(x_1, \ldots, x_n) &= P(\widetilde{X}_1 \leq x_1, \ldots, \widetilde{X}_n \leq x_n) \\
&= C(P(\widetilde{X}_1 \leq x_1), \ldots, P(\widetilde{X}_n \leq x_n)) \\
&= C(F_{\widetilde{X}_1}(x_1), \ldots, F_{\widetilde{X}_n}(x_n))
\end{aligned}
$$

where $F_{\widetilde{X}_1}(x_1), \ldots, F_{\widetilde{X}_n}(x_n)$ are the marginal cumulative distribution functions of the random variables $\widetilde{X}_1, \ldots, \widetilde{X}_n$. If each of the marginal distributions is continuous, the copula function C is unique.

On an intuitive level, the values $F_{\widetilde{X}_i}(x_i) = P(\widetilde{X}_i \leq x_i)$ all vary between 0 and 1 (because probabilities are always between 0 and 1) and can be thought of as uniformly distributed.[14] The copula function is the joint cumulative distribution function of those n uniform random variables. It captures all the

---

[12] See, for example, Embrechts, Lindskog, and McNeil (2003).

[13] See Chapter 2.5 for an introduction to cumulative probability distribution function (CDF).

[14] See Exhibit 2.12 for an illustration of what the uniform distribution looks like.

information on the dependence between the random variables $\widetilde{X}_1, \ldots, \widetilde{X}_n$, while the probability distribution of the random variables $\widetilde{X}_1, \ldots, \widetilde{X}_n$ is provided by their marginal distributions.

If the random variables $\widetilde{X}_1, \ldots, \widetilde{X}_n$ are independent, then the PDF of the copula function is a constant (it is 1), and the copula C_0 has the following simple form:

$$C_0(u_1, \ldots, u_n) = u_1 \cdot \ldots \cdot u_n$$

In the general case, the PDF of the copula can be expressed by means of the PDFs of the random variables as follows:

$$c(F_{\widetilde{X}_1}(x_1), \ldots, F_{\widetilde{X}_n}(x_n)) = \frac{f_{\widetilde{X}_1, \ldots, \widetilde{X}_n}(x_1, \ldots, x_n)}{f_{\widetilde{X}_1}(x_1) \cdot \ldots \cdot f_{\widetilde{X}_n}(x_n)}$$

The numerator in the formula above contains the joint PDF of the random variables $\widetilde{X}_1, \ldots, \widetilde{X}_n$, and the denominator contains the joint PDF of the random variables $\widetilde{X}_1, \ldots, \widetilde{X}_n$ if they were independent, in which case it would just be the product of the marginal distributions.

By fixing the marginal distributions and varying the copula function, one can obtain all possible distributions with the given marginal distributions. Consider two random variables, $\widetilde{X}_1$ and $\widetilde{X}_2$, which are both standard normal random variables. The PDFs of the multivariate distributions that can be constructed with four different types of copula functions (Normal, Clayton, Frank, and Gumbel)[15] are shown in Exhibit 2.14.[16]

Exhibit 2.15 shows the contours (projections) of the PDFs from Exhibit 2.14. It is easier to notice from the contours that the multivariate distributions constructed with different copulas are not necessarily symmetric even though the marginal distributions are. The copula density function can impose a local dependence structure on the random variables.

Exhibit 2.16 shows the PDFs for the Normal and the Clayton copulas themselves.

---

[15]The Normal (Gaussian) copula is one of the most widely used copulas. The Clayton, Frank, and Gumbel copulas are all part of the Archimedean copula family.
[16]The illustrations of copulas in this section were created with the R package `copula` by Marius Hofert, Ivan Kojadinovic, Martin Maechler, and Jun Yan. See http://cran .r-project.org/web/packages/copula/copula.pdf.

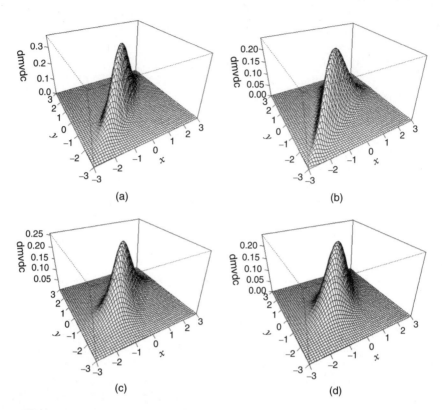

Exhibit 2.14 PDFs of multivariate probability distributions obtained from two standard normal marginals and four different types of copula functions: (a) Normal copula, (b) Clayton copula, (c) Frank copula, and (d) Gumbel copula.

2.11 FROM PROBABILITY THEORY TO STATISTICAL MEASUREMENT: PROBABILITY DISTRIBUTIONS AND SAMPLING

More often than not, modelers are faced with data from which they try to deduce how uncertainty should be modeled, rather than knowing the exact probability distribution that these data should follow. Suppose you have collected a sample of n independent observations $X_1, \ldots, X_n$. You can imagine grouping similar observations together into "bins" (the bins can be as small as a single number), and creating a histogram of observed values. This histogram will be an *empirical* probability distribution. All of the concepts explained in Sections 2.5–2.6 (for describing central tendency, spread, skew, covariability, etc.) are valid for empirical distributions derived from samples

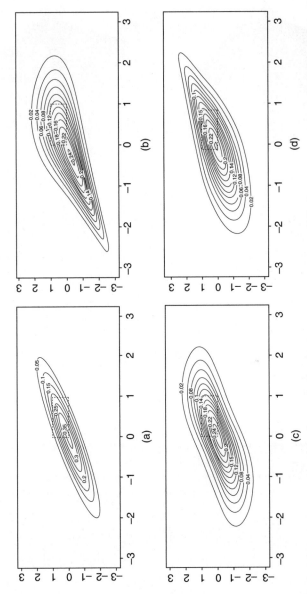

Exhibit 2.15 Contours of multivariate probability distributions obtained from two standard normal marginals and four different types of copula functions: (a) Normal copula, (b) Clayton copula, (c) Frank copula, and (d) Gumbel copula.

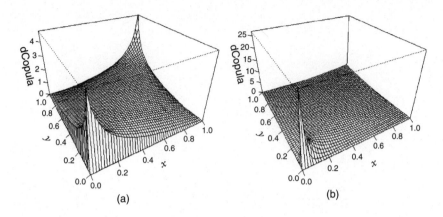

Exhibit 2.16 PDFs of (a) the Normal copula and (b) the Clayton copula.

of data. The difference is that when dealing with real-world data, we need to take into consideration the fact that there is inevitably some "noise." This noise may come from many sources, including inaccuracies in recording or handling the data, but a substantial source of imprecision in estimation is the limited number of observations. With financial data in particular, we can never observe or anticipate everything that can happen. We are not only limited in our ability to reconstruct a probability distribution from a fixed number of observations and forecasts, but also need to worry about rare events, which are difficult to observe, and thus are not necessarily a part of the sample. Hence, our estimates of the parameters of the "underlying" probability distribution for the empirical data are inherently inaccurate.

We refer to means, standard deviations, correlations, covariances, and other quantities estimated from data as *descriptive statistics* or simply *statistics*, while we refer to their "real" values (assumed to come from a specific underlying probability distribution that we cannot observe exactly because of the noise) as *parameters*. Different notations are used to differentiate between the two concepts. Parameters are usually denoted by Greek letters such as μ (for mean), σ (for standard deviation), σ^2 (for variance), and ρ (for correlation). Statistics are usually denoted by Latin letters, such as $\overline{X}$ (for sample mean), s (for sample standard deviation), s^2 (for sample variance), and r (for sample correlation).

To compute these sample statistics, we use formulas very similar to the formulas for the corresponding parameters:

Sample mean: $\overline{X} = \dfrac{1}{n} \cdot \displaystyle\sum_{i=1}^{n} X_n$

Sample variance: $s^2 = \dfrac{1}{n-1} \cdot \sum\limits_{i=1}^{n} (X_n - \overline{X})^2$

Sample standard deviation: $s = \sqrt{\dfrac{1}{n-1} \cdot \sum\limits_{i=1}^{n} (X_n - \overline{X})^2}$

Sample covariance: $\text{SCov}(\widetilde{X}, \widetilde{Y}) = \dfrac{1}{n-1} \cdot \sum\limits_{i=1}^{n} (X_n - \overline{X})(Y_n - \overline{Y})$

Sample correlation: $r(\widetilde{X}, \widetilde{Y}) = \dfrac{\text{SCoV}(\widetilde{X}, \widetilde{Y})}{s_X s_Y}$

Note, for example, that the principle behind computing the sample mean is very similar to the principle behind computing the mean of a general distribution. The mean is still a weighted average of the possible values of the random variable. It is just that our sample contains n independent observations, so the probability of each of them must be $1/n$ (otherwise, the total probability would not add up to 1). Therefore, to compute the mean, we are weighing each observation by its probability of occurrence ($1/n$), and adding up over all observations.

A substantial amount of research in statistics has been dedicated to finding ways to make the estimation of parameters through sampling accurate. For example, covariance and correlation estimates are widely used in forecasting the return on assets for portfolio management purposes, and are notoriously inaccurate because, as surprising as it seems, there are not actually enough data to estimate them reliably. (This is complicated by the fact that they vary over time.) The correlation coefficient we described in Section 2.7 is the classical Pearson correlation coefficient. Another kind of correlation coefficient is the Spearman correlation. The Spearman correlation is a *rank* correlation. In other words, instead of considering the *values* of the random variables, it computes the correlation between the ranks of the observations in a sample. The mean of the random variable is replaced by the mean of the rank. The Spearman correlation does not incorporate as much information about the data as the Pearson correlation coefficient but tends to be more stable than the Pearson correlation when there is noise in the data.

Additionally, inferential statistics is concerned with evaluating the degree of accuracy of sample estimates. Some powerful and far-reaching concepts in this context include the Central Limit Theorem, confidence intervals estimates, bootstrapping, and hypothesis testing. These concepts are also widely used in simulation modeling for risk management purposes.

2.11.1   Central Limit Theorem

Suppose that we have a sample of n independent observations $X_1, \ldots, X_n$ drawn from the same underlying distribution. (The shorthand for this statement is that $X_1, \ldots, X_n$ are IID, that is, independent and identically distributed.) Let us assume that the mean of the underlying distribution is μ_X and its standard deviation is σ_X. Let S_n denote the sum of the n observations, that is,

$$S_n = \sum_{i=1}^{n} X_n$$

Then, as long as the sample size n is moderately large (greater than 30), and under some relatively mild technical conditions on the underlying probability distribution, the distribution of the sum S_n is normal with mean equal to $\mu_S = n \cdot \mu_X$ and standard deviation $\sigma_S = \sigma_X \cdot \sqrt{n}$. This means that if we are to take many, many samples (always of size n) from this distribution, compute the sums of the n observations for each of these samples, and plot these sums, we would obtain a graph that looks very much like the normal distribution.

The expressions for the mean and the standard deviation of the sum of IID random variables in the *Central Limit Theorem* (CLT) follow easily from the rules in Section 2.8. However, the fact that the distribution of the sum approaches the normal distribution is not at all obvious. It is one of the greatest demonstrated links between probability theory and applied statistics, and is to a large extent the reason for the popularity of the normal distribution in practice. The power of the CLT is the conclusion that many real-world phenomena should be well described by the normal distribution, even if the underlying random process that generates them is unknown.

The CLT result serves as the justification for many practitioners to use the normal distribution as an approximation when they analyze the risk of their investments. The argument is that as returns accumulate over time, "things become normal." The problem arises, however, if the assumptions behind the CLT are not satisfied in practice. For example, the underlying distributions from which samples are drawn change over time depending on market conditions, and there can be correlation across returns from different time periods, so the IID assumption does not necessarily hold. The nonnormality of returns is especially pronounced in high-frequency trading, as the time intervals between trades are too short to allow for "things to approach" the normal distribution. This kind of reasoning can lead to a gross underestimation of investment risk.

2.11.2 Confidence Intervals

One of the consequences of the CLT is that it allows us to make statements about the accuracy of our estimate of the sample mean, which in our context is typically the average portfolio return. The sample mean $\overline{X}$ we introduced earlier in this section can be expressed as a sum of n IID variables, $X_1/n, \ldots, X_n/n$. Therefore, the CLT applies. Using the rules in Section 2.8, it can be shown that the sample mean $\overline{X}$ follows an approximately normal distribution with mean $\mu_{\overline{X}} = \mu_X$ and standard deviation $\sigma_{\overline{X}} = \sigma_X/\sqrt{n}$.

Therefore, we know the variability of our sample mean estimate. The standard deviation of $\overline{X}$, also called *standard error* of the estimate, is inversely proportional to the square root of the number of observations in the sample. Not surprisingly, the more observations we have, the more accurate our estimate of the true average of the distribution will be. In practice, of course, we do not know the true standard deviation σ_X (if we knew it, we would know the mean as well, so we would not be trying to estimate the mean). So, we need to make some adjustments—use the standard deviation s from the sample to approximate σ_X—and modify the estimation slightly to account for the additional inaccuracy that using a sample statistic in the formula brings.[17]

The concept of *confidence interval* (CI) estimates is to present not only a point estimate for the parameter of interest (in this case, one value for the sample mean $\overline{X}$), but also to state something about how far away this estimate will be from the true parameter (the true mean of the underlying distribution). This is achieved by stating an interval centered at $\overline{X}$ whose length depends on

1. The *variability* of the estimate (the larger the standard error of $\overline{X}$, the less likely it is that we will get the correct estimate for the true mean from the sample).
2. The degree of *confidence* we have that this interval will cover the true mean.

Typical values for the confidence level include 90%, 95%, and 99%. The exact formula for a $(100 - \alpha)\%$ CI for the sample mean $\overline{X}$ is

$$\left[\overline{X} - t_{(100 - \alpha/2), n-1} \frac{s}{\sqrt{n}}, \overline{X} + t_{(100 - \alpha/2), n-1} \frac{s}{\sqrt{n}} \right]$$

---

[17]This is where the discovery of Student's t distribution (usually referred to simply as t distribution) made a substantial contribution to modern statistics.

where $t_{(100-\alpha/2),n-1}$ is $(100-\alpha)$th percentile (the value on the x-axis) of a t distribution with $n-1$ degrees of freedom.[18] (We describe the t distribution in detail in Chapter 3.) In words, the $(100-\alpha)\%$ CI for the sample mean $\overline{X}$ states that the probability that the interval computed from the formula above covers the true mean μ is $(100-\alpha)\%$.

The t distribution becomes very close to the normal distribution as the parameter for degrees of freedom (which here equals $n-1$) becomes large. In the context of simulation, where sample sizes would generally be large, replacing the value of the percentile from the t distribution with the value of the percentile from the normal distribution will make no difference for all practical purposes. However, in the context of assessing probability distributions that can fit observed asset returns, the t distribution often provides much better fit than the normal distribution.

2.11.3 Bootstrapping

The CI estimate for the mean is the confidence interval most widely used in practice. However, sometimes we need to evaluate the accuracy of other parameter estimates for one or more distributions. For example, we may be concerned about how accurate our estimates of the distribution percentiles or skewness are. (This kind of application is relevant in portfolio risk management.) Alternatively, suppose that you have computed the correlation between historical returns on Investment A and Investment B from Exhibit 2.9, and have discovered that it is 0.6. Is this a strong correlation in a statistical sense, that is, does it appear to be strong just by chance (because we picked a good sample), or can we expect that it will remain strong in other samples, given the overall variability in this sample's data?

The procedure for computing the CI estimate of the mean is representative of classical methods in statistics, which relied on mathematical formulas to describe the accuracy of a sample statistic estimate. There are some theoretical results on confidence interval estimates for distribution parameters other than the mean, but in general, the results are not as easy to summarize as the closed-form expression for the CI estimate for the mean from Section 2.11.2.

---

[18] A number of software packages have commands for computing the value of t, including Excel and R. For example, in R (and most statistical packages) one would use a command of the kind tinv($100-\alpha/2$, degrees of freedom). Excel has a similar command (= TINV(α,degrees of freedom)), but it is a bit inconsistent. It takes in as an argument α, not $100-\alpha/2$, to compute the $(100-\alpha/2)$th percentile of the t distribution.

Bootstrapping[19] is a statistical technique that is useful in such situations. It involves drawing multiple samples (say, k samples) of the same size at random from the observations in the original sample of n observations. Each of the k samples is drawn with replacement—that is, every time an observation is drawn, it is placed back in the original sample, and is eligible to be drawn again, in the same sample or in future samples.

After drawing k samples from the original sample, the statistic corresponding to the parameter we are interested in estimating (whether it is percentile, skewness, correlation, or a general function of the random variable) is computed for each of the k samples. The so-obtained k values for the sample statistic are used to form an approximation for the parameter's *sampling distribution*. This sampling distribution can be used, for example, to determine what values of the sample statistic are most likely to occur, what is the variability of the estimate, and what the 5th and the 95th percentile of the approximate sampling distribution are. These percentiles provide an approximation for the confidence interval for the true parameter we are trying to estimate.

At first glance, this technique appears pointless. Why do we not collect k more samples instead of reusing the same data set k times? The reason is that it is expensive to collect data, and that sometimes additional data collection is not an option, especially with financial data.

Bootstrapping is used not only for evaluating the accuracy in the estimate of a probability distribution parameter, but also as a simple method for generating forecasts for uncertain quantities based on a set of historical observations for risk management purposes. The concept of simulation is necessary to understand how the bootstrap method is actually applied, as the random draws from the original sample need to be generated with a random number generator.

2.11.4   Hypothesis Testing

Hypothesis testing is a fundamental concept in statistics. The procedure is as follows. We start out by stating a hypothesis (the *null hypothesis*) about a parameter of the distribution that is of interest. For example, we claim that the skew of the distribution for the returns of the S&P 500 index is 0. (While often unjustified, making assumptions like these substantially simplifies risk measurement but could lead to the construction of a portfolio

---

[19]There is a methodology commonly used in bond analysis to derive the term structure of interest rates that is also referred to as *bootstrapping*. The statistical concept of bootstrapping described in this chapter has nothing to do with that methodology.

that has greater exposure to the market than was expected.) Then we take a sample of S&P 500 returns, and estimate the skew for that sample. Suppose we get a skew of -0.11. The statistical hypothesis testing methodology allows us to test whether the value obtained from the sample (-0.11) is sufficiently "close" to the hypothesized value (0) to conclude that in fact, the "real" skew could indeed be 0, and that the difference is only a consequence of sampling error.

To test whether the difference between the hypothesized and the observed value is *statistically significant*, that is, large enough to be considered a reason to reject the null hypothesis, we would compute a quantity called a *test statistic*, which is a function of observed and hypothesized parameters. In some cases, this test statistic follows a known probability distribution. For example, if we are testing a hypothesis about the sample mean, then the test statistic is called the *t-statistic*, because it follows a t distribution with degrees of freedom equal to the sample size minus one. Knowing that the test statistic follows a specific distribution, we can see whether the test statistic obtained from the sample is "very far" from the center of the distribution, which tells us whether the sample estimate we obtained would be a rare occurrence if the hypothesized value were true.

There are different ways to measure the rarity of the observed statistic. Modern statistical software packages typically report a *p-value*, which is the probability that, if the null hypothesis were true, we would get a more extreme sample statistic than the one we observed. If the p-value is "small" (the actual cutoff is arbitrary, but the values typically used are 1%, 5%, or 10%), then we would reject the null hypothesis. This is because a small p-value means that there is very small probability that we would have obtained a sample statistic as extreme as the one we obtained if the hypothesis were true, that is, that the current test statistic is in the tails of the distribution.

The hypothesis tests we described so far are called *one-sample hypothesis tests* because they interpret the information only for one sample. There are *two-sample hypothesis tests* that compare observed statistics from two samples with the goal of testing whether two populations are statistically different. They could be used, for example, to compare whether the returns on one investment have been statistically better on average than the returns on another investment.

Finally, more sophisticated hypothesis tests are used in the background for a number of important applications in financial modeling. Multivariate regression analysis, which we discuss in the context of factor model estimation later in the book, uses hypothesis testing to determine whether a forecasting model is statistically significant. Goodness-of-fit tests, which are used in the context of fitting probability distributions to observed data, use statistical hypothesis testing to determine whether the observed data are statistically "significantly close" to a hypothesized probability distribution. See also the discussion on selecting probability distributions as inputs for simulation models in Chapter 5.

Summary

- Uncertainty can be represented by random variables with associated probability distributions.
- Probability distributions can be viewed as "listings" of all possible values that can happen and the corresponding probability of occurrence, and are conveniently represented in graphs (histograms and bar charts).
- Probability distributions can be discrete or continuous. Discrete distributions are defined over a countable number of values, whereas continuous distributions are defined over a range.
- Discrete distributions are described by probability mass functions (PMFs), whereas continuous distributions are described by probability density functions (PDFs).
- A continuous random variable can take an infinite number of values, and the probability of each individual value is 0. In the context of continuous distributions, we replace the concept of probability of a value with the concept of probability of an interval of values, and the probability is the area under the PDF.
- Probability distributions can be summarized in terms of central tendency (mean, median, and mode), variability (standard deviation, variance, coefficient of variance [CV], range, percentile, etc.), skewness, and kurtosis.
- Value-at-risk (VaR) and conditional value-at-risk (CVaR) are widely used portfolio risk measures related to the percentiles of the portfolio loss distribution.
- The mean, variance, skew, and kurtosis of a probability distribution are related to the first, second, third, and fourth moment of the distribution. The moments of a probability distribution can be computed from its moment generating function. Inversely, if the moments of a probability distribution are known, most generally the distribution can be uniquely identified. However, sometimes the moments do not exist.
- Covariance and correlation are measures of average codependence of two random variables. Copulas enable incorporating dependencies between random variables even if the relationship between the random variables is not linear.
- Empirical distributions are derived from data. All summary measures for probability distributions apply to empirical distributions.

- The Central Limit Theorem states that the probability distribution of a sum of n independent and identically distributed observations tends to a normal distribution with a specific mean and standard deviation.
- Confidence intervals allow us to state both our estimate of a parameter of an unknown probability distribution and our confidence in that estimate.
- Bootstrapping is a statistical technique for evaluating the accuracy of sample statistics based on one sample of observations. It involves drawing multiple samples from the original sample, calculating the sample statistic in each of them, and analyzing the resulting distribution of the sample statistic. Bootstrapping can also be used as a simple way to generate future forecasts for uncertain quantities based on a sample of past observations.
- Hypothesis testing is a statistical methodology for evaluating whether a statistic observed in a sample is significantly different from the expected value of a parameter of interest. It is used in many applications, including goodness-of-fit tests, multivariate regression analysis, and comparisons of two populations.

CHAPTER 3

Important Probability Distributions

To model financial market risks, one needs to (1) understand how financial data behave and (2) select probability distributions that incorporate the important characteristics of the data. Chapter 2 reviewed useful statistical terminology, described the normal distribution, and introduced the concept of risk measures. This chapter presents further examples of probability distributions and continues the discussion with an emphasis on their use for simulation and risk management.

The normal distribution was and continues to be one of the most widely used distributions for modeling financial risk. It implicitly underlies Modern Portfolio Theory (MPT), which we discuss in Chapter 8, and continues to be used even in the calculation of tail-risk measures such as value-at-risk and conditional value-at-risk.[1] However, it has been known for a long time (at least as far back as the influential papers of Mandelbrot (1963) and Fama (1963)) that extreme events in the financial markets happen a lot more frequently than the assumption that financial returns follow a normal distribution would lead one to believe. Observed characteristics of financial data include:[2]

- The empirical distributions of financial returns are leptokurtic,[3] or in other words they have "fat tails"[4] compared to the tails of the normal distribution.
- The empirical distribution of returns is left-skewed, that is, large negative returns are possible.

---

[1] See Chapter 2.
[2] See Mandelbrot (1963), Campbell, Lo, and MacKinlay (1997), and McNeil, Frey, and Embrechts (2005).
[3] See Chapter 2.
[4] "Fat tails" are also commonly referred to as "heavy tails." However, there is a technical difference between the two terms that we will not discuss here. A fat-tailed distribution is a special case of a heavy-tail distribution.

- There is a difference in the behavior of short-term returns such as daily returns, and longer-term returns such as monthly or quarterly returns.
- Extreme returns tend happen in clusters, that is, closely in time. (This is referred to as *volatility clustering*.)

These observed characteristics are referred to as stylized facts[5] about financial markets.

To model the characteristics of observed return distributions, approaches generally fall into one of three categories:

1. Assume that returns have stable distributions of infinite variance.
2. Assume that returns have distributions that are more fat-tailed and/or skewed than the normal distribution.
3. Assume that the distributions of returns are normal at each instant of time, but look fat tailed due to fluctuations in the variance (volatility) of these distributions. Incorporate the fluctuations in the volatility using ARCH/GARCH or other models.

This chapter explains the concepts behind the first two approaches in more detail. The third approach, and specifically ARCH/GARCH models, is explained in Chapter 4.

We begin by listing examples of some discrete and continuous probability distributions useful for simulation and risk modeling, their probability mass functions (PMFs) or probability density functions (PDFs), and select summary measures.[6] We then summarize important "superclasses" or "families" of probability distributions, which are used in approaches 1 and 2 above for modeling returns, such as the stable Paretian distributions and the generalized lambda distribution. As a comparison, we also cover the elliptical distributions family, of which the normal distribution is a member and which has an important role in Modern Portfolio Theory.[7]

Sometimes, portfolio risk management focuses only on tail (extreme) risks. This is especially relevant in cases when one tries to estimate possible

---

[5]The term *stylized facts* is used to describe well-known characteristics or empirical irregularities of financial return series. For example, as we mentioned, daily stock index returns display volatility clustering, fat tails, and almost no autocorrelation. These specific three stylized facts can be explained with the ARCH family of models, which we discuss in Chapter 4. Additional stylized facts include leverage effect and long memory effect.

[6]For a more detailed overview of some of these probability distributions, see, for example, Forbes, Evans, Hastings, and Peacock (2011).

[7]We discuss Modern Portfolio Theory in Chapter 8.

losses that could happen with very small probability, such as 1 in 1,000 occurrences, which translates into the portfolio's 99.9% VaR (see Chapter 2). In such cases, one can use theoretical results to analyze the tail of the distribution of returns. Analysis of the tail distribution involves understanding the distribution of the maxima as well as the distribution of the size of the excess over a given threshold. These two lines of analysis are referred to as *extreme value theory*. Despite the fact that the most important developments in extreme value theory can be traced as far back as the 1920s, extreme value theory has only gained popularity among finance practitioners in the past 10 to 15 years, likely because of the increased frequency of financial crises. We discuss the family of extreme value distributions as well as extreme value theory in the last section of this chapter.

3.1 EXAMPLES OF PROBABILITY DISTRIBUTIONS

In Chapter 2, we introduced two discrete distributions, the binomial distribution and the Bernoulli distribution. We also introduced one continuous distribution (the normal distribution) and mentioned the uniform distribution and the *t* distribution. In this section, we give examples of two other discrete distributions, the discrete uniform and the Poisson distribution, as well as multiple continuous distributions, including

- Continuous uniform distribution
- Student's *t* distribution
- Lognormal distribution
- Gamma distribution
- Exponential distribution
- Chi-square distribution
- Gamma distribution
- Beta distribution

3.1.1 Notation Used in Describing Continuous Probability Distributions

When we describe continuous probability distributions, we will encounter the following notation:

The gamma function is defined as

$$\Gamma(y) = \int_0^\infty t^{y-1} e^{-t} \, dt$$

The beta function, also called the *Euler integral* of the first kind, is defined as

$$B(x, y) = \int_0^1 t^{x-1}(1 - t)^{y-1} \, dt$$

Most continuous probability distributions are described by three types of parameters that have geometrical meaning: a *location* parameter, which can be the mean or some other relevant point on the horizontal axis; a *scale* parameter, which generally describes the "spread" of the distribution; and a *shape* parameter that determines the form of the distribution.

We will generally denote these three parameters with the Greek letters δ, θ, and ξ, respectively. However, some distributions have fewer than three parameters, some have more, and for some widely used distributions the conventions for naming these parameters are different, so we will use the conventions. For example, the normal distribution is defined in its entirety by only two parameters—a location and a scale parameter—which enter the formula for the normal PDF (see Chapter 2). The location parameter is actually μ, the mean of a normal distribution, and the scale parameter is σ, the standard deviation of the normal distribution. At the same time, some distributions, such as the beta distribution, have multiple shape parameters. In the case of the beta distribution, the shape parameters are often denoted by α and β rather than ξ.

We show illustrations of the PMFs/PDFs of the distributions in order to provide intuition for the circumstances under which such distributions can be a good fit for financial data.

3.1.2 Discrete and Continuous Uniform Distributions

The *uniform distribution* is a fundamental building block for modeling with probability distributions. It is also one of the easiest distributions to understand on an intuitive level.

The *discrete uniform distribution* represents a situation in which a random variable can take a prespecified number of discrete values, and each value has an equal chance of occurring. A simple example of such distribution is a roll of a fair die: there are six possible outcomes, 1, 2, 3, 4, 5, 6, and each of them happens with the same probability (see Exhibit 3.1).

It can be seen that if the random variable can take N values and if the total probability needs to be 1, then the probability of each individual value should be $1/N$. Therefore, the PMF of the discrete uniform distribution is

$$P(\widetilde{X} = x) = \frac{1}{N}$$

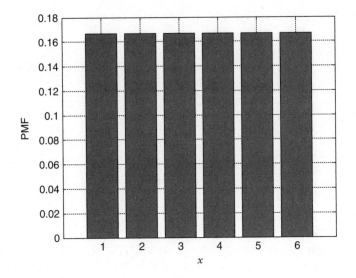

Exhibit 3.1 PMF of a discrete uniform distribution.

The *continuous uniform distribution* represents a situation in which a random variable can take a continuum of values on a *range* (say, between two numbers a and b) with equal probability. This distribution presents a simple example of why the value of the PDF $f(x)$ at a point x should not be treated as the probability of x. Since the total probability mass under the PDF needs to be 1, the height of the line on the graph of the uniform distribution (i.e., the value of the PDF at each point on the range $[a,b]$) is $1/(b-a)$. This number can be greater than 1, depending on the values of a and b, which is not allowed for a probability. For example, if a is 3 and b is 3.5, then $(b-a) = 0.5$, and the PDF $f(x)$ at any point x between 3 and 3.5 is $1/0.5 = 2$ (see Exhibit 3.2(a)).

To summarize, the PDF of the continuous uniform distribution is:

$$f(x) = \frac{1}{b-a}, \quad a \leq x \leq b$$

While uniform distributions are not particularly applicable to modeling financial returns, they represent a fundamental probability distribution type that is useful for other applications in finance. Specifically, the "standard" continuous uniform distribution on the interval $[0,1]$ (i.e., when $a = 0$ and $b = 1$) plays a very important role in simulation, and simulation is an important tool for portfolio risk estimation. We discuss simulation in Chapter 5.

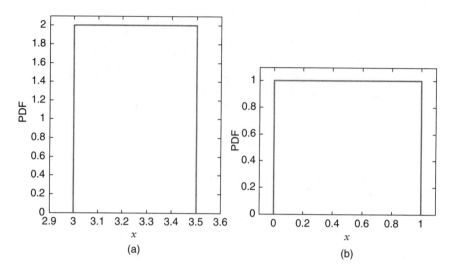

Exhibit 3.2   (a) Continuous uniform distribution on [3,3.5] and (b) Standard continuous uniform distribution.

3.1.3   Student's *t* Distribution

The *Student's t distribution* (or simply the *t* distribution) looks very much like the normal distribution in shape, but the weight in the tails is determined by a parameter k, which is associated with degrees of freedom in statistics.[8] Examples of *t* distributions for different values of k are shown in Exhibit 3.3. For large values of the parameter k, the *t* distribution approaches the normal distribution with the same mean and variance. However, the *t* distribution has fatter tails than the normal distribution for small values of k. For this reason, it is often used to model financial data.[9] The PDF for the *t* distribution is

$$f(x) = \frac{\Gamma\left(\frac{k+1}{2}\right)}{\Gamma\left(\frac{k}{2}\right)} \frac{1}{\sqrt{k\pi}} \frac{1}{\left(1 + \frac{x^2}{k}\right)^{\frac{k+1}{2}}}$$

where $\Gamma(.)$ is the gamma function defined in Section 3.1.1.

---

[8]W. S. Gossett stumbled across this distribution while working for the Guinness brewery in Dublin. At the time, he was not allowed to publish his discovery under his own name, so he used the pseudonym *Student*, and this is how the distribution is known today.
[9]Blattberg and Gonedes (1974) were among the first to propose this distribution for describing returns.

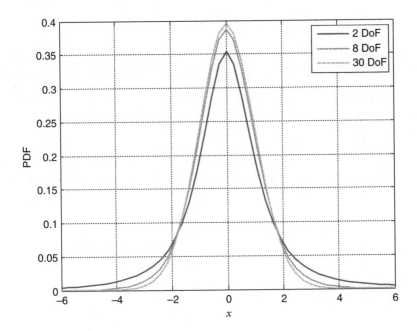

Exhibit 3.3 Examples of PDFs of t distributions for different degrees of freedom.

In addition to its applications for modeling financial returns, the t distribution also arises in important applications in statistics, in particular, in calculating confidence interval estimates for the true mean of a distribution and hypothesis testing (see Chapter 2). Since simulation bears strong resemblance to statistical sampling, we will encounter the t distribution when we discuss simulation in Chapter 5.

3.1.4 Lognormal Distribution

The *lognormal distribution* has one of the most prominent uses in finance. It arises when values for the random variable cannot be negative, and tends to be asymmetrically distributed, which has been observed for stock prices and prices for other asset classes (see Exhibit 3.4). The PDF of the lognormal distribution is

$$f(x) = \frac{1}{x\sigma\sqrt{2\pi}} e^{-\frac{(\ln(x)-\mu)^2}{2\sigma^2}}, \quad x > 0$$

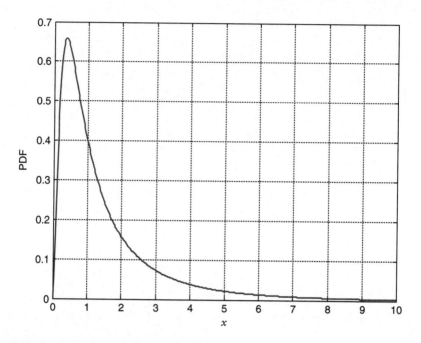

Exhibit 3.4 PDF of a lognormal distribution.

Here μ is the location parameter and σ is a scale parameter, but they are not the mean and the standard deviation of the lognormal distribution. They can in fact be thought of as the mean and the standard deviation of a normal random variable related to the lognormal random variable in a very specific way. (Note the resemblance to the PDF of the normal distribution from Chapter 2.4 and Exhibit 2.6.) Specifically, if $\widetilde{Y}$ is a normal random variable with mean μ and standard deviation σ, then the random variable $\widetilde{X} = e^{\widetilde{Y}}$ is lognormal with the PDF above.

In addition to its skew and its nonnegativity, another reason why the lognormal random variable is so widely used in finance is because products of lognormal random variables are also lognormal random variables. This is very convenient for building models of asset price dynamics—it means that models for returns can be built without worrying about the length of the time period.

Let us explain this last point in more detail. We will show that if the price S_0 of an asset today is known and that if asset prices $S_1, \ldots, S_{t-1}$ at times $1, 2, \ldots, t-1$ are lognormal random variables, then the price S_t at time t is also a lognormal random variable.

The asset price S_t at time t can be expressed in terms of the known initial price S_0. Specifically,

$$S_t = S_0 \cdot \frac{S_1}{S_0} \cdot \ \ldots \ \cdot \frac{S_{t-1}}{S_{t-2}} \cdot \frac{S_t}{S_{t-1}}$$

Therefore,

$$S_t = S_0 \cdot (1 + \tilde{r}_0) \cdot \ \ldots \ \cdot (1 + \tilde{r}_{t-1})$$

where $\tilde{r}_t$ is the return between time period t and time period $t + 1$. (This is because $\frac{S_{j+1}}{S_j} = 1 + \frac{S_{j+1} - S_j}{S_j} = 1 + \tilde{r}_j$.)

If we take logarithms of both sides of the equation for S_t, we get

$$\ln(S_t) = \ln(S_0 \cdot (1 + \tilde{r}_0) \cdot \ \ldots \ \cdot (1 + \tilde{r}_{t-1}))$$
$$= \ln(S_0) + \ln(1 + \tilde{r}_0) + \ldots + \ln(1 + \tilde{r}_{t-1})$$

The terms of the sum above are called *log returns*:

$$\ln(1 + r_t) = \ln\left(1 + \frac{S_{t+1} - S_t}{S_t}\right)$$
$$= \ln\left(\frac{S_{t+1}}{S_t}\right)$$
$$= \ln(S_{t+1}) - \ln(S_t)$$

Based on the definition of a lognormal random variable, if financial returns $(1 + \tilde{r}_t)$ are lognormally distributed, then the logarithms of returns $\ln(1 + \tilde{r}_t)$ are normally distributed (because $(1 + \tilde{r}_t) = e^{\ln(1 + \tilde{r}_t)}$). Sums of normal random variables $(\ln(1 + \tilde{r}_0) + \ln(1 + \tilde{r}_1) + \ldots + \ln(1 + \tilde{r}_t))$ are also normal random variables, and this does not change if a known constant $(\ln(S_0))$ is added. Therefore, $\ln(S_t)$ is a normal random variable, and the price S_t is a lognormal random variable.

This situation arises when asset prices follow a so-called geometric random walk.[10]

3.1.5 Poisson Distribution

The *Poisson distribution* applies in situations in which one is concerned about the probability of having a given number of arrivals in a

---

[10]For more details, see Chapter 12 in Pachamanova and Fabozzi (2010).

prespecified time interval, where these arrivals are assumed to be independent of one another. In finance, the Poisson distribution is widely used for modeling jumps in electricity prices (referred to as "spikes," because prices typically return to their original levels), in extreme event modeling (see Section 3.3), as well as in credit risk modeling, because defaults or other credit-related events can be modeled as "arrivals" in a random process.

The Poisson PMF is given by

$$f(x) = \frac{\lambda^x}{x!}e^{-\lambda}$$

It requires an input parameter, λ, that corresponds to the average number of arrivals during the time period.

A graph of the PMF of a Poisson distribution with $\lambda = 5$ is shown in Exhibit 3.5. Imagine incorporating the distribution into a model for the process followed by the price of electricity, in which the price spikes on average five times per day because of transmission constraints or unexpected outages. The Poisson distribution in the picture is slightly skewed, which means

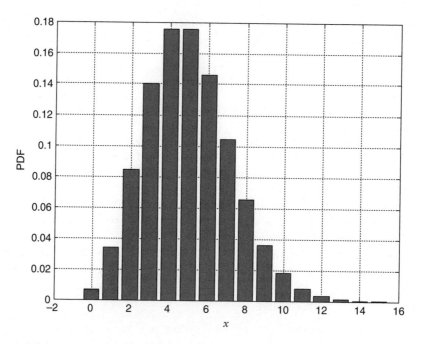

Exhibit 3.5   PMF of a Poisson distribution (with $\lambda = 5$).

that the probability that fewer than five spikes occur in a day is slightly more than the probability that more than five spikes occur in a day.

The Poisson distribution has a number of interesting properties. Notably, it looks very much like a binomial distribution if the number of trials in the binomial distribution is large, and the probability of success at every trial is adjusted so that the probability of success remains constant as the number of trials grows large. More precisely, a binomial random variable with number of trials n and probability of success λ/n at every trial approaches a Poisson distribution with parameter λ as n grows large.

Furthermore, the Poisson distribution looks like the normal distribution if the parameter λ (mean arrivals per unit time) grows large. In fact, the effect is noticeable for λ as small as 20 arrivals. As λ increases, the Poisson distribution approaches a normal distribution with mean λ and standard deviation $\sqrt{\lambda}$. These facts are often exploited in financial models for asset price dynamics.

3.1.6   Exponential Distribution

The *exponential distribution* has an interesting relationship with the Poisson distribution. While the Poisson distribution measures the number of arrivals in a given period of time (assuming arrivals are independent), the exponential distribution measures the time between independent arrivals. The PDF of the exponential distribution is

$$f(x) = \lambda e^{-\lambda x}, \quad x \geq 0$$

and its cumulative distribution function (CDF) is

$$F(x) = 1 - e^{-\lambda x}, \quad x \geq 0$$

The parameter λ is the same parameter we saw in the definition of the Poisson distribution. Specifically, if we expect an average of λ arrivals during a unit time period, then the average time we would expect between arrivals is $1/\lambda$ (which happens to be the mean of the exponential distribution). A picture of the exponential distribution is shown in Exhibit 3.6. Note that if we slice the distribution vertically and consider the piece of the curve to the right of the value at which we sliced, that piece has the same shape as

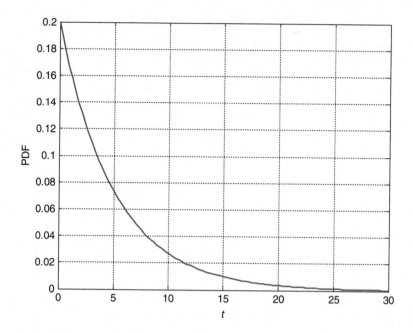

Exhibit 3.6 PDF of an exponential distribution (with $\lambda = 0.2$).

the original distribution. This is the so-called *memoryless property* of the exponential distribution, which, counterintuitively, means that the distribution of the time until the next arrival does not depend on how long you have waited. Specifically, if 30 minutes have already elapsed, the probability that you will see an arrival after 10 minutes is the same as the probability you would have seen an arrival after 10 minutes at the beginning of the first time period of 30 minutes.

Similarly to the Poisson distribution, the exponential distribution is used in credit risk modeling and in modeling of high-frequency arrival times between orders in financial markets (referred to as *trade duration*).

3.1.7 Chi-Square Distribution

The *chi-square distribution* (often denoted χ^2 *distribution*) is used predominantly in hypothesis testing in statistics. The reason we list it here, given our focus on financial applications, is because it is the basis for goodness-of-fit tests that decide whether a particular distribution is appropriate for modeling an observed set of data. The sum of k independent squared

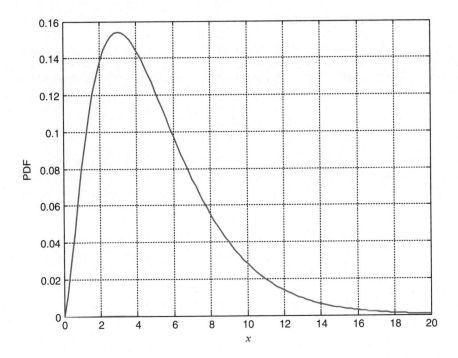

Exhibit 3.7 PDF of a chi-square distribution (with 5 degrees of freedom).

normal random variables follows a chi-square distribution with k degrees of freedom.[11]

The PDF of the chi-square distribution is given by

$$f(x) = \frac{2^{-k/2}}{\Gamma(k/2)} x^{k/2-1} e^{-x/2}, \quad x > 0$$

where Γ is the gamma function, as defined earlier in this section, and k is the degrees of freedom. A picture of the distribution is shown in Exhibit 3.7.

---

[11]The squared random variables arise when computing squared differences between observed values (which vary because the sample is random) and expected values. Chi-square goodness-of-fit tests consider the sum of the total squared differences between the observed frequencies of values in a sample and the expected frequencies if the sample came from a particular distribution. Whether the difference between what was observed and what was expected is statistically "large" depends on the value of the difference relative to the critical value of the chi-square test statistic, which is computed from the chi-square distribution. See the brief introduction to hypothesis testing in Chapter 2.

3.1.8 Gamma Distribution

The gamma distribution is sometimes used for modeling skewness in financial returns. Outside the financial context, it is used for modeling lifetimes in reliability applications. The gamma distribution has the following PDF:

$$f(x) = \frac{x^{k-1}e^{-\frac{x}{\theta}}}{\theta^k \Gamma(k)}$$

for $x > 0$ and $k,\ \theta > 0$. The graph of the PDF is shown in Exhibit 3.8. The exponential and the chi-square distributions are a special case of the gamma distribution.

3.1.9 Beta Distribution

The *beta distribution* is very flexible in terms of shape, and is useful for representing a variety of models of uncertainty. In contrast to other distributions that have a distinctive skew, the beta distribution is defined by two parameters, α and β, which define the shape and the skew of the distribution. The precise formula for the PDF is

$$f(x) = \frac{x^{\alpha-1}(1-x)^{\beta-1}}{\frac{\Gamma(\alpha)\Gamma(\beta)}{\Gamma(\alpha+\beta)}}, \quad x > 0,\ \alpha > 0,\ \beta > 0$$

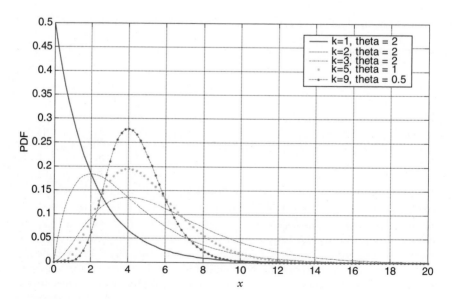

Exhibit 3.8 The PDF of the gamma distribution for different values of the parameters k and θ.

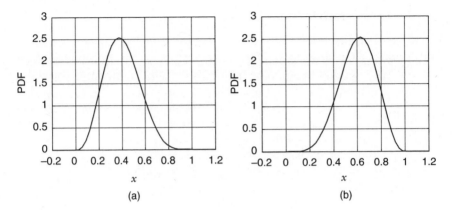

Exhibit 3.9 PDFs of examples of beta distributions with values for shape parameters equal to (a) 4 and 6 and (b) 6 and 4.

Equivalently, the beta distribution PDF can be expressed through the beta function B(x,y) introduced in Section 3.1.1:

$$f(x) = \frac{1}{B(\alpha, \beta)} x^{\alpha-1}(1 - x)^{\beta-1}, \quad x > 0, \quad \alpha > 0, \quad \beta > 0$$

The beta function is a normalization constant to make sure that the total probability adds up to one.

Exhibit 3.9 illustrates the shape of the beta distribution with parameter values equal to 4 and 6 (panel a), and 6 and 4 (panel b). One can observe that the skew of the beta distribution changes depending on the relative magnitudes of α and β.

3.2 MODELING FINANCIAL RETURN DISTRIBUTIONS

After presenting some examples of useful probability distributions, we generalize the discussion by considering "superclasses" or "families" of probability distributions useful for incorporating the observed characteristics of financial return distributions. A *superclass* or a *family* of distributions contains different kinds of distributions that can be described through a single form. These distributions do not necessarily look "similar" in shape. For example, the exponential family of distributions contains the normal, exponential, chi-square, beta, Bernoulli, and Poisson distributions as special cases. As we have seen from the graphs in this chapter, their shapes are very different. At the same time, probability distributions with similar shapes may not belong to the same family. For example, even though the normal distribution (Exhibit 2.6) belongs to the exponential family of distributions, the *t* distribution (Exhibit 3.3) does not.

In this section, we review the following three important families of distributions:

1. *Elliptical* distributions can be thought of as generalizations of the multivariate normal distribution. They are the only family of distributions for which correlation and covariance are the correct ways to measure dependence, and historically have had an important place in the context of portfolio allocation and risk management.

2. *Stable Paretian distributions* were suggested by Mandelbrot (1963) as a way to address the fat tails in observed financial data.

3. The *generalized lambda distribution family* allows modeling a wide range of distribution shapes, and because it uses a quantile function in its definition, it makes the calculation of tail portfolio risk measures such as VaR and CVaR easy once the distribution has been fitted to observed returns.

While these families of distributions cover a wide range of useful probability distributions used for risk management, the list is by no means exhaustive. Other interesting families of distributions, for example, include the *generalized beta distribution* and the *exponential generalized beta distribution*. The former distribution family is used for modeling stock returns distributions, whereas the latter distribution family is used in time series models and GARCH/ARCH type models.[12] Because the *t* distribution is often used to model financial returns, the *generalized hyperbolic distribution* family may be of interest as well. It includes the *t* distribution as a special case, and is particularly useful for modeling return distributions with heavy tails, that is, when the observed behavior of returns shows that extreme observations in the tails are much more likely than in the case of a normal distribution.

3.2.1 Elliptical Distributions

Elliptical distributions are a special class of multivariate symmetric distributions and have a number of desirable properties.[13] Examples of elliptically distributed random variables include all multivariate normal distributions, multivariate *t*-distributions, logistic distributions, Laplace distributions, and some of the multivariate stable distributions described in Section 3.2.2. A vector $\tilde{x}$ of random variables with PDF f is elliptically distributed if the set of all points where the density function f admits a certain value c has the form of an ellipse. (In mathematical jargon, the *level curves* look like ellipses.) In the special case when the vector $\tilde{x}$ is two-dimensional, the PDF

---

[12]See Chapter 4 for a brief introduction to GARCH/ARCH type models.
[13]See Chapter 2 for a definition of multivariate distribution.

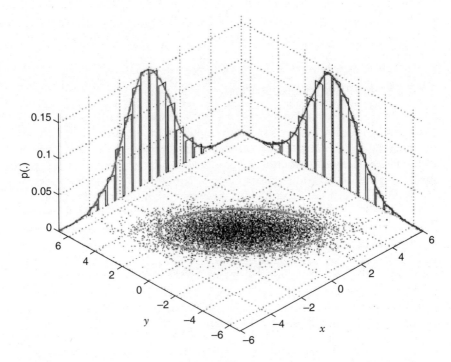

Exhibit 3.10 An example of a bivariate elliptic distribution: simulated values for a bivariate normal distribution (in the scatterplot), a level curve at 0 (appears as an ellipse), and the marginal distributions for the two random variables (in this example, standard normal distributions).

level curves for the resulting bivariate elliptic distribution can be visualized easily (Exhibit 3.10).

The PDF of elliptical distributions is described by a triple (μ, Σ, g), where μ and Σ are parameters that play a similar role to the mean and the covariance matrix in the case of multivariate normal distributions, and g is called the *density generator*. The PDF is given by

$$f(x) = \frac{c}{\sqrt{|\Sigma|}} g((x - \mu)' \Sigma^{-1} (x - \mu))$$

In the formula above, c is a normalizing constant, x and μ are vectors, and Σ is a matrix (Σ^{-1} is its inverse; see the Appendix). A special case, the multivariate normal distribution, has the PDF

$$f(x) = \frac{1}{\sqrt{(2\pi)^N |\Sigma|}} e^{-\frac{1}{2}(x-\mu)' \Sigma^{-1}(x-\mu)}$$

where N is the dimension of the random vector x. One can observe that in this case, $c = \frac{1}{\sqrt{(2\pi)^N}}$ and g is the exponential function e with a specific parameter.

3.2.2 Stable Paretian Distributions

After Mandelbrot (1963) pointed out that financial returns tend to exhibit "fat tails," studies of market returns attempted to capture the excess kurtosis by modeling financial returns as members of the family of stable Paretian (or stable Pareto-Lévy) distributions. The normal distribution is a member of this family but all remaining probability distributions in the stable Paretian family have fatter tails than the normal distribution. In fact, their tails are so fat that all nonnormal stable Paretian distributions have infinite variances and infinite higher moments, which means that their variance, skewness, and kurtosis are not defined.

Members of the Paretian distribution can all be characterized through an explicit form of their characteristic function;[14] however, only three members of the stable Paretian distribution family have closed-form PDFs: the normal, Cauchy, and Lévy distributions.

The Cauchy distribution's PDF is given by

$$f(x) = \frac{1}{\pi\theta \left(1 + \left(\frac{x-\delta}{\theta} \right)^2 \right)}$$

where δ is the location parameter (shows where the peak of the distribution is) and θ is the scale parameter. A Cauchy distribution is followed, for instance, by the random variable formed as a ratio of two independent normal random variables. An example of a Cauchy distribution, the standard Cauchy distribution with $\delta = 0$ and $\theta = 1$, is given in Exhibit 3.11. The standard Cauchy distribution is actually a special case of the t distribution (Section 3.1.3) with parameter $k = 1$. The standard normal distribution is superimposed to illustrate the lower peak and the fatter tails of the Cauchy distribution relative to the normal distribution.

The Lévy distribution's PDF is given by

$$f(x) = \sqrt{\frac{\theta}{2\pi}} \frac{e^{-\frac{\theta}{2(x-\delta)}}}{(x-\delta)^{3/2}}$$

---

[14]Working with characteristic functions is beyond the scope of this book; see the original derivation by Lévy (1924) or Rachev and Mittnik (2000).

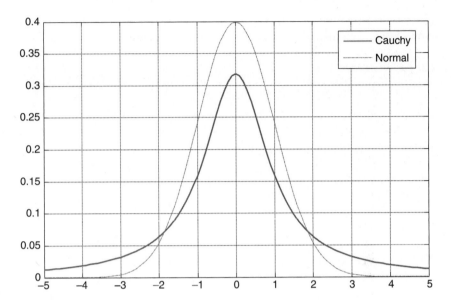

Exhibit 3.11 Comparison of the PDF of the standard Cauchy distribution and the PDF of the standard normal distribution.

Here again δ is the location parameter and θ is the scale parameter. The Lévy distribution is right-skewed and its right "wing" exhibits heavy-tail behavior.

A differentiating property of the stable family of distributions is that sums of stable random variables are also stable random variables. This makes it convenient for modeling financial returns (specifically, log-returns) because one can create the same models for daily, monthly, or annual returns, and not worry about the unit of time. However, there are also problems with using this assumption in practice. For example, it implies that long-term returns behave in the same way as short-term returns. This is not what has been observed in practice; specifically, long-term returns tend to follow distributions that are much closer to normal than short-term returns. Another reason why the use of stable Paretian distributions in practice has been problematic is that so much of finance theory and applications depend on the assumption of finite variances and higher moments. For example, Modern Portfolio Theory, which we discuss in Chapter 8, assumes that asset returns have finite variances, leading to the principle of diversification. Most practitioners agree that at least some level of portfolio diversification is useful; however, the assumption that financial returns have infinite variances would invalidate this principle because adding multiple assets to a portfolio would increase its risk infinitely. Dealing with distributions with infinite higher moments can thus be difficult in practice.

Studies of stable Paretian distributions and how they apply to financial returns were very popular in the 1960s and 1970s,[15] and enjoyed a revival in the 1990s and 2000s. A good reference on the subject is the book by Rachev and Mittnik (2000), which provides some powerful arguments for including stable distributions in one's financial risk modeling toolbox.

3.2.3 Generalized Lambda Distribution

The four-parameter generalized lambda distribution (GLD) family is an extension of the lambda distribution originally proposed by Tukey (1962). The lambda distribution can be expressed through the inverse of the cumulative distribution function F (that is, through its quantile function Q):

$$
F^{-1}(p) = Q(p) = \begin{cases} \frac{p^{\lambda} - (1-p)^{\lambda}}{\lambda}, & \lambda \neq 0 \\ \frac{\log p}{1-p}, & \lambda = 0 \end{cases}
$$

where p is a probability; $p \in [0,1]$. There is no simple closed form for the PDF and the CDF for almost any values of λ, so the PDF and the CDF typically need to be calculated numerically.

The Tukey lambda distribution is rarely fitted directly to data. Instead, it is used to estimate what kind of distribution may fit the data best. (This is somewhat restricted to only symmetric distributions because the Tukey lambda PDF and quantile function are symmetric.) Different values of the parameter λ result in distributions that approximate well-known distributions; for example:

- $\lambda = 0.14$ approximates the normal distribution.
- $\lambda = -1$ approximates the Cauchy distribution (Section 3.2.2).
- $\lambda = 0$ corresponds exactly to the logistic distribution (not covered in this book but widely used in statistical modeling, for instance, in applications such as logistic regression).
- $\lambda = 1$ corresponds exactly to the uniform distribution (Section 3.1.2).
- $\lambda = 0.5$ is U-shaped.

---

[15] See, for example, Fama (1965), Fama and Roll (1968), and Blattberg and Gonedes (1974).

Splitting the parameter λ in the definition of the Tukey lambda distribution into several parameters results in the GLD, which can incorporate additional distribution features such as skewness. The GLD family is defined by the quantile function again:

$$F^{-1}_{GLD}(p) = Q_{GLD}(p) = \lambda_1 + \frac{p^{\lambda_3} - (1-p)^{\lambda_4}}{\lambda_2}$$

where λ_1 is a location parameter, λ_2 is a scale parameter, and λ_3 and λ_4 are shape parameters related to the strengths of the lower and upper tails, respectively. Not all values for λ_1, λ_2, λ_3, and λ_4 result in valid probability distributions; one can identify six regions for the parameters over which a valid probability distribution is defined. When $\lambda_1 = 0$ and $\lambda_2 = \lambda_3 = \lambda_4 = \lambda$, one obtains the Tukey lambda distribution.

Ramberg and Schmeiser (1972, 1974) as well as Ramberg et al. (1979) studied the GLD and derived some of its important properties. Chalabi, Scott, and Würtz (2010) specifically study the application of the GLD as an alternative distribution for modeling financial return series, and derive expressions for special cases of the distribution, random number generation, and financial risk measures such as VaR. Calculating VaR is relatively easy to do once the GLD has been fitted because the GLD is defined through its quantile function. The only consideration to keep in mind is that the GLD is fitted to financial returns. So, the VaR and the CVaR will be evaluated in terms of the percentiles of the distributions of returns (rather than the percentiles of the loss distributions). For example, to evaluate 95% VaR, we should estimate the negative of the 5th percentile of the distribution of returns. Specifically,

$$(100 - \epsilon)\% \ \text{VaR} = -F^{-1}_{GLD}(\epsilon/100) = -\left(\lambda_1 + \frac{(\epsilon/100)^{\lambda_3} - (1 - \epsilon/100)^{\lambda_4}}{\lambda_2}\right)_1$$

For 95% VaR, we calculate

$$95\% \ \text{VaR} = -F^{-1}_{GLD}(5/100) = \lambda_1 + \frac{(0.05)^{\lambda_3} - (0.95)^{\lambda_4}}{\lambda_2}$$

The $(100 - \epsilon)\%$ CVaR will be the negative of the average return from negative infinity to the ϵth percentile of the distribution of returns. It can be calculated to be

$$(100 - \epsilon)\% \ \text{CVaR} = -\left(\lambda_1\left(\frac{\epsilon}{100}\right) + \frac{1}{\lambda_2(\lambda_3 + 1)}\left(\frac{\epsilon}{100}\right)^{\lambda_3+1}\right.$$

$$\left. + \frac{1}{\lambda_2(\lambda_4 + 1)}\left[\left(1 - \frac{\epsilon}{100}\right)^{\lambda_4-1} - 1\right]\right)$$

3.3 MODELING TAILS OF FINANCIAL RETURN DISTRIBUTIONS

As we mentioned in the introduction to this chapter, modeling the tail of the distribution of financial returns is often of greater concern for the purposes of risk modeling than modeling the entire distribution. *Extreme Value Theory* (EVT) is a branch of statistics that provides the tools for doing so. EVT is concerned with studying events that happen far from the "middle" of the distribution of outcomes. In financial risk management, EVT is used in two particular applications:[16]

1. The asymptotic probability distribution of extremes (maxima or minima) is modeled and, amazingly, for a large class of probability distributions it is approximated by one of three specific types of extreme value distributions.
2. The probability distribution of the excess over a given threshold is modeled.

In this section, we introduce the two families of probability distributions that have a critical role in EVT, specifically, the generalized extreme value distribution family and the generalized Pareto distribution family. According to the *Extreme Value Theorem* (also called the Fisher–Tippett–Gnedenko Theorem), the generalized extreme value distribution family is the only possible limit distribution of the properly renormalized maximum of a sample of independent and identically distributed (i.i.d.) random variables, and is used for modeling extreme events (the first application above). The generalized Pareto distribution is used in the second application above. We then explain how these distributions are estimated and used for financial risk modeling in the context of estimating VaR and other risk measures.

3.3.1 Generalized Extreme Value Distribution

The generalized extreme value (GEV) distribution is a standard form that combines three distributions: Gumbel, Fréchet, and Weibull. These three distributions are also known as type I, II, and III extreme value distributions, respectively. The GEV distribution arises in the modeling of the maximum of a series of i.i.d. random variables, and is useful for modeling extreme risks. Specifically, according to the Extreme Value Theorem, appropriately normalized maxima of a series of i.i.d. random variables converge to one of the three types of extreme value distributions. The set of classes of distributions for which this is true is rather large—virtually all commonly encountered

---

[16]See, for example, Bensalah (2000).

continuous distributions show the required "regular" behavior for sample maxima.

The GEV distribution PDF can be written as follows:

$$
f(x) = \begin{cases}
\dfrac{1}{\theta}\left[1 + \xi\left(\frac{x-\delta}{\theta}\right)\right]^{\left(-\frac{1}{\xi}-1\right)} e^{-\left[1+\xi\left(\frac{x-\delta}{\theta}\right)\right]^{-\frac{1}{\xi}}} & \text{for } \xi > 0,\ x > \delta - \frac{\theta}{\xi} \\[2ex]
\dfrac{1}{\theta}\left[1 + \xi\left(\frac{x-\delta}{\theta}\right)\right]^{\left(-\frac{1}{\xi}-1\right)} e^{-\left[1+\xi\left(\frac{x-\delta}{\theta}\right)\right]^{-\frac{1}{\xi}}} & \text{for } \xi < 0,\ x < \delta - \frac{\theta}{\xi} \\[2ex]
\dfrac{1}{\theta} e^{-\left(\frac{x-\delta}{\theta}\right)} e^{-\left[e^{-\left(\frac{x-\delta}{\theta}\right)}\right]} & \text{for } \xi = 0,\ \text{any real } x
\end{cases}
$$

Here δ is the location parameter, θ is the scale parameter, and ξ is the shape parameter. The PDF is 0 everywhere else. The Gumbel, Fréchet, and Weibull distributions correspond to the cases $\xi = 0$, $\xi > 0$, and $\xi < 0$, respectively.

The distribution PDF for a sequence of minima can be written analogously by using $(-x)$ instead of x in the PDF above.

The CDF has the following form:

$$
F(x) = \begin{cases}
e^{-\left[1+\xi\left(\frac{x-\delta}{\theta}\right)\right]^{-\frac{1}{\xi}}} & \text{for } \xi > 0,\ x > \delta - \frac{\theta}{\xi} \\[2ex]
e^{-\left[1+\xi\left(\frac{x-\delta}{\theta}\right)\right]^{-\frac{1}{\xi}}} & \text{for } \xi < 0,\ x < \delta - \frac{\theta}{\xi} \\[2ex]
e^{-\left[e^{-\left(\frac{x-\delta}{\theta}\right)}\right]} & \text{for } \xi = 0,\ \text{any real } x
\end{cases}
$$

The three types of extreme distributions are illustrated in Exhibit 3.12.

3.3.2 Generalized Pareto Distribution

The Generalized Pareto distribution (GPD) is a family of distributions that also arise in the modeling of extremes, but apply to the modeling of the distribution of the excess over a threshold rather than the distribution of the maximum. The GPD's use is based on a theorem[17] that states that as long as a probability distribution is in a class that satisfies the conditions for convergence to a GEV distribution, the GPD is the limiting distribution of

---

[17] See Balkema and de Haan (1974) and Pickands (1975).

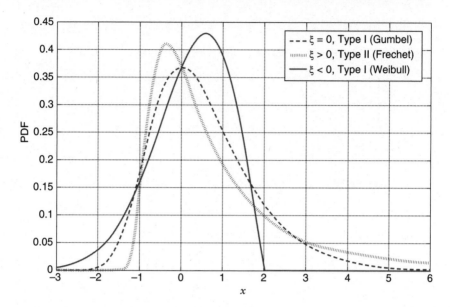

Exhibit 3.12   The PDFs of the standard forms (shape parameter $\delta = 0$, scale parameter $\theta = 1$) of the three types of extreme value distributions.

excesses over a threshold as the threshold tends to the rightmost point of the distribution.

The Generalized Pareto distribution's PDF is

$$f(x) = \frac{1}{\theta}\left[1 + \xi\left(\frac{x-\delta}{\theta}\right)\right]^{\left(-\frac{1}{\xi}-1\right)} \text{ for } \xi \geq 0, \ x \geq \delta \text{ or } \xi < 0, \delta \leq x < \delta - \frac{\theta}{\xi}$$

where, as before, δ is the location parameter, $\theta > 0$ is the scale parameter, and ξ is the shape parameter. The GPD incorporates three distributions: $\xi > 0$ and $\xi < 0$ correspond to the so-called Pareto (Type I) and Pareto (Type II) distributions, and $\xi = 0$ corresponds to the exponential distribution (Section 3.1.6).

The Generalized Pareto distribution's CDF has the following form:

$$F(x) = \begin{cases} 1 - \left[1 + \xi\left(\frac{x-\delta}{\theta}\right)\right]^{\left(-\frac{1}{\xi}\right)} & \text{for } \xi > 0, \ x \geq \delta \\ 1 - \left[1 + \xi\left(\frac{x-\delta}{\theta}\right)\right]^{\left(-\frac{1}{\xi}\right)} & \text{for } \xi < 0, \delta \leq x < \delta - \frac{\theta}{\xi} \\ 1 - e^{-\left(\frac{x-\delta}{\theta}\right)} & \text{for } \xi = 0, \ x \geq \delta \end{cases}$$

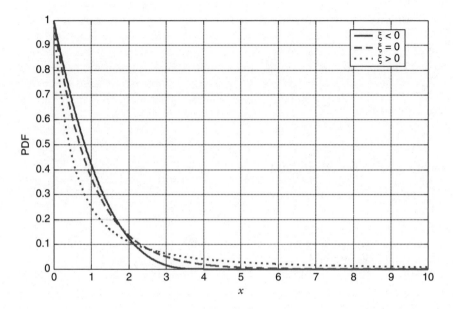

Exhibit 3.13 PDFs for Generalized Pareto distribution.

The PDF of the GPD for different values of the shape parameter ξ is shown in Exhibit 3.13.

3.3.3 Extreme Value Models

The GEV and the GPD families of distributions reviewed in the previous two subsections form the foundations of Extreme Value Theory. Some useful results exist about the convergence of the maxima for different classes of probability distributions to specific GEV and GPD type distributions.[18] For example, the normal, exponential, gamma, and lognormal distributions maxima converge to the Gumbel extreme value distribution, and the distribution of excesses over sufficiently high thresholds for these distributions may be approximated by an exponential distribution, which is the GPD with $\xi = 0$. More heavy-tailed distributions for which the tail decays like a power function (for instance, the Pareto, Cauchy, and t distributions) converge to the Fréchet extreme value distribution, and the distribution of the excesses can be approximated by a GPD with a positive shape parameter ξ. Finally, the maxima for short-tailed probability distributions such as the uniform and beta distributions converge to the Weibull extreme value distribution.

---

[18]See McNeil and Saladin (1997), Falk, Hüsler, and Reiss (1994), and Gnedenko (1943).

Although these theoretical results guide the selection of estimation methods, the application of EVT in practice requires a lot of preliminary data exploration and can be an art. There are two general approaches to applying EVT. The first one is to work with the distribution of extremes. The *block maxima* method is often used to produce the sample of extreme points for estimation. The block maxima method divides the data into nonoverlapping blocks of equal sizes, and records the maximum loss within each block. A distribution is then fitted to the maxima recorded from each block. Obviously, there are problems with this approach—the type of fitted distribution and the estimated distribution parameters can vary greatly with the selection of the blocks and the size of the blocks. Another problem is that, given the fact that extreme events often happen in clusters in time, dividing the data into blocks may cause data points during blocks of non-extreme time periods to be selected. Such data points are "extreme" within the block, but not necessarily extreme in terms of the behavior of the entire time series. Finally, only a limited number of observations can be used for the extreme distribution fitting. In addition to thinking through these issues while determining the selection of the blocks, in practice, one also looks at Q-Q plots to determine if the current sample of maxima fits well a particular probability distribution.[19] (Of particular interest is whether it fits well one of the GEV distributions.) Depending on the results and the parameter estimates, one may vary the size of the block or the way in which observations in a block are selected.

The second approach is to work with the distribution of the excess losses over a threshold, and estimate the metrics of interest (such as the value of high quantiles) from that distribution. The theoretical justification for this approach is that if the normalized maxima converge to a GEV distribution, then the distribution of the excesses should converge to the GPD (the Pickands–Balkema–deHaan theorem). The method is called the *peaks-over-threshold* (POT) approach, and does not split the data into blocks.[20] Instead, it considers all losses in the data that are above a certain threshold. This helps ameliorate some of the problems with the block maxima approach—for example, the sample size is not as limited. However, for the POT approach to work well, one needs to be able to find a suitable

---

[19] Q-Q (quantile–quantile) plots are graphs in which the quantiles of the empirical distribution (determined from the data) are plotted against the quantiles of the theoretical distribution. If the fit is good, then the plot approximates a straight line. The Q-Q plot also helps identify if the tails of the empirical distribution are very different from the theoretical distribution tails. If they are, then the plot will show a curve at the top right end or the bottom left end.

[20] See McNeil and Saladin (1997).

high threshold above which the approximation of the distribution of excesses suggested by the Pickands-Balkema-deHaan Theorem is good and above which there are still sufficient data to produce accurate estimates of the unknown probability distribution parameters. McNeil (1997) addresses these practical issues.

To check whether GPD is a good approximation for the distribution of excesses, one can look at the sample mean excess plot, which has the data values (observations) in increasing order on the horizontal axis, and the average of the excesses above each value on the vertical axis. (The last few points on the right side of the scatterplot are averages of very few remaining data points, and may have higher variability, so they are sometimes omitted from the analysis.) If the scatterplot appears reasonably linear (like a straight line) above a certain value on the horizontal axis, has a positive gradient (i.e., is increasing), and appears to increase "infinitely," then this is an indication that the excesses over this threshold value follow a generalized Pareto distribution with a positive shape parameter $\xi > 0$. (Most financial loss data have a positive shape parameter because financial return distributions are more likely to be skewed negatively, and loss distributions are more likely to be skewed positively.) Alternatively, to select a good threshold, one may pick a value for the threshold so that the estimated shape parameter for the GPD "plateaus," that is, does not vary "a lot" as the threshold changes by a little bit.

To fit the GPD to the data, the GPD parameters are typically estimated with maximum likelihood estimation (MLE).[21] After a GPD is fitted to the data, quantile risk measures such as VaR and CVaR can be estimated directly using the parameters of the GPD. Specifically,

$$(100 - \epsilon)\% \text{ VaR} = u + \frac{\theta}{\xi}\left(\left(\frac{n}{N_u}(1 - \epsilon/100)\right)^{-\xi} - 1\right)$$

where u is the threshold, n is the total number of observations, N_u is the number of observations that exceed the threshold u, and θ and ξ are the scale and shape parameter of the fitted GPD.

$$(100 - \epsilon)\% \text{ CVaR} = \frac{(100 - \epsilon)\% \text{ VaR}}{1 - \xi} + \frac{\theta - \xi u}{1 - \xi}$$

---

[21]MLE involves writing a function called the maximum likelihood function that represents the probability that a given set of data were obtained if the actual probability distribution was of the hypothesized type. One then optimizes the maximum likelihood function to find the values of the parameters of the hypothesized distribution that fit the empirical distribution the best.

The interested reader is referred to Embrechts, Klüppelberg, and Mikosch (1997) for a detailed introduction to EVT.

Summary

- Observed characteristics of financial returns include: (a) the empirical distributions of financial returns exhibit "fat tails"; (b) the empirical distribution of returns is often left-skewed; (c) there is a difference in the behavior of short-term returns such as daily returns, and longer-term returns such as monthly or quarterly returns, and (d) extreme returns tend happen in clusters (i.e., closely in time).
- To model the characteristics of observed distributions, approaches generally fall into one of three categories: (1) assume that returns have stable distributions of infinite variance; (2) assume that returns have distributions that are more fat-tailed and/or skewed than the normal distribution; and (3) assume that the distributions of returns are normal at each instant of time, but look fat tailed due to fluctuations in the variance (volatility) of these distributions.
- Important discrete probability distributions include the binomial distribution, the Bernoulli distribution, the discrete uniform distribution, and the Poisson distribution.
- Important continuous probability distributions include the normal distribution, the continuous uniform distribution, the t distribution, the lognormal distribution, the exponential distribution, the chi-square distribution, the gamma distribution, and the beta distribution.
- Families of distributions used for modeling financial returns include stable Paretian distributions and the generalized lambda distribution family.
- Stable Paretian distributions were suggested by Mandelbrot (1963) as a way to address the fat tails in observed financial data. The normal distribution is a member of this family but all remaining probability distributions in the stable Paretian family have fatter tails than the normal distribution. All nonnormal stable Paretian distributions have infinite variances and infinite higher moments, which means that their variance, skewness, and kurtosis are not defined.
- The form of the generalized lambda distribution family allows for modeling a wide range of distribution shapes, and because it uses a quantile function in its definition, it makes the calculation of tail portfolio risk measures such as VaR and CVaR easy once the distribution has been fitted to observed returns.

- Sometimes, portfolio risk management focuses only on tail (extreme) risks. This is especially relevant in cases when one tries to estimate possible losses that could happen with very small probability, such as 1 in 1,000 occurrences, which translates into the portfolio 99.9%VaR. Extreme Value Theory (EVT) is a branch of statistics that provides the tools for doing so.
- In financial risk management, the use of EVT is based on two significant applications: (1) the asymptotic probability distribution of extremes (maxima or minima) is modeled and, for a large class of probability distributions, it is approximated by one of three very specific types of generalized extreme value (GEV) distributions—Gumbel, Fréchet, or Weibull—and (2) the probability distribution of the excess over a given threshold is modeled.
- When a probability distribution is in a class that satisfies the conditions for convergence to a GEV distribution, the generalized Pareto distribution (GPD) is the limiting distribution of excesses over a threshold as the threshold tends to the rightmost point of the distribution.
- The block maxima method is often used to produce the sample of extreme points for estimation of the GEV. It divides the data into nonoverlapping blocks of equal sizes and records the maximum loss within each block. A distribution is then fitted to the maxima recorded from each block.
- The peaks-over-threshold (POT) approach does not split the data into blocks. Instead, it considers all losses in the data that are above a certain threshold, and uses the information to fit a GPD for the distribution of excesses over the threshold.
- For the POT approach to work well, one needs to be able to find a suitable high threshold above which the approximation of the distribution of excesses suggested by the Pickands–Balkema–deHaan theorem is good and above which there are still sufficient data to produce accurate estimates of the unknown probability distribution parameters.

CHAPTER 4

Statistical Estimation Models

When modeling portfolio risk, one can think about the distribution of financial returns at a particular point in time. This is the approach we took in Chapter 3—we reviewed probability distributions that can be used to represent observed characteristics of financial returns. A complementary approach is to use statistical models for asset return dynamics. Such models do not look at returns at a particular point in time in isolation—they identify factors that drive returns, or model the asset price process over time.

In this chapter, we review the most widely used statistical estimation models in portfolio management and explain how they are estimated and applied. We begin with a general discussion about return estimation models in finance followed by a review of linear regression analysis, factor analysis, and principal components analysis. We then discuss ARCH and GARCH models. The level of the chapter is intended to be introductory, and the emphasis is specifically on concepts that are useful in portfolio construction.[1]

4.1 COMMONLY USED RETURN ESTIMATION MODELS

By far the most widely used return models in finance are models of the form

$$\tilde{r}_i = \alpha_i + \beta_{i1}f_1 + \cdots + \beta_{iK}f_K + \tilde{\epsilon}_i$$

where

$\tilde{r}_i$ is the rate of return on security i,
f_k, $k = 1, \ldots, K$ are factors,
β_{ik} is the sensitivity of asset i to factor k,
α_i is a constant, and
$\tilde{\epsilon}_i$ is a random shock.

---

[1]For more in-depth treatment of financial econometric models, we refer the reader to Fabozzi, Focardi, Rachev, and Arshanapalli (2014).

The models are a mathematical expression of the assumption that financial return movements can be represented as a sum of predictable movements based on factor influences and a *random (white) noise* or *error* term. Despite their simple form, such models have remarkable flexibility. A fundamental model of this type is the regression model in which the values of all variables are recorded at the same time period and the random shock $\tilde{\epsilon}_i$ follows a normal distribution, making $\tilde{r}_i$ normally distributed as well. This is a classical static regression model, which is often used to explain asset returns in terms of factors. Such factors can be macroeconomic variables (gross domestic product, level of interest rates) and/or company fundamentals (industry group, various financial ratios), and we discuss them in more detail in Chapter 9.

In regression models, the factors are identified by the modeler, and a hypothesis is tested to verify that these factors explain returns in a statistically significant way. Two other kinds of statistical models covered in this chapter—*factor analysis* and *principal component analysis*—look very similar in terms of the equation estimated for returns; however, they extract factors from the data and do not treat them as exogenous.

The form of the model above is linear,[2] which makes its estimation easier. However, nonlinear relationships between factors and the response variable (in this context, returns) can be incorporated as well. For example, the factors in the model can be modeled as nonlinear functions (such as a square or a logarithm) of observable variables.

The models can be made dynamic, too. For example, it may take some time for the market to respond to a change in a macroeconomic variable. The lag is measured in a certain number of time units, such as five months or two weeks. To incorporate such dynamics, one can include *lagged* values of factors in the equation above. Lagged values are values realized a certain number of time periods before the current time period. An example model of this kind is one in which the return on an asset i is determined by factor values from one time period ago (note the addition of the subscript t to the variables in the equation):

$$\tilde{r}_{i,t+1} = \alpha_i + \beta_{i1} f_{1t} + \cdots + \beta_{iK} f_{Kt} + \tilde{\epsilon}_{it}$$

and a special model of this kind is one in which the return on an asset is determined by its own return values between 1 and p time periods ago:

$$\tilde{r}_{i,t+1} = \alpha_i + \beta_1 r_{i,t} + \cdots + \beta_p r_{i,t-p+1} + \tilde{\epsilon}_{it}$$

---

[2]Linear expressions involve sums and differences of terms of the kind (constant · variable), and exclude expressions like (constant · variable^2), (variable 1 · variable 2), (variable 1 / variable 2), log(variable), and so on. We will see more uses of the term in the context of optimization modeling in Chapters 6 and 7.

This is an *autoregressive* (AR) *model* of order p, a special case of the more general ARMA(p,q) (*AutoRegressive Moving Average*) model, which incorporates both lag terms and moving average[3] terms:

$$\tilde{r}_{i,t+1} = \alpha_i + \underbrace{\beta_1 r_{i,t} + \cdots + \beta_p r_{i,t-p+1}}_{\text{autoregressive}} + \underbrace{\theta_1 r_{i,t} + \cdots + \theta_q r_{i,t-p+1}}_{\text{moving average}} + \tilde{\epsilon}_{it}$$

Dynamics can be incorporated in the expectation of factor models as well, by assuming an autoregressive model for the factors themselves.[4] Finally, one can incorporate dynamics in the white noise term $\tilde{\epsilon}_{it}$. ARCH and GARCH models do just that, allowing for some important observed characteristics ("stylized facts") of asset returns such as heavy tails and volatility clustering to be incorporated in the models.

4.2 REGRESSION ANALYSIS

In regression analysis, a modeler specifies the factors that are thought to drive the co-variation in asset returns, and the statistical analysis confirms or rejects this hypothesis. As explained in the introduction, a regression equation assumes that the return on a particular stock i can be represented as

$$\tilde{r}_i = \alpha_i + \beta_{i1} f_1 + \cdots + \beta_{iK} f_K + \tilde{\epsilon}_i$$

where

α_i	is the mean return,
$f_1, \ldots, f_K$	are the K factors,
β_{ik}	are the coefficients in front of the factors, and
$\tilde{\epsilon}_i$	is the residual error.

In practice, the linearity assumption is not very restrictive, because nonlinear relationships can be represented by transforming the data as explained earlier.

---

[3] A moving average is the average of a prespecified number of previous observations. The calculations "move along"—for instance, to calculate a moving average of three observations at time t, one calculates the average of observations $t - 1$, $t - 2$, and $t - 3$; to calculate the moving average at time $t + 1$, one calculates the average of observations t, $t - 1$, and $t - 2$, and so on. One can also assign weights to the previous observations if, for example, more recent observations are considered more important than observations further in the past.

[4] See Engle, Ng, and Rothschild (1990).

The factors f_k in this regression are the *explanatory variables* (also called *independent* or *predictor variables*). They help explain the variability in the *response variable* (also called *dependent variable*) r_i.

4.2.1 A Simple Regression Example

Let us consider a simple example of a regression model with a single explanatory variable. Suppose we are trying to understand how the returns of a stock, say Procter & Gamble (P&G), are impacted by the returns of a market index (the S&P 500).[5] The model we are trying to estimate looks as follows:

$$\tilde{r}_{P\&G} = \alpha + \beta \cdot r_{S\&P500} + \tilde{\varepsilon}$$

where $\tilde{r}_{P\&G}$ is the return on P&G stock and $r_{S\&P500}$ is the return on the S&P 500. The data used for the estimation are pairs of observations for the explanatory variable $r_{S\&P500}$ and the response variable $\tilde{r}_{P\&G}$. Suppose there are $T = 78$ such pairs of monthly observations. The data can be represented in a graph, referred to as a *scatterplot*, like the one in Exhibit 4.1, where the coordinates of each point are the observed values of the two variables ($r_{S\&P500}$ and $r_{P\&G}$).

Building the model requires finding coefficients α and β so that the line determined by the regression equation is "as close" as possible to all the observations. There are different measures of proximity but the classical measure is that the sum of the squared deviations from all the points (observations) to the line is the smallest possible. This is referred to as an *ordinary least squares* (OLS) regression. The line obtained using the OLS regression is plotted in Exhibit 4.1.

Because linear regression is the most fundamental statistical estimation model, virtually every statistical package (and many not specifically statistical ones such as Excel) contains functions for estimating a regression model. The only inputs one needs to specify are which variable is the response and which variable(s) are the explanatory variables. The calculations for the regression model output typically use the OLS method, where the formula for calculating the parameters is derived using calculus to minimize the sum of squared residuals from the regression, or maximum likelihood estimation, which maximizes a log-likelihood function.[6] Even though the output formats for different statistical packages differ, the information conveyed in them is standard, so we will use the Excel output in Exhibit 4.2 to discuss the most important terminology associated with regression models.

---

[5]For this example, we used the returns on an exchange-traded fund, the SPDR S&P500 ETF (SPY), as a proxy for the S&P 500 returns.
[6]See, for example, Rachev, Mittnik, Fabozzi, Focardi, and Jašić (2007).

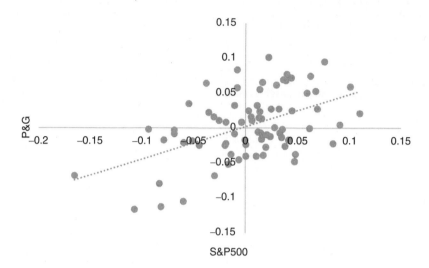

Exhibit 4.1 Determining a linear relationship between returns on a market index (the S&P 500) and returns on P&G stock.

The value for the coefficient beta in front of the explanatory variable (the S&P 500 excess return in our example) is 0.4617 (cell B18). This value tells us the amount of change in the response variable when the explanatory variable increases by one unit. (In a regression with multiple explanatory variables, this interpretation is still valid if we hold the values of the other explanatory variables constant.) In this case, the return of the P&G stock will change by about half (0.4617) of the amount of change in the return on the S&P 500.

The value of the intercept alpha is −0.0021 (cell B17). The intercept tells us the value of the response variable if the values for all explanatory variables are zero.

The estimated model equation based on this regression is

$$r_{P\&G} = 0.0021 + 0.4617 \cdot r_{S\&P500}$$

For example, if the monthly return on the S&P 500 is 0.0400, we would expect the return on P&G to be, on average, $0.0021 + 0.4617 \cdot 0.04 = 0.0206$. Before this model can be used, however, it needs to be validated by testing for statistical significance and explanatory power. We show how this is done next.

	A	B	C	D	E	F	G
1	SUMMARY OUTPUT						
2							
3	*Regression Statistics*						
4	Multiple R	0.4951					
5	R Square	0.2451					
6	Adjusted R Square	0.2352					
7	Standard Error	0.0403					
8	Observations	78					
9							
10	ANOVA						
11		*df*	*SS*	*MS*	*F*	*Significance F*	
12	Regression	1	0.0401	0.0401	24.6744	4.0709E-06	
13	Residual	76	0.1235	0.0016			
14	Total	77	0.1635				
15							
16		*Coefficients*	*Standard Error*	*t Stat*	*P-value*	*Lower 95%*	*Upper 95%*
17	Intercept	0.0021	0.0046	0.4676	0.6414	–0.0070	0.0113
18	S&P500	0.4617	0.0929	4.9673	4.0709E-06	0.2766	0.6468

Exhibit 4.2 Excel regression output for the P&G example.

If the regression coefficient beta is statistically different from 0, the explanatory variable to which the regression coefficient corresponds will be significant for explaining the response variable. To check whether the regression coefficient is statistically significant (which means that it is statistically different from zero), we can check its *p-value* (cell E18) or the confidence interval associated with the coefficient (cells F18:G18). If the p-value is small (generally, less than 5% is considered small enough), then the beta coefficient is statistically different from zero. In this example, the p-value is 0.0000040709 ($=4.0709 \cdot 10^{-6}$, or 4.0709E-06 in Excel's notation), which is very small, so we can conclude that the S&P 500 excess return is a significant factor for forecasting P&G's stock returns. The same conclusion can be reached by checking whether zero is contained in the confidence interval for the regression coefficient. In this case, the 95% confidence interval for beta is (0.2766, 0.6468). Zero is not contained in the interval; therefore, the beta coefficient is statistically different from zero, and the S&P 500 return is a significant factor for explaining the P&G stock returns.

There are several other statistics we should consider in evaluating the regression model. The p-value for the F-statistic (cell F12), which in Excel appears as "Significance F," tells us whether the regression model as a whole is statistically significant. Because in our example the p-value for the F-statistic is small (0.0000040709), the regression model is significant.

Three measures of goodness of fit are reported as standard output for a regression. The coefficient of determination R^2 (which in Excel appears as "R Square" in cell B5) tells us what percentage of the variability of the response variable is explained by the explanatory variable. The higher the number is, the better. (It ranges from 0% to 100%.) In this example, 24.51% of the variability in P&G returns can be explained by the variability in the S&P 500 returns. The problem with R^2 is that if we add more explanatory variables (factors), R^2 will stay the same or continue to increase, even if the additional factors are not important. To control for this, in multiple regression models one looks also at the Adjusted R^2 (cell B6), which imposes a penalty for having too many explanatory variables.

Another measure of goodness of fit is the *standard error* of the regression (cell B7), which equals the standard deviation of the *regression residuals*, the errors left after the model is fitted. The units of the standard error are the units of the residuals, which are also the units of the response variable. In our example, a standard error of 0.0403 tells us that the forecasts for the S&P 500 returns based on this regression model will be on average 0.0403 off from the observed S&P 500 returns.

In order for the regression model to be valid, we need to check that three assumptions that are made in regression analysis regarding the *residuals* (ϵ) are satisfied:

Assumption 1: The residuals ϵ follow a normal distribution.

Assumption 2: The residuals ϵ exhibit *homoscedasticity* (i.e., they have the same variability regardless of the values of the response and the explanatory variables).

Assumption 3: The residuals ϵ are not autocorrelated (i.e., they do not exhibit patterns that depend on the order of the data in the data set).

Assumption 1 can be checked visually by creating a histogram of the residuals from the regression, and examining whether the distribution is bell-shaped and close to a normal curve fitted to the distribution (with the same mean and variance). One can also use a normal probability plot or quantile–quantile (Q-Q) plot that shows the standardized values of the residuals from the regression against the corresponding quantile values for a standard normal distribution.

Assumption 2 can be checked visually from graphs of the residuals against the response variable values predicted from the regression as well as against individual explanatory variables. A fan-shaped pattern with residuals farther away from the fitted regression line as, say, values for the response variable increase, is a typical indication that the homoscedasticity assumption is not satisfied by the regression model.

Assumption 3 can be checked visually by plotting a time series of the residuals from the regression. With observations collected over time, a cyclical pattern, for example, would indicate autocorrelation. In addition, the Durbin-Watson statistic or the Dickey-Fuller test are often used to evaluate the degree of autocorrelation in the residuals.

Many statistical software packages produce graphs and summary metrics that allow for checking these assumptions as part of the standard regression output. When the assumptions are not satisfied, the modeling exercise is not completed, since one may be able to improve the explanatory power of the model. Onc should consider

- Transforming the explanatory variables by using functions such as logarithm, square, square root (this may fix the statistical problems associated with the violation of the first two assumptions about the residuals).
- Incorporating lagged explanatory variables or modeling the changing variability of the error term explicitly (this may fix the statistical problems associated with the last two assumptions about the residuals).

In regression models with multiple explanatory variables, we are also concerned about *multicollinearity*, which happens when the explanatory variables are highly correlated among themselves. In the specific context of forecasting asset returns, an example of factors that could be correlated, for example, is the level of interest rates and stock market returns, or credit spreads and stock market returns. Strong correlation between the factors means that it is difficult to isolate the effect of one variable from the effect of the other. This makes the estimates of the regression coefficients (the betas) misleading because they can take on multiple values, it inflates the value of the R^2 of the regression artificially, and leads to estimates for the p-values and other measures of the significance of the regression coefficients that cannot be trusted.[7] To check for multicollinearity, one examines the correlation matrix of the explanatory variables and other measures of co-dependence such as the *variance inflation factors* (VIFs), which are standard output in more advanced statistical packages. Unfortunately, there is not much that

---

[7]Technically, when we talk about correlation between two explanatory variables, we describe *collinearity*. Multicollinearity occurs when one explanatory variable is explained by a group of other explanatory variables. The main point, however, remains the same.

can be done if multicollinearity is observed. Sometimes, explanatory variables can be dropped or transformed.

Finally, when we build regression models, there is a trade-off between finding a model with good explanatory power and *parsimony* (i.e., limiting the number of factors that go into the model). On the one hand, we want to include all factors that are significant for explaining the response variable (in many finance applications, this is typically returns). On the other hand, including too many factors requires collecting a lot of data, and increases the risk of problems with the regression model, such as multicollinearity.

4.2.2 Regression Applications in the Investment Management Process

Regression analysis is the workhorse of quantitative finance. It is used in virtually every stage of the quantitative equity investment management process, as well as in a number of interesting bond portfolio applications. This section provides a brief overview of the applications of regression in the four stages of the investment management process described in Chapter 1.

4.2.2.1 Setting an Investment Policy Setting an investment policy begins with the asset allocation decision. Although there is a wide variety of asset allocation models, they all require the expected returns for different asset classes. (Some, like the Markowitz mean-variance model we describe in Chapter 8, require also the variances and covariances.) These expected returns and other inputs are typically calculated using regression analysis. We explain the estimation process in more detail in Chapter 9 but here we mention that the regression models that are used establish links between returns and their lagged values or exogenous variables. These variables are referred to as "factors." The justification for the models that are used is primarily empirical, that is, they are considered valid insofar as they fit empirical data.

4.2.2.2 Selecting a Portfolio Strategy Clients can request a money manager for a particular asset class to pursue an active (also referred to as alpha) or passive (also referred to as beta) strategy. As we explained in Chapter 1, an active portfolio strategy uses available information and forecasting techniques to seek a better performance than a portfolio that is simply diversified broadly. A passive portfolio strategy involves minimal input when it comes to forecasts, and instead relies on diversification to match the performance of some market index. There are also hybrid strategies.

Whether a client selects an active or a passive strategy depends on his or her belief that the market is efficient for an asset class. If the market is not efficient, the client needs to believe that the manager will be able to out-perform the benchmark for the asset class that is believed to be inefficient. Regression analysis is used in most tests of the pricing efficiency of the market. The tests examine whether it is possible to generate abnormal returns. An abnormal return is defined as the difference between the actual return and the expected return from an investment strategy. The expected return used in empirical tests is the return predicted from a regression model after adjustment for transaction costs. The model itself adjusts for risk. To show price inefficiency, the abnormal return (or alpha) must be shown to be statistically significant.[8]

4.2.2.3 Selecting the Specific Assets Given a portfolio strategy, portfolio construction involves the selection of the specific assets to be included in the portfolio. This step in the investment management process requires an estimate of expected returns as well as the variance and covariances of returns. Regression analysis is often used to identify factors that impact asset returns. In bond portfolio management, regression-based durations (key measures of interest rate exposures) are estimated to evaluate portfolio risk. Regression-based durations can be estimated also for equities. These are important, for example, in the case of defined-benefit pension funds, which match the duration of their asset portfolio to the duration of their pension liabilities. We explain some of these concepts in more detail in later chapters.

4.2.2.4 Measuring and Evaluating Performance In evaluating the performance of a money manager, one must adjust for the risks accepted by the manager in generating the return. Regression (factor) models provide such information. The process of decomposing the performance of a money manager relative to each factor that has been found through multifactor models is called *return* (or *performance*) *attribution analysis*.

---

[8]This basically reduces to testing whether the intercept term in the regression is statistically significant. We were not concerned with the intercept term in the example in Section 4.2.1 but to test whether the intercept term is statistically significant, one would look at its p-value, which shows the results from the hypothesis test that the intercept term is statistically 0. The p-value for the intercept term of the example in Section 4.2.1 (Exhibit 4.2) was 0.6414, too large for the intercept term to be statistically significant. To prove significance, the p-value should be less than 0.05.

4.3 FACTOR ANALYSIS

To illustrate the main idea behind factor analysis, let us begin with a simple nonfinance example provided by Kritzman (1993). Suppose that we have the grades for 1,000 students in nine different subjects: literature, composition, Spanish, algebra, calculus, geometry, physics, biology, and chemistry. If we compute the pairwise correlations for grades in each subject, we would expect to find higher correlations between grades within the literature, composition, Spanish group than between grades in, say, literature and calculus. Suppose we observe that we have (1) high correlations for grades in the literature, composition, Spanish group, (2) high correlations for grades in the algebra, calculus, geometry group, and (3) high correlations for grades in the physics, biology, chemistry group. There will still be some correlations between grades in different groups, but suppose that they are not nearly as high as the correlations within the groups. This may indicate that there are three factors that determine a student's performance in these subjects: a verbal aptitude, an aptitude for math, and an aptitude for science. A single factor does not necessarily determine a student's performance; otherwise all correlations would be 0 or 1. However, some factors will be weighted more than others for a particular student. Note, by the way, that these factors (the aptitudes for different subjects) are invisible. We can only observe the strength of the correlations within the groups and between them, and we need to provide interpretation for what the factors might be based on our intuition.

How does this example translate for financial applications? Suppose we have data on the returns of N assets. One can think of them as the grades recorded for the different students. We compute the pairwise correlations between the different asset returns, and look for patterns. There may be a group of assets for which the returns are highly correlated. If all assets in the group receive a large portion of their earnings from foreign operations, we may conclude that exchange risk is one underlying factor. Another group of highly correlated assets may have high debt-to-equity ratios, so we may conclude that the level of interest rates is another underlying factor. We proceed in the same way, and try to identify common factors from groups that exhibit high correlations in returns.

There is a specific statistical technique for computing such underlying factors. Most advanced statistical packages have a function that can perform the calculations. Excel's statistical capabilities are unfortunately not as advanced, but the open source statistical language R and other specialized statistical packages and modeling environments have this ability. The user provides the data, specifies the number of factors (which the user can try to guess based on the preliminary analysis and economic theory), and obtains the factor loadings. The *factor loadings* are the coefficients in front of the factors that determine how to compute the value of the observation (the grade or the asset return) from the hidden factors, and can be interpreted as the sensitivities of the asset returns to the different factors. A factor model equation in fact looks like the familiar regression equation; the difference is in the way the factors are computed. The output from running factor analysis with statistical software on our data set of asset returns will be a model

$$\tilde{r}_i = \alpha_i + \beta_{i1}f_1 + \cdots + \beta_{iK}f_K + \tilde{\epsilon}_i$$

or, in terms of the vector of returns for the assets in the portfolio,

$$\mathbf{r} = \boldsymbol{\alpha} + \mathbf{B} \cdot \mathbf{f} + \boldsymbol{\epsilon}$$

where $\boldsymbol{\alpha}$ is the N-dimensional vector of mean returns, $\mathbf{f}$ is the K-dimensional vector of factors, $\mathbf{B}$ is the $N \times K$ matrix of factor loadings (the coefficients in front of every factor), and $\boldsymbol{\epsilon}$ is the N-dimensional vector of residual errors.

Factor analysis assumes that an underlying causal model exists and has a particular strict factor structure in the sense that the covariance matrix of the data can be represented as a function of the covariances between factors plus idiosyncratic variances:

$$\boldsymbol{\Sigma} = \mathbf{B}\boldsymbol{\Sigma}_{\mathbf{f}}\mathbf{B}' + \boldsymbol{\Sigma}_{\epsilon}$$

Because there are multiple ways to represent the covariance structure, however, the factors identified from a factor model are not unique. If the factors and the noise terms are uncorrelated, and the noise terms are uncorrelated among themselves (which means that $\boldsymbol{\Sigma}_{\epsilon}$ is a diagonal matrix that contains the variances in the noise terms in its diagonal), then the factors are determined up to a nonsingular linear transformation.[9] In other words, if we multiply the vector that represents the set of factors by a nonsingular matrix, we obtain a new factor model that fits the original data. In order to make the model uniquely identifiable, one can require that the factors are orthonormal variables and that the matrix of factor loadings is diagonal (with zeros in off-diagonal elements). Even then, the factors are unique only up to a rotation.[10]

The problem with the factor analysis procedure is that even if we have accounted for all the variability in the data and have identified the factors numerically, we may not be able to provide a good interpretation of their meaning. In addition, factor analysis may work if we are considering asset prices at a single point in time but is difficult to transfer between

---

[9]In practice, these assumptions can be very restrictive, and one often uses approximate factor models. See, for example, Bai (2003).
[10]See the Appendix.

samples or time periods. For example, factor 1 in one data set may be factor 5 in another data set, or not discovered at all. In addition, the factors discovered through factor analysis are not necessarily independent. This makes factor analysis challenging to apply for portfolio construction and risk management purposes.

4.4 PRINCIPAL COMPONENTS ANALYSIS

Principal components analysis (PCA) is similar to factor analysis in the sense that the goal of the statistical procedure is to extract factors (*principal components*) out of a given set of data that explain the variability in the data. The factors are statistical; that is, the factors are not input by the user, but computed by software. The difference between PCA and factor analysis is that the main goal of PCA is to find *uncorrelated* factors in such a way that the first factor explains as much of the variability in the data as possible, the second factor explains as much of the remaining variability as possible, and so on. Mathematically, this is accomplished by finding the eigenvectors and the eigenvalues[11] of the covariance matrix or the correlation matrix of the original data. (The results are different depending on which matrix is used.) PCA is principally a dimensionality reduction technique[12] and does not require starting out with a particular hypothesis. Factor analysis, on the other hand, assumes that an underlying causal model exists. This assumption needs to be verified for factor analysis to be applied.

Consider a data set that, as we mentioned, is often encountered in finance: time series of returns on N assets over T time periods, that is, column vectors r_i, $i = 1, \ldots, N$ that contain T entries each. In this context, PCA reduces to the following. Consider a linear combination of these assets (that is, a weighted sum of their returns). The latter can be thought of as a portfolio of these assets with percentage weights $\mathbf{w} = (w_1, \ldots, w_N)$. This portfolio has variance σ_p^2, which depends on the portfolio weights, as we will see in Chapter 8. Consider a normalized portfolio with the largest possible variance.[13] Let $\mathbf{\Sigma}$ be the covariance matrix of the data, that is, the

---

[11]See the Appendix.

[12]In other words, its goal is to reduce the number of factors used in the model by finding (a smaller number of) combinations of them that explain almost as much of the variability in returns as the original factors.

[13]In this context, a normalized portfolio is a portfolio such that the squares of the weights sum to one. On an intuitive level, one needs to normalize the weights to restrict their total magnitude because otherwise, one can always find a portfolio with a higher variance by just increasing the weights themselves to infinity.

matrix that measures the covariances of the returns of the N assets. PCA involves solving an optimization problem of the kind

$$\text{Max} \quad \mathbf{w}'\mathbf{\Sigma}\mathbf{w}$$

subject to the normalization condition on the weights:

$$\mathbf{w}'\mathbf{w} = 1$$

It turns out that the optimal solution to this problem is the eigenvector corresponding to the largest eigenvalue of the covariance matrix $\mathbf{\Sigma}$. The eigenvalues and eigenvectors can be found with numerical methods for matrix decomposition.[14]

Before running PCA, the data are usually centered at 0 (i.e., the means are subtracted) and divided by their standard deviations.[15] This is not as important in the case of returns because they are all of the same units but it makes a difference when the variables under consideration have very different magnitudes.

Each subsequent principal component explains a smaller portion of the variability in the original data. After we are done finding the principal components, the representation of the data will in a sense be "inverse" to the original representation: each principal component will be expressed as a linear combination of the original data. For example, if we are given N stock returns $r_1, \ldots, r_N$, the principal components $x_1, \ldots, x_N$ will be given by

$$x_k = \sum_{i=1}^{N} \beta_{ik} \cdot r_i, \, k = 1, \ldots, N$$

This is what is referred to as a *linear transformation* of the original data. We calculate the principal components $x_1, \ldots, x_N$ as combinations (again, think of them as portfolios) of the original variables, which are often returns in the financial context. If there are N initial variables (e.g., we have the time series for the returns on N assets), there will be N principal components in total.

If we observe that a large percentage of the variability in the original data is explained by the first few principal components, we can drop the remaining components from consideration. This is the process of *dimensionality*

---

[14]See the Appendix.
[15]In other words, the z-scores for the original data are often used. We defined z-scores in Chapter 2.4.

reduction. For example, if we have data for the returns on 1,000 stocks and find that the first seven principal components explain 99% of the variability, we can drop the other principal components, and model only with seven variables (instead of the original 1,000). How do we determine which principal components are "important" and which are "not as important"? A popular method for doing this is the *scree plot*, first suggested by Cattell (1988). The horizontal axis of the scree plot lists the number of principal components, and the vertical axis lists the eigenvalues. The plot of the eigenvalues against the number of principal components is examined for an "elbow," that is, a place where there is a dramatic change in slope, and the marginal benefit of adding more principal components diminishes. This is the point at which the number of principal components should be sufficient.

The principal components may not have a straightforward interpretation, and PCA is even less concerned with interpretation of the factors than factor analysis is. However, the principal components are guaranteed to be uncorrelated, which has a number of advantages for modeling purposes, such as when simulating future portfolio performance. The principal components are helpful for building factors models (e.g., to reduce the dimensionality of the data and to capture hidden factors in hybrid factor models, as we will see in Chapter 9), and are often used as input variables for other statistical techniques, such as clustering, regression, and discriminant analysis. PCA models also help eliminate sources of possible noise in the data, by removing components that do not account for a large portion of the variance in the data.

Similarly to the case of factor analysis, most advanced statistical packages have a function that can compute the principal components for a set of data. There is no such function in Excel; however, R's functions `prcomp()` and `princomp()` that come with the default R package "stats," as well as a number of other functions available from other packages such as `FactoMineR`, `ade4` and `amap`, allow a user to input the data and obtain useful output such as the coefficients in front of the original data, that is, β_{ik} in the equation above, the *scores* (i.e., the values of the principal components themselves), and the percentage of the variability of the original data explained by each principal component.

Let us provide a simple example to illustrate how PCA is performed. Consider the returns of 10 stocks (tickers AXP, T, BA, CAT, CVX, CSCO, KO, DD, XOM, GE) over 78 months (from August 2008 until September 2014). The time series of the returns are plotted in Exhibit 4.3.

The principal components are calculated using the `prcomp` function in R. The resulting principal components (that is, the weights of the original stocks in the portfolios that are now the new variables) are shown in Exhibit 4.4. The eigenvalues of the covariance matrix are the variances of the new variables. The square roots of those variances (that is, the standard

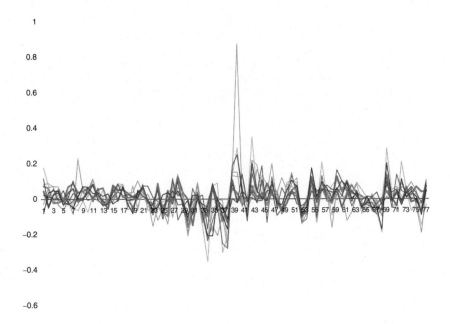

Exhibit 4.3   Ten stock return processes.

deviations of the principal components) are given in Exhibit 4.5. Exhibit 4.5 also shows the proportion and the cumulative proportion of total variance explained by each consecutive principal component. One can observe that the first principal component explains 52.91% of the total variance of the returns, the second principal component explains 13.74% of the total variance, and so on. Together, the first three principal components explain about three quarters (74.80%) of the total variance. There is a large gain with the first three components. After the sixth component, the gains are marginal.

The scree plot (Exhibit 4.6) helps visualize the contribution of each principal component. However, a considerable amount of subjectivity is involved in identifying the "elbow." In this example, the elbow appears to be around the second principal component, that is, we could employ only two principal components. Fortunately, there is a procedure for deciding how many principal components to keep, known as Kaiser's criterion. For standardized data, Kaiser's criterion for retaining principal components specifies that one should only retain principal components with variance (that is, standard deviation squared) that exceeds 1.[16] In this example, only the first two principal components meet this criterion.

---

[16]See Kaiser (1960).

EXHIBIT 4.4 Principal components.

	PC1	PC2	PC3	PC4	PC5	PC6	PC7	PC8	PC9	PC10
AXP	-0.3125	-0.3965	-0.0053	-0.1065	0.2329	-0.3591	0.7197	-0.0855	-0.0244	0.1563
T	-0.262	0.2583	-0.5274	-0.5126	0.5049	0.2171	-0.0773	0.0167	0.0072	-0.1233
BA	-0.319	-0.1623	0.3003	0.4218	0.51	0.3489	-0.2128	-0.2478	-0.3287	0.0829
CAT	-0.3592	-0.0749	0.0022	-0.3208	-0.3152	-0.3924	-0.4024	-0.092	-0.5604	0.1562
CVX	-0.316	0.4582	0.2953	-0.0732	0.0018	-0.0931	-0.0679	-0.1833	0.4842	0.5622
CSCO	-0.3206	-0.1258	0.1474	-0.2682	-0.4821	0.6971	0.2597	0.0245	-0.0325	-0.0057
KO	-0.2625	0.2633	-0.5851	0.5335	-0.3049	-0.0072	0.1629	-0.3324	-0.0654	-0.0178
DD	-0.3654	-0.3085	0.081	-0.0091	-0.0691	-0.162	-0.2745	-0.2502	0.5104	-0.5788
XOM	-0.2559	0.5627	0.3717	0.0788	0.0302	-0.1638	0.256	0.2926	-0.2266	-0.4931
GE	-0.3634	-0.1923	-0.1883	0.2768	-0.0081	-0.0166	-0.1704	0.7934	0.1595	0.1854

EXHIBIT 4.5 Standard deviations of the 10 principal components.

	PC1	PC2	PC3	PC4	PC5	PC6	PC7	PC8	PC9	PC10
Standard deviation	2.3003	1.1724	0.9020	0.7931	0.7036	0.6943	0.5649	0.4933	0.4500	0.3865
Proportion of variance	0.5291	0.1374	0.0814	0.0629	0.0495	0.0482	0.0319	0.0243	0.0203	0.0149
Cumulative proportion	0.5291	0.6666	0.7480	0.8109	0.8604	0.9086	0.9405	0.9648	0.9851	1.0000

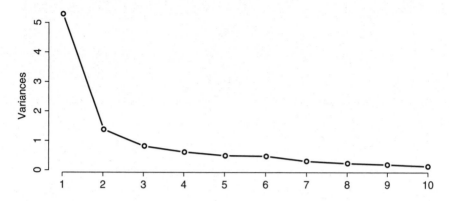

Exhibit 4.6 Scree plot.

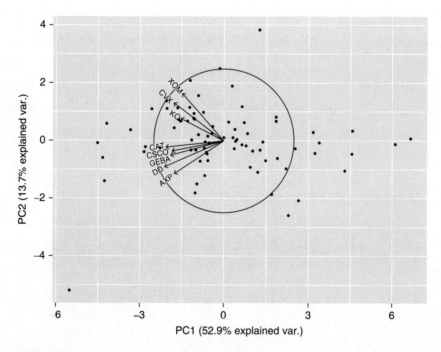

Exhibit 4.7 Representation of the original data for the 10 stocks (78 data points, one for each time period) in terms of the first two principal components.

Once the number of principal components to use is determined, one can compute the principal components scores, that is, the values of the principal components in terms of the original variables through the formula

$$x_k = \sum_{i=1}^{N} \beta_{ik} \cdot r_i$$

using the coefficients from Exhibit 4.4. If we retain the first two principal components and plot them, we get the picture in Exhibit 4.7. It is difficult to discern specific patterns in this graph but often the principal components are then used as inputs into clustering algorithms that help separate a universe of stocks into particular groups (one can imagine such groups as clusters of points on the graph), or into statistical factor models.

4.5 AUTOREGRESSIVE CONDITIONAL HETEROSCEDASTIC MODELS

As we explained in Section 4.2, one of the main assumptions regarding the residuals in regression models is *homoscedasticity*, that is, the assumption that the variance of the error terms is the same regardless of the magnitudes of the response and explanatory variables. (When the variance of the error terms is different, this is referred to as *heteroscedasticity*.) Another assumption is that there is no autocorrelation in the residuals from the regression. Financial returns, however, tend to exhibit the following characteristics:

1. The amplitude of financial returns tends to vary over time; large changes in asset prices are more likely to be followed by large changes and small changes are more likely to be followed by small changes. This is referred to as *volatility clustering*, and it violates both regression assumptions mentioned above.
2. Higher-frequency (e.g., daily) asset returns data exhibit heavy tails. This violates the normality assumption of regression models.

Application of regression models to financial data needs to be able to handle these stylized facts. Autoregressive Conditional Heteroscedastic (ARCH) models, suggested in a seminal work by Engle (1982) and followed by the important generalization to Generalized Conditional Heteroscedastic (GARCH) models by Bollerslev (1986, 1987), are used to address both of these issues. Robert Engle received the Nobel Memorial Prize in Economic Sciences in 2003 for this contribution.

ARCH and GARCH models address the problem of forecasting the mean and the variance (volatility) of future returns based on past information.

They focus on modeling the error process, and specifically on modeling its variance. We should note that the error process is not directly observable. The only time series that is actually observable is the time series of asset returns, $\tilde{r}_t$. The error process needs to be implied from the observed values for $\tilde{r}_t$ and will depend both on the observed values and on the assumption for the model describing the dynamics of $\tilde{r}_t$. For example, if one assumes that returns have a constant mean μ and follow a model

$$\tilde{r}_t = \mu + \tilde{\epsilon}_t$$

where $\tilde{\epsilon}_t$ are the error terms, then the error process will be determined from the differences between the returns and their constant mean. If, instead, one discovers that accounting for a factor f helps predict returns better, that is, that the returns can be modeled as

$$\tilde{r}_t = \mu + \beta \cdot f_{t-1} + \tilde{\epsilon}_t$$

then the process for $\tilde{\epsilon}_t$ should be implied from the differences between the returns and $\mu + \beta \cdot f_{t-1}$.

In the original ARCH model formulation (Engle 1982), the errors are assumed to have the form

$$\tilde{\epsilon}_t = \sqrt{h_t}\, \tilde{z}_t$$

where $\tilde{z}_t$ are independent standard normal variables (with mean of 0 and standard deviation of 1).[17] The conditional variance of the error terms (that is, the variance based on past information) is therefore h_t; in the ARCH(q) model it is forecasted as a weighted moving average of q past error terms:[18]

$$h_t = \omega + \sum_{j=1}^{q} \alpha_j \epsilon_{t-j}^2$$

The weights α_j for the squares of the past error terms ϵ_{t-j}^2 are estimated from data to provide the best fit.

---

[17] The $\tilde{z}_t$s are typically assumed to be normal in most models used in practice; this normality assumption does not preclude modeling fat tails in the returns, as we will explain shortly.

[18] As we explained in the introduction, a moving average is the average of a pre-specified number of previous observations. A weighted moving average is calculated similarly but weights are assigned to the previous observations. A commonly used type of weighted moving average is the exponential moving average, in which all previous observations are taken into consideration but the weights decrease exponentially as the observations are further in the past.

The GARCH(p,q) model adds flexibility to the ARCH(q) model by allowing for the conditional variance to depend not only on the past error terms but also on p lagged conditional variances. The conditional variance can be written as

$$h_t = \omega + \sum_{j=1}^{q} \alpha_j \epsilon_{t-j}^2 + \sum_{j=1}^{p} \beta_j h_{t-j}$$

As pointed out by Bollerslev (1986), the GARCH(p,q) process can be interpreted as an autoregressive moving average process in ϵ_t^2. The majority of volatility forecasting models used in practice are GARCH models. The GARCH(1,1) model in particular, with one lag for the squared error and one lag for the conditional variance, is one of the most robust volatility models:

$$h_t = \omega + \alpha \epsilon_{t-1}^2 + \beta h_{t-1}$$

The parameters α_j and β_j in GARCH models are estimated with maximum likelihood methods. A variety of statistical software packages, such as R, EViews, and SAS, have functions that can estimate the GARCH process directly. For example, in R one can use the `garchFit` function from the `fGarch` library.

The ARCH/GARCH framework has been very successful at capturing volatility changes in practice, and it is widely used in portfolio risk management in particular. It is successful at modeling fat tails observed in return distributions.[19]

The ARCH/GARCH framework also allows for accounting for the time-varying nature of volatility in portfolio risk calculations, such as the calculation of value-at-risk (VaR) and conditional value-at-risk (CVaR). As we explained in Chapter 2, VaR and CVaR are typically reported for 1 or 10 days ahead. VaR at the $(1 - \epsilon)\%$ level is calculated either through simulation (by observing the $(1 - \epsilon)$ percentile of the simulated distribution of future portfolio losses) or through the normal approximation,

$$\text{VaR}_{(1-\epsilon)} = (-\mu_r + q_{(1-\epsilon)} \cdot \sigma_r) \cdot V_t$$

In the expression above, μ_r is the expected return, σ_r is the standard deviation of the return, V_t is the current portfolio value, and $q_{(1-\epsilon)}$ is the $100(1 - \epsilon)$th percentile of a standard normal distribution.[20]

Similarly, CVaR at the $(1 - \epsilon)\%$ level can be calculated either through simulation (by observing the average of the $(1 - \epsilon)$ percentile of the

---

[19] See McNeil, Frey, and Embrechts (2005) for a derivation.
[20] See Chapter 2.6.2.5 for how to calculate this expression with software.

simulated distribution of future portfolio losses) or through the normal approximation,

$$\text{CVaR}_{(1-\epsilon)} = \left(-\mu_r + \frac{\phi\left(q_{(1-\epsilon)}\right)}{\epsilon} \cdot \sigma_r \right) \cdot V_t$$

The number $q_{(1-\epsilon)}$ is the $100(1-\epsilon)$th percentile of a standard normal distribution, as before, and we use $\varphi(q_{(1-\epsilon)})$ to denote the value of the normal probability density at the point $q_{(1-\epsilon)}$.[21]

It is the estimate of σ_r based on forecasting models that is improved by using ARCH/GARCH models to estimate the volatility of the error in that estimate and linking it to the volatility of the estimate itself. For example, in the simple model mentioned earlier in this section,

$$\tilde{r}_t = \mu + \tilde{\epsilon}_t$$

the standard deviation of the error σ_ϵ is actually the standard deviation of the return σ_r. This is because the mean return is assumed to be constant. This is not the case for general econometric models of returns but forecasts for the volatility of returns can be created based on forecasts for the volatility of the error.

Before ARCH/GARCH models became mainstream, the primary tool for capturing past information in the calculation of σ_r was the rolling standard deviation. The rolling standard deviation is the standard deviation of returns over a prespecified number of time periods under consideration, calculated as the square root of the average of the squared differences of the returns during the prespecified time period from the mean return during that period. For example, the rolling standard deviation could be calculated every day using the daily returns from the 22 previous trading days to capture one month of observations. The rolling standard deviation approach is still sometimes used but it suffers from a number of problems, including the issues of picking exactly a certain number of days for estimation (e.g., 22), and attributing the same importance to the returns in all 22 days (virtually, ignoring information about more recent momentum). ARCH/GARCH models let the weights of the observations be estimated from the data so that they can explain the variance in the data the best, and capture the volatility dynamics in a more flexible way. This makes them particularly valuable in the context of modeling portfolio risk.

---

[21] See Chapter 2.6.2.6 for how to calculate this expression with software.

Many additional uses of ARCH and GARCH models have been addressed in the literature. For example, multivariate extensions of ARCH/GARCH models (in which the volatilities of multiple asset return processes are modeled simultaneously) are of particular interest in portfolio risk modeling because one needs to account for changes in volatility both across time and across assets.[22]

Summary

- Regression analysis models the relationship between a variable of interest and exogenous factors specified by the modeler. It is the most widely used statistical technique in finance, and is used at virtually every stage of the quantitative portfolio management process.
- Regression analysis has especially important applications in portfolio construction, risk attribution, and performance measurement.
- In regression models with multiple explanatory variables, muliticollinearity must be checked. Multicollinearity happens when the explanatory variables are highly correlated among themselves.
- Assumptions made in a regression model regarding the residuals are that they (1) follow a normal distribution, (2) exhibit homoscedasticity, and (3) are not autocorrelated.
- Homoscedasticity means that the variance of the residuals is the same regardless of the values of the response and the explanatory variables. When the variance of the residuals is not constant, the residuals are said to exhibit heteroscedasticity.
- Nonautocorrelated residuals means that residuals do not exhibit patterns that depend on the order of the data in the data set.
- Factor analysis is a statistical technique for identifying unobservable factors that drive correlations between observable quantities.
- Principal components analysis is a statistical technique for identifying uncorrelated factors that are linear combinations of the original data. The first principal component is constructed in such a way as to explain the largest portion of the variability in the data, the second factor is constructed in such a way as to explain the largest portion of the remaining variability in the data, and so on.
- ARCH and GARCH models address the problem of forecasting the mean and the variance (volatility) of future returns based on past information. They focus on modeling the error process, and specifically on modeling its variance.

---

[22] Interested readers are referred to Engle, Focardi, and Fabozzi (2008) for an accessible introduction to the theory and uses of ARCH/GARCH models.

Simulation and Optimization Modeling

CHAPTER 5

Simulation Modeling

Simulation is a widely used technique for portfolio risk assessment and management. Portfolio exposure to different factors is often evaluated over multiple scenarios, and portfolio risk measures such as value-at-risk are estimated. Generating meaningful scenarios is an art as much as a science, and presents a number of modeling and computational challenges.

This chapter reviews the main ideas behind Monte Carlo simulation and discusses important issues in its application to portfolio management, such as the number of scenarios to generate and the interpretation of output.

5.1 MONTE CARLO SIMULATION: A SIMPLE EXAMPLE

As we explained in Chapter 2, the analysis of risk is based on modeling uncertainty, and uncertainty can be represented mathematically by probability distributions. These probability distributions are the building blocks for simulation models. Namely, simulation models take probability distribution assumptions on the uncertainties as inputs, and generate scenarios (often referred to as *trials*) that happen with probabilities described by the probability distributions. They then record what happens to variables of interest (called "output variables") over these scenarios, and let us analyze the characteristics of the output probability distributions (see Exhibit 5.1). In the financial context, inputs may be interest rate levels, market returns, and so on, and the output variable can be a portfolio return or the return on a financial instrument.

Let us start with a simple example. Suppose you want to invest $1,000 in the U.S. stock market for one year. To do so, you decide that you want to invest in a stock index that represents the performance of the stock market. You invest in a mutual fund whose investment objective is to reproduce the return performance on the S&P 500. A mutual fund with such an objective is referred to as an *index fund*. We will denote the initial investment, or capital, invested in the index fund as C_0 (i.e., $C_0 = \$1,000$). How much money do

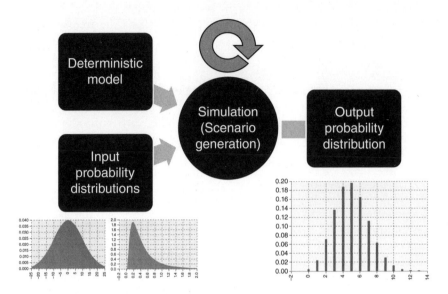

Exhibit 5.1 A typical Monte Carlo simulation system.

you expect to have at the end of the year? Let us label the amount of capital at the end of the year by $\widetilde{C}_1$.[1] Note that $\widetilde{C}_1$ will be a random variable because it will depend on how the market (i.e., the S&P 500) performs over the year. In fact, if we let $\widetilde{r}_{0,1}$ denote the market return over the time period [0,1], then $\widetilde{C}_1$ will equal

$$C_0 + \widetilde{r}_{0,1} C_0$$

or, equivalently,

$$(1 + \widetilde{r}_{0,1}) C_0$$

The return r_t over a time period $[t, t + 1]$ can be computed as

$$\frac{P_{t+1} - P_t + D_t}{P_t}$$

where P_t and P_{t+1} are the values of the S&P 500 at times t and $t + 1$, respectively, and D_t is the amount of dividends paid over that time period. In this example, we can think of P_t and P_{t+1} as the S&P 500 index levels at the beginning ($t = 0$) and at the end of the year ($t = 1$), respectively, and D_t is 0.

---

[1]Recall from Chapter 2 that we use tilde ("~") to denote uncertain quantities and random variables.

To estimate the end-of-year capital, you can guess the return on the market, and compute the resulting value for $\tilde{C}_1$. However, this would give you only a point estimate of the possible values for your investment. A more sophisticated approach is to generate scenarios for the market return over the year, and compute $\tilde{C}_1$ in each of these scenarios. In other words, you can represent future market returns by a probability distribution,[2] generate scenarios that are representative of this probability distribution, and then analyze the resulting distribution of your end-of-year capital. The resulting probability distribution of $\tilde{C}_1$ will be a set of scenarios itself. You can create a histogram of the outcomes, that is, collect the outcomes of the scenarios into nonoverlapping bins and draw bars above all bins with heights corresponding to the percentage of times outcomes in each bin were obtained in the simulation. This will allow you to visualize the approximate probability distribution of $\tilde{C}_1$, and analyze it with the statistical measures described in Chapter 2.6 (central tendency, skew, variability, and so on). The distribution for $\tilde{C}_1$ from the simulation will be only an approximation, because it will depend both on the number of scenarios and on the set of scenarios you generated for $\tilde{r}_{0,1}$. Intuitively, if you generate 1,000 scenarios that cover the possible values for $\tilde{r}_{0,1}$ well, you would expect to obtain a better representation of the distribution of $\tilde{C}_1$ than if you generated only two scenarios.

5.1.1   Selecting Probability Distributions for the Inputs

In the simple simulation example we just discussed, the estimate of the probability distribution of $\tilde{C}_1$ is affected by the assumptions made about the probability distribution of the input $\tilde{r}_{0,1}$. How should you select the probability distribution of the input $\tilde{r}_{0,1}$ to the simulation?

One possible starting point is to look at a historical distribution of past returns, and assume that the future will behave in the same way. When creating scenarios for future realizations, then, you can draw randomly from historical scenarios.

Another possibility is to assume a particular probability distribution for future returns, and use historical data to estimate the parameters of this distribution, that is, the parameters that determine the specific shape of the distribution, such as the expected value (μ) and standard deviation (σ) for a

---

[2]Note that, in practice, there are an infinite number of values a return can take because it is expressed as a percentage. So, while you can certainly input a discrete set of possible scenarios for return, it is not unnatural to assume that the actual realization of the return is drawn from a continuous probability distribution.

normal distribution (see Chapter 2.4); λ_1, λ_2, λ_3, and λ_4 for a generalized lambda distribution (see Chapter 3.2.3); or α and β for a beta distribution (see Chapter 3.1.9). For example, if you assume a normal distribution for returns, then you can use the historical variability of returns as a measure of the standard deviation σ of this normal distribution, and the historical average (mean) as the expected return μ of the normal distribution.

A third approach is not to start out with a particular distribution, but to use historical data to find a distribution for returns that provides the best fit to the data. As we mentioned in Chapter 2.11.4, the chi-square hypothesis test is one possible goodness-of-fit test. Other goodness-of-fit tests include the Kolmogorov-Smirnov (K-S) test, the Anderson-Darling (A-D) test, and root-mean-squared-error (RMSE).[3] Many software packages, including R, have commands that can test the goodness of fit for different probability distributions.

Yet a fourth way is to ignore the past and look forward, constructing a probability distribution based on your subjective guess about how the uncertain variable in your model will behave. For example, using the beta distribution from Exhibit 3.9(a) to model the future market return will express a more pessimistic view about the market than using the beta distribution in Exhibit 3.9(b) or a normal distribution, because most of the probability mass in the distribution in (a) is to the left, so low values for return will happen more often when scenarios are generated.

It is important to realize that none of these approaches will provide "the answer." Simulation is a very useful tool for modeling uncertainty, but the outcome is only as good as the inputs provided to the model. The art of simulation modeling is in providing good inputs and interpreting the results carefully.

---

[3]There is no rule for which goodness-of-fit test is "best." Each of them has advantages and disadvantages. The chi-square test is the most general one, and can be used for data that come from both continuous and discrete distributions; however, to calculate the chi-square test statistic, one needs to divide the data into "bins," and the results depend strongly on how the bins are determined. The K-S and the A-D tests apply only for continuous distributions. They do not depend on dividing the data into bins, so their results are less arbitrary. The K-S statistic is concerned primarily with whether the *centers* of the empirical and the expected distribution are "close," whereas A-D focuses on the discrepancy between the *tails* of the observed and the expected distribution. For all three tests, the smaller the value of the test statistic, the closer the fit is. (As mentioned in Chapter 2.11.4, most statistical software packages report a p-value, that is, a "probability," in addition to a test statistic. The larger the p-value, the closer the fit.) Finally, the RMSE measures the squared error of the differences between observed and the expected values. The smaller the number, the better, but the actual magnitude of the RMSE depends on the distribution and data at hand.

5.1.2 Interpreting Monte Carlo Simulation Output

For purposes of our example, let us assume that the return on the market over the next year will follow a normal distribution. (This is a widely used assumption in practice, despite the fact that few empirical studies find evidence to support it.) Suppose that the S&P 500 has historically returned 8.79% per annum on average, with a standard deviation of 14.65%. We will use these numbers as approximations for the average return and the standard deviation of the return on your investment in the stock market over the next year. Relying on historical data is flawed, but is a reasonable starting point.

Let us discuss the output one would obtain after generating 100 scenarios for the market return over the next year. (Note that to generate these scenarios, we simply need to draw 100 numbers from a normal distribution with mean 8.79% and standard deviation 14.65%.[4]) The input to the simulation would then be a sequence of 100 numbers such as

$$0.0245$$
$$-0.1561$$
$$0.1063$$
$$0.1300$$
$$-0.0801$$
$$0.2624$$
$$0.2621$$
$$0.0824$$
$$0.1358$$
$$0.1135$$
$$0.0605$$
$$\dots$$

---

[4]These scenarios can be generated with a number of software packages. If one uses only Excel, for example, then a random number from a normal distribution with mean μ and standard deviation σ can be generated with the formula =NORMINV(RAND(),μ,σ), or =NORMINV(RAND(),0.0879,0.1465) in this example. Excel has limited simulation capabilities but there are simulation add-ins to Excel such as @RISK and Crystal Ball that make the simulation of a wide range of probability distributions easy. In R, one can use the rnorm function. Specifically, the command scen <- rnorm(100, 0.0879, 0.1465) will generate 100 random numbers from a normal distribution with mean 0.0879 and standard deviation 0.1465, and will store them in the array scen for further analysis.

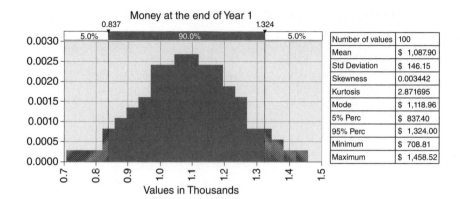

Exhibit 5.2 Histogram and summary statistics for the end-of-year distribution of 100 simulated values for $1,000 invested at the beginning of the year.

The output graph would look like Exhibit 5.2. Summary statistics obtained based on the 100 values of the distribution are provided to the right of the graph.[5]

If historical trends hold, you would expect to have $1,087.90 on average at the end of the first year. The standard deviation of the end-of-year capital you would expect is $146.15, that is, on average, you would expect to be $146.15 off the mean value. With 5% probability, you will not be able to make more than $837 (the 5th percentile of the distribution), and with 95% probability you will make less than $1,324 (the 95th percentile of the distribution). The skewness is close to 0 and the kurtosis is close to 3, which means that the simulated distribution is close to normal. (In fact, the output distribution is normal. This is because the input distribution we provided for the simulation of this simple relationship was normal and the relationship between the market return and the end-of-year capital is a simple linear expression. However, the estimate from the simulation will never be perfectly accurate.)

Be careful with the interpretation of minima and maxima in a simulation. Theoretically, the minimum and maximum we could have obtained in this simulation are negative and positive infinity because the probability distribution for the return (the normal distribution) has an infinite range.

---

[5]Note that, depending on the specific set of 100 scenarios we have generated, the graph will look different. Therefore, the descriptive statistics and the look of the graph we present here will only be close to what you would obtain if you try to repeat this experiment.

We did not obtain a particularly small minimum or a particularly large maximum because we only simulated 100 values. While not completely accurate mathematically, a rule of thumb is that an event in the tail of the distribution with probability of occurring of roughly less than 1/100 would be unlikely to appear in this set of simulated values. The minimum and the maximum are highly sensitive to the number of simulated values and whether the simulated values in the tails of the distribution provide good representation for the tails of the distribution. There are smart ways to simulate scenarios so that the tails are well represented but the minimum and the maximum values obtained in a simulation should nevertheless be interpreted with care.

In Chapter 2.11, we explained the statistical concept of confidence interval (CI) estimates. The main idea was the following: in statistics, when we want to estimate a specific parameter of a distribution, such as the mean, we take a sample and observe what the value of the parameter is in the sample (in technical terms, we record the value of the *sample statistic* for the mean). Instead of reporting a single value for our estimate for the mean, however, we could report an interval whose length is related to the probability that the true distribution parameter indeed lies in that interval.

Simulation is very similar to statistical sampling in that we try to represent the uncertainty by generating scenarios, that is, "sampling" values for the output parameter of interest from an underlying probability distribution. When we estimate the average (or any other parameter of interest) of the sample of scenarios, we run into the same issue statisticians do—we need to worry about the accuracy of the estimate. To compute a 95% CI estimate for the average end-of-year capital, we use the 95% CI formula from Chapter 2.11.2, and substitute the values obtained from the simulation statistics: $n = 100$, $\overline{X} = 1{,}087.90$ and $s = 146.15$. The value for $t_{(100-\alpha/2)\%,n-1}$ for 95% CI is the value of the 97.5th percentile of the standard t-distribution with 99 degrees of freedom, which is 1.98. The 95% CI is therefore

$$\left(1087.90 - 1.98 \cdot \frac{146.15}{\sqrt{100}}, 1087.90 + 1.98 \cdot \frac{146.15}{\sqrt{100}}\right)$$

$$= (\$1{,}058.90, \$1{,}116.90)$$

Therefore, if the 100 scenarios were *independent* when generated, we can be 95% confident that the true average end-of-year capital will be between \$1,058.90 and \$1,116.90. It just happens that because of the simplicity of the example, we know exactly what the true mean is. It is $(1 + 0.0879) \cdot 1{,}000 = \$1087.90$, because 8.79% was assumed to be the true mean of the distribution of returns (see Chapter 2.8 for calculating means of functions of random variables), and it is indeed contained inside the 95% CI. In 5% of all possible collections of 100 scenarios, however, we will be unlucky to draw a very extreme sample of scenarios, and the true mean will not be contained in the confidence interval we calculate. Note that if we had calculated a 99% confidence interval, then the true mean will not be contained in the confidence interval in only 1% of the cases. If we generated $4n$ (instead of n) scenarios, then the 95% confidence interval's length would be half of the current length. (This is because the square root of the number of scenarios is contained in the denominator of the expression that determines the length of the confidence interval.) We revisit the issue of confidence interval estimation and the implications for accuracy again later in this chapter when we talk about the number of scenarios needed in a simulation.

Drawing "independent" samples from distributions is not the most efficient way to simulate random numbers that provide good representation of the underlying probability distribution. Most simulation engines nowadays use sophisticated methodology that estimates parameters from the distribution of output variables of interest a lot more accurately. The CI formula we used above is a conservative bound, rather than an exact estimate, for the actual accuracy in estimating the mean. Still, it is a useful benchmark to have.

5.2　WHY USE SIMULATION?

The example in the previous section illustrated a very basic Monte Carlo simulation system. We started out with a deterministic model that involved a relationship between an input variable (market return $\tilde{r}_{0,1}$) and an output variable of interest (capital at the end of one year $\tilde{C}_1$). We modeled the input variable as a realization of a probability distribution (we assumed a normal distribution), generated scenarios for that input variable, and tracked what the value of the output variable was in every scenario by computing it through the formula that defines the relationship between $\tilde{C}_1$ and $\tilde{r}_{0,1}$. This is the general form of simulation models illustrated in Exhibit 5.1.

Despite its simplicity, this example allows us to point out one of the advantages of simulation modeling over pure mathematical modeling. Simulation enables you to evaluate (approximately) a *function* of a random variable. In this case, the function is very simple—your end-of-year capital, $\tilde{C}_1$, is dependent on the realization of the returns through the equation $(1 + \tilde{r}_{0,1})C_0$. If you are given a probability distribution for $\tilde{r}_{0,1}$, in some cases you can compute the probability distribution for $\tilde{C}_1$ in closed form. For example, if $\tilde{r}_{0,1}$ followed a normal distribution with mean $\mu_{0,1}$ and standard deviation $\sigma_{0,1}$, then $\tilde{C}_1$ would follow a normal distribution, too, with mean $(1 + \mu_{0,1})C_0$ and standard deviation $\sigma_{0,1}C_0$.

However, if $\tilde{r}_{0,1}$ did not follow a normal distribution, or if the output variable $\tilde{C}_1$ were a more complex function of the input variable $\tilde{r}_{0,1}$, it would be difficult and in some cases impossible to derive the probability distribution of $\tilde{C}_1$ from the probability distribution of $\tilde{r}_{0,1}$ in closed form. Using simulation simplifies matters substantially.

There are three other important advantages of simulation that can only be appreciated in more complex situations. The first one is that simulation enables us to visualize a probability distribution resulting from compounding probability distributions for multiple input variables. The second is that it allows us to incorporate correlations between input variables. The third is that simulation is a low-cost tool for checking the effect of changing a strategy on an output variable of interest. Next, we extend the investment example to provide illustrations of such situations.

5.2.1 Multiple Input Variables and Compounding Distributions

Suppose now that you are planning for retirement and decide to invest in the stock market for the next 30 years (instead of only the next year). Suppose that your initial capital is still $1,000. You are interested in the return (and, ultimately, in the end-of-year capital, $\tilde{C}_{30}$) you will have after 30 years.

Let us assume that every year, your investment returns from investing in the S&P 500 will follow a normal distribution with the mean and standard deviation from the example in Section 5.1.2. The final capital you have will depend on the realizations of 30 random variables—one for each year you are invested in the market.[6] We found through simulation in Section 5.1.2 that the probability distribution of the capital at the end of the first year will be normal. What do you think the probability distributions for the total return and the capital at the end of the 30th year will look like? Will they be normal?

An investment of $1 at time 0 will grow to $(1 + \tilde{r}_{0,1})(1 + \tilde{r}_{1,2})\ldots$ $(1 + \tilde{r}_{t-1,t})$ dollars at the end of year t, and the total return $\tilde{r}_{0,t}$ from time 0 to time t equals

$$\tilde{r}_{0,t} = (1 + \tilde{r}_{0,1})(1 + \tilde{r}_{1,2})\ldots(1 + \tilde{r}_{t-1,t}) - 1$$

Interestingly, the probability distribution of $\tilde{r}_{0,t}$ is not normal, and neither is the distribution of the capital at the end of 30 years. (The distribution

---

[6]We do not discuss the possibility that returns in different years may be correlated here. More sophisticated models for asset returns can, of course, be created.

of the capital is basically a scaled version of the distribution of total return, since it can be obtained as $\tilde{C}_{0,t} = (1 + \tilde{r}_{0,t}) \cdot C_0$, and the initial capital C_0 is a constant (nonrandom) number.) In general, here are some useful facts to keep in mind when dealing with multiple input probability distributions:

- When a constant is added to a random variable, as in 1 added to the random variable $\tilde{r}_{0,1}$, the distribution of $(1 + \tilde{r}_{0,1})$ has the same shape as the distribution of $\tilde{r}_{0,1}$; however, it is shifted to the right by 1.
- As we saw in Chapter 2.8, when a random variable is added to another random variable (e.g., $\tilde{r}_{0,1} + \tilde{r}_{1,2}$), we cannot simply "add" the two probability distributions. In fact, even in cases when the two distributions have the same shape, the probability distribution of the sum of the random variables does not necessarily have the same shape. There are some exceptions—for instance, if we add two independent normal random variables, the probability distribution of the sum is normal. However, holding aside this case, this is not true in general.

In our example, we are *multiplying* two random variables, $(1 + \tilde{r}_{0,1})$ and $(1 + \tilde{r}_{1,2})$, in order to obtain the total return. Products of random variables are even more difficult to visualize than sums of random variables. Again, it virtually never happens that a product of several random variables, even if the random variables all follow the same probability distributions, results in a random variable with that same probability distribution. The lognormal distribution, which we introduced in Chapter 3.1.4, is a rare exception, and this is one of the reasons that the lognormal distribution is used very often in financial modeling.

Fortunately, simulation makes visualizing the probability distribution of the product easy. Exhibit 5.3 presents the output distribution of the capital at the end of 30 years. We can observe (both from the graph and from the statistics for skewness and kurtosis) that the distribution is very skewed, even though the distributions for individual returns in each of the 30 years were symmetric (normal).

5.2.2 Incorporating Correlations

Let us now complicate the situation more. Suppose that you have the opportunity to invest in stocks and Treasury bonds over the next 30 years. Suppose that today you allocate 50% of your capital to the stock market by investing in the index fund, and 50% in bonds. Furthermore, suppose over the 30 years you never rebalance your portfolio (i.e., you do not change the allocation between stocks and bonds). What will be the total amount in your portfolio after 30 years?

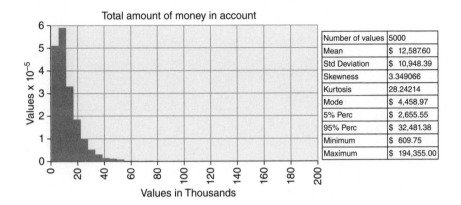

Total amount of money in account

Number of values	5000
Mean	$ 12,587.60
Std Deviation	$ 10,948.39
Skewness	3.349066
Kurtosis	28.24214
Mode	$ 4,458.97
5% Perc	$ 2,655.55
95% Perc	$ 32,481.38
Minimum	$ 609.75
Maximum	$ 194,355.00

Exhibit 5.3 Output distribution for amount of capital after 30 years.

Historically, stock market and the Treasury bond market returns have exhibited extremely low, but often statistically significant, negative correlation. This is because these two asset classes tend to move in opposite directions. When the stock market is performing poorly, investors tend to move their money to what they perceive to be safer investments such as bonds; conversely, when the stock market is performing well, investors tend to reallocate their portfolios, increasing their allocation to the stock market and reducing their allocation to bonds.

Visualizing the impact of multiple input variables at the same time and incorporating correlations between these variables is very difficult to do in an analytical way. Simulation eliminates the need for complex mathematics but preserves the benefits of creating richer and more accurate models. Correlations can be incorporated both implicitly (by generating joint scenarios for realizations of input variables, for example, by sampling from observed past data) and explicitly (by specifying a correlations matrix as an input to the simulation). Here, we give an example in which the correlations are specified as an input.

Let us assume that the correlation between the stock market and the Treasury bond market returns will be about -0.2. Let us also assume for the purpose of this exercise that the annualized return on the Treasury bonds in your portfolio will be normally distributed with mean 4% and standard deviation 7%. Therefore, the returns on the stock market and the bond market follow a multivariate normal distribution with correlation coefficient -0.2.

Exhibit 5.4 shows the output distribution for the total amount of money in your account after generating 5,000 scenarios for stock market (as measured by the S&P 500) returns and Treasury bond returns over 30 years. The shape of the distribution of the capital available after 30 years is similar to

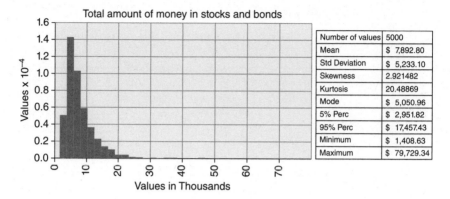

Exhibit 5.4 Histogram and summary statistics of the capital after 30 years from investing in the S&P 500 and Treasury bonds, taking into account the correlation between the returns on stocks and bonds.

the shape of the distribution from Exhibit 5.3; however, the variability (in terms of standard deviation) is smaller.

5.2.3 Evaluating Decisions

In the end, the goal of using simulation is to help us make decisions. Is a 50–50 portfolio allocation in stocks and bonds "better" than a 30–70 allocation? We refer to the former allocation as Strategy A, and to the latter as Strategy B. Let us evaluate the distribution of the capital at the end of 30 years for each allocation strategy, and use that knowledge to decide on the "better" allocation. Notice that it is unclear what "better" means in the context of uncertainty. We need to think about whether "better" for us means higher return on average, lower risk, acceptable trade-off between the two, and so on. Exhibit 5.5 contains the summary statistics of the simulated capital at the end of 30 years with each allocation over 5,000 scenarios.

We can observe that although Strategy A performs better than Strategy B as evaluated based on the mean capital at the end of 30 years ($7,905.30 for Strategy A versus $6,040.17 for Strategy B), Strategy A's standard deviation is higher ($5,341.57 versus $3,219.06). In terms of risk/return trade-off, as measured by the coefficient of variation,[7] Strategy A's CV is 67.57% (= $5,341.57/$7,905.30), whereas Strategy B's CV is 53.29% (= $3,219.06/$6,040.17), which makes Strategy A appear riskier than Strategy B. This is apparent also from the overlay chart shown in

---

[7]See Chapter 2.6.2.2 for a definition of coefficient of variation.

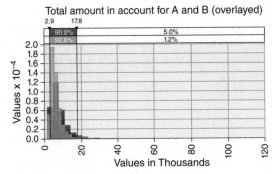

	Strategy A	Strategy B
Number of values	5000	5000
Mean	$ 7,905.30	$6,040.17
Std Deviation	$ 5,341.57	$3,219.06
Skewness	3.698306	3.514493
Kurtosis	43.44567	41.09948
Mode	$ 4,856.33	$4,389.39
5% Perc	$ 2,930.51	$2,809.56
95% Perc	$ 17,834.32	$11,940.22
Minimum	$ 1,131.24	$1,287.31
Maximum	$ 116,550.20	$70,578.09

Exhibit 5.5 Comparison of Strategy A (equal allocation to stocks and bonds, in dark gray) and Strategy B (allocation of 30% to stocks and 70% to bonds, in light gray).

Exhibit 5.5—much of the mass of the histogram for Strategy B is contained within the histogram for Strategy A, which means that Strategy B has less variability and results in less extreme outcomes than Strategy A.

The standard deviation may not be a good measure of risk when the underlying distributions are asymmetric. Strategy A's 5th percentile ($2,930.51), for example, is higher than Strategy B's 5th percentile ($2,809.56), meaning that if you are concerned with events that happen with 5% probability, Strategy A would be less risky. Strategy A also has a higher upside—its 95th percentile ($17,834.32) is higher than Strategy B's 95th percentile ($11,940.22).[8] The fact that Strategy A has a high upside "penalizes" its standard deviation relative to the standard deviation of Strategy B because it results in more outcomes that are far away from the mean. A high standard deviation is not necessarily a bad thing if the largest deviations from the mean happen on the upside.

It should be clear from the discussion so far that the summary statistics do not tell the whole story. It is important to look at the entire distribution of outcomes. Suppose now that we would like to compare Strategy A to Strategy B on a scenario-by-scenario basis. In what percentage of scenarios does Strategy B perform better than Strategy A? One efficient way to answer this question is to create an additional variable, Difference (A-B), that keeps track of the difference between the capital at the end of 30 years from Strategy A

---

[8] We could be looking at the minimum and maximum realized outcomes as measures of the "riskiness" of Strategy A and Strategy B as well, but recall that those are very sensitive to the number of trials in the simulation, and should be interpreted with care.

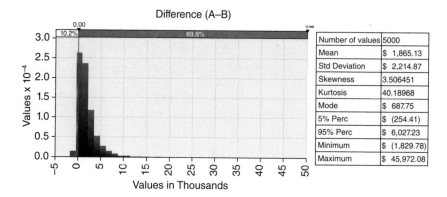

Exhibit 5.6 Histogram and summary statistics for the difference between the capital at the end of 30 years with Strategy A and with Strategy B.

and from Strategy B during the simulation. Exhibit 5.6 shows a histogram of Difference (A-B) and presents its summary statistics.[9]

It is interesting to observe that even though Strategy A appeared riskier than Strategy B based on the summary statistics in Exhibit 5.5 (Strategy A's standard deviation was almost twice the standard deviation of Strategy B), Strategy A results in lower realized outcomes than Strategy B in only 10.2% of the 5,000 generated scenarios. (As the graph in Exhibit 5.6 illustrates, 10.2% of the 5,000 scenarios for Difference (A–B) have values less than zero.) This perspective on the risk of one strategy versus the risk of another is valuable because it can substantially impact the final decision on which strategy to choose. For example, the problematic scenarios can be specifically identified, and in some situations, managerial action can be taken to avoid them. A strategy that appears riskier may therefore be selected if it is desirable for other qualitative reasons.

When comparing two alternative decisions under uncertainty, it is technically correct (and fair) to evaluate them under the same set of scenarios. For example, when obtaining the summary statistics for Strategy A and Strategy B earlier, we should have used the same set of 5,000 scenarios for both. This would eliminate circumstances in which we happened to generate more favorable scenarios when evaluating one of the strategies than the other, which would lead us to conclude erroneously that the strategy evaluated over the more favorable set of scenarios is better.

---

[9]Note that this is a histogram of the differences between the total amount of capital realized with Strategy A and the total amount of capital realized with Strategy B in each of the 5,000 scenarios generated.

In principle, if we generate a huge number of scenarios for the two strategies, even if the two sets of scenarios are not the same, the estimates will be quite accurate. However, generating a large number of scenarios is time consuming. Moreover, even a difference of a few digits after the decimal point may be significant in some financial applications.

One way to simulate the same set of scenarios multiple times is to specify the *seed* of the simulation. The seed determines the first random number that gets generated in the simulation. We explain what the seed of the simulation is in Section 5.4. For now, it is only important to understand that it determines the first random number that gets generated in a simulation.

By default, most simulation packages change the seed every time they run a simulation. If we enter a particular number for the seed (depending on the software, different ranges for possible seed values are available), we will be fixing the first scenario that will be generated, which would enable the software to generate the same sequence of scenarios again the next time it runs the simulation.[10]

Alternatively, in a statistical modeling language like R, we can dedicate variables in our program that store the generated scenarios, and then evaluate all the different strategies (Strategy A and Strategy B in this example) over that same set of scenarios. Storing 5,000 scenarios is not a problem, but if there are multiple variables and the number of scenarios increases substantially, we could run into memory problems.

5.3 HOW MANY SCENARIOS?

A simulation may not be able to capture all possible realizations of uncertainties in the model. For instance, think about the distribution of the end-of-year capital in Section 5.1.1. As we explained in Section 5.1.2, the possible number of values for the simulation output variable—the end-of-year capital—is technically infinite. Thus, we could never obtain the exact distribution of $\tilde{C}_1$ or the exact expected value of $\tilde{C}_1$ by simulation. We can, however, get close. The accuracy of the estimation will depend on the number of generated scenarios. As we discussed in Section 5.1.2, if the scenario generation is truly random, then the variability (the standard error) of the estimate of the true expected value will be $s/\sqrt{n}$, where s is the standard deviation of the simulated values for the output variable and n is the number of scenarios.

---

[10]To set the seed in R, one uses the command `set.seed`, for example, `set.seed(123)`. In Excel, this is not straightforward because one can only generate one random variable at the time. Excel add-ins for simulation all have the ability to set the seed by modifying the simulation settings.

Hence, to double the accuracy of estimating the mean of the output distribution, we would need to quadruple (roughly) the number of scenarios. For instance, in the example in Section 5.1.2, we generated 100 scenarios, calculated that the average capital after one year is $1,087.90, and estimated the 95% CI for the average capital as ($1,058.90, $1,116.90). We concluded that we can be 95% confident that the true expected capital will be between $1,058.90 and $1,116.90; that is, that the true mean will not be further than $29 from the mean estimated from the simulation ($1,087.90). Now suppose that we had obtained the same numbers for sample mean ($1,087.90) and sample standard deviation ($146.15) but we had generated four times as many scenarios (400). The 95% CI would have been

$$\left(1087.90 - 1.97 \cdot \frac{146.15}{\sqrt{400}}, 1087.90 + 1.97 \cdot \frac{146.15}{\sqrt{400}} \right)$$
$$= (\$1,073.53, \ \$1102.27).[11]$$

This means that we could be 95% confident that the true mean would not be more than $14.37 from the simulated mean of $1,087.90, which is about half of the amount by which we could be off ($29) when we generate 100 scenarios. Therefore, our accuracy has increased about twofold after quadrupling the number of generated scenarios.

Increasing the number of scenarios to improve accuracy can get expensive computationally, especially in more complicated multiperiod situations such as the simulation of a 30-year investment in Section 5.2.1. Fortunately, there are modern methods for generation of random numbers and scenarios that can help reduce the computational burden.

Although the average output from a simulation is important, it is often not the only quantity of interest, something that practitioners tend to forget when using simulation to value complex financial instruments. When evaluating the value-at-risk or the conditional value-at-risk of a portfolio, for example, a portfolio manager may be interested in the percentiles of the distribution of possible portfolio returns. Unfortunately, it is not as straightforward to determine the accuracy of estimates of percentiles and other sample statistics from a simulation. There are some useful results from probability theory that apply,[12] and we can use bootstrapping, as described in

---

[11] Note that the value for $t_{(100-\alpha/2)\%, \, n-1}$ has decreased slightly as well—this is because we now have more observations, that is, more degrees of freedom, so the t distribution is less spread out, and is closer to the normal distribution. See Chapter 3.1.3 for more information on the t distribution.

[12] See, for example, Chapter 9 in Glasserman (2004).

Chapter 2.11.3. However, in general, the question of how many scenarios one should generate to get a good representation of the output distribution does not have an easy answer. This issue is complicated further by the fact that results from probability theory do not necessarily apply to many of the scenario-generating methods used in practice, which do not simulate "pure" random samples of observations, but instead use smarter simulation methods that reduce the number of scenarios needed to achieve good estimate accuracy.

5.4 RANDOM NUMBER GENERATION

Contrary to what many would imagine, coming up with truly random numbers is difficult and time consuming. Moreover, the ability to reproduce the random number sequence and to analyze the random number characteristics is actually a desirable property for random number generators. In particular, the ability to reproduce a sequence of random numbers allows for reducing the variance of estimates and for debugging computer code by rerunning experiments in the same conditions in which they were run in previous iterations of code development.

Most simulation software employs random number generation algorithms that produce streams of numbers that appear to be random, but in fact are a result of a clearly defined series of calculation steps in which the next "random number" x_n in the sequence is a function of the previous "random number" x_{n-1}, that is, $x_n = g(x_{n-1})$. As mentioned earlier, the sequence starts with a number called the seed, and if the same seed is used in several simulations, each simulation sequence will contain exactly the same numbers, which is helpful for running fair comparisons between different strategies evaluated under uncertainty. It is quite an amazing statistical fact that some of these recursion formulas (named *pseudo-random number generators*) define sequences of numbers that imitate random behavior well and appear to obey (roughly) some major laws of probability, such as the Central Limit Theorem (Chapter 2.11.1).

Generating random numbers from a wide variety of distributions reduces to generating random numbers from the continuous uniform distribution on the unit interval [0,1], that is, to generating random numbers on the interval [0,1] in such a way that each value between 0 and 1 is equally likely to occur.[13] Many computer languages and software packages have a command for generating a random number between 0 and 1: =RAND()

---

[13]See Pachamanova and Fabozzi (2010).

in Microsoft Excel, `runif(n, min=0, max=1)` in R, `rand(1)` in MATLAB and FORTRAN, and `rand()` in C++.

A truly random number generator may produce clustered observations, which necessitates generating many scenarios in order to obtain a good representation of the output distribution of interest. *Quasi-random* (also called *low discrepancy*) sequences as well as a variety of so-called variance reduction techniques are used to speed up execution and improve accuracy in simulations. Most simulation packages implement such techniques. The interested reader is referred to Chapters 4 and 14 in Pachamanova and Fabozzi (2010) for more information.

Summary

- Monte Carlo simulation is a valuable tool for evaluating functional relationships between variables, visualizing the effect of multiple correlated variables, and testing strategies.
- Monte Carlo simulation involves creating scenarios for output variables of interest by generating scenarios for input variables for which we have more information.
- The art of Monte Carlo simulation modeling is in selecting input probability distributions wisely and interpreting output distributions carefully.
- The distributions of output variables can be analyzed through statistical summaries. Statistics of interest include measures of central tendency (average, median, mode), measures of volatility (standard deviation, percentiles), skewness, and kurtosis.
- Minima and maxima from simulations should be interpreted with care because they often depend on the input assumptions and are very sensitive to the number of trials in the simulation.
- The accuracy of estimation through simulation is related to the number of generated scenarios. Unfortunately, the relationship is nonlinear—in order to double the accuracy, we need to more than quadruple the number of scenarios.
- Random number generation is not trivial, and simulation software packages do not produce truly "random" numbers. There is value, however, in generating random number sequences that are replicable, and thus not completely random.

CHAPTER 6

Optimization Modeling

This chapter introduces optimization—a methodology for selecting an optimal strategy given an objective and a set of constraints. Optimization appears in a variety of financial applications, including portfolio allocation, trading strategies, identifying arbitrage opportunities, and pricing financial derivatives. In this chapter, we motivate the discussion with a simple example, and describe how optimization problems are formulated and solved.

Let us recall the retirement example from Chapter 5.2.3. We showed how to compute the realized return on the portfolio of stocks and bonds if we allocate 50% of the capital in each of the two investments. Can we obtain a "better" portfolio return with a different allocation? (As we discussed in Chapter 5, a "better" return is not well defined in the context of uncertainty, so for the sake of argument, let us assume that "better" means higher expected return.) We found that if the allocation in stocks and bonds is 30% and 70%, respectively, rather than 50% and 50%, we end up with a lower portfolio expected return, but also lower portfolio standard deviation. What about an allocation of (60%, 40%)? Of (80%, 20%)?

In this example, we are dealing with only two investments (the two asset classes), and we have no additional requirements on the portfolio structure. It is, however, still difficult to enumerate all the possibilities and find those that provide the optimal tradeoff of return and risk. In practice, portfolio managers are considering thousands of potential investments and need to worry about transaction costs, requirements on the portfolio composition, and trading constraints, which makes it impossible to find the "best" portfolio allocation by trial-and-error. The optimization methodology provides a disciplined way to approach the problem of optimal asset allocation. Problems such as the most cost-effective way to balance a portfolio can also be cast in the optimization framework.

6.1 OPTIMIZATION FORMULATIONS

The increase in computational power and the tremendous pace of developments in the operations research field in the past 20 to 25 years has led to highly efficient algorithms and user-friendly software for solving optimization problems of many different kinds. To a large extent, the art of optimization modeling is in framing a situation so that the formulation fits within recognized frameworks for problem specifications, and can be passed to optimization solvers. It is important to understand the main building blocks of optimization formulations, as well as the limitations of the software and the insights that can be gained from the output of optimization solvers.

An optimization problem formulation consists of three parts:[1]

1. A set of *decision variables* (usually represented as an $N \times 1$–dimensional vector array[2] $\mathbf{x}$),
2. An *objective function*, which is a function of the decision variables ($f(\mathbf{x})$), and
3. A set of *constraints* defined by functions ($g_i(\mathbf{x})$, $h_j(\mathbf{x})$), $i = 1, \ldots, I$, $j = 1, \ldots J$ of the general form $g_i(\mathbf{x}) \leq 0$ (inequality constraints) and $h_j(\mathbf{x}) = 0$ (equality constraints).

The decision variables are numerical quantities that represent the decisions to be made. In the portfolio example, the decision variables could be the portfolio weights. Alternatively, they could represent the dollar amount to allocate to each asset class. The objective function is a mathematical expression of the goal, and the constraints are mathematical expressions of the limitations in the business situation. In our example, the objective function could be an expression that computes the expected portfolio return, and the constraints could include an expression that computes the total portfolio risk. We can then maximize the expression of the objective function subject to an upper limit on the risk we are willing to tolerate.

Optimization software expects users to specify all three components of an optimization problem, although it is sometimes possible to have optimization problems with no constraints. The latter kind of optimization problems is referred to as *unconstrained* optimization. Unconstrained optimization problems are typically solved with standard techniques from calculus,[3] and

---

[1] See the Appendix for a review of matrix-vector notation.
[2] Optimization formulations can handle decision variables that are matrix arrays as well, but these types of problems are too advanced for the purposes of this book. This area of optimization is called semi-definite programming. See Fabozzi, Kolm, Pachamanova, and Focardi (2007) for a discussion of its applications in finance.
[3] In other words, by setting the derivative of the objective function to zero.

the optimal solution is selected from all possible points in the N-dimensional space of the decision variables **x**. When there are constraints, only some points in that space will be *feasible*, that is, only some will satisfy the constraints. The values of the decision variables that are feasible and result in the best value for the objective function are called the *optimal solution*. Optimization solvers typically return only one optimal solution. However, it is possible to have multiple optimal solutions, that is, multiple feasible solutions **x** that produce the same optimal value for the objective function.[4]

When formulating optimization problems, it is important to realize that the decision variables need to participate in the mathematical expressions for the objective function and the constraints that are passed to an optimization solver. Optimization algorithms then tweak the values of the decision variables in these expressions in a smart, computationally efficient way in order to produce the best value for the objective function with values for the decision variables that satisfy all of the constraints. In other words, we cannot simply pass the expression

$$\text{Maximize} \quad \textit{Portfolio Expected Return}$$

to an optimization solver, unless *Portfolio Expected Return* is expressed as a function of the decision variables (the portfolio weights). As we show in Chapter 8, the expected portfolio return can be expressed in terms of the portfolio weights as $\mathbf{w}'\boldsymbol{\mu}$, where $\mathbf{w} = (w_1, \ldots, w_N)'$ and $\boldsymbol{\mu} = (\mu_1, \ldots, \mu_N)'$ are N-dimensional arrays containing the weights and the expected returns of the N assets in the portfolio, respectively. So, the objective function should be written as

$$\max_{\mathbf{w}} \quad \mathbf{w}'\boldsymbol{\mu}$$

which is interpreted as "maximize the value of $\mathbf{w}'\boldsymbol{\mu}$ over the possible values for **w**."

In addition, the input data in a classical optimization problem formulation need to be fixed numbers, not random variables. For example, the objective function of an optimization problem cannot be passed to a solver as

$$\text{Maximize} \quad \textit{Portfolio Return}$$

---

[4]Unfortunately, there is no straightforward way to request that all optimal solutions be listed in optimization software output. If we are interested in checking whether there is another optimal solution, we need to modify the optimization problem formulation to exclude the current optimal solution, and rerun the optimization solver again. If a second optimal solution exists, it will be found by the solver when the first optimal solution is no longer a feasible option.

where *Portfolio Return* = $\mathbf{w}'\,\tilde{\mathbf{r}}$, and $\tilde{\mathbf{r}} = (\tilde{r}_1, \ldots, \tilde{r}_N)'$ is the N-dimensional array with (uncertain) asset returns with some probability distributions. Some areas in optimization, such as *robust optimization* and *stochastic programming*, study methodologies for solving optimization problems in which the input data are subject to uncertainty and follow theoretical or empirical probability distributions. However, in the end, the methods for solving such problems reduce to specifying the coefficients in the optimization problem as fixed numbers that are representative of the underlying probability distributions.

6.1.1 Minimization versus Maximization

Most generally, optimization solvers require an optimization problem formulation to be of the kind

$$\min_{\mathbf{x}} \quad f(\mathbf{x})$$

$$\text{subject to} \quad g_i(\mathbf{x}) \le 0 \quad i = 1, \ldots, I$$
$$h_j(\mathbf{x}) = 0 \quad j = 1, \ldots, J$$

There are variations on this formulation, and some have to do with whether the optimization problem falls in a specific class. (We discuss different categories of optimization problems based on the form of their objective function and the shape of their feasible set in Section 6.2.) Some optimization software syntax allows for specifying only minimization problems, while other optimization software packages are more flexible, and accept both minimization and maximization problems.

Standard formulation requirements are not as restrictive as they appear at first sight. For example, an optimization problem that involves finding the maximum of a function $f(\mathbf{x})$ can be recast as a minimization problem by minimizing the expression $-f(\mathbf{x})$, and vice versa: an optimization problem that involves finding the minimum of a function $f(\mathbf{x})$ can be recast as a maximization problem by maximizing the expression $-f(\mathbf{x})$. To obtain the actual value of the objective function, one then flips the sign of the optimal value. Exhibit 6.1 illustrates the situation for a quadratic function of one variable x. The optimal value for max $f(x)$ is obtained at the optimal solution x^*. The optimal value for min $-f(x)$ is obtained at x^* as well. It also holds that

$$\max_{x} \quad f(x) = -\min_{x} \quad -f(x)$$

For the portfolio expected return maximization example above, stating the objective function as

$$\max_{\mathbf{w}} \quad \mathbf{w}'\boldsymbol{\mu}$$

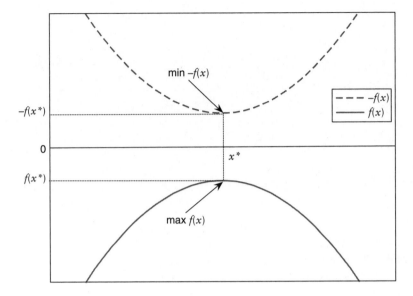

Exhibit 6.1 An example of the optimal objective function values for $\max_x f(x)$ and $\min_x -f(x)$ for a quadratic objective function $f(x)$ of a single decision variable x.

or

$$\min_{\mathbf{w}} \quad -\mathbf{w}'\boldsymbol{\mu}$$

will produce the same optimal values for the decision variables $\mathbf{w}$. To get the actual optimal objective function value for $\max_\mathbf{w} \mathbf{w}'\boldsymbol{\mu}$, we would flip the sign of the optimal objective function value obtained after minimizing $-\mathbf{w}'\boldsymbol{\mu}$.

6.1.2 Local versus Global Optima

In optimization, we distinguish between two types of optimal solutions: *global* and *local* optimal solutions. A global optimal solution is the "best" solution for any value of the decision variables vector $\mathbf{x}$ in the set of *all* feasible solutions. A local optimal solution is the best solution in a *neighborhood* of feasible solutions. In the latter case, the objective function value at any point "close" to a local optimal solution is worse than the objective function value at the local optimal solution. Exhibit 6.2 illustrates the global (point A) and local (point B) optimal solution for the unconstrained minimization of a function of two variables.

Most classical optimization algorithms can only find local optima. They start at a point, and go through solutions in a direction in which the objective function value improves. Their performance has an element of luck that has

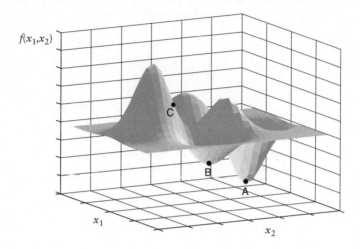

Exhibit 6.2 Global (point A) versus local (point B) minimum for a function of two variables x_1 and x_2.

to do with picking a good starting point for the algorithm. For example, if a nonlinear optimization algorithm starts at point C in Exhibit 6.2, it may find the local minimum B first, and never get to the global minimum A. In the general case, finding the global optimal solution can be difficult and time consuming, and involves finding all local optimal solutions first, and then picking the best one among them.

The good news is that in some cases, optimization algorithms can explore the special structure of the objective function and the constraints to deliver stronger results. In addition, for some categories of optimization problems, a local optimal solution is in fact guaranteed to be the global optimal solution, and many optimization problems in finance have that property. (We review the most important kinds of such "nice" optimization problems in Section 6.2.) This makes the ability to recognize the type of optimization problem in a given situation and to formulate the optimization problem in a way that enables optimization algorithms to take advantage of the special problem structure even more critical.

6.1.3 Multiple Objectives

In practice, one often encounters situations in which one would like to optimize several objectives at the same time. For example, a portfolio manager may want to maximize the portfolio expected return and positive skew while minimizing the portfolio variance and kurtosis. There is no straightforward way to pass several objectives to an optimization solver. A multiobjective optimization problem needs to be reformulated as an optimization problem with a single objective. There are two commonly used methods to do this. The first is to assign weights to the different objectives, and optimize the weighted sum of objectives as a single objective function. The second is to optimize the most important objective, and include the other objectives as constraints, after assigning to each of them a bound on the value one is willing to tolerate.

6.2 IMPORTANT TYPES OF OPTIMIZATION PROBLEMS

Optimization problems can be categorized based on the form of their objective function and constraints as well as the kind of decision variables. The type of optimization problem with which one is faced determines what software is appropriate, the efficiency of the algorithm for solving the problem, and the degree to which the optimal solution returned by the optimization solver is trustworthy and useful. Awareness of this fact is particularly helpful in situations in which there are multiple ways to formulate the optimization problem. The way in which one states the formulation will determine whether the optimization solver can exploit any special structure in the problem and achieve stronger results.

6.2.1 Convex Programming

As we mentioned in Section 6.1.2, some general optimization problems have "nice" structure in the sense that a local optimal solution is guaranteed to be the global optimal solution. *Convex optimization problems* have that property. A general convex optimization problem is of the form

$$\min_{\mathbf{x}} \quad f(\mathbf{x})$$

$$\text{subject to} \quad g_i(\mathbf{x}) \leq 0 \quad i = 1, \ldots, I$$

$$\mathbf{A}\mathbf{x} = \mathbf{b}$$

where both $f(\mathbf{x})$ and $g_i(\mathbf{x})$ are convex functions and $\mathbf{A}\mathbf{x} = \mathbf{b}$ is a system of linear equalities. A *convex function* of a single variable x has the shape in Exhibit 6.3(a). For a convex function, a line that connects any two points on the curve is always above the curve. The "opposite" of a convex function is a *concave function* (see Exhibit 6.3[b]), which looks like a "cave." For a concave function, a line that connects any two points on the curve is always below the curve.

Convex programming problems encompass several classes of problems with special structure, including *linear programming* (LP), some *quadratic programming* (QP), *second-order cone programming* (SOCP),

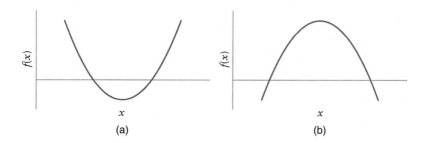

Exhibit 6.3 Examples of (a) a convex function; (b) a concave function.

and *semidefinite programming* (SDP). Algorithms for solving convex optimization problems are more efficient than algorithms for solving general nonlinear problems but it is important to keep in mind that even within the class of convex problems, some convex problems are computationally more challenging than others. LP problems are best studied and easiest to solve with commercial solvers, followed by convex QP problems, SOCP problems, and SDP problems.

We introduce LP, QP, and SOCP in more detail next. Many classical problems in finance involve linear and quadratic programming, including asset-liability problems, portfolio allocation problems, and some financial derivative pricing applications. SDP problems are advanced formulations that have become more widely used in financial applications with recent advances in the field of robust optimization. They are beyond the scope of this book, but we refer interested readers to Fabozzi, Kolm, Pachamanova, and Focardi (2007) for a detailed overview of robust optimization formulations.

6.2.2 Linear Programming

Linear programming refers to optimization problems in which both the objective function and the constraints are linear expressions in the decision variables.[5] The standard formulation statement for linear optimization

_____

[5]As we explained in Chapter 4, linear expressions involve sums and differences of terms of the kind (*constant* · *decision variable*), and exclude expressions like (*constant* · *decision variable*^{2}), (*decision variable 1* · *decision variable 2*), (*decision variable 1 / decision variable 2*), log(*decision variable*), and so on. Note that an expression of the kind (*constant*^{2} · *decision variable*) is still a linear expression in the decision variable, even if it is not a linear expression in the constant. Linear optimization formulations are concerned only with whether the expressions in the objective function and constraints are linear expressions in the decision variables.

problems is

$$\min_{\mathbf{x}} \quad \mathbf{c}'\mathbf{x}$$

$$\text{subject to} \quad \mathbf{Ax} = \mathbf{b}$$

$$\mathbf{x} \geq \mathbf{0}$$

All optimization problems involving linear expressions for the objective function and the decision variables can be converted to this standard form. We will see an example in Section 6.3.

Linear optimization problems are the easiest kind of problems to solve. Modern specialized optimization software can handle LP formulations with hundreds of thousands of decision variables and constraints in a matter of seconds. In addition, linear optimization problems belong to the class of convex problems for which a local optimal solution is guaranteed to be the global optimal solution. (We discuss this in more detail in Section 6.4.) LPs arise in a number of finance applications, such as asset allocation among asset classes, the construction of portfolios of securities within an asset class, and identification of arbitrage opportunities. The sample optimization problem formulation we provide in Section 6.3 is a linear optimization problem.

6.2.3 Quadratic Programming

Quadratic programming problems have an objective function that is a quadratic expression in the decision variables and constraints that are linear expressions in the decision variables. The standard form of a quadratic optimization problem is

$$\min_{\mathbf{x}} \quad \tfrac{1}{2}\mathbf{x}'\mathbf{Qx} + \mathbf{c}'\mathbf{x}$$

$$\text{subject to} \quad \mathbf{Ax} = \mathbf{b}$$

$$\mathbf{x} \geq \mathbf{0}$$

where $\mathbf{x}$ is an N-dimensional vector of decision variables as before, and the other arrays are input data:

$\mathbf{Q}$ is an $N \times N$ matrix,

$\mathbf{c}$ is an N-dimensional vector,

$\mathbf{A}$ is a $J \times N$ matrix,

$\mathbf{b}$ is a J-dimensional vector.

When the matrix $\mathbf{Q}$ is positive semi-definite,[6] the objective function is convex. (It is a sum of a convex quadratic term and a linear function, and

---

[6]See the Appendix for the definition of a positive semi-definite matrix.

a linear function is both convex and concave.) Since the objective function is convex and the constraints are linear expressions, we have a convex optimization problem. The problem can be solved by efficient algorithms, and we can trust that any local optimum they find is in fact the global optimum. When Q is not positive semi-definite, however, the quadratic problem can have several local optimal solutions and stationary points, and is therefore more difficult to solve.

The most prominent use of quadratic programming in finance is for asset allocation and trading models. We will see examples in Chapter 8.

6.2.4 Second-Order Cone Programming

Second-order cone programs (SOCPs) have the general form

$$\min_{\mathbf{x}} \quad \mathbf{c}'\mathbf{x}$$

$$\text{subject to} \quad \mathbf{A}\mathbf{x} = \mathbf{b}$$

$$||\mathbf{C}_i\mathbf{x} + \mathbf{d}_i|| \leq \mathbf{c}_i'\mathbf{x} + e_i, \quad i = 1, \ldots, I$$

where $\mathbf{x}$ is an N-dimensional vector of decision variables as before and the other arrays are input data:

$\mathbf{c}$ is an N-dimensional vector,

$\mathbf{A}$ is a $J \times N$ matrix,

$\mathbf{b}$ is a J-dimensional vector,

$\mathbf{C}_i$ are $I_i \times N$ matrices,

$\mathbf{d}_i$ are I_i-dimensional vectors,

e_i are scalars.

The notation $||\cdot||$ stands for second norm, or Euclidean norm. (It is sometimes denoted $||\cdot||_2$ to differentiate it from other types of norms.) The Euclidean norm of an N-dimensional vector $\mathbf{x}$ is defined as[7]

$$||\mathbf{x}|| = \sqrt{x_1^2 + \cdots + x_N^2}$$

The SOCP class of problems is more general than the classes covered in Sections 6.2.2 and 6.2.3. LPs, convex QPs, and convex problems with quadratic objective function and quadratic constraints can be reformulated as SOCPs with some algebra.

---

[7] See also Section A.4 in the Appendix.

It turns out that SOCP problems share many nice properties with linear programs, so algorithms for their optimization are very efficient. SOCP formulations in finance arise mostly in robust optimization applications. We discuss such formulations in Chapter 7.

6.2.5 Integer and Mixed Integer Programming

So far, we have classified optimization problems according to the form of the objective function and the constraints. Optimization problems can be classified also according to the type of decision variables **x**. Namely, when the decision variables are restricted to be integer (or, more generally, discrete) values, we refer to the corresponding optimization problem as an *integer programming* (IP) or a *discrete problem*. When some decision variables are discrete and some are continuous, we refer to the optimization problem as a *mixed integer programming* (MIP) problem. In special cases of integer problems in which the decision variables can only take values 0 or 1, we refer to the optimization problem as a *binary optimization problem*.

Integer and mixed integer optimization formulations are useful for formulating extensions to classical portfolio allocation problems. Index-tracking formulations and many constraints on portfolio structure faced by managers in practice require modeling with discrete decision variables. Examples of constraints include maximum number of assets to be held in the portfolio (so-called cardinality constraints), maximum number of trades, round-lot constraints (constraints on the size of the orders in which assets can be traded in the market),[8] and fixed transaction costs. We discuss such formulations further in Chapter 11.

6.3 A SIMPLE OPTIMIZATION PROBLEM FORMULATION EXAMPLE: PORTFOLIO ALLOCATION

To provide better intuition for how optimization problems are formulated, we give a simplified example of an asset allocation problem formulation. We will see more advanced nonlinear problems formulations in the context of portfolio applications in Chapters 8 and 11.

We explain the derivation of the optimization problem formulation in detail, so that the process of optimization problem formulation can be explicitly outlined. The problem formulation is the crucial step—once we are able to map a situation to one of the optimization problem types

---

[8]In the stock market, a round lot is 100 shares. In the bond market, a round lot varies with the type of bond.

reviewed in Section 6.2, we can find the optimal solution with optimization software. Later in this chapter, we explain how optimization formulations can be input into a solver, and how the output can be retrieved and interpreted.

Suppose that the portfolio manager at a large university in the United States is tasked with investing a $10 million donation to the university endowment. He has decided to invest these funds only in mutual funds[9] and is considering the following four types of mutual funds: an aggressive growth fund (Fund 1), an index fund (Fund 2), a corporate bond fund (Fund 3), and a money market fund (Fund 4), each with a different expected annual return and risk level.[10] The investment guidelines established by the Board of Trustees limit the percentage of the funds that can be allocated to any single type of investment to 40% of the total amount. The data for the portfolio manager's task are provided in Exhibit 6.4. In addition, in order to contain the risk of the investment to an acceptable level, the amount of money allocated to the aggressive growth and the corporate bond funds cannot exceed 60% of the portfolio, and the aggregate average risk level of the portfolio cannot exceed 2. What is the optimal portfolio allocation for achieving the maximum expected return at the end of the year if no short selling is allowed?[11]

EXHIBIT 6.4   Data for the portfolio manager's problem.

Fund Type	Growth	Index	Bond	Money Market
Fund #	1	2	3	4
Expected return	20.69%	5.87%	10.52%	2.43%
Risk level	4	2	2	1
Max investment	40%	40%	40%	40%

---

[9]A mutual fund, more specifically an open-end investment company, uses proceeds from the sale of shares to the public to invest in various securities. The value of one share of a mutual fund is computed by dividing the difference between the mutual fund's assets and liabilities by the number of shares outstanding. This value is called the net asset value (NAV). Mutual funds have different investment objectives. In the case of a money market fund, the fund manager can only invest in short-term high-quality investments (money market instruments). This type of mutual fund has the lowest risk and therefore the lowest expected return (see Exhibit 6.4).

[10]This is just a simplified example of portfolio allocation with risk considerations. We discuss more sophisticated portfolio allocation schemes in Chapters 10 through 14.

[11]*Short selling* is when an investor borrows a security from a broker and sells it, with the understanding that the security must be returned later. Alternatively, the investor

To formulate the optimization problem, the first thing we need to ask is what the objective is. In this case, the logical objective is to maximize the expected portfolio return. The second step is to think of how to define the decision variables. The decision variables need to be specified in such a way as to allow for expressing the objective as a mathematical expression of the quantities the manager can control to achieve his objective. The latter point is obvious, but sometimes missed when formulating optimization problems for the first time. For example, although the market return on the assets is variable and increasing market returns will increase the portfolio's return, changing the behavior of the market is not under the manager's control. The manager, however, can change the amounts he invests in different assets in order to achieve his objective.[12] Thus, the vector of decision variables can be defined as

$$\mathbf{x} = (x_1, x_2, x_3, x_4): \text{amounts (in \$) invested in Funds 1, 2, 3,}$$

$$\text{and 4, respectively.}$$

Let the vector of expected returns be $\boldsymbol{\mu} = (20.69\%, 5.87\%, 10.52\%, 2.43\%)$. Then, the objective function can be written as

$$f(x) = \boldsymbol{\mu}'\mathbf{x} = (20.69\%) \cdot x_1 + (5.87\%) \cdot x_2 + (10.52\%) \cdot x_3 + (2.43\%) \cdot x_4$$

It is always a good idea to write down the actual description and the units for the decision variables, the objective function, and the constraints. For example, the units of the objective function value in this example are dollars.

Finally, there are several constraints.

1. The total amount invested should be $10 million. This can be formulated as $x_1 + x_2 + x_3 + x_4 = 10,000,000$.
2. The total amount invested in Fund 1 and Fund 3 cannot be more than 60% of the total investment ($6 million). This can be written as

$$x_1 + x_3 \leq 6,000,000$$

---

is said to have taken a *short position* in the security. An investor may pursue a short sale if the investor believes that the price of the security will fall, making the future purchase of the security cheaper and realizing a profit from the sale of the security today.

[12] As we mentioned earlier, there are often different ways to formulate an optimization problem for the same business situation. For example, the decision variables for this example can be defined as the percentages invested (rather than the dollar amounts invested) in each fund. The problem formulation will be very similar, and the optimal solution will qualitatively be the same.

3. The average risk level of the portfolio cannot be more than 2. This constraint can be expressed as

4*(proportion of investment with risk level 4) + 2*(proportion of investment with risk level 2) + 1*(proportion of investment with risk level 1) ≤ 2 or, mathematically, as

$$\frac{4 \cdot x_1 + 2 \cdot x_2 + 2 \cdot x_3 + 1 \cdot x_4}{x_1 + x_2 + x_3 + x_4} \leq 2$$

Note that this is not a linear constraint. (We are dividing decision variables by decision variables.) Based on our discussion in Section 6.2, from a computational perspective, it is better to have linear constraints whenever we can. There are different ways to convert this particular constraint into a linear constraint. For example, we can multiply both sides of the inequality by $x_1 + x_2 + x_3 + x_4$, which is a nonnegative number and will preserve the sign of the inequality as is. In addition, in this particular example we know that the total amount $x_1 + x_2 + x_3 + x_4 = 10,000,000$, so the constraint can be formulated as

$$4 \cdot x_1 + 2 \cdot x_2 + 2 \cdot x_3 + 1 \cdot x_4 \leq 2 \cdot 10,000,000$$

4. The maximum investment in each fund cannot be more than 40% of the total amount ($4,000,000). These constraints can be written as

$$x_1 \leq 4,000,000, \; x_2 \leq 4,000,000, \; x_3 \leq 4,000,000, \; x_4 \leq 4,000,000$$

5. Finally, given the no-short-selling requirement, the amounts invested in each fund cannot be negative. (Note we are assuming that the portfolio manager can invest only the $10,000,000, and cannot borrow additional money.)

$$x_1 \geq 0, \; x_2 \geq 0, \; x_3 \geq 0, \; x_4 \geq 0$$

These are *nonnegativity constraints*. Even though they seem obvious in this example, they still need to be specified explicitly for the optimization solver.

The final optimization formulation can be written in matrix form. The objective function is

$$\max_{x_1, x_2, x_3, x_4} \begin{bmatrix} 0.2069 & 0.0587 & 0.1052 & 0.0243 \end{bmatrix} \cdot \begin{bmatrix} x_1 \\ x_2 \\ x_3 \\ x_4 \end{bmatrix}$$

Let us organize the constraints together into groups according to their signs. (This will be useful when we discuss solving the problem with optimization software later.)

$$\text{Equality} (=): \begin{bmatrix} 1 & 1 & 1 & 1 \end{bmatrix} \cdot \begin{bmatrix} x_1 \\ x_2 \\ x_3 \\ x_4 \end{bmatrix} = 10{,}000{,}000$$

$$\text{Inequality} (\le): \begin{bmatrix} 1 & 0 & 1 & 0 \\ 4 & 2 & 2 & 1 \\ 1 & 0 & 0 & 0 \\ 0 & 1 & 0 & 0 \\ 0 & 0 & 1 & 0 \\ 0 & 0 & 0 & 1 \end{bmatrix} \cdot \begin{bmatrix} x_1 \\ x_2 \\ x_3 \\ x_4 \end{bmatrix} \le \begin{bmatrix} 6{,}000{,}000 \\ 20{,}000{,}000 \\ 4{,}000{,}000 \\ 4{,}000{,}000 \\ 4{,}000{,}000 \\ 4{,}000{,}000 \end{bmatrix}$$

$$\text{Nonnegativity} (\ge): \begin{bmatrix} x_1 \\ x_2 \\ x_3 \\ x_4 \end{bmatrix} \ge \begin{bmatrix} 0 \\ 0 \\ 0 \\ 0 \end{bmatrix}$$

This problem is an LP. It would look like the standard form in Section 6.2.2, except for the inequality ($\le$) constraints. We can rewrite the LP in standard form by converting them to equality constraints. We introduce six additional nonnegative variables $\mathbf{s} = (s_1, \ldots, s_6)$ (called *slack variables*), one for each constraint in the group Inequality ($\le$):

$$\begin{bmatrix} 1 & 0 & 1 & 0 & 1 & 0 & 0 & 0 & 0 & 0 \\ 4 & 2 & 2 & 1 & 0 & 1 & 0 & 0 & 0 & 0 \\ 1 & 0 & 0 & 0 & 0 & 0 & 1 & 0 & 0 & 0 \\ 0 & 1 & 0 & 0 & 0 & 0 & 0 & 1 & 0 & 0 \\ 0 & 0 & 1 & 0 & 0 & 0 & 0 & 0 & 1 & 0 \\ 0 & 0 & 0 & 1 & 0 & 0 & 0 & 0 & 0 & 1 \end{bmatrix} \cdot \begin{bmatrix} x_1 \\ x_2 \\ x_3 \\ x_4 \\ s_1 \\ s_2 \\ s_3 \\ s_4 \\ s_5 \\ s_6 \end{bmatrix} = \begin{bmatrix} 6{,}000{,}000 \\ 20{,}000{,}000 \\ 4{,}000{,}000 \\ 4{,}000{,}000 \\ 4{,}000{,}000 \\ 4{,}000{,}000 \end{bmatrix}$$

Then, we add the nonnegativity constraints on the slack variables to the problem formulation:

$$[x_1, x_2, x_3, x_4, s_1, s_2, s_3, s_4, s_5, s_6]' \ge \mathbf{0}$$

Optimization solvers in the past required that the problem be passed in standard form; however, solvers and optimization languages are much more flexible today, and do their own conversion to standard form. In any case, as this example illustrates, it is easy to go from a general linear problem formulation to the standard form.

6.4   OPTIMIZATION ALGORITHMS

How do optimization solvers actually find the optimal solution for a problem? As a general rule, optimization algorithms are iterative. They start with an initial solution and generate a sequence of intermediate solutions until they get "close" to the optimal solution. The degree of "closeness" is determined by a parameter called *tolerance*, which usually has some default value, but can often be modified by the user. Often, the tolerance parameter is linked to a measure of the distance between the current and the subsequent solution, or to the incremental progress made by subsequent iterations of the algorithm in improving the objective function value. If subsequent iterations of the algorithm bring very little change relative to the status quo, the algorithm is terminated.

The algorithms for optimization in today's optimization software are rather sophisticated and an extensive introduction to these algorithms is beyond the scope of this book. However, many optimization solvers let the user select which optimization algorithm to apply to a specific problem, and some basic knowledge of what algorithms are used for different classes of optimization solvers is helpful for deciding what optimization software to use and what options to select for the problem at hand.

The first optimization algorithm, called the *simplex algorithm*, was developed by George Dantzig in 1947. It finds optimal solutions to linear optimization problems by iteratively solving systems of linear equations to find intermediate feasible solutions in a way that continually improves the value of the objective function. Despite its age, the simplex algorithm is still widely used for linear optimization, and is remarkably efficient in practice.

In the 1980s, inspired by a new algorithm Narendra Karmakar created for linear programming problems, another class of efficient algorithms called *interior point methods* was developed. The advantage of interior point methods is that they can be applied not only to linear optimization problems but also to a wider class of convex optimization problems.

Many nonlinear optimization algorithms are based on using information from a special set of equations that represent necessary conditions that a solution $\mathbf{x}$ is optimal. These conditions are the Karush-Kuhn-Tucker (KKT) conditions for optimality. The KKT conditions for a solution $\mathbf{x}^*$ to be the optimum are necessary but not sufficient, meaning that they need to be satisfied at the optimal solution; however, a solution that satisfies them is not necessarily the global optimum. Hence, the user is not guaranteed that the solution returned by the optimization algorithm is indeed the global optimum solution. The KKT conditions are, fortunately, necessary and sufficient for optimality in the case of convex optimization problems. They take a special form in the case of linear optimization problems and some other classes of convex problems, which is exploited in interior point algorithms for finding the optimal solution.

The importance of the KKT conditions for general nonlinear optimization is that they enable a nonlinear optimization problem to be reduced to a system of nonlinear equations, whose solution can be attained by using successive approximations. Widely used algorithms for nonlinear optimization include barrier methods, primal-dual interior point methods, and sequential quadratic programming methods. The latter try to solve the KKT conditions for the original nonlinear problem by optimizing a quadratic approximation to a function derived from the objective function and the constraints of the original problem.[13]

Integer programming problems, that is, problems with integer decision variables, are typically solved by branch-and-bound algorithms, branch-and-cut routines, and heuristics[14] that exploit the special structure of the problem.[15] The main idea behind many of these algorithms is to start by solving a *relaxation* of the optimization problem in which the decision variables are not restricted to be integer numbers. The algorithms then begin with the solution found in the initial stage and narrow down the choices of integer solutions. In practice, a simple rounding of the initial fractional optimal solution is sometimes good enough. However, it can lead to an integer solution that is very far from the actual optimal solution, and the problem is more pronounced when the number of integer decision variables is large.

Integer programming problems are generally more difficult and take longer to solve than problems with continuous decision variables. In addition, not every optimization solver can handle them, so it is important to check the specifications of the solver before trying to solve such problems.

---

[13] For more details, see, for example, Freund (2004).

[14] A *heuristic* is a logical, approximate way to solve an optimization problem that, however, is not necessarily guaranteed to produce the optimal result.

[15] For an intuitive overview of some of these algorithms, see Chapter 9 in Fabozzi, Kolm, Pachamanova, and Focardi (2007). For a complete mathematical treatment of the subject, see, for example, Bertsimas and Tsitsiklis (1997) or Nemhauser and Wolsey (1999).

There are some good commercial optimization solvers that can handle linear and convex quadratic mixed-integer optimization problems, but there are virtually no solvers that can handle more general nonlinear mixed-integer problems efficiently.

A number of algorithms incorporate an element of randomness in their search. Specifically, they allow moves to feasible solutions with worse value of the objective function to happen with some probability, rather than pursuing always a direction in which the objective function improves. Although there are no guarantees, the hope is that this will prevent the algorithm from getting stuck in a local optimum so that the algorithm finds the global optimum in the case of multiple local optima.

Randomized search algorithms for optimization fall into several classes, including *simulated annealing, tabu search*, and *genetic algorithms*. Genetic algorithms in particular have become an option in several popular Microsoft Excel add-ins for optimization, such as Premium Solver and Palisade's Evolver. Package GA in R[16] is designed for optimization using genetic algorithms. MATLAB also has a Genetic Algorithms and Direct Search Toolbox, which contains simulated annealing and genetic algorithms.

Randomized search algorithms have their drawbacks—they can be slow, and provide no guarantee that they will find the global optimum. However, they are appropriate for handling difficult integer problems, nonlinear problems, and problems with discontinuities, when traditional optimization solvers fail.

6.5 OPTIMIZATION SOFTWARE

When selecting an optimization software product, it is important to differentiate between *optimization solvers* and *optimization modeling languages*.

An optimization solver is software that implements numerical routines for finding the optimal solution of an optimization problem. Well-known commercial optimization solvers include MOSEK[17] and IBM ILOG CPLEX[18] for linear, mixed-integer, and quadratic problems, and MINOS, SNOPT, and CONOPT for general nonlinear problems,[19] but there are a number of other commercial and free solvers available.

Optimization modeling languages have emerged as user-friendly platforms that allow the user to specify optimization problems in a more intuitive

---

[16] See http://cran.r-project.org/web/packages/GA/GA.pdf.
[17] See www.mosek.com.
[18] See www.ilog.com/products/cplex.
[19] See www.aimms.com/aimms/product/solvers/.

generic fashion, regardless of the specific algorithmic and input requirements of optimization routines. Typically, optimization language software automates the underlying mathematical details of the optimization model formulation, but does not actually solve the problem. It passes the formulation to a solver, and retrieves the results from the solver in a convenient format. Popular optimization languages include AMPL[20] and GAMS.[21] The Computational Infrastructure for Operations Research[22] project (COIN-OR, or simply COIN) is a great resource for information about solvers and modeling languages available for optimization.

Optimization solvers and modeling languages are often part of *modeling environments* that handle not only the optimization, but also the input and output processing, statistical analysis, and perform other functions a user may need for a comprehensive analysis of a situation. MATLAB is an example of a high-level technical computing and interactive environment for model development that also enables data visualization, data analysis, and numerical simulation. The optimization solvers in MATLAB's Optimization Toolbox can solve a variety of constrained and unconstrained optimization problems for linear programming, quadratic programming, nonlinear optimization, and binary integer programming. Other examples of modeling environments include IBM ILOG OPL Studio, which allows users to build optimization models that are then accessed from a subroutine library using VBA, Java, or C/C++. Thus, a user can connect optimization systems directly to data sources, and make calls to optimization subroutines repeatedly.

Free open-source alternatives for modeling environments include R[23] and Python.[24] Although such open source alternatives may not always be as user-friendly as commercial alternatives, they have the advantage that new algorithms are constantly developed and implemented by contributors to the projects, and sometimes one can find functionality that commercial software companies have not yet had the time to develop.

Excel's inherent capabilities for optimization are rather limited. Excel Solver, which ships with Excel, can handle only optimization problems of small size, up to a few hundred variables and constraints. It is a perfectly acceptable solver for linear optimization problems, but its performance (and the output one would obtain from it) is unreliable for more complex problems of the general nonlinear or integer programming type. Premium Solver

---

[20] See www.ampl.com.
[21] See www.gams.com.
[22] See www.coin-or.org/.
[23] See http://cran.r-project.org/web/views/Optimization.html.
[24] See http://docs.scipy.org/doc/scipy/reference/tutorial/optimize.html.

Platform,[25] which is sold by the developers of Excel Solver, is an extended and improved version of the standard Excel Solver, and can handle linear, integer, and quadratic problems of larger size. It employs efficient interior point methods for solving classical optimization formulations and genetic algorithms for arbitrary Excel optimization models that contain spreadsheet functions such as IF, INDEX, and COUNTIF (such functions are not recognized in traditional optimization problem formulations). Palisade's Evolver is another add-in for Excel that uses genetic algorithms to solve optimization problems. The Palisade Decision Tools Suite[26] also contains RiskOptimizer, which is a tool for optimization given possible scenarios for the uncertain parameters in the problem. Premium Solver Platform is part of Analytics Solver Platform,[27] which also offers tools for statistics, simulation, and data mining. Analytics Solver Platform and Palisade's Decision Tools Suite are examples of modeling environments for Excel: they contain a number of software add-ins for optimization, statistical analysis, and sensitivity analysis that use a spreadsheet program—MS Excel—as the underlying platform.

It should be mentioned that there are numerous optimization software packages that target financial applications in particular, especially portfolio management applications. Established vendors of portfolio management software include Axioma,[28] MSCI Barra,[29] ITG,[30] and Northfield Information Services.[31] More recently, traditional financial data providers such as Bloomberg and FactSet have added portfolio optimization capabilities to their offerings. Bloomberg introduced Portfolio Optimizer to its Portfolio and Risk Analytics Platform and fully integrated it with the data feeds. FactSet offers the ability to integrate its data feeds with portfolio optimization software vendors such as Axioma, MSCI Barra, and Northfield.

6.6 A SOFTWARE IMPLEMENTATION EXAMPLE

Modeling environments employ very different approaches to the formulation and output formatting of optimization problems. For example, array-based modeling languages like R and MATLAB expect optimization formulations to be passed to solvers in an array form, and contain functions

---

[25] See www.solver.com.
[26] See www.palisade.com/.
[27] See www.solver.com/products-overview.
[28] See www.axiomainc.com.
[29] See https://www.msci.com/.
[30] See www.itginc.com.
[31] See www.northinfo.com.

that call specific solvers for specific types of optimization problems. In particular, R has a number of application programming interfaces (commonly referred to as APIs) to both commercial and free optimization solvers.[32] Examples of APIs for leading commercial packages include cplexAPI[33] and Rcplex[34] (an interface to the CPLEX optimization package from IBM) and Rmosek[35] (an interface to the MOSEK solver). Free optimization packages for R include linprog[36] (for linear programming) and quadprog (for quadratic programming, which is often used in portfolio optimization), as well as the package Rglpk,[37] which provides an interface to the free GNU Linear Programming Kit.[38]

Optimization modeling with spreadsheets requires a different approach. Microsoft Excel's Solver and other Excel optimization add-ins use spreadsheet values and formulas as inputs, and return output to the spreadsheet.

In order to provide a concrete example, in this section we show how the portfolio allocation problem from Section 6.3 can be formulated and solved with Excel Solver. We begin with a general description of how optimization works with Excel Solver, and then show the specific inputs and outputs for the portfolio allocation example.

6.6.1 Optimization with Excel Solver

Excel Solver comes prepackaged with Excel.[39] Its main dialog box is shown in Exhibit 6.5. Excel Solver expects users to input an objective cell, changing variable cells, and constraints, and specify whether the optimization problem is a maximization or a minimization problem.

The entry for the *objective cell* should be a reference to a cell that contains a formula for the objective function of the optimization problem. This formula should link the objective cell and the *changing variable cells*. The changing variable cells are cells dedicated to the decision variables—they can be left empty, or have some initial values that the solver will eventually replace with the optimal values. The initial values of the changing variable

---

[32] http://cran.r-project.org/web/views/Optimization.html.

[33] See http://cran.r-project.org/web/packages/clpAPI/index.html.

[34] See http://cran.r-project.org/web/packages/Rcplex/index.html.

[35] See http://cran.r-project.org/web/packages/Rmosek/index.html.

[36] See http://cran.r-project.org/web/packages/linprog/index.html.

[37] See https://cran.r-project.org/web/packages/Rglpk/Rglpk.pdf.

[38] See http://cran.r-project.org/web/packages/quadprog/index.html.

[39] Excel Solver should be available under the **Data** tab in Excel. If you do not see it there, go to the main Excel button (in the top left corner), click on **Excel Options** at the bottom, click on **Add-Ins**, select **Solver Add-In**, then **Go**, and Solver should appear in the **Data** tab.

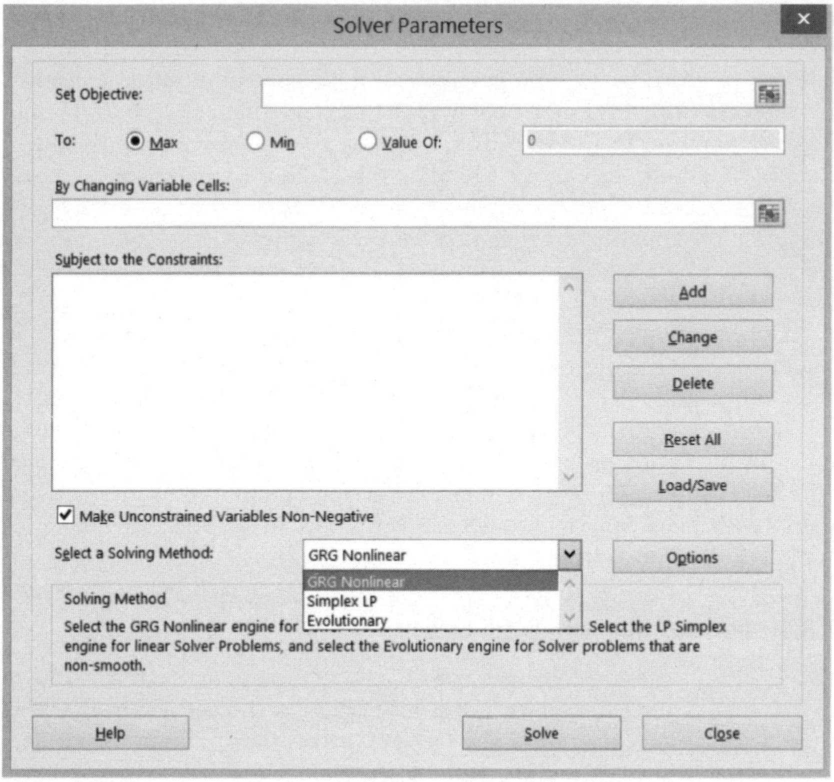

Exhibit 6.5 Excel Solver dialog box.

cells are used by Solver as the starting point of the algorithm. They do not really matter when the optimization problem is linear, but they can cause Solver to find very different solutions if the problem is nonlinear or contains integer variables.

Constraints can be specified by clicking on the **Add** button, then entering the left-hand side and the right-hand side of a constraint, as well as the sign of the constraint. The constraint dialog box is shown in Exhibit 6.6. By clicking on the middle button, the user can specify inequality constraints ($\leq$ or $\geq$) or equality constraints ($=$). Solver also lets the user specify whether a set of decision variables is integer (int) or binary (bin). To do that, the user must have designated the cells corresponding to these decision variables as changing cells, and then add the int or bin constraint through the **Add Constraint** dialog box. The last option, dif, stands for "alldifferent." It imposes the constraint that if there are N decision variables (changing variable cells), they all take different integer values between 1 and N.

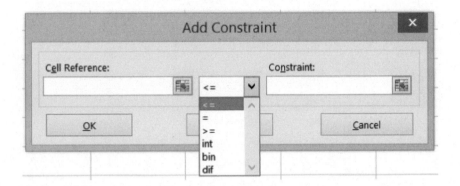

Exhibit 6.6 Solver constraint dialog box.

Solver expects constraints to be entered as cell comparisons, that is, it can only compare the value of one cell to the value of another cell in the spreadsheet. One cannot type a formula directly into the constraint dialog box—the formula needs to be already contained in the cell that is referenced. A good way to organize an optimization formulation in Excel is to create a column of cells containing the formulas on the left-hand side of all constraints, and a column of cells containing the right-hand sides (the limits) of all constraints. That allows for groups of constraints to be entered simultaneously. For example, if there are three constraints that all have equal signs, one can enter an array reference to the range of three cells with the left-hand sides of these constraints, and an array reference to the range of three cells with the right-hand sides. Solver will compare each cell in the first array to the corresponding cell in the second array.

Solver also allows users to specify options for the algorithms it uses to find the optimal solution. This can be done by clicking on the **Select a Solving Method** drop-down menu as well as on the **Options** button in Solver's main dialog box. The **Select a Solving Method** drop-down menu is shown in Exhibit 6.5, and the **Options** dialog box is shown in Exhibit 6.7. For most problems, leaving the defaults in works fine; however, it is always helpful to provide as much information to the solver as possible to ensure optimal performance. For example, if we know that the optimization problem is linear, we should select **Simplex LP** from the **Select a Solving Method** drop-down menu. (**GRG Nonlinear** is a more general solver for nonlinear optimization problems, and **Evolutionary** is a solver based on genetic algorithms which use some randomization to find better solutions for difficult types of optimization models, such as problems with integer variables.)

The **Make Unconstrained Variables Nonnegative** option is a shortcut to declaring all decision variables nonnegative (rather than entering separate

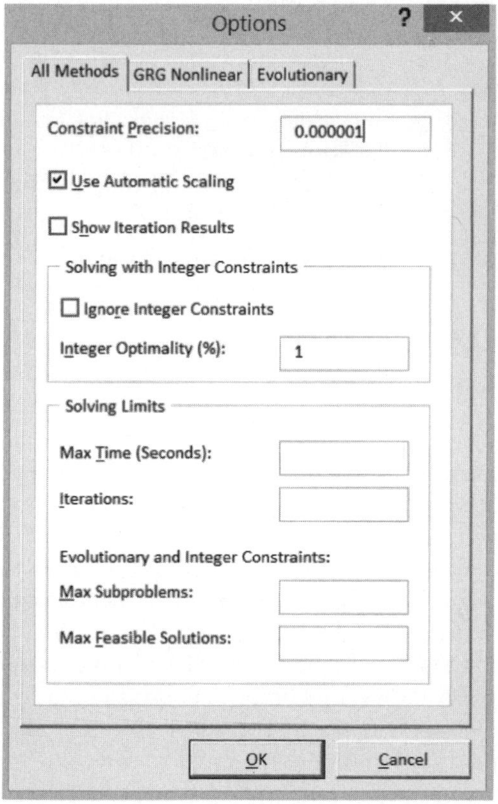

Exhibit 6.7 Excel Solver Options dialog box.

constraints for each decision variable). The **Show Iteration Results** option in the **Options** dialog box lets the user step through the search for the optimal solution. The **Use Automatic Scaling** option is helpful when there is big difference between the magnitudes of decision variables and input data, because sometimes that leads to computational issues due to poor scaling. An optimization problem is poorly scaled if changes in the decision variables produce large changes in the objective or constraint functions for some components of the vector of decision variables more than for others. (For example, if we are trying to find the optimal percentages to invest, but the rest of the data in the problem is measured in millions of dollars, the solver may run into numerical difficulties because a small change in a value measured in percentages will have a very different magnitude than a small change in a value measured in millions.) Some optimization techniques are very sensitive to poor scaling. In that case, checking the **Use Automatic Scaling** option instructs it to scale the data so the effect can be minimized.

The remaining options in the **Options** dialog box have to do with the numerical details of the algorithm used, and can be left at their default values. For example, **Max Time** lets the user specify the maximum amount of time for the algorithm to run in search of the optimal solution.

6.6.2 Solution to the Portfolio Allocation Example

Let us now solve the portfolio allocation problem in Section 6.3. Exhibit 6.8 shows a snapshot of an Excel spreadsheet with the model.

Cells B4:E4 are dedicated to storage of the values of the decision variables, and will be the changing variable cells for Solver. It is convenient then to keep the column corresponding to each variable dedicated to storing data for that particular variable. For example, row 7 contains the coefficients in front of each decision variable in the objective function (the expected returns). Similarly, the cell array B10:E16 contains the coefficients in front of each variable in each constraint in the problem. Cells H10:H16 contain the right-hand side limits of all constraints. (In fact, we are entering the data in matrix form.)

In cell F7, we enter the formula for calculating the objective function value in terms of the decision variables:

```
=SUMPRODUCT($B$4:$E$4,B7:E7)
```

The SUMPRODUCT function in Excel takes as inputs two arrays, and returns the sum of the products of the corresponding elements in each array. In this case, the SUMPRODUCT formula is equivalent to the formula

```
=B7*B4+C7*C4+D7*D4+E7*E4
```

but the SUMPRODUCT formula is clearly a lot more efficient to enter, especially when there are more decision variables.

Cells F10:F16 contain the formulas for the left-hand sides of the seven constraints. For example, cell F10 contains the formula

```
=SUMPRODUCT($B$4:$E$4,B10:E10)
```

Now the advantage of organizing the data in this array form in the spreadsheet is apparent. When creating the optimization model, we can copy the formula in cell F10 down to all cells until cell F16. Thus, we can enter the information for multiple constraints very quickly.

	A	B	C	D	E	F	G	H
1	Portfolio allocation problem							
2								
3	Decision variables	Fund 1	Fund 2	Fund 3	Fund 4			
4	amounts	$ 2,000,000.00	$ 0.00	$ 4,000,000.00	$ 4,000,000.00			
5								
6	Objective function							
7	Maximize expected return ($)	20.69%	5.87%	10.52%	2.43%	$ 931,800.00		
8								
9	Constraints							Limits
10	Total investment	1	1	1	1	$ 10,000,000.00	=	$ 10,000,000.00
11	Fund 1 + Fund 3 <= 60%	1	0	1	0	$ 6,000,000.00	<=	$ 6,000,000.00
12	Max average risk level	4	2	2	1	$ 20,000,000.00	<=	$ 20,000,000.00
13	Max investment Fund 1	1				$ 2,000,000.00	<=	$ 4,000,000.00
14	Max investment Fund 2		1			$ 0.00	<=	$ 4,000,000.00
15	Max investment Fund 3			1		$ 4,000,000.00	<=	$ 4,000,000.00
16	Max investment Fund 4				1	$ 4,000,000.00	<=	$ 4,000,000.00

Exhibit 6.8 Snapshot of an Excel model of the portfolio allocation example from Section 6.3.

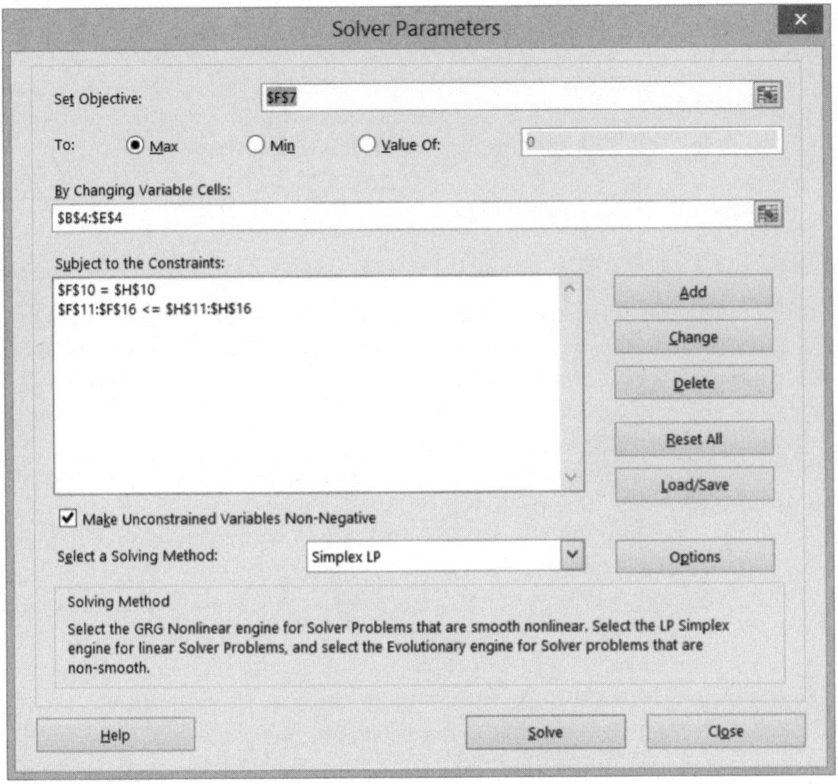

Exhibit 6.9 Excel Solver inputs for the portfolio allocation problem.

We select **Data | Solver**, and enter the information in Exhibit 6.9.

Our goal is to maximize the expression stored in cell F7 by changing the values in cells B4:E4, subject to a set of constraints. Note that since all constraints in rows 11–16 have the same sign ($\geq$), we can pass them to Solver as one entry. Solver interprets the constraint

```
$F$11:$F$16 <= $H$11:$H$16
```

equivalently to the set of constraints

```
$F$11<= $H$11
$F$12<= $H$12
$F$13<= $H$13
$F$14<= $H$14
$F$15<= $H$15
$F$16<= $H$16
```

We use the **Simplex LP** and the **Make Unconstrained Variables Nonnegative** options. The optimal solution is contained in the spreadsheet snapshot in Exhibit 6.8. To attain the optimal return of $931,800 while satisfying all required constraints, the manager should invest $2,000,000 in Fund 1, $0 in Fund 2, $4,000,000 in Fund 3, and $4,000,000 in Fund 4.

Summary

- An optimization formulation consists of three parts: (1) an objective function, (2) a set of decision variables, and (3) a set of constraints.
- A solution is feasible if it satisfies all constraints. A solution is optimal if it is feasible and produces the best value of the objective function among all feasible solutions.
- A solution is a local optimum if it produces the best value of the objective function among all feasible solutions in its neighborhood. There may be multiple local optima depending on the type of optimization problem.
- Optimization problems are categorized according to: (1) the form of the objective function and the constraints, and (2) the type of decision variables (discrete or continuous).
- Important classes of optimization problems include linear programming, quadratic programming, convex programming, integer programming, and mixed-integer programming.
- For convex optimization problems, a local optimal solution is also the global optimal solution.
- The Karush-Kuhn-Tucker conditions are necessary conditions for local optima of constrained optimization problems. Their structure is exploited by numerous algorithms for convex and general nonlinear optimization.
- Most optimization algorithms are iterative in nature. The number of iterations taken by the algorithm is determined by the stopping criteria specified by the user, such as the tolerance level.
- Important types of optimization algorithms include the simplex algorithm (for linear problems), interior point methods (for linear and convex problems), branch-and-bound or branch-and-cut algorithms (for integer programs), and randomized search algorithms (for all types of optimization problems).
- Randomized search algorithms, such as genetic algorithms, simulated annealing, and tabu search, do not guarantee the optimality of the solution they return. Neither do general optimization algorithms when applied to nonlinear optimization problems that do not have special structure.

- Linear problems are the "easiest" class of optimization problems in the sense that today, linear problems with hundreds of thousands of decision variables and constraints can be solved efficiently.
- Convex problems (which include linear problems) have nice structure, and are typically more efficient to solve than general nonlinear programming. Integer and mixed-integer problems are challenging, and require specialized optimization software.
- An optimization solver is software that implements numerical routines for finding the optimal solution of an optimization problem. Different solvers are typically used to handle different kinds of optimization problems.
- An optimization modeling language automates the underlying mathematical details of the optimization model formulation, but typically does not actually solve the problem. It passes the formulation to a solver, and retrieves the results from the solver in a convenient format. The advantage of using optimization languages is that the user can formulate the problem only once, and use different options for solvers.

CHAPTER 7

Optimization under Uncertainty

The optimization framework presented in Chapter 6 has numerous applications in finance and other fields. However, our discussion omitted an important aspect of realistic optimization modeling. We assumed that the input data, such as the coefficients in front of the decision variables in the objective function and the constraints, are certain. In practice, however, optimization often needs to be performed under conditions in which the input data are random, or represent statistical estimates and subjective guesses. Models in which all input data are fixed, or nonrandom, are referred to as *deterministic*. Models that contain parameters that vary are referred to as *nondeterministic, probabilistic*, or *stochastic*.

Concepts from probability theory, statistics, and simulation (Chapters 2, 3, and 5) can be used to extend the basic framework of deterministic optimization to deal with uncertainty. Randomness, however, adds a high level of complexity to optimization formulations, and the output of the resulting models needs to be interpreted carefully.

There are three general approaches for incorporating uncertainty into optimization problems: *dynamic programming, stochastic programming*, and *robust optimization*. Dynamic programming methods date back to Bellman (1957) and are specifically designed to deal with stochastic uncertain systems over multiple stages. The optimization problem is solved recursively, going backwards from the last state, and computing the optimal solution for each possible state of the system at a particular stage. In finance, dynamic programming is used in the context of pricing of some derivative instruments, in investment strategies such as statistical arbitrage, and in long-term corporate financial planning.

Stochastic programming methods can be used in both single-period and multiperiod settings. They rely on representing the uncertain data with scenarios and focus on finding a strategy so that the expected value of the objective function over all scenarios (sometimes, penalized for some measure of risk) is optimal. Stochastic algorithms have been successfully applied in a variety of financial contexts, such as management of portfolios of fixed income securities, corporate risk management, security selection, and asset/liability management for individuals as well as for financial entities such as banks, pension funds, and insurance companies.[1] They are particularly useful in situations in which modeling complicated dependencies in a number of uncertain parameters over multiple time periods is required. Such situations often arise, for example, in managing callable bond portfolios or international asset portfolios, where the callable feature of the bonds, interest rate risk, default risk, or currency risk needs to be taken into consideration.

Robust optimization is a technique whose applications in finance have been explored more recently. It can be used to address the same type of problems as dynamic programming and stochastic programming do; however, it takes a worst-case approach to optimization formulations. In addition, in robust optimization one typically makes relatively general assumptions on the probability distributions of the uncertain parameters in order to work with problem formulations that are more tractable computationally.

The fields of dynamic programming, stochastic programming, and robust optimization have some overlap; however, historically, they have evolved independently of each other. This chapter explains these three techniques for optimization under uncertainty in more detail.

7.1 DYNAMIC PROGRAMMING

Dynamic programming solves a large multistage optimization problem sequentially, starting at the last stage and proceeding backward, thus keeping track only of the optimal paths from any given time period onward.

Dynamic programming under uncertainty is sometimes also called *stochastic control*.[2] There is an underlying dynamic system and an objective function (called a *reward* or a *cost* function depending on whether the problem is a maximization or a minimization) that is additive over time. The dynamic system at any point in time t is described by a vector of state

---

[1] See, for example, Ziemba and Mulvey (1998), Consigli and Dempster (1996), Zenios and Kang (1993), Carino and Ziemba (1998), Bogentoft, Romeijn, and Uryasev (2001), Ziemba (2003), Hillier and Eckstein (1993), Ferstl and Weissensteiner (2011), Consiglio, Cocco, and Zenios (2006); Boender, Dert, Heemskerk, and Hoek (2005), and Kouwenberg (2001).

[2] Modern treatment of the dynamic programming field with applications in engineering, finance, and operations research is provided in Bertsekas (2005, 2012). Applications of dynamic programming to optimal consumption and portfolio selection are discussed, for example, in Merton (1995), and Ingersoll (1987).

variables $\mathbf{x}_t$ that summarizes all past information about the system. The state variable evolves according to the relationship

$$\mathbf{x}_{t+1} = g_t(\mathbf{x}_t, \mathbf{u}_t, \xi_t)$$

where $\mathbf{u}_t$ is a vector of *control*, or *policy*, variables to be selected by the decision-maker, and ξ_t is a random variable (also called disturbance or noise depending on the context). The reward at time t, which we will denote by $f_t(\mathbf{x}_t, \mathbf{u}_t, \xi_t)$, accumulates over time.

Dynamic programming problems can be defined over a finite horizon (e.g., over a period of time T) or over an infinite horizon. In most financial applications, we encounter finite horizon dynamic programming systems, so we will assume that the horizon is finite and time is discrete. The total reward/cost can then be written as

$$\sum_{t=0}^{T} f_t(\mathbf{x}_t, \mathbf{u}_t, \xi_t)$$

Assuming that we would like to maximize the total reward, at every state our goal is to find a policy vector $\mathbf{u}_t$ so that

$$V_t(\mathbf{x}_t) = \max_{\mathbf{u}_t} \ \{c(\mathbf{u}_t) + d \cdot V_{t+1}^*(\mathbf{u}_t)\}$$

In other words, we select $\mathbf{u}_t$ so that the value of the reward from the current stage forward is the highest. This is the expression for the dynamic programming recursion. Suppose now that there is uncertainty, that is, our actions do not determine an exact outcome but instead there is some probabilistic component in the realization of future rewards. In that case, a logical goal is to select $\mathbf{u}_t$ so that the expected value of the reward from the current stage forward is the highest, where the expected value is the weighted average of possible outcomes from some probability distribution of the future values. We write

$$V_t(\mathbf{x}_t) = \max_{\mathbf{u}_t} \ \{c(\mathbf{u}_t) + d \cdot E[V_{t+1}^*(\mathbf{u}_t)|\mathbf{x}_t]\}$$

where $E[V_{t+1}^*(\mathbf{u}_t)|\mathbf{x}_t]$ is the expected value of the optimal reward from the current stage forward, given that we are currently at state $\mathbf{x}_t$.

Approximation algorithms are often used in order to reduce the size and complexity of dynamic programming problems. Instead of evaluating the exact optimal policy in every state of the world, they approximate the form of the optimal policy as a function of the current state.[3] There is no general recipe for how the approximation should be selected.

7.2 STOCHASTIC PROGRAMMING

Perhaps the easiest way to think of a stochastic programming formulation is to imagine writing an optimization problem formulation of one of the kinds described in Chapter 6.2 and searching for an optimal solution over *scenarios* for the input data. Consider a general stochastic optimization (say, maximization) problem, in which we have an objective function $F(\mathbf{x}, \xi)$ that depends on a decision vector $\mathbf{x}$ of dimension N and a vector of uncertain parameters ξ of dimension d. Such optimization problems are not well defined because the objective depends on the unknown value of ξ. Namely, every realization of the vector of random variables ξ corresponds to a different realization of the objective function. Thus, we have a different probability distribution of objective function values for every feasible solution $\mathbf{x}$. It is incorrect to say that one probability distribution is "better" than another unless we specify what "better" means. Hence, it is impossible to state what the optimal solution $\mathbf{x}^*$ is, since by definition the optimal solution is the one that gives the "best" value of the objective function. The simplest way to make the objective well defined is to optimize it on average:

$$\max_{\mathbf{x}} f(\mathbf{x}) = E[F(\mathbf{x}, \xi)]$$

where the expectation is taken over scenarios for ξ.[4] This means that we define the optimal solution $\mathbf{x}^*$ as the solution that results in a probability distribution for the objective function value with the highest mean of all probability distributions of objective function values.

What if uncertainty is present in the constraints? In some cases we can formulate such problems by introducing penalties for violating the constraints, thus defining a mean-risk objective function.[5] An alternative

---

[3] See, for example, Chryssikou (1998) for a development of approximate dynamic programming approaches that characterize the optimal investment policy for multi-stage portfolio optimization problems. Bertsekas (2012) provides a comprehensive review of approximate dynamic algorithms.

[4] In other words, we maximize a weighted average of objective functions, where each weight is the probability that the scenario that results in that particular objective function will occur.

[5] See, for example, Mulvey, Vanderbei, and Zenios (1995), and Ruszczynski and Shapiro (2003).

approach is to require that the constraints be satisfied for all possible (in particular, the worst-case) values of the uncertain parameters. This is a stochastic programming method whose philosophy overlaps with the philosophy of robust optimization, which we will explain in the next section. Finally, we may impose the requirement that the constraints be satisfied with a high probability. This leads to a stochastic programming formulation with chance constraints.

In summary, stochastic programming can be used to address the presence of uncertain input data in three types of optimization problems:

- Expected value for single-stage and multistage models.
- Models involving risk measures.
- Chance-constrained models.

We discuss each type of model next.

7.2.1 Multistage Models

In *multistage stochastic programming models*, decision variables and constraints are divided into groups corresponding to time periods, or stages $t = 1, \ldots, T$. The information structure of the model (i.e., what is known at each stage) is specified in advance. The standard form of a multistage stochastic linear program is[6]

$$
\min_{\mathbf{x}} \ \tilde{c}_0' \mathbf{x}_0 + E_{\xi_1}\left[\left(\tilde{c}_1^{\xi_1}\right)' \mathbf{x}_1^{\xi_1} + \ldots + E_{\xi_{T-1}|\xi_{T-2}}\left[\left(\tilde{c}_{T-1}^{\xi_1,\ldots,\xi_{T-1}}\right)' \mathbf{x}_{T-1}^{\xi_1,\ldots,\xi_{T-1}}\right.\right.
$$

$$
\left.\left. + E_{\xi_T|\xi_{T-1}}\left[\left(\tilde{c}_T^{\xi_1,\ldots,\xi_T}\right)' \mathbf{x}_T^{\xi_1,\ldots,\xi_T}\right]\right]\right]
$$

s.t.

$$
\begin{array}{llll}
\mathbf{A}_0 \mathbf{x}_0 & & & = \mathbf{b}_0 \\
\mathbf{B}_0^{\xi_1} \mathbf{x}_0 + & & \mathbf{A}_1^{\xi_1} \mathbf{x}_1^{\xi_1} & = \mathbf{b}_1^{\xi_1} \\
& \ddots & & \vdots \\
& \mathbf{B}_{T-1}^{\xi_T} \mathbf{x}_{T-1}^{\xi_1,\ldots,\xi_{T-1}} + & \mathbf{A}_T^{\xi_T} \mathbf{x}_T^{\xi_1,\ldots,\xi_T} & = \mathbf{b}_T^{\xi_T} \\
\end{array}
$$

$$
\mathbf{x}_0, \mathbf{x}_1^{\xi_1}, \ldots, \mathbf{x}_{T-1}^{\xi_1,\ldots,\xi_{T-1}}, \mathbf{x}_T^{\xi_1,\ldots,\xi_T} \geq \mathbf{0}
$$

Here the array $\xi = \{\xi_1, \ldots, \xi_T\}$ represents the realizations of an underlying process that drives the uncertainty in the coefficients of the objective

---

[6]The notation $E_{\xi_t|\xi_{t-1}}[.]$ means "expectation of the expression inside the brackets over realizations of the uncertain variable ξ_t at time t conditional on the realizations of ξ_{t-1} at time $t - 1$."

function, and A and B are matrices with data. Note that the vectors of solutions x are indexed off the vectors of uncertainty ξ_t at each stage t except at the beginning (stage 0). In stochastic programming, decision variables can be divided into two categories: anticipative and adaptive. *Anticipative decision variables* (such as x_0 in the above formulation) correspond to decisions that must be made at that particular stage, and all information for making the decision is available. *Adaptive decision variables* (such as $x_t^{\xi_1,\ldots,\xi_t}$ in the formulation above) depend on future realizations of the random parameters.

A large number of financial applications—asset–liability management, index tracking, active investment management—can be treated as a sequence of decisions and observations, and represented in this form. The "block" formulation of the stochastic optimization problem is preferable because specialized software (stochastic optimization packages in particular) can take advantage of the structure when applying decomposition algorithms for solving the problem. In order to complete the multistage stochastic programming model, we need to specify the structure of the random process for the uncertain coefficients, which is typically reduced to a set of scenarios. The scenarios are organized in an event tree, which at each stage describes the unfolding of the uncertainties with respect to possible values of the uncertain parameters. The values of these realizations (denoted ξ above) are then plugged into the problem formulation above.

Exhibit 7.1 shows an example of such a tree if only one uncertain parameter is modeled. There are three time periods and two optimization stages. The nodes represent points in time at which the information about the

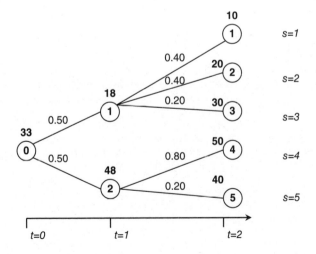

Exhibit 7.1 A simplified example of a scenario tree.

realizations of the uncertain parameter is updated. They are numbered for each stage t. The numbers in bold above the nodes denote the specific realizations of the uncertain parameter. At time 0, its value is known and unique (it is 33 in this example). At that time, there is only one node (node 0), which is called the *root* of the tree. At the last stage, there are $S_T = 5$ possible scenarios, represented by the paths from the root to the *leaves* (the last-stage nodes) of the tree. The numbers above the arcs of the tree represent the probabilities of moving to the next node *conditional* on having reached its ancestor node. Note that the probabilities on all branches emanating from the same node add up to 1.

Given this scenario tree, we can create the block stochastic programming formulation as follows:

i. Define decision variables $\mathbf{x}_t^{(s)}$ for each possible scenario s at each time period t. There are different ways to define a set of decision variables, but one possibility is to have eight of them: $\mathbf{x}_0^{(0)}$ for stage 0; $\mathbf{x}_1^{(1)}$ and $\mathbf{x}_1^{(2)}$ for stage 1; and $\mathbf{x}_2^{(1)}, \mathbf{x}_2^{(2)}, \mathbf{x}_2^{(3)}, \mathbf{x}_2^{(4)}, \mathbf{x}_2^{(5)}$ for stage 2. In this example, the number of scenarios at each stage is equal to the number of nodes at that stage because the tree does not recombine.

ii. Write out the objective as a function of these decision variables and the uncertain data:

$$\max_{\mathbf{x}} \quad (\mathbf{c}_0)'\mathbf{x}_0 + \pi_1^{(1)} \left(\mathbf{c}_1^{(1)}\right)' \mathbf{x}_1^{(1)} + \pi_1^{(2)} \left(\mathbf{c}_1^{(2)}\right)' \mathbf{x}_1^{(2)} + \pi_2^{(1)} \left(\mathbf{c}_2^{(1)}\right)' \mathbf{x}_2^{(1)}$$

$$+ \pi_2^{(2)} \left(\mathbf{c}_2^{(2)}\right)' \mathbf{x}_2^{(2)} + \pi_2^{(3)} \left(\mathbf{c}_2^{(3)}\right)' \mathbf{x}_2^{(3)}$$

$$+ \pi_2^{(4)} \left(\mathbf{c}_2^{(4)}\right)' \mathbf{x}_2^{(4)} + \pi_2^{(5)} \left(\mathbf{c}_2^{(5)}\right)' \mathbf{x}_2^{(5)}$$

The objective is a sum of the reward at the initial node and the expected rewards at all remaining nodes. In the expression above, $\pi_t^{(s)}$ denotes the probability of scenario s at time t. For example, $\pi_1^{(1)} = 0.50$ and $\pi_2^{(4)} = (0.50)(0.80) = 0.40$.

iii. Write a set of constraints for each stage and each scenario:

$$\text{Stage 0:} \quad \mathbf{A}_0^{(0)}\mathbf{x}_0^{(0)} = \mathbf{b}_0^{(0)}$$

$$\text{Stage 1:} \quad \mathbf{B}_0^{(1)}\mathbf{x}_0^{(0)} + \mathbf{A}_1^{(1)}\mathbf{x}_1^{(1)} = \mathbf{b}_1^{(1)}$$

$$\mathbf{B}_0^{(2)}\mathbf{x}_0^{(0)} + \mathbf{A}_1^{(2)}\mathbf{x}_1^{(2)} = \mathbf{b}_1^{(2)}$$

$$\text{Stage 2:} \quad \mathbf{B}_1^{(1)}\mathbf{x}_1^{(1)} + \mathbf{A}_2^{(1)}\mathbf{x}_2^{(1)} = \mathbf{b}_2^{(1)}$$

$$\mathbf{B}_1^{(2)}\mathbf{x}_1^{(1)} + \mathbf{A}_2^{(2)}\mathbf{x}_2^{(2)} = \mathbf{b}_2^{(2)}$$

$$\mathbf{B}_1^{(3)}\mathbf{x}_1^{(1)} + \mathbf{A}_2^{(3)}\mathbf{x}_2^{(3)} = \mathbf{b}_2^{(3)}$$

$$\mathbf{B}_1^{(4)}\mathbf{x}_1^{(2)} + \mathbf{A}_2^{(4)}\mathbf{x}_2^{(4)} = \mathbf{b}_2^{(4)}$$

$$\mathbf{B}_1^{(5)}\mathbf{x}_1^{(2)} + \mathbf{A}_2^{(5)}\mathbf{x}_2^{(5)} = \mathbf{b}_2^{(5)}$$

Note that the constraints keep track of the ancestor of each node. For example, nodes 1, 2, and 3 at stage 2 have a common ancestor: node 1 from stage 1. So, the decision variables associated with the scenarios ending at those nodes ($\mathbf{x}_2^{(1)}$, $\mathbf{x}_2^{(2)}$, and $\mathbf{x}_2^{(3)}$) are linked to the decision variable associated with node 1 from stage 1 ($\mathbf{x}_1^{(1)}$) via the first three constraints from stage 2.

iv. Write the so-called nonanticipativity conditions, if applicable. Nonanticipativity conditions make sure that scenarios with the same past have identical decisions up to the stage at which they have the same history. In this case, the nonanticipativity conditions are incorporated implicitly by our choice of decision variables and the fact that only one scenario corresponds to each node. Some formulations that involve alternative definitions of the decision variables, such as the original non-block formulation of the portfolio problem, require stating the nonanticipativity constraints explicitly.[7]

---

[7]For example, in an alternative formulation we could associate two variables with every given node: one variable at stage t and a copy of that decision variable for each particular "child" of that node. This kind of representation may be convenient for formulating the problem in a modeling language, depending on how the scenario data are stored. In the scenario tree in Exhibit 7.1, we could have two copies of the variable $\mathbf{x}_1^{(2)}$ (associated with node 2 at stage 1): $\mathbf{x}_1^{(2,4)}$ for its "child" node 4 at stage 2, and $\mathbf{x}_1^{(2,5)}$ for its "child" node 5 at stage 2. Then, the constraints

$$\mathbf{B}_1^{(4)}\mathbf{x}_1^{(2)} + \mathbf{A}_2^{(4)}\mathbf{x}_2^{(4)} = \mathbf{b}_2^{(4)} \quad \text{and} \quad \mathbf{B}_1^{(5)}\mathbf{x}_1^{(2)} + \mathbf{A}_2^{(5)}\mathbf{x}_2^{(5)} = \mathbf{b}_2^{(5)}$$

should be written as

$$\mathbf{B}_1^{(4)}\mathbf{x}_1^{(2,4)} + \mathbf{A}_2^{(4)}\mathbf{x}_2^{(4)} = \mathbf{b}_2^{(4)} \quad \text{and} \quad \mathbf{B}_1^{(5)}\mathbf{x}_1^{(2,5)} + \mathbf{A}_2^{(5)}\mathbf{x}_2^{(5)} = \mathbf{b}_2^{(5)}$$

We must specify explicitly that $\mathbf{x}_1^{(2,4)} = \mathbf{x}_1^{(2,5)}$ to make sure that the nonanticipativity condition is satisfied. For further details, see, for example, Fragniere and Gondzio (2005).

Four common ways to create scenario trees for the uncertain parameters are[8]

1. Bootstrapping historical data.
2. Using parametric models in which one assumes specific probability distributions and then estimates their parameters from data.
3. Generating simple discrete distributions whose moments are then matched to moments of real data distributions.
4. Constructing vector autoregressive models.

We need to use caution when creating the tree. Its dimension becomes unmanageable very quickly. This is a problem because, as the simple example above illustrated, the number of decision variables and constraints in the optimization problem is directly related to the number of scenarios. If you are managing a portfolio and you allow the possible returns for the N assets in the portfolio to have just two possible realizations at each stage, the total number of scenarios at the last stage is 2^{NT}. If your portfolio consists of only 10 assets and is rebalanced monthly over one year, you would need to work with 2^{120} scenarios for the possible asset returns. Needless to say, optimization problems of such dimension are impossible to solve. Because the size of the problem tends to grow exponentially with the number of nodes, it is important to represent the underlying stochastic process with as few nodes as possible. However, it is also important to take into consideration the trade-off between the dimension of the problem and the accuracy of approximation of the underlying stochastic process, otherwise little insight is gained from solving the optimization problem.

The dimension of realistic multistage stochastic programming problems is typically very large, and optimization is challenging even with today's advanced technology. For certain types of stochastic problems, and linear optimization problems in particular, techniques such as nested *Benders decomposition*[9] and *importance sampling* can be used. The idea behind Benders decomposition is to split the multistage problem into a series of two-stage relations. Subproblems of much smaller size than the original problem are solved at each stage and scenario—these subproblems receive a trial solution from their ancestors, and communicate a trial solution to their successors. Some stochastic programming software packages contain

---

[8]For a survey of stochastic programming applications in financial optimization and scenario generation techniques, see Yu, Ji, and Wang (2003), and Gulpinar, Rustem, and Settergren (2004). For a description of the different econometric techniques used in scenario generation, see Fabozzi, Focardi, and Kolm (2006).
[9]See Birge (1985).

subroutines for decomposition of large stochastic programming problems that can be called directly.[10] However, to use standard optimization solvers, one would need to implement the decomposition in a modeling environment by calling the optimization solver repeatedly for each different subproblem.

Because the number of scenarios substantially impacts the speed with which multistage stochastic optimization problems can be solved, a significant amount of research has been dedicated to developing methodologies for effective scenario generation. The main idea is that scenario generation should try to approximate well not the probability distributions of the uncertain parameters but rather the optimal value of the optimization problem. It has been shown that stochastic programming problems with two stages can be solved very efficiently, and with proven accuracy, by employing Monte Carlo simulation methods.[11] However, little is known about the computational complexity and the quality of approximation of Monte Carlo sampling methods for multistage problems. In the financial modeling context, factor models and bundling of similar sample paths (as opposed to building entire scenario trees) have been used in order to reduce the dimension of such multistage problems.[12] We discuss factor models in more detail in Chapters 9, 10, 12, and 14.

7.2.2 Mean-Risk Stochastic Models

Mean-risk stochastic models use an objective function that is composed of two parts: the expectation and some measure of risk.[13] As explained earlier in this section, when there is uncertainty in the coefficients in the optimization formulation, finding the optimal solution reduces to finding the solution that results in the "best" probability distribution for the objective function values. We mentioned one definition of best probability distribution—the probability distribution with the highest mean. There are other plausible definitions, however. In particular, if we are also concerned about the degree of variability in the probability distribution of the objective function values, we can include a term in the objective function that penalizes for risk.

For example, suppose there are N assets with random returns $\tilde{r}_1, \tilde{r}_2, \ldots, \tilde{r}_N$ over the next year. We would like to invest percentages

---

[10]For example, OSL/SE by IBM and SPInE by the CHARISMA research center at Brunel University.

[11]See Chapter 5 for an introduction to Monte Carlo simulation. A good overview of stochastic programming and importance sampling in particular is available in Ruszczynski and Shapiro (2003).

[12]See Bogentoft, Romeijn, and Uryasev (2001) and Mulvey, Rush, Mitchell, and Willemain (2000).

[13]See Chapter 2.6.2 for an introduction to variability and risk measures.

$w_1, w_2, \ldots, w_N$ of our capital so as to maximize the portfolio expected return and penalize for the variance of the distribution of possible portfolio returns. Suppose we are given a set of S possible scenarios for returns and μ_i are the average returns for assets $i = 1, \ldots, N$ over the scenarios. Let r_i^s be the realization of the return of security i in scenario s. The return of the portfolio in scenario s is simply the sum of the individual asset returns multiplied by their weights in the portfolio, that is,

$$\sum_{i=1}^{N} r_i^s w_i$$

Let us denote the probabilities of the S scenarios by $\pi_1, \ldots, \pi_S$, where

$$\sum_{s=1}^{S} \pi_s = 1$$

The expected return on a portfolio with weights $w_1, w_2, \ldots, w_N$ over the N scenarios equals

$$\sum_{i=1}^{N} \mu_i w_i$$

and the variance of the portfolio return over the S scenarios is[14]

$$\sum_{s=1}^{S} \pi_s \left(\underbrace{\sum_{i=1}^{N} r_i^s w_i}_{\text{portfolio return in scenario } s} - \underbrace{\sum_{i=1}^{N} \mu_i w_i}_{\text{expected portfolio return}} \right)^2$$

Therefore, we can define the following objective for our portfolio optimization problem under uncertainty:

$$\max_{w} \sum_{i=1}^{N} \mu_i w_i - \kappa \left[\sum_{s=1}^{S} \pi_s \left(\underbrace{\sum_{i=1}^{N} r_i^s w_i}_{\text{portfolio return in scenario } s} - \underbrace{\sum_{i=1}^{N} \mu_i w_i}_{\text{expected portfolio return}} \right)^2 \right]$$

---

[14]The definition of variance of a discrete probability distribution is provided in Chapter 2.6.2.

EXHIBIT 7.2 Scenarios for the returns of the four funds.

Fund #	1	2	3	4
Scenario 1	50.39%	15.69%	23.29%	2.50%
Scenario 2	−9.02%	−3.96%	−2.25%	2.36%
Mean return	20.69%	5.87%	10.52%	2.43%

Here, κ is a penalty coefficient that is determined by the user—the more tolerance we have for uncertainty, the smaller the coefficient is. If we only cared about the expected portfolio return over the S scenarios, we would set κ to 0. We can specify additional constraints, as we would do in any optimization problem.

To gain some intuition, let us consider a simplified extension of the portfolio allocation example in Chapter 6.3. Suppose that the expected returns of the four funds are the same but we believe that their returns could end up in one of two scenarios: a "good" scenario, Scenario 1, or a "bad" scenario, Scenario 2 (see Exhibit 7.2). Suppose also that we believe that the probability of Scenario 1 is 0.30, and the probability of Scenario 2 is 0.70.

The stochastic programming mean-risk formulation of this problem is

$$\max_{w} 20.69 \cdot w_1 + 5.87 \cdot w_2 + 10.52 \cdot w_3 + 2.43 \cdot w_4$$

$$- \kappa \cdot 0.30 \cdot \big(50.39 \cdot w_1 + 15.69 \cdot w_2 + 23.29 \cdot w_3 + 2.50 \cdot w_4$$

$$- (20.69 \cdot w_1 + 5.87 \cdot w_2 + 10.52 \cdot w_3 + 2.43 \cdot w_4) \big)^2$$

$$- \kappa \cdot 0.70 \cdot \big(-9.02 \cdot w_1 - 3.96 \cdot w_2 - 2.25 \cdot w_3 + 2.36 \cdot w_4$$

$$- (20.69 \cdot w_1 + 5.87 \cdot w_2 + 10.52 \cdot w_3 + 2.43 \cdot w_4) \big)^2$$

subject to the remaining other constraints in the problem.

Different risk measures can, of course, be used as well.

7.2.3 Chance-Constrained Models

Chance-constrained stochastic optimization problems contain requirements on the probability that the solution will satisfy the constraints for all realizations of the random parameters in the problem. If the original constraint is

$$\tilde{a}' x \leq b$$

where x is the vector of decision variables and $\tilde{a}$ is a vector of uncertain coefficients, then the general form of the chance constraint is

$$P(\tilde{a}' x > b) \leq \epsilon$$

where P denotes probability and ϵ is some small number, such as 0.05 (5%). In order for the probabilistic constraint above to be satisfied, we need to find such a solution $\mathbf{x}$ such that the original constraint $\tilde{\mathbf{a}}'\mathbf{x} \leq b$ is violated for at most ϵ% of all possible values for the uncertain coefficients. An important example of a chance-constrained stochastic programming problem in the portfolio management context is portfolio value-at-risk (VaR) optimization.

Based on our introduction to optimization models in Chapter 6.2, it is clear that a probabilistic constraint is not part of any of the standard optimization formulations. We need to apply tricks to convert the constraint into a form that can be passed to an optimization solver, and this involves making different assumptions. In the case in which we are given S scenarios for the vector of uncertain coefficients $\tilde{\mathbf{a}}$, we would replace this probabilistic constraint with an equivalent group of constraints:

$$(\mathbf{a}^{(s)})'\mathbf{x} \leq b + M \cdot y_s, \qquad s = 1, \ldots, S$$

$$\sum_{s=1}^{S} y_s \leq \lfloor \epsilon \cdot S \rfloor$$

$$y_s \in \{0,1\}, \qquad s = 1, \ldots, S$$

In the formulation above, M is a large constant relative to the size of the problem that is specified by the user. We have introduced S new binary decision variables y_s and have $S + 1$ constraints instead of the original one probabilistic constraint. If $y_s = 0$, this forces the constraint

$$(\mathbf{a}^{(s)})'\mathbf{x} \leq b$$

to be satisfied, that is, the constraint $\tilde{\mathbf{a}}'\mathbf{x} \leq b$ to be satisfied in scenario s. However, if $y_s = 1$, the term $M \cdot y_s$ is large, that is, the right-hand side of the constraint is no longer restrictive and the constraint no longer needs to be satisfied.

The additional constraint

$$\sum_{s=1}^{S} y_s \leq \lfloor \epsilon \cdot S \rfloor$$

limits the number of binary variables that are 1 to at most $\lfloor \epsilon \cdot S \rfloor$ (which is the integer part of $\epsilon \cdot S$). For example, if we are given 115 scenarios for $\tilde{\mathbf{a}}$ and $\epsilon = 5\%$, it is guaranteed that at most 5 ($= \lfloor 0.05 \cdot 115 \rfloor = \lfloor 5.75 \rfloor$) of the y's are 1 (i.e., the constraint is not violated in more than 95% of the scenarios).

The introduction of binary variables and additional constraints increases the size and complexity of the original optimization problem significantly and can overwhelm even the best solvers when the number of scenarios (and, hence the number of binary variables) is large. Moreover, the optimization problem type is now nonconvex, which means that if the solver returns a solution, we cannot be confident that it is the optimal one. Therefore, probabilistic constraints need to be handled with care.

Note that a chance constraint basically requires that the $100(1 - \epsilon)$th percentile of the distribution of the random variable $\tilde{a}'x$ be less than the right-hand-side limit b. Therefore, in rare cases in which we know the distribution of $\tilde{a}'x$ and can compute a closed-form expression for its $100(1 - \epsilon)$th percentile, we can convert a probabilistic constraint directly into a single nonprobabilistic constraint.

This is the case when all uncertain coefficients $\tilde{a}_1, \ldots, \tilde{a}_N$ in the chance constraint are assumed to come from a multivariate normal distribution. We can compute the exact $100(1 - \epsilon)$th percentile of the probability distribution $\tilde{a}'x$ in terms of the means of the uncertain coefficients $\tilde{a}$, the standard deviations and the covariance structure of the uncertain coefficients $\tilde{a}$, and the solution vector x.

The $100(1 - \epsilon)$th percentile of the distribution of a normal random variable with a mean μ and standard deviation σ is given by $\mu + q_{(1-\epsilon)}(1 - \epsilon) \cdot \sigma$, where $q_{(1-\epsilon)}$ is the $100(1 - \epsilon)$th percentile of a standard normal distribution.[15] From the equations for expectation and variance of a sum of random variables, we can compute the mean of the normal random variable $\tilde{a}'x$ as $\hat{a}'x$ and its standard deviation as $\sqrt{x'\Sigma x}$, where $\hat{a}$ are the expected values of the coefficients $\tilde{a}$ and Σ is the covariance matrix of the coefficients $\tilde{a}$.[16] Therefore, the deterministic constraint equivalent of the chance constraint under the assumption of normally distributed uncertain coefficients is

$$\hat{a}'x + q_{(1-\epsilon)} \cdot \sqrt{x'\Sigma x} \leq b$$

This is a second-order cone programming (SOCP) constraint, which we discussed in Chapter 6.2.4. This type of constraint is easier to handle than a large set of constraints involving mixed-integer decision variables if one has the right solver. Robust optimization techniques have been also successfully applied for approximating the optimal solutions of problems with chance constraints in stochastic programming.[17]

---

[15] See Chapters 2.4, 2.6.2.5, and 4.5.

[16] This can be shown by writing out the expressions for expected values and variances of sums of random variables when the random variables are given in a vector/matrix form. (See the Appendix.) We discuss this in more detail in Chapter 8.

[17] See Chen, Sim, and Sun (2007) and Natarajan, Pachamanova, and Sim (2008).

7.3 ROBUST OPTIMIZATION

A major problem with dynamic and stochastic programming formulations is that in practice it is often difficult to obtain detailed information about the probability distributions of the uncertainties in the model. At the same time, depending on the number of scenarios involved in the formulation, dynamic and stochastic programming methods can be prohibitively costly computationally. *Robust optimization* makes optimization models robust with respect to uncertainty in the input data of optimization problems by solving so-called robust counterparts of these problems for appropriately defined *uncertainty sets* for the random parameters. The robust counterparts contain no uncertain coefficients; they are deterministic optimization problems. The robust counterparts are worst-case formulations of the original optimization problems, where the worst-case is computed over the possible values the input parameters could take within their uncertainty sets. Typically, the uncertainty sets are defined in smart ways that do not lead to overly conservative or computationally challenging formulations. If the uncertainty sets are defined as a set of scenarios for the uncertain coefficients, robust optimization shares some features with stochastic programming. However, classical robust optimization focuses on the worst case, whereas classical stochastic programming focuses on the average over these scenarios.

To provide intuition for the robust optimization philosophy, let us consider a linear constraint of the kind

$$\tilde{\mathbf{a}}'\mathbf{x} \leq b$$

Let us assume that we use a statistical procedure to estimate nominal, or expected, values for the elements of the vector of coefficients $\tilde{\mathbf{a}}$. We obtain estimates (let us denote them by $\hat{\mathbf{a}} = (\hat{a}_1, \ldots, \hat{a}_N)$) and 95% confidence intervals for the true parameter values, $(\hat{a}_i - \delta_i, \hat{a}_i + \delta_i)$ for $i = 1, \ldots, N$.[18] A natural choice for an uncertainty set for $\tilde{\mathbf{a}}$ is the collection of confidence intervals, which can be written as

$$U_\delta(\hat{\mathbf{a}}) = \left\{ \mathbf{a} \mid |a_i - \hat{a}_i| \leq \delta_i, \ i = 1, \ldots, N \right\}$$

This mathematical expression states that the coefficient a_i can take any value between $\hat{a}_i - \delta_i$ and $\hat{a}_i + \delta_i$, where δ_i is a nonnegative number

---

[18]See Chapter 2.11.2 for a definition of confidence intervals and Chapter 5.1.2 for their use in simulation.

representing the half-length of the confidence interval formed around the estimate $\hat{a}_i$.

The robust counterpart of the linear constraint above is the following expression:

$$\max_{a \in U_\delta(\hat{a})} \{a'x\} \leq b$$

In other words, we require that the constraint be satisfied even for the worst-case value of the expression $a'x$ when a varies in the specified uncertainty set $U_\delta(\hat{a})$. In this case, the worst-case value is obtained at the maximum because if the maximum value of $a'x$ is less than or equal to b, then the constraint is clearly satisfied for all smaller values of $a'x$. If the inequality were in the opposite direction, that is,

$$\tilde{a}'x \geq b$$

then the worst case would happen at the minimum of the expression $a'x$, that is, the robust counterpart would be

$$\min_{a \in U_\delta(\hat{a})} \{a'x\} \geq b$$

The robust counterpart of the constraint can be written in a form that can be passed to an optimization solver. The maximum of the expression $a'x$ when a varies in $U_\delta(\hat{a})$ is given by

$$\hat{a}'x + \delta'|x|$$

This can be seen without any advanced mathematics. If the value of a particular decision variable x_i is nonnegative, then $|x_i| = x_i$ and the maximum value of $a_i \cdot x_i$ is obtained by multiplying the maximum possible value of a_i in the uncertainty set, $\hat{a}_i + \delta_i$, by x_i. If the value of x_i is negative, then $|x_i| = -x_i$, which is a positive number, and the maximum value of $a_i \cdot x_i$ is obtained by multiplying the maximum possible value of a_i in the uncertainty set, $\hat{a}_i + \delta_i$, by $-x_i$.

The uncertainty set we considered above, $U_\delta(\hat{a})$, is very simple, and in fact its applications in finance have been limited because it is too conservative. The shape of the uncertainty set is a rectangle in two dimensions, and looks like a box in more dimensions (see Exhibit 7.3(a)). The robust optimization approach finds the optimal solution when a is at one of the corners of the "box"—the corner in which all elements of a are at their "worst" values in terms of constraint violation, and result in the maximum value for the expression $a'x$.

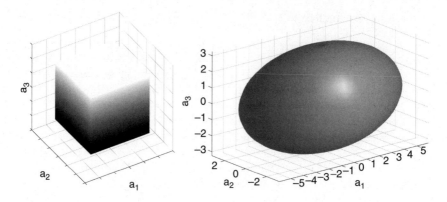

Exhibit 7.3 (a) A "box" uncertainty set in three dimensions; (b) an ellipsoidal uncertainty set in three dimensions.

It may be realistic to be less conservative and assume that not all uncertain coefficients will take their worst-case values at the same time. In addition, we may have information about the standard deviations and the covariance structure of the uncertain coefficients. More advanced uncertainty sets can be specified to capture this information. A classical uncertainty set in robust optimization is the ellipsoidal uncertainty set (see Exhibit 7.3(b)), which mathematically can be represented as

$$U_\delta(\hat{a}) = \left\{ a \mid (a - \hat{a})' \Sigma^{-1} (a - \hat{a}) \le \delta^2 \right\}$$

Here, Σ is the covariance matrix of the uncertain coefficients $\tilde{a}$ and δ is a budget (tolerance) for robustness that is specified by the user. This uncertainty set states that the constraint should be satisfied for all values of a whose total squared distances from their nominal estimated values $\hat{a}$, scaled by their variability, are less than or equal to δ^2. Often, this uncertainty set is seen in the literature as

$$U_\delta(\hat{a}) = \left\{ a \mid \left\| \Sigma^{-1/2} (a - \hat{a}) \right\| \le \delta \right\}$$

where $\| \cdot \|$ stands for second, or Euclidean, norm.[19] The two expressions for the ellipsoidal uncertainty set are equivalent.

---

[19]See Chapter 6.2.4 and the Appendix.

It turns out that the robust counterpart of the constraint

$$\tilde{a}'x \leq b$$

when the vector of uncertain coefficients $\tilde{a}$ varies in the ellipsoidal uncertainty set is

$$\hat{a}'x + \kappa \cdot \left\| \Sigma^{1/2}x \right\| \leq b$$

This can be proved using optimization duality.[20] Now the formulation is in a form that can be passed to an optimization solver because all coefficients are certain. Nonlinear solvers such as MINOS can handle it. Alternatively, since we are dealing with a SOCP, a solver such as SeDuMi,[21] SDP3,[22] or IBM ILOG CPLEX would be able to take advantage of its structure and solve it more efficiently.

To summarize, the methodology for creating a single optimization problem to represent the robust counterpart of a constraint is based on a trick from optimization duality. We first formulate a problem in which the original variables x are treated as fixed and try to find the worst-case value for the expression containing the vector of uncertain parameters $\tilde{a}$. We then use optimization duality to convert the expression with uncertain coefficients into a constraint that does not contain uncertain parameters, and plug it into the original constraint. Finally, we solve the original optimization problem with the modified constraint and with x as a vector of decision variables again. While a certain amount of preprocessing is involved in formulating the robust problem, there is only one call to an optimization solver once the robust counterpart problem is formulated correctly.

The shape of the uncertainty set and the calibration of the different parameters that enter its specification is a very important part of ensuring that the robust counterpart has a good performance in practice. The uncertainty sets we saw in these examples were symmetric, that is, we assumed that the uncertain coefficients could deviate from their nominal values by the same amount in each direction. In theory, we could select uncertainty sets that represent better the probability distributions of the

---

[20]The proof is beyond the scope of this book. See Chapter 5 in Pachamanova and Fabozzi (2010).
[21]See http://sedumi.ie.lehigh.edu/.
[22]See www.math.nus.edu.sg/~mattohkc/sdpt3.html.

uncertain coefficients when these probability distributions are skewed.[23] There has also been interest in developing "structured" uncertainty sets, that is, uncertainty sets that are intersections of elementary uncertainty sets, or are constructed for a specific purpose.[24]

Robust optimization formulations can be used also in multistage settings to replace dynamic programming or stochastic programming algorithms. Namely, instead of considering scenarios with realizations of the different uncertain parameters in a multistage problem, robust optimization formulations specify uncertainty sets around these parameters at each stage.[25]

Summary

- Dynamic programming, stochastic programming, and robust optimization are all methodologies for optimization under uncertainty. Although there is overlap among the three approaches, historically they have evolved independently of each other.
- The dynamic programming approach is used for optimization over multiple stages. Its main idea is to break up the large multistage problem into a sequence of smaller optimization problems, starting from the last stage and proceeding backward.
- The stochastic programming approach deals with optimization problems in which scenarios are generated for the values of the uncertain parameters. The optimization may be performed so that the objective function is optimized on average, or may include penalties for constraint violation and risk considerations. Stochastic programming can be applied to both single- and multistage optimization problems.
- In most real-world applications, the dimensions of dynamic and stochastic programming methods are too large, and the problems are difficult to handle computationally. Often, approximation algorithms are used;

---

[23]See, for example, Natarajan, Pachamanova, and Sim (2008).
[24]For more details, see Chapters 10 and 12 in Fabozzi, Kolm, Pachamanova, and Focardi (2007).
[25]See, for example, Ben-Tal, Margalit, and Nemirovski (2000), Bertsimas and Pachamanova (2008), Gulpinar and Pachamanova (2013), and Gulpinar, Pachamanova, and Canakoglu (2014).

some such algorithms employ Monte Carlo simulation and sample the state space efficiently.

- Robust optimization handles uncertainty in the coefficients of optimization problems by solving so-called robust counterparts of these problems. The robust counterparts are optimization problems that are formulated in terms of the worst-case realizations of the uncertain parameters within prespecified uncertainty sets.

Portfolio Theory

CHAPTER 8

Asset Diversification

The concepts of portfolio risk management and diversification have been instrumental in the development of modern financial decision making. These breakthrough ideas originated in an article by Harry Markowitz that appeared in 1952. Before Markowitz's publication, the focus in the investment industry was on identifying and investing in "winners"—stocks that appear undervalued relative to some measure of their potential or promise sustainable growth, that is, stocks with high expected returns. Markowitz reasoned that investors should decide based on both the expected return from their investment, and the risk from that investment. He defined risk as the variance of future returns. The idea of incorporating risk in investment decisions and applying a disciplined quantitative framework to investment management was novel at the time.[1] Originally, this investment philosophy generated little interest, but eventually, the finance community adopted it. Over the years, the theory of portfolio selection formulated by Markowitz has been extended and reinvented based on a modification of the assumptions made in the original model that limited its application. It has also introduced a whole new terminology, which is now the norm in the investment management community. Markowitz's investment theory is popularly referred to as *mean-variance analysis*, *mean-variance portfolio optimization*, and *Modern Portfolio Theory* (MPT). In 1990, Markowitz was awarded the Nobel Memorial Prize in Economic Sciences in recognition of his seminal work.

As we will see in this chapter, the definition of risk as the variance of returns leads to the conclusion that *diversification* is preferable as an investment strategy. Markowitz's framework in essence quantified the conventional wisdom of "not putting all of your eggs in one basket."

---

[1] We need to clarify here that *utility theory*, which was developed in the economics literature before Markowitz's publication, allowed for incorporating risk implicitly by considering special kinds of investor utility functions that described risk averseness. However, Markowitz's publication suggested the first tangible and practical quantitative framework that defined investment decision making explicitly as a tradeoff between risk and return. See Section 8.6 for a brief introduction to utility theory.

Mathematically, the portfolio variance is a sum of terms including both the variances of the returns of the individual assets and the covariances (equivalently, the correlations) between those returns. Investing all of your money in assets that are strongly correlated is not considered a prudent strategy, even if individually each of the assets appears to be a "winner" based on preliminary analysis. If any single asset performs worse than expectations, it is likely, due to its high correlation with the other assets, that the other assets will also perform poorly, decreasing substantially the value of the entire portfolio.

In this chapter, we explain the basic assumptions in Markowitz's model. We also show that the mean-variance approach is consistent with two different frameworks: expected utility maximization under certain conditions, and the assumption that future security returns are jointly normally distributed. It is worth noting that in recent years, especially in light of the financial crisis of 2007–2008 when asset class return correlations moved closely together, the concept of diversification has been questioned and reconsidered. Specifically, practitioners and academics have been interested in new ways to define diversification and measure the degree of diversification in a portfolio, leading to substantial interest in *risk-based allocation* strategies. The last section in this chapter (Section 8.7) is dedicated to these new developments.

In practice, the Markowitz framework has been applied to portfolio construction in two ways: (1) at the asset class level (in order to make an asset allocation decision), and (2) to select the securities in a portfolio within an asset class. With regard to allocation of funds among asset classes, there has been a recent shift away by some asset management firms from asset-based portfolio optimization to factor-based portfolio optimization. We discuss factor models and their applications to portfolio construction in Chapters 10, 12, and 14. With regard to security selection within an asset class to construct a portfolio, we should clarify that although the Markowitz framework has been used in equity portfolio management for many years, it has seen limited application in the management of fixed income portfolios. Thus, much of the discussion and most of the examples in this chapter refer to stocks. However, some of the terminology that was created based on Markowitz's framework is used in the risk management of both equity and fixed income portfolios; hence, understanding the material in this chapter is important for both types of applications.

8.1 THE CASE FOR DIVERSIFICATION

Consider an investor who is evaluating an investment in two stocks over the next year, Stock 1 and Stock 2. The stocks' expected returns are $E[\tilde{r}_1] = \mu_1 = 9.1\%$ and $E[\tilde{r}_2] = \mu_2 = 12.1\%$, and their standard deviations are $\sigma_1 = 16.5\%$ and $\sigma_2 = 15.8\%$.

At first glance, Stock 2 is the clear winner. Its expected return is higher than Stock 1's and its standard deviation is lower than Stock 1's. Thus, by investing 100% of his wealth in Stock 2, the investor could achieve a better return for less risk, if risk is defined as the standard deviation of possible outcomes.

Now suppose the investor is given the additional information that the correlation coefficient between the two stocks' returns is $\rho_{12} = -0.22$. Let us denote the weight of Stock 1 in the portfolio by w_1, and the weight of Stock 2 by w_2. Note that the sum of the weights of the two stocks must be 100%, that is, $w_2 = 1 - w_1$.

The portfolio return $\tilde{r}_p$ is a random variable as denoted by a tilde ($\sim$), and can be expressed as

$$\tilde{r}_p = w_1 \tilde{r}_1 + w_2 \tilde{r}_2$$

The portfolio's expected return and the variance can be computed from the rules listed in Chapter 2.8. In particular, the portfolio expected return is

$$E[\tilde{r}_p] = E[w_1 \tilde{r}_1 + w_2 \tilde{r}_2] = E[w_1 \tilde{r}_1] + E[w_2 \tilde{r}_2] = w_1 E[\tilde{r}_1] + w_2 E[\tilde{r}_2]$$

$$= w_1 \mu_1 + w_2 \mu_2$$

The portfolio variance is

$$\sigma_p^2 = \text{Var}(w_1 \tilde{r}_1 + w_2 \tilde{r}_2) = \text{Var}(w_1 \tilde{r}_1) + \text{Var}(w_2 \tilde{r}_2) + 2 \cdot \text{Covar}(w_1 \tilde{r}_1, w_2 \tilde{r}_2)$$

$$= w_1^2 \sigma_1^2 + w_2^2 \sigma_2^2 + 2 w_1 w_2 \sigma_{12}$$

Because we have estimated the correlation coefficient instead of the covariance, we can express the portfolio variance through the correlation coefficient[2]

$$\sigma_p^2 = w_1^2 \sigma_1^2 + w_2^2 \sigma_2^2 + 2 w_1 w_2 \sigma_1 \sigma_2 \rho_{12}$$

The portfolio standard deviation is simply the square root of the portfolio variance computed above.

Exhibits 8.1(a) and 8.1(b) illustrate how the portfolio return and standard deviation change with the fraction of the portfolio invested in Stock 1. We can observe that although the portfolio expected return is highest when 0% is invested in Stock 1, the portfolio standard deviation when the weight of Stock 1 is 0% is not the lowest possible. By investing in both Stock 1 and Stock 2, the investor can reduce the portfolio standard deviation to a level that is less than the level of any of the individual stocks' standard deviations.

---

[2] See the definition for the correlation coefficient in Chapter 2.7.

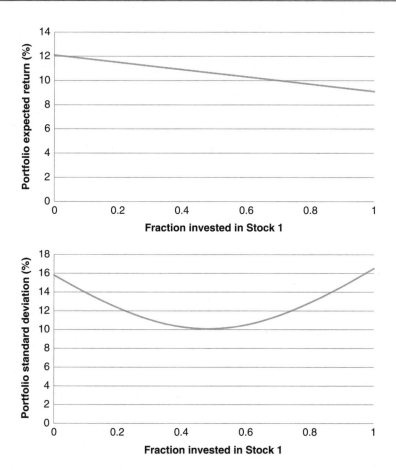

Exhibit 8.1 (a) Change in portfolio expected return as the fraction invested in Stock 1 increases from 0 to 1; (b) change in portfolio standard deviation as the fraction invested in Stock 1 increases from 0 to 1.

In the two-stock example above, the fact that the stocks were negatively correlated made the effect of diversification on reducing the overall portfolio standard deviation particularly dramatic. The same conclusion, however—that diversification decreases the portfolio standard deviation—holds when stock returns are uncorrelated or exhibit weak correlations. The conclusion tends to hold true in observed stock return behavior as well. Exhibit 8.2 contains a chart of the mean and the standard deviation of portfolio returns for equally weighted portfolios containing between 1 and 25 stocks picked at random from the S&P 500. The average correlation of these stocks is slightly positive. Yet, as the graph

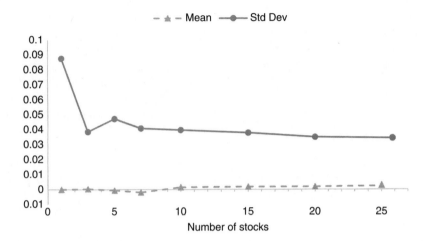

Exhibit 8.2   Mean and standard deviation for the returns of equally weighted portfolios of S&P 500 stocks picked at random. Note: The random selection started with a portfolio of a single stock (Caterpillar) followed by a portfolio of three stocks (Caterpillar, Boeing, and AT&T) and ended with a portfolio of 25 stocks. The portfolio mean and standard deviation were computed based on 12 monthly returns for each stock included in the portfolios between January 2013 and December 2013. The graph illustrates the decrease in the realized standard deviation of an equally weighted portfolio as the number of stocks in the portfolio increases.

in Exhibit 8.2 illustrates, the standard deviation of a portfolio obtained by weighting equally a selected number of stocks decreases as the number of stocks grows larger. Diversification in this case is beneficial even for a portfolio whose weights were determined casually—by weighting each stock equally. We could do even better by selecting the portfolio weights in a more deliberate way—by using optimization to calculate the weights that minimize the portfolio risk as measured by its variance.

   A fact worth noting here is that diversification cannot necessarily eliminate risk completely. For example, as the graph in Exhibit 8.2 shows, we reach a point (about 20 stocks in this particular example), beyond which adding more stocks does not reduce the standard deviation of the portfolio. A study by Evans and Archer (1968), the first of its kind, suggested that the major benefits of diversification can be obtained with 10 to 20 stocks. More recent studies by Campbell, Lettau, Malkiel, and Xu (2001) and Malkiel (2002) show that the volatility of individual stocks has increased between the 1960s and the 1990s. On the other hand, the correlations between individual stocks have decreased over the same time period. Together, these two effects have canceled each other out, leaving the overall market volatility the same. However, Malkiel's study suggests that it now takes almost 200 individual equities to obtain the same amount of diversification that was historically possible with as few as 10 individual equities.

As we mentioned in Chapter 3.2.2, several studies have suggested that the behavior of real-world asset returns can be mapped to a probability distribution known as the *stable Paretian distribution*. Mandelbrot (1963) was the first to make this observation. The variance of a random variable following a stable Paretian distribution is not bounded (i.e., it is infinite and therefore does not exist). This fact calls into question the principle of diversification. Adding assets with very large or infinite variances to a portfolio cannot reduce the overall portfolio standard deviation. In particular, Fama (1965) demonstrated that if asset returns behave like a stable Paretian distribution, diversification may no longer be meaningful. In general, however, most practitioners agree that a certain degree of diversification is preferable and attainable in the market.

8.2   THE CLASSICAL MEAN-VARIANCE OPTIMIZATION FRAMEWORK

Suppose that an investor would like to invest in N risky assets. The investor's choice can be represented as an $N \times 1$ vector array $\mathbf{w} = (w_1, \ldots, w_N)'$ of asset weights.[3] Each weight w_i represents the proportion of asset i held in the portfolio and the total portfolio weight needs to be 100%, that is,

$$\sum_{i=1}^{N} w_i = 1$$

In vector notation, the above requirement can be written as[4]

$$\mathbf{w}' \, \iota = 1$$

where ι is an $N \times 1$ vector array of ones. If short-selling is allowed, then the weights can be negative.

Markowitz's framework assumes that the investor is making a decision for his investment over one time period of a prespecified length. The investor is concerned with the return on his portfolio at the end of that time period,

---

[3]See the Appendix for a review of matrix notation and definition of matrix transpose (').
[4]See the Appendix for a review of matrix array multiplication.

but not during it or after the end of it. The returns of the N assets in the portfolio during that time period can be represented as a vector array of random variables: $\tilde{\mathbf{r}} = (\tilde{r}_1, \ldots, \tilde{r}_N)'$. Suppose the expected returns on the N assets are $\boldsymbol{\mu} = (\mu_1, \ldots, \mu_N)'$ and the covariance matrix of returns is

$$\boldsymbol{\Sigma} = \begin{bmatrix} \sigma_{11} & \cdots & \sigma_{1N} \\ \vdots & \ddots & \vdots \\ \sigma_{N1} & \cdots & \sigma_{NN} \end{bmatrix}$$

where σ_{ij} denotes the covariance between asset i and asset j, and the diagonal element σ_{ii} is the variance of asset i, that is, $\sigma_{ii} = \sigma_i^2$. (Note that $\sigma_{ij} = \sigma_{ji}$, that is, the covariance matrix is symmetric because the covariance between i and j is the same as the covariance between j and i.) Then, the expected return on a portfolio that has allocations of $\mathbf{w} = (w_1, \ldots, w_N)'$ is

$$\mu_p = \sum_{i=1}^{N} \mu_i \cdot w_i = \boldsymbol{\mu}' \mathbf{w}$$

and the portfolio variance σ_p^2 is

$$\sigma_p^2 = \mathbf{w}' \boldsymbol{\Sigma} \mathbf{w}$$

If, instead of the covariance matrix, we know the correlation matrix

$$\mathbf{C} = \begin{bmatrix} 1 & \cdots & \rho_{1N} \\ \vdots & \ddots & \vdots \\ \rho_{N1} & \cdots & 1 \end{bmatrix}$$

and the standard deviations of the individual assets, we can either convert the correlation matrix into a covariance matrix element-by-element by using the relationship[5]

$$\rho_{ij} = \frac{\sigma_{ij}}{\sigma_i \sigma_j}$$

or we can use directly the correlation matrix in the expression for portfolio variance. To do that, we need to construct a vector $\mathbf{w}^s$ of products of the weights of the assets and the corresponding standard deviations, $\mathbf{w}^s = (w_1 \sigma_1, \ldots, w_N \sigma_N)'$. Then, the portfolio variance can be computed as

$$\sigma_p^2 = (\mathbf{w}^s)' \mathbf{C} \mathbf{w}^s$$

---

[5]See Chapter 2.7.

To provide intuition, let us go back to the case of two assets with weights w_1 and w_2. The portfolio return can be written in vector notation as

$$\tilde{r}_p = \begin{bmatrix} w_1 & w_2 \end{bmatrix} \cdot \begin{bmatrix} \tilde{r}_1 \\ \tilde{r}_2 \end{bmatrix} = \mathbf{w}' \tilde{\mathbf{r}}$$

The portfolio expected return in matrix notation is

$$E[\tilde{r}_p] = E[\mathbf{w}' \tilde{\mathbf{r}}] = \mathbf{w}' E[\tilde{\mathbf{r}}] = \begin{bmatrix} w_1 & w_2 \end{bmatrix} \cdot \begin{bmatrix} E[\tilde{r}_1] \\ E[\tilde{r}_2] \end{bmatrix} = \mathbf{w}' \boldsymbol{\mu}$$

The portfolio variance in matrix notation is

$$\sigma_p^2 = \mathbf{w}' \boldsymbol{\Sigma} \mathbf{w} = \begin{bmatrix} w_1 & w_2 \end{bmatrix} \cdot \begin{bmatrix} \sigma_1^2 & \sigma_{12} \\ \sigma_{21} & \sigma_2^2 \end{bmatrix} \cdot \begin{bmatrix} w_1 \\ w_2 \end{bmatrix}$$

$$= \begin{bmatrix} w_1 \sigma_1^2 + w_2 \sigma_{21} & w_1 \sigma_{12} + w_2 \sigma_2^2 \end{bmatrix} \cdot \begin{bmatrix} w_1 \\ w_2 \end{bmatrix}$$

Note that the last expression equals

$$w_1^2 \sigma_1^2 + w_2^2 \sigma_2^2 + 2 w_1 w_2 \sigma_{12}$$

which is the same expression as the expression for variance we derived in Section 8.1.

If we have the correlation matrix rather than the covariance matrix, then we can compute the portfolio variance as

$$\sigma_p^2 = \begin{bmatrix} w_1 \sigma_1 & w_2 \sigma_2 \end{bmatrix} \cdot \begin{bmatrix} 1 & \rho_{12} \\ \rho_{21} & 1 \end{bmatrix} \cdot \begin{bmatrix} w_1 \sigma_1 \\ w_2 \sigma_2 \end{bmatrix}$$

$$= \begin{bmatrix} w_1 \sigma_1 + w_2 \sigma_2 \rho_{21} & w_1 \sigma_1 \rho_{12} + w_2 \sigma_2 \end{bmatrix} \cdot \begin{bmatrix} w_1 \sigma_1 \\ w_2 \sigma_2 \end{bmatrix}$$

$$= w_1^2 \sigma_1^2 + w_2^2 \sigma_2^2 + 2 w_1 w_2 \sigma_1 \sigma_2 \rho_{12}$$

which again is equivalent to the expression for variance we derived in Section 8.1 because $\sigma_1 \sigma_2 \rho_{12} = \sigma_{12}$.

The classical mean-variance portfolio allocation problem is formulated as follows:

$$\min_{\mathbf{w}} \quad \mathbf{w}' \boldsymbol{\Sigma} \mathbf{w}$$

$$\text{s. t.} \quad \mathbf{w}' \boldsymbol{\mu} = r_{\text{target}}$$

$$\mathbf{w}' \boldsymbol{\iota} = 1$$

Note that the objective function of this optimization problem is quadratic in the decision variables **w**.[6] This minimization problem is convex because the objective function is convex and all the constraints are linear functions of the decision variables.[7] To see that the objective function is a convex function of the decision variables **w**, consider the portfolio of two assets. The weight of the second asset, w_2, can be expressed through the weight of the first asset, w_1, as $w_2 = 1 - w_1$. Plugging into the expression for the portfolio variance, we obtain

$$\sigma_p^2 = w_1^2 \sigma_1^2 + (1 - w_1)^2 \sigma_2^2 + 2w_1(1 - w_1)\rho_{12}\sigma_1\sigma_2$$

$$= w_1^2(\sigma_1^2 + \sigma_2^2 - 2\rho_{12}\sigma_1\sigma_2) + w_1(-2\sigma_2^2 + 2\rho_{12}\sigma_1\sigma_2) + \sigma_2^2$$

The sign of the coefficient in front of the decision variable w_1^2 determines whether the quadratic objective function will be concave or convex (see Exhibit 6.3). Note that the coefficient can be written as

$$\sigma_1^2 + \sigma_2^2 - 2\sigma_1\sigma_2 + 2\sigma_1\sigma_2 - 2\rho_{12}\sigma_1\sigma_2$$

$$= (\sigma_1^2 + \sigma_2^2 - 2\sigma_1\sigma_2) + 2\sigma_1\sigma_2(1 - \rho_{12})$$

$$= \underbrace{(\sigma_1 - \sigma_2)^2}_{\geq 0 \text{ (squared term)}} + \underbrace{2\sigma_1\sigma_2(1 - \rho_{12})}_{\geq 0 \text{ (because } -1 \leq \rho_{12} \leq 1)}$$

so it is always nonnegative. Therefore, the objective function has the shape in Exhibit 6.3(a) and, as a result, minimization will bring us to the global minimum at the tip of the curve.[8]

The optimal solution for the classical mean-variance portfolio allocation problem can be found in closed form by using Lagrange multipliers. The optimal weights are

$$\mathbf{w}^* = \mathbf{g} + \mathbf{h} \cdot r_{\text{target}}$$

where

$$\mathbf{g} = \frac{1}{ac - b^2} \cdot \boldsymbol{\Sigma}^{-1} \cdot [c \cdot \boldsymbol{\imath} - b \cdot \boldsymbol{\mu}]$$

$$\mathbf{h} = \frac{1}{ac - b^2} \cdot \boldsymbol{\Sigma}^{-1} \cdot [a \cdot \boldsymbol{\mu} - b \cdot \boldsymbol{\imath}]$$

---

[6] See Chapter 6 for a review of optimization problem formulations, classification, and terminology.

[7] See Chapter 6 for use of convex functions in optimization.

[8] This statement is a bit simplified because the function plotted in Exhibit 6.3 is a function of a single variable x, whereas here we have a function of two variables, so the visualization would be three-dimensional. The general conclusion, however, is the same.

and

$$a = \iota' \Sigma^{-1} \iota$$
$$b = \iota' \Sigma^{-1} \mu$$
$$c = \mu' \Sigma^{-1} \mu$$

Typically, however, the classical mean-variance optimization is modified to include additional constraints or to express the objective in a different way, so no closed-form solution exists, and an optimization solver must be used to solve for the optimal weights.

The problem of minimizing the portfolio variance is equivalent to the problem of minimizing the portfolio standard deviation (which is the square root of the portfolio variance) in the sense that the optimal weights will be the same. Minimizing the portfolio variance, however, is more solver-friendly. It is preferable that the minimum variance formulation is implemented with optimization software. The optimal portfolio standard deviation can then be easily derived from the optimal portfolio variance.

8.3   EFFICIENT FRONTIERS

Let us consider again the two-stock example from Section 8.1. As the weight of Stock 1 in the portfolio increases, the portfolio expected return and risk trace out the solid curve in Exhibit 8.2(a). Each point on this curve is obtained for a different combination of stock weights. The point at the top right part of the curve is the portfolio obtained if 100% is invested in Stock 2. Note that that portfolio's expected return is 12.1% (the expected return of Stock 2) and its standard deviation is 15.8% (the standard deviation of Stock 2). At the other end (the point at the bottom right part of the curve) is a portfolio in which 100% is invested in Stock 1.

As we trace the curve between its top rightmost point and its bottom rightmost point, we obtain different portfolio risk-return characteristics. In principle, we cannot say which risk-return combination is "optimal"—it will depend on the individual's risk tolerance. What we can say, however, is that no rational investor would prefer portfolios located on the lower part of the curve, such as Portfolio B in Exhibit 8.3(a). For the same level of

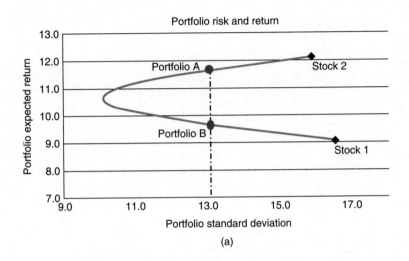

(a)

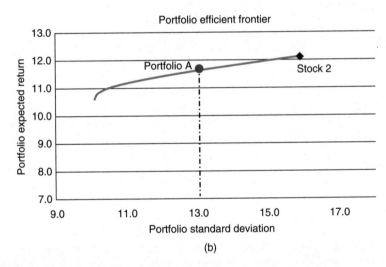

(b)

Exhibit 8.3 (a) Possible pairings of portfolio expected return and standard deviation as the weights of the two stocks vary between 0 and 1; (b) portfolio efficient frontier.

portfolio risk (standard deviation of 13.0%), the investor could obtain a much higher expected return—that of Portfolio A. Therefore, Portfolio A dominates Portfolio B. Exhibit 8.3(b) illustrates the *efficient frontier*—the upper part of the curve, which contains the set of portfolios that dominate all other portfolios given a specific tolerance for the level of risk or the level of expected return.[9]

Consider now a portfolio of N assets, where N is greater than two. The set of all portfolio risk-return pairs obtained when varying the weights of the individual assets fills the shaded area in Exhibit 8.4. The Markowitz mean-variance formulation explained in Section 8.2 helps us find the portfolios along the upper part of the curve (between Portfolio D and Portfolio E on the graph)—that is, the portfolios along the efficient frontier. Those portfolios offer the lowest standard deviation for a given level of expected return, and provide the best possible tradeoff between return and risk. All portfolios in the shaded area (such as Portfolio C) and along

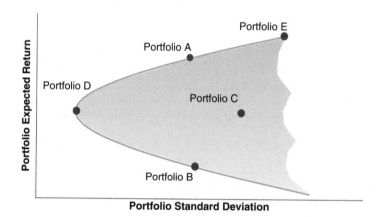

Exhibit 8.4   Feasible and mean-variance efficient portfolios.

---

[9]To construct the efficient frontier, we solve the portfolio optimization problem from Section 8.2 and plot the optimal standard deviation obtained for any level of target expected return. The interested reader is referred to Chapter 7 in Pachamanova and Fabozzi (2010) for instructions and code for solving the mean-variance problems and plotting the efficient frontier with Excel Solver. There is a variety of packages in R that can be used to implement the basic mean-variance problem and plot the efficient frontier as well. A well-known one is **fportfolio**, which is part of the RMetrics financial modeling tools suite. (See the documentation at https://cran.r-project.org/web/packages/fPortfolio/fPortfolio.pdf.) An alternative is the package **tseries** (https://cran.r-project.org/web/packages/tseries/tseries.pdf). It contains the core function `portfolio.optim`, which can be used in the functions `effFrontier` and `maxSharpe` to calculate the efficient frontier and the maximum Sharpe ratio, respectively. A nice list of tutorials for implementation of portfolio optimization with different R packages is available from www.finance-r.com/.

the lower part of the curve (such as Portfolio B) are dominated by the portfolios on the efficient frontier. All portfolios above the efficient frontier (higher on the graph than the curve defined by Portfolios A, D, and E) are unattainable. Portfolio D has the lowest possible standard deviation among all combinations of weights for the assets in the portfolio. It is called the *minimum variance portfolio* or the *global minimum variance portfolio* (GMV).

If more assets are added to the portfolio, there is obviously a higher number of possible combinations of weights for these assets in the portfolio. The feasible set in Exhibit 8.4 widens and the efficient frontier gets pushed outward to reflect the fact that there are now more possibilities for diversification.

8.4 ALTERNATIVE FORMULATIONS OF THE CLASSICAL MEAN-VARIANCE OPTIMIZATION PROBLEM

The mean-variance optimization problem we introduced in Section 8.2 has two alternative equivalent formulations that are used in practice.

8.4.1 Expected Return Formulation

Instead of imposing a constraint on the expected return and minimizing the portfolio variance, we could impose a constraint on the portfolio variance and maximize the expected return. The optimization formulation is then

$$
\begin{aligned}
\max_{\mathbf{w}} \quad & \mathbf{w}' \boldsymbol{\mu} \\
\text{s. t.} \quad & \mathbf{w}' \Sigma \mathbf{w} = \sigma_{\text{target}}^2 \\
& \mathbf{w}' \iota = 1
\end{aligned}
$$

This formulation, which we refer to as the *expected return maximization formulation* of the classical mean-variance optimization problem, is particularly widely used by portfolio managers whose goal is to limit their risk relative to a benchmark. We discuss such applications in Chapter 10.

8.4.2 Risk Aversion Formulation

Another possible formulation is to model the trade-off between risk and return directly through the objective function. This can be accomplished by assigning a penalty term for high portfolio variance, that is, a risk-aversion coefficient λ. The *risk aversion mean-variance formulation* is stated as

$$\max_{\mathbf{w}} \quad \mathbf{w}'\boldsymbol{\mu} - \lambda \cdot \mathbf{w}'\boldsymbol{\Sigma}\mathbf{w}$$

$$\text{s. t.} \quad \mathbf{w}'\boldsymbol{\iota} = 1$$

The risk aversion coefficient λ is referred to as the *Arrow-Pratt risk aversion coefficient*. When λ is small, the aversion to risk is also small, leading to more risky portfolios because the portfolio variance is not penalized as much in the objective function of the optimization problem. If we gradually increase λ starting from 0 and we solve the optimization problem for each value of λ, we in fact calculate every portfolio along the efficient frontier. It is common practice to calibrate λ so that the portfolio has the desired risk-return characteristics ("risk profile"). The calibration is often performed via backtests with historical data. For most portfolio allocation decisions in practice, the risk aversion coefficient is somewhere between 2 and 4.

8.5   THE CAPITAL MARKET LINE

So far, we described Markowitz's framework for selecting an optimal portfolio of risky assets. As demonstrated by Sharpe (1964), Lintner (1965), and Tobin (1958), however, the efficient set of portfolios available to investors who can in addition invest in a risk-free asset (think of it as borrowing or lending money) is superior to the efficient set of portfolios available to investors who can only invest in risky assets.

Let us assume that there is a risk-free asset with a risk-free return denoted by r_f and that the investor can borrow and lend at this rate.[10] The investor still needs to select weights $\mathbf{w} = (w_1, \ldots, w_N)$ for the N risky assets, but the weights for the risky assets no longer need to add up to 1 because the remainder can be absorbed by the risk-free asset. Therefore, the total portfolio return is

$$\mathbf{w}'\mathbf{r} + (1 - \mathbf{w}'\boldsymbol{\iota}) \cdot r_f$$

---

[10]In practice, this assumption is not valid for most investors. Specifically, an investor may not be able to borrow and lend at the same interest rate, or may only be permitted to lend. If there are no short-selling restrictions on the risky assets, however, the theoretical conclusions under such conditions are similar to the results presented in this section. See, for example, Black (1972) and Ingersoll (1987).

Since the return on the risk-free asset is assumed to be known and fixed, the total expected portfolio return is

$$\mathbf{w}' \boldsymbol{\mu} + (1 - \mathbf{w}' \boldsymbol{\iota}) \cdot r_f$$

and the portfolio variance is

$$\mathbf{w}' \boldsymbol{\Sigma} \mathbf{w}$$

Note that the portfolio variance is the same as in the case of a portfolio of all risky assets because the risk-free asset does not contribute to the total portfolio risk.

The minimum variance portfolio optimization problem can therefore be formulated as

$$\min_{\mathbf{w}} \quad \mathbf{w}' \boldsymbol{\Sigma} \mathbf{w}$$

$$\text{s. t.} \quad \mathbf{w}' \boldsymbol{\mu} + r_f \cdot (1 - \mathbf{w}' \boldsymbol{\iota}) = r_{\text{target}}$$

and, similarly to the case with no risk-free asset, the optimal solution can be found by using an optimizer or computed in closed form. The optimal portfolio weights are given by the formula

$$\mathbf{w} = C \cdot \boldsymbol{\Sigma}^{-1} \cdot (\boldsymbol{\mu} - r_f \cdot \boldsymbol{\iota})$$

where

$$C = \frac{r_{\text{target}} - r_f}{(\boldsymbol{\mu} - r_f \cdot \boldsymbol{\iota})' \, \boldsymbol{\Sigma}^{-1} (\boldsymbol{\mu} - r_f \cdot \boldsymbol{\iota})}$$

This formula suggests that the weights of the risky assets are proportional to the vector $\boldsymbol{\Sigma}^{-1} \cdot (\boldsymbol{\mu} - r_f \cdot \boldsymbol{\iota})$, with a proportionality constant C. Therefore, with a risk-free asset, all minimum variance portfolios are a combination of the risk-free asset and a given risky portfolio. This risky portfolio is called the *tangency portfolio*. Under certain assumptions, it can be shown that the tangency portfolio must consist of all assets available to investors, and each asset must be held in proportion to its market value relative to the total market value of all assets.[11] Hence, the tangency portfolio is often referred to as the *market portfolio*, or simply *the market*.

---

[11] See Fama (1970).

The composition of the market portfolio, $\mathbf{w}^M$, can be computed explicitly as[12]

$$\mathbf{w}^M = \frac{1}{\boldsymbol{\iota}' \ \boldsymbol{\Sigma}(\boldsymbol{\mu} - r_f \cdot \boldsymbol{\iota})} \cdot \boldsymbol{\Sigma}^{-1}(\boldsymbol{\mu} - r_f \cdot \boldsymbol{\iota})$$

It turns out, actually, that the market portfolio is also the optimal solution for the following optimization problem:

$$\max_{\mathbf{w}} \quad \frac{\mathbf{w}' \boldsymbol{\mu} - r_f}{\sqrt{\mathbf{w}' \boldsymbol{\Sigma} \mathbf{w}}}$$

$$\text{s. t.} \quad \mathbf{w}' \boldsymbol{\iota} = 1$$

The expression in the objective function is called the *Sharpe ratio*.[13] It is the ratio of the portfolio excess return (relative to the risk-free asset) to the portfolio variance, that is, it represents the tradeoff between return ($\mathbf{w}' \boldsymbol{\mu} - r_f$) and risk ($\sqrt{\mathbf{w}' \boldsymbol{\Sigma} \mathbf{w}}$). The Sharpe ratio is widely used in the context of evaluating portfolio performance.

The fact that all risky portfolios available to the investor are linear combinations of the market portfolio and the risk-free rate means that they all lie on a line. (See Exhibit 8.5.) This line is called the *Capital Market Line* (CML). Observe that all portfolios that lie on the Markowitz efficient frontier are inferior to the portfolios on the CML in the sense that they result

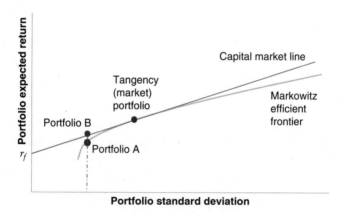

Exhibit 8.5   Capital market line.

[12]See Chapter 2 in Fabozzi, Kolm, Pachamanova, and Focardi (2007), 37.
[13]See, for example, Sharpe (1994).

in a lower expected return for the same amount of risk. For example, in Exhibit 8.5, Portfolio A, which is on the Markowitz efficient frontier, has a lower expected return than Portfolio B, which is on the CML. The only portfolio on the Markowitz efficient frontier that is not dominated by portfolios on the CML is the tangency portfolio.

If we assume that all investors use the mean-variance framework, then every investor will select a portfolio on the CML that represents a combination of the market portfolio and borrowing or lending at the risk-free rate. This important property of the mean-variance framework is called *separation*. Portfolios on the CML to the left of the market portfolio represent combinations of risky assets and the risk-free asset. Portfolios on the CML to the right of the market portfolio represent purchases of risky assets made with funds borrowed at the risk-free rate.

The separation property also has important implications in practice. Practical portfolio construction usually reduces to the following two steps:

1. *Asset allocation*: Decide how to allocate the investor's wealth between the risk-free asset and the set of risky assets.
2. *Risky portfolio construction*: Decide how to distribute the risky portion of the investment among the set of risky assets.

We can derive a formula for the CML algebraically. The reason for going through this exercise will become clear in Chapter 10, when we link the CML to an important modeling tool used in practical portfolio management: factor models.

If all investors invest a portion w_{rf} of their portfolio in the risk-free asset and a portion w_M in the market portfolio, then their expected portfolio returns, $E[r_p]$, are equal to the weighted averages of the expected returns of the two assets:

$$E[r_p] = w_{rf} \cdot r_f + w_M \cdot E[r_M]$$

Because the two portfolio weights must add up to 1, we can rewrite the above equality as

$$E[r_p] = r_f + w_M \cdot (E[r_M] - r_f)$$

The return on the risk-free asset and the return on the market portfolio are uncorrelated and the variance of the risk-free asset is equal to zero. Therefore, the variance of the portfolio consisting of the risk-free asset and the market portfolio is given by (see Section 8.1):

$$\sigma_p^2 = w_{rf}^2 \sigma_{rf}^2 + w_M^2 \sigma_M^2 + 2 w_{rf} w_M \sigma_{rf} \sigma_M \rho_{(rf,M)}$$

$$= w_M^2 \sigma_M^2$$

Because the standard deviation is the square root of the variance, we can write

$$\sigma_p = w_M \sigma_M$$

Hence, the weight of the market portfolio can be expressed as

$$w_M = \frac{\sigma_p}{\sigma_M}$$

If we substitute the above result and rearrange terms, we get an explicit line equation for the CML:

$$E[r_p] = r_f + \left(\frac{E[r_M] - r_f}{\sigma_M} \right) \cdot \sigma_p$$

The bracketed expression in the second term in the equation for the CML,

$$\left(\frac{E[r_M] - r_f}{\sigma_M} \right)$$

is referred to as the *risk premium*. It is also referred to as the *equilibrium market price of risk*, because it, being the slope of the CML, determines the additional expected return needed to compensate for a unit change in risk (when risk is defined as standard deviation).

8.6 EXPECTED UTILITY THEORY

In the classical Markowitz framework, the investor chooses a desired tradeoff between risk and return and solves an optimization problem to find the portfolio weights that result in a portfolio with the desired risk profile. Alternatively, risk preferences can be expressed through *utility functions*. An investor's utility function assigns values to levels of wealth. The *expected utility framework* is based on the idea that a rational investor would choose his portfolio allocation **w** so as to maximize his expected utility one time period ahead. More formally, let the investor's utility function be denoted by u, and let $\widetilde{W}$ denote his end-of-period wealth. The investor's goal is to maximize $E[u(\widetilde{W})]$, the "weighted average" of the values for the investor's utility evaluated at the possible outcomes for his wealth at the end of the time period. If his wealth at time 0 is W_0, then his expected utility optimization problem can be formulated as

$$\max_{\mathbf{w}} \quad E[u(W_0 \cdot (1 + \mathbf{w}'\tilde{\mathbf{r}})]$$

$$\text{s. t.} \quad \mathbf{w}'\boldsymbol{\iota} = 1$$

The Markowitz framework is consistent with expected utility theory in two cases. The first case is when asset returns are assumed to follow elliptical distributions, of which the normal distribution is a special case.[14] When returns follow elliptical distributions, randomness is completely described by the returns' means, variances, and covariances. Therefore, $\mathbf{w}'\tilde{\mathbf{r}}$ can be written as a function of means, variances, and covariances. The utility $u(W_0 \cdot (1 + \mathbf{w}'\tilde{\mathbf{r}}))$ also depends entirely on the means, variances, and covariances, and so does its expected value E. This is consistent with the mean-variance optimization philosophy.

The second case is when investors are assumed to have quadratic utility functions. We explain the quadratic utility function in more detail below.

8.6.1 Quadratic Utility Function

A quadratic utility function has the form

$$u(x) = x - \frac{b}{2}x^2, \quad b > 0$$

If we plug in $x = W_0 \cdot (1 + \mathbf{w}'\tilde{\mathbf{r}})$, we get the following expression for expected utility:

$$E[u(W_0 \cdot (1 + \mathbf{w}'\tilde{\mathbf{r}}))] = E\left[W_0 \cdot (1 + \mathbf{w}'\tilde{\mathbf{r}}) - \frac{b}{2} \cdot W_0^2 \cdot (1 + \mathbf{w}'\tilde{\mathbf{r}})^2\right]$$

$$= E\left[W_0 + W_0 \cdot \mathbf{w}'\tilde{\mathbf{r}} - \frac{b}{2} \cdot W_0^2 - \frac{b}{2} \cdot W_0^2 \cdot (\mathbf{w}'\tilde{\mathbf{r}})^2 - \frac{b}{2} \cdot 2 \cdot W_0^2 \cdot \mathbf{w}'\tilde{\mathbf{r}}\right]$$

$$= W_0 + W_0 \cdot E\left[\mathbf{w}'\tilde{\mathbf{r}}\right] - \frac{b}{2} \cdot W_0^2 - \frac{b}{2} \cdot W_0^2 \cdot E\left[(\mathbf{w}'\tilde{\mathbf{r}})^2\right] - \frac{b}{2} \cdot 2 \cdot W_0^2 \cdot E[\mathbf{w}'\tilde{\mathbf{r}}]$$

$$= W_0 - \frac{b}{2} \cdot W_0^2 + W_0 \cdot E\left[\mathbf{w}'\tilde{\mathbf{r}}\right] - \frac{b}{2} \cdot W_0^2 \cdot (E\left[(\mathbf{w}'\tilde{\mathbf{r}})^2\right] + 2 \cdot E\left[\mathbf{w}'\tilde{\mathbf{r}}\right])$$

---

[14]See Chapter 3.2.1 for an introduction to elliptical distributions.

$$= u(W_0) + W_0 \cdot \mu_p - \frac{b}{2} \cdot W_0^2 \cdot \left(E\left[(\mathbf{w}'\tilde{\mathbf{r}})^2 \right] + 2 \cdot \mu_p] \right)$$

$$= u(W_0) + W_0 \cdot \mu_p - \frac{b}{2} \cdot W_0^2 \cdot 2 \cdot \mu_p - \frac{b}{2} \cdot W_0^2 \cdot \left(\underbrace{E[(\mathbf{w}'\tilde{\mathbf{r}})^2] + \mu_p^2}_{\sigma_p^2} - \mu_p^2 \right)$$

$$= u(W_0) + W_0 \cdot \mu_p \cdot (1 - b \cdot W_0) - \frac{b}{2} \cdot W_0^2 \cdot (\sigma_p^2 - \mu_p^2)$$

Here μ_p and σ_p^2 denote the mean and the variance of the end-of-period portfolio return, respectively. The expression above illustrates that the portfolio mean and variance are sufficient for describing the expected utility of an investor with a quadratic utility function. Moreover, increasing the expected return of the portfolio increases the investor's expected utility, and decreasing the portfolio standard deviation decreases the investor's expected utility, which is consistent with the mean-variance optimization framework.

The general shape of the quadratic utility function is illustrated in Exhibit 8.6. As the graph shows, the quadratic utility function makes

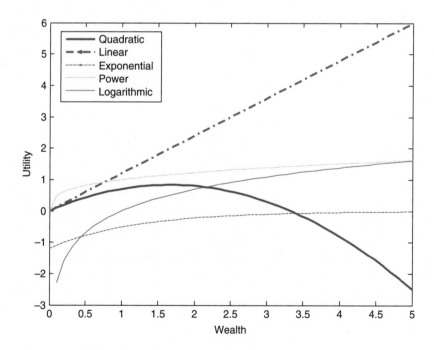

Exhibit 8.6   Examples of different utility functions.

some unrealistic assumptions on investor behavior. The function is not monotonically increasing. At some level of wealth (specifically at values greater than $1/b$), investors' utility decreases as their wealth increases, which is a fairly unnatural assumption. A justification for the use of Markowitz's model, however, has been the assumption that asset returns follow normal distributions, even though many studies indicate otherwise. In the case of normal distributions for returns, a mean-variance approach makes sense regardless of the shape of the investors' utility functions.

The Markowitz model is useful also because it provides an approximation to other utility functions. Before we discuss approximating general utility functions, let us introduce a few more examples of utility functions. As a general rule, the shapes of most used utility functions are based on the assumption that investors are risk averse. A risk-averse investor is somebody who is indifferent or unwilling to accept a risky payoff at its expected value. Instead, a risk-averse investor requires additional compensation for accepting a risky payoff instead of a certain payoff, even if the expected values of the two payoffs are the same. In other words, the expected utility from an uncertain payoff of a risk-averse investor is always less than or equal to the utility of the expected payoff. Mathematically, risk-averseness translates into concave utility function shapes.[15] A "straight-line" utility function corresponds to indifference to risk, or *risk neutrality*, because it represents a situation in which the expected utility of the uncertain payoff equals the utility of the expected payoff. The more "curved" (the less "flat") the utility functions are, the more risk-averse investors are assumed to be. The quadratic utility function (explained earlier) and the exponential, power, logarithmic utility functions (explained later) all assume risk averseness.

8.6.2 Linear Utility Function

The linear utility function is the simplest kind of utility function. It has the form

$$u(x) = a + b \cdot x$$

for some parameters a and b. As we mentioned earlier, the linear utility function assumes that investors are *risk-neutral*, that is, that they are concerned only with expected return, not with risk. Recall from Chapter 2.8 that the expected value of a linear function of a random variable is a linear function of the expected value of the random variable. The expected utility of the end-of-period wealth is

$$E[u(\widetilde{W})] = E[a + b \cdot \widetilde{W}] = a + b \cdot E[\widetilde{W}]$$

---

[15] See, for example, Chapter 1 in Huang and Litzenberger (1988).

whereas the utility of the expected end-of-period wealth is

$$u(E[\widetilde{W}]) = a + b \cdot E[\widetilde{W}]$$

Therefore, $E[u(\widetilde{W})] = u(E[\widetilde{W}])$. An investor with a linear utility function is indifferent between receiving a certain outcome of $E[\widetilde{W}]$ and an uncertain outcome that is "on average" equal to $E[\widetilde{W}]$. See Exhibit 8.6. for an illustration of the shape of the linear utility function.

8.6.3 Exponential Utility Function

The exponential utility function has the form

$$u(x) = -\frac{1}{a}e^{-ax}, \quad a > 0$$

Note that the exponential utility has negative values; however, this does not matter because the function is monotonically increasing (see Exhibit 8.6), and it is possible to compare the relative utilities for different levels of wealth.

8.6.4 Power Utility Function

The power utility function (Exhibit 8.6) is of the form

$$u(x) = ax^a, \quad 0 < a \leq 1$$

8.6.5 Logarithmic Utility Function

The logarithmic utility function has the form

$$u(x) = \ln(x)$$

Note that this function is only defined for $x > 0$ (Exhibit 8.6).

In practice, it is very difficult to determine the utility function of an investor, and the situation is further complicated by the fact that the investor's utility function type and the degree of risk averseness may change depending on circumstances. The choice of utility function for portfolio allocation depends on the application as well as computational considerations. For example, the exponential utility function is widely used because it is generally easier to optimize than some of the other utility functions.

The problem of expected utility optimization is not as intractable as it used to be, given the advances in computational power today. However, virtually no practitioners rely on a full-scale utility optimization approach.

Typically, practitioners work with a mean-variance approximation of a selected utility function. A general utility function can be approximated by mean-variance optimization by expanding the expression for expected utility using Taylor series around the expected end-of-period wealth.[16] Jean (1971) was the first to suggest this approach. Later, more general and rigorous discussion was provided by several authors. The main idea is as follows.

Let us denote the expected end-of-period wealth by $\hat{W}$. Note that

$$\hat{W} = E[W_0 \cdot (1 + \mathbf{w}'\tilde{\mathbf{r}})] = E[W_0] + E[W_0 \cdot (\mathbf{w}'\tilde{\mathbf{r}})] = W_0 + W_0 \cdot \mathbf{w}'\boldsymbol{\mu}$$

The end-of-period expected utility can be expanded in a Taylor series around the expected end-of-period wealth $\hat{W}$:

$$E[u(\widetilde{W})] = u(\hat{W}) + u'(\hat{W}) \cdot E[\widetilde{W} - \hat{W}] + \frac{1}{2!} \cdot u''(\hat{W}) \cdot E[(\widetilde{W} - \hat{W})^2]$$

$$+ \frac{1}{3!} \cdot u'''(\hat{W}) \cdot E[(\widetilde{W} - \hat{W})^3] + \frac{1}{4!} \cdot u''''(\hat{W}) \cdot E[(\widetilde{W} - \hat{W})^4] + O((\widetilde{W} - \hat{W})^5)$$

The functions $E[(\widetilde{W} - \hat{W})^k]$, $k = 1, 2, 3, \ldots$ are called the *central moments* of the random variable $\widetilde{W}$. They are related to the moments of the distribution of the random variable $\widetilde{W}$.[17] It is easy to see that the second central moment, $E[(\widetilde{W} - \hat{W})^2]$, is actually the variance of the random variable $\widetilde{W}$.[18] Since $E[W - \hat{W}] = E[W] - \hat{W} = 0$, we can write

$$E[u(\widetilde{W})] = u(\hat{W}) + \frac{1}{2!} \cdot u''(\hat{W}) \cdot E[(\widetilde{W} - \hat{W})^2]$$

$$+ \frac{1}{3!} \cdot u'''(\hat{W}) \cdot E[(\widetilde{W} - \hat{W})^3] + \frac{1}{4!} \cdot u''''(\hat{W}) \cdot E[(\widetilde{W} - \hat{W})^4] + O((\widetilde{W} - \hat{W})^5)$$

An approximation for the problem of maximizing the expected utility of an investor can be achieved by using only the first two terms of the expression above. These expressions involve the expected end-of-period wealth and

---

[16]The Taylor series is a representation of a function as an infinite sum of terms calculated from the values of its derivatives at a single point. The Taylor series expansion of a function $f(x)$ around a point a is given by

$$f(a) + \frac{f'(a)}{1!} \cdot (x - a) + \frac{f''(a)}{2!} \cdot (x - a)^2 + \ldots$$

where $f'(a), f''(a), \ldots$ are the first, second, $\ldots$ derivatives of the function f evaluated at the point a, and $n! = 1 \cdot 2 \cdot 3 \cdot \ldots \cdot n$.

[17]See Chapter 2.6.

[18]See Chapter 2.6.

the variance of the expected end-of-period wealth in a way consistent with the classical mean-variance framework. A complete formulation of the optimization problem would, of course, involve the third term (which is related to skewness), the fourth term (which is related to kurtosis), and all other higher-order central moment terms.

Levy and Markowitz (1979) compared the performance of portfolio allocations obtained by maximizing expected power utility with that of portfolio allocations obtained with standard mean-variance optimization, and found that the mean-variance approximation worked quite well. Cremers, Kritzman, and Page (2003, 2005) showed empirically that the log and the power utility functions are fairly insensitive to higher moments, and, therefore, mean-variance optimization performs quite well for investors with logarithmic or power utility. However, for discontinuous or S-shape utility functions, this result no longer holds, and mean-variance optimization leads to a significant loss in utility compared to an optimization of the full utility function.[19]

8.7 DIVERSIFICATION REDEFINED

Markowitz's seminal paper has made "diversification" one of the most used terms in investing, but in practice the term is used loosely and its meaning is not always clear. In the Markowitz framework, the riskiness of the assets in the portfolio and the dependencies between them are measured by the variance-covariance matrix, so diversification translates into decreasing the overall portfolio risk (as measured by the portfolio variance) by holding multiple assets. Bouchard, Potters, and Aguilar (1997) suggest using "diversification indicators" that measure the concentration of the portfolio.

Choueifaty and Coignard (2008) consider one such measure of the degree of portfolio diversification, the diversification ratio (DR):

$$DR(\mathbf{w}) = \frac{\mathbf{w}'\boldsymbol{\sigma}}{\sqrt{\mathbf{w}'\boldsymbol{\Sigma}\mathbf{w}}}$$

where $\boldsymbol{\sigma}$ is the vector of asset standard deviations, $\boldsymbol{\Sigma}$ is the asset covariance matrix, and $\mathbf{w}$ is the vector of asset weights. The numerator is the weighted average standard deviation of the individual assets in the portfolio and the denominator is the portfolio standard deviation. In other words, DR calculates the ratio of the weighted average portfolio volatility to the overall portfolio volatility. It tries to capture the nature of diversification in the Markowitz sense, in that the overall portfolio volatility should be less than

---

[19]See Kahneman and Tversky (1979).

the weighted average volatility of the individual assets if the portfolio were properly diversified. The DR should be 1 for a portfolio consisting of a single asset. For a long-only, well-diversified portfolio, the ratio should be greater than 1. For example, an equally weighted portfolio consisting of N independent assets with the same individual volatility (standard deviation) has a DR of $\sqrt{N}$.

Choueifaty, Froidure, and Reynier (2011) derive the mathematical properties of the portfolio that results from maximizing the diversification ratio defined above. It turns out that the optimal portfolio can be obtained by minimizing $\mathbf{w}'\mathbf{Cw}$, where $\mathbf{C}$ is the correlation (rather than the covariance) matrix of asset returns. Hence, maximization of the DR is reminiscent of the minimization of the portfolio variance in the Markowitz framework. The resulting portfolios, however, are not equivalent. The maximum-DR portfolio (which Choueifaty, Froidure, and Reynier (2011) call the MDP) is obtained by first finding an allocation that produces the least correlated asset mix. Then, the solution is inversely adjusted by the asset standard deviations. The impact of the individual assets' volatilities is smaller for the MDP than for the minimum variance portfolio. The MDP possesses the following core properties:[20]

- "Any stock not held by the MDP is more correlated to the MDP than any of the stocks that belong to it. Furthermore, all stocks belonging to the MDP have the same correlation to it."
- "The long-only MDP is the long-only portfolio such that the correlation between any other long-only portfolio and itself is greater than or equal to the ratio of their DRs."

The first core property implies that all assets in the investment universe are effectively represented in the MDP, even if they are not actually included in it. For example, an MDP portfolio constructed from the 500-stock universe of the S&P 500 may contain only 50 stocks. This is because the 50 stocks it actually holds are less correlated to the MDP than the 450 stocks it does not hold. (In other words, the correlations for the remaining 450 stocks are taken into consideration.)

The second core property implies that the more a long-only portfolio is diversified, the higher the correlation of the portfolio's returns with that of the MDP.

While the diversification ratio proposed by Choueifaty and Coignard (2008) attempts to quantify the diversification concept of Markowitz's framework, one can think of diversification also as applied to the portfolio risk itself, where the measure of risk can be the portfolio variance or a

---

[20]Choueifaty, Froidure, and Reynier (2011).

tail risk measure such as conditional value-at-risk.[21] A number of studies have examined the empirical properties of this class of alternative asset allocation approaches, collectively categorized as *risk-based asset allocation* (Lee, 2011). The main idea of such approaches is to diversify across sources of risk in the portfolio. The simplest way to achieve diversification is to invest capital equally, and such a strategy may have its merits. Specifically, DeMiguel, Garlappi, and Uppal (2009), evaluating the "1/N" portfolio allocation strategy against 14 popular allocation models and seven empirical data sets, show that it outperforms the other models out of sample. They conclude that "that there are still many miles to go before the gains promised by optimal portfolio choice can actually be realized out of sample."

Another approach is to make use of a risk model rather than a return model, for instance, by investing in the global minimum variance portfolio (see Section 8.3). Since such a strategy does not use information on the expected returns, it is generally recognized as robust; however, it is also known to suffer from the problem of portfolio concentration. Imposing constraints on the size of the positions in the portfolio is one way to handle portfolio concentration heuristically. This strategy is very common in practice, and we will discuss it in detail in Chapter 11. A related strategy which addresses the issue of portfolio concentration heuristically and has recently moved into the spotlight is *risk parity*.[22] A risk parity asset allocation scheme represents the middle ground between the equally weighted and the minimum variance portfolio. The main idea is to equalize the risk contributions from the different portfolio components.

The risk contribution of an individual position in the portfolio can be defined in different ways. One common way to express it is as the difference between the risk of the portfolio with and without the individual position. This is also the approach outlined in CreditMetrics (J.P. Morgan & Co., 1997). Another way is as follows. The *marginal risk contribution* (*MRC*) of asset *i* can be thought of as the rate of change in the portfolio risk as the weight of asset *i* increases:

$$MRC_i(\mathbf{w}) = \frac{\partial \sigma(\mathbf{w})}{\partial w_i} = \frac{(\mathbf{\Sigma w})_i}{\sigma(\mathbf{w})}$$

where $(\mathbf{\Sigma w})_i$ is the *i*th component of the vector $\mathbf{\Sigma w}$.

---

[21] See Chapter 2.6.2.6 for a definition of conditional value-at-risk.
[22] See, for example, Asness, Frazzini, and Pedersen (2012), Lee (2011), Chaves, Hsu, Li, and Shakernia (2011), and Qian (2005, 2006).

The *risk contribution* (RC) of asset i can then be defined as

$$RC_i(\mathbf{w}) = w_i \, MRC_i(\mathbf{w}) = \frac{w_i(\Sigma\mathbf{w})_i}{\sigma(\mathbf{w})}$$

This definition of risk contribution ensures that the sum of the risk contributions of the individual assets equals the total risk of the portfolio, that is, the portfolio variance $\sigma(\mathbf{w})$.

A risk parity portfolio with respect to the covariance matrix Σ is one in which the risk contributions of the individual assets are equal, that is, the portfolio variance is equally allocated among the N assets in the portfolio:

$$RC_i(\mathbf{w}) = \frac{1}{N_i}\sigma(\mathbf{w})$$

It turns out that while risk parity portfolios are easy to explain on an intuitive level, they are difficult to find from a computational point of view. In one special case, the calculation can be done in closed form. Specifically, in the case of a long-only portfolio, Maillard, Roncalli, and Teiletche (2010) derive the optimal portfolio allocation by considering the following problem:

$$\min_{\mathbf{w} > \mathbf{0}} f(\mathbf{w}) = \mathbf{w}'\Sigma\mathbf{w} - \sum_{i=1}^{N} \ln w_i$$

This is a well-known problem formulation in optimization, and is widely used in the context of interior point algorithms.[23] The problem can be solved by writing out the optimality conditions,[24] and it can be confirmed that the risk contributions of the individual assets for the optimal portfolio end up equal.

Instead of asking for equal risk contributions, one could allocate different risk budgets to different portfolio components. The computational burden of finding the optimal portfolio then becomes greater, as there is no known closed-form solution.

Further, the risk-based portfolio allocation approach can be extended to include a different measure of portfolio risk—the conditional value-at-risk. Again, the computation of the optimal portfolio is more challenging computationally. The approach is described in Boudt, Carl, and Peterson (2010), and is based on results in Boudt, Peterson, and Croux (2008).

---

[23] See, for example, Boyd and Vandenberghe (2004) or Bazaraa, Sharali, and Shetty (1993).
[24] See Maillard, Roncalli, and Teiletche (2010) or Kolm, Tutuncu, and Fabozzi (2014).

Risk-based asset allocation methods are part of a broad family of asset allocation strategies referred to as *smart beta* strategies, which we discuss in more detail in Chapters 10, 12, and 14.

Summary

- The basic principle of modern portfolio theory, which originated in Harry Markowitz's work from 1952, is that for a given level of expected return, a rational investor would select the portfolio with the minimum variance among all possible portfolios.
- There are three equivalent formulations of this principle: (1) the portfolio variance minimization formulation; (2) the expected return maximization formulation; and (3) the risk-aversion formulation.
- Markowitz's mean-variance framework in effect quantified the idea of diversification as a prudent strategy. Mathematically, the portfolio variance is a sum of terms including both the variances of the returns of the individual assets and the covariances (equivalently, the correlations) between those returns.
- In a well-diversified portfolio, the potential weak performance of a single asset will be compensated by the performance of other assets that are not strongly correlated with that asset.
- Portfolio allocations obtained by minimizing the portfolio variance are called mean-variance efficient portfolios. The set of all mean-variance efficient portfolios is called the efficient frontier.
- The portfolio on the efficient frontier with the smallest variance is called the global minimum variance portfolio.
- A utility function assigns a value to all possible outcomes faced by an investor. The expected utility is the weighted average of these values over all possible outcomes, where the weights correspond to the probabilities of these outcomes. The concept of expected utility maximization allows for generalizing the framework of optimal portfolio choice.
- Although it is difficult to produce the utility function for a specific investor, commonly used types of utility functions include exponential, logarithmic, power, and quadratic. These functions all incorporate risk averseness. The linear utility function represents the preferences of an investor who is risk neutral, that is, who is concerned only with expected outcome, and not with the risk associated with that outcome.
- The Markowitz mean-variance portfolio optimization framework is consistent with the expected utility maximization framework in two cases: when future asset returns are assumed to follow elliptical distributions, or when investors are assumed to have quadratic utility

functions. In addition, the Markowitz framework works well as an approximation to expected utility maximization for several important types of utility functions.

- While the Markowitz model provided support for portfolio diversification, the way the term "diversification" is used in the financial industry today is inconsistent.
- A variety of new approaches have been developed in recent years for (1) identifying better metrics for describing the concentration of portfolios, and (2) diversifying portfolios based on risk allocation budgets.

CHAPTER 9

Factor Models

This chapter introduces factor models—equations that establish links between security returns and their lagged values or exogenous variables. The latter variables are referred to as *factors*. The theoretical foundations of factor models stem from the idea that a part of the security's risk is shared by groups of other securities (referred to as *systematic risk*), while another part is unique to the individual security (referred to as *idiosyncratic, nonsystematic,* or *specific* risk).

Factor models are widely applied in the practice of investment management, and this chapter outlines some of their main uses. First introduced in the context of solving practical problems with portfolio optimization, factor models simplify portfolio optimization routines and make their input estimation more stable and computationally efficient. They have now broader applications in helping portfolio managers isolate and manage sources of risk (beta) and excess return (alpha) for the portfolio, and are used in portfolio performance attribution and stress testing.[1] They are also used in forecasting for implementing active portfolio management strategies.

In order to provide context, we begin this chapter by introducing the classical pricing models from the financial literature. We then discuss practical aspects of the estimation and use of factor models in industry. We review statistical techniques for building factor models as well as the process of selecting the right type of factor model depending on specific investment goals. Finally, we explain how factor models are used for risk decomposition, risk attribution, performance attribution, as well as active and semi-active (smart beta) investment strategies.

---

[1] "Alpha" and "beta" have specific interpretations in the context of factor models but, as we have already seen in the book, informally beta is the risk one takes simply by investing in a particular category of risky assets. Alpha is the excess return (relative to a benchmark) from noticing something other investors have missed.

9.1 FACTOR MODELS IN THE FINANCIAL ECONOMICS LITERATURE

Linear factor models represent the vast majority of factor models used in finance. As we explained in Chapter 4, the general form of a linear factor model is

$$\tilde{r}_i = \alpha_i + \beta_{i1}f_1 + \ldots + \beta_{iK}f_K + \tilde{\epsilon}_i$$

where in the context of factor models

$\tilde{r}_i$ is the rate of return on security i,

β_{ik} is the sensitivity (*factor loading*) of security i to factor k,

f_k is the rate of return (*factor return*) on factor k, and

$\alpha_i + \tilde{\epsilon}_i$ is the *specific* (nonfactor) *return* on security i, with α_i as the expected return and $\tilde{\epsilon}_i$ as a random shock.

The simplest linear factor model, the *single-index model*, was suggested by Markowitz (1959) with the goal of simplifying mean-variance portfolio analysis. While the approach was mentioned by Markowitz in a footnote in his book, it was Sharpe (1963) who investigated it further. The model contains a single factor called the index. In theory, the index is the value-weighted portfolio of all assets in the economy, where "value-weighted" means that the weight given to each asset's return in the portfolio is the fraction that the asset's market value (the number of shares outstanding times the price per share) represents of the total market value of all assets in the economy. In practice, any of several broad-based market indices (such as the S&P 500) are used. The version of the model that assumes that the factor is the return on a market index such as the S&P 500 is referred to as the *single-index market model*.

In the single-index market model, the security's sensitivity with respect to changes in the market (the security's *beta*) is estimated from a set of observed returns for the security and the market return using simple linear regression:[2]

$$\tilde{r}_i = \alpha_i + \beta_i \tilde{r}_M + \tilde{\epsilon}_i$$

where

$\tilde{r}_i$ is the random (uncertain) total return on security i,

α_i is *alpha*, the nonrandom component of security i's return that is unique (firm-specific) to security i,

---

[2]See Chapter 4.2.1 for an example of estimating and assessing the validity of a simple linear regression model.

β_i is *beta*, a measure of the sensitivity of security i's return to the return on the market portfolio,

$\tilde{r}_M$ is the random (uncertain) total return on the market portfolio, and

$\tilde{\varepsilon}_i$ is epsilon, the random component of security i's return that is unique (firm-specific) to security i, with mean value of 0.

The single-index model makes three assumptions:

1. All random variables in the model have finite means and variances.
2. The covariance between the market index's random return and the security's random error term (epsilon) is zero.
3. The covariance of the unique components of return for any two securities i and j is zero, that is, the epsilon terms $\tilde{\varepsilon}_i$ and $\tilde{\varepsilon}_j$ are uncorrelated.

The first assumption allows one to calculate the expected return of a security given the market return. Namely, the expected return of a security i is the sum of the security-specific return α_i and the market-determined return $\beta_i \cdot E(\tilde{r}_M)$:

$$E(\tilde{r}_i) = E(\alpha_i + \beta_i \tilde{r}_M + \tilde{\varepsilon}_i) = \alpha_i + \beta_i \cdot E(\tilde{r}_M)$$

The second assumption allows one to decompose the risk (as measured by the variance) of the security's return, σ_i^2, into two components: the security-specific risk, and the market risk (the covariance term is 0):

$$\sigma_i^2 = \text{Var}(\alpha_i + \beta_i \tilde{r}_M + \tilde{\varepsilon}_i) = \beta_i^2 \sigma_M^2 + \beta_i \cdot \underbrace{\text{Cov}(\tilde{r}_M, \tilde{\varepsilon}_i)}_{0} + \sigma_\varepsilon^2 = \beta_i^2 \sigma_M^2 + \sigma_{\varepsilon_i}^2$$

The last assumption means that the reason for any two securities' total returns to move systematically together is because of the securities' common sensitivity to the market portfolio. There are no additional factors or influences, such as specific industry effects, that will make the returns of two securities move together. If the third assumption is satisfied, then the covariance between any two securities i and j can be represented in terms of the betas of the securities and the variance of the market index:

$$\text{Cov}(\tilde{r}_i, \tilde{r}_j) = \text{Cov}(\beta_i \tilde{r}_M, \beta_j \tilde{r}_M) = \beta_i \cdot \beta_j \cdot \sigma_M^2$$

It can be also shown that if the third assumption holds and a portfolio is well-diversified (contains many securities), the risk (variance) of the portfolio is only determined by the securities' individual betas and the market index variance—the individual security's risk gets diversified away.

The single-index model allows for capturing the complex covariance structure between multiple portfolio securities through their relationship with a single factor, and simplifies it substantially. As we will see in Section 9.2, this representation significantly reduces the number of parameters that need to be estimated from data to create the inputs to the Markowitz portfolio optimization problem formulation. Sharpe (1963) estimates that using the single-index model allows for achieving the same results as the Markowitz portfolio model but with about 2% of the computational resources needed for implementing the optimization.

The single-index market model is sometimes confused with the Capital Asset Pricing Model (CAPM), which is well known and is widely used in the financial industry, for example, for estimating the cost of equity capital for firms and evaluating the performance of managed portfolios. However, the two models start out with different assumptions. The CAPM model, derived independently by Sharpe (1964), Lintner (1965), and Mossin (1966), is a statement about expected returns in equilibrium when every investor optimizes a portfolio's allocation by taking into consideration only the portfolio's mean and the variance, subject to some additional assumptions, such as

1. Investors are rational and risk-averse, and they completely agree on the joint probability distribution of securities' returns (and their estimate of the distribution is correct).
2. Investors all invest for the same period of time.
3. There is a risk-free asset.
4. All investors can borrow or lend any amount at the risk-free rate.
5. Capital markets are perfectly competitive and frictionless.

The Sharpe-Lintner-Mossin model builds on the Markowitz model, rather than addressing its efficient computation as the single-index model does. Specifically, the Markowitz portfolio optimization model derives a condition for the asset weights in mean-variance-efficient portfolios, and the CAPM turns this condition into a prediction about the relationship between risk and expected return by identifying a portfolio that must be efficient if asset prices are to clear the market of all assets (Fama and French 2004). The assumed investor behavior implies something very specific about the excess returns of assets in equilibrium. For prices to clear, the expected return $E(\tilde{r}_i)$ on any security i in the market should follow the equality

$$E(\tilde{r}_i) = r_f + \beta_i(E(\tilde{r}_M) - r_f) + \tilde{\epsilon}_i$$

Here r_f is the risk-free return (the return on a Treasury bill), $\tilde{r}_M$ is the return on the market, $\tilde{\epsilon}_i$ is an asset-specific noise term, and

$$\beta_i = \frac{\text{Cov}(\tilde{r}_i, \tilde{r}_M)}{\text{Var}(\tilde{r}_M)}$$

There is a relationship between the CAPM and the single-index model: if we take expectations of both sides of the single-index model, we get

$$E(\tilde{r}_i) = E(\alpha_i + \beta_i\tilde{r}_M + \tilde{\epsilon}_i) = \alpha_i + \beta_i \cdot E(\tilde{r}_M)$$

and when $\alpha_i = r_f(1 - \beta_i)$ and the market portfolio is the tangency portfolio (see Chapter 8.5), the CAPM and the single-index model equations are the same. However, the assumptions and the purpose of each of the models are different.

The single-index model continues to be used but it is generally recognized that the assumption that a single factor accounts for the covariance structure of asset returns is too simplistic. Ross (1976) derived the Arbitrage Pricing Theory (APT), which uses theoretical arguments (nonexistence of arbitrage opportunities) to arrive at the following equation for asset returns:

$$\tilde{r}_i = E(\tilde{r}_i) + \beta_{i1}\tilde{f}_1 + \cdots + \beta_{iK}\tilde{f}_K + \tilde{\epsilon}_i$$

where $\tilde{r}_i$ is the uncertain return on security i, $E(\tilde{r}_i)$ is the expected return on the security, $\tilde{f}_1, \tilde{f}_2, \ldots, \tilde{f}_K$ are factors, and $\tilde{\epsilon}_i$ is the risky security's specific (idiosyncratic) return, which is 0 on average. The coefficients $\beta_{i1}, \ldots, \beta_{iK}$ measure the sensitivity, or exposure, of security i to each of the K factors, and are also referred to as the *factor loadings*. Conceptually, the APT has strong appeal: it prices securities on the basis of the prices of other securities, does not assume anything about the probability distributions of securities' returns, and is based on relatively unrestrictive assumptions about investor preferences toward risk and return. Because the actual factors are not known, however, the APT is not testable, and its implementation in practice is not unique. Practitioners and portfolio management software vendors create different versions of factor models to fit the main equation, as we discuss later in this chapter.

9.2 MEAN-VARIANCE OPTIMIZATION WITH FACTOR MODELS

As we mentioned in Section 9.1, the imperative for introducing the simplest factor model (the single-index factor model) was to simplify the implementation of mean-variance portfolio optimization. This section elaborates on the estimation of risk and return when using factor models and illustrates the computational savings.

Consider a portfolio of N assets with a vector of expected returns $\boldsymbol{\mu} = (\mu_1, \ldots, \mu_N)'$ and return covariance matrix $\boldsymbol{\Sigma}$. If the weights of the assets are

$w_1, \ldots, w_N$, then recall from Chapter 8 that the portfolio expected return and variance can be written as $\boldsymbol{\mu}' \cdot \mathbf{w}$ and $\mathbf{w}' \boldsymbol{\Sigma} \mathbf{w}$, respectively.

To compute the inputs necessary to estimate the portfolio risk (defined as the portfolio variance) for a portfolio of N securities without using factor models, one would need to find the covariance matrix of the N securities. That would require estimating N variances (one for each of the N securities) and $N \cdot (N-1)/2$ covariances. One would also need to estimate the expected returns—there will be N of them, one for each security. This is a total of $2 \cdot N + N \cdot (N-1)/2$ estimates.

Suppose a portfolio manager is considering constructing a portfolio and there are 1,000 candidate securities to include in the portfolio (i.e., $N = 1,000$). In order to calculate the portfolio variance, the portfolio manager would need to estimate 1,000 variances and 499,500 covariances. Adding the 1,000 estimates of expected returns, this is a total of 501,500 values to estimate, a very difficult undertaking. In addition to the difficulty of coming up with the data to be used for the estimation, the estimates will be unstable. A security's sensitivity to a particular factor may be a lot more stable over time than the security's sensitivity to other securities in the portfolio. If one uses covariance estimates based on the direct relationships between securities, the output from the portfolio optimization routines will be unreliable and unstable. A small change in input parameters can cause big swings in the optimal portfolio allocation.[3]

Now suppose that the portfolio manager would like to construct a portfolio out of N securities, and the vector[4] of N security returns $\mathbf{r}$ can be expressed through a factor model as

$$\mathbf{r} = \boldsymbol{\alpha} + \mathbf{B} \cdot \mathbf{f} + \boldsymbol{\epsilon}$$

where

$\boldsymbol{\alpha}$ is the N-dimensional vector of mean returns of the N securities,

$$\boldsymbol{\alpha} = \begin{bmatrix} \alpha_1 \\ \vdots \\ \alpha_N \end{bmatrix},$$

$\mathbf{f}$ is the K-dimensional vector of factors, $\mathbf{f} = \begin{bmatrix} f_1 \\ \vdots \\ f_K \end{bmatrix},$

$\mathbf{B}$ is the $N \times K$ matrix of factor loadings (the coefficients in front of every factor), $\mathbf{B} = \begin{bmatrix} \beta_{1,1} & \cdots & \beta_{1,K} \\ \vdots & \ddots & \vdots \\ \beta_{N,1} & \cdots & \beta_{N,K} \end{bmatrix},$

---

[3] See Chapter 7.
[4] See the Appendix for a review of vector and matrix notation.

and

$\boldsymbol{\epsilon}$ is the N-dimensional vector of residual errors, $\boldsymbol{\epsilon} = \begin{bmatrix} \epsilon_1 \\ \vdots \\ \epsilon_N \end{bmatrix}$.

In this case, the expected portfolio return can be written as

$$\boldsymbol{\alpha}' \cdot \mathbf{w} + \mathbf{B} \cdot E(\mathbf{f})$$

where $E(\mathbf{f})$ is the vector of factor means.

The expected excess portfolio return can be written as

$$\boldsymbol{\alpha}' \cdot \mathbf{w}$$

Finally, the variance of the portfolio return can be written as

$$\mathbf{w}'(\mathbf{B}\boldsymbol{\Sigma}_\mathbf{f}\mathbf{B}' + \boldsymbol{\Sigma}_\epsilon)\mathbf{w}$$

where

$\boldsymbol{\Sigma}_\mathbf{f}$ is the factor covariance matrix, $\boldsymbol{\Sigma}_\mathbf{f} = \begin{bmatrix} \text{Var}(f_1) & \cdots & \text{Cov}(f_1, f_K) \\ \vdots & \ddots & \vdots \\ \text{Cov}(f_K, f_1) & \cdots & \text{Var}(f_K) \end{bmatrix}$

and

$\boldsymbol{\Sigma}_\epsilon$ is the diagonal matrix (with zeros in all off-diagonal elements) containing the variance of the error terms,

$$\boldsymbol{\Sigma}_\epsilon = \begin{bmatrix} \text{Var}(\epsilon_1) & 0 & 0 \\ 0 & \ddots & 0 \\ 0 & 0 & \text{Var}(\epsilon_N) \end{bmatrix}$$

Suppose that the portfolio manager uses the single-index model to estimate the inputs. As shown in the previous section, the expected return, variance, and covariances for security i in a portfolio can be calculated as $\alpha_i + \beta_i \cdot E(\tilde{r}_M)$, $\beta_i^2 \sigma_M^2 + \sigma_{\epsilon_i}^2$, and $\beta_i \cdot \beta_j \cdot \sigma_M^2$, respectively. A portfolio of N securities would then require the estimation of the following parameters in order to perform mean-variance optimization:

- N alphas (one α_i for each security i) to calculate the expected returns.
- N betas (one β_i for each security i) to calculate the expected returns, the variances, and the covariances.
- 1 estimate of the index's variance σ_M^2 to calculate the variances and the covariances.
- N estimates of the residual (security-specific) variances $\sigma_{\epsilon_i}^2$ to calculate the variances.

This is a total of $3 \cdot N + 1$ estimates. For a portfolio with 1,000 candidate securities (i.e., $N = 1,000$), this translates to 3,001 estimates, which is much more manageable than the 501,500 estimates needed without using a factor model.

Now suppose the portfolio manager uses a factor model with K factors. The logic will be similar, except that the factor covariance matrix, which was not needed in the case of a single factor model, would need to be estimated. With K factors, one would need to estimate the:

- K factor loadings (the beta coefficients) for each of the N securities (that is, $K \cdot N$ values).
- $K \cdot (K - 1)/2$ factor covariances.
- K factor variances.
- N residual (security-specific) variances.

This is a total of $K \cdot N + K \cdot (K - 1)/2 + K + N$ estimates. For a portfolio with $N = 1,000$ candidate securities whose returns are explained by $K = 3$ factors, one would need to estimate $3 \cdot 1,000 + 3(3 - 1)/2 + 3 + 1,000 = 4,006$ values. This represents a 99% reduction from the original number of 501,500 values, and not a substantial increase from the case of the single-factor model. Hence, with well-chosen factors, one can substantially reduce the work involved in estimating a portfolio's risk. From a statistical estimation point of view, factor covariance matrices also tend to be much more stable and reliable than security covariance matrices.

9.3 FACTOR SELECTION IN PRACTICE

The APT (described in Section 9.1) provided the theoretical framework for asset pricing models that improve risk measurement and estimation by attributing it to multiple factors. Unfortunately, the APT does not explain what these factors are, or how one may find them. Anything could be considered a factor, including whole asset classes. Harvey, Liu, and Zhu (2014) list 314 known empirical factors. A key requirement for using a particular factor in the investment process, however, is that there is sound economic intuition for why the factor should represent systematic risk and how it should drive returns.

Practitioners employ sophisticated empirical methods for factor identification and model construction. The general form of the equation that gets estimated from data is

$$r_i = \alpha_i + \beta_{i1} f_1 + \cdots + \beta_{iK} f_K + \epsilon_i$$

The coefficients in the above equation are interpreted as excess return (alpha) and risk exposure (beta).

The factors that affect returns significantly can be different depending on the asset class. For example, stock returns may be affected by factors related to company size and industry. Fixed income security returns tend to be impacted by company fundamentals as well but other factors may have a much larger effect on them than on equities: for example, duration, changes in the term structure, yield spread, and currency fluctuations if the securities are denominated in a particular currency. Many factors cut across multiple asset classes. Exhibit 9.1 shows an example of how that can happen.

Most generally, empirical factors used in factor models fall into the following three categories:

1. *External (macroeconomic) factors*, such as gross domestic product (GDP), consumer price index (CPI), unemployment rate, credit spreads on bonds, and the steepness of the yield curve.
2. *Fundamental factors (firm characteristics)*, such as the price-earnings ratio, the dividend-payout ratio, the earnings growth forecast, and financial leverage.[5]
3. *Extracted (statistical) factors*, such as the return on the market portfolio (computed as the compilation of returns on the individual securities), the average of the returns of stocks in a particular industry (utilities, transportation, aerospace), and so on. Some such factors are computed using principal component analysis (see Chapter 4.4).

Well-known empirical factor models for the equity market in particular are the models developed by Chen, Roll, and Ross (1986), who proposed a macroeconomic factor model, and Fama and French (1993, 1995, 1996, 1998), who studied fundamental factor models.

Fundamental company characteristics are not technically "factors" in the sense of the APT. However, including such factors in models in practice reduces the estimation error. It can actually be shown that the fundamental and macroeconomic factor models should be equivalent (that is, produce the same results) if expected asset returns are linear functions of the fundamental factor exposures.[6] If asset returns are not linear functions of the fundamental factor exposures, however (that is, the equation above is not actually correct for the fundamental factor model), then the macroeconomic factor model should theoretically be used, as it has a stronger foundation in

---

[5]These characteristics are not technically "factors" in the sense of the APT, but they help reduce the variance of the error in the regression.
[6]See Chapter 3 in Chincarini and Kim (2006).

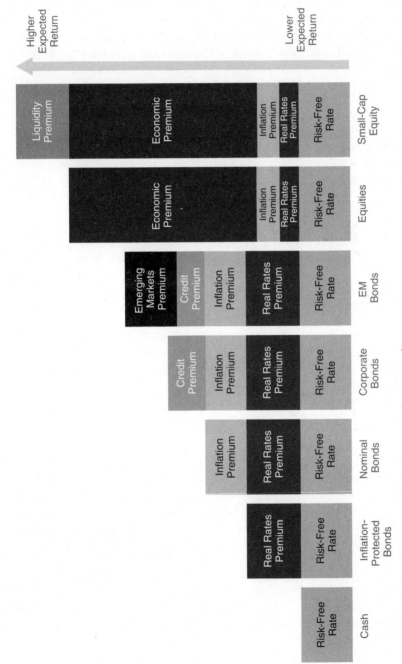

Exhibit 9.1 An example of breaking down asset classes into factors.
Source: Hogan, Hodges, Potts, and Ransenberg (2015). Reprinted with permission.

economic theory than the fundamental factor model. We discuss the choice of factor models later in this chapter.

A number of portfolio management software vendors offer factor models as part of their product suite. Well-known commercial factor model vendors include MSCI Barra,[7] Northfield Information Services,[8] Axioma,[9] SunGard's APT,[10] and R-Squared.[11] Some traditional financial data providers such as Bloomberg and FactSet have added factor models to their offerings. FactSet has also made the integration between its data and various vendor factor models seamless so that clients can have a single portfolio analysis tool.

It is worth mentioning that practitioners often use separate factor models for predicting excess, or specific, return (alpha) and risk (beta). There is no theoretical basis for doing so, and in fact, separating the models introduces misalignment problems in portfolio optimization routines.[12] However, there are some practical reasons for this. The construction of factor models requires multiple stages of data preparation and very careful modeling, which can be resource-intensive. Quantitative investment managers typically spend their energy and time on the development of alpha models for forecasting returns—those are typically proprietary, and are built based on a manager's unique understanding of the fundamental characteristics of securities and market behavior. Risk is often assessed by a separate group within the organization, and vendor-provided factor models for risk estimation are employed to analyze and report portfolio risk.

Alpha construction, which is explained in Section 9.4, is concerned with capturing and exploiting signals that can lead to excess return. Factor models for risk estimation, which are explained in Section 9.5, are concerned primarily with breaking down the sources of risk in the portfolio and imposing some structure to focus on meaningful correlations rather than on noise. The latter boils down to representing the covariance structure of asset returns as two contributions: the contributions of factors underlying asset return correlations ($\mathbf{B\Sigma_f B'}$) and a residual risk matrix $\mathbf{\Sigma_\epsilon}$:

$$\mathbf{\Sigma} = \mathbf{B\Sigma_f B'} + \mathbf{\Sigma_\epsilon}$$

An example from Ceria, Saxena, and Stubbs (2012) illustrates the difference between using factors for excess return prediction versus risk

---

[7] See www.msci.com.
[8] See www.factset.com.
[9] See www.axioma.com.
[10] See www.sungard.com.
[11] See www.rsquaredriskmanagement.com.
[12] See Saxena, Martin, and Stubbs (2012).

estimation. The earnings yield (E/P) is a widely quoted and used valuation factor. But E/P is not calculated identically for all companies. Adjustments may be made due to the use of different accounting principles (U.S. Generally Accepted Accounting Principles versus International Financial Reporting Standards), different treatment of income sheet entries (nonrecurring, unusual, and infrequent items, and nonoperating gains and losses), and different views on depreciation, amortization, and so on. The differences in these E/P calculations should enter models created for the purpose of predicting excess returns, as the differentials in calculations between asset returns and adjustments can be exploited. At the same time, they make little difference for factor models built specifically for predicting risk. As we will see in Section 9.5, such models focus more on explaining the variability in different securities' returns at a particular point in time than on return forecasts.

9.4   FACTOR MODELS FOR ALPHA CONSTRUCTION

Alpha construction has been at the core of active quantitative investment management for decades. The main idea is to identify empirically drivers of return (factors) that lead to outperformance.

In technical terms, alpha is the expected residual return after accounting for the impact of all factors. From a modeling perspective, the goal is to produce a statistical model that accurately captures this information. In the statistical model equation in Section 9.2 ($r = \alpha + B \cdot f + \epsilon$), the alphas for individual assets are represented by the vector α and the error term ϵ has zero mean. Sometimes, the statistical estimation models are written as $r = B \cdot f + \epsilon$ (without an intercept term), in which case the information about alpha is contained in the error term vector ϵ: α is the vector of expected values of the entries of ϵ. Alpha models are proprietary; however typically statistical methods such as regressions are used to determine α.

In practice, the process of alpha construction begins with an observation or a *signal*, such as "small cap stocks outperform large cap stocks," "low volatility stocks outperform high volatility stocks," or "firms with high earnings per share outperform firms with low earnings per share." Behind each of these examples of observations is a factor (size, volatility, earnings per share) that a portfolio manager then tries to represent using a factor-mimicking portfolio (FMP).

The Fama and French (1992) factors, size and book-to-price, are examples of such analysis. To create an FMP for size, for instance, one method is to rank all companies by size and divide them into equally sized groups (e.g., deciles). A dollar-neutral long–short *signal portfolio* is then constructed by taking a long position in the top decile and an equal-sized short position in the bottom decile. The return of the FMP is analyzed and the quality of the factor is judged by its return-to-risk ratio.

Obviously, there can be many other factors that can affect the performance of an FMP created with the method described above. For example, if some companies are based in different countries or are from different industries, those factors may be responsible for some of the out- or under-performance. Fama and French (1992) suggest a procedure for dealing with the joint effects of their two factors, SMB (small cap minus big cap) and HML (high minus low book-to-price ratio). To construct a portfolio with exposure only to the SMB factor, instead of considering the top and bottom decile of the ranking for each factor, they split the candidate companies into two groups for size (small and big) and three groups for book-to-price (value, neutral, and growth). The intersections between the groups are considered to create six portfolios: small value, small neutral, small growth, large value, large neutral, and large growth. The SMB FMP portfolio is then created by taking equal long positions in the three small portfolios and short positions in the three big portfolios. This neutralizes the effect of HML on the SMB portfolio.

This procedure is intuitive but is difficult to generalize to multiple factors. Stubbs (2013) suggests instead formulating the problem of an FMP as an optimization problem in which one imposes constraints to ensure that the exposure of the portfolio to factors different from the one with the positive alpha signal is zero. Let us assume that a portfolio manager has no reason to expect return from the factors other than the one factor that has been identified. Let $\mathbf{B}$ be the factor loadings matrix for the factors (without the factor under consideration) and $\boldsymbol{\alpha}$ be a vector containing the alpha signal, that is, the excess returns expected from the unique factor the portfolio manager has identified. Then, the optimization problem can be written as

$$\text{Min} \quad \mathbf{w}'\boldsymbol{\Sigma}\mathbf{w}$$

$$\text{s.t.} \quad \mathbf{B}'\mathbf{w} = 0$$

$$\boldsymbol{\alpha}'\mathbf{w} = 1$$

Stubbs (2013) explains in detail why the same statistical model should be used to calculate both $\mathbf{B}$ and $\boldsymbol{\alpha}$. As we mentioned earlier, however, this is often not the case in practice. Building separate statistical models for alpha and beta can lead to misalignment in optimization routines, and overexpose portfolios to sources of risk that are not present in both models.[13]

---

[13] See Ceria, Saxena, and Stubbs (2012) and Saxena, Martin, and Stubbs (2012).

9.5 FACTOR MODELS FOR RISK ESTIMATION

As mentioned earlier in this chapter, when factor models are used for risk management purposes, the primary focus is on estimating the covariance structure of security returns. This means that the goal is to come up with a good estimate of $B\Sigma_f B'$ in particular. Depending on the type of factor model under consideration, we may have information about B, about Σ_f, or can extract information about underlying factors without modeling them explicitly.

Factor model construction is typically based on theory and various regression techniques or on statistical methods such as principal component analysis and factor analysis.[14] In the remainder of this section, we provide a high-level overview of the quantitative approaches used for the three basic types of factor models for risk estimation. The data used for the models can be cross-sectional or time-series data. As we explained in Chapter 1, *cross-sectional data* are data across multiple securities at the same time period, representing a "cross-section" of the securities at that time period. *Time-series* or *longitudinal data* are collected over a certain amount of time—an example is data on returns and fundamental factors for the same company over a period of 10 years.

9.5.1 Macroeconomic Factor Models

It is logical that asset returns should be impacted by macroeconomic factors. For example, if the U.S. Fed cuts interest rates, both the bond and the stock market respond. The reason is that when interest rates are lower, investors require a lower rate of return for their investments. A lower required rate of return generally results in the appreciation of the value of securities, although the sensitivity of the price of a stock to interest rate changes in particular varies by company. Some industries, such as banking, are adversely impacted by lower interest rates, whereas others are impacted favorably.[15]

Among the first macroeconomic factor models developed in practice were the Solomon Brothers (now Citigroup) model and the Northfield model. Macroeconomic factors in these models included an overall market factor (the CAPM beta), exchange rate movements, small-cap premia, inflation, risky bond spreads (credit), long-term rates, short-term rates, and economic growth. As macroeconomic variables are often related (for example, as we just explained, a change in interest rates impacts the overall market), one needs to take special care to minimize multicollinearity effects.[16]

---

[14]See Chapter 4 for an introduction to these statistical estimation models.

[15]We explain the relationship between bond prices and interest rates in detail in Chapter 13.3.1.

[16]See Chapter 4.2.1 for a definition of multicollinearity.

The beta coefficients of each security on each factor in macroeconomic models are typically estimated from time-series regressions. Specifically, because the macroeconomic factor values $f_1, \ldots, f_K$ are known at each time period, one can estimate the factor covariance matrix Σ_f directly from the time series data and run time-series regressions of the returns of each individual security over time on the returns of the different factors to estimate the matrix **B** as well as Σ_ϵ. The model looks similar to the model at the beginning of this chapter, with a time period t subscript:

$$r_{it} = \beta_{i1} f_{1t} + \cdots + \beta_{iK} f_{Kt} + \epsilon_{it}$$

Another way to think about the estimation is to imagine that there are $t = 1, \ldots, T$ observations for a particular security i's returns over time. The time series of factor returns is available and the beta coefficients $\beta_{i1}, \ldots, \beta_{iK}$ for each security i need to be estimated:

$$\begin{bmatrix} r_{i1} \\ r_{i2} \\ \vdots \\ r_{iT} \end{bmatrix} = \begin{bmatrix} f_{11} & f_{21} & \cdots & f_{K1} \\ f_{12} & r_{i2} & \cdots & r_{K1} \\ \vdots & \vdots & \vdots & \vdots \\ f_{1T} & f_{2T} & \cdots & f_{KT} \end{bmatrix} \begin{bmatrix} \beta_{i1} \\ \beta_{i2} \\ \vdots \\ \beta_{iK} \end{bmatrix} + \begin{bmatrix} \epsilon_{i1} \\ \epsilon_{i2} \\ \vdots \\ \epsilon_{iT} \end{bmatrix}$$

The betas $\beta_{i1}, \ldots, \beta_{iK}$ are then put together in a factor exposure matrix **B** that can be used for the estimation of portfolio variance in the formula $\mathbf{B}\Sigma_f \mathbf{B}'$. The covariance matrix of residuals Σ_f is evaluated from the time series of the residuals $[\epsilon_{i1}, \ldots, \epsilon_{iT}]'$, $i = 1, \ldots, N$ securities, in the time series regressions, and Σ_f is evaluated directly from the time series of factor returns $[f_{j1}, \ldots, f_{jT}]'$ for $j = 1, \ldots, K$.

9.5.2 Fundamental Factor Models

Fundamental factor models rely on fundamental research—combing through industry and individual company data to find company characteristics that are valued by the market. Such company characteristics may have to do with company valuation or with investor expectations and are often referred to as *style* factors. They may include company size, financial ratios such as P/E (price-to-earnings ratio), dividend yield, momentum, growth, financial leverage, earnings variability, and volatility. Industry factors (e.g., which industry group the issuer of a security belongs to) are another group of factors that are part of fundamental factor models. Often, risk indices that are a compilation of fundamental factors rather than single financial ratios are used for modeling purposes in order to handle multicollinearity effects and improve the explanatory power of the model.

In contrast to macroeconomic factor models, fundamental factor models require estimating the factor returns f_k rather than the factor exposures β_{ik}. This is because the factor exposures are in fact the values of the observable or easily obtainable company metrics and financial ratios, so the matrix **B** in the portfolio covariance matrix formula is available. These metrics obviously change over time, and one needs to use care in updating them to the correct values. (It is standard practice to use factor exposures from the beginning of each time period within the data estimation window.) To calculate the factor covariance matrix, on the other hand, one goes through a two-step procedure similar to a well-known procedure by Fama and MacBeth (1976).

In the first stage of the procedure, factor returns are estimated based on data from multiple companies. The technique used for this estimation is *cross-sectional regression*. In other words, a regression is run on data on returns and fundamental factor exposures for multiple companies at the same point in time. Typically, one normalizes the values of the factor exposures before running the regression to avoid scaling issues. Specifically, if there are N securities under consideration, one calculates the mean and the standard deviation of the exposures of all securities for each particular factor.[17] Then, the normalized exposure of each security to this particular factor is calculated by subtracting the mean and dividing by the standard deviation. The equation to be estimated for a particular time period t is

$$r_{it} = \beta_{i1t} f_{1t} + \cdots + \beta_{iKt} f_{Kt} + \epsilon_i$$

where, with a slight abuse of notation, we use r_{it} to denote security i's return over time period t, $\beta_{i1t}, \ldots, \beta_{iKt}$ to denote the factor exposures (known) at the beginning of time period t, ϵ_i to denote the specific risk for security i, and f_{kt} to denote the factor return for factor k over time period t (to be estimated based on the regression). In other words, given factor exposures and returns for N securities at time t, one estimates f_k for each $t = 1, \ldots, T$:

$$
\begin{bmatrix} r_1 \\ r_2 \\ \vdots \\ r_N \end{bmatrix}
=
\begin{bmatrix}
\beta_{11} & \beta_{12} & \cdots & \beta_{1K} \\
\beta_{21} & \beta_{22} & \cdots & \beta_{2K} \\
\vdots & \vdots & \ddots & \vdots \\
\beta_{N1} & \beta_{N2} & \cdots & \beta_{NK}
\end{bmatrix}
\begin{bmatrix} f_1 \\ f_2 \\ \vdots \\ f_K \end{bmatrix}
+
\begin{bmatrix} \epsilon_1 \\ \epsilon_2 \\ \vdots \\ \epsilon_N \end{bmatrix}
$$

In the second stage of the procedure, the outputs from the cross-sectional regression—the regression coefficients that are in fact the returns on the factors (i.e., the f_{kt}) for the time period t under consideration—are compiled

---

[17]We will see examples of normalization in Chapter 12.

for multiple time periods, and a time series of factor returns is created. The time series of factor returns can then be used to calculate the covariance structure of factor returns, Σ_f.

To calculate the security-specific risk (i.e., to create matrix Σ_ϵ in our notation), one could use information from the first stage of the procedure. In particular, the value of ϵ_i at time t for each security i can be calculated from the cross-sectional regression, stored so that a time series of it is available, and the covariance matrix Σ_ϵ of the ϵ_i for all the securities can be calculated from the time series of all the individual ϵ_i put together. In practice, this procedure, however, runs into estimation issues, and often alternative methods are used to estimate the security-specific risks.

9.5.3 Statistical Factor Models

As we mentioned earlier, statistical factor models do not involve specification of factors in advance. Instead, they work directly with the covariance matrix of the securities. From the covariance matrix, they try to extract information on hidden factors that allows one to explain as much of the variability in security returns as possible with as few factors as possible.

Mathematically, the principal components of the security return covariance matrix will be extracted by decomposing the covariance matrix Σ of security returns as

$$\Sigma = P \Lambda P'$$

where P contains the eigenvectors[18] of Σ and is an orthogonal matrix ($PP' = I$, the identity matrix), and Λ is a diagonal matrix that contains the eigenvalues of the matrix Σ. Row j of the matrix P is the exposure (factor loadings) of the jth security to N factors. (Note that the number of possible factors N here is the same as the number of securities under consideration for inclusion in the portfolio.) The entry λ_k with index (k,k) in the diagonal matrix Λ is the variance of the kth factor.

Recall from Chapter 4.4 that principal component analysis (PCA) works in the following way with financial time series. Suppose there are N time series of security returns over T time periods. PCA basically identifies portfolios with weight-vectors (of dimension N) that break down the variance of returns. These portfolios are called the principal components, and there will be N of them in total. The first principal component will be a portfolio with specific weights that has the largest amount of variance within

---

[18]See the Appendix for a definition of eigenvectors, eigenvalues, and eigendecomposition.

the set of returns. The next principal component is a portfolio that has the second-largest variance, and so on. These principal components are vectors that are linear combinations of the original time series of security returns (that is, they are weighted combinations of the security returns that can be thought of as portfolios of the securities), and are obtained by multiplying the matrix of the original time series of N security returns over T time periods by the matrix of the eigenvectors.

The result of PCA is N portfolios (combinations of securities) that can be thought of as factors, and are uncorrelated. In addition, PCA can help reduce *dimensionality*—that is, it may be able to capture the majority of the information in the time series with a reduced number of principal components. If one ends up selecting K factors (out of the N obtained with PCA), then the percentage of variance that is captured by the model is

$$\sum_{k=1}^{K} \lambda_k \bigg/ \sum_{i=1}^{N} \lambda_i$$

As we mentioned in Chapter 4.4, the number of principal components (factors) to leave in the model could be found using tools such as the scree plot and Kaiser's criterion. Alternatively, the optimal number can be found by using the theory of random matrices.[19]

An alternative technique for determining hidden statistical factors is factor analysis. Factor analysis is more appropriate than principal components analysis when there is a theoretical basis for the underlying factor model. One typically declares a certain number of factors to be constructed.[20] As explained in Chapter 4.3, factor analysis typically uses regression to estimate a factor loadings matrix so that security returns can be represented as

$$\mathbf{r} = \boldsymbol{\alpha} + \mathbf{B} \cdot \mathbf{f} + \boldsymbol{\epsilon}$$

where $\boldsymbol{\alpha}$ is the N-dimensional vector of returns, $\mathbf{f}$ is the K-dimensional vector of factors, $\mathbf{B}$ is the $K \times N$ matrix of factor loadings (the coefficients in front of every factor), and $\boldsymbol{\epsilon}$ is the N-dimensional vector of residual errors. The covariance matrix to be estimated is assumed to be

$$\Sigma = \mathbf{B}\mathbf{B}' + \Sigma_\epsilon$$

---

[19]See Chapter 12 in Focardi and Fabozzi (2004) for a description of the theory of random matrices.
[20]There are methods for testing out different values for the number of factors; see, for example, Rachev, Mittnik, Fabozzi, Focardi, and Jašić (2007).

The estimation procedure is performed in two steps. In the first step, one estimates the covariance matrix and the factor loadings by linear regression or maximum likelihood estimation methods. In the second step, one estimates factors using the covariance matrix and the factor loadings. The vector of factors $\hat{f}_t$ at each point in time t is estimated as

$$\hat{f}_t = (\mathbf{B}'\mathbf{\Sigma}_\epsilon^{-1}\mathbf{B})^{-1}\mathbf{B}'\mathbf{\Sigma}_\epsilon^{-1}(\mathbf{r}_t - \boldsymbol{\alpha})$$

9.5.4 Hybrid Factor Models

Several factor model vendors are now offering *hybrid factor models*. These models use traditional groups of factors (currency, industry, country, etc.) to explain as much of the variability in returns as possible, and then use statistical factors (obtained with principal component analysis) to soak up the residual risk in the factor model, that is, the variability left over in the error term of the factor model.

On the one hand, using a fundamental/macroeconomic model provides context for risk and portfolio management. On the other hand, using a statistical model allows for capturing any remaining hidden factors in the residual returns. Hybrid factor models hence try to deliver the best of both worlds: they impose some structure but they also mine the data for additional information that was not anticipated in the theoretical model.

9.5.5 Selecting the "Right" Factor Model

As we mentioned earlier, many asset management companies use factor models provided by software vendors. There are "fundamental" factor models that use only information about company fundamentals. There are "global" factor models that incorporate information about currencies and spreads around the world. There are "hybrid" factor models that combine fundamental and/or macroeconomic models with statistical models.

Which factor model is "the best"? There is no single answer, but the specifics of the portfolio manager's investment strategy can narrow down the choices.[21]

First, an investment manager should select a factor model that covers his or her investment universe: single country, regional, or global. This is because global factor models take into consideration currency and other factors that are not as important when investing regionally.

---

[21]We thank FactSet for providing us with materials related to the discussion in this section.

Second, an investment manager should think about the portfolio investment horizon. Vendor factor models typically have a target horizon—short, medium, or long—where the investment horizon is the average turnover time of the portfolio. Different factors are significant over the short term and over the long term. Short-term factor models are more appropriate for investors with a horizon of one day to two months, such as hedge funds. Long horizon is an investment horizon that is longer than a year, and medium horizon is any horizon between short and long.

The statistical estimation of short-, medium- and long-horizon factor models differs, and hence the signals captured in the models will be different. For example, many long-horizon factor models are estimated using monthly return data going five years back. Short-horizon factor models may use only a year of daily returns for model estimation.

Finally, when selecting a factor model, an investment manager should think about the investment approach: Is the portfolio quantitatively or fundamentally managed? Is the investment strategy bottom-up or top-down? A *bottom-up investment strategy* focuses on individual stocks rather than the industry or the economy as a whole, so a fundamental factor model would be a good fit. A *top-down investment strategy* looks at the economy as a whole and then breaks down economic trends by industry sectors, selecting investments in a way that can capitalize on which industries are likely to beat the market. A more comprehensive factor model that includes macroeconomic factors may be a better fit in this case.

9.6 DATA MANAGEMENT AND QUALITY ISSUES

Powerful analytics and continuous research are critical for executing factor-based investment strategies. A very important preliminary step in the process is the acquisition, standardization, and cleaning of data. The significance of understanding and managing the data used for building factor models cannot be overstated.[22] In this section, we outline a few common challenges with data preparation and model building, including data alignment, survival bias, look-ahead bias, and data snooping.

---

[22]To build and update its factor models, MSCI Barra, for example, compiles market and fundamental data from more than 100 data feeds supplied by 56 data vendors. Market information is collected daily, and fundamental company data are derived from quarterly and annual financial statements. Data are analyzed for inconsistencies, and special attention is paid to capital restructurings and other atypical events. Information is also compared across data sources (Barra on Campus 2003).

9.6.1 Data Alignment

Data are often stored in multiple databases and need to be merged in order to run the analysis. For example, price and return data may be collected from University of Chicago's Center for Research in Security Prices (CRSP) database; fundamental data may be extracted from Standard and Poor's Capital IQ Compustat database; macroeconomic data may be retrieved from government sites or Bloomberg; analyst data may be obtained from the Institutional Broker Estimates System (IBES) database, and social issues data may be acquired from KLD Research and Analytics, Inc. Merging data from different databases can be very challenging. For instance, sometimes different identifiers are used for the same company in the different databases, making it difficult to align records. Even when common identifiers such as CUSIPs or ticker symbols are used, the latter may change over time and are sometimes reused when a company is no longer in the database, so it may be difficult to link correctly all companies across databases.

A more nuanced problem with data alignment is that alternative ways to calculate model inputs based on data records of different variables may not lead to consistent estimates because of data discrepancies. Fabozzi, Focardi, and Kolm (2010) illustrate how two alternative but equivalent ways of calculating a fundamental factor (EBITDA/EV) from records in the Capital IQ Compustat Point-In-Time database lead to very different estimates of EBITDA/EV. The two approaches differ by the data items used in calculating the numerator (EBITDA):

Method 1: EBITDA = Sales (Compustat data item 2) – Cost of Goods Sold (Compustat data item 30) – Selling and General Administrative Expenses (Compustat data item 1)

Method 2: EBITDA = Operating Income before Depreciation (Compustat data item 21)

The relationship:

Operating Income before Depreciation = Sales – Cost of Goods Sold – Selling and General Administrative Expenses

should hold; however, this is not the case when the data are pulled from the database. Fabozzi, Focardi, and Kolm (2010) list multiple reasons for such data inconsistencies. First, there may be a problem with rounding and minor inaccuracies. Second, there can be errors in the records. Third, different data items are sometimes combined. For example, sometimes depreciation and amortization expenses are not a separate line item on an income statement; instead they are included in cost of goods sold. Fourth, data items may be inconsistently reported across different companies, sectors, or industries. This happens also when the financial data provider incorrectly maps financial measures from company reports to the specific database items.

The final result is the two mathematically equivalent approaches for calculating EBITDA above do not deliver the same empirical results. Thus, two investment managers using the two different approaches for calculating the ratio may decide on very different portfolio allocations. Fabozzi, Focardi, and Kolm (2010) illustrate that the percentage of companies in the Russell 1000 with different ranking according to this factor was as high as 30% over the time period 1989–2008.

9.6.2 Survival Bias

If companies are removed from the database when they no longer exist and only data on the surviving companies are used for analysis, *survival bias* occurs. (Companies may stop existing for different reasons, such as a bankruptcy or a merger.) Survival bias leads to faulty analysis. By focusing only on survivors and ignoring those that did not make it, one may omit important information from the analysis. This problem can be understood by considering the following example. Suppose that one looks at the 3,000 largest (highest market capitalization) companies in 2005, and then again at the 3,000 largest companies in 2015, and finds that the value of the 3,000 largest companies went up by 40%. One might be tempted to conclude that the percentage return on a portfolio including these companies would be 40%. However, if some of the companies that existed in 2005 are no longer there (or on the list of the 3,000 largest companies in 2015), one cannot actually construct a portfolio that contains the largest companies and realize the 40% return. To avoid survival bias and obtain a more accurate picture of the factors that determined performance, one would need to track the original 3,000 companies from 2005, regardless of whether they were on the list of the 3,000 largest companies in 2015.

9.6.3 Look-Ahead Bias

Look-ahead bias occurs when predictive models use data that would not be available at the time at which the prediction occurs. For example, suppose that end-of-year earnings are used as a factor in a predictive model for returns in January. Those earnings are not reported until at least a month after the end of the year. Thus, they cannot be used to forecast January earnings—they would not be available at the beginning of January. The look-ahead bias can be made worse by backfilling and restatements. *Backfilling* is when previously missing data are entered into the database upon receipt, which may happen much later than the time that is necessary to use the information for prediction purposes. *Restatements* can happen when, for example, a company revises its initial earnings release. Many database companies (for example, Capital IQ) overwrite the number that was originally recorded. However, if the information were to be used in predictive models, only the original number would have been available. Using the updated information for building predictive models introduces bias because it does not reflect correctly the information available at the time when the investment decision needs to be made.

9.6.4 Data Snooping

Data snooping is finding "patterns" in data even though they do not actually exist. It is a particular problem in situations in which one cannot conduct a controlled experiment but instead must rely on recorded data and statistical inference to identify patterns. This is exactly the case with financial data.

With sufficient time and enough data, one can find any data pattern one sets out to find. It is therefore important to make sure that any analytical model a portfolio manager uses is grounded in sound economic theory and common sense rather than just empirical evidence.

9.7 RISK DECOMPOSITION, RISK ATTRIBUTION, AND PERFORMANCE ATTRIBUTION

Portfolio standard deviation (Chapter 8) and portfolio tracking error relative to a benchmark (to be explained in Chapter 10) are often used as measures of portfolio risk. However, they provide only a limited view of portfolio risk. Factor models are useful for determining not only whether a portfolio has risk but also whether it has the right kinds of risks. Risk decomposition, risk attribution, and performance attribution are the most useful applications of factor models for practical purposes. In Chapters 12 and 14, we provide explicit examples of how such analysis is conducted for an equity and a fixed income portfolio. In this chapter, we set up the discussion by introducing the terminology and methodology behind the analysis.

Risk decomposition is the decomposition of the portfolio variance into individual contributions by either holdings or types of risks. In the case of risk decomposition with factor models, one determines the exposure of the portfolio to different factors in the factor model.

Risk attribution determines the exposure of the portfolio to factors that are not necessarily in the factor model. For example, many portfolio managers calculate the portfolio's exposure to a benchmark but the benchmark itself is rarely one of the factors in the factor model.

While risk decomposition and risk attribution are primarily forward looking (that is, they help a portfolio manager assess the current level of portfolio risk), *performance attribution* is primarily backward looking—it helps the portfolio manager assess which factors' performance (among the factors that were part of the factor model) was responsible for the portfolio performance over a particular time period.

The portfolio exposure to a particular factor is simply the weighted average of the exposure of each security in the portfolio to that factor. For example, suppose a portfolio has 42 securities with individual exposures to factor k equal to $\beta_{i,k}$. Suppose further that securities 1 through 40 are equally weighted in the portfolio at 2.2%, security 41 is 5% of the portfolio, and security 42 is 7% of the portfolio. Then the exposure of the portfolio to factor k is

$$0.022 \cdot \beta_{1,k} + 0.022 \cdot \beta_{2,k} + \cdots + 0.022 \cdot \beta_{40,k} + 0.050 \cdot \beta_{41,k} + 0.070 \cdot \beta_{42,k}$$

In the case of risk decomposition, the betas are obtained as the factor loadings from the factor model as part of the estimation. In the case of risk attribution and performance attribution, the portfolio performance is tracked over time and regressed against the returns of the factor of interest (factor k in this case). The beta coefficient in the regression is the exposure (sensitivity) of the portfolio to the factor.

Another useful way to look at risk decomposition, risk attribution and performance attribution is in terms of the percentage of portfolio risk that is contributed by different factors or by security-specific risks. This percentage can be calculated given a factor model.

Portfolio risk could be measured as *total risk* (the portfolio variance, as explained in Chapter 8) or *portfolio active risk* (the portfolio tracking error with respect to a benchmark, which we will explain in detail in Chapter 10).

Knowing that the total portfolio variance is $\mathbf{w}'(\mathbf{B}\Sigma_f\mathbf{B}' + \Sigma_\epsilon)\mathbf{w}$, one can calculate the ratio

$$\frac{\mathbf{w}' \cdot (\Sigma_\epsilon) \cdot \mathbf{w}}{\mathbf{w}' \cdot (\mathbf{B} \cdot \Sigma_f \cdot \mathbf{B}' + \Sigma_\epsilon) \cdot \mathbf{w}}$$

as the estimate of the fraction of portfolio total risk that is security-specific (not factor-contributed) risk.

In Chapter 10, we will talk about measuring portfolio risk relative to a benchmark. In that case, what is of interest is the deviation of the portfolio return from the benchmark return. The total variance of portfolio return relative to the benchmark return is

$$(\mathbf{w} - \mathbf{w}_b)'(\mathbf{B}\Sigma_f\mathbf{B}' + \Sigma_\epsilon)(\mathbf{w} - \mathbf{w}_b)$$

where $\mathbf{w}_b$ are the benchmark weights.[23] The ratio

$$\frac{(\mathbf{w} - \mathbf{w}_b)' \cdot (\Sigma_\epsilon) \cdot (\mathbf{w} - \mathbf{w}_b)}{(\mathbf{w} - \mathbf{w}_b)' \cdot (\mathbf{B} \cdot \Sigma_f \cdot \mathbf{B}' + \Sigma_\epsilon) \cdot (\mathbf{w} - \mathbf{w}_b)}$$

is then the estimate of the fraction of portfolio active risk that is security-specific (not factor-contributed) risk.

In some cases, these ratios are calculated as the ratios of the standard deviations or volatilities (that is, a square root is taken from the expression in the numerator and a square root is taken from the expression in the denominator).

9.8 FACTOR INVESTING

Factor models have been around since the 1970s and were used in the context of alpha construction and risk management but the adoption of factor models for constructing investment strategies experienced particularly strong growth in the 2000s. This trend has been magnified by the recent difficulty in differentiating between sources of alpha (security-specific) and beta (systematic) returns. As more and more sources of excess return are being identified and broadly exploited by quantitative models, alpha has been turning into beta. Much attention has now been focused on smart investment when it comes to systematic risk, or beta. Such strategies are a part of the *smart beta* strategies family which will be discussed more broadly in Chapter 10. Some have argued that the careful selection of factors in which to invest is a form of alpha in itself.[24]

Factor investing strategies—sometimes referred to as *smart beta, scientific beta, factor-based investing,* or *fundamental indexing*—have tremendous variety but what they all share is constant exposures to factors which have performed well historically or which investment managers believe are likely to continue to add risk-adjusted returns.[25] Factor investing has changed both traditional asset allocation and portfolio selection within a particular asset class.

In traditional asset allocation strategies, portfolios were diversified across asset classes (e.g., a 60/40 portfolio would contain 60% of capital invested in equities and 40% invested in bonds). However, such portfolios are not necessarily well diversified—the correlations between asset classes

---

[23] We provide a mathematical derivation of this expression in Chapter 10.4.1.
[24] Um (2014).
[25] For a brief overview of smart beta strategies, see Kahn and Lemmon (2015).

tend to be high, and in fact spike during difficult markets. For example, during "normal" markets such as the time period 2009–2014, U.S. large-cap stocks were perfectly correlated with the S&P 500; U.S. mid-cap stocks had a correlation of 0.96 with the S&P 500; and U.S. small-cap stocks had a correlation of 0.93 with the S&P 500. According to Morningstar, these correlations were 1.00, 0.97, and 0.96, respectively, after the financial crisis in 2008–2009. The same high degree of correlation and the same phenomena hold true for developed and emerging equity markets.

A more disciplined investment approach arguably requires breaking down asset classes into common factors that can explain their correlations and return/risk characteristics. BlackRock, a vendor of smart-beta products, for example, identifies six factors that span different asset classes: economic (risks associated with uncertainty in economic growth), credit (the risk of default), real rates (the risk of exposure to changes in real interest rates), inflation (the risk of exposure to price changes), emerging markets (risks of political turmoil), and liquidity (the risk that one will not be able to sell the investment at certain times). By allocating investments to such factors rather than asset classes, investment managers could avoid concentrations of risk that result from overlap in the factor exposures of asset classes. The factors themselves exhibit lower correlations, which allows for better portfolio diversification. (The exact mechanics of how low correlations between the portfolio securities result in lower total portfolio risk were explained in Chapter 8.1.) Exhibit 9.2 shows correlations between factors identified by BlackRock.

When it comes to portfolio selection within a particular asset class, factor investment strategies typically explore the opportunities associated with tracking custom designed indexes that emphasize specific factors. In equities, for example, investors may desire exposure to some combination of value, momentum, size (with small caps outperforming large caps), quality, and volatility (with low-volatility stocks outperforming high-volatility stocks).[26] This kind of exposure cannot be obtained from traditional market indexes. We discuss the construction of customized indexes in detail in Chapter 10.

The first two prototypes of factor-based investment products came out in May 2000, and were iShares Exchange-Traded Funds aimed at growth and value. According to Bloomberg Intelligence (2015), there are now almost 400 smart-beta funds in the United States, and they account for $400 billion (20% of all assets) in U.S. exchange-traded funds. Although most such products are in the equity space, there are now also some fixed-income smart-beta products as well as multi-asset smart-beta products.

---

[26]Kahn and Lemmon (2015).

	ECONOMIC	CREDIT	REAL RATES	INFLATION	EMERGING MARKETS	LIQUIDITY
ECONOMIC	1					
CREDIT	0.58	1				
REAL RATES	0.16	−0.09	1			
INFLATION	−0.37	−0.34	−0.14	1		
EMERGING MARKETS	0.52	0.51	0.08	−0.28	1	
LIQUIDITY	0.44	0.44	0.09	−0.31	0.38	1

Exhibit 9.2 Correlations of major factors that explain asset class returns and co-movements. Correlations measured over the period August 1988 through September 2014.

Source: Hogan, Hodges, Potts, and Ransenberg (2015). Reprinted with permission.

Summary

- The single-index model was suggested to simplify mean-variance portfolio analysis. It involves estimating a security's sensitivity to the market from a set of observed returns for the security and the market.
- The Capital Asset Pricing Model is an equilibrium model of asset prices that links the expected return on an asset or a portfolio to the expected return on the market.
- The Arbitrage Pricing Theory states that investors want to be compensated for the factors that systematically affect the return on a portfolio. The compensation in this theory is the sum of the products of each factor's systematic risk and the risk premium assigned to it by the market.
- Factors used in factor models can be external (macroeconomic), fundamental (firm characteristics), and extracted (statistical).
- Factor models are most widely used for portfolio risk decomposition and portfolio performance evaluation but they are also used for modeling signals that lead to outperformance (alpha construction).
- Factor models are also useful for obtaining more stable estimates of the inputs to statistical and optimization models for portfolio allocation.
- The selection of the "right" factor model has to do with the investment universe, the investment horizon, and the investment philosophy.
- Factor models are typically constructed using regression analysis, factor analysis, or principal component analysis.
- A very important preliminary step in the factor model construction process is the acquisition, standardization, and cleaning of data. Common challenges with data preparation and model building include data alignment, survival bias, look-ahead bias, and data snooping.
- Factor investing—sometimes also referred to as smart beta, scientific beta, factor-based investing, or fundamental indexing—involves portfolio investment strategies that create exposures to factors which have performed well historically or which investment managers believe likely to continue to add risk-adjusted returns.

CHAPTER 10

Benchmarks and the Use of Tracking Error in Portfolio Construction

Expected portfolio return maximization under the mean-variance framework introduced in Chapter 8 is an example of an active investment strategy—a strategy that identifies a universe of potentially attractive investments and ignores inferior investments opportunities. As we mentioned in Chapter 1, a different approach to investing, referred to as a *passive investment strategy*, or *indexing*, argues that in the absence of any superior forecasting ability, investors might as well resign themselves to the fact that they cannot outperform the market after adjusting for transaction costs and management fees. From a theoretical perspective, the analytics of portfolio theory tell investors to hold a broadly diversified portfolio. Hence, many mutual funds and equity portfolios are managed relative to a particular benchmark, market index, or stock universe, such as the S&P 500 or the Russell 1000. Bond portfolios are also benchmarked against fixed income indexes with particular characteristics regarding credit quality and maturity. For benchmarked portfolios, portfolio risk is evaluated based on the standard deviation of the portfolio deviations from the benchmark, or the *tracking error*, rather than the portfolio's overall standard deviation.

The selection of a benchmark is very important for effective portfolio management, and we spend a substantial amount of time in this chapter discussing the types of indexes that are used as benchmarks. We cover both traditional market capitalization-based indexes as well as alternative indexes, leading into a discussion of smart beta strategies, which use smart indexing to implement strategies that fall between active and passive strategies. But first, we set up the discussion by describing the fundamentals of the concept of tracking error and explaining its role in predicting and evaluating portfolio performance.

10.1 TRACKING ERROR VERSUS ALPHA: CALCULATION AND INTERPRETATION

As we mentioned in the introduction to this chapter, tracking error measures the dispersion of a portfolio's returns relative to the returns of a specified benchmark. Mathematically, *tracking error* is calculated as the standard deviation of the portfolio's *active return*, where

Active return = Portfolio's actual return − Benchmark's actual return

If a portfolio such as an index fund created to match the benchmark regularly has zero active returns (that is, always matches the benchmark's actual return), it would have a tracking error of zero. But if a portfolio is actively managed and takes positions substantially different from the benchmark, it would likely have large active returns, both positive and negative, and thus would have an annual tracking error of, say, 2% to 5%.

Note that because the tracking error measures return variability rather than absolute return, a portfolio does not have tracking error simply because of outperformance or underperformance. For instance, consider a portfolio that underperforms its benchmark by exactly 10 basis points every month. This portfolio would have a tracking error of zero because there is no variability in the portfolio's active returns. On the other hand, the portfolio's average active return, also referred to as *alpha*, will be negative 10 basis points. It will signal that the portfolio is underperforming the benchmark. However, the tracking error itself is not indicative of outperformance or underperformance—it just measures the degree of variability of the portfolio performance relative to the benchmark performance.

In contrast, consider a portfolio that outperforms its benchmark by 10 basis points during half the months and underperforms by 10 basis points during the other months. This portfolio would have a tracking error that is positive because there is variability in the active returns. The alpha of the portfolio in this case will be zero since no active return has been realized.

Exhibit 10.1 presents the information necessary to calculate the tracking error for a hypothetical portfolio and benchmark using 12 monthly observations. The fourth column in the table shows the active return for the month. The mean (average) and the standard deviation of the monthly active returns are 0.21% and 0.96%, respectively.[1] These values are then annualized.

---

[1] The average and the standard deviation for a set of data can be calculated with any statistical or spreadsheet software; for example, one can use the AVERAGE and STDEV formulas in Microsoft Excel. In R, there are a variety of options but two possible formulas are `sapply(mydata, mean, na.rm=TRUE)` (for mean) and `sapply(mydata, sd, na.rm=TRUE)` (for standard deviation). The data here are stored in a data frame `mydata`, and the commands as written (with the argument `na.rm=TRUE`) remove missing observations from the calculations.

Month	Portfolio	Benchmark	Active
1	3.19%	3.82%	−0.63%
2	−0.89%	0.00%	−0.89%
3	5.84%	6.68%	−0.84%
4	2.15%	2.34%	−0.19%
5	2.97%	3.47%	−0.50%
6	0.17%	0.01%	0.16%
7	4.50%	2.90%	1.59%
8	−1.28%	−1.13%	−0.15%
9	−0.85%	−1.68%	0.83%
10	−2.14%	−2.00%	−0.14%
11	−3.69%	−5.50%	1.81%
12	−5.53%	−6.94%	1.41%

Exhibit 10.1   Data and calculation of tracking error.

To annualize average returns computed for a time period of length $1/t$ years, one multiplies the average returns by t. For example, to annualize average monthly returns (computed for a time period of 1/12 years), one multiplies the average monthly returns by the number of months in a year (12).

To annualize the standard deviation of returns computed for a time period of length $1/t$ years, one multiplies the standard deviation by the square root of t (i.e., by $\sqrt{t}$). For example, to annualize the standard deviation of monthly returns, one multiplies the monthly standard deviation by the square root of the number of months in a year ($\sqrt{12}$).

To compute the annual average active return (alpha) in our example, one multiplies the monthly active return (0.21%) by the number of months in a year (12). The annualized active return is

$$\text{Alpha} = (0.21\%) \cdot (12) = 2.47\%$$

To calculate the annualized tracking error, one multiplies the monthly standard deviation (0.96%) by the square root of the number of months in a year. Hence

$$\text{Annualized tracking error} = (0.96\%) \cdot (\sqrt{12}) = 3.34\%$$

If the observations were weekly rather than monthly, the weekly tracking error would be annualized by multiplying by the square root of the number of weeks in a year, that is, by $\sqrt{52}$. Alpha in that case would be annualized by multiplying by 52.

If one could assume that the active returns are normally distributed, one can estimate a range for the possible portfolio active return and a corresponding range for the portfolio return given the tracking error. For example, assume the following:

Benchmark = S&P 500

Expected return on S&P 500 = 20%

Tracking error relative to S&P 500 = 2%

If active normal returns followed a normal distribution, then 68% of them would fall within one standard deviation of the mean return, 95% would fall within approximately two standard deviations from the mean return, and 99% would fall within approximately three standard deviations from the mean return. Given these well-known facts about the normal distribution,[2] one would estimate that the portfolio return has

- A 68% chance of being within one standard deviation (2%) of the expected return (20%) of the S&P 500, that is, between 18% and 22%.
- A 95% chance to be within two standard deviations (2 × 2%) of the expected return of the S&P 500, that is, between 16% and 24%.
- A 99% chance to be within three standard deviations of the expected return of the S&P 500, that is, between 14% and 26%.

Various factors affect the portfolio tracking error. The effects of different factors are investigated in Vardharaj, Fabozzi, and Jones (2004) for the case of equity portfolios in particular. Noteworthy findings include:

- Portfolio tracking error generally decreases with the number of securities from the benchmark included in the portfolio.
- Portfolio tracking error increases as the average market capitalization of the portfolio deviates from that of the benchmark.
- Portfolio tracking error increases when the portfolio beta (measure of market risk) deviates from the benchmark beta.

The fact that tracking error increases due to a particular factor is not necessarily a cause for concern. For example, a portfolio manager may pursue an *enhanced indexing strategy* in which the portfolio holdings deviate from the index holdings in small amounts in the hope that these bets (or views) will allow for the portfolio to outperform the index slightly. A portfolio manager

---

[2] See Chapter 2.4–2.5.

may also pursue an *active/passive strategy*, that is, a blend of active and passive strategies, in which a part of the portfolio may be actively managed while another part may be indexed to a benchmark index.

10.2 FORWARD-LOOKING VERSUS BACKWARD-LOOKING TRACKING ERROR

In Exhibit 10.1, we showed the calculation of portfolio tracking error based on realized active portfolio returns over 12 months. The realized portfolio performance is the result of the portfolio manager's decisions during those 12 months with respect to portfolio positioning issues such as beta, sector allocations, style tilt (value versus growth),[3] and individual security selection. The tracking error calculated in this manner from historical active returns is referred to as *backward-looking tracking error*, *ex post tracking error*, and *actual tracking error*.

The backward-looking tracking error has its use in portfolio performance evaluation but has little predictive value and can be misleading when it comes to assessing portfolio risk. This is because it does not reflect the effect of the portfolio manager's current decisions (e.g., a change in sector allocations) on the future active returns and the tracking error that may be realized in the future.

Portfolio managers need forward-looking estimates of tracking error to assess future portfolio performance. In practice, this is accomplished by using a multifactor model[4] from a commercial vendor that has identified and defined the factors driving the return on the benchmark, or by building such a model in-house. Statistical analysis of historical return data for the securities in the benchmark are used to obtain the factors and to quantify the risks. Using the manager's current portfolio holdings, the portfolio's current exposure to the various factors is calculated and compared to the benchmark's exposures to the factors. From the differential factor exposures, a *forward-looking tracking error* for the portfolio can be computed. This tracking error is also referred to as *ex ante tracking error* and *predicted tracking error*. We provide more detail on the calculation of forward-looking tracking error in Section 10.4 of this chapter.

There is no guarantee that the forward-looking tracking error will match exactly the tracking error realized over the future time period of interest. However, this calculation of the tracking error has its use in risk control and portfolio construction. By performing a simulation analysis on the factors that enter the calculation, the manager can evaluate the potential

---

[3]See Chapter 1.1 for a definition of value and growth stocks.
[4]See Chapter 9.

performance of portfolio strategies relative to the benchmark, and eliminate those that result in tracking errors beyond the client-imposed tolerance for risk. As we mentioned, the backward-looking tracking error, in contrast, is useful for assessing actual performance relative to a benchmark, and enters into the calculation of various performance metrics of concern to investors, such as the information ratio (covered in the next section).

10.3 TRACKING ERROR AND INFORMATION RATIO

The *information ratio* (IR) is a widely used reward/risk performance metric. It is calculated as follows:

$$\text{Information ratio} = \frac{\text{Alpha}}{\text{Backward-looking tracking error}}$$

As we illustrated in Section 10.1, the alpha realized by a portfolio manager historically is the average active return over a time period. The backward-looking tracking error is calculated as explained in Section 10.1.

The IR is essentially a reward–risk ratio. The reward is the average of the active return (alpha). The risk is the standard deviation of the active return (the tracking error), and, more specifically, the backward-looking tracking error. The higher the IR, the better the manager performed relative to the risk assumed. The IR also attempts to measure consistency. A high IR ratio indicates that the portfolio manager outperformed the benchmark by a little every month (as opposed to by a lot in just some of the months). Consistency in performance is considered a desirable trait in a portfolio manager.

To illustrate the calculation of the IR, consider the active returns for the hypothetical portfolio shown in Exhibit 10.1. As we showed in Section 10.1, the annualized average active return is 2.47%. The backward-looking tracking error (annualized) is 3.34%. Therefore, the information ratio is 2.47%/3.34% = 0.74.

10.4 PREDICTED TRACKING ERROR CALCULATION

Section 10.1 illustrated the calculation of backward-looking tracking error for the purpose of portfolio performance evaluation. In this section, we illustrate the methodology for calculating forward-looking tracking error for the purpose of portfolio optimization or risk estimation. Specifically, we describe the variance-covariance calculation method for the tracking error and illustrate the calculation using a multifactor model.

Mathematically, determining the optimal portfolio selection for a passive investment strategy involves changing the objective function of the portfolio allocation problem from Chapter 8 so that instead of minimizing the portfolio variance, one minimizes the tracking error with respect to the benchmark. Alternatively, a limit on the tracking error may be included as a constraint in the optimization formulations for active investment strategies. The variance-covariance representation of the tracking error reviewed in this section is useful both in forward-looking portfolio optimization schemes and for estimating the portfolio risk by simulating possible values for the factors influencing future portfolio returns.

10.4.1   Variance-Covariance Method for Tracking Error Calculation

Given a benchmark, the forward-looking tracking error can be calculated using the covariance matrix of returns. Specifically, the tracking error is the standard deviation of the difference between the portfolio return, $\mathbf{w}'\tilde{\mathbf{r}}$, and the return on the benchmark, $\mathbf{w}'_b\tilde{\mathbf{r}}$. Here, $\mathbf{w}$ is the vector of portfolio weights and $\mathbf{w}_b$ is the vector of benchmark weights. The vector $(\mathbf{w}'\tilde{\mathbf{r}} - \mathbf{w}'_b\tilde{\mathbf{r}})$ is the vector of *exposures*.

The variance-covariance (VcV) method calculates the tracking error as follows:

$$
\begin{aligned}
\text{TE} &= \sqrt{\text{Var}(\mathbf{w}'\tilde{\mathbf{r}} - \mathbf{w}'_b\tilde{\mathbf{r}})} \\
&= \sqrt{\text{Var}((\mathbf{w} - \mathbf{w}_b)'\tilde{\mathbf{r}})} \\
&= \sqrt{(\mathbf{w} - \mathbf{w}_b)'\text{Var}(\tilde{\mathbf{r}})(\mathbf{w} - \mathbf{w}_b)} \\
&= \sqrt{(\mathbf{w} - \mathbf{w}_b)'\boldsymbol{\Sigma}(\mathbf{w} - \mathbf{w}_b)}
\end{aligned}
$$

where $\boldsymbol{\Sigma}$ is the covariance matrix of the security returns. One can observe that the formula is very similar to the formula for the portfolio variance derived in Chapter 8.1; however, the portfolio weights in the formula from Chapter 8.1 are replaced by the active weights, that is, by the differences between the weights of the securities in the portfolio and the weights of the securities in the benchmark.

10.4.2   Tracking Error Calculation Based on a Multifactor Model

Using factor models in the context of tracking error calculation has important advantages for reducing security pricing errors. As we explained in Chapter 9, a general factor model has the form

$$
\tilde{r}_i = \beta_{i1}f_1 + \ldots + \beta_{iK}f_K + \tilde{\epsilon}_i
$$

where

$\tilde{r}_i$ is the rate of return on security i,

β_{ik} is the sensitivity (*factor loading*) of security i to factor k,

f_k is the rate of return (*factor return*) on factor k, and

$\tilde{\epsilon}_i$ is the residual error of security i, a random shock with expected value of α_i.[5]

Suppose there are N securities in the portfolio and K factors, and the weight of each security i is w_i. The portfolio variance σ_p^2 can be expressed as

$$\sigma_p^2 = \sum_{k=1}^{K}\sum_{l=1}^{K}\beta_{pk}\beta_{pl}\sigma_{kl}^2 + \sum_{i=1}^{N}\sigma_{\epsilon_i}^2 w_i^2$$

where

$\sigma_{\epsilon_i}^2$ is the variance of $\tilde{\epsilon}_i$,

σ_{kl}^2 is the covariance of factors k and l, and

β_{pk} is the portfolio sensitivity to factor k, calculated as the weighted sum of the individual securities' sensitivities to factor k:

$$\beta_{pk} = \left(\sum_{i=1}^{N}\beta_{ik}w_i\right)$$

The tracking error based on the multifactor model is

$$\sigma_{TE} = \sqrt{\sum_{k=1}^{M}\sum_{l=1}^{M}\overline{\beta}_{pk}\overline{\beta}_{pl}\sigma_{kl}^2 + \sum_{i=1}^{N}\sigma_{\epsilon_i}^2(w_i - w_{ib})^2}$$

where $\overline{\beta}_{pk}$ is the *net*, or *active*, sensitivity to factor k, calculated as

$$\overline{\beta}_{pk} = \left(\sum_{i=1}^{N}\beta_{ik}w_i\right) - \left(\sum_{j=1}^{N_b}\beta_{jk}w_{jb}\right)$$

---

[5] An equivalent form is

$$\tilde{r}_i = \alpha_i + \beta_{i1}f_1 + \ldots + \beta_{iK}f_K + \tilde{\epsilon}_i$$

where the expected value of the residual error, α_i, is specifically pulled out of $\tilde{\epsilon}_i$, and $\tilde{\epsilon}_i$ is assumed to have a mean of 0.

In the above formulas, N_b is the number of securities in the benchmark and w_{ib} is the weight of security i in the benchmark.

10.5 BENCHMARKS AND INDEXES

As we mentioned in the introduction to this chapter, selecting an appropriate benchmark for the purposes of portfolio management and performance evaluation is critical. In this section, we discuss the process of selecting a benchmark and the type of benchmarks used by investment managers and financial advisors.

When institutional investors engage the services of professional asset managers, they usually specify the benchmark by which the manager's performance will be evaluated. Typically, asset managers are hired to manage client assets within an asset class such as equities or fixed income. In fact, the client will often specify not just the major asset class but also a sub-class within the asset class. So, for example, a client seeking an equity portfolio manager might specify a manager who specializes in large capitalization companies or growth-oriented companies. In seeking a bond portfolio manager, a client may specify a manager who specializes in investment-grade bonds or in noninvestment-grade (i.e., high-yield) bonds.

Once a client sets forth the risk exposure and the asset class (and possible sub-asset class), a benchmark represents the portfolio that has the highest expected return given the desired risk exposure. The benchmark's construction requires that a set of rules be specified for the purpose of determining which specific securities from a universe of the asset class (or sub-asset class) should be included and excluded from the benchmark.

Benchmarks can be classified as either market indexes or customized indexes. Historically, investors have required their asset managers to use as a benchmark a market index. However, due to certain limitations of market indexes, since the turn of the century more institutional investors have turned to customized indexes.

10.5.1 Market Indexes

Market indexes can be classified into three groups:

1. Those produced by exchanges based on all securities traded on the exchanges.
2. Those produced by organizations that subjectively select the securities to be included in the benchmark.
3. Those for which security selection is based on an objective measure, such as market capitalization or, in the case of bonds, a minimum credit rating and issue size.

The first group, *exchange-provided market indexes*, are typically only available for equities because bonds are primarily traded over-the-counter. The more popular equity market indexes that fall into this category include the New York Stock Exchange Composite Index. Although the Nasdaq is not an exchange, the Nasdaq Composite Index falls into this category, too, because the index represents all stocks tracked by the Nasdaq system.

The most popular market index that falls into the second group for equities is the Standard & Poor's 500 (S&P 500). The S&P 500 represents stocks that are chosen from the two major national stock exchanges and the over-the-counter market. The stocks in the index at any given time are determined by a committee of the Standard & Poor's Corporation, which periodically adds or deletes individual stocks or the stocks of entire industry groups. The aim of the committee is to capture overall stock market conditions as reflected in a broad range of economic indicators. Two other market indexes that fall into this group but are rarely used as benchmarks for evaluating the performance of an asset manager are the Value Line Composite Index and the Dow Jones Industrial Average (DJIA). The former market index, produced by Value Line Inc., covers a broad range of widely held and actively traded companies selected by Value Line. The DJIA is constructed from 30 of the largest and most widely held U.S. industrial companies selected by the Dow Jones & Company (publisher of the *Wall Street Journal*).

Representative examples from the third group are the Wilshire indexes (produced by Wilshire Associates and published jointly with Dow Jones) and the Russell indexes (produced by the Frank Russell Company, a firm that consults to pension funds and other institutional investors). The criterion for inclusion in each of these market indexes is solely a firm's market capitalization. The most comprehensive index is the Wilshire 5000. The Wilshire 4500 includes all stocks of companies in the Wilshire 5000 except for those in the S&P 500. Thus, the stocks of companies in the Wilshire 4500 have smaller capitalization than those in the Wilshire 5000. The Russell 3000 encompasses the 3,000 largest companies in terms of their market capitalization. The Russell 1000 is limited to the largest 1,000 companies of those, and the Russell 2000 has the remaining smaller firms.

For bond benchmarks, the most common market indexes are those used by investment banking firms such as Barclays Capital, Merrill Lynch, JP Morgan, and Morgan Stanley. The broad-based U.S. bond market index most commonly used is the Barclays Capital U.S. Aggregate Bond Index. There are more than 6,000 bond issues in this index, which includes only investment-grade securities. The index is computed daily. The pricing of the securities in each index is either trader priced or model priced. Each broad-based bond index is broken into sectors. The sector breakdown for the Barclays Capital U.S. Aggregate Bond Index is Treasury securities, government agency securities, corporate bonds, agency mortgage-backed securities, commercial mortgage-backed securities, and asset-backed securities. There are then market indexes created for each of these sectors.

The securities included in a market index must be combined in certain proportions, and each security must be given a weight. The two main weighting scheme methodologies are

1. Weighting by market capitalization.
2. Equal weighting for each security.

Market capitalization weighting (also referred to as *value weighting*) means that the weight assigned to a company's stock is found by dividing that company's market capitalization by the total market capitalization of the universe of stocks included in the index.[6] Market capitalization in the case of a bond market index is calculated differently—in terms of individual bond issues rather than market capitalization for the entire company. One deals with individual bond issues rather than companies since a company typically has more than one bond issue outstanding. The market capitalization for a bond issue is equal to the total par value of a bond issue outstanding multiplied by the price per bond (expressed as a percentage of par value). Market indexes created using the market capitalization weighting scheme are referred to as *market-capitalization market indexes*.

The equal weighting methodology, the second weighting scheme listed above, is easier. In the case of an equity benchmark, if there are N candidate companies, then the weight assigned to each company's market capitalization is simply $1/N$. In the case of a bond benchmark, if there are B bond issues that are candidate securities, then the weight assigned to each bond issue is $1/B$.

10.5.2 Noncapitalization Weighted Indexes

Historically, a market index that is market-capitalization weighted has been the benchmark of choice for clients. The theoretical justification for using a market index that is market-capitalization weighted is provided by capital market theory. If a market is price efficient and satisfies the restrictive conditions of the capital asset pricing model (CAPM),[7] then the best way to capture the efficiency of the market is to hold the market portfolio that is a market-capitalization-weighted portfolio such an index purports

---

[6]As we explained in Chapter 1.1, the market capitalization of a company is equal to the number of shares of a company's stock outstanding multiplied by the price per share.

[7]See Chapter 9.1 for a listing of these conditions.

to represent. However, in recent years, research has questioned whether market-capitalization market indexes offer the highest expected return given a client's desired risk exposure and therefore whether such indexes are suitable benchmarks for evaluating portfolio managers.

For example, constructing a portfolio that matches a cap-weighted index such as the S&P 500 can be viewed as an (inefficient) strategy of buying high and selling low (*The Economist,* July 6, 2013). This is because companies increase their weight in the index when their stock price rises faster than the rest of the market, and decrease their weight when their stock price falls. This and other shortcomings of cap-weighted indexes have been documented in a number of recent studies.[8]

The limitations of market indexes that are market-capitalization weighted have led to the development of alternative indexes and customized indexes, more generally referred to as *noncapitalization weighted indexes.*

Alternative indexes can be classified as heuristic-based weighted indexes and optimization-based-weighted indexes. The former include equally weighted indexes, risk-based indexes, fundamental-based indexes, and diversity-based indexes. These indexes seek to weight candidate securities (stocks in the case of an equity index and bond issues in the case of a bond index) by one or more factors that drive asset class returns. Two examples for equity indexes are the Research Affiliates Fundamental Indexes and the MSCI Factor Indexes. Company fundamentals that are used in fundamental-based indexes include cash flow, book-to-value ratio, dividend per share, sales growth, and the like. The MSCI Factor Indexes are a family of factor indexes that are weighted by value style, momentum, and volatility. These alternative equity indexes are referred to as *ad-hoc indexes* because of the subjective elements involved in constructing them (i.e., in selecting the weights).

We build on an example from Arnott, Hsu, and Moore (2005) to illustrate how one constructs an ad-hoc index. Suppose we would like to create a fundamental-based index that represents company size.[9] Arnott, Hsu, and Moore (2005) use the following metrics of company size:

- Book value
- Trailing five-year average cash flow

---

[8]See, for example Amenc, Goltz, Martellini, and Retkowsky (2011), Arnott, Hsu, and Moore (2005), and Maillard, Roncalli, and Teiletche (2010).

[9]Note that this is not accomplished by an index like the S&P 500 because the S&P 500 uses market capitalization, which is calculated as the number of company shares times the value of the one share—so, to a large extent it is a measure of what investors think about the company.

- Trailing five-year average revenue
- Trailing five-year average gross sales
- Trailing five-year average gross dividends
- Total employment

After ranking the companies according to each metric, one can calculate the relative weight of each stock within the ranking and select, for example, the largest 1,000 according to each metric. The final result could be a Composite Fundamental Index, in which the ranking of the stocks is determined by an equally weighted sum of the stocks' relative weights in each of the metrics for the size factor.

In contrast to ad-hoc constructed indexes, optimization-based indexes are constructed using optimization methodologies to create a diversified index that takes into account the systematic factors that drive returns and thereby a better benchmark that should be used for achieving client objectives and then to evaluate manager performance. The best known example of optimization-based equity indexes is what is popularly referred to as smart beta indexes, which we will discuss in Section 10.6.

Nonweighted market capitalization indexes also include customized indexes where an asset manager in consultation with clients creates customized indexes that can be used to provide tailor-made benchmarks that better reflect a client's investment objectives and risk tolerance or to remove the concentration risk of large issuers dominating the index. To deal with concentration risk for the purpose of avoiding idiosyncratic risk, an index can be created that imposes a maximum allocation constraint on the weight for a given company in the case of an equity customized index, on the weight of the issuer of a corporate bond index in the case of a bond customized index, or on the weight of a given country in the case of a customized international government bond index. An increasing number of corporate sponsors of defined benefit plans create a customized index to reflect better their objectives and risk tolerance when liabilities must be taken into account (i.e., when a liability-driven strategy is pursued). These customized indexes are referred to as *liability indexes*.

10.6   SMART BETA INVESTING

We have encountered the term *beta* in multiple chapters already. Beta is a measure of the sensitivity of a particular security to the market. For example, a stock with a beta of one moves in line with the market—when the market return increases by 1%, the return on the stock with a beta of 1 would be expected to increase by 1% as well (on average). One can buy beta cheaply by investing in an index fund. For example, the largest exchange-traded fund

(ETF), the SPDR S&P 500 ETF Trust (SPY), tracks the S&P 500. Alpha, on the other hand, captures the moves in the return of a security that cannot be explained by the market.

A new term—*smart beta*—has grown in use tremendously in the last few years. To most finance professionals, smart beta investing is about index-like fund management to keep costs down; however, the indexes themselves are "smarter" than the market-capitalization weighted indexes that have been used historically. In Chapter 9.8, we characterized factor investing as a smart beta strategy, and in Section 10.5, we discussed the link to customized indexes. Providers of smart beta indexes include Research Affiliates, BlackRock, Russell, EDHEC-Risk Institute, and STOXX, among others. Several financial institutions are now offering smart beta funds.

The term *smart beta* is now an umbrella term that encompasses a wide range of strategies, the investment style for which falls between active and passive. In fact, the term is so imprecise that apparently it makes Nobel Prize-winning economist William Sharpe "definitionally sick."[10] The smart beta opportunity set can include (Thomas 2014):

- Alternatives to cap weighting (such as valuation-based, low-volatility, or equal-weighted portfolios).
- Investments in nontraditional asset classes such as commodities, breakeven inflation, volatility, currency carry.
- Alternative asset class payoffs such as collars and leveraged strategies.
- Specialized rules-based strategies such as merger arbitrage, trend-following, convertible arbitrage, and active manager emulation.

Many smart beta indexes employ simple heuristics, such as the fundamental weighting scheme described in Section 10.5. Other heuristic weighting methods include equal weighting, risk-cluster equal weighting (where risk clusters, instead of individual securities, are equally weighted), and diversity weighting (which combines equal weighting and cap weighting).

However, there can be added layers of complexity. Smart beta strategies could combine various proxies for optimal portfolios (e.g., the minimum-variance portfolio calculated with optimization methods) and other portfolios that explore factor exposures that do well under certain conditions. Portfolios based on mixes of different strategies often benefit from the effect of diversification, and appear to do better than single smart beta strategies.[11]

---

[10] Authers (2014).
[11] Amenc, Goltz, Lodh, and Martellini (2012).

For some, risk-parity-based strategies (strategies that attempt to allocate risk, rather than capital, equally among investments) are also part of the smart beta strategies family.[12] Smart beta index providers list a variety of possible methodologies used for constructing smart beta indexes, including equal weight, minimum variance, dividend, risk weighted (equal risk, low beta, etc.), style, environmental, and sustainability.[13]

Amenc, Goltz, and Lodh (2012) suggest that the problem of creating a smart beta investment portfolio be separated into two stages: (1) a constituent selection, that is, which characteristics of securities are desirable to hold, and (2) a diversification scheme within the chosen universe of securities. The first stage takes into account stand-alone properties of the securities whereas the second stage attempts to achieve a particular objective by taking into account how the securities interact within the portfolio. Some smart beta index providers focus on the first stage, selecting securities with particular characteristics such as the ad-hoc fundamental weighting scheme described in Section 10.5 or ranking securities based on the output from factor models. Others add optimization to come up with the optimal diversification scheme. Amenc, Goltz, and Lodh (2012) claim that there is a "key distinction between the stock selection decision, which helps tilt the portfolio towards the relevant characteristics, and the choice of diversification scheme which is more effective in attaining the relevant diversification objective than a pure stock selection strategy."

Consider the creation of the Russell 1000 Low Beta Factor Index offered by Frank Russell Company.[14] The first stage reduces to the calculation of a "naive" factor index that delivers exposure to stocks that have low predicted betas according to a screening and ranking methodology applied to the output of the Axioma U.S. Equity Medium Horizon Fundamental Factor Risk Model. The betas are the sensitivities of the stocks to a change in the market price level as measured by the Russell 1000 Index.

The Russell 1000 stocks are ranked based on their predicted betas from the Axioma U.S. Equity Medium Horizon Fundamental Factor Risk Model. The naive target index is then created by starting with the lowest beta stock and adding the next lowest beta stocks until the target portfolio has a total capitalization of 35% of the Russell 1000 Index.

The second stage involves selecting a portfolio of up to 200 stocks from the Russell 1000 Index to track optimally the returns of the naive factor index while managing turnover and neutralizing exposure to other factors,

---

[12]Maillard, Roncalli, and Teiletche (2010). See also Chapter 8.7 for a description of risk-parity-based investment strategies.

[13]See, for example, www.stoxx.com/indices/types/smart&uscore;beta.html.

[14]Russell Investments (2014).

such as volatility and momentum. This is accomplished by solving an optimization problem in which the tracking error between the Russell-Axioma Factor Index and the naive factor index is minimized[15] and constraints are added to ensure

1. *Factor neutrality* to factors that are not the target of the index.
2. *Controlled turnover* so that the monthly turnover is not too high.
3. *Limits on the exposure* to the target factor (in this case, the beta).
4. *Limits on the number of stocks* in the portfolio.

We explain the mathematical formulation of such constraints in detail in Chapters 11 and 12.

There can be a variety of alternative diversification schemes for the securities included in the naive index. Amenc, Goltz, and Lodh (2012) study three in particular:

1. *A minimum volatility weighting with norm constraints*: The overall portfolio volatility (standard deviation) is minimized, subject to a constraint on portfolio concentration, which is also known as a norm constraint.[16]
2. *Efficient maximum Sharpe ratio weighting*: The portfolio Sharpe ratio[17] is maximized, where the expected returns are estimated indirectly by assuming that they are proportional to the median downside risk of the risk group a stock belongs to.[18]
3. *Maximum de-correlation weighting*: The overall portfolio volatility is minimized under the assumption that the individual volatilities are identical across stocks.[19] The idea is to combine stocks so as to exploit the risk reduction effect stemming from low correlations between the stocks in the portfolio rather than reducing risk by concentrating in stocks with low volatilities (standard deviations).

---

[15] See Section 10.4 for how the tracking error is calculated based on the factor model for the purposes of the optimization problem formulation. In this example, $\mathbf{w}$ is the vector of weights of the stocks in the customized index, and $\mathbf{w}_b$ is the vector of weights of the naïve factor index.

[16] For research on norm constraints as a more flexible alternative to weight constraints, see DeMiguel, Garlappi, Nogales, and Uppal (2009).

[17] The Sharpe ratio was introduced in Chapter 8.5.

[18] See Amenc, Goltz, Martellini, and Retkowsky (2011) for a detailed description of the methodology.

[19] See Christoffersen, Errunza, Jacobs, and Xisong (2012) for a description of the methodology.

Each of these diversification schemes performs differently in bull and bear markets and in high- and low-volatility regimes. As Amenc, Goltz, and Lodh (2012) note, both the systematic (constituent selection) component of the smart beta strategies and the strategy-specific (diversification) component display characteristics that can be exploited by investors.

Smart-beta funds have been utilizing ever-more-complex investment rules. ProShares Large Cap Core Plus, for instance, uses leverage (that is, it borrows money) to buy stocks that target 10 different factors, including value, growth, and price momentum.[20] The reason why leverage may be helpful is illustrated in Exhibit 10.2. Suppose factor models are used to create a diversified equity portfolio with best risk/return trade-off (Portfolio A). An investor who wants higher returns generally has two options: (1) invest more in equities, taking on more risk in equities (Portfolio C), or (2) apply leverage to the diversified portfolio to achieve specific target return levels (Portfolio B). A leveraged portfolio—Portfolio B—is one of the options to achieve the target return.

ProShares Core Plus also identifies underperforming stocks. If some stocks miss the targets, ProShares Core Plus sells them short, betting they'll decline. The resulting product is not an ETF but more of an exchange-traded hedge fund, illustrating the variety of smart-beta products available today.

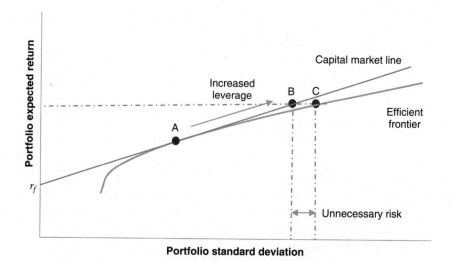

Exhibit 10.2   Illustration of the effect of leverage on investment risk and return.

---

[20] See Effinger and Balchunas (2015).

Summary

- The active return of a portfolio is the difference between the portfolio's actual return and the actual return on a benchmark.
- Tracking error is the standard deviation of a portfolio's active return.
- Backward-looking tracking error, also referred to as ex-post tracking error or actual tracking error, is calculated as the standard deviation of realized historical active portfolio returns.
- Although backward-looking tracking error is used in portfolio performance evaluation, it is not helpful for predicting future portfolio risk.
- Portfolio managers need estimates of forward-looking tracking error (also referred to as ex-ante tracking error or predicted tracking error) to reflect future portfolio performance more accurately for risk management purposes.
- Estimates of forward-looking tracking error can be obtained by using the services of a commercial vendor that has a multifactor model that has identified and defined the risks associated with the benchmark, or by building such a model in-house.
- One method for calculating the forward-looking tracking error is the variance-covariance method.
- The information ratio utilizes tracking error to calculate a portfolio performance metric defined as alpha divided by the backward-looking tracking error, where alpha is the average active return over the time period under evaluation.
- The information ratio is a risk–reward ratio. The higher it is, the better the manager performed relative to the risk assumed.
- A benchmark is used to determine whether the performance of a portfolio satisfied certain criteria. There are two general types of benchmarks: a market index and a customized benchmark.
- Market indexes can be (1) produced by exchanges, (2) produced by organizations, and (3) selected by an objective measure such as market capitalization or, in the case of bonds, minimum credit rating or issue size.
- Market indexes can be (1) market-capitalization-weighted and (2) equally weighted.
- Custom-designed indexes include (1) ad-hoc indexes and (2) optimization-based indexes.
- Liability indexes are customized indexes that reflect manager objectives and risk tolerance when liabilities need to be taken into account.
- The term *smart beta* encompasses a wide range of strategies, the investment style for which falls between active and passive.

- To most investment professionals, smart beta investing is about index-like fund management to keep costs down; however, the indexes themselves are "smarter."
- The problem of creating a smart beta investment portfolio can be separated into two stages: (1) a constituent selection, that is, which characteristics of securities are desirable to hold, and (2) a diversification scheme within the chosen universe of securities. The first stage takes into account stand-alone properties of the securities whereas the second stage attempts to achieve a particular objective by taking into account how the securities interact within the portfolio.

PART Four

Equity Portfolio
Management

CHAPTER 11

Advances in Quantitative Equity Portfolio Management

The mean-variance portfolio optimization framework introduced in Chapter 8 suggested that quantitative investment management can be formulated as the question of determining an appropriate probability distribution of portfolio returns and engineering the optimal trade-off between risk and return as a function of individual risk preferences. More than 60 years after Harry Markowitz came up with the framework, the investment management community is divided over its adoption. Some portfolio managers reject the idea of quantitative portfolio management on principle. Others have given quantitative portfolio management a chance but have given up after growing frustrated with some of the significant shortcomings of the Markowitz framework, such as the sensitivity of portfolio allocation schemes to errors in the inputs to the problem and the limitations of portfolio variance as a measure of risk. A third group has faced the latter problems but has decided to invest in finding solutions that can correct for them because it believes that there is a benefit to the ability to quantify, measure, and allocate risks in an optimal way. Elements of advanced tools from multiple analytical fields—robust statistics, Bayesian methods, simulation, robust optimization—have been employed to address some of the issues with the mean-variance framework. For example, the framework has been expanded to include practical approaches for parameter estimation through factor models (introduced in Chapter 9), considerations for transaction costs and taxes, and different constraints that take specific investment guidelines and institutional features into account, such as maximum exposure to an industry, or maximum active risk.

This chapter reviews some of the more recent analytical developments in equity portfolio management.[1] We begin by providing a classification of

---

[1] As we mentioned in Chapter 8, the mean-variance framework has seen only limited application in the management of fixed income portfolios.

the most common portfolio constraints used in practice and a discussion of the misalignment problems that may come with them. We then give an overview of extensions such as the inclusion of transaction costs, optimization of trades across multiple client accounts, tax-aware strategies, and incorporating robustness in portfolio allocation procedures by using robust statistics, simulation, and robust optimization techniques.

In this chapter, we take a single-period view of investing, in the sense that the goal of the portfolio allocation procedure is to invest optimally over a single predetermined period of interest, such as one month.[2] Many institutional investors, especially sponsors of defined benefit pension plans and insurance companies, have a long investment horizon. However, they treat that horizon as a sequence of shorter period horizons. Risk budgets are often stated over a time period of a year, and return performance is monitored quarterly or monthly.

11.1 PORTFOLIO CONSTRAINTS COMMONLY USED IN PRACTICE

As explained in Chapter 8, the optimal portfolio weights in the Markowitz mean-variance model can be calculated in closed form. The Markowitz model, however, is virtually never used in its basic form. Practical extensions of the model include modifying the objective to reflect different investment priorities, and incorporating constraints of importance to portfolio managers, such as constraints on the tracking error relative to a benchmark, on the size of the portfolio, on the allowed turnover, on the amount of transaction costs, on the portfolio leverage, or related to tax considerations. Some of these constraints are imposed by clients while others are imposed by regulators. For example, in the case of regulated investment companies, restrictions on asset allocation are set forth in the prospectus and may be changed only with the approval of the fund's shareholders. Pension funds must comply with Employee Retirement Income Security Act (ERISA)[3] requirements. These constraints can be stated in mathematical terms (or entered into a user-friendly graphical user interface, or GUI), and the resulting optimization problem can be solved with advanced optimization algorithms.

---

[2]Multiperiod portfolio optimization models are still rarely used in practice, not because the value of multiperiod modeling is questioned, but because multiperiod models are often too intractable from a computational perspective.

[3]ERISA was enacted in 1974 as a federal regulatory scheme for private sector employee benefit pension plans, including healthcare plans. It sets forth requirements for benefit plan participation, funding, and vesting.

We will use $\mathbf{w}_0$ to denote the vector array of stock weights in the portfolio at the beginning of the period and $\mathbf{w}$ to denote the weights at the end of the period. (The weights $\mathbf{w}$ are to be determined.) We assume that the dimension of the vector array $\mathbf{w}$ is N, that is, there are N candidate stocks to choose from during the portfolio selection process. Stocks not selected for the final portfolio will still be part of the vector $\mathbf{w}$ but will have weights of 0.

11.1.1 Long-Only (No-Short-Selling) Constraints

Many funds and institutional investors face restrictions or outright prohibitions on the amount of short selling they can do. When short selling is not allowed, the portfolio allocation optimization model contains the constraints $\mathbf{w} \geq 0$.

11.1.2 Holding Constraints

Diversification principles argue against investing a large proportion of the portfolio in a single asset, or having a large concentration of assets in a specific industry, sector, or country. Limits on the holdings of a specific stock can be imposed with the constraints

$$\mathbf{l} \leq \mathbf{w} \leq \mathbf{u}$$

where $\mathbf{l}$ and $\mathbf{u}$ are vectors of lower and upper bounds of the holdings of each stock in the portfolio.

Consider a portfolio of 10 stocks. Suppose that the stocks of companies 1, 3, and 5 are in the same industry, and that we would like to limit the portfolio exposure to that industry to be at least 20% but at most 40%. To limit exposure to that industry, we add the constraint

$$0.20 \leq w_1 + w_3 + w_5 \leq 0.40$$

to the portfolio allocation optimization problem.

More generally, if we have a specific set of stocks I_j out of the investment universe I consisting of stocks of companies in the same category (such as industry or country), we can write the constraint

$$L_j \leq \sum_{j \in I_j} w_j \leq U_j$$

In words, this constraint requires that the sum of all stock weights in the particular category of investments with indices I_j is greater than or equal to a lower bound L_j and less than or equal to a maximum exposure of U_j.

11.1.3 Turnover Constraints

High portfolio turnover can result in large transaction costs that make portfolio rebalancing inefficient and costly. Thus, some portfolio managers limit the amount of turnover allowed when trading their portfolio. (Another way to control for transaction costs is to minimize them explicitly; we discuss the appropriate formulations later in this chapter.)

Turnover constraints are typically imposed for each stock:

$$|w_i - w_{0,i}| \leq u_i$$

that is, the absolute magnitude of the difference between the final and the initial weight of stock i in the portfolio is restricted to be less than some upper bound u_i. Sometimes, a constraint is imposed to minimize the portfolio turnover as a whole:

$$\sum_{all\ i} |w_i - w_{0,i}| \leq U$$

that is, the total absolute difference between the initial and the final weights of the stocks in the portfolio is restricted to be less than or equal to an upper bound U. Under this constraint, some stock weights may deviate a lot more than others from their initial weights, but the total deviation is limited.

Turnover constraints are often imposed relative to the *average daily volume* (ADV) of a stock.[4] For example, we may want to restrict turnover to be no more than 5% of the ADV. (In the latter case, the upper bound u_i is set to a value equal to 5% of the ADV.) Modifications of these constraints, such as limiting turnover in a specific industry or sector, are also often applied.

11.1.4 Factor Constraints

As discussed earlier, it is very common for quantitatively oriented portfolio managers to use factor models to control for the portfolio risk exposure to different factors. The estimation of the inputs for portfolio optimization models and the optimization itself are more stable and efficient when using factor models as explained in Chapter 9.2.

---

[4]The ADV measures the total amount of a given stock traded in a day on average, where the average is taken over a prespecified time period.

Assuming that the return on stock i has a factor structure with K factors, that is, can be expressed through the equality

$$r_i = \alpha_i + \sum_{k=1}^{K} \beta_{ik} \cdot f_k + \epsilon_i$$

the following constraint limits the exposure of a portfolio of N stocks to the kth risk factor:

$$\sum_{i=1}^{N} \beta_{ik} \cdot w_i \leq U_k$$

In words, the weighted sum of the sensitivities (betas) of the individual stocks to factor k should be at most U_k.

To understand this constraint, note that based on the factor models for the returns of the individual stocks, the total return on the portfolio can be written as

$$\sum_{i=1}^{N} w_i \cdot r_i = \sum_{i=1}^{N} w_i \cdot \left(\alpha_i + \sum_{k=1}^{K} \beta_{ik} \cdot f_k + \epsilon_i \right)$$

$$= \sum_{i=1}^{N} w_i \cdot \alpha_i + \sum_{i=1}^{N} \left(w_i \cdot \left(\sum_{k=1}^{K} \beta_{ik} \cdot f_k \right) \right) + \sum_{i=1}^{N} w_i \cdot \epsilon_i$$

The sensitivity of the portfolio to the different factors is represented by the second term, which can be also written as

$$\sum_{k=1}^{K} \left(\left(\sum_{i=1}^{N} w_i \cdot \beta_{ik} \right) \cdot f_k \right)$$

Therefore, the exposure to a particular factor k is the coefficient in front of f_k, that is,

$$\sum_{i=1}^{N} \beta_{ik} \cdot w_i$$

Intuitively, the sensitivity of the portfolio to a factor k will be larger the larger the presence of factor k in the portfolio through the exposure of the individual stocks. Thus, when the total exposure of the portfolio to factor k is calculated, one needs to take into consideration both how important this factor is for determining the return on each of the stocks in the portfolio and how much of each stock there is in the portfolio.

A version of the maximum factor exposure constraint commonly used in practice is

$$\sum_{i=1}^{N} \beta_{ik} \cdot w_i = 0$$

This constraint forces the portfolio optimization algorithm to find portfolio weights so that the overall risk exposure to factor k is 0 (i.e., so that the portfolio is neutral with respect to changes in factor k). Portfolio allocation strategies that claim to be "market-neutral" often employ this constraint, and the factor is the return on the equity market.

11.1.5 Cardinality Constraints

Depending on the portfolio allocation model used, sometimes the optimization subroutine recommends holding small amounts of a large number of stocks, which can be costly when one takes into consideration the transaction costs incurred when acquiring these positions. Alternatively, a portfolio manager may be interested in limiting the number of stocks used to track a benchmark. To formulate the constraint on the number of stocks to be held in the portfolio (called a *cardinality constraint*), we introduce binary variables, one for each of the N stocks in the portfolio. Let us denote these binary variables as $\delta_1, \ldots, \delta_N$. Variable δ_i will take a value of 1 if stock i is included in the portfolio, and 0 otherwise.

Suppose that out of the N stocks in the investment universe, we would like to include a maximum of K stocks in the final portfolio. K here is a positive integer and is less than N. This constraint can be formulated as

$$\sum_{i=1}^{N} \delta_i \leq K$$

$$\delta_i \text{ binary}, \quad i = 1, \ldots, N$$

We need to make sure, however, that if a stock is not selected in the portfolio, then the binary variable that corresponds to that stock is set to 0, so that the stock is not counted as one of the K stocks left in the portfolio. When the portfolio weights are restricted to be nonnegative, this can be achieved by imposing the additional constraints

$$0 \leq w_i \leq \delta_i, \, i = 1, \ldots, N$$

If the optimal weight for stock i turns out to be different from 0, then the binary variable δ_i associated with stock i is forced to take value 1, and stock i will be counted as one of the K stocks to be kept in the portfolio. If the optimal weight for stock i is 0, then the binary variable δ_i associated with stock i can be either 0 or 1, but that will not matter for all practical purposes because the solver will set it to 0 if there are too many other attractive stocks that will be counted as the K stocks to be kept in the portfolio. At the same time, since the portfolio weights w_i are between 0 and 1 and δ_i is 0 or 1, the constraint $w_i \le \delta_i$ does not restrict the values that the stock weight w_i can take.

The constraints are a little different if short sales are allowed, in which case some of the weights w_i may be negative. We have

$$-M \cdot \delta_i \le w_i \le M \cdot \delta_i, \quad i = 1, \ldots, N$$

where M is a "large" constant (large relative to the size of the inputs in the problem; so in this portfolio optimization application $M = 10$ can be considered "large"). Observe that if the weight w_i is anything but 0, the value of the binary variable δ_i will be forced to be different from 0, that is, δ_i will need to be 1, since it can only take values 0 or 1.

11.1.6 Minimum Holding and Transaction Size Constraints

Cardinality constraints are often used in conjunction with minimum holding/trading constraints. Minimum holding/trading constraints set a minimum limit on the amount of a stock that can be held in the portfolio or the amount of a stock that can be traded, effectively eliminating small trades. Both cardinality and minimum holding/trading constraints aim to reduce the amount of transaction costs.

Threshold constraints on the amount of stock i to be held in the portfolio can be imposed with the constraint

$$|w_i| \ge L_i \cdot \delta_i$$

where L_i is the smallest holding size allowed for stock i and δ_i is a binary variable, analogous to the binary variables δ_i defined in Section 11.1.5—it equals 1 if stock i is included in the portfolio, and 0 otherwise. (All additional constraints relating δ_i and w_i described in the previous section still apply.)

Similarly, constraints can be imposed on the minimum trading amount for stock i. As we explained earlier in this section, the size of the trade for stock i is determined by the absolute value of the difference between the current weight of the stock, $w_{0,i}$, and the new weight w_i that will be found by the solver: $|w_i - w_{0,i}|$. The minimum trading size constraint formulation is

$$|w_i - w_{0,i}| \geq L_i^{\text{trade}} \cdot \delta_i$$

where L_i^{trade} is the smallest trading size allowed for stock i.

As we explained in Chapter 6.2.5, adding binary variables to an optimization problem makes the problem more difficult for the solver, and can increase the computation time substantially. That is why in practice, portfolio managers often omit minimum holding and transaction-size constraints from the optimization problem formulation, selecting instead manually to eliminate weights and/or trades that appear too small, after the optimal portfolio is determined by the optimization solver. It is important to realize, however, that modifying the optimal solution for the simpler portfolio allocation problem (the optimal solution in this case is the weights/trades for the different stocks) by eliminating small positions manually does not necessarily produce the optimal solution to the optimization problem. In fact, there can be pathological cases in which the rounded solution is very different from the true optimal solution. However, for most practical cases, the small manual adjustments to the optimal portfolio allocation do not cause tremendous discrepancies or inconsistencies.

11.1.7 Round Lot Constraints

So far, we have assumed that stocks are infinitely divisible, that is, that we can trade and invest in fractions of stocks. This is, of course, not true—in reality, stocks are traded in multiples of minimum transaction lots, or *rounds* (e.g., 100 or 500 shares).

In order to represent the condition that stocks should be traded in rounds, we need to introduce additional decision variables (let us call them z_i, $i = 1, \ldots, N$) that are integer and will correspond to the number of lots of a particular stock that will be purchased. Each z_i will then be linked to the corresponding portfolio weight w_i through the equality

$$w_i = z_i \cdot f_i, \quad i = 1, \ldots, N$$

where f_i is measured in dollars, and is a fraction of the total amount to be invested. For example, suppose there is a total of $100 million to be invested, and stock i trades at $50 in round lots of 100. Then

$$f_i = \frac{50 \cdot 100}{100,000,000} = 5 \cdot 10^{-7}$$

All remaining constraints in the portfolio allocation can be expressed through the weights w_i, as usual. However, we also need to specify for the solver that the decision variables z_i are integers.

An issue with imposing round lot constraints is that the constraint that the total weight of the stocks in the portfolio should be 100%,

$$\mathbf{w}'\boldsymbol{\iota} = 1$$

which is in fact

$$\sum_{i=1}^{N} z_i \cdot f_i = 1$$

may not be satisfied exactly. This is because we are adding up specific chunks, and no combination of them may add up to exactly 1.

One possibility to handle this problem is to relax the constraint on the total weight. For example, we can state the constraint as

$$\mathbf{w}'\boldsymbol{\iota} \le 1$$

or, equivalently,

$$\sum_{i=1}^{N} z_i \cdot f_i \le 1$$

This will ensure that we do not go over budget.

If our objective is stated as expected return maximization, the optimization solver will attempt to make this constraint as tight as possible, that is, we will end up using up as much of the budget as we can. Depending on the objective function and the other constraints in the formulation, however, this may not always happen. We can try to force the solver to minimize the slack in the budget constraint by introducing a pair of nonnegative decision variables (let us call them ϵ^+ and ϵ^-) that account for the amount that is "overinvested" or "underinvested." These variables will pick up the slack left over because of the inability to round the amounts for the different investments. Namely, we impose the constraints

$$\sum_{i=1}^{N} z_i \cdot f_i + \epsilon^- - \epsilon^+ = 1$$

$$\epsilon^- \ge 0, \quad \epsilon^+ \ge 0$$

and subtract the following term from the objective function:

$$\lambda_{rl} \cdot (\epsilon^- + \epsilon^+)$$

where λ_{rl} is a penalty term associated with the amount of over- or under-investment the portfolio manager is willing to tolerate (selected by the portfolio manager). In the final solution, the violation of the budget constraint will be minimized. Note, however, that this formulation technically allows for the budget to be overinvested.[5]

The optimal portfolio allocation we obtain after solving this optimization problem will not be the same as the allocation we would obtain if we solve an optimization problem without round lot constraints, and then round the amounts to fit the lots that can be traded in the market.

Cardinality constraints, minimum holding/trading constraints, and especially round lot constraints, require more sophisticated binary and integer programming solvers, and are difficult problems to solve in the case of large portfolios.

11.1.8   Tracking Error Constraints

In Chapter 10, we introduced the concept of tracking error relative to a benchmark. Restrictions on the tracking error of a portfolio are often imposed as a constraint. The tracking error constraint takes the form

$$(\mathbf{w} - \mathbf{w}_b)' \, \boldsymbol{\Sigma} \, (\mathbf{w} - \mathbf{w}_b) \leq \sigma_{\text{TE}}^2$$

where σ_{TE}^2 is a limit (imposed by the investor) on the amount of variance of deviations from the benchmark the investor is willing to tolerate. This is a quadratic constraint, which is convex and computationally tractable, but requires specialized optimization software.

A question that may be on some readers' minds is why we need to optimize portfolio weights in order to track a benchmark, when technically the most effective way to track a benchmark is by investing the portfolio in the securities in the benchmark portfolio in the same proportions as the proportions of these securities in the benchmark. The problem with this approach is that, especially with large benchmarks such as the Russell 3000, the transaction costs of a proportional investment and the subsequent rebalancing of the portfolio can be prohibitive (that is, dramatically adversely impact the performance of the portfolio relative to the benchmark). Furthermore, in practice securities are not infinitely divisible, so investing in a portfolio of a limited size in the same proportions as the composition of the benchmark will still not achieve zero tracking error. Thus, the optimal formulation is to require that the portfolio follows the benchmark as closely as possible.

---

[5]The idea of introducing additional decision variables to account for deviations in the limits imposed by the constraints is also used for modeling soft constraints, which we discuss in Section 11.1.9.

11.1.9 Soft Constraints

Traditional optimization formulations treat constraints as hard; that is, they are required to be satisfied. Some vendor software (e.g., Bloomberg L.P.) allows portfolio managers to specify soft constraints; that is, constraints that would be "nice" to satisfy, but could be violated given a particular penalty. Mathematically, such constraints are formulated by setting "constraint violation tolerance" limits on additionally introduced decision variables similar to the ϵ^+ and ϵ^- we saw in Section 11.1.7. Soft constraints allow a portfolio manager to specify his priorities, and understand which of them cannot be satisfied if the objective is to be met.

11.1.10 Misalignment Caused by Constraints

Portfolio optimization relies on three key components: (1) an expected returns model, (2) a factor model, and (3) constraints. These components are typically determined separately from each other, often by different groups within the portfolio management team. When they are then used together in a common portfolio optimization framework, misalignment problems may occur. As we mentioned in Chapter 9.4, this issue has attracted attention recently.[6] Specifically, when the outputs from different factor models for risk and return are used as inputs to portfolio optimization, the optimization algorithm tends to take advantage of the misalignment by producing strategies that appear to provide excess returns without incurring extra risk exposure but in fact they exploit the difference in the factors used in the two models. The result is a downward bias in portfolio risk prediction. The situation gets even more complicated in the presence of constraints. Care needs to be exercised in structuring the portfolio optimization problems and determining their inputs.

11.2 PORTFOLIO OPTIMIZATION WITH TAIL RISK MEASURES

The use of portfolio variance as a risk measure has been a subject of considerable debate in both academia and practice. As explained in Chapter 8.6, mean-variance portfolio allocation is optimal in two cases: when investors have quadratic utility functions, or when asset returns follow elliptical probability distributions. The former condition is difficult to verify empirically;

---

[6]See, for example, Lee and Stefek (2008), Ceria, Saxena, and Stubbs (2012), and Saxena, Martin, and Stubbs (2012).

it is also likely that investors' utility functions vary with market conditions. The latter condition is also not supported empirically. It is particularly not true during financial crises such as the 1997 Asian financial crisis, the 1998 Russian financial crisis, the 2007 subprime mortgage crisis, and more recent turmoil in the financial markets.

As we saw in Chapter 2.6.2.1, variance is a measure of the spread, or the dispersion of a probability distribution. Using the variance as a measure of risk in the context of portfolio optimization means that outcomes above the expected portfolio return are deemed as risky as outcomes below the expected portfolio return. This is counterintuitive to many, as investors are more likely to be concerned about outcomes that fall short of expectations rather than outcomes that exceed expectations.

Markowitz himself acknowledged the shortcomings of the portfolio variance, and suggested semi-deviation as an alternative measure of portfolio risk.[7] While there has been research showing that mean-variance optimization actually aligns portfolio investments in a very similar way to utility-maximizing schemes for a number of different investor utility functions,[8] there is also recognition that portfolio allocation can be done using other risk measures. In this section, we show how one can formulate the problem of optimal portfolio allocation with two important tail risk measures, value-at-risk and conditional value-at-risk, which were introduced in Chapter 2.6.2.

11.2.1 Portfolio Value-at-Risk Optimization

Value-at-risk (VaR) measures the maximum portfolio dollar loss at a specified probability level over a certain time horizon. A portfolio allocation that aims to reduce losses therefore generally aims to reduce the VaR.

The portfolio VaR minimization problem can be represented as a stochastic problem with chance constraints.[9] Its optimization formulation is

$$\min_{\gamma, \mathbf{w}} \quad \gamma$$
$$\text{s.t.} \quad P(-\tilde{\mathbf{r}}'\mathbf{w} > \gamma) \le \epsilon$$
$$\mathbf{w}'\iota = 1$$

[7]See Markowitz (1959). Semi-deviation is the weighted sum of the squared deviations of values in a probability distribution that are below the mean; in other words, it is only concerned with outcomes that underperform expectations.
[8]See Cremers, Kritzman, and Page (2005).
[9]See Chapter 7.2.3.

where $\tilde{r}$ is the N-dimensional vector of (uncertain) stock returns over the time horizon for portfolio optimization, $\mathbf{w}$ is the N-dimensional vector of stock weights in the portfolio, and ι is a vector of ones. In words, this optimization formulation states that we would like to minimize a number γ (which is a decision variable) so that the probability that the portfolio losses (calculated in terms of return) exceed γ is less than or equal to a small number ϵ. We also have the standard budget constraint that the portfolio weights must add up to 1, or 100%.[10]

Given our discussion about optimization problems with chance constraints in Chapter 7.2.3, optimizing a portfolio allocation so that the resulting VaR is the lowest among all possible distributions is nontrivial. Suppose, for example, that we are given data on S possible scenarios for vectors of individual stock returns $\mathbf{r}^{(1)}, \ldots, \mathbf{r}^{(S)}$. The VaR optimization problem can be rewritten as[11]

$$\min_{\gamma, \mathbf{w}} \quad \gamma$$

$$\text{s.t.} \quad (-\mathbf{r}^{(s)})'\mathbf{w} \leq \gamma + M \cdot y_s, \qquad s = 1, \ldots, S$$

$$\sum_{s=1}^{S} y_s \leq \lfloor \epsilon \cdot S \rfloor$$

$$\mathbf{w}'\iota = 1$$

$$y_s \in \{0,1\}, \qquad s = 1, \ldots, S$$

where $\lfloor \epsilon \cdot S \rfloor$ denotes the integer part of $\epsilon \cdot S$, and M is a "large" constant. The optimal value of γ returned by the solver will be the minimum possible value for the VaR expressed in terms of return. (It can be converted to a dollar amount by multiplying the value returned by the solver by the initial value of the portfolio.)

Note that for a data set consisting of 1,000 scenarios, this problem formulation involves solving a mixed-integer program[12] with 1,000 binary variables, which can take a very long time. In practice, the optimization of VaR can be done with approximations, or with additional assumptions. For example, if we assume that the stock returns follow a multivariate normal

---

[10]See Chapter 8 for the fundamental portfolio optimization problem formulation.
[11]See Chapter 7.2.3.
[12]See Chapter 6.2.5.

distribution with a vector of means μ and a covariance matrix Σ, then the portfolio VaR optimization problem can be written as

$$\min_{\gamma, \mathbf{w}} \quad \gamma$$
$$\text{s.t.} \quad -\mu'\mathbf{w} + q_{(1-\epsilon)} \cdot \sqrt{\mathbf{w}'\Sigma\mathbf{w}} \leq \gamma$$
$$\mathbf{w}'\iota = 1$$

where $q_{(1-\epsilon)}$ is the $100(1 - \epsilon)$th percentile of a standard normal distribution.[13] The formulation above is equivalent to the optimization formulation

$$\min_{\mathbf{w}} \quad -\mu'\mathbf{w} + q_{(1-\epsilon)} \cdot \sqrt{\mathbf{w}'\Sigma\mathbf{w}}$$
$$\text{s.t.} \quad \mathbf{w}'\iota = 1$$

which can also be written as

$$\max_{\mathbf{w}} \quad \mu'\mathbf{w} - q_{(1-\epsilon)} \cdot \sqrt{\mathbf{w}'\Sigma\mathbf{w}}$$
$$\text{s.t.} \quad \mathbf{w}'\iota = 1$$

This formulation involves optimizing the portfolio allocation using only the portfolio mean ($\mu'\mathbf{w}$) and the portfolio standard deviation ($\sqrt{\mathbf{w}'\Sigma\mathbf{w}}$). Thus, the portfolio allocations resulting from solving the approximation to the VaR optimization problem with the assumption that asset returns follow normal distributions have the same characteristics, and in particular suffer from the same drawbacks, as allocations obtained with mean-variance formulations.

11.2.2 Portfolio Conditional Value-at-Risk Optimization

Conditional value-at-risk (CVaR) measures the average portfolio loss that happens with at most ϵ probability, that is, the average loss in the tail of the probability distribution for portfolio returns. The CVaR of a portfolio of N stocks is a function of both the uncertain returns of the different stocks in the portfolio (the N-dimensional vector $\tilde{\mathbf{r}}$) and the weights $\mathbf{w}$ these stocks have in the portfolio. For any given set of weights $\mathbf{w}$, the portfolio return is given by $\tilde{r}_p = \tilde{\mathbf{r}}'\mathbf{w}$. Suppose the portfolio return $\tilde{r}_p$ follows a probability

---

[13]See Chapters 2.4, 2.6.2.5, 4.5, and 7.2.3.

distribution with density function f. Then, we can express the $100(1 - \epsilon)\%$ CVaR mathematically as

$$\text{CVaR}_{(1-\epsilon)} = \frac{1}{\epsilon} \cdot \int_{-r \geq \text{VaR}_{(1-\epsilon)}} (-r) \cdot f(r) \ dr$$

The term inside the integral is the expected value of the portfolio loss (as a percentage of amount invested) in the tail of the distribution.

This definition of CVaR in terms of VaR makes it difficult to optimize the CVaR because we need to first calculate the VaR, which, as we mentioned in Section 11.2.1, is itself difficult to calculate. Rockafellar and Uryasev (2000) suggest using an auxiliary objective function instead of CVaR that has better computational properties. Namely, consider the function

$$F_{1-\epsilon}(\mathbf{w}, \xi) = \xi + \frac{1}{\epsilon} \cdot \int_{-r \geq \xi} (-r - \xi) \cdot f(r) \ dr$$

which can be equivalently written as

$$F_{1-\epsilon}(\mathbf{w}, \xi) = \xi + \frac{1}{\epsilon} \cdot \int_{-\infty}^{\infty} \max\{-r - \xi, 0\} \cdot f(r) \ dr$$

It turns out that if we try to minimize this function by varying $\mathbf{w}$ and ξ, the minimum value of the function will in fact equal the $100(1 - \epsilon)\%$ CVaR.[14]

Hence, we can find the minimum value of CVaR without finding VaR first. The value of ξ in the optimal solution will actually equal the VaR of the portfolio with the optimal weights found by optimizing the CVaR. However, the weights for the portfolio that results in minimum CVaR will not necessarily be the weights for the portfolio that results in minimum VaR.

There is a specific case in which the minimization of CVaR is a very tractable optimization problem: when the joint probability density function of the returns for the stocks in the portfolio is represented in a set of scenarios. This is typically the kind of data we have in practice: we can use

---

[14]There is an alternative way to derive this function using optimization duality theory but it is beyond the scope of this book. See Chapter 8 in Pachamanova and Fabozzi (2010).

historical data or generate scenarios by simulation. Suppose also that each scenario in the set is equally likely. In that case, the function can be written as

$$F_{(1-\epsilon)}(\mathbf{w}, \xi) = \xi + \frac{1}{\lfloor \epsilon \cdot S \rfloor} \cdot \sum_{s=1}^{S} \max \left\{ -\left(\mathbf{r}^{(s)} \right)' \mathbf{w} - \xi, 0 \right\}$$

where the N-dimensional vector $\mathbf{r}^{(s)}$ is the vector of returns on the N stocks in the sth scenario. (So, $(\mathbf{r}^{(s)})'\mathbf{w}$ is the portfolio return in the sth scenario.)

To make this function more optimization-solver friendly, we get rid of the expression

$$\max\{-(\mathbf{r}^{(s)})'\mathbf{w} - \xi, 0\}$$

by introducing additional decision variables $y_1, \ldots, y_S$, one for each scenario. The portfolio CVaR minimization problem can be written as

$$
\begin{aligned}
\min_{\mathbf{w}, \xi, \mathbf{y}} \quad & \xi + \frac{1}{\lfloor \epsilon \cdot S \rfloor} \cdot \sum_{s=1}^{S} y_s \\
\text{s.t.} \quad & y_s \geq -(\mathbf{r}^{(s)})'\mathbf{w} - \xi, \quad s = 1, \ldots, S \\
& y_s \geq 0, \quad s = 1, \ldots, S \\
& \mathbf{w}'\iota = 1
\end{aligned}
$$

To understand the meaning of the first two sets of constraints, note that the objective function contains a minimization of the sum of the variables y_s. The optimization solver will try to make the values of these variables as small as possible. The first two sets of constraints, however, restrict the auxiliary variables y_s to be greater than both $-(\mathbf{r}^{(s)})'\mathbf{w} - \xi$ and 0. Thus, in order to satisfy both sets of constraints, the solver will set them equal to the larger of the two values, that is, to the maximum of $-(\mathbf{r}^{(s)})'\mathbf{w} - \xi$ and 0, which is the expression in $F_{(1-\epsilon)}(\mathbf{w}, \xi)$.

The formulation above is a linear optimization problem, which makes scenario CVaR optimization a particularly attractive option from a computational perspective.[15] Adding portfolio constraints such as number of positions, trading costs, and so on (see Section 11.1) results in equally tractable (linear or mixed-integer) optimization formulations.

In some situations, it may be more desirable to specify the CVaR of the portfolio as part of a constraint. The optimization formulation below

---

[15]See Chapter 6.2.2 for a definition of linear optimization problems.

maximizes the expected portfolio return subject to a constraint on the portfolio CVaR by rewriting the problem above as

$$\max_{\mathbf{w},\xi,\mathbf{y}} \quad \boldsymbol{\mu}'\mathbf{w}$$

$$\text{s.t.} \quad \xi + \frac{1}{\lfloor \epsilon \cdot S \rfloor} \cdot \sum_{s=1}^{S} y_s \leq b_{1-\epsilon}$$

$$y_s \geq -(\mathbf{r}^{(s)})'\mathbf{w} - \xi, \quad s = 1, \ldots, S$$

$$y_s \geq 0, \quad s = 1, \ldots, S$$

$$\mathbf{w}'\boldsymbol{\iota} = 1$$

where $\boldsymbol{\mu}$ is the N-dimensional vector of expected returns on the N stocks and $b_{1-\epsilon}$ is the average loss in the tail the portfolio manager is willing to tolerate.

Because of its linear structure, CVaR optimization over scenarios can be performed with any portfolio optimization software. Chapter 8 in Pachamanova and Fabozzi (2010) shows the implementation of the CVaR optimization problem with Excel Solver and MATLAB. With R, one can use the **Rglpk** package,[16] which provides a high-level interface to the free GNU Linear Programming Kit (GLPK).

11.3   INCORPORATING TRANSACTION COSTS

The typical portfolio allocation models are built on top of one or several forecasting models for expected returns and risk. Small changes in these forecasts can result in reallocations that would not occur if transaction costs are taken into account. Transaction costs can be generally divided into two categories: explicit (such as bid–ask spreads, commissions and fees), and implicit (such as price movement risk costs[17] and market impact costs[18]). The effect of transaction costs on portfolio performance in practice can be very significant. If transaction costs are not taken into consideration in allocation

---

[16]See https://cran.r-project.org/web/packages/Rglpk/Rglpk.pdf.
[17]Price movement risk costs are the costs resulting from the potential for a change in market price between the time the decision to trade is made and the time the trade is actually executed.
[18]Market impact is the effect a trader has on the market price of an asset when it sells or buys the asset. It is the extent to which the price moves up or down in response to the trader's actions. For example, a trader who tries to sell a large number of shares of a particular stock may drive down the stock's market price.

and rebalancing decisions, they can lead to poor portfolio performance. This is the reason for multiple portfolio optimization software vendors (Northfield Information Services, MSCI Barra, FactSet, Axioma, Bloomberg LP) to offer portfolio managers the ability to incorporate transaction cost models of various degrees of complexity in their decision making.[19]

This section describes the mathematics behind some common transaction cost models for portfolio rebalancing. We use the mean-variance framework as the basis for describing the different approaches. However, it is straightforward to extend the transaction cost models into other portfolio allocation frameworks. In fact, in practice, transaction cost models are most relevant for portfolio rebalancing, not portfolio allocation.

The earliest, and most widely used, model for transaction costs is the mean-variance risk-aversion formulation with transaction costs.[20] The optimization problem has the following objective function:

$$\max_{\mathbf{w}} \quad \mathbf{w}'\boldsymbol{\mu} - \lambda \cdot \mathbf{w}'\boldsymbol{\Sigma}\mathbf{w} - \lambda_{TC} \cdot TC$$

where TC is a transaction cost penalty function and λ_{TC} is the transaction cost aversion parameter. In other words, the objective is to maximize the expected portfolio return less the cost of risk and transaction costs. We can imagine that as the transaction costs increase, at some point it becomes optimal to keep the current portfolio rather than to rebalance. Variations of this formulation exist. For example, it is common to maximize expected portfolio return minus transaction costs, and impose limits on the risk as a constraint (i.e., to move the second term in the objective function in the constraints).

Transaction costs models can involve complicated nonlinear functions. Although software exists for general nonlinear optimization problems, the computational time required for solving such problems is often too long for realistic investment applications, and, as we explained in Chapter 6, the quality of the solution is not guaranteed. An observed complex nonlinear transaction costs function can, however, be approximated with a computationally tractable function that is assumed to be separable in the portfolio weights, that is, a function that assumes that the transaction costs for each

---

[19]See Kopman and Liu (2011) and Northfield Information Services (2015) for an overview of transaction cost models used in MSCI Barra and Northfield portfolio management software. Northfield Information Services (2015) and Axioma (2007) contain detailed instructions on how to incorporate transaction costs with Northfield's and Axioma's portfolio management software, respectively.
[20]Versions of this model have been suggested in Pogue (1970), Adcock and Meade (1994), Lobo, Fazel, and Boyd (2007), and Mitchell and Braun (2013).

individual stock are independent of the transaction costs for another stock. For the rest of this section, we denote the individual cost function for stock i by TC_i.

11.3.1 Linear Transaction Costs

Let us start simple. Suppose that the transaction costs are proportional, that is, they are a percentage c_i of the transaction size $|t_i| = |w_i - w_{0,i}|$.[21] Then, the portfolio allocation problem with transaction costs can be written simply as

$$\max_{\mathbf{w}} \quad \mathbf{w}'\boldsymbol{\mu} - \lambda \cdot \mathbf{w}'\boldsymbol{\Sigma}\mathbf{w} - \lambda_{TC} \cdot \sum_{i=1}^{N} c_i \cdot |w_i - w_{0,i}|$$

The problem can be made solver-friendly by replacing the absolute value terms with new decision variables y_i and adding two sets of constraints. Hence, we rewrite the objective function as

$$\max_{\mathbf{w},\mathbf{y}} \quad \mathbf{w}'\boldsymbol{\mu} - \lambda \cdot \mathbf{w}'\boldsymbol{\Sigma}\mathbf{w} - \lambda_{TC} \cdot \sum_{i=1}^{N} c_i \cdot y_i$$

and add the constraints

$$y_i \geq w_i - w_{0,i}$$

$$y_i \geq -(w_i - w_{0,i})$$

This preserves the quadratic optimization problem formulation because the constraints are linear expressions, and the objective function contains only linear and quadratic terms.[22]

In the optimal solution, the optimization solver will set the value for y_i to $|w_i - w_{0,i}|$. This is because this is a maximization problem and y_i occurs with a negative sign in the objective function, so the solver will try to set y_i to the minimum value possible. That minimum value will be the maximum of $(w_i - w_{0,i})$ or $-(w_i - w_{0,i})$, which is in fact the absolute value $|w_i - w_{0,i}|$.

---

[21] Here we are thinking of w_i as the portfolio weights, but in fact it may be more intuitive to think of the transaction costs as a percentage of the amount traded. It is easy to go back and forth between portfolio weights and portfolio amounts by simply multiplying w_i by the total amount in the portfolio. In fact, we can switch the whole portfolio optimization formulation around, and write it in terms of allocation of dollars instead of weights. We just need to replace the vector of weights $\mathbf{w}$ by a vector $\mathbf{x}$ of dollar holdings.

[22] See Chapter 6.2.3.

11.3.2 Piecewise-Linear Transaction Costs

Taking the model in Section 11.3.1 a step further, we can introduce piecewise-linear approximations to transaction cost function models. This kind of function is more realistic than the linear cost function, especially for large trades. As the trading size increases, it becomes increasingly more costly to trade because of the market impact of the trade.

An example of a piecewise-linear function of transaction costs for a trade of size t of a particular stock is illustrated in Exhibit 11.1. The transaction cost function in the graph assumes that the rate of increase of transaction costs (reflected in the slope of the function) changes at certain threshold points. For example, it is smaller in the range 0 to 15% of daily volume than in the range 15% to 40% of daily volume (or some other trading volume index). Mathematically, the transaction cost function in Exhibit 11.1 can be expressed as

$$TC(t) = \begin{cases} s_1 t, & 0 \le t \le 0.15 \cdot \text{Vol} \\ s_1\left(0.15 \cdot \text{Vol}\right) + s_2(t - 0.15 \cdot \text{Vol}), & 0.15 \cdot \text{Vol} \le t \le 0.40 \cdot \text{Vol} \\ s_1(0.15 \cdot \text{Vol}) + s_2(0.25 \cdot \text{Vol}) & 0.40 \cdot \text{Vol} \le t \le 0.50 \cdot \text{Vol} \\ \quad + s_3(t - 0.40 \cdot \text{Vol}), \end{cases}$$

where s_1, s_2, s_3 are the slopes of the three linear segments on the graph. (They are given data.)

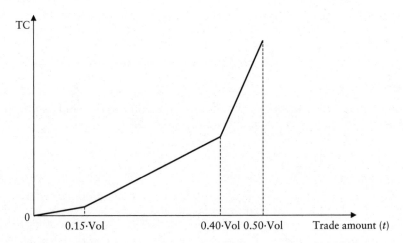

Exhibit 11.1 An example of modeling transaction costs (TC) as a piecewise-linear function of trade size t.

To include piecewise-linear functions for transaction costs in the objective function of a mean-variance (or any general mean-risk) portfolio optimization problem, we need to introduce new decision variables that correspond to the number of pieces in the piecewise-linear approximation of the transaction cost function (in this case, there are three linear segments, so we introduce three variables z_1, z_2, z_3). We write the penalty term in the objective function for an individual stock as[23]

$$\lambda_{TC} \cdot (s_1 \cdot z_1 + s_2 \cdot z_2 + s_3 \cdot z_3)$$

If there are N stocks in the portfolio, the total transaction cost will be the sum of the transaction costs for each individual stock; that is, the penalty term that involves transaction costs in the objective function becomes

$$-\lambda_{TC} \sum_{i=1}^{N} (s_{1,i} \cdot z_{1,i} + s_{2,i} \cdot z_{2,i} + s_{3,i} \cdot z_{3,i})$$

In addition, we specify the following constraints on the new decision variables:

$$0 \leq z_{1,i} \leq 0.15 \cdot \text{Vol}_i$$

$$0 \leq z_{2,i} \leq 0.25 \cdot \text{Vol}_i$$

$$0 \leq z_{3,i} \leq 0.10 \cdot \text{Vol}_i$$

Because of the increasing slopes of the linear segments and the goal of making the penalty term as small as possible in the objective function, the optimizer will never set the decision variable corresponding to the second segment, $z_{2,i}$, to a number greater than 0 unless the decision variable corresponding to the first segment, $z_{1,i}$, is at its upper bound. Similarly, the optimizer would never set $z_{3,i}$ to a number greater than 0 unless both $z_{1,i}$ and $z_{2,i}$ are at their upper bounds. So, this set of constraints allows us to compute the amount of transaction costs incurred in the trading of stock i as $z_{1,i} + z_{2,i} + z_{3,i}$.

We also need to link the amount of transaction costs incurred in the trading of stock i to the optimal portfolio allocation. This can be done by adding a few more variables and constraints. We introduce variables y_i, one for each stock in the portfolio, that would represent the amount traded (but

---

[23] See, for example, Bertsimas, Darnell, and Soucy (1999).

not the direction of the trade), and would be nonnegative. Then, we require that

$$y_i = z_{1,i} + z_{2,i} + z_{3,i} \quad \text{for each stock } i$$

and also that y_i equals the change in the portfolio position of stock i. This condition can be imposed by writing the constraint

$$y_i = |w_i - w_{0,i}|$$

where $w_{0,i}$ and w_i are the initial and the final amount of stock i in the portfolio, respectively.[24]

11.3.3 Quadratic Transaction Costs

The transaction cost function is often parameterized as a quadratic function of the form

$$\text{TC}_i(t) = c_i \cdot |t| + d_i \cdot |t|^2$$

The coefficients c_i and d_i are calibrated from data—for example, by fitting a quadratic function to an observed pattern of transaction costs realized for trading a particular stock under normal conditions.[25]

Including this function in the objective function of the portfolio optimization problem results in a quadratic program that can be solved with widely available quadratic optimization software.

11.3.4 Fixed Transaction Costs

Fixed transaction costs are incurred regardless of the magnitude of the trade. To include such costs in the portfolio optimization problem, we need to introduce binary variables $\delta_1, \ldots, \delta_N$ corresponding to each of N stocks in a portfolio, where δ_i equals 0 if the amount traded of stock i is 0, and 1 otherwise. The idea is similar to the idea we used in Section 11.1.5 to model the requirement that only a given number of stocks can be included in the portfolio.

Suppose the fixed transaction cost for stock i is a_i. Then, the transaction cost function is

$$\text{TC}_i = a_i \cdot \delta_i$$

---

[24]As we explained earlier, this constraint can be written in an equivalent, solver-friendly form, namely,

$$y_i \geq w_i - w_{0,i}$$
$$y_i \geq -(w_i - w_{0,i})$$

[25]Both Microsoft Excel and R have tools for fitting quadratic functions to data.

The objective function formulation is

$$\max_{\mathbf{w}, \boldsymbol{\delta}} \quad \mathbf{w}'\boldsymbol{\mu} - \lambda \cdot \mathbf{w}'\boldsymbol{\Sigma}\mathbf{w} - \lambda_{\text{TC}} \cdot \sum_{i=1}^{N} a_i \cdot \delta_i$$

and we need to add the following constraints to make sure that the binary variables are linked to the trade amounts $| w_i - w_{0,i} |$:

$$|w_i - w_{0,i}| \leq M \cdot \delta_i, \quad i = 1, \ldots, N$$

$$\delta_i \text{ binary}$$

where M is a "large" constant. When the trade amount $| w_i - w_{0,i} |$ is nonzero, δ_i will be forced to be 1. When the trade amount is 0, then δ_i can be either 0 or 1, but the optimizer will set it to 0 since it will try to make its value the minimum possible in the objective function.

Combinations of different trading cost models can be used. For example, if the trade involves both a fixed and a variable quadratic transaction cost, then we could use a transaction cost function of the kind

$$\text{TC}_i(t) = a_i \cdot \delta_i + c_i \cdot |t| + d_i \cdot |t|^2$$

11.3.5 Market Impact Costs

Market impact costs result from the trade itself. The price of a security is generally pushed upward when buying and downward when selling. The market impact can be substantial when the ratio of the trade size to the average trade volume is high.

A variety of market impact cost models have been suggested in the academic literature and in publications by portfolio software vendors.[26] The models typically start off with a power law function[27] of the kind

$$g(t) = \pm \gamma \, |t|^\alpha$$

---

[26]See, for example, Hasbrouck (1991), Almgren and Chriss (2000), Lillo, Farmer, and Mantegna (2003), and Almgren, Thum, Hauptmann, and Li (2005).

[27]The class of power law functions includes concave functions (when the exponent is less than 1), convex functions (when the exponent is greater than 1), and linear functions (when the exponent equals 1). The power law function is the functional form that is implicitly assumed by fitting a straight line on a log-log plot (i.e., a plot of the logarithms of the variables on the horizontal and the vertical axes). See Lillo, Farmer, and Mantegna (2003) and Almgren, Thum, Hauptmann, and Li (2005).

where $g(t)$ is the expected price movement (in %), and the numerical values of the coefficient γ and the exponent α are to be determined by linear and nonlinear regressions on the data. The sign is to be chosen so $g(t)$ has the same sign as the trade t.[28]

Almgren, Thum, Hauptmann, and Li (2005), for example, split the impact into a permanent and a temporary component, and estimate the following transaction cost function:

$$TC_i(x_i) = a_i \cdot |x_i|^{8/5} + b_i \cdot x_i^2$$

where x_i is the number of shares traded.

Adding over all securities in the portfolio, one can obtain the total cost of market impact given trades of $x_1, \ldots, x_N$ shares of stocks $1, \ldots, N$, and incorporate the expression for total cost in a portfolio optimization formulation.

11.4 MULTIACCOUNT OPTIMIZATION

Portfolio managers who handle multiple accounts face an important practical issue. When individual clients' portfolios are managed, portfolio managers incorporate their clients' preferences and constraints. However, on any given trading day, the necessary trades for multiple diverse accounts are pooled and executed simultaneously. Moreover, typically trades may not be crossed, that is, it is not simply permissible to transfer an asset that should be sold on behalf of one client into the account of another client for whom the asset should be bought.[29] The trades should be executed in the market. Thus, each client's trades implicitly impact the results for the other clients: the market impact of the combined trades may be such that the benefits

---

[28]We note that it is not easy to find data to estimate the parameters in market impact models. Almgren, Thum, Hauptmann, and Li (2005), for example, use a proprietary data set obtained from Citigroup's equity trading desk in which the trade's direction (whether the trade is initiated by a buyer or a seller) is known. For most public data sets, information about trade direction is not available. Classification algorithms have been used to understand the direction of particular trades (Lee and Ready, 1991); however, the classification error introduces a bias that typically overestimates the true trading cost (Ellis, Michaely, and O'Hara, 2000).

[29]The Securities and Exchange Commission (SEC) in general prohibits cross-trading but does provide exemptions if prior to the execution of the cross trade the asset manager can demonstrate to the SEC that a particular cross trade benefits both parties. Similarly, Section 406(b)(3) of the Employee Retirement Income Security Act of 1974 (ERISA) forbids cross-trading but there is a cross-trading exemption in Section 408(b)(19) adopted in the Pension Protection Act of 2006.

sought for individual accounts through trading are lost due to increased overall transaction costs. A robust multiaccount management process should ensure accurate accounting and fair distribution of transaction costs among the individual accounts.

One approach to handling the effect of trading in multiple accounts suggested by Khodadadi, Tutuncu, and Zangari (2006) is to use an iterative process, in which at each iteration the market impact of the trades in previous iterations is taken into account. More precisely, single clients' accounts are optimized as usual, and once the optimal allocations are obtained, the portfolio manager aggregates the trades and computes the actual marginal transaction costs based on the aggregate level of trading. The portfolio manager then reoptimizes individual accounts using these marginal transaction costs, and aggregates the resulting trades again to compute new marginal transaction costs, and so on. The advantage of this approach is that little needs to be changed in the way individual accounts are typically handled, so the existing single-account optimization and management infrastructure can be reused. The disadvantage is that most generally, this iterative approach does not guarantee a convergence (or its convergence may be slow) to a "fair equilibrium," in which clients' portfolios receive an unbiased treatment with respect to the size and the constraint structure of their accounts.[30] The latter equilibrium is the one that would be attained if all clients traded independently and competitively in the market for liquidity, and is thus the correct and fair solution to the aggregate trading problem.

An alternative, more comprehensive, approach is to optimize trades across all accounts simultaneously. O'Cinneide, Scherer, and Xu (2006) describe such a model, and show that it attains the fair equilibrium mentioned above.[31] Assume that client k's utility function is given by u_k, and is in the form of a dollar return penalized for risk. Assume also that a transaction cost model τ gives the cost of trading in dollars, and that τ is a convex increasing function. Its exact form will depend on the details of how trading is implemented. Let $\mathbf{t}$ be the vector of trades. It will typically have the form $(t_1^+, \ldots, t_N^+, t_1^-, \ldots, t_N^-)$, that is, it will specify the aggregate buys t_i^+ and the aggregate sells t_i^- for each stock $i = 1, \ldots, N$, but it may also incorporate information about how the trade could be carried out.[32]

---

[30]The iterative procedure is known to converge to the equilibrium, however, under special conditions; see O'Cinneide, Scherer, and Xu (2006).

[31]The issue of considering transaction costs in multiaccount optimization has been discussed by others as well. See, for example, Bertsimas, Darnell, and Soucy (1999).

[32]For example, if asset i is a euro-pound forward, then a trade in that asset can also be implemented as a euro-dollar forward plus a dollar-pound forward, so there will be two additional assets in the aggregate trade vector $\mathbf{t}$. Such concepts will become more intuitive after the introduction to financial derivatives in Chapters 16 through 18.

The multiaccount optimization problem can be formulated as

$$\max_{w_1,\ldots,w_K,t} \quad E[u_1(\mathbf{w}_1)] + \cdots + E[u_K(\mathbf{w}_K)] - \tau(\mathbf{t})$$

$$s.t. \quad \mathbf{w}_k \in C_k, \quad k = 1, \ldots, K$$

where $\mathbf{w}_k$ is the N-dimensional vector of stock holdings (or weights) of client k, and C_k is the collection of constraints on the portfolio structure of client k. The objective can be interpreted as maximization of net expected utility, that is, as maximization of the expected dollar return penalized for risk and net of transaction costs.

The problem can be simplified by making some reasonable assumptions. For example, it can be assumed that the transaction cost function τ is additive across different stocks, that is, that trades in one stock do not influence trading costs in another. In such a case, the trading cost function can be split into more manageable terms, that is,

$$\tau(\mathbf{t}) = \sum_{i=1}^{N} \tau_i(t_i^+, t_i^-)$$

where $\tau_i(t_i^+, t_i^-)$ is the cost of trading stock i as a function of the aggregate buys and sells of that stock. Splitting the terms $\tau_i(t_i^+, t_i^-)$ further into separate costs of buying and selling, however, is not a reasonable assumption because simultaneous buying and selling of a stock tends to have an offsetting effect on its price.

To formulate the problem completely, let $\mathbf{w}_k^0$ be the vector of original holdings (or weights) of client k's portfolio, $\mathbf{w}_k$ be the vector of decision variables for the optimal holdings (or weights) of client k's portfolio, and $\eta_{k,i}$ be constants that convert the holdings (or weight) of each stock i in client i's portfolio $w_{k,i}$ to dollars, that is, $\eta_{k,i}w_{k,i}$ is client k's dollar holdings of asset i.[33] We also introduce new variables $\mathbf{w}_k^+$ to represent an upper bound on the weight of each stock that client k will buy:

$$w_{k,i} - w_{k,i}^0 \leq w_{k,i}^+, \quad i = 1, \ldots, N, \quad k = 1, \ldots, K$$

The aggregate amount of stock i bought for all clients can then be computed as

$$t_i^+ = \sum_{k=1}^{K} \eta_{k,i} \cdot w_{k,i}^+$$

---

[33]Note that $\eta_{k,i}$ equals 1 if $w_{k,i}$ is the actual dollar holdings.

The aggregate amount of stock i sold for all clients can be easily expressed by noticing that the difference between the amounts bought and sold of each stock is exactly equal to the total amount of trades needed to get from the original position $w_{k,i}^0$ to the final position $w_{k,i}$ of that stock:[34]

$$t_i^+ - t_i^- = \sum_{k=1}^{K} \eta_{k,i} \cdot \left(w_{k,i} - w_{k,i}^0 \right)$$

Here t_i^+ and t_i^- are nonnegative variables.

The multiaccount optimization problem then takes the form

$$\max_{w_1,\ldots,w_K,t^+,t^-} E[u_1(\mathbf{w}_1)] + \cdots + E[u_K(\mathbf{w}_K)] - \sum_{i=1}^{N} \tau_i(t_i^+, t_i^-)$$

$$\text{s.t.} \quad \mathbf{w}_k \in C_k, \quad k = 1, \ldots, K$$

$$w_{k,i} - w_{k,i}^0 \leq w_{k,i}^+, \quad i = 1, \ldots, N, \quad k = 1, \ldots, K$$

$$t_i^+ = \sum_{k=1}^{K} \eta_{k,i} w_{k,i}^+, \quad i = 1, \ldots, N$$

$$t_i^+ - t_i^- = \sum_{k=1}^{K} \eta_{k,i} \cdot (w_{k,i} - w_{k,i}^0), \quad i = 1, \ldots, N$$

$$t_i^+ \geq 0, \quad t_i^- \geq 0, \quad w_{k,i}^+ \geq 0, \quad i = 1, \ldots, N, \quad k = 1, \ldots, K$$

O'Cinneide, Scherer, and Xu (2006) study the behavior of the model in simulated experiments with a simple model for the transaction cost function, namely one in which

$$\tau(t) = \theta \cdot t^\gamma$$

where t is the trade size and θ and γ are constants satisfying $\theta \geq 0$ and $\gamma \geq 1$.[35] θ and γ are specified in advance and calibrated to fit observed

---

[34]Note that, similarly to $\mathbf{w}_k^+$, we could introduce additional sell variables $\mathbf{w}_k^-$, but this is not necessary. By expressing aggregate sales through aggregate buys and total trades, we reduce the dimension of the optimization problem because there are fewer decision variables. This would make a difference for the speed of obtaining a solution, especially in the case of large portfolios and complicated representation of transaction costs.

[35]Note that $\gamma = 1$ defines linear transaction costs. For linear transaction costs, multiaccount optimization produces the same allocation as single-account optimization, because linear transaction costs assume that an increased aggregate amount of trading does not have an impact on prices.

trading costs in the market. The transaction costs for each client k can therefore be expressed as

$$\tau_k = \theta \sum_{i=1}^{N} \left| w_{k,i} - w_{k,i}^0 \right|^{\gamma}$$

O'Cinneide, Scherer, and Xu (2006) observe that key portfolio performance measures such as the information ratio,[36] turnover, and total transaction costs change under this model relative to the traditional approach. Not surprisingly, the turnover and the net information ratios of the portfolios obtained with multiaccount optimization are lower than those obtained with single-account optimization under the assumption that accounts are traded separately while transaction costs are higher. These results are more realistic and are a better representation of the post-optimization performance of multiple client accounts in practice.

11.5 INCORPORATING TAXES

In the United States, when stocks in a portfolio appreciate or depreciate in value, *capital gains* (respectively, *capital losses*) accumulate. When stocks are sold, investors pay taxes on the realized net capital gains. The taxes are computed as a percentage of the difference between the current market value of the stocks and their tax basis, where the *tax basis* is the price at which the stocks were bought originally.[37] The percentage is less for long-term capital gains (when stocks have been held for more than a year) than it is for short-term capital gains (when stocks have been held for less than a year).[38] Because shares of the same stock could have been bought at different points in time (in different *lots*), selling one lot of the stock as opposed to another could incur a different amount of tax. In addition to capital gains taxes, investors who are not exempt from taxes owe taxes on the dividends paid on stocks in their portfolios. Dividends have been historically taxed at a higher rate than capital gains, and are currently taxed as ordinary income, that is, at the investor's personal tax rate.[39] The tax liability of a particular portfolio

---

[36] See Chapter 10.3.

[37] There are special rules for computing the tax basis for bonds.

[38] The exact rates vary depending on the current version of the tax code, but the main idea behind the preferential treatment of long-term capital gains compared to short-term capital gains is to encourage long-term capital investments and promote entrepreneurial activity.

[39] Qualified dividends are an exception—they are taxed at the long-term capital gains rate. To treat dividends as qualified, the IRS requires that the stock investment be held for more than 60 days during the 121-day period that begins 60 days prior to the day after a corporation's board declares a dividend payment to shareholders.

therefore depends on the timing of the execution of trades, on the tax basis of the portfolio, on the accumulated short-term and long-term capital gains, and on the tax bracket of the investor.

More than two-thirds of portfolio assets in the United States are held by individuals, insurance, and other companies who pay taxes on their returns. (Exceptions are, for example, pension funds, which do not pay taxes year-to-year.) Studies have indicated that taxes are the greatest expense investors face—greater than commissions and investment management fees. To gain some intuition about the effect of taxes on the income of an investor over the investor's lifetime, consider a portfolio that has a capital appreciation of 6% per year. After 30 years, $1,000 invested in that portfolio will turn into $1,000 \cdot (1 + 0.06)^{30} = $5,743.49$. Now suppose that the capital gains are realized each year, a tax of 20% is paid on the gains, and the remainder is reinvested. After 30 years, $1,000 invested in the portfolio will turn into $1,000 \cdot (1 + (1 - 0.20) \cdot 0.06)^{30} = $4,081.68$, about 30% less than the amount without taxes even when the tax is one fifth of the capital gains. In fact, in order to provide the same return as the portfolio with no taxes, the portfolio with annual realized capital gains would need to generate a capital appreciation of 7.5% per year. You can imagine that the same logic would make benchmark tracking and performance measurement very difficult on an after-tax basis.

As investors have become more aware of the dramatic impact of taxes on their returns, there is increasing pressure on portfolio managers to include tax considerations in their portfolio rebalancing decisions and to report after-tax performance. Consequently, the demand for computationally efficient and quantitatively rigorous methods for taking taxes into consideration in portfolio allocation decisions has grown in recent years. The complexity of the problem of incorporating taxes, however, is considerable, both from a theoretical and from practical perspective:

1. The presence of tax liabilities changes the interpretation of even fundamental portfolio performance summary measures such as market value and risk. Thus, well-established methods for evaluating portfolio performance on a pretax basis do not work well in the case of tax-aware portfolio optimization. For example, in traditional portfolio management a loss is associated with risk, and is therefore minimized whenever possible. However, in the presence of taxes, losses may be less damaging because they can be used to offset capital gains and reduce the tax burden of portfolio rebalancing strategies. Benchmarking is also not obvious in the presence of taxes: two portfolios that have exactly the same current holdings are not equivalent if the holdings have a different tax basis.[40]

---

[40]See Stein (1998).

2. Tax considerations are too complex to implement in a nonautomated fashion; at the same time, their automatic inclusion in portfolio rebalancing algorithms requires the ability to solve very difficult, large-scale optimization problems.

3. The best approach for portfolio management with tax considerations is optimization problem formulations that look at return forecasts over several time periods (e.g., until the end of the year) before recommending new portfolio weights. However, this multiperiod view of the portfolio optimization problem is very difficult to handle computationally—the dimension of the optimization problem, that is, the number of variables and constraints, increases exponentially with the number of time periods under consideration.

We need to emphasize that while many of the techniques described in the previous sections of this chapter are widely known, there are no standard established practices for tax-aware portfolio management. Different asset management firms approach the problem differently. To some firms, minimizing turnover,[41] for example, by investing in index funds or selecting strategies that minimize the portfolio dividend yield[42] qualify as tax-aware portfolio strategies. Other asset management firms employ complex optimization algorithms that incorporate tax considerations directly into portfolio rebalancing decisions so that they can keep up with the considerable burden of keeping track of thousands of managed accounts and their tax preferences. The fact is, even using simple rules of thumb, such as always selling stocks from the oldest lots after rebalancing the portfolio with classical portfolio optimization routines, can have a positive effect on after-tax portfolio returns. Such strategies minimize the likelihood that short-term capital gains will be incurred, which in turn reduces taxes, because short-term capital gains are taxed at a higher rate than long-term capital gains.

Apelfeld, Fowler, and Gordon (1996) suggested a tax-aware portfolio rebalancing framework that incorporates taxes directly into the portfolio optimization process. The main idea of the approach was to treat different lots of the same stock as different securities, and then penalize for taxes as if they were different transaction costs associated with the sale of each

---

[41] Apelfeld, Fowler, and Gordon (1996) showed that a manager can outperform on an after-tax basis with high turnover as well, as long as the turnover does not result in net capital gains taxes. (There are other issues with high turnover, however, such as higher transaction costs that may result in a lower overall portfolio return.)

[42] Dividends are taxed as ordinary income, i.e., at a higher rate than capital gains, so minimizing the portfolio dividend yield should theoretically result in a lower tax burden for the investor.

lot. (This means, for example, that Microsoft stock bought on Date 1 is treated as a different security from Microsoft stock bought on Date 2.) Many tax-aware quantitative investment strategies employ versions of this approach, but there are a few issues to beware of when using it in practice:

- The first one is a general problem for all tax-aware approaches when they are used in the context of active portfolio management. For a portfolio manager who handles hundreds of different accounts with different tax exposures, it is virtually impossible to pay attention to the tax cost incurred by each individual investor. While the tax-aware method described above minimizes the overall tax burden by reducing the amount of realized short-term sales, it has no provisions for differentiating between investors in different tax brackets because it is difficult to think of each trade as divided between all investors, and adjusted for each individual investor's tax circumstances. This issue is so intractable that in practice it is not really brought under consideration.
- The dimension of the problem can become unmanageable very quickly. For example, a portfolio of 1,000 securities, each of which has 10 different lots, is equivalent to a portfolio of 10,000 securities when each lot is treated as a different security. Every time a new purchase is realized, a new security is added to the portfolio since a new lot is created. One needs to exercise care and "clean up" lots that have been sold and therefore have holdings of zero each time the portfolio is rebalanced.
- As we explained in Chapter 9, factor models are typically used for forecasting returns, estimating risk, and portfolio optimization. One of the assumptions with factor models is that the specific risk of a particular security is uncorrelated with the specific risk of other securities. (The only risk they share is the risk expressed through the factors in the factor model.) This assumption clearly does not hold when different "securities" are in fact different lots of the same stock.

DiBartolomeo (2000) described a modification to the model used by Northfield Information Service's portfolio management software that eliminates the last two problems. Instead of treating each lot as a separate security, the software imposes a piecewise-linear transaction cost (see Exhibit 11.1) where the breakpoints on the horizontal axis correspond to the current size of different lots of the same security. The portfolio rebalancing algorithm goes through several iterations for the portfolio weights, and at each iteration, only the shares in the highest cost basis tax lot can be traded. Other shares of the same stock can be traded in subsequent iterations of the algorithm, with their appropriate tax costs attached.

The approaches we described so far take into consideration the short-term or long-term nature of capital gains, but do not incorporate the possibility of offsetting capital gains and losses accumulated over the year. This is an inherent limitation of single-period portfolio rebalancing approaches, and is a strong argument in favor of adopting more realistic multiperiod portfolio optimization approaches. The rebalancing of the portfolio at each point in time should be made not only by considering the immediate consequences for the market value of the portfolio, but also the opportunity to correct for tax liabilities by realizing other capital gains or losses by the end of the taxable year. The scarce theoretical literature on multiperiod tax-aware portfolio optimization contains some characterizations of optimal portfolio strategies but they make numerous simplifying assumptions.[43] Even under such simplifying assumptions, the dimension of the problem grows exponentially with the number of stocks in a portfolio, and it is difficult to come up with computationally viable algorithms for portfolios of realistic size.

11.6   ROBUST PARAMETER ESTIMATION

The most commonly used approach for estimating security expected returns, covariances, and other parameters that are inputs to portfolio optimization models is to calculate the sample analogues from historical data.[44] These are sample estimates for the parameters we need.

When we rely on historical data for estimation purposes, we assume that the past provides a good representation of the future. It is well known, however, that expected returns exhibit significant time variation (referred to as *nonstationarity*). They are impacted by changes in markets and economic conditions, such as interest rates, the political environment, consumer confidence, and the business cycles of different industry sectors and geographical regions. Consequently, extrapolated historical returns are typically poor forecasts of future returns.

Similarly, the covariance matrix is unstable over time. Moreover, sample estimates of covariances for thousands of stocks are notoriously unreliable because one needs large data sets to estimate them and such large data sets of relevant data are difficult to procure.

In practice, portfolio managers often alter historical estimates of different parameters subjectively or objectively, ·based on their expectations and

---

[43]See Constantinides (1984), Dammon and Spatt (1996), and Dammon, Spatt, and Zhang (2001, 2004).
[44]See Chapter 2.6 and 3.11 for information on how to obtain sample estimates.

forecasting models for future trends. They also use statistical methods for finding estimators that are less sensitive to outliers and other sampling errors, such as Bayesian and shrinkage estimators. A complete review of advanced statistical estimation topics is beyond the scope of this book. We provide a brief overview of the most widely used concepts.[45]

Shrinkage is a form of averaging different estimators. The shrinkage estimator typically consists of three components: (1) an estimator with little or no structure (like the sample mean); (2) an estimator with a lot of structure (the shrinkage target); and (3) a coefficient that reflects the shrinkage intensity. Probably the most well-known estimator for expected returns in the financial literature was proposed by Jorion (1986). The shrinkage target in Jorion's model is a vector array with the return on the minimum variance portfolio,[46] and the shrinkage intensity is determined from a specific formula.[47] Shrinkage estimators are used for estimates of the covariance matrix of returns as well,[48] although equally weighted portfolios of covariance matrix estimators have been shown to be equally effective as shrinkage estimators as well.[49]

Bayesian estimation approaches are based on subjective interpretations of the probability that a particular event will occur. A probability distribution, called the *prior distribution*, is used to represent the investor's knowledge about the probability before any data are observed. After more information is gathered (e.g., data are observed), a formula known as Bayes' rule (named after the English mathematician Thomas Bayes) is used to compute the new probability distribution, called the *posterior distribution*.

In the portfolio parameter estimation context, a posterior distribution of expected returns is derived by combining the forecast from the empirical data with a prior distribution. One of the most well-known examples of the application of the Bayesian framework in this context is the *Black-Litterman model*,[50] which produces an estimate of future expected returns by combining the market equilibrium returns (i.e., returns that are derived from pricing models and observable data) with the investor's subjective views. The investor's views are expressed as absolute or relative deviations from the equilibrium together with confidence levels of the views (as measured by the standard deviation of the views).

---

[45] For further details, see Chapters 6 and 8 in Fabozzi, Kolm, Pachamanova, and Focardi (2007) and Kim, Kim, and Fabozzi (2016).

[46] See Chapter 8.3 for a definition of the minimum variance portfolio.

[47] See Chapter 8 in Fabozzi, Kolm, Pachamanova, and Focardi (2007), p. 217.

[48] See, for example, Ledoit and Wolf (2003).

[49] See Disatnik and Benninga (2007) for an overview of such models.

[50] See Chapter 8 in Fabozzi, Kolm, Pachamanova, and Focardi (2007) for a step-by-step description of the Black-Litterman model.

The ability to incorporate exogenous insight such as a portfolio manager's opinion into quantitative forecasting models is important; this insight may be the most valuable input to the model. The Bayesian framework provides a mechanism for forecasting systems to use both important traditional information sources such as proprietary market data and subjective external information sources such as analysts' forecasts.

Regardless of how sophisticated the estimation and forecasting methods are, they are always subject to estimation error. What makes matters worse, however, is that different estimation errors can accumulate over the different activities of the portfolio management process, resulting in large aggregate errors at the final stage. It is critical that the inputs evaluated at each stage are reliable and robust so that the aggregate impact of estimation errors is minimized.

11.7   PORTFOLIO RESAMPLING

Robust parameter estimation is only one aspect of an analytical portfolio management process. It has been observed that portfolio allocation schemes are very sensitive to small changes in the inputs that go into the optimizer. In particular, a well-known study by Black and Litterman (1992) demonstrated that in the case of mean-variance optimization, small changes in the inputs for expected returns had a substantial impact on the portfolio composition. "Optimal" portfolios constructed under conditions of uncertainty can have extreme or nonintuitive weights for some stocks.

With advances in computational capabilities and new research in the area of optimization under uncertainty, practitioners in recent years have been able to incorporate considerations for uncertainty not only at the estimation stage but also at the portfolio optimization stage. Methods for taking into consideration inaccuracies in the inputs to the portfolio optimization problem include simulation (resampling) and robust optimization. We explain portfolio resampling in this section, and robust portfolio optimization in the following section.

A logical approach to making portfolio allocation more robust with respect to changes in the input parameters is to generate different scenarios for the values these parameters can take and find weights that remain stable for small changes in the input parameters. Simulation[51] is therefore a natural technique to use in this context. In the literature, using simulation

---

[51] See Chapter 5.

to generate robust portfolio weights has been referred to as *portfolio resampling*.[52] To illustrate the resampling technique, we explain how it is applied to portfolio mean-variance optimization as an example.

Suppose that we have initial estimates for the expected stock returns, $\hat{\mu}$, and covariance matrix, $\hat{\Sigma}$, for N candidate stocks for a portfolio. (As before, we use "hat" to denote a statistical estimate.)

1. We simulate S samples of N returns from a multivariate normal distribution with mean $\hat{\mu}$ and covariance matrix $\hat{\Sigma}$.
2. We use the S samples we generated in (1) to compute S new estimates of vectors of expected returns $\hat{\mu}_1, \ldots, \hat{\mu}_S$ and covariance matrices $\hat{\Sigma}_1, \ldots, \hat{\Sigma}_S$.
3. We solve S portfolio optimization problems, one for each estimated pair of expected returns and covariances $(\hat{\mu}_s, \hat{\Sigma}_s)$, and save the weights for the N stocks in a vector array $\mathbf{w}^{(s)}$, where $s = 1, \ldots, S$. (The optimization problem itself could be any of the standard mean-variance formulations: maximize expected return subject to constraints on risk, minimize risk subject to constraints on the expected return, or maximize the utility function.[53])
4. To find the final portfolio weights, we average out the weight for each stock over the S weights found for that stock in each of the S optimization problems. In other words,

$$\mathbf{w} = \frac{1}{S} \sum_{s=1}^{S} \mathbf{w}^{(s)}$$

For example, stock i in the portfolio has final weight

$$w_i = \frac{w_i^{(1)} + \cdots + w_i^{(S)}}{S}$$

Perhaps even more valuable than the average estimate of the weights obtained from the simulation and optimization iterations is the probability distribution we obtain for the portfolio weights. If we plot the weights for each stock obtained over the S iterations, $w_i^{(1)}, \ldots, w_i^{(S)}$, we can get a sense for how variable this stock weight is in the portfolio. A large standard

---

[52] See Michaud (1998), Jorion (1992), and Scherer (2002).
[53] See Chapter 8.

deviation computed from the distribution of portfolio weight i will be an indication that the original portfolio weight was not very precise due to estimation error.

An important question, of course, is how large is "large enough." Do we have evidence that the portfolios we obtained through resampling are statistically different from one another? We can evaluate that by using a test statistic.[54] For example, it can be shown that the test statistic

$$d(\mathbf{w}^*, \mathbf{w}) = (\mathbf{w}^* - \mathbf{w})' \, \boldsymbol{\Sigma} (\mathbf{w}^* - \mathbf{w})$$

follows a chi-square (χ^2) distribution[55] with degrees of freedom equal to the number of securities in the portfolio. If the value of this statistic is statistically "large," then there will be evidence that the portfolio weights $\mathbf{w}^*$ and $\mathbf{w}$ are statistically different. This is an important insight for the portfolio manager, and its applications extend beyond resampling. Let us provide intuition as to why.

Suppose that we are considering rebalancing our current portfolio. Given our forecasts of expected returns and risk, we could calculate a set of new portfolios through the resampling procedure. Using the test statistic above, we determine whether the new set of portfolio weights are statistically different from our current weights and, therefore, whether it would be worthwhile to rebalance or not. If we decide that it is worthwhile to rebalance, we could choose any of the resampled portfolios that are statistically different from our current portfolio. Which one should we choose? A natural choice would be to select the portfolio that would lead to the lowest transaction costs. The idea of determining statistically equivalent portfolios, therefore, has much wider implications than the ones illustrated in the context of resampling.

Resampling has its drawbacks:

- Because the resampled portfolio is calculated through a simulation procedure in which a portfolio optimization problem needs to be solved at each step, the approach is computationally cumbersome, especially for large portfolios. There is a trade-off between the number of resampling steps and the accuracy of estimation of the effect of errors on the portfolio composition.
- Due to the averaging in the calculation of the final portfolio weights, it is highly likely that all stocks will end up with nonzero weights. This has

---

[54]See Chapter 3.11.4 for a brief introduction to statistical hypothesis testing.
[55]See Chapter 3.1.7.

implications for the amount of transaction costs that will be incurred if the final portfolio is to be attained. One possibility is to include constraints that limit both the turnover and the number of stocks with nonzero weights. As we saw in Section 11.1, however, the inclusion of such constraints adds another level of complexity to the optimization problem, and may slow down the resampling procedure.

- Because the averaging process happens after the optimization problems are solved, the final weights may not actually satisfy some of the constraints in the optimization formulation. In general, only convex (e.g., linear) constraints are guaranteed to be satisfied by the averaged final weights. Turnover constraints, for example, may not be satisfied. This is a serious limitation of the resampling approach for practical applications.

Despite these limitations, resampling has advantages, and presents a good alternative to using only point estimates as inputs to the optimization problem.

11.8 ROBUST PORTFOLIO OPTIMIZATION

Another way in which uncertainty about the inputs can be modeled is by incorporating it directly into the optimization process. Robust optimization, the technique we introduced in Chapter 7.3, is an intuitive and efficient way to deal with uncertainty. Robust portfolio optimization does not use the traditional forecasts such as expected returns and stock covariances, but rather uncertainty sets containing these point estimates. A simple example of such an uncertainty set is a confidence interval around the forecast for expected returns, but we can also formulate advanced uncertainty sets that incorporate more knowledge about the estimation error. For example, as we explained in Chapter 7.3, a widely used uncertainty set is the ellipsoidal uncertainty set, which takes into consideration the covariance structure of the estimation errors.

Let us give a specific example of how the robust optimization framework can be applied in the portfolio optimization context. Consider the utility function formulation of the classical mean-variance portfolio allocation problem from Chapter 8.4.2:

$$\max_{\mathbf{w}} \quad \mathbf{w}'\boldsymbol{\mu} - \lambda \cdot \mathbf{w}'\Sigma\mathbf{w}$$
$$\text{s.t.} \quad \mathbf{w}'\boldsymbol{\iota} = 1$$

Suppose that we have estimates $\hat{\boldsymbol{\mu}}$ and $\hat{\boldsymbol{\Sigma}}$ of the vector of expected returns and the covariance matrix. Instead of the estimate $\hat{\boldsymbol{\mu}}$, however, we will consider a set of vectors $\boldsymbol{\mu}$ that are "close" to $\hat{\boldsymbol{\mu}}$. We define the "box" uncertainty set[56]

$$U_\delta(\hat{\boldsymbol{\mu}}) = \{\boldsymbol{\mu} \mid |\mu_i - \hat{\mu}_i| \leq \delta_i, \; i = 1, \ldots, N\}$$

In words, the set $U_\delta(\hat{\boldsymbol{\mu}})$ contains all vectors $\boldsymbol{\mu} = (\mu_1, \ldots, \mu_N)$ such that each component μ_i is in the interval $[\hat{\mu}_i - \delta_i, \hat{\mu}_i + \delta_i]$. The robust counterpart of the classical mean-variance problem with this uncertainty set can be found using the ideas from Chapter 7.3 where we explained how to find the robust counterpart of a constraint. In this case, the uncertainty is in the objective function. We can introduce a new decision variable v, and write the expression in the objective function as a constraint:

$$\begin{aligned} \max_{\mathbf{w}} \quad & v \\ \text{s.t.} \quad & \mathbf{w}'\boldsymbol{\mu} - \lambda \cdot \mathbf{w}'\boldsymbol{\Sigma}\mathbf{w} \geq v \\ & \mathbf{w}'\boldsymbol{\iota} = 1 \end{aligned}$$

This is a standard trick in optimization: the value of the decision variable v is to be maximized, but it is constrained from above by the expression $\mathbf{w}'\boldsymbol{\mu} - \lambda \cdot \mathbf{w}'\boldsymbol{\Sigma}\mathbf{w}$, so the optimizer will try to make $\mathbf{w}'\boldsymbol{\mu} - \lambda \cdot \mathbf{w}'\boldsymbol{\Sigma}\mathbf{w}$ as large as possible (i.e., maximize it) as well. The optimal solution to the problem does not change, but now we can compute the robust counterpart of the constraint

$$\mathbf{w}'\boldsymbol{\mu} - \lambda \cdot \mathbf{w}'\boldsymbol{\Sigma}\mathbf{w} \geq v$$

in the same way as we did for a constraint of the general type

$$\tilde{\mathbf{a}}'\mathbf{x} \leq b$$

in Chapter 7.3. Namely, we first solve an optimization problem of the kind

$$\max_{\boldsymbol{\mu} \in U_\delta(\hat{\boldsymbol{\mu}})} \{-\mathbf{w}'\boldsymbol{\mu} + \lambda \cdot \mathbf{w}'\boldsymbol{\Sigma}\mathbf{w}\} \leq -v$$

(Note here that we multiplied both sides of the constraint by -1, which reversed the sign of the constraint. This is just to demonstrate that we can

---

[56]See Exhibit 7.3(a).

bring the constraint exactly into the general form $\tilde{a}'x \leq b$.) This problem is equivalent to

$$\max_{\mu \in U_\delta(\hat{\mu})} \{-w'\mu\} \leq -v - \lambda \cdot w'\Sigma w$$

and because there is no μ in the expression on the right-hand side of the constraint, we can treat the whole expression as if it was a constant (with respect to μ). In other words, we have the constraint $\tilde{a}'x \leq b$, where $\tilde{a} = \mu$, $x = w$, and $b = -v - \lambda \cdot w'\Sigma w$.[57]

The robust counterpart of the mean-variance optimization problem with the box uncertainty set for expected returns is

$$\max_{w} \quad w'\mu - \delta'|w| - \lambda \cdot w'\Sigma w$$

$$\text{s.t.} \quad w'\iota = 1$$

where $|w|$ denotes the absolute value of the entries of the vector of weights w. To gain some intuition, notice that if the weight of stock i in the portfolio is negative, the worst-case expected return for stock i is $\mu_i + \delta_i$ (we lose the largest amount possible). If the weight of stock i in the portfolio is positive, then the worst-case expected return for stock i is $\mu_i - \delta_i$ (we gain the smallest amount possible). Observe that $\mu_i w_i - \delta_i |w_i|$ equals $(\mu_i - \delta_i)w_i$ if the weight w_i is positive and $(\mu_i + \delta_i)w_i$ if the weight w_i is negative. Hence, the mathematical expression in the objective agrees with intuition: it minimizes the worst-case expected portfolio return. In this robust version of the mean-variance formulation, stocks whose mean return estimates are less accurate (i.e., have a larger estimation error δ_i) are therefore penalized in the objective function and will tend to have a smaller weight in the optimal portfolio allocation.

This optimization problem has the same computational complexity as the nonrobust mean-variance formulation—namely, it can be stated as a

---

[57]Observe that this model incorporates the notion of aversion to estimation error in the following sense. When the interval $[\hat{\mu}_i - \delta_i, \hat{\mu}_i + \delta_i]$ for the expected return of the ith asset is large, meaning that the expected return has been estimated with large estimation error, then the minimization problem over μ is less constrained. Consequently, the minimum will be smaller than it would be in situations when the interval for the expected return is smaller. Obviously, when the interval is small enough, the minimization problem will be so tightly constrained that it would deliver a solution that is close to the optimal solution of the classical portfolio optimization problem in which estimation errors are ignored. In other words, it is the size of the intervals (in general, the size of the uncertainty set) that controls the aversion to the uncertainty that comes from estimation errors.

quadratic optimization problem. This can be achieved by using the trick we used in Section 11.1 to get rid of the absolute values for the weights. Namely, we introduce an N-dimensional vector of additional variables ψ to replace the absolute values $|\mathbf{w}|$, and write an equivalent version of the optimization problem,

$$\max_{\mathbf{w}, \psi} \quad \mathbf{w}'\hat{\mu} - \delta'\psi - \lambda \mathbf{w}'\Sigma\mathbf{w}$$

$$\text{s.t.} \quad \mathbf{w}'\iota = 1$$

$$\psi_i \geq w_i; \quad \psi_i \geq -w_i, \quad i = 1, \ldots, N$$

Therefore, incorporating considerations about the uncertainty in the estimates of the expected returns in this example has virtually no computational cost.

We can view the effect of this particular "robustification" of the mean-variance portfolio optimization formulation in two different ways. On the one hand, we can see that the values of the expected returns for the different stocks have been adjusted downward in the objective function of the optimization problem. That is, the robust optimization model "shrinks" the expected return of stocks with large estimation error. In this case the robust formulation is related to statistical shrinkage methods.[58] On the other hand, we can interpret the additional term in the objective function as a "risk-like" term that represents a penalty for estimation error. The size of the penalty is determined by the investor's aversion to estimation risk, and it is reflected in the magnitude of the δ.

More complicated specifications for uncertainty sets have more involved mathematical representations but can still be selected so that they preserve an easy computational structure for the robust optimization problem. For example, as we mentioned in Chapter 7.3, a commonly used uncertainty set is the ellipsoidal uncertainty set[59]

$$U_\delta(\hat{\mu}) = \{\mu \mid (\mu - \hat{\mu})'\Sigma_\mu^{-1}(\mu - \hat{\mu}) \leq \delta^2 \}$$

where Σ_μ is the covariance matrix of estimation errors for the vector of expected returns μ. This uncertainty set represents the requirement that the scaled sum of squares (scaled by the inverse of the covariance matrix of estimation errors) between all elements in the set and the point estimates

---

[58]See Section 11.7 for a definition of statistical shrinkage.
[59]See Exhibit 7.3(b).

$\hat{\mu}_1, \hat{\mu}_2, \ldots, \hat{\mu}_N$ can be no larger than δ^2. Note that this uncertainty set cannot be interpreted as individual confidence intervals around each point estimate. Instead, it captures the idea of a joint confidence region. In practical applications, the covariance matrix of estimation errors is often assumed to be diagonal, that is, errors are assumed not to be correlated with each other. For this particular case, the set contains all vectors of expected returns that are within a certain number of standard deviations from the point estimate of the vector of expected returns.

The robust counterpart of the mean-variance portfolio optimization problem with an ellipsoidal uncertainty set for the expected return estimates turns out to be the following optimization problem formulation:

$$\max_{\mathbf{w}} \quad \mathbf{w}'\boldsymbol{\mu} - \lambda \cdot \mathbf{w}'\boldsymbol{\Sigma}\mathbf{w} - \delta\sqrt{\mathbf{w}'\boldsymbol{\Sigma}_{\mu}\mathbf{w}}$$

$$\text{s.t.} \quad \mathbf{w}'\boldsymbol{\iota} = 1$$

This is a second-order cone problem and it requires specialized software to solve, but the methods for solving it are very efficient.[60]

Just as in the robust counterpart with a box uncertainty set, we can interpret the extra term in the objective function $(\delta\sqrt{\mathbf{w}'\boldsymbol{\Sigma}_{\mu}\mathbf{w}})$ as the penalty for estimation risk, where δ incorporates the degree of the investor's aversion to estimation risk. Note, by the way, that the covariance matrix in the estimation error penalty term, $\boldsymbol{\Sigma}_{\mu}$, is not necessarily the same as the covariance matrix of returns $\boldsymbol{\Sigma}$. In fact, it is not immediately obvious how $\boldsymbol{\Sigma}_{\mu}$ can be estimated from data. $\boldsymbol{\Sigma}_{\mu}$ is the covariance matrix of the errors in the estimation of the expected (average) returns. Thus, if a portfolio manager forecasts 5% active return over the next time period, but gets 1%, he cannot argue that there was a 4% error in his expected return—the actual error would consist of both an estimation error in the expected return and the inherent volatility in actual realized returns. In fact, critics of the approach have argued that the realized returns typically have large stochastic components that dwarf the expected returns, and hence estimating $\boldsymbol{\Sigma}_{\mu}$ from data is very difficult, if not impossible.[61]

Several approximate methods for estimating $\boldsymbol{\Sigma}_{\mu}$ have been found to work well in practice. For example, it has been observed that simpler estimation approaches, such as using just the diagonal matrix containing the variances of the estimates (as opposed to the complete error covariance

---

[60] See Chapter 6.2.4.
[61] See Lee, Stefek, and Zhelenyak (2006).

matrix), often provide most of the benefit in robust portfolio optimization.[62] In addition, standard approaches for estimating expected returns, such as Bayesian statistics and regression-based methods, can produce estimates for the estimation error covariance matrix in the process of generating the estimates themselves.[63]

Among practitioners, the notion of robust portfolio optimization is often equated with the robust mean-variance model we discussed in this section, with the box or the ellipsoidal uncertainty sets for the expected stock returns. While robust optimization applications often involve one form or another of this model, the actual scope of robust optimization can be much broader. We note that the term *robust optimization* refers to the technique of incorporating information about uncertainty sets for the parameters in the optimization model, and not to the specific definitions of uncertainty sets or the choice of parameters to model as uncertain. For example, we can use the robust optimization methodology to incorporate considerations for uncertainty in the estimate of the covariance matrix in addition to the uncertainty in expected returns, and obtain a different robust portfolio allocation formulation. Robust optimization can be applied also to portfolio allocation models that are different from the mean-variance framework, such as Sharpe ratio optimization and value-at-risk optimization.[64] Finally, robust optimization has the potential to provide a computationally efficient way to handle portfolio optimization over multiple stages—a problem for which so far there have been few satisfactory solutions.[65] There are numerous useful robust formulations, but a complete review is beyond the scope of this book.[66]

Is implementing robust optimization formulations worthwhile? Some tests with simulated and real market data indicate that robust optimization, when inaccuracy is assumed in the expected return estimates, outperforms classical mean-variance optimization in terms of total excess return a large percentage (70–80%) of the time.[67] Other tests have not been as

---

[62]See Stubbs and Vance (2005).

[63]See Chapter 12 in Fabozzi, Kolm, Pachamanova, and Focardi (2007) for a more in-depth coverage of the topic of estimating input parameters for robust optimization formulations.

[64]See, for example, Goldfarb and Iyengar (2003) and Natarajan, Pachamanova, and Sim (2008).

[65]See Ben-Tal, Margalit, and Nemirovski (2000) and Bertsimas and Pachamanova (2008).

[66]See Chapters 6 and 8 in Fabozzi, Kolm, Pachamanova, and Focardi (2007) and Kim, Kim, and Fabozzi (2016).

[67]See Ceria and Stubbs (2006).

conclusive (Lee, Stefek, and Zhelenyak, 2006). The factor that accounts for much of the difference is how the uncertainty in parameters is modeled. Therefore, finding a suitable degree of robustness and appropriate definitions of uncertainty sets can have a significant impact on portfolio performance.

Independent tests by practitioners and academics using both simulated and market data appear to confirm that robust optimization generally results in more stable portfolio weights, that is, that it eliminates the extreme corner solutions resulting from traditional mean-variance optimization. This fact has implications for portfolio rebalancing in the presence of transaction costs and taxes, as transaction costs and taxes can add substantial expenses when the portfolio is rebalanced. Depending on the particular robust formulations employed, robust mean-variance optimization also appears to improve worst-case portfolio performance, and results in smoother and more consistent portfolio returns. Finally, by preventing large swings in positions, robust optimization typically makes better use of the turnover budget and risk constraints.

Robust optimization, however, is not a panacea. By using robust portfolio optimization formulations, investors are likely to trade off the optimality of their portfolio allocation in cases in which nature behaves as they predicted for protection against the risk of inaccurate estimation. Therefore, investors using the technique should not expect to do better than classical portfolio optimization when estimation errors have little impact, or when typical scenarios occur. They should, however, expect insurance in scenarios in which their estimates deviate from the actual realized values by up to the amount they have prespecified in the modeling process.

Summary

- Quantitative equity portfolio management in practice may involve advanced portfolio optimization formulations that contain constraints, objective functions that may not be the same as in the mean-variance framework, considerations for transaction costs and taxes, and robustness in estimation and optimization routines.
- Commonly used constraints in practice include long-only (no short-selling) constraints, turnover constraints, holding constraints, risk factor constraints, and tracking error constraints.
- Minimum holding constraints, transaction size constraints, cardinality constraints, and round-lot constraints are also widely used in practice but their nature is such that they require binary and integer modeling, which necessitates the use of mixed-integer and other specialized optimization solvers.

- Transaction costs can be incorporated into standard portfolio allocation models. Typical functions for representing transaction costs include linear, piecewise linear, and quadratic.
- For investment managers who handle multiple accounts, increased transaction costs—because of the market impact of simultaneous trades—can be an important practical issue, and should be taken into consideration when individual clients' portfolio allocation decisions are made to ensure fairness across accounts.
- Taxes can have a dramatic effect on portfolio returns; however, it is difficult to incorporate them into the classical portfolio optimization framework. Their importance to the individual investor is a strong argument for taking a multiperiod view of investments but the computational burden of multiperiod portfolio optimization formulations with taxes is very high.
- Considerations for estimation risk and model risk in portfolio allocation schemes have been growing in importance.
- Methods for robust statistical estimation of parameters include shrinkage and Bayesian techniques.
- Portfolio resampling is a technique that uses simulation to generate multiple scenarios for possible values of the input parameters in the portfolio optimization problem, and aims to determine portfolio weights that remain stable with respect to small changes in model parameters.
- Robust portfolio optimization incorporates uncertainty directly into the portfolio optimization process.
- The uncertain parameters in the optimization problem are assumed to vary in prespecified uncertainty sets that are selected subjectively or based on data.

CHAPTER 12

Factor-Based Equity Portfolio Construction and Performance Evaluation

The analytic approaches described in Chapter 11 are better suited for equity portfolio managers who are comfortable with the idea of quantitative portfolio management. Even equity portfolio managers who do not consider themselves quantitatively oriented, however, use portfolio analytics to some degree. For example, they may not use optimization for portfolio allocation and rebalancing, but they may use data and analysis for stock screening, or simulation in the portfolio performance evaluation process.

Factor models have become a key driver for the use of analytics in portfolio construction and risk management. Equity investment strategies are often based on factor groupings, where the factors can include value, growth, volatility, and liquidity. Portfolio diversification across managers pursuing various alpha strategies has given way to diversification across betas for multiple strategically selected factors. Identifying and incorporating such factors in the investment process requires deeper comfort with analytical techniques than has been traditionally required.

This chapter describes in detail how factors enter into the process for selecting equity investments, portfolio construction, and portfolio evaluation. We begin with a list of typical factors used in equity portfolio construction and then show explicit examples of how factors are used for stock screening, portfolio construction, stress testing, and portfolio performance evaluation.

12.1 EQUITY FACTORS USED IN PRACTICE

As explained in Chapter 9, equity portfolio managers can use a variety of factors to account for the sources of return in their portfolios. The exact factors used depend on the investment style and the selection of a factor model vendor. This section describes factors used in equity factor models in more detail.[1]

12.1.1 Fundamental Factors

Fundamental factors describe the financial condition of the company and are usually financial ratios that can be read or calculated in a straightforward way from financial statements. Many of these financial ratios are correlated as they represent similar characteristics of the company, so it is not necessary to consider all. Investment managers often consider subsets or composite indexes of the following metrics that proxy for factors when they make investment decisions:

- *Valuation* or *value* factors can include market capitalization, price-to-earnings (P/E) ratio, price-to-book (P/B) ratio, price-to-sales (P/S) ratio, dividend yield (D/P), price-to-cash-flow (P/CF) ratio, and price-to-EBITDA (P/EBITDA) ratio. For example, it has been observed that small-cap stocks outperform large-cap stocks over the long term. Some studies claim that companies with high dividend yields and low P/B, P/S, P/CV, and P/EBITDA ratios tend to outperform stocks with low dividend yields and high P/B, P/S, P/CV, and P/EBITDA ratios.
- *Growth potential* or *growth* factors can include price-to-earnings-to-growth (PEG) ratio, R&D-expenditure-to-sales ratio, advertising-expenditure-to-sales ratio, and capital-expenditure-to-sales ratio. PEG ratio, for example, can be considered in conjunction with P/E ratio. A high P/E ratio by itself may mean that the stock is overvalued, but when accompanied by a low PEG ratio, the high P/E ratio may appear reasonable given the potential for company growth.
- *Operating efficiency* factors can include cost-of-goods-sold-to-average-inventory ratio (inventory turnover (IT) ratio), total asset turnover (TAT) ratio, equity turnover (ET) ratio, and fixed-asset turnover (FAT) ratio. For example, a high IT ratio is an indication that the company's products are in high demand.
- *Solvency* factors can include debt-to-equity (D/E) ratio, interest coverage ratio (ICR), current (CUR) ratio, quick ratio (QR), and cash ratio (CR). For example, a high D/E ratio generally can mean higher risk of financial distress. A high CUR ratio (the ratio of current assets to current liabilities) generally indicates high liquidity; however, it should be

---

[1]See also Chincarini and Kim (2006) and Barra on Campus (2003).

examined in conjunction with the IT ratio because large inventories (which generally inflate the current ratio) may also mean that the company's products are not selling.

- *Operating profitability* factors can include gross profit margin (GPM), operating profit margin (OPM), net profit margin (NPM), return on total capital (ROTC), and return on total equity (ROTE).
- *Liquidity* factors such as trading turnover (TT) give an indication for how easy it is to trade the stock. Higher liquidity generally translates into higher returns because investors are more willing to hold liquid stocks.

12.1.2 Macroeconomic Factors

Asset Pricing Theory, the theory that gave rise to the spread of factor models in industry, was based on macroeconomic factors of asset returns such as inflation, real interest rates, and risk premiums calculated as the spread in returns between Baa-rated bonds and government bonds.[2] Other economic and market factors used to assess asset returns include gross domestic product (GDP), consumer sentiment index, business confidence index, investor sentiment index, and broad market indices such as the S&P 500 Index.

12.1.3 Technical Factors

Technical factors are constructed based on information about past prices, trading volume, and bid–ask spreads. Perhaps the most widely used technical factor is momentum, which can, for example, be measured as the stock return over the past year. Studies have found positive autocorrelation in stock returns, although the conclusion does not always hold for individual stocks and over small time periods. Portfolio managers use technical factors in order to take into consideration possible short-term effects on the stock price.

12.1.4 Additional Factors

Additional factors that can be taken into consideration include analysts' forecasts, corporate finance policy factors such as stock buybacks and insider purchases, as well as social responsibility factors such as employee relations, environment, or human rights.[3]

---

[2] See Ross (1976) and Chapter 9.1.
[3] See Chincarini and Kim (2006).

12.2 STOCK SCREENS

Equity investment managers use stock screens to rank stocks in the investment universe according to one or multiple criteria in such a way that it makes it possible to differentiate between desirable and undesirable investments. These criteria are often based on the factors investment managers consider important for portfolio performance. For example, suppose that an investment manager believes that a low price-to-earnings (P/E) ratio is indicative of a company's hidden value. The manager could rank all companies in the investment universe by their P/E ratio, and pick a prespecified number of stocks with the lowest P/E ratios.

A famous example of a screen is the *Peter Lynch growth screen*, named after former Fidelity Magellan fund manager Peter Lynch, which identifies companies that are generating strong growth relative to their current market valuation. Two of the main criteria used are a P/E ratio that is less than the industry average and a PEG ratio that is less than 1.0.[4]

Stock screens are not the most sophisticated method for portfolio construction, but they are intuitive and are a good starting point. More sophisticated analytical tools used in stock screens include *z-score rankings*, aggregating such rankings based on the underlying factor models built to identify portfolio risk and return contributors, and econometric and optimization tools for constructing portfolios with desired characteristics and "optimal" performance according to a particular criterion.

The concept of a z-score was introduced briefly in Chapter 2.4. A z-score calculates how many standard deviations away an observation is from the average of a probability distribution. In the context of stock screens, the z-score of a company for a particular metric such as a P/E ratio gives a sense of the outperformance or underperformance of the company relative to the other companies in the investment universe according to that metric. Suppose, for example, that an investment manager is considering 10 companies for investment in March, and the average P/E ratio for the 10 companies for February is 25 while the standard deviation of their P/E ratios is 13. Suppose that Company A's P/E ratio is 23. Company A's z-score is

$$\frac{\text{Individual P/E Ratio} - \text{Mean P/E Ratio}}{\text{Standard Deviation of P/E Ratios}} = \frac{23 - 25}{13} = -0.15$$

---

[4]See Fidelity's website https://research2.fidelity.com/fidelity/screeners/commonstock/landing.asp? for a description of the Lynch screen (listed as Growth at a Reasonable Price) and a number of other stock screens.

This means that company A's P/E ratio is lower than the average P/E ratio of the 10 companies under consideration by 0.15 standard deviations. Because a low P/E ratio is an indication of company strength, the companies with negative z-scores of the 10 companies in the sample may be considered more desirable than the companies with positive z-scores.

A z-score is helpful also when a portfolio manager would like to use multiple criteria to rank stocks simultaneously. These criteria are often expressed through metrics of different magnitudes. For example, the manager may be interested in high-momentum stocks as measured by the high returns over the past 12 months, or in large companies as measured by the companies' market caps. While returns are measured in percentage points, company size can be in the millions or billions of dollars. Calculating the z-scores for the different metrics according to which the ranking will be performed allows the manager to combine rankings and come up with an aggregate score for a particular company. For example, suppose that company A's momentum z-score (within the investment universe of 10 stocks) is -1.35, and its size z-score is 2.50.

The manager can combine the z-scores for the three metrics: P/E ratio, momentum, and size. When combining individual factor's z-scores, the portfolio manager needs to take into consideration whether a low or a high z-score is preferable for a particular metric. For example, if the portfolio manager likes stocks with low P/E ratio but large market capitalization and high momentum, then he could multiply the z-score corresponding to P/E ratio by (-1) while keeping the z-scores for size and momentum with their original signs. This will ensure that stocks with high P/E ratio are discounted for purposes of overall stock ranking and stocks with large market capitalization and high momentum are ranked higher. If the portfolio manager considers all three factors (P/E ratio, momentum, and size) equally important, he can weigh each z-score by 1/3 (one over the number of factors in a more general setting) after adjusting its sign. In this example, the manager could use

$$\frac{1}{3}(-z_{A,P/E} + z_{A,Size} + z_{A,Momentum}) = \frac{1}{3}(-(-0.15) + (2.50) + (-1.35))$$

$$= 0.43$$

Alternatively, the manager can redefine his metrics in a way that removes the need to keep track of positive and negative signs in the calculation of the overall z-score. For example, if the manager would like a high aggregate z-score to correspond to desirable investments, and a low z-score to correspond to undesirable investments, he can keep track of, and calculate the z-scores for, the E/P (rather than P/E) ratios of the stocks in the investment universe. Then, the highest-ranked stocks according to their E/P ratio z-score would be the most attractive investments, and Company A's aggregate z-score can then be calculated as

$$\frac{1}{3}(z_{A,E/P} + z_{A,Size} + z_{A,Momentum})$$

Instead of an equal weighting of all the factors, a portfolio manager may determine an "optimal" set of weights that best corresponds to a set of historical returns or economic scenarios of interest. For example, suppose that there are data for T time periods (scenarios) of returns $r_{i,t}$ for stocks $i = 1, \ldots, N$, and K factor z-scores calculated for each stock i for each time period $t = 1, \ldots, T$. Then one can run a regression to determine coefficients $w_1, \ldots, w_K$ such that

$$r_{i,t} = m_i + w_1 \cdot z_{i,1,t-1} + w_2 \cdot z_{i,2,t-1} + \ldots + w_K \cdot z_{i,K,t-1} + \epsilon_{i,t-1}$$

The coefficients $w_1, \ldots, w_K$ can then be used as relative weights for the different factors in calculating the aggregate z-score of a particular stock.

As we mentioned in Section 12.1, portfolio managers sometimes group similar factors together, and calculate aggregate z-scores within each factor group before computing an overall z-score. Examples of factor groups are[5]

- Valuation metrics (Price-to-Earnings [P/E] ratio, Return-on-Equity [ROE], Price-to-Book [P/B] ratio, Price-to-Sales [P/S] ratio).
- Profitability metrics (Gross Profit Margin [GPM]), financial soundness metrics (Interest Coverage Ratio [ICR], Debt-to-Equity [D/E] ratio).
- Risk metrics (previous 12 month's standard deviation of returns, standard deviation of cash flows).
- Technical or momentum metrics (previous one month's return, previous six months' return, previous 12 months' return, return on a major index such as the S&P 500).

Grouping metrics of performance together has several advantages. First, looking at several metrics that represent the same concept (e.g., P/E and P/S to analyze the company valuation) provides a more complete picture than a single metric such as P/E. Second, an investment manager can change the

---

[5]See Chincarini and Kim (2006) and Barra on Campus (2003).

relative weights of the different groups of factors depending on his views of how the market prioritizes these factors at a particular moment in time.

A number of financial data providers (e.g., Bloomberg) have made access to data on company fundamentals easy and convenient for investment professionals. User-friendly graphical user interfaces (GUIs) allow for narrowing down the investment universe according to a set of predetermined criteria as well as the ranking of stocks within that universe.

Stock screens are appealing in their simplicity, but they also have the drawback of providing only a relative ranking of stocks without an actual estimate of the expected stock return. Excess return, outperformance, or alpha is what most investment managers pursue, and factor models provide the quantitative framework within which such out- and underperformance can be evaluated.

12.3 PORTFOLIO SELECTION

In Chapters 8, 10, and 11 we discussed optimization-based methods for portfolio selection. There is also a variety of ad-hoc and heuristic methods used in practice. This section discusses such methods in the context of portfolio selection relative to a benchmark. While passive managers use such methods to match the return on a benchmark, active managers may use them to make bets relative to the benchmark.

12.3.1 Ad-Hoc Portfolio Selection

For portfolio managers who manage relative to a benchmark, a simplistic approach to imitating the return on the benchmark is to select the largest holdings in the benchmark and keep them in the portfolio. For example, if the portfolio manager would like to hold 30 stocks, the 30 stocks with the largest weights from the benchmark can be included. Further, if the portfolio manager would like to *tilt* the portfolio toward stocks that he prefers, the portfolio manager can, for example, rank the 30 stocks to include in the portfolio according to their aggregate z-scores (or any other ranking method), and use a mathematical method to calculate the weights for the 30 stocks in the portfolio in such a way that the weights add up to 1 but are higher for stocks with "good" z-scores.

Note that this kind of selection would make the portfolio vulnerable to a particular factor—namely, size. It also does not control well for portfolio exposure to other factors. Stratification, a method described next, attempts to take more than one factor explicitly into consideration in deciding on portfolio allocation.

12.3.2 Stratification

Stratification is the selection of stocks in such a way that the primary factors from a benchmark are represented in the portfolio.[6] To get intuition about the mechanics of stratification, let us consider the following example.

Suppose a portfolio manager would like to match the industry composition factor of the benchmark. Suppose there are 10 industries represented in the benchmark: Information Technology, Consumer Discretionary, Energy, Healthcare, Telecommunications Services, Industrials, Financials, Consumer Staples, Utilities, and Materials. A passive manager selects a few stocks from each of these 10 industries in such a way that the relative weight of all the stocks in a particular industry in his portfolio is the same as the relative weight of the industry in the benchmark. A manager following an enhanced indexing strategy may choose to tilt the portfolio to an industry that is expected to outperform, and increase the relative percentage of stocks from that industry in the portfolio.

Now suppose that the manager would like to take a second factor into consideration, such as P/E ratio. He considers "buckets" or "cells" of stocks within each industry with, say "small" (e.g., below-average), "medium" (average), and "large" (above-average) P/E ratio. An easy way to visualize the buckets is to imagine a two-dimensional matrix (table), each column of which is an industry group, and each row of which represents a P/E category (Exhibit 12.1). The stocks in the index are assigned to the buckets depending on their specific characteristics. The passive manager then picks among the stocks in each bucket (cell of the table) and makes sure that the relative weight of the representative stocks from a bucket is the same as the relative weight of all the stocks in the bucket is in the benchmark. A manager following an enhanced indexing strategy may tilt the portfolio by selecting a percentage of the portfolio from some buckets that is deliberately higher or lower than the percentage they represent in the benchmark.

As the number of factors increases, the determination of buckets becomes quite cumbersome. Also, it is very difficult to implement the stratified sampling approach when large, diversified portfolios are considered

---

[6]In statistics, stratification is used in the context of sampling. *Stratified sampling* is a method for obtaining better information about a population by breaking up the population into nonoverlapping groups first, and then sampling observations within each group. This is done because purely random sampling of the entire population tends to miss observations from groups that are underrepresented in the population, and such groups may not get a chance to appear in the sample. By including such groups by design and sampling within them, stratified sampling achieves a better representation of the population as a whole with a smaller sample size than pure random sampling. The main idea of stratified sampling in statistics—using representative groups of the population and sampling within those—carries over to the use of stratification in the portfolio management process.

EXHIBIT 12.1   Example of stratification with two factors (industry and P/E ratio).

	Small P/E	Medium P/E	Large P/E
Information Technology	...	...	...
Consumer Discretionary	...	...	...
Energy	...	...	...
Healthcare	...	...	...
Telecommunications Services	...	...	...
Industrials	...	...	...
Financials	...	...	...
Consumer Staples	...	...	...
Utilities	...	...	...
Materials	...	...	...

the benchmark. Because the handpicking of stocks to match each bucket is subjective, tracking error results. Finally, a portfolio manager using stratification would not have a clear picture of how risk is reduced relative to not using the method.

Some portfolio managers use stratification in combination with optimization to produce more precise matching of the buckets with stocks, to impose additional portfolio constraints, and to optimize an objective, such as minimization of tracking error. Additional constraints may include not purchasing certain stocks or not purchasing more than a certain amount within a particular category of stocks. While the optimization routine helps with the matching problem, the burden of coming up with subjective buckets and allocating stocks from a large benchmark to the buckets can still be formidable.

12.3.3   Factor Exposure Targeting

Factor exposure targeting uses the betas from factor models to control a portfolio's exposure to particular factors.[7] To accomplish this, one imposes factor type constraints inside portfolio optimization routines.[8]

For example, if the benchmark is one of the factors, one can set the portfolio beta with respect to the benchmark to 1, or set limits on the deviation of the portfolio beta from 1:

$$0.9 \leq \beta_{p, \, benchmark} \leq 1.1$$

---

[7]Recall from Chapter 9.7 that the portfolio beta for a particular factor k is simply the sum of the betas of the individual stocks with respect to the factor weighted by the weight of these stocks in the portfolio, that is, $\beta_{p, \, k} = \sum_{i=1}^{N} w_i \beta_{i,k}$.

[8]See Chapter 11.1.4.

Note that when the portfolio beta with respect to the benchmark is less than 1, the portfolio is underexposed to the benchmark factor.

One can specify limits on factor exposures for multiple factors. This allows for tilting the portfolio toward or away from specific factors in accordance with the portfolio manager's beliefs about market trends for these factors. If there are K factors and N stocks in the portfolio, one imposes the following set of constraints:

$$\beta_{p,1}^L \leq \sum_{i=1}^N w_i \beta_{i,1} \leq \beta_{p,1}^U$$

$$\cdots$$

$$\beta_{p,K}^L \leq \sum_{i=1}^N w_i \beta_{i,K} \leq \beta_{p,K}^U$$

where $\beta_{p,k}^L$ and $\beta_{p,k}^U$ are the upper and lower limits on the portfolio exposure to factor k, respectively.

12.4 RISK DECOMPOSITION

An important part of the portfolio construction and management process is understanding the sources of risk in the portfolio. In practice, this reduces to estimating to what extent the variability in different factors contributes to the variability in portfolio returns. Sometimes portfolio risk management software vendors refer to factors as *risk factors* to emphasize their use in understanding portfolio variability. The process of breaking down a particular measure of portfolio risk into contributions by factors is referred to as *portfolio risk decomposition*. In this section, we provide an example of how an investment manager can perform risk decomposition.[9] To be specific, we consider a U.S. large-cap portfolio, and are concerned with decomposing the active risk relative to a benchmark (the S&P 500).

In this particular example, the active risk will be measured as the variance of the deviations of the portfolio returns from the benchmark returns,

---

[9]We thank Andrew Geer, Ed Reis, Rick Barrett, and Bill McCoy of FactSet for creating this example. In addition, we thank Ed Reis for generating the exhibits and for his careful proofreading of this section. FactSet is a data provider and a portfolio management software vendor that has its own factor models, and also integrates several factor models provided by other vendors, such as Axioma (fundamental and statistical factor models for short and medium horizon), MSCI Barra (fundamental factor models for short and long horizon), Northfield (fundamental, hybrid, and macroeconomic models for short and long horizon), SunGard APT (statistical factor models), and R-squared (hybrid models).

that is, by the square of the tracking error. We begin by decomposing portfolio active risk into risk contributed by three sources: specific (variability attributable to individual securities), style (variability attributable to factors in the style category, which we will review shortly), and industry (variability attributable to the performance of various industries represented in the portfolio). The percentage stacked bar chart visualization in Exhibit 12.2 shows what percentage of total active risk is represented by specific, style, and industry factors. One can observe that stock specific risk is the largest component of the portfolio active risk, and that style factors variability has been increasing over the past three months (the portion of active risk, that is, the portion of the bar at each date corresponding to style risk has been increasing).

We can drill down into the specific factors that contribute to style factor variability. The stacked bar chart in Exhibit 12.3 helps illustrate both the active portfolio risk at each point in time (the total height of each bar) and the amount of active risk that is attributable to style factors such as size, short-term momentum, volatility, exchange rate sensitivity, medium-term momentum, market sensitivity, growth, leverage, liquidity, and value (the length of the corresponding piece in the bar at each date). Size and volatility (the top two portions of each bar) are by far the largest contributors to active risk.

Time series visualizations such as the one in Exhibit 12.4 show whether the portfolio has been historically overexposed or underexposed to the style factors that contribute the most to its active risk. In this case, it appears that there has been a systematic bet on volatility (the portfolio has had a consistently high exposure to it over the previous year and a half), and a systematic bet against size (the portfolio has had a consistent negative exposure to it that has become even more negative in the last two months). The exposure to another style factor, Value (the lightest line, in the middle of the graph), has remained stable and small.

Let us drill deeper into the role size plays in the portfolio active risk. The table of risk decomposed by sector and market cap (Exhibit 12.5) shows that the majority of the portfolio active risk (51.30%) is contributed by small-cap stocks (with a cap of less than $10 billion). The largest risk contributor among all sectors is Information Technology, with 18.79% of active risk.

What factors are responsible for the variability within the Information Technology sector? Exhibit 12.6 shows tornado graphs of the active weight of each industry sector and the percentage of active risk it represents (left graph) as well as the active weight of each industry within the Information Technology sector and the percentage of active risk it represents (right graph). Tornado graphs illustrate both the magnitude and the sign of a quantity, and sort the categories in decreasing order. If a bar points to the left, it is negative. The length of the bar corresponds to the magnitude. In this case, looking at the tornado graph on the left, we can see that the Information Technology sector not only accounts for the largest percentage of active

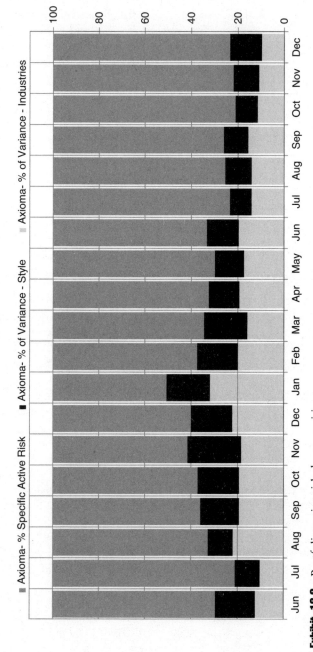

Exhibit 12.2 Portfolio active risk decomposition.
Source: FactSet.

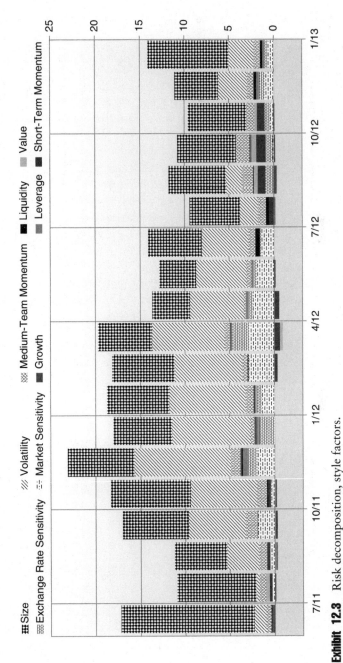

Exhibit 12.3 Risk decomposition, style factors.
Source: FactSet.

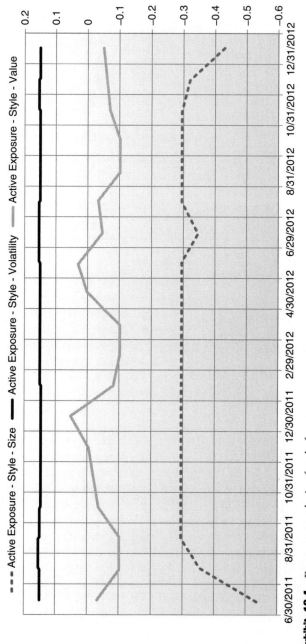

Exhibit 12.4 Exposure analysis of style factors.
Source: FactSet.

EXHIBIT 12.5   Risk decomposition, sector by market cap (in billions of dollars).

	100B+ % of Active Risk	25B–100B % of Active Risk	10B–25B % of Active Risk	<10B % of Active Risk	Total % of Active Risk
Total	9.70	17.35	21.65	51.30	100.00
Information Technology	9.86	−0.80	2.43	7.31	18.79
Consumer Discretionary	−0.34	2.23	0.44	15.31	17.63
Energy	−0.86	10.57	2.33	4.31	16.35
Health Care	−0.20	9.42	2.50	0.98	12.71
Telecommunication Services	−0.13	0.00	−0.25	12.72	12.35
Industrial	−0.41	−1.36	5.67	8.09	11.99
Financials	−0.12	−1.04	4.54	0.92	4.30
Consumer Staples	1.91	−0.58	1.87	0.69	3.88
Utilities	0.00	−0.10	−0.22	1.50	1.17
Materials	0.00	−0.98	2.34	−0.53	0.84

Source: FactSet.

portfolio risk (the first gray bar on the positive side of the vertical axis), but is also the largest underweighted industry sector (the first black bar on the negative side of the vertical axis). Looking at the tornado graph on the right, the largest contributor to active risk within the Information Technology sector is Technology Hardware Storage & Peripherals, with about 7% of active risk (the first gray bar on the positive side of the vertical axis). The active weight for Technology Hardware Storage & Peripherals is about −5% (the first black bar on the negative side of the vertical axis).

Which stocks within Technology Hardware Storage & Peripherals are the largest risk contributors? The visualization in Exhibit 12.7 allows us to drill down to the individual stock level. The tornado graph on the left shows that the largest percentage of active risk by far (almost 8%) is attributable to Apple. Apple is also heavily underweighted in the portfolio (−4%). The bar chart on the right shows that the majority of Apple's risk comes from its specific risk. The next largest source of risk is the size factor. The volatility factor is actually acting as a hedge—its negative active risk (−0.72%) shows that it is diversifying away some of the risk. Most likely, this is because the portfolio has a positive exposure to volatility (Exhibit 12.4), and Apple has a positive exposure to volatility as well (but is underweighted in the portfolio).

Further visualizations can illustrate the raw factor exposures of each stock in the portfolio. (Recall from Chapter 10 that the factor exposures are the beta coefficients in the factor model; they reflect the sensitivity of the stock's return to changes in factor levels.) Exhibit 12.8 uses conditional formatting to indicate stocks (listed as titles in the first column) with large positive and large negative exposures to style factors (listed as titles in

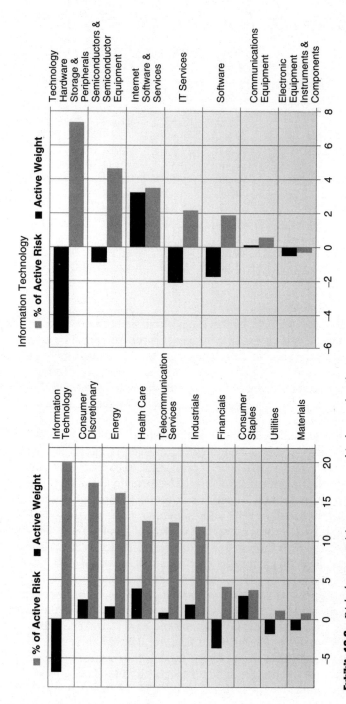

Exhibit 12.6 Risk decomposition, sector, and industry detail.

Source: FactSet.

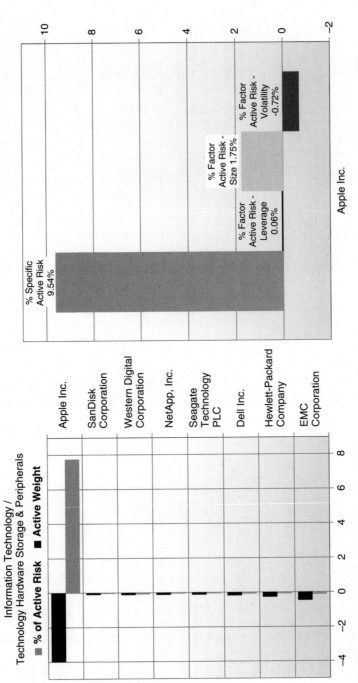

Exhibit 12.7 Risk decomposition, asset detail.
Source: FactSet.

EXHIBIT 12.8 Raw factor exposures.

Security Name	Exchange Rate Sensitivity	Growth	Leverage	Liquidity	Market Sensitivity	Medium-Term Momentum	Short-Term Momentum	Size	Value	Volatility
Apple, Inc.	-0.56	1.73	-0.74	1.59	0.29	0.90	-1.64	2.12	-0.60	0.96
Exxon Mobil Corporation	0.11	0.67	-0.69	0.17	-0.48	-0.33	-0.60	2.01	-0.24	-0.90
Wal-Mart Stores, Inc.	1.27	0.39	-0.34	0.06	-1.13	0.18	-1.03	1.76	-0.44	-0.66
Microsoft Corporation	-0.07	0.25	-0.66	0.53	0.33	-0.37	-0.28	1.75	-0.46	-0.20
General Electric Company	-0.07	-0.15	2.45	0.31	-0.15	0.12	-0.30	1.74	0.04	-0.48
International Business Machines	0.21	2.36	-0.50	0.17	-0.49	-0.38	-0.22	1.73	-0.89	-0.78
Chevron Corporation	0.01	0.26	-0.65	0.10	-0.18	-0.45	0.00	1.71	0.20	-0.44
Johnson & Johnson	0.52	-0.28	-0.60	0.28	-1.09	-0.22	-0.26	1.68	-0.42	-1.47
AT&T, Inc.	0.62	-0.46	-0.20	0.31	-0.63	0.06	-0.52	1.67	-0.02	-0.71
Procter & Gamble Company	0.59	-0.24	-0.47	0.10	-0.58	-0.28	-0.74	1.67	-0.39	-1.10
Pfizer, Inc.	1.11	-0.27	-0.40	0.25	-1.08	0.09	-0.30	1.66	-0.19	-0.99
Google Inc. Class A	0.21	0.45	-0.69	0.74	-0.23	-0.28	-0.11	1.66	-0.34	-0.42
Wells Fargo & Company	-0.38	0.07	0.95	0.30	-0.06	0.18	0.18	1.64	0.55	-0.34
Coca-Cola Company	0.85	0.21	-0.42	0.01	-0.96	-0.18	-0.98	1.60	-0.68	-1.11
JPMorgan Chase & Co.	-0.61	-0.04	3.01	0.51	-0.09	0.32	0.69	1.59	1.28	-0.35
Oracle Corporation	-0.45	0.67	-0.53	0.41	0.23	0.28	0.30	1.58	-0.52	-0.51
Philip Morris International Inc.	0.96	2.36	-0.49	0.05	-0.59	0.02	-1.21	1.54	-1.10	-0.53
Merck & Co., Inc.	1.02	-0.30	-0.50	0.24	-0.15	0.13	-1.31	1.49	-0.22	-0.64
Verizon Communications, Inc.	1.00	-0.46	-0.05	0.22	-0.87	-0.05	-0.62	1.47	-0.47	-0.56
Bank of America Corporation	-0.93	-0.34	3.01	1.18	0.63	1.90	2.25	1.44	2.71	0.70
Amazon.com, Inc.	0.01	-0.43	-0.71	0.55	0.86	0.34	-0.39	1.43	-0.94	0.28
Citigroup, Inc.	-1.39	-0.25	3.01	1.02	1.23	0.45	1.76	1.42	2.30	0.65
PepsiCo, Inc.	0.93	0.18	-0.32	-0.01	-1.18	-0.28	-0.60	1.40	-0.67	-1.72
QUALCOMM, Inc.	-0.01	0.20	-0.74	0.59	-0.21	0.02	-0.65	1.40	-0.44	0.00
Cisco Systems, Inc.	-0.32	0.23	-0.49	0.60	0.44	-0.31	0.23	1.39	-0.06	-0.33
Abbott Laboratories	1.32	0.24	-0.48	0.23	-0.70	0.07	-0.23	1.38	-0.55	-0.60
Intel Corporation	0.18	0.42	-0.63	0.67	-0.46	-1.05	0.45	1.37	-0.11	-0.08
Berkshire Hathaway, Inc. Class B	0.58	-0.05	0.31	0.25	-0.81	-0.05	-0.07	1.36	2.74	-1.18
Schlumberger, NV	-0.87	0.19	-0.55	0.35	0.05	-0.33	-0.81	1.34	-0.34	-0.04
Home Depot, Inc.	0.52	0.26	-0.55	0.27	-0.39	1.28	-1.06	1.34	-0.69	-0.24
McDonald's Corporation	0.81	0.45	-0.50	0.39	-0.69	-0.86	-0.14	1.31	-0.76	-1.12
Walt Disney Company	0.53	0.16	-0.47	0.22	-0.10	0.48	-0.08	1.31	-0.16	-0.44

Source: FactSet.

the first row). This is useful in several ways. First, we can identify the underlying properties of each stock in the portfolio across a variety of metrics. For example, Apple is large, liquid, growth-oriented, and has negative short-term momentum. Second, this visualization can help us find stocks that can increase or decrease our exposure to a particular factor. For example, the portfolio has been consistently underweighted in Size (Exhibit 12.4). If we would like to increase exposure to this factor, we can focus on stocks with high exposure to Size; in this example, they are Exxon Mobil, Wal-Mart Stores, Inc., and Microsoft Corporation.

Some risk management software, including FactSet's, allow for assessing security exposures also firm-wide. As seen in the top graph in Exhibit 12.9, Apple represents 1.02% of the overall holdings of the firm. The bottom graph in Exhibit 12.9 shows that Apple's weight across all portfolios managed by this asset management firm, however, has been decreasing, from 1.4% in August 2012 to 1% in December 2012.

To summarize, this example illustrated how one can look into different sources of active risk in a portfolio and drill down to individual factor and security level.

12.5 STRESS TESTING

Stress testing is another important component of a robust portfolio risk management strategy. It involves subjecting the portfolio to hypothetical scenarios to see how the portfolio would perform if such scenarios were to occur. Factor models are widely used in this context as well. Stress testing can involve factor shocks or extreme scenarios. An example of a factor shock is when the market goes down by 30%, or gold goes up by 30% (when the market or gold are used as factors in the factor model). An example of an extreme event is the market crash of October 2008.

Exhibit 12.10 illustrates the analysis that can be conducted. The top graph shows the performance of the portfolio from Section 12.4 over the previous year and a half, to give a sense for the typical values realized for the portfolio return. The bottom graph shows 10 stress scenarios, such as the demise of Long Term Capital Management in August 1998 (labeled "LTCM 8/1998"), the credit crisis of October 2008 (labeled "Credit Crisis (10/2008)"), and a 30% drop in the S&P 500 (labeled "S&P 500 −30%"). Because the portfolio is overweighed in small-cap stocks, we test what happens when large-cap stocks outperform small-cap stocks. The portfolio is also overweighed in volatility, so we test what happens when volatility goes up (scenario "Volatility Up"). We can see that some of these scenarios do not generate portfolio returns that are significantly different from recent returns. For example, increased volatility results in an active portfolio return

Security Exposures
31-Dec-2012
U.S. Dollar

Portfolios	Portfolio Description	Shares	Market Value	% of Portfolio Weight	% of Benchmark Weight	Active Weight	% of Total Weight
Apple Inc. (03783310)							**1.02**
CLIENT:/DEMO_SEA/ABCFUND.ACCT	ABC FUND	11,913,712	905,736,411	6.22	0.56	5.66	0.83
CLIENT:/DEMO_SEA/ALASKA.ACCT	ALASKA	–	–	–	3.16	–3.16	–
CLIENT:/DEMO_SEA/CALIFORNIA.ACCT	CALIFORNIA	153,867	11,697,692	0.46	3.16	–2.70	0.01
CLIENT:/DEMO_SEA/DEFFUND.ACCT	DEF FUND	–	–	–	0.56	–0.56	–
CLIENT:/DEMO_SEA/EUROPEANOPPORTUNITIES.ACCT	EUROPEAN OPPORTUNITIES	232,848	17,702,198	3.87	–	3.87	0.02
CLIENT:/DEMO_SEA/GHIFUND.ACCT	GHI FUND	–	–	–	0.56	–0.56	–
CLIENT:/DEMO_SEA/GLOBALGROWTH.ACCT	GLOBAL GROWTH	–	–	–	0.24	–0.24	–
CLIENT:/DEMO_SEA/GLOBALOPPORTUNITIES.ACCT	GLOBAL OPPORTUNITIES	–	–	–	0.24	–0.24	–
CLIENT:/DEMO_SEA/GLOBALSMALLCAP.ACCT	GLOBAL SMALL CAP	–	–	–	0.24	–0.24	–
CLIENT:/DEMO_SEA/GLOBALVALUE.ACCT	GLOBAL VALUE	–	–	–	0.24	–0.24	–
CLIENT:/DEMO_SEA/HAWAII.ACCT	HAWAII	–	–	–	3.16	–3.16	–
CLIENT:/DEMO_SEA/IDAHO.ACCT	IDAHO	130,200	9,895,415	3.96	3.16	0.80	0.01
CLIENT:/DEMO_SEA/INTERNATIONALCORE.ACCT	INTERNATIONAL CORE	16,065	1,221,337	5.96	–	5.96	0.00
CLIENT:/DEMO_SEA/INTERNATIONALGROWTH.ACCT	INTERNATIONAL GROWTH	111,832	8,501,994	4.49	–	4.49	0.01
CLIENT:/DEMO_SEA/INTERNATIONALVALUE.ACCT	INTERNATIONAL VALUE	46,620	3,544,271	1.71	–	1.71	0.00

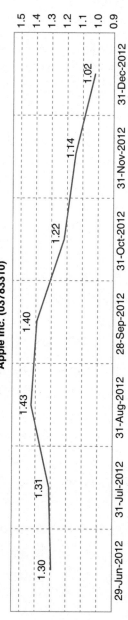

% of Total Weight
Apple Inc. (03783310)

Exhibit 12.9 Firm-wide security exposure.
Source: FactSet.

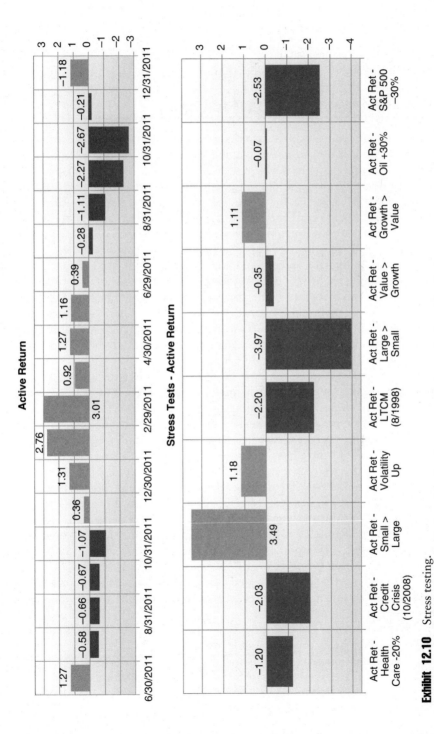

Exhibit 12.10 Stress testing.

Note: All stress testing returns displayed in the charts are relative to the benchmark.

Source: FactSet.

of 1.18%. The biggest downside exposure for the portfolio is when large cap stocks outperform small cap stocks (–3.97%), followed by the scenario when the S&P 500 drops 30% (–2.53%).

12.6 PORTFOLIO PERFORMANCE EVALUATION

Portfolio performance gets tracked and evaluated at regular intervals. We consider the portfolio from the example in Section 12.4 to illustrate how a portfolio manager could perform risk attribution.[10] A portfolio manager would begin by looking at overall portfolio performance. In this example (see Exhibit 12.11), the manager is looking at total active return (the medium gray line) over a time period of a year and a half (from June 2011 to December 2012). The portfolio active return has dropped significantly over the past year. By plotting stock-specific (light gray line) and factor-explained (darkest gray line) return on the same graph, the portfolio manager can observe that most of the underperformance is because of wrong factor allocation. (This is because the part of the return explained by factors is consistently negative.) Stock-specific return, on the other hand, is accept-able, which means that the portfolio manager is doing a reasonably good job of selecting individual stocks. The portfolio manager should probably reevaluate his factor allocation decision.

Let us perform more granular analysis on the factor allocation ques-tion. Specifically, let us look at the investment decisions by industry sector. Exhibit 12.12 shows the risk attribution by sectors.

The tornado graph in Exhibit 12.12 shows that stock selection was pos-itive within the Energy, Consumer Discretionary, Materials, and Utilities sectors. (The light gray bars, corresponding to a stock-specific effect, are all on the positive side for these sectors.) However, in all of these sectors the manager made poor factor allocation decisions. (For those sectors, the darkest gray bars, indicating factor effects, are all on the negative side of the graph.) For some of these sectors, such as the Energy and the Consumer Discretionary sectors, good stock selection made up for the problems with factor allocation. (The total effect, represented by the medium gray bars, is positive.) However, for other sectors, such as the Materials and the Utilities sectors, faulty factor selection erased all gains from the superior stock selec-tion within the sector. (The total effect, as represented by the medium gray bars, is negative.)

Which factors are to blame for this performance? Let us perform factor attribution for the factors in the style category.

The tornado graph in the left panel in Exhibit 12.13 shows that Volatility was by far the largest factor contributing negatively to cumulative portfolio

---

[10]See Chapter 9.7 for definition of risk attribution.

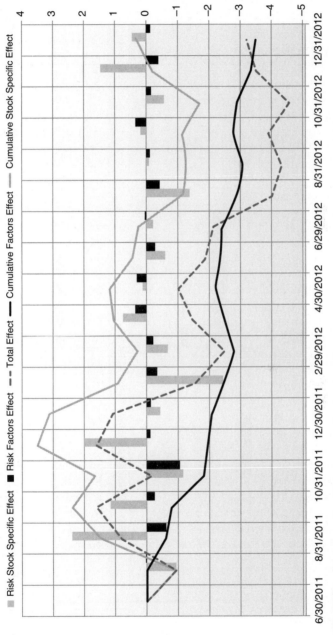

Exhibit 12.11 Risk-based performance attribution (total).

Source: FactSet.

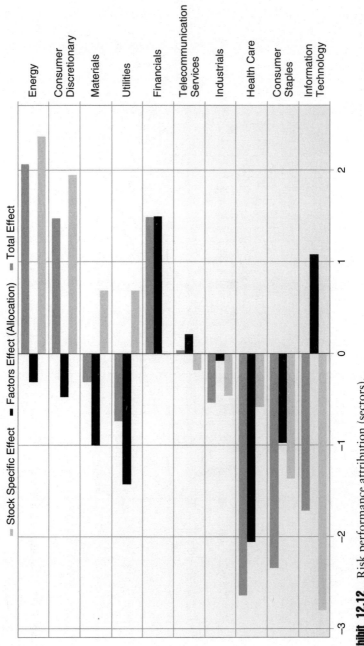

Exhibit 12.12 Risk performance attribution (sectors).
Source: FactSet.

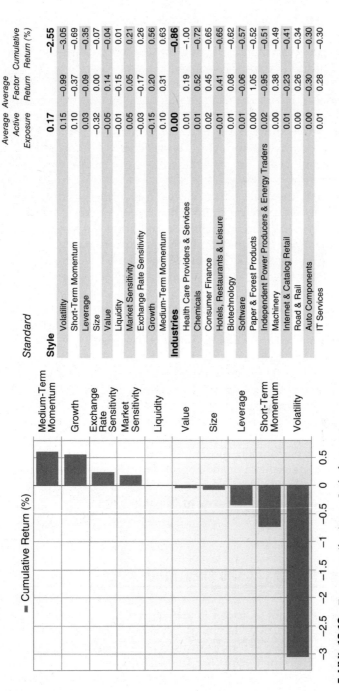

Standard	Average Active Exposure	Average Factor Return	Cumulative Return (%)
Style	**0.17**		**-2.55**
Volatility	0.15	-0.99	-3.05
Short-Term Momentum	0.10	-0.37	-0.69
Leverage	0.03	-0.09	-0.35
Size	-0.32	0.00	-0.07
Value	-0.05	0.14	-0.04
Liquidity	-0.01	-0.15	0.01
Market Sensitivity	0.05	0.05	0.21
Exchange Rate Sensitivity	-0.03	-0.17	0.26
Growth	-0.15	0.20	0.56
Medium-Term Momentum	0.10	0.31	0.63
Industries	**0.00**		**-0.86**
Health Care Providers & Services	0.01	0.19	-1.00
Chemicals	0.01	0.52	-0.72
Consumer Finance	0.02	0.45	-0.65
Hotels, Restaurants & Leisure	-0.01	0.41	-0.65
Biotechnology	0.01	0.08	-0.62
Software	0.01	-0.06	-0.57
Paper & Forest Products	0.00	1.05	-0.52
Independent Power Producers & Energy Traders	0.02	-0.95	-0.51
Machinery	0.00	0.38	-0.49
Internet & Catalog Retail	0.01	-0.23	-0.41
Road & Rail	0.00	0.26	-0.34
Auto Components	0.00	-0.30	-0.30
IT Services	0.01	0.28	-0.30

Exhibit 12.13 Factor attribution—Style factors.

Source: FactSet.

return. Short-Term Momentum, Leverage, Size, and Value all contributed negatively as well, but to a lesser extent. Medium-Term Momentum and Growth, on the other hand, were the two largest positive contributors to cumulative portfolio return. A systematic bet on Growth appears to have paid off.

The table in the right panel in Exhibit 12.13 shows how weighting each decision on each factor contributed to performance. The portfolio was overweighed in the Volatility factor (the average active exposure was 0.15%), which had a negative factor return on average (−0.99%) relative to the benchmark, and hence the cumulative negative active portfolio return attributable to this factor was −3.05%.

At the same time, the portfolio was overweighed in the Growth factor (+0.15% in active weight), and it had a positive factor return on average (+0.20%) relative to the benchmark, and hence the cumulative positive active portfolio return attributable to this factor was +0.56%.

Further time series analysis of the Growth factor (Exhibit 12.14) reveals that the systematic bet on Growth was consistently a positive contributor to portfolio active return. Specifically, the graph in the top panel shows that the portfolio was consistently overweighed in the Growth factor (the dark gray bars are all positive) and the factor impact (represented by the medium gray bars in the top graph) was mostly positive. The cumulative factor impact, represented by the light gray line in the top graph, was overwhelmingly positive, as it followed the general positive factor return for Growth in the market as a whole (the bottom panel in Exhibit 12.14).

Finally, the time series graph in Exhibit 12.15 allows for comparison of the general market performance for all factors in the Style category over the year-and-a-half period under consideration. As one can observe from the graph, Volatility performed consistently worse (it was consistently more negative) than the other Style factors. Short-Term Momentum, Liquidity, and Leverage were also negative performers, albeit to a lesser extent. Consistent positive performance was achieved by Medium-Term Momentum, Growth, and Value.

12.7   RISK FORECASTS AND SIMULATION

Factor models are not as useful for return forecasting as they are for risk decomposition. However, they may still provide meaningful information when trying to glimpse at future portfolio performance. Portfolio managers need to be aware that short-horizon factor models can only provide short-term forecasts, and long-horizon factor models are not necessarily

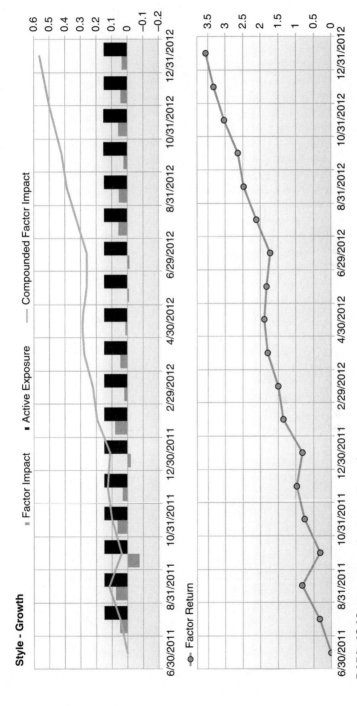

Exhibit 12.14 Factor attribution—Growth.

Source: FactSet.

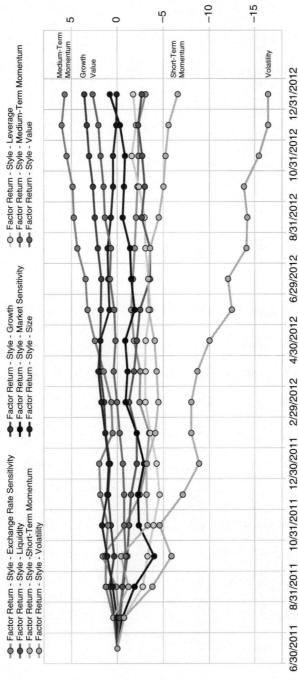

Exhibit 12.15 Factor returns (historical performance).

Source: FactSet.

good at predicting short-term performance.[11] In general, the reliability of factor model predictions decreases dramatically as one tries to look further into the future.[12]

Still, factors are more likely to exhibit consistent behavior than individual stocks. Understanding the factors that contribute to the variability of the portfolio and how they have behaved historically can help simulate meaningful scenarios about how the portfolio may perform in the future.

Forecasts of future portfolio risk and return are often done by Monte Carlo simulation.[13] By breaking down the sources of portfolio return, building models to explain them, and simulating the returns of the individual factors to calculate total portfolio return, managers can obtain a distribution for possible future portfolio returns, which includes the values of the returns at a particular date in the future, and the probabilities that they will happen. On this basis, one can calculate metrics of portfolio performance, such as value-at-risk (VaR) and conditional value-at-risk (CVaR).[14]

The output typically looks like the histogram of simulated future portfolio returns in Exhibit 12.16. Based on the histogram, the 20 Trading Day 95% VaR for the portfolio example from Section 12.4 (labeled 95% on the graph) is 7.36%. This is interpreted as follows: the portfolio loss after 20 trading days will be at most 7.36% of the portfolio value with 95% probability. The 20 Trading Day 95% CVaR, the average of the simulated portfolio returns in the shaded left area of the histogram in Exhibit 12.16, is 9.25% (not shown on the graph). The interpretation is that there is a 95% probability that the average portfolio loss after 20 trading days will be at most 9.25%. The 20 Trading Day 90% VaR is 5.72%.

Simulation can be used also to generate portfolio returns under unusual market conditions. If an extreme event such as the market crash of October 2008 is included in the simulation for our portfolio example, then the 95% VaR under such an extreme scenario is almost double the 95% VaR for typical market conditions: 14.65% instead of 7.36%. The 95% CVaR

---

[11]See also the discussion in Chapter 9.5.5.

[12]This can be compared to predicting the weather. Just a couple of decades ago, next-day weather forecasts used to be very unreliable. Now weather forecasting models have gotten much more sophisticated, and one can predict the weather within three or four days quite reliably. But we have reached the limit. Building more sophisticated models and collecting more data do not help predict the weather 10 days out reliably. The reason for this is that sometimes, a tiny change in conditions in one part of the world can dramatically change the weather in another part. This is in fact the definition of chaos.

[13]See Chapter 5.

[14]See Chapters 2.6.2.5, 2.6.2.6, and 11.2.

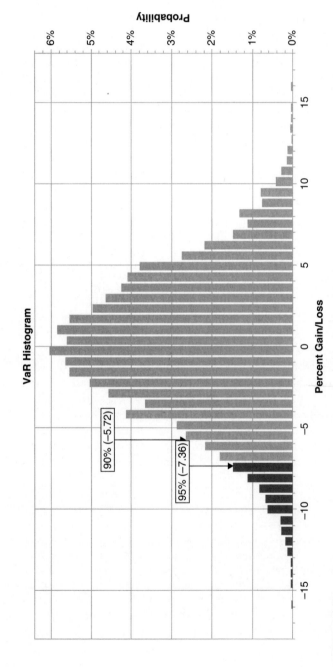

Exhibit 12.16 Simulated value-at-risk for the portfolio example from Section 12.4.
Source: FactSet.

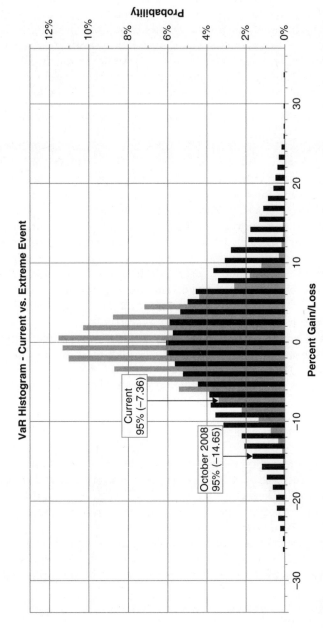

Exhibit 12.17 Simulated value-at-risk under current and "extreme" (October 2008) market conditions for the portfolio example from Section 12.4.

Source: FactSet.

is also much larger: 18.41% instead of 9.25%. The actual way in which extreme simulation is done varies among portfolio risk management software vendors, but in the calculation of the VaR and CVaR for this example the covariance matrix relevant for the market conditions of October 2008 is used to simulate future factor returns and then evaluate the future portfolio return. Exhibit 12.17 illustrates the difference in the distributions of returns obtained by simulation under current market conditions (light gray histogram) and the market conditions of October 2008 (dark gray histogram).

Summary

- Factors are used at many stages of the equity portfolio management process, including for fundamental screening, portfolio selection, risk decomposition, and performance attribution analysis.
- The most common groups of factors used in equity investments include fundamental factors (such as value, growth, liquidity), macroeconomic factors (such as GDP, consumer sentiment index, broad market indices such as the S&P 500 index), technical factors (such as momentum), social responsibility factors (such as employee relations, environment, or human rights), corporate finance policy factors (such as stock buybacks and insider purchases), and analysts' forecasts.
- Stock screens are methods for ranking stocks in the investment universe so that it is possible to differentiate between desirable and undesirable investments.
- Rankings based on z-scores provide a simple analytical framework for ranking stocks based on one or several criteria.
- Ad-hoc methods for portfolio selection relative to a benchmark include selecting the largest-weight stocks from the benchmark and stratification.
- Stratification is a method for dividing stocks in a benchmark in nonoverlapping "buckets" according to common characteristics, and selecting stocks from the buckets either to mirror the characteristics of the benchmark or to tilt the portfolio away from certain characteristics of the benchmark based on the portfolio manager's views.
- Factor exposure targeting uses the betas from factor models to control a portfolio's exposure to particular factors. To accomplish this, one imposes factor-type constraints inside portfolio optimization routines.
- Risk decomposition breaks down portfolio risk into its components. For example, a portfolio manager could use risk decomposition to identify

what percentage of portfolio risk (variability) is due to style factor risk (variability), and then look into which style factors contribute the most to that risk (variability).

- Stress testing involves running the portfolio through hypothetical scenarios to see how the portfolio would perform if such scenarios were to occur. Stress testing can be based on factor shocks or extreme scenarios.
- Portfolio performance evaluation can be done by performing risk attribution or assessing performance according to metrics of tail risk such as value-at-risk and conditional value-at-risk.
- Risk attribution breaks down the total risk (volatility) realized by the portfolio over a specified evaluation period to estimate the contributions of different sources of risk.
- Value-at-risk and conditional value-at-risk measure the extreme risks associated with the current portfolio composition based on the distribution of portfolio returns over the evaluation period.

PART

Five

Fixed Income Portfolio Management

CHAPTER 13

Fundamentals of Fixed Income Portfolio Management

This chapter introduces fixed income portfolio management in practice. We begin by describing the different sectors of the bond market. We then review fundamental fixed income terminology, including features of fixed income securities (term to maturity, maturity, coupon rate, par value, yield, provisions for paying off bonds, and bondholder option provisions) as well as major sources of risk for a bond investor. Important fixed income analytics concepts for measuring bond portfolio risk, including duration, convexity, key rate duration, and spread duration, are discussed next. We conclude with an overview of the spectrum of bond portfolio strategies. The next chapter shows explicit examples of how these concepts are used in the context of fixed income portfolio construction and risk decomposition with factor models.

13.1 FIXED INCOME INSTRUMENTS AND MAJOR SECTORS OF THE BOND MARKET

A fixed income security is a financial instrument whereby an entity agrees to make specified payments to the holder of the security. The key feature is that the entity issuing the security (i.e., the issuer) will be making contractually specified payments according to a schedule. Bear in mind that the payments need not be fixed in dollar amounts. The amounts can vary over time but what is important is that the holder of the security cannot receive more than the scheduled amount.

Fixed income securities are classified as either a debt instrument or a form of equity called *preferred stock*. Debt instruments include bonds, notes, and loans. These instruments obligate the issuer of the obligation to make interest payments over time and repay the amount borrowed. Failure to satisfy the payment obligation by the issuer will result in a default, which then requires the immediate repayment of the debt obligation. Failure to do so by the issuer allows the holder of the security to force the issuer into bankruptcy proceedings.

Debt obligations also include *asset-backed securities* (ABS), which are securities backed by pools of loans—mortgages or receivables (e.g., credit card receivables or automobile receivables). The assets in ABS pools are typically too small or illiquid to be sold individually. Pooling the assets allows them to be sold in pieces to investors, a process known as *securitization*. The largest sector of the ABS market by far is securities backed by pools of mortgages, referred to as *mortgage-backed securities* (MBS).

In the case of preferred stock, which is a form of equity, the issuer agrees to make dividend payments and pay a stated amount to the security holder at some future date. Failure of the issuer to make dividend payments and/or the stated amount does not allow the security holder to force the issuer into bankruptcy. The reason is that preferred stock is just a special type of equity giving preferred stockholders priority of distribution of dividends (when declared by the board of directors) over the common stockholders and priority in receipt of proceeds in the case of a bankruptcy.

In this chapter and those to follow, our focus is on debt obligations. Although debt obligations include bonds, notes, and loans, we refer to them as simply bonds, and also use the terms "fixed income security" and "bond" interchangeably.

The major sectors of the U.S. bond market are the (1) Treasury securities market, (2) federal agency securities market, (3) corporate bond market, (4) municipal bonds market, (5) non-U.S. bond market, (6) agency residential mortgage-backed securities market, (7) nonagency residential mortgage securities market, (8) commercial mortgage-backed securities market, and (9) asset-backed securities market. The last four bond sectors are collectively referred to as the *structured product sector* because these bonds are more complex than the typical bond structure.

13.1.1   Treasury Securities

Treasury securities are issued by the U.S. Department of the Treasury (U.S. Treasury hereafter). Because they are backed by the full faith and credit of the U.S. government, market participants throughout the world view them as having little default risk and therefore the yields offered on these securities are used as a benchmark to measure credit spreads offered on non-Treasury securities.

The U.S. Treasury does not issue zero-coupon notes or bonds. However, because of the demand for zero-coupon instruments with minimal perceived default risk, the private sector has created such securities as part of the U.S. Treasury's Separate Trading of Registered Interest and Principal of Securities (STRIPS) program.[1]

13.1.2 Federal Agency Securities

Federal agency securities can be classified by the type of issuer—federally related institutions and government-sponsored enterprises. Federal agencies that provide credit for certain sectors of the credit market issue two types of securities: debentures and mortgage-backed securities.

Federally related institutions are arms of the federal government and generally do not issue securities directly into the marketplace. Examples of federally related institutions that issue securities are the Tennessee Valley Authority and the Private Export Funding Corporation. With certain exceptions (e.g., securities of the Tennessee Valley Authority and the Private Export Funding Corporation), securities issued by federally related institutions are backed by the full faith and credit of the U.S. government.

Government-sponsored enterprises (GSEs) are privately owned, publicly chartered entities. They were created by Congress to reduce the cost of capital for certain borrowing sectors of the economy deemed to be important enough to warrant assistance. GSEs issue securities directly in the marketplace. With the exception of the securities issued by the Farm Credit Financial Assistance Corporation, GSE securities are not backed by the full faith and credit of the U.S. government, as is the case with Treasury securities. Consequently, investors purchasing GSEs are exposed to credit risk.

13.1.3 Corporate Bonds

Corporate bonds are classified into three sectors: utilities, financials, and industries. *Utilities* include investor-owned companies that are involved in the generation, transmission, and distribution of electricity, gas, and water. *Financials* include bonds issued by a wide range of financial institutions—banks, insurance companies, securities firms, brokerage firms, mortgage firms, and finance companies. The *industrials* sector is the catchall category. It includes companies that are not utilities or financials.

---

[1]These securities are created via a process referred to as *coupon stripping*.

13.1.4 Municipal Bonds

Municipal bonds are bonds issued by states, municipalities, counties, towns and townships, school districts, and special service system districts. There are tax-exempt and taxable municipal securities. "Tax-exempt" means that interest on a municipal security is exempt from federal income taxation. The tax exemption of municipal securities applies to interest income, not capital gains. The exemption may or may not extend to taxation at the state and local levels. Most municipal securities that have been issued are tax exempt.

Municipal bonds are issued for various purposes. There are basically two types of municipal security structures: tax-backed debt and revenue bonds. Tax-backed debt obligations are secured by some form of tax revenue. The broadest type of tax-backed debt obligation is the general obligation debt. Revenue bonds are issued for enterprise financings that are secured by the revenues generated by the completed projects themselves.

13.1.5 Structured Products

As we mentioned earlier, an asset-backed security (ABS) is a debt instrument backed by a pool of loans or receivables. ABSs are also referred to as *structured products*. The process for the creation of asset-backed securities, referred to as *securitization*, begins when the owner of assets sells a *pool of assets* (an aggregation of large numbers of loans such as mortgages with similar but not identical characteristics) to a bankruptcy remote vehicle called a *special purpose entity* (SPE). The SPE obtains the proceeds to acquire the asset pool, referred to as the *collateral*, by issuing debt instruments. The cash flow of the asset pool is used to satisfy the obligations of the debt instruments issued by the SPE. With the creation of an ABS, loans are transformed from a heterogeneous group of disparate assets into sizeable and homogeneous securities that trade in a liquid market.

ABSs issued in a single securitization can have different credit exposure and, based on the priority for receiving payments and absorbing credit losses, such securities are described as *senior notes* and *junior notes* (*subordinate notes*). There are rules that are used to allocate the collateral's cash flow among the different classes of investors.

There is considerable diversity in the types of assets that have been securitized. These assets can be classified as mortgage assets and nonmortgage assets. Securities backed by residential and commercial mortgage loans are referred to as residential mortgage–backed securities (RMBS) and commercial mortgage–backed securities (CMBS), respectively. In turn, RMBS can be further classified as agency RMBS and private-label (or nonagency)

RMBS. Agency RMBS are those issued by three government-related entities (Ginnie Mae, Fannie Mae, and Freddie Mac)[2] and is by far the largest sector in the investment-grade bond market. They include (1) mortgage-passthrough securities, (2) collateralized mortgage obligations, and (3) stripped mortgage-backed securities. In the case of mortgage passthrough securities, the monthly cash flow from the pool of mortgage loans is distributed on a pro rata basis to the security holders. The monthly cash flow distributed consists of three components: (1) interest, (2) regularly scheduled principal payments (amortization), and (3) prepayments.

Private-label RMBS are issued by any other entity. Because of the credit risk associated with private-label RMBS, they require credit enhancement to provide some form of credit protection against default on the pool of assets backing a transaction. Credit enhancement mechanisms are typical in ABS transactions.

13.2 FEATURES OF FIXED INCOME SECURITIES

Having reviewed the types of debt obligations and the sectors of the bond market, we provide an overview of bond features to set up the discussion of fixed income portfolio analytics. Features of a bond include (1) maturity, (2) par value, (3) coupon rate, (4) yield, and (5) provisions for paying off a bond issue.

13.2.1 Term to Maturity and Maturity

Unlike common stock, which has a perpetual life, bonds have a date on which they mature. The number of years over which the issuer has promised to meet the conditions of the obligation is referred to as the *term to maturity*. The *maturity* of a bond refers to the date on which the debt will cease to exist, at which time the issuer will redeem the bond by paying the amount borrowed.

There are provisions that may be included in the indenture that grant either the issuer or the bondholder the right to alter a bond's term to maturity. These provisions include call provisions, put provisions, and conversion provisions, which we describe later because of how they impact the potential price performance of a bond.

---

[2]Ginnie Mae (Government National Mortgage Association) is an agency of the U.S. government, carrying the full faith and credit of U.S. government. Fannie Mae and Freddie Mac are GSEs.

The term to maturity of a bond is important. The first reason is that the yield[3] on a bond depends on it. At any given point in time, the relationship between the yield and the maturity of a bond indicates how bondholders are compensated for investing in bonds with different maturities. This relationship is referred to as the *term structure of interest rates*. The second reason is that the price of a bond will fluctuate over its life as interest rates in the market change. The degree of price volatility of a bond is dependent on its term to maturity as well.

13.2.2 Par Value

The *par value* of a bond is the amount that the issuer agrees to repay the bondholder by the maturity date. This amount is also referred to as the *principal*, *notional*, *face value*, *redemption value*, or *maturity value*.

Because bonds can have a different par value, the practice is to quote the price of a bond as a percentage of its par value. A value of 100 means 100% of par value. So, for example, if a bond has a par value of $1,000 and is selling for $950, this bond would be said to be selling at 95. If a bond with a par value of $100,000 is selling for $103,000, the bond is said to be selling for 103.

13.2.3 Coupon Rate

The coupon rate is the annual interest rate that the issuer agrees to pay each year. The annual amount of the interest payment made to bondholders during the term of the bond is called the *coupon* and is determined by multiplying the coupon rate by the par value of the bond. For example, a bond with a 4% coupon rate and a par value of $1,000 will pay annual interest of $40.

For bonds issued in the United States, the usual practice is for the issuer to pay the coupon in two semiannual installments. Mortgage-backed securities and asset-backed securities typically pay interest monthly. For bonds issued in some markets outside the United States, coupon payments are made only once per year.

Not all bonds make periodic coupon payments. Zero-coupon bonds, as the name indicates, do not make periodic coupon payments. Instead, the holder of a zero-coupon bond realizes interest at the maturity date. The aggregate interest earned is the difference between the maturity value and the purchase price. For example, if an investor purchases a zero-coupon bond for 73, the aggregate interest at the maturity date is 27, the difference

---

[3]We explain yield in more detail in Section 13.2.4.

between the par value (100) and the price paid (73). The reason why certain investors like zero-coupon bonds is that they eliminate *reinvestment risk*: the risk of having to reinvest the proceeds from coupons at a lower interest rate than the interest rate on the bond. The disadvantage of a zero-coupon bond is that the accrued interest earned each year is taxed despite the fact that no actual cash payment is made.

A coupon-bearing security need not have a fixed interest rate over the term of the bond. There are bonds that have an interest rate that is variable. These bonds are referred to as *floating-rate securities*. In fact, another way to classify bond markets is as the fixed-rate bond market and the floating-rate bond market. For a floating-rate security the interest rate is adjusted on specific dates, referred to as the *coupon reset dates*. There is a formula for the new coupon rate, referred to as the *coupon reset formula*, which has the following generic form:

Coupon reset formula = Reference rate + Quoted margin

The quoted margin is the additional amount that the issuer agrees to pay above the reference rate. The most common reference rate is the London Interbank Offered Rate (LIBOR). LIBOR is the interest rate that major international banks offer each other on Eurodollar certificates of deposit with given maturities. While the reference rate for most floating-rate securities is an interest rate or an interest rate index, there are some issues for which this is not the case. Instead, the reference rate can be some financial index such as the return on the Standard & Poor's 500 index or a nonfinancial index such as the price of a commodity or the consumer price index.

The coupon rate affects the bond's price sensitivity to changes in market interest rates, as we explain later in this chapter.

13.2.4 Bond Valuation and Yield

The value of a bond B_0 is the discounted sum of its payments. In other words,

$$B_0 = \frac{C_1}{(1+r)} + \frac{C_2}{(1+r)^2} + \frac{C_3}{(1+r)^3} + \cdots + \frac{C_T}{(1+r)^T}$$

where C_t denotes the cash flow (coupons or coupon plus principal) paid at date t. Although the concept is simple, the details of its implementation, including how to determine an appropriate discount rate, can lead to different valuations. The minimum interest rate r an investor should require is the prevalent discount rate in the marketplace on a default-free cash flow.[4]

---

[4]In the United States, U.S. Treasuries are considered the norm for default-free securities. This is one of the reasons the Treasury market is closely watched.

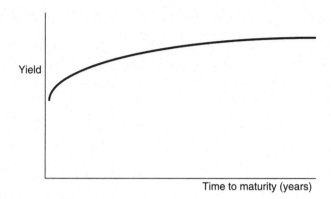

Exhibit 13.1 An upward-sloping yield curve.

The implied interest rate that makes the present value of the stream of cash flows equal to the bond price observed in the market is called the *yield to maturity* (YTM), or simply *yield*. It is quoted on an annual basis.

As we mentioned earlier, observed bond yields tend to be different depending on the time to maturity. The plot of bond yields versus the length of time corresponding to these yields is referred to as the *yield curve*.[5] An example of a yield curve is given in Exhibit 13.1. The usual shape of the yield curve is upward-sloping; however, the yield curve can have different shapes depending on market conditions. The reason why an upward-sloping curve is considered "normal" is because investors are assumed to demand more yield for long-term investments than for short-term investments. Long-term investments are subject to more uncertainty. However, sometimes long-term bonds have lower yields than short-term bonds. In the latter case, we refer to the yield curve as an *inverted yield curve*. If the yields for all maturities were the same, of course, the yield curve would simply be a flat horizontal line.

13.2.5 Provisions for Paying Off Bonds

The issuer of a bond agrees to repay the principal by the stated maturity date. The issuer can repay the entire amount borrowed in one lump sum payment at the maturity date. That is, the issuer is not required to make any

---

[5]A related term is the term structure of interest rates. The term structure of interest rates is in fact a yield curve but its meaning is a bit more academic, as it focuses on pure interest rates for default-free securities rather than bond yields.

principal repayments prior to the maturity date. Such bonds are said to have a *bullet maturity*.

Bonds backed by pools of loans (mortgage-backed securities and asset-backed securities) often have a schedule of principal repayments. Such bonds are said to be *amortizing securities*. For many loans, the payments are structured so that when the last loan payment is made, the entire amount owed is fully paid off.

A bond issue may have a call provision granting the issuer an option to retire all or part of the issue prior to the stated maturity date. Some issues specify that the issuer must retire a predetermined amount of the issue periodically. These provisions include (1) call and refunding provisions and (2) prepayment provisions.

13.2.5.1 Call and Refunding Provisions A call provision grants the issuer the right to retire the issue prior to the stated maturity date. This provision is basically a call option granted to the issuer and hence a bond with this provision is referred to as a *callable bond*. The call price is the price that an issuer must pay to call the bond issue.

When a bond is issued, the issuer may be restricted from calling the bond for a number of years. In such situations, the bond is said to have a deferred call. If a bond issue does not have any protection against early call, then it is said to be a currently callable issue. But most new bond issues, even if currently callable, usually have some restrictions against certain types of early redemption.

A provision that gives an issuer the right to retire a bond issue prior to the stated maturity date is an advantage to the issuer and a disadvantage to the bondholder. Typically, the issuer will exercise this right if interest rate declines sufficiently below the issue's coupon rate to justify the costs associated with paying off the issue and replacing it with another bond issue with a lower coupon rate. There are two disadvantages to a bondholder. First, since proceeds received must be reinvested at a lower interest rate when the issuer calls the bond when interest rates are lower, the bondholder is exposed to reinvestment risk. The second disadvantage is in terms of price performance. Because there is the risk of a bond being called, its price has limited price appreciation when interest rates decline since, if called, the issue will only pay the call price to pay off the bond issue.

The most common restriction is prohibiting the refunding of the bonds for a certain number of years. Refunding a bond issue means redeeming bonds with funds obtained through the sale of a new bond issue.

When a bond is callable, there are multiple yield measures computed, referred to as the *yield to call*. Each yield to call measure assumes a particular date at which the bond will be called and the cash flows are computed accordingly. Once the cash flows are determined, the yield is calculated in the same way as the yield to maturity. Commonly used yield-to-call measures are *yield to first call* and *yield to first par call*.

For a callable bond, therefore, there may be more than one yield measure. A common practice that provides a conservative measure of yield is to calculate the lowest of all the yield measures. This measure is referred to as the *yield to worst*.

13.2.5.2 Prepayment Provisions Amortizing securities backed by loans have a schedule of principal repayments. However, individual borrowers typically have the option to pay off all or part of their loan prior to the scheduled principal repayment date. Any principal repayment prior to the scheduled date is called a *prepayment*. The right of borrowers to prepay is called the *prepayment option*.

The prepayment option is similar to a call option. However, unlike a call option, there is not a call price that depends on when the borrower pays off the issue. Typically, the price at which a loan is prepaid is at par value.

In the case of ABS and MBS, prepayment options are typically granted to all borrowers in a pool of loans. A yield measure can be calculated; however, this measure is not referred to as yield to maturity by most market participants. Instead, because it is based on a cash flow generated from an assumed prepayment rate, it is called a *cash flow yield*.

As for the maturity of an ABS and MBS, there is a legal maturity which is based on the maturity of the longest loan in the loan pool. Typically, investors ignore the legal maturity. Instead, they use a measure called *average life* or *weighted average life*, which is the average time to receipt of principal payments. To determine the average life, it is necessary to determine the principal payments over the security's life. Principal payments include regularly scheduled principal payments plus prepayments. To obtain prepayments, it is necessary to assume a prepayment rate. The principal payments are monthly. The average life is the time-weighted average maturity of the stream of principal payments, and is calculated as

$$\text{Average life} = \sum_{t=1}^{T} \frac{t \times (\text{Projected principal received at time } t)}{12 \times (\text{Total principal})}$$

where T is the legal maturity in months.

13.2.6 Bondholder Option Provisions

The most common type of option embedded in a bond is a call option, discussed already. This option is granted to the issuer. There are two options that can be granted to the bondholder: the right to put the issue and the right to convert the issue to the issuer's common stock.

A bond with a put provision grants the bondholder the right to sell the bond (that is, force the issuer to redeem the bond) at a specified price on designated dates. A bond with this provision is referred to as a *putable bond*. The specified price is called the *put price*. The advantage of the put provision to the bondholder is that if after the issue date market rates rise above the issue's coupon rate, the bondholder can force the issuer to redeem the bond at the put price and then reinvest the proceeds at the prevailing higher rate.

A *convertible bond* is an issue giving the bondholder the right to exchange the bond for a specified number of shares of the issuer's common stock. Such a feature allows the bondholder to take advantage of favorable movements in the price of the issuer's common stock. An *exchangeable bond* allows the bondholder to exchange the issue for a specified number of shares of common stock of a corporation different from the issuer of the bond.

13.3 MAJOR RISKS ASSOCIATED WITH INVESTING IN BONDS

It is obvious from the valuation formula in Section 13.2.4 that the value of a bond depends on the interest rates for discounting the cash flows, the amount and timing of the cash flows, and a variety of other considerations such as liquidity and the ability to reinvest payments at the same rate. The interest rate depends on the credit quality of the issuer. Bonds may therefore expose an investor to one or more of the following risks: (1) interest rate risk, (2) call and prepayment risk, (3) credit risk, and (4) liquidity risk. This section explains the risks in more detail. Factor models for fixed income portfolio management, which we discuss in Chapter 14, attempt to capture these risks.

13.3.1 Interest Rate Risk

The price of a bond will change in the opposite direction from a change in interest rates. That is, when interest rates rise, a bond's price will fall; when interest rates fall, a bond's price will rise. To see this, consider the example of a bond with a \$100 principal, a coupon rate of 10% paid annually, and a term to maturity of three years. Assume a discount rate of 6%. Today's value of the bond is

$$\frac{10}{(1+0.06)} + \frac{10}{(1+0.06)^2} + \frac{110}{(1+0.06)^3} = \$110.69$$

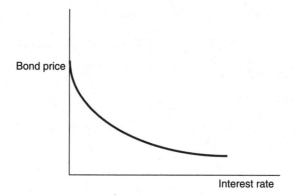

Exhibit 13.2   Relationship between bond price and interest rate.

If a 12% annual discount rate was used, the bond value today would have been

$$\frac{10}{(1+0.12)} + \frac{10}{(1+0.12)^2} + \frac{110}{(1+0.12)^3} = \$95.20$$

The value of the bond is lower when the required interest rate is higher. The relationship between bond prices and interest rates is actually nonlinear: the bond price is a convex function of interest rates (see Exhibit 13.2).

The degree of sensitivity of a bond's price to changes in market interest rates depends on various characteristics of the issue, such as maturity and coupon rate. Consider first maturity. All other factors constant, the longer the maturity is, the greater the bond's price sensitivity to changes in interest rates. Next consider the coupon rate. A property of a bond is that, all other factors constant, the lower the coupon rate, the greater the bond's price sensitivity to changes in interest rates. An implication of these two properties is that zero-coupon bonds have greater price sensitivity to interest rate changes than same-maturity bonds bearing a coupon rate and trading at the same yield. Finally, for a given coupon rate and maturity, the lower the level of interest rates, the greater the bond's price sensitivity to changes in market interest rates. So during periods of low interest rates, bond prices will be highly sensitive to changes in interest rates.

A bond's price sensitivity will also depend on any options embedded in the issue. This is explained below when we discuss call risk.

13.3.2   Call and Prepayment Risk

As explained earlier, a bond may include a provision that allows the issuer to retire or call all or part of the issue before the maturity date. We mentioned the two disadvantages of the inclusion of the call provision from the investor's perspective: (1) the risk of having to reinvest proceeds at a lower interest rate and (2) the capital appreciation potential of a bond will be reduced because the price of a callable bond may not rise much above the price at which the issuer is entitled to call the bond. Because of these disadvantages faced by the investor, a callable bond is said to expose the investor to *call risk*. The same disadvantages apply to asset-based and mortgage-backed securities that can prepay. In this case, the risk is referred to as *prepayment risk*.

13.3.3 Credit Risk

Credit risk refers to three forms of risk: default risk, credit spread risk, and downgrade risk.

13.3.3.1 Default Risk *Default risk* is the risk that the issuer will fail to satisfy the terms of the obligation with respect to the timely payment of interest and repayment of the amount borrowed. To gauge default risk, portfolio managers use as a screening process the credit ratings of nationally recognized statistical rating organizations (more popularly known as *rating agencies*) that perform credit analysis of bond issues and issuers and express their conclusions in the form of a credit rating. The three major rating agencies include Moody's Investors Service (Moody's), Standard & Poor's Corporation (S&P), and Fitch Ratings (Fitch).

The rating systems of the three rating agencies use similar symbols. Separate categories are used by each rating agency for short-term debt (with original maturity of 12 months or less) and long-term debt (over one year of original maturity). With respect to long-term debt ratings, with all rating systems the term "high grade" means low credit risk or, equivalently, high probability of future payments. The highest-grade bonds are designated by Moody's with the letters Aaa, and by the other rating agencies as AAA. The next highest grade is designated as Aa by Moody's, and by the others as AA; for the third grade, all rating agencies use A. The next three grades are Baa, Ba, and B by Moody's and BBB, BB, and B by S&P and Fitch. There are also C grades. S&P and Fitch use plus or minus signs to provide a narrower credit quality breakdown within each class. Moody's uses 1, 2, or 3 for the same purpose. Bonds rated triple A (AAA or Aaa) are said to be "prime"; double A (AA or Aa) are of "high quality"; single A issues are called "upper medium grade"; and triple B are "medium grade." Lower-rated bonds are said to have "speculative" elements or be "distinctly speculative."

Bond issues that are assigned a rating in the top four categories are referred to as *investment-grade bonds*. Bond issues that carry a rating below the top four categories are referred to as *noninvestment-grade bonds* or more popularly as *high-yield bonds* or *junk bonds*. Thus, the bond market can be divided into two sectors: the investment-grade sector and the noninvestment-grade sector. Distressed debt is a subcategory of noninvestment-grade bonds. These bonds may be in bankruptcy proceedings, may be in default of coupon payments, or may be in some other form of distress.

13.3.3.2 Credit Spread Risk The credit spread is the premium over the government or risk-free rate required by the market for taking on a certain perceived credit exposure. The benchmark is often the U.S. Treasury issue for the given maturity. The higher the credit rating, the smaller the credit spread to the benchmark rate, all other factors constant. *Credit spread risk* is the risk of financial loss resulting from changes in the level of credit spreads used in the marking-to-market of a debt instrument. Changes in market credit spreads affect the value of a fixed income portfolio and the performance relative to a portfolio manager's benchmark.

13.3.3.3 Downgrade Risk Once a credit rating is assigned to a debt obligation, a rating agency monitors the credit quality of the issuer and can reassign a different credit rating. An improvement in the credit quality of an issue or issuer is rewarded with a better credit rating, referred to as an *upgrade*; deterioration in the credit rating of an issue or issuer is penalized by the assignment of an inferior credit rating, referred to as a *downgrade*. The actual or anticipated downgrading of an issue or issuer increases the credit spread and results in a decline in the price of the issue or the issuer's bonds. This risk is referred to as *downgrade risk* and is closely related to credit spread risk. A rating agency may announce in advance that it is reviewing a particular credit rating, and may go further and state that the review is a precursor to a possible downgrade or upgrade. This announcement is referred to as "putting the issue under credit watch."

13.3.4 Liquidity Risk

Investors who want to sell a bond prior to the maturity date are concerned about whether the price that can be obtained from dealers is close to the true value of the issue. For example, if recent trades in the market for a particular issue have been between 97.25 and 97.75 and market conditions have not changed, investors would expect to sell the bond somewhere in the 97.25 to 97.75 range.

Liquidity risk is the risk that an investor will have to sell a bond below its true value, where the true value is indicated by recent transactions. The primary measure of liquidity is the size of the spread between the bid price (the price at which a dealer is willing to buy a security) and the ask price (the price at which a dealer is willing to sell a security). The wider the bid–ask spread, the greater the liquidity risk.

13.4 FIXED INCOME ANALYTICS

This section builds on Section 13.2 to explain fundamental concepts in measuring risk for individual fixed income securities and for bond portfolios. Concepts covered include duration, convexity, key rate duration, spread duration, and portfolio value-at-risk or conditional value-at-risk assessment using simulation.

13.4.1 Measuring Interest Rate Risk

As we mentioned earlier, the value of a bond investment is sensitive to changes in interest rates. Duration is the fundamental measure used to describe the sensitivity of a bond's price with respect to changes in interest rates. In mathematical terms, *duration* is the derivative of the bond price with respect to interest rates, that is, it measures *first-order sensitivity*. As Exhibit 13.1 shows, the relationship between the bond price and interest rates is in fact nonlinear, so the duration would not explain the exact change in bond prices for a given change in interest rates. Convexity, which we describe later, complements duration to provide a more accurate description.

It is important to note that both duration and convexity describe the sensitivity of bond prices to interest rates when there is a *parallel shift in the yield curve*, that is, when the rates for all maturities move up or down simultaneously and by the same number of basis points.[6] This clearly places a limitation on the usefulness of duration and convexity as measures of bond interest rate risk. Nevertheless, duration and convexity are very popular, fundamental tools for fixed income analytics.

13.4.1.1 Duration Defining duration as the first derivative of the price/yield function is mathematically correct; however, it is not really used in practice, because it is difficult to explain to clients what the relevance of such mathematical concept is to measuring actual investment risk.[7] Instead, duration is typically explained as the approximate price sensitivity of a bond to a

---

[6]One basis point is 1/100th of a percent, that is, 0.0001 or 0.01%.
[7]Moreover, for bonds that have embedded options such as callable bonds and mortgage-backed securities, there is no closed form solution for the price and hence referring to a first derivative for the duration of such securities offers little insight.

100 basis point change in rates. Thus, a bond with a duration of 5 will change by approximately 5% for a 100 basis point change in interest rates (that is, if the yield required for this bond changes by 100 basis points). For a 50 basis point change in interest rates, the bond's price will change by approximately 2.5%; for a 25 basis point change in interest rates, 1.25%, and so on.

Let us now define duration more rigorously. The exact formulation is

$$\frac{\text{Price if yields decline} - \text{Price if yields rise}}{2 \cdot (\text{Initial price}) \cdot (\text{Change in yield in decimal})}$$

Let D denote duration, B_0 denote the initial price, Δy denote the change in yield, B_- denote the price if yields decrease by Δy, and B_+ denote the price if yields increase by Δy. We have

$$D = \frac{B_- - B_+}{2 \cdot B_0 \cdot \Delta y}$$

It is important to understand that the two values in the numerator of the equation above, B_+ and B_-, are the estimated values obtained from a valuation model if interest rates change. Consequently, the duration measure is only as good as the valuation model employed to obtain these estimated values. The more difficult it is to estimate the value of a bond, the less confidence a portfolio manager may have in the estimated duration. The duration of a portfolio is nothing more than a market-weighted average of the duration of the bonds comprising the portfolio. Hence, a portfolio's duration is sensitive to the estimated duration of the individual bonds.

To illustrate the duration calculation, consider the following bond: a 6% coupon five-year bond trading at par value to yield 6%. The current price is $100. Suppose the yield is changed by 50 basis points. Thus, $\Delta y = 0.005$ and $B_0 = \$100$. This is a simple bond to value if interest rates or the yield change. If the yield is decreased to 5.5%, the value of this bond would be $102.1600. If the yield is increased to 6.5%, the value of this bond would be $97.8944. Therefore, $B_- = \$102.1600$ and $B_+ = \$97.8944$. Substituting into the equation for duration, we obtain

$$\text{Duration} = \frac{102.1600 - 97.8944}{2 \cdot (100) \cdot (0.005)} = 4.27$$

Dollar Duration In estimating the sensitivity of the price of bond to changes in interest rates, we looked at the percentage price change. However, for two bonds with the same duration but trading at different prices, the dollar price change will not be the same. To see this, suppose that we have two bonds,

A and B, that both have durations of 5. Suppose further that the current prices of A and B are $100 and $90, respectively. A 100 basis point change for both bonds will change the price by approximately 5%. This means a price change of $5 (5% times $100) for A, and a price change of $4.5 (5% times $90) for B.

The dollar price change of a bond can be measured by multiplying duration by the full dollar price and the number of basis points (in decimal form) and is called the *dollar duration*. That is,

Dollar duration = (Duration) · (Dollar price) · (Change in rates in decimal)

The dollar duration for a 100 basis point change in rates is

Dollar duration = (Duration) · (Dollar price) · 0.01

So, for bonds A and B, the dollar duration for a 100 basis point change in rates is

For bond A: Dollar duration = 5 · $100 · 0.01 = $5.00
For bond B: Dollar duration = 5 · $90 · 0.01 = $4.50

Knowing the dollar duration allows a trader to neutralize the risk of a bond position. For example, consider a position in bond B. If a trader wants to eliminate the interest rate risk exposure of this bond,[8] the trader will look for a position in one or more other financial instruments, such as an interest rate derivative, whose value will change in the opposite direction to bond B's price by an amount equal to $4.50. So, if the trader has a long position in (i.e., owns) bond B, the position will decline in value by $4.50 for a 100 basis point increase in interest rates. To eliminate this risk exposure, the trader can take a position in another financial instrument whose value increases by $4.50 if interest rates increase by 100 basis points.

The dollar duration can also be computed without knowing a bond's duration. This is done by simply looking at the average price change for a bond when interest rates are increased and decreased by the same number of basis points.

Modified Duration, Macaulay Duration, and Effective Duration A popular form of duration that is used by practitioners is modified duration. *Modified duration* is the approximate percentage change in a bond's price for a 100 basis point change in interest rates, assuming that the bond's cash

---

[8] A strategy that reduces or eliminates risk is called *hedging*.

flows do not change when interest rates change. What this means is that in calculating the values used in the numerator of the duration formula, the cash flows used to calculate the current price are assumed constant. Therefore, the change in the bond's value when interest rates change by a small number of basis points is due solely to discounting at the new yield level.

Modified duration is related to another measure commonly cited in the bond market: *Macaulay duration*. The formula for this measure, first used by Frederick Macaulay in 1938, is rarely used in practice, so it will not be produced here. For a bond that pays coupon interest semiannually, modified duration is related to Macaulay duration as follows:

$$\text{Modified duration} = \text{Macaulay duration}/(1 + \text{yield}/2)$$

where yield is the bond's yield to maturity in decimal form. Practically speaking, there is very little difference in the computed values for modified duration and Macaulay duration.

The assumption that the cash flows will not change when interest rates change makes sense for option-free bonds because the payments by the issuer are not altered when interest rates change. This is not the case for bonds with embedded options, mortgage-backed securities, and certain types of asset-backed securities. For these securities, a change in interest rates may alter the expected cash flows.

For such bonds, there are specific valuation models that take into account how changes in interest rates will affect cash flows. When the values used in the numerator of the equation for duration are obtained from a valuation model that takes into account both the discounting at different interest rates and how the cash flows can change, the resulting duration is referred to as *effective duration* or *option-adjusted duration*.

Duration of a Bond Portfolio   The interpretation of the duration of a portfolio is the same as for a single bond. A portfolio duration of 4, for example, means that the portfolio's market value will change by approximately 4% for a 100 basis point change in the interest rate for all maturities. A portfolio's duration is obtained by calculating the weighted average of the durations of the bonds in the portfolio. The weight for a bond is the proportion of the market value of the portfolio represented by the bond. Mathematically, we have

$$D_p = w_1 \cdot D_1 + w_2 \cdot D_2 + \ldots + w_N \cdot D_N$$

where N is the number of bonds in the portfolio, w_i is the weight of the ith bond, D_i is the duration of the ith bond, and D_p is the duration of the portfolio. The duration of a bond index is computed in the same way, since an index is simply a portfolio with particular weights.

A measure of the portfolio exposure to an individual issue or sector is given by its *contribution to portfolio duration*. This contribution is found by multiplying the percentage of the market value of the portfolio represented by the individual issue or sector times the duration of the individual issue or sector. That is,

Contribution to portfolio duration =
    (Weight of issue or sector in portfolio) × (Duration of issue or sector)

13.4.1.2 Convexity The duration measure indicates that regardless of whether interest rates increase or decrease, the approximate percentage price change is the same. However, although for small changes in yield the percentage price change will be the same for an increase or decrease in yield, for large changes in yield this is not true. Duration is only a good approximation of the percentage price change for a small change in yield.

The reason for this is that duration is in fact a first approximation for a small change in yield. The approximation can be improved by using a *second-order approximation*. This approximation is referred to as *convexity*. The use of this term in the industry is unfortunate since the term "convexity" is also used to describe the shape or curvature of the price/yield relationship. The convexity measure of a security can be used to approximate the change in price that is not explained by duration.

Convexity Measure   The convexity measure of a bond can be approximated using the following formula:

$$\text{Convexity measure} = \frac{B_+ + B_- - 2 \cdot B_0}{2 \cdot B_0 \cdot (\Delta y)^2}$$

where the notation is the same as used earlier for defining duration.

For a hypothetical 6%, 25-year bond selling to yield 9%, we can compute that for a 10 basis point change in yield ($\Delta y = 0.001$), we have $B_0 = 70.3570$, $B_- = 71.1105$, and $B_+ = 69.6164$. Substituting these values into the convexity measure given by the equation above, we obtain

$$\text{Convexity measure} = \frac{69.6164 + 71.1105 - 2 \cdot 70.3570}{2 \cdot 70.3570 \cdot (0.001)^2} = 91.67$$

We will see how to use this convexity measure shortly. Before doing so, there are three points that should be noted. First, there is no simple interpretation of the convexity measure as there is for duration.[9] Second, it is more common for market participants to refer to the value computed in the equation above as the "convexity of a bond" rather than the "convexity measure of a bond." Finally, the convexity measures reported by dealers and vendors will differ. The reason is that the convexity value obtained from the equation above will be scaled for the reason explained later.

Convexity Adjustment to Percentage Price Change Given the convexity measure, the approximate percentage price change adjustment due to the bond's convexity (i.e., the percentage price change not explained by duration) is

Convexity adjustment to percentage price change =
$$\text{Convexity measure} \cdot (\Delta y)^2 \cdot 100$$

For example, for the 6%, 25-year bond selling to yield 9%, the convexity adjustment to the percentage price change based on duration if the yield increases from 9% to 11% is

$$91.67 \cdot (0.02)^2 \cdot 100 = 3.67$$

If the yield decreases from 9% to 7%, the convexity adjustment to the approximate percentage price change based on duration would also be 3.67%.

The approximate percentage price change based on duration and the convexity adjustment is found by adding the two estimates. So, for example, if yields change from 9% to 11%, the estimated percentage price change would be:

Estimated change approximated by duration = −21.20%

Convexity adjustment = +3.66%

Total estimated percentage price change = −17.54%

The actual percentage price change can be computed to be −18.03%. Hence, the approximation has improved compared to using only duration.

---

[9]The intuition is mostly mathematical—convexity represents a quadratic approximation to the relative curvature at a given point of the price-yield curve, whereas duration represents a linear approximation. In effect, we are constructing the Taylor series of the bond price around a specific point of the price-yield curve, and considering the first two terms in the approximation.

For a decrease of 200 basis points, from 9% to 7%, the approximate percentage price change would be as follows:

$$\text{Estimated change approximated by duration} = +21.20\%$$

$$\text{Convexity adjustment} = +3.66\%$$

$$\text{Total estimated percentage price change} = +24.86\%$$

The actual percentage price change can be computed to be +25.46%. Once again, we see that duration combined with the convexity adjustment does a good job of estimating the sensitivity of a bond's price change to large changes in yield.

Scaling the Convexity Measure The convexity measure means nothing in isolation. It is the substitution of the computed convexity measure into the equation for the convexity adjustment that provides the necessary information. Therefore, it is possible to scale the convexity measure in any way and obtain the same convexity adjustment.

For example, the convexity measure is defined as follows:

$$\text{Convexity measure} = \frac{B_+ + B_- - 2 \cdot B_0}{B_0 \cdot (\Delta y)^2}$$

The equation above differs from the definition provided earlier because it does not include 2 in the denominator. Thus, the convexity measure computed using the equation above will be double the convexity measure using our earlier definition. So, for our earlier illustration, instead of a convexity measure of 91.67, we would obtain a convexity measure of 183.34.

Which is correct, 91.67 or 183.24? Both are correct. The reason is that the corresponding equation for computing the convexity adjustment can be adjusted accordingly.

Some dealers and vendors scale in a different way. Consequently, the convexity measure for our hypothetical bond could be reported as 9.17 or 18.3. It is the modification of the equation for the convexity adjustment that assures that regardless of how the convexity measure is scaled, it will produce the same approximate percentage change in bond price due to convexity.

Standard Convexity and Effective Convexity The bond prices used to calculate the convexity measure can be obtained by assuming either that when the yield changes the expected cash flows do not change, or that they do change. In the former case, the resulting convexity is the standard convexity, although in the industry the adjective "standard" is dropped.

Effective convexity, in contrast, assumes that the cash flows do change when yields change. The distinction is the same as the one made for duration and effective duration.

As with duration, for bonds with embedded options there can be a large difference between the calculated standard convexity and effective convexity. In fact, for all option-free bonds, either convexity measure will have a positive value. For bonds with embedded options, the calculated effective convexity can be negative when the calculated modified convexity is positive.

13.4.1.3 Key Rate Duration As we mentioned earlier, duration assumes that when interest rates change, all yields on the yield curve change by the same amount. This is a problem when using duration for a portfolio that will typically have bonds with different maturities. Consequently, it is necessary to be able to measure the exposure of a bond or bond portfolio to shifts in the yield curve. There have been several approaches to measuring yield curve risk. The most commonly used measure is *key rate duration* introduced by Ho (1992).

The basic principle of key rate duration is to change the yield for a particular maturity of the yield curve and determine the sensitivity of either an individual bond or a portfolio to that change holding all other yields constant. The sensitivity of the change in the bond's value or portfolio's value to a particular change in yield is called *rate duration*. There is a rate duration for every point on the yield curve. Consequently, there is not just one rate duration. Rather, there is a set of durations representing each maturity on the yield curve. Note that the total change in the value of a bond or a portfolio if all rates change by the same number of basis points is in fact the standard duration of a bond or portfolio.

Ho's approach focuses on 11 key maturities of the Treasury yield curve. These rate durations are called *key rate durations*. The specific maturities on the spot rate curve for which a key rate duration is measured are three months, one year, two years, three years, five years, seven years, 10 years, 15 years, 20 years, 25 years, and 30 years. Changes in rates between any two key rates are calculated using a linear approximation.

A key rate duration for a particular portfolio maturity should be interpreted as follows: holding the yield for all other maturities constant, the key rate duration is the approximate percentage change in the value of a portfolio (or bond) for a 100-basis-point change in the yield for the maturity whose rate has been changed. Thus, a key rate duration is quantified by changing the yield of the maturity of interest and determining how the value or price changes. In fact, the equation we introduced for duration is used. The prices denoted by B_- and B_+ in the equation are the prices a bond (in the case of a single security) and the portfolio values (in the case of a bond portfolio) found by holding all other interest rates constant and changing the yield for the maturity whose key rate duration is sought.

13.4.1.4 Yield Curve Scenario Analysis In addition to calculating key rate durations, when evaluating the yield curve risk of a portfolio, a more comprehensive picture of the risk exposure resulting from yield curve shifts is obtained by analyzing the distribution of the present values of the cash flows for the portfolio under different scenarios for the yield curve.

13.4.2 Measuring Spread Risk

Duration is a measure of the change in the value of a bond when rates change. The interest rate that is assumed to shift is the Treasury rate. However, for non-Treasury securities, the yield is equal to the Treasury yield plus a spread to the Treasury yield curve. The price of a bond exposed to credit risk can change even when Treasury yields are unchanged because the spread required by the market changes. A measure of how a non-Treasury issue's price will change if the spread sought by the market changes is called *spread duration* and is a measure of credit spread risk, which we described earlier in this chapter. There are three spread duration measures: nominal spread, zero-volatility spread, and option-adjusted spread.

The *nominal spread* is the traditional spread measure. That is, it is the difference between the yield on a spread product and the yield on a comparable maturity Treasury issue. Thus, when spread is defined as the nominal spread, spread duration indicates the approximate percentage change in price for a 100 basis point change in the nominal spread, holding the Treasury yield constant. It is important to note that, for any spread product, spread duration is the same as duration if the nominal spread is used. For example, suppose that the duration of a corporate bond is 5. This means that for a 100 basis point change in interest rates, the value of the corporate bond changes by approximately 5%. It does not matter whether the change in rates is due to a change in the level of rates (i.e., a change in the Treasury rate) or a change in the nominal spread.

The *zero-volatility spread*, *z-spread*, or *static spread*, is the spread that, when added to the Treasury spot rate curve, makes the present value of the cash flows (when discounted at the spot rates plus the spread) equal to the price of the bond plus accrued interest. It is a measure of the spread over the entire Treasury yield curve the investor would realize if the bond is held to maturity, rather than off one point on the Treasury yield curve, like the nominal spread. When spread is defined in this way, spread duration is the approximate percentage change in price for a 100 basis point change in the zero-volatility spread, holding the Treasury spot rate curve constant.

The *option-adjusted spread* (OAS) is another spread measure that can be interpreted as the approximate percentage change in price of a spread product for a 100 basis point change in the OAS, holding Treasury rates constant. The spread is called "option-adjusted" because the OAS attempts to take into consideration how the cash flows for bonds with embedded options could change if the spread changes. The OAS calculation relies on a valuation model that estimates the "fair" price of the fixed income security. The OAS (measured in basis points) is the spread that would make the market price of a security equal to the fair price. OAS models differ considerably in how they forecast interest rate changes, so the OAS could vary significantly as well. Two modeling assumptions having particularly strong impact on the value of the OAS are:

1. The OAS is the spread over the Treasury yield curve or over the benchmark curve used in the analysis. The curve itself is created based on a series of assumptions, and different models may lead to different values for the OAS.
2. The volatility in interest rates is a critical assumption. The higher the volatility assumed, the lower the OAS. The assumptions on volatility need to be compared when comparing the OAS calculated by dealer firms.

The zero-volatility spread is sometimes referred to as the *zero-volatility OAS* because it ignores the fact that interest rate changes can affect cash flows. In essence, it assumes that interest rate volatility is zero.

13.4.3 Measuring Credit Risk

The credit risk of a portfolio on a stand-alone basis or relative to a benchmark can be gauged by the portfolio allocation to each credit rating category. Another gauge is the contribution to duration by credit rating. Basically, the portfolio is divided into groups of bonds with the same credit rating, and the contribution to duration for each group is computed.

Additional metrics include percentage of portfolio volatility due to the probability of default of the securities in the portfolio. We will see an example in Chapter 14.

13.4.4 Estimating Fixed Income Portfolio Risk Using Simulation

Even though the measures described in the previous sections in this chapter are classical measures in bond portfolio management, many bond portfolio managers use additional measures, such as value-at-risk (VaR) and conditional value-at-risk (CVaR),[10] to obtain a fuller picture of portfolio risk.

To estimate the VaR or the CVaR of a bond portfolio, one needs to simulate the distribution of possible values for the portfolio (or the total return of the portfolio) at the end of the holding period. To understand the intuition behind the procedure, consider a simple example: suppose that a portfolio manager is trying to estimate the VaR of a $1 position in a bond with 10 years to maturity after a one-year investment. The steps are as follows:

1. The initial price of the bond is calculated (given the yield curve observable today).
2. Scenarios for the future values of interest rates are generated and the price of the bond (given those future interest rates) after one year is estimated. Let us call this price the "terminal price," because it is at the end of the investment horizon.
3. In each interest rate scenario, the losses from the position are calculated as the difference between the initial price and the terminal price (plus any coupon payments, appropriately discounted, that happen between today and one year from now).
4. There is now a series of observations from losses for the bond position. The VaR or the CVaR can be estimated using the techniques described in Chapters 2.6.2.5 and 2.6.2.6.

Suppose the portfolio manager would like to incorporate not only interest rate risk, but also credit risk in the VaR or CVaR estimate. To do that, the following additional factors should be taken into consideration during the simulation:

1. *The default process.* A default is a binary event, and the cash flows associated with default are distributed far from normal.
2. *The recovery rate.* The recovery rate is the amount recovered in the event of default. (The exact specification of recovery rate depends on the credit risk model used. For example, it could be measured as a percentage of the expected cash flows.)
3. *The dependence between market and default risk.* Even though the two are assumed to be independent in many pricing models, the reality is that the price difference between credit risky and riskless bonds will depend

---

[10]See Chapters 2.6.2.5 and 2.6.2.6.

on both types of risks in a complex way. In addition, the default probability may change over time.

4. *The complicated nature of credit enhancement agreements that often accompany credit risky positions.* Such agreements include collateral requirements, credit triggers, credit guarantee arrangements, and so on. In practice, these agreements help the institution manage its credit risk, but they make it more complicated to assess the actual impact of a credit event on a bond portfolio.

These complications make simulation a useful tool for approaching the modeling of credit-risky positions. The procedure for evaluating the VaR or CVaR of a credit risky bond is similar to the procedure for a nondefaultable bond described earlier in this section. However, to evaluate future cash flows, one would simulate the realizations of binary random variables that indicate whether the cash flows were received and how much was recovered if they were not received in full. (Once a bond has defaulted, the model should make sure that no future cash flows are received.)

Estimating the VaR or the CVaR of a portfolio of credit-risky bonds (as opposed to a position in a single bond) is more complicated, as one needs to simulate the dependencies between the defaults of the different bonds. Such dependencies can be modeled through different types of copula functions.[11] Calibrating (that is, finding the input parameters for) such models is very difficult in practice because historically there have been few observations of multiple defaults happening simultaneously.

13.5 THE SPECTRUM OF FIXED INCOME PORTFOLIO STRATEGIES

We conclude this chapter with an overview of the spectrum of fixed income portfolio strategies. In Chapter 14, we give examples of analytical approaches used to create these strategies.

A good way to think about the spectrum of bond portfolio strategies and the key elements of each strategy is in terms of the benchmark established by the client. This is depicted in Exhibit 13.3. Volpert (1997) classifies the strategies as follows:

- Pure bond index matching
- Enhanced indexing/primary factor matching
- Enhanced indexing/minor factor mismatches

---

[11]See Chapter 2.10 and Chapter 9 in Glasserman (2004).

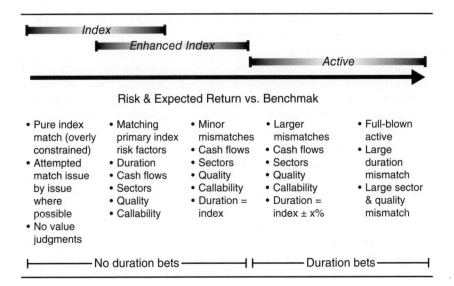

Exhibit 13.3 Spectrum of bond portfolio management strategies.
Source: Exhibit 7 in Volpert (1997). Used with permission of John Wiley & Sons, Inc.

- Active management/larger factor mismatches
- Active management/full-blown active

More recently, there has also been a discussion of using smart beta strategies for bond portfolio management. We discuss each of these strategies next.

13.5.1 Pure Bond Indexing Strategy

A *pure bond index matching strategy* tracks the composition and returns of a given benchmark as closely as possible. In terms of risk and return, it involves the least risk of underperforming the benchmark. Bond indexing strategies are very popular, and several factors contribute to their popularity. First, the empirical evidence suggests that historically the overall performance of active bond managers has been poor. Second, advisory management fees are lower for an indexed portfolio than for an actively managed one. Advisory fees charged by active managers typically range from 15 to 50 basis points. The range for indexed portfolios, in contrast, is 1 to 20 basis points (with the upper range representing the fees for enhanced indexing, discussed later). Some pension plan sponsors have decided to do away with advisory fees and to manage some or all of their funds in-house following an indexing strategy. Lower nonadvisory fees, such as custodial fees, is the third reason for the popularity of bond indexing.

Critics of indexing point out that while an indexing strategy matches the performance of some benchmark, the performance of that benchmark, which is typically some bond index, does not necessarily represent optimal performance. Moreover, matching an index does not mean that the manager will satisfy a client's return requirement objective. For example, if the objective of a life insurance company or a pension fund is to have sufficient funds to satisfy a predetermined liability, indexing only reduces the likelihood that performance will not be materially worse than the benchmark index. The return on the benchmark index is not necessarily related to the liability.

A portfolio manager pursuing an indexing strategy will encounter several logistical problems as well. First, the prices for the bond issues used by the organization that publishes the index may not be execution prices available to the portfolio manager. In fact, they may be materially different from the prices offered by some dealers. In addition, the prices used by organizations reporting the value of indexes are based on bid prices. Dealer ask prices, however, are the ones that the manager would have to transact at when constructing or rebalancing the indexed portfolio. Thus there will be at least some discrepancy between the performance of the index and the indexed portfolio that is equal to the bid–ask spread.

Furthermore, there are logistical problems unique to certain sectors in the bond market. Consider first the corporate bond market. There are typically more than 5,000 issues in the corporate bond sector of a broad-based bond market index. Because of the illiquidity for many of the issues, not only may the prices used by the organization that publishes the index be unreliable, but also many of the issues may not be available for purchase.

Next, consider the mortgage sector. There are more than 800,000 agency passthrough issues. The organizations that publish indexes aggregate all these issues into a few hundred generic issues. The manager is then faced with the difficult task of finding passthrough securities with the same risk-return profile as these hypothetical generic issues.

Finally, the total return depends on the reinvestment rate available on interim cash flows received prior to month end. If the organization publishing the index regularly overestimates the reinvestment rate, then the indexed portfolio could underperform the index.

13.5.2 Enhanced Indexing/Primary Factor Matching

An enhanced indexing strategy can be pursued so as to construct a portfolio to match the primary risk factors without acquiring each issue in the index.

This is a common strategy used by smaller funds because of the difficulties of acquiring all of the issues comprising the index. While this strategy is called an "enhanced strategy" in Exhibit 13.3, some investors refer to it as simply an "indexing strategy." Similarly to the case of equities, there are two methodologies used to construct a portfolio to replicate an index: stratification and optimization. Both methodologies assume that the performance of an individual security depends on a number of systematic factors that affect the performance of all securities and on a factor unique to the individual issue. We explain how these methodologies work in the case of fixed income portfolio management in Chapter 14. Some mismatches are tolerated in an enhanced indexing strategy not because the portfolio manager deliberately expresses views but because of recognition that perfect matching of the benchmark index is not possible with the purchase of only a limited number of securities.

13.5.3 Enhanced Indexing/Minor Factor Mismatches

Another enhanced strategy is one in which the portfolio is constructed so as to have minor deviations from the factors that affect the performance of the benchmark index. For example, there might be a slight overweighting of issues or sectors where the portfolio manager believes there is relative value. However, it is important to point out that the duration of the constructed portfolio is matched to the duration of the index. This is shown also in Exhibit 13.3, which places enhanced indexing/minor risk factor mismatches strategies in the "no duration bets" part of the spectrum of bond portfolio strategies.

13.5.4 Active Management/Larger Factor Mismatches

Active bond strategies attempt to outperform the market by intentionally constructing a portfolio that will have a greater index mismatch than in the case of enhanced indexing. The decision to pursue an active strategy or to engage a client to request a portfolio manager to pursue an active strategy must be based on the belief that there is some type of gain from such costly efforts; for there to be a gain, pricing inefficiencies must exist. The particular strategy chosen depends on why the portfolio manager believes this is the case.

An active management/larger risk factor mismatches strategy is the more conservative of the two types of active strategies. The portfolio manager creates larger mismatches relative to the index in terms of risk factors. This includes minor mismatches of duration. Typically, there will be a limitation as to the degree of duration mismatch. For example, the portfolio manager may be constrained to be within ±1 of the duration of the index. So, if the duration of the index is 4, the portfolio manager may have a duration between 3 and 5.

A portfolio manager may use an active management/larger risk factor mismatches strategy to take advantage of an anticipated reshaping of the yield curve, and there can be significant differences in the cash flow distribution between the index and the portfolio constructed by the portfolio manager. As another example, if a portfolio manager believes that, within the corporate sector, issues rated A will outperform issues rated AA, the portfolio manager may overweight the A issues and underweight AA issues relative to the weights these sectors have in the benchmark index.

13.5.5 Active Management/Full-Blown Active

In the case of full-blown active management, the portfolio manager is permitted to make a significant duration bet without any constraint. The portfolio manager can have a duration of zero (i.e., be all in cash) or can leverage the portfolio to a high multiple of the duration of the index. The portfolio manager can decide not to invest in one or more of the major sectors of the broad-based bond market indexes. The portfolio manager can make a significant allocation to sectors not included in the index. For example, there can be a substantial allocation to nonagency mortgage-backed securities.

We discuss various strategies used in active portfolio management in the next section.

13.5.6 Smart Beta Strategies for Fixed Income Portfolios

As we mentioned in Chapters 9 and 10, smart beta strategies fall between active and passive. They are not as widespread in fixed income portfolio management as they are in equity portfolio management but there are new products and research that indicate that such strategies show promise. Shepherd (2014), for example, reported the creation and testing of a smart-beta bond index that determined issuer weights on the basis of economic fundamentals. Such an index has a built-in preference for low-credit-risk securities because it bases allocations on measures of debt service capacity: corporate cash flow and long-term assets. In contrast, a typical benchmark weighs bond issues by the value of company debt outstanding. Over the 17-year period between 1997 and 2013, the hypothetical fundamentally weighted corporate bond index outperformed a market-value-weighted benchmark by 39 basis points per year, for a cumulative excess return over the entire period of 6.86%. The fundamentally weighted index had lower volatility and performed better on a risk-adjusted basis, with a Sharpe ratio of 0.67 compared to the benchmark's Sharpe ratio of 0.55.

13.6   VALUE-ADDED FIXED INCOME STRATEGIES

Active portfolio strategies seek to generate additional return after adjusting for risk. This additional return is popularly referred to as alpha. We refer to such strategies as *value-added strategies*. These strategies can be classified as *strategic strategies* and *tactical strategies*.

Strategic strategies, sometimes referred to as *top-down value-added strategies*, fall into the following categories:

- Interest rate expectations strategies
- Yield curve strategies
- Inter- and intra-sector allocation strategies

Tactical strategies, sometimes referred to as *relative value strategies*, are short-term trading strategies. They include:

- Strategies based on rich/cheap analysis
- Yield curve trading strategies
- Return enhancing strategies employing futures and options

This section provides an overview of some of the most widely used value-added strategies.

13.6.1   Interest Rate Expectations Strategies

A portfolio manager who believes that he or she can accurately forecast the future level of interest rates will alter the portfolio's duration based on the forecast. Because duration is a measure of interest rate sensitivity, this involves increasing a portfolio's duration if interest rates are expected to fall and reducing duration if interest rates are expected to rise. For those portfolio managers whose benchmark is a bond market index, this means increasing the portfolio duration relative to the benchmark index if interest rates are expected to fall and reducing it if interest rates are expected to rise. The degree to which the duration of the managed portfolio is permitted to diverge from that of the benchmark index may be limited by the client. Interest rate expectations strategies are commonly referred to as *duration strategies*.

A portfolio's duration may be altered in the cash market by swapping (or exchanging) bonds in the portfolio for other bonds that will achieve the target portfolio duration. Alternatively, a more efficient means for altering the duration of a bond portfolio is to use interest rate futures contracts. As we explain in Chapter 18, buying futures increases a portfolio's duration, while selling futures decreases it.

The key to this active strategy is, of course, an ability to forecast the direction of future interest rates. The academic literature does not support the view that interest rates can be forecasted so that risk-adjusted excess returns can be consistently realized. It is doubtful whether betting on future interest rates will provide a consistently superior return.

13.6.2 Yield Curve Strategies

As we explained earlier in this chapter, the yield curve for U.S. Treasury securities shows the relationship between maturity and yield. The shape of the yield curve changes over time. A shift in the yield curve refers to the relative change in the yield for each Treasury maturity. A parallel shift in the yield curve refers to a shift in which the change in the yield for all maturities is the same. A nonparallel shift in the yield curve means that the yield for every maturity does not change by the same number of basis points.

Top-down yield curve strategies involve positioning a portfolio to capitalize on expected changes in the shape of the Treasury yield curve. There are three yield curve strategies: (1) bullet strategies, (2) barbell strategies, and (3) ladder strategies. In a *bullet strategy*, the portfolio is constructed so that the maturities of the bonds in the portfolio are highly concentrated at one point on the yield curve. In a *barbell strategy*, the maturities of the bonds included in the portfolio are concentrated at two extreme maturities. Actually, in practice when managers refer to a barbell strategy, it is relative to a bullet strategy. For example, a bullet strategy might be to create a portfolio with maturities concentrated around 10 years while a corresponding barbell strategy might be a portfolio with 5-year and 20-year maturities. In a *ladder strategy* the portfolio is constructed to have approximately equal amounts of each maturity. So, for example, a portfolio might have equal amounts of bonds with one year to maturity, two years to maturity, and so on.

Each of these strategies will result in different performance when the yield curve shifts. The actual performance will depend on both the type of shift and the magnitude of the shift. Thus, no general statements can be made about the optimal yield curve strategy. When this strategy is applied by a portfolio manager whose benchmark is a broad-based bond market index, there may be a mismatching of maturities relative to the index in one or more of the bond sectors.

13.6.3 Inter- and Intra-sector Allocation Strategies

A portfolio manager may allocate funds among the major bond sectors in a way that is different from the allocation in the benchmark index. This is referred to as an *inter-sector allocation strategy*. In an *intra-sector allocation strategy*, the portfolio manager's allocation of funds within a sector differs from that of the index.

In making inter- and intra-sector allocations, a portfolio manager is anticipating how spreads will change. Spreads reflect differences in credit risk, call risk (or prepayment risk), and liquidity risk. When the spread for a particular sector or subsector is expected to decline or "narrow," a portfolio manager may decide to overweight that particular sector or subsector. It will be underweighted if the portfolio manager expects the spread to increase or "widen."

Credit spreads change because of expected changes in economic prospects. Credit spreads between Treasury and non-Treasury issues widen in a declining or contracting economy and narrow during economic expansion. The economic rationale is that in a declining or contracting economy, corporations experience a decline in revenue and cash flow, making it difficult for corporate issuers to service their contractual debt obligations. To induce investors to hold non-Treasury securities, the yield spread relative to Treasury securities must widen. The converse is that during economic expansion and brisk economic activity, revenue and cash flow pick up, increasing the likelihood that corporate issuers will have the capacity to service their contractual debt obligations. Yield spreads between Treasury and federal agency securities will vary depending on investor expectations about the prospects that an implicit government guarantee will be honored.

Consequently, a portfolio manager can use economic forecasts of the economy in developing forecasts of credit spreads. Also, some portfolio managers base forecasts on historical credit spreads. The underlying principle is that there is a "normal" credit spread relationship that exists. If the current credit spread in the market differs materially from that normal credit spread, then the portfolio manager should position the portfolio so as to benefit from a return to the normal credit spread. The assumption is that the normal credit spread is some type of average or mean value and that mean reversion will occur. If, in fact, there has been a structural shift in the marketplace, this may not occur as the normal spread may change.

A portfolio manager will also look at technical factors to assess relative value. For example, a portfolio manager may analyze the prospective supply and demand for new issues on spreads in individual sectors or issuers to determine whether they should be overweighted or underweighted. This commonly used tactical strategy is referred to as *primary market analysis.*

Now let's look at spreads due to call or prepayment risk. Expectations about how these spreads will change will affect the inter-sector allocation decision between Treasury securities (with noncallable securities) and spread products that have call risk. Corporate and agency bonds have callable and noncallable issues, all mortgages are prepayable, and asset-backed securities have products that are callable but borrowers may be unlikely to exercise the call. Consequently, with sectors having different degrees of call risk, expectations about how spreads will change will also affect intra-sector decisions. They will affect (1) the allocation between callable and noncallable bonds within the corporate bond sector and (2) within the agency, corporate, mortgage, and ABS sectors the allocation among premium (i.e., high coupon), par, and discount (i.e., low coupon) bonds.

Spreads due to call risk will change as a result of expected changes in (1) the direction of the change in interest rates and (2) interest rate volatility. An expected drop in the level of interest rates will widen the yield spread between callable bonds and noncallable bonds as the prospects that the issuer will exercise the call option increase. The reverse is true, too: the spread narrows if interest rates are expected to rise. An increase in interest rate volatility increases the value of the embedded call option and thereby increases the spread between (1) callable bonds and noncallable bonds and (2) premium and discount bonds. Trades where the portfolio manager anticipates better performance due to the embedded option of individual issues or sectors are referred to as *structure trades.*

13.6.4 Individual Security Selection Strategies

Once the allocation to a sector or subsector has been made, the portfolio manager must decide on the specific issues to select. This is because a portfolio manager will typically not invest in all issues within a sector or subsector. Instead, depending on the dollar size of the portfolio, the manager will select a representative number of issues.

It is at this stage that a portfolio manager makes an intra-sector allocation decision to the specific issues. The portfolio manager may believe that there are securities that are mispriced within a subsector and therefore will outperform over the investment horizon other issues within the same sector. There are several active strategies that portfolio managers pursue to identify mispriced securities. The most common strategy identifies an issue as undervalued because either (1) its yield is higher than that of comparably rated issues; or (2) its yield is expected to decline (and price therefore rise) because credit analysis indicates that its rating will be upgraded.

Once a portfolio is constructed, a portfolio manager may exchange one bond for another bond that is similar in terms of coupon, maturity, and credit quality, but offers a higher yield. This is called a *substitution swap* and depends on a capital market imperfection. Such situations sometimes exist in the bond market owing to temporary market imbalances and the fragmented nature of the non-Treasury bond market. The risk the portfolio manager faces in making a substitution swap is that the bond purchased may not be truly identical to the bond for which it is exchanged. Moreover, typically bonds will have similar but not identical maturities and coupon. This could lead to differences in the convexity of the two bonds.

What is critical in assessing any potential substitution swaps is to compare positions that have the same dollar duration. To understand why, consider two bonds, X and Y. Suppose that bond X has a price of 80 and a duration of 5 while bond Y has a price of 90 and a duration of 4. Since duration is the approximate percentage change per 100 basis point change in yield, a 100 basis points change in yield for bond X would change its price by about 5%. Based on a price of 80, its price will change by about $4 per $80 of market value. Thus, its dollar duration for a 100 basis point change in yield is $4 per $80 of market value. Similarly, for bond Y, its dollar duration for a 100 basis point change in yield per $90 of market value can be determined. In this case it is $3.6. So, if bonds X and Y are being considered as alternative investments or in some swap transaction other than one based on anticipating interest rate movements, the amount of each bond involved should be such that they will both have the same dollar duration.

To illustrate this, suppose that a portfolio manager owns $10 million par value of bond X, which has a market value of $8 million. The dollar duration of bond X per 100 basis point change in yield for the $8 million market value is $400,000. Suppose further that this manager is considering exchanging bond X that he owns in his portfolio for bond Y. If the portfolio manager wants to have the same interest rate exposure (i.e., dollar duration) for bond Y that the manager currently has for bond X, she will buy a market value amount of bond Y with the same dollar duration. If the portfolio manager purchased $10 million of par value of bond Y and therefore $9 million of market value of bond Y, the dollar price change per 100 basis point change in yield would be only $360,000. If, instead, the portfolio manager purchased $10 million of market value of bond Y, the dollar duration per 100 basis point change in yield would be $400,000. Since bond Y is trading at 90, $11.11 million of par value of bond Y must be purchased to keep the dollar duration of the position for bond Y the same as for bond X.

Mathematically, this problem can be expressed as follows. Let

$\$D_X$ = dollar duration per 100 basis point change in yield for bond X
for the market value of bond X held

D_Y = duration for bond Y

MV_Y = market value of bond Y needed to obtain the same dollar duration
as bond X

Then, the following equation sets the dollar duration for bond X equal to the dollar duration for bond Y:

$$\$D_X = (D_Y/100)MV_Y$$

Solving for MV_Y,

$$MV_Y = \$D_X/(D_Y/100)$$

Dividing by the price per \$1 of par value of bond Y gives the par value of bond Y, which has approximately equivalent dollar duration as bond X.

Failure to adjust a substitution swap so as to hold the dollar duration the same means that the return will be affected by not only the expected change in the spread but also a change in the yield level. Thus, a portfolio manager would be making a conscious spread bet and possibly an unintentional bet on changes in the level of interest rates.

The example in Chapter 14 will illustrate how optimization can be used to take multiple considerations into account when making trades to accomplish a particular goal.

Summary

- The major sectors of the U.S. bond market are the (1) Treasury securities market, (2) federal agency securities market, (3) corporate bond market, (4) municipal bonds market, (5) non-U.S. bond market, (6) agency residential mortgage-backed securities market, (7) nonagency residential mortgage securities market, (8) commercial mortgage-backed securities market, and (9) asset-backed securities market.
- Features of a bond include (1) maturity, (2) par value, (3) coupon rate, (4) yield, and (5) provisions for paying off a bond issue.
- Observed bond yields tend to be different depending on the time to maturity. The plot of bond yields versus the length of time corresponding to these yields is referred to as the yield curve.

- Bonds may expose an investor to one or more of the following risks: (1) interest rate risk, (2) call and prepayment risk, (3) credit risk, and (4) liquidity risk.
- Measures of interest rate risk include duration, convexity, and key rate duration.
- Spread risk is measured using spread duration, where the spread can be of three different types: nominal spread, zero-volatility spread, and option-adjusted spread.
- A comprehensive picture of bond portfolio performance under different scenarios can be obtained using simulation.
- The spectrum of bond portfolio strategies includes (1) pure bond index matching, (2) enhanced indexing/primary factor matching, (3) enhanced indexing/minor factor mismatches, (4) active management/ larger factor mismatches, and (5) active management/full-blown active. These strategies range from passive to active. Smart beta strategies for bond portfolio management are also becoming popular.
- Value-added (or alpha) bond portfolio strategies are active strategies that incorporate a portfolio manager's view.
- Value-added bond strategies include interest rate expectation strategies, yield curve strategies, inter- and intra-sector allocation strategies, and substitution swap strategies.

CHAPTER 14

Factor-Based Fixed Income Portfolio Construction and Evaluation

Chapter 13 introduced fundamental fixed income terminology and discussed sources of bond portfolio risk. In this chapter, we describe analytical frameworks for fixed income portfolio management and focus on the use of factor models for fixed income portfolio construction and risk decomposition.

We begin the chapter with a list of commonly used fixed income factors that represent potential sources of risk, as we described in Chapter 12. We then review analytics-based bond portfolio construction strategies, including stratification and optimization-based approaches. Finally, we present a detailed example of the use of factor models for portfolio construction and risk decomposition.

14.1 FIXED INCOME FACTORS USED IN PRACTICE

In Chapters 9 and 12, we explained that the main groups of factors used in equity portfolio management include fundamental, macroeconomic, and statistical. Many of the factors used in equity portfolio construction impact fixed income securities' returns as well. In this section, we elaborate on factors most useful for fixed income portfolio construction, including interest rate levels, credit quality, currency rates, the volatility of interest rates, and the possibility of prepayments.[1]

---

[1] Our exposition in this section is influenced by the MSCI Barra fixed income factor model. See Barra on Campus (2003) and Breger and Cheyette (2005) for more details.

14.1.1 Term Structure Factors

Changes in the term structure—the curve representing the relationship between yields and time to maturity—are a very significant component of the overall risk of a fixed income portfolio. Common ways to represent term structure risk include average change in interest rates, key rates, and "shift-twist-butterfly" factors. We explain the reasoning behind these modeling choices next.

The portfolio return attributed to interest rate changes is approximately the product of effective duration and the average change in rates, that is,

$$r_{\text{portfolio}} \approx (\Delta y) \cdot D_{\text{effective}}$$

This is the reason for the average change in interest rates (Δy) to be sometimes used as a factor in bond return models. The disadvantage of using this single factor is that the resulting factor model does not capture the change and reshaping of the entire term structure.

The yield curve risk component due to changes in the shape of the yield curve can be accounted for by using key rate durations. As explained in Chapter 13, key rates are the interest rates for a prespecified set of maturities. Shifts in the term structure are represented as a discrete vector, the elements of which are the changes in the key zero-coupon rates of various maturities. Interest rate changes at other maturities are derived from the key rates via linear interpolation. Key rate durations are then defined as the sensitivity of the portfolio value to the given key rates at different points along the term structure. Typical key rates are the 6-month, 1-year, 2-year, 5-year, 10-year, 20-year, and 30-year rates but factor models using key rate durations vary in the choice of key rates. Ho (1992) proposed using as many as 11 key rates to hedge interest rate risk effectively. Later in this chapter, we show an example of how key rates are used for portfolio risk decomposition with the Barclays POINT system.

Neighboring key rates are often more than 90% correlated; hence there is an argument for not using so many factors to explain movements in the yield curve.[2] Some models are based on a compromise approach, which does not treat the term structure in terms of specific key rates but in terms of factors that describe the way the term structure moves.[3] The three factors commonly used include *shift* (when rates move in parallel), *twist* (when the curve steepens or flattens, that is, when the ends of the curve move in

---

[2]Breger and Cheyette (2005).
[3]Barra on Campus (2003).

opposite directions), and *butterfly* (when the curvature changes or flexes). These factors are derived using principal components analysis[4] applied to the key rate covariance matrix, and have been found to explain as much as 98% of the variability for portfolios of Treasury securities.

In addition to the selection of factors to represent the term structure of interest rates, an important issue is the selection of the benchmark curve itself. Domestic government bonds (e.g., the U.S. Treasury yield curve in the case of the United States) are the choice in most markets but there are important exceptions. For example, in the case of the Eurozone, there is no natural government yield curve but there is a liquid swap market, so the LIBOR/swap curve is typically used for corporate debt.[5] At the same time, domestic government debt trades relative to its local government yield curve. As long as the term structure factors completely span the interest rate risk and the risk relative to the benchmark, the choice of a benchmark should technically not matter for modeling the complete interest rate risk exposure of a bond portfolio. However, selecting a particular benchmark may have implications for correctly identifying and hedging critical factors.

14.1.2 Credit Spread Factors

All taxable non-U.S. Treasury securities[6] trade at a spread relative to U.S. Treasury securities due to credit risk. That is, for every maturity, non-U.S. Treasury securities require that the issuer pay a different—typically larger—interest rate to borrow funds than the U.S. government. Hence, non-U.S. Treasury securities are referred to as "spread products." As we explained in Chapter 13, the spread is due to several sources of credit risk: market-wide credit spread risk, credit event risk, and downgrade risk. Market-wide credit spread risk arises when events in the market affect the general level of credit spreads in a particular industry or rating category. Credit event risk happens when the issuer suffers changes that affect the

---

[4]See Chapter 4.4.

[5]The swap yield curve shows the relationship between interest rate swap rates at different maturities and is used in a similar manner to the bond yield curve. Interest rate swaps are financial derivative instruments in which periodic exchange of cash flows happens between two counterparties over a specified time period. One party typically pays a fixed rate whereas the counterparty's cash flows are linked to the performance of a financial security, index, a reference interest rate, or something else. Swap rates are the rates paid on the fixed portions of interest rate swaps. We discuss interest rate swaps in more detail in Chapter 16.

[6]Sectors of the fixed income market include corporate bonds, mortgage-backed securities, and foreign debt.

company's fundamentals or the fundamentals of a sector. Downgrade risk is the risk that the issuer's credit rating will be downgraded.

Market-wide credit spread factors can include the average spread between swap rates and the Treasury curve. Credit event risk factors can, for example, be based on a historical rating migration matrix and average yield spreads estimated for bonds bucketed by rating,[7] or by using the Merton (1974) framework for linking issuer credit quality to prices observed in the equity market.[8]

14.1.3 Currency Factors

A bond portfolio consisting of issues whose cash flow is not denominated in the domestic currency is subject to currency risk. However, the extent to which the variability in currencies affects the portfolio risk depends on the portfolio exposure relative to the benchmark's exposure to currency risk. The variability in currencies is often modeled using GARCH models.[9] Factors that can represent currency risk typically include a volatility model such as GARCH, and may include a correlation model.[10]

14.1.4 Emerging Market Factors

Emerging market debt can be issued either in the local currency or in an external currency. The two types of debt are typically considered separately. Debt issued in the local currency is subject to local interest rate and spread factors. Debt issued in an external currency is considered riskier because, in contrast to debt issued in the local currency, the government cannot service it by raising taxes or printing money.

Emerging market debt is subject to risk due to the creditworthiness of the issuer, and the credit risk associated with an emerging market sovereign may be larger than the interest rate and all the other sources of risk combined. This risk can be gleaned from relative spreads of other debt issued by the particular issuer.

Emerging market spreads are typically measured relative to the swap curve. An emerging market bond denominated in U.S. dollars would be exposed to interest rate and spread factors in its local market as well as its emerging market credit spread.

---

[7]Barra on Campus (2003).
[8]Northfield Information Services (2009).
[9]See Chapter 4.5 for an introduction to GARCH models.
[10]Barra on Campus (2003).

14.1.5   Volatility Factors

Fixed income securities with embedded options are subject not only to term structure and credit risk but also to interest rate volatility risk because their returns depend on the market expectations about future interest rate volatility. The main idea in modeling volatility risk factors is to calibrate a stochastic interest rate model to match market prices observed for traded interest rate options. The variation over time of the model parameters can be used to determine the implied factors.[11] In the MSCI Barra (2003) model implementation, for example, the factor is the logarithm of the 10-year yield, which captures the volatility in the portion of the yield curve most relevant for mortgage-backed securities (MBSs) and bonds with embedded options. The exposure of a security to the volatility risk factor is the percentage change in price per percentage increase in the 10-year yield volatility.

14.1.6   Prepayment Factors

Certain fixed income securities such as securitized mortgages (MBS) are subject to prepayment risk. Because borrowers have the option to prepay the underlying loans, MBSs have characteristics similar to callable bonds. Prepayment models are typically used to project the prepayment rate on an MBS as a function of the security's characteristics and the current and past state of the market. To incorporate prepayment risk into the valuation model, one would calculate an implied prepayment model that uses market valuations to adjust modeled prepayment rates to match market expectations. Incorporating prepayment risk into a factor model reduces to introducing one or more factors to capture the changes in expectations of the market price of prepayment risk.

14.2   PORTFOLIO SELECTION

In Chapter 12, we described various ad-hoc and structured approaches to equity portfolio selection. As in the case of equities, bond portfolio characteristics can be selected to either match or deviate from the characteristics of a designated benchmark. When characteristics of the benchmark are matched, the portfolio manager would be following a *bond indexing strategy*. Such a strategy is today commonly referred to as a beta strategy. When the portfolio manager intentionally chooses to deviate from the characteristics of the benchmark based on his or her view, the portfolio manager would be following an active (alpha) strategy.

---

[11] See Breger and Cheyette (2005) for more details.

In this section, we focus on two popular approaches for fixed income portfolio selection: *stratification* (also referred to as a *cell-based approach*) and *optimization*. We discuss their application in conjunction with multifactor models, which is consistent with the way they are typically used in practice. Because the definition of a factor is broad (as we mentioned in Chapter 9, an entire asset class can be considered a factor), our discussion is not limited to situations in which portfolio managers use particular multifactor models.

14.2.1 Stratification Approach

In Chapter 12, we gave an example of how an equity portfolio manager could use a stratification strategy with two factors: industry composition and size. In the case of fixed income portfolios, commonly used factors are (1) duration, (2) coupon, (3) maturity, (4) market sectors, (5) credit quality, (6) call features, and (7) sinking fund features.[12]

Consider, for example, the case of a portfolio manager who would like to match the credit quality of an investment-grade benchmark. The portfolio manager could consider four "buckets" or "cells" for credit quality: (1) AAA, (2) AA, (3) A, and (4) BBB. Remember that such benchmark could include as many as 6,000 bonds issues. From this large universe of bonds, the portfolio manager selects a few bonds from each of the four categories for credit quality in such a way that the relative weight of all the bonds in a particular bucket in the portfolio is the same as the relative weight of bonds with the corresponding credit quality in the benchmark.

Suppose the portfolio manager would like to include a second characteristic: duration. The portfolio manager could consider two buckets for effective duration: (1) less than or equal to five years, and (2) greater than five years. There will be a total of 8 (= 4 × 2) buckets or cells. (See Exhibit 14.1.) The portfolio manager can then select a few bonds from these 8 categories in such a way that the relative weight of all the stocks in a particular industry in his portfolio is the same as the relative weight of the industry in the benchmark.

The portfolio manager could use this framework to place bets on important factors. For example, the portfolio manager may overweight

---

[12]With sinking fund bonds, the issuer of the bond makes periodic payments to a trustee who retires part of the issue by purchasing the bonds in the open market. From the investor's point of view, a sinking fund makes the bond issue safer: the bond issuer is less likely to default on the payment of the principal upon maturity since the amount of the final repayment is substantially less than it would be without the sinking fund feature.

EXHIBIT 14.1 Example of stratification with two factors (credit quality and effective duration).

	Duration ≤ 5 Years	Duration > 5 Years
AAA	. . .	. . .
AA	. . .	. . .
A	. . .	. . .
BBB	. . .	. . .

AAA bonds with duration greater than five years by increasing the percentage of his portfolio allocated to issues in this bucket (upper-right cell in Exhibit 14.1) compared to the percentage of AAA bonds with duration greater than five years in the benchmark.

Note that when the allocation to a bucket is the same percentage as the percentage of the benchmark this bucket represents, the allocation is said to be neutral. When all of the buckets match the benchmark, this is an indexing strategy. Unfortunately, indexing when it comes to fixed income securities is not as simple as equity indexing because of the cost of purchasing a large enough number of issues in a bucket to increase the likelihood that the performance of a portfolio's bucket matches the performance of the corresponding bucket in the benchmark. When the portfolio manager tolerates minor mismatches in the primary risk factors between the portfolio and the benchmark buckets with the exception of duration (i.e., duration must be neutral), the strategy is referred to as an *enhanced indexing strategy*.

While stratification helps fixed income portfolio managers structure their decisions, it has a number of shortcomings.

First, the number of buckets increases quickly with the addition of factors. For example, suppose the portfolio manager adds two more factors: Maturity with 3 buckets ([1] less than 5 years, [2] between 5 and 15 years, and [3] greater than 15 years) and Market Sectors with 4 buckets ([1] Treasury, [2] agencies, [3] corporate, and [4] agency MBS). The total number of buckets to consider becomes 96 (= 4 × 2 × 3 × 4). In a portfolio of less than \$100 million, including representative issues in each cell would require buying odd lots of issues and would increase transaction costs considerably.

Second, a portfolio allocation using the stratification approach does not make it easy to understand how the risk profile of the portfolio changes with changes in the allocation of issues to cells. It is difficult to assess immediately if a particular selection of a bond issue adds to or decreases overall portfolio risk relative to the benchmark, and how that compares to the selection of a different bond issue. Correlations between bond issues in different cells are also not taken into account—but it is possible that the selection of two issues in different buckets reduces overall risk even if by themselves the issues do not represent as attractive investments as other issues.

The optimization approach, described in the next section, addresses some of these issues.

14.2.2 Optimization Approach

An optimization formulation of the portfolio allocation problem requires a specification of[13]

1. Decision variables
2. Objective function
3. Constraints

A typical objective is to minimize the tracking error between the portfolio and a benchmark, but one can also, for example, maximize expected total return, and instead limit the tracking error to be within a prespecified risk budget by stating the limit as a constraint.

The decision variables are the amounts that should be allocated to different bond issues. These bond issues are a part of a tradable universe specified by the portfolio manager. The tradable universe may or may not include only issues from the benchmark; if it does not, then portfolio managers often specify as a constraint the maximum percentage of the portfolio that can be allocated to securities not in the benchmark (i.e., nonbenchmark issues).

By specifying a set of constraints, the portfolio manager can express views on the various factors that drive the return on the benchmark, or limit the risk by restricting the portfolio tracking error to be within a particular risk budget. As in the case of equities (see Chapter 11.1), a fixed income portfolio manager may specify upper and lower bounds on the amounts to be invested in individual securities or sectors, or on the maximum number of securities to be held in the portfolio.

Let us consider the following illustration.[14] Suppose we are trying to allocate $100 million among 50 securities so as to track a composite index (specified by a client) made up of the Barclays Capital U.S. Treasury Index, the Barclays Capital U.S. Credit Index, and the Barclays Capital U.S. MBS Index on an equally weighted basis.[15] The tradable universe is the securities in these three indexes.

---

[13]See Chapter 6.
[14]We are very grateful to Anthony Lazanas and Cenk Ural of Barclays Capital for preparing this illustration.
[15]In other words, each index has one-third of the benchmark weight.

To allocate the $100 million among 50 securities, we solve the following optimization problem:

Minimize the tracking error between the portfolio and the benchmark subject to the following constraints:

1. Total invested amount (sum of all allocations) = $100 million.
2. No more than 50 securities in the portfolio.[16]
3. No short sales.
4. The duration of the portfolio must not exceed the duration of the benchmark by more than 0.30 and must not be more than 0.15 below the benchmark duration.
5. Spreads should be between 50 and 80 basis points higher than the benchmark.
6. The monthly tracking error should not exceed 15 basis points.
7. The maximum active (under- or over-) weight relative to the benchmark should be no more than 3% per issuer.

Constraints (1)–(3) are typical constraints that are specified in a manner similar to the specifications in Chapter 11.1. Constraint (5) expresses the portfolio manager's view: it tilts the portfolio in the direction of the portfolio manager's view so that there is a mismatch between the benchmark and the portfolio when it comes to risk factors representing credit risk. Constraint (6) represents the risk budget, and Constraint (7) is imposed for diversification purposes.

The tracking error is calculated based on the covariances between the primary risk factors used in the model.[17] Because of this, correlations between the securities in the portfolio and their impact on portfolio risk are taken into consideration during portfolio construction. This is an advantage to the optimization method compared to the stratification method described in the previous section.

The optimal portfolio with position amounts obtained from the optimal values of the decision variables and with a market value of $100 million is displayed in Exhibit 14.2. The portfolio has 50 securities, as was requested in the portfolio optimization formulation.

The portfolio allocations to different sectors are summarized in Exhibit 14.3. It is clear that the portfolio manager has taken a positive view on the government-related and corporate (specifically, industrials and

[16]This constraint requires the introduction of binary variables, as explained in Chapter 11.1.5.
[17]We showed the general form of the calculation in Chapter 9 and discuss it later in this chapter.

EXHIBIT 14.2 Example portfolio as of April 24, 2015.

Identifier	Description	Position Amount	Market Value
912828SH	U.S. TREASURY NOTES	876,432	886,952
912828RP	U.S. TREASURY NOTES	1,073,611	1,110,015
018490AQ	ALLERGAN INC	1,243,903	1,190,836
912828A7	U.S. TREASURY NOTES	1,247,650	1,273,196
900123BA	TURKEY (REPUBLIC OF) GLOBAL	1,165,348	1,293,973
172967GK	CITIGROUP INC	1,291,748	1,354,490
626717AE	MURPHY OIL CORP	1,363,337	1,356,196
887315AM	TIME WARNER INC	988,883	1,382,289
460146CJ	INTERNATIONAL PAPER	1,340,939	1,387,463
472319AK	JEFFERIES GROUP INC	1,336,613	1,411,561
71644EAB	PETRO-CANADA	1,052,874	1,436,107
552081AK	LYONDELLBASELL IND NV	1,233,801	1,466,603
744320AK	PRUDENTIAL FINANCIAL INC	1,227,074	1,487,274
195325AU	COLOMBIA (REP OF) GLOBAL	1,087,010	1,524,078
907818EB	UNION PACIFIC CORP	1,560,696	1,525,660
912810FJ	U.S. TREASURY BONDS	1,022,264	1,525,693
912810FG	U.S. TREASURY BONDS	1,123,720	1,543,808
19075QAB	COBANK ACB	1,348,117	1,543,823
21987AAB	CORPBANCA	1,541,266	1,568,132
961214AH	WESTPAC BANKING CORP	1,462,237	1,577,821
912828A3	U.S. TREASURY NOTES	1,562,508	1,581,904
912810RK	U.S. TREASURY BONDS	1,649,808	1,617,777
912828KD	U.S. TREASURY NOTES	1,518,878	1,620,220
05958AAF	BANCO DO BRASIL SA	1,589,927	1,637,470
478160BK	JOHNSON & JOHNSON	1,362,096	1,638,772
64966TFD	NEW YORK N Y CITY HSG DEV CORP	1,596,300	1,692,206
912828WD	U.S. TREASURY NOTES	1,734,632	1,759,120
FGB04015	FHLM Gold Guar Single F. 30yr	1,642,874	1,762,564
912828QT	U.S. TREASURY NOTES	1,680,365	1,769,987
904764AH	UNILEVER CAPITAL CORP GLOBAL	1,265,643	1,783,867
912828VK	U.S. TREASURY NOTES	1,796,513	1,830,266
912828RY	U.S. TREASURY NOTES	1,856,634	1,885,278
88732JAP	TIME WARNER CABLE INC	1,610,496	1,947,952
06406HDA	BANK OF NEW YORK	1,923,706	1,958,215
912828RH	U.S. TREASURY NOTES	1,945,596	1,972,677
71654QAU	PETROLEOS MEXICANOS	1,657,696	2,048,452
912828VE	U.S. TREASURY NOTES	2,142,903	2,158,762
GNA03015	GNMA I Single Family 30yr	2,094,452	2,171,008
912828RE	U.S. TREASURY NOTES	2,353,888	2,400,666

(continued)

EXHIBIT 14.2 (*Continued*)

Identifier	Description	Position Amount	Market Value
912810RB	U.S. TREASURY BONDS	2,280,980	2,425,837
FNA03015	FNMA Conventional Long T. 30yr	2,459,119	2,526,148
FGB03015	FHLM Gold Guar Single F. 30yr	2,803,612	2,874,357
912828VQ	U.S. TREASURY NOTES	2,888,362	2,937,842
912920AL	U.S. WEST COMMUNICATIONS	2,908,056	3,014,840
293791AV	ENTERPRISE PRODUCTS OPER	2,896,660	3,127,065
FGB02412	FHLM Gold Guar Single F. 30yr	3,191,438	3,165,783
FNA04015	FNMA Conventional Long T. 30yr	2,974,254	3,196,294
71647NAC	PETROBRAS GLOBAL FINANCE BV	3,241,703	3,210,186
GNB06408	GNMA II Single Family 30yr	3,303,219	3,845,964
FNA02413	FNMA Conventional Long T. 30yr	6,632,518	6,592,550

EXHIBIT 14.3 Portfolio and benchmark sector allocation.

	Portfolio (%)	Benchmark (%)	Difference (%)
Market Value [%]	100.00	100.00	0.00
Treasury	30.30	33.30	−3.00
Gov-Related	11.41	6.93	4.48
Corp Industrials	21.26	15.88	5.38
Corp Utilities	0.00	2.00	−2.00
Corp Fin Inst	10.90	8.58	2.32
MBS	26.13	33.30	−7.17

financials) sectors. Their active weights in the portfolio are positive: 4.48%, 5.38%, and 2.32%, respectively. The other sectors are underweighted relative to the benchmark.

This portfolio allocation has a tracking error (optimal objective function value) of 7.48 basis points (bps) per month, which is within the risk budget of 15 bps set in the constraints, and is the minimum possible given the set of constraints imposed on the portfolio composition.

14.2.3 Portfolio Rebalancing

While portfolio construction provides a setting within which the stratification and the optimization approaches can be illustrated, as we have mentioned earlier in the book, in practice it happens more often that one needs to solve a different problem: how to rebalance an existing portfolio so that the same level of tracking error is maintained while the transaction costs of the rebalancing are as low as possible. This is because even portfolios constructed to have an initial tracking error within a prespecified range may drift away from the required characteristics to achieve that range over time as different events take place. Four common types of such events include:

1. The portfolio manager changes views.
2. Funds are added to or withdrawn from the portfolio.
3. Some of the attributes of the issues in the portfolio change (e.g., there is an upgrade or a downgrade for some of the securities, or there is a change in the duration of some of the issues in the portfolio).
4. Some of the attributes of the benchmark change.

A portfolio manager could apply the stratification approach and identify "buckets" within which the portfolio weights are beginning to deviate substantially from the target weights desired. However, a portfolio manager using this approach would not necessarily have a clear idea of the best way to prioritize correcting these deviations so as to reduce tracking error at a minimal cost to implement the rebalancing strategy. It is in situations like these—in which there are multiple possible transactions that should be considered to achieve a particular goal—that the optimization approach has clear advantages over the stratification approach because it is designed to weigh multiple alternatives, assess the trade-offs, and produce the optimal strategy.

When using an optimizer to rebalance a portfolio, one typically sets as an objective the minimization of transaction costs. A new set of constraints may be imposed, including a risk budget constraint on the amount of tracking error, a constraint on the maximum number of trades allowed, or a new set of requirements on the total portfolio allocation to particular sectors. The optimizer is able to identify optimal packages of transactions (sales and purchases) and calculate the resulting change in portfolio risk so that the portfolio manager can understand the risk adjustment benefit relative to the cost of executing the transactions.

Let us consider a portfolio rebalancing example based on the portfolio example from Section 14.2.2. The sector allocation summary in Exhibit 14.3 shows that corporate industrials were overweighted in the portfolio. Suppose the portfolio manager's view has changed, and he or she would like to rebalance the portfolio so that corporate industrials are not overweighted by more than 3%. He or she would also like to achieve this with 15 or fewer trades. These two constraints (corporate industrials active weight of less than or equal to 3% and number of trades less than or equal to 15) must be added to the optimization. Exhibit 14.4 shows the trades that accomplish the portfolio manager's goal. For example, the optimizer suggests selling some corporate industrial bonds and replacing them primarily with bonds in

EXHIBIT 14.4 Optimal set of 15 trades for portfolio rebalancing.

		Sells	
Identifier	Description	Trade Position Amount	Market Value
FGB02412	FHLM Gold Guar Single F. 30yr	−1,769,795	−1,755,568
912810RB	US TREASURY BONDS	−1,472,774	−1,566,304
GNB06408	GNMA II Single Family 30yr	−1,268,339	−1,476,738
88732JAP	TIME WARNER CABLE INC	−1,187,967	−1,436,888
FNA02413	FNMA Conventional Long T. 30yr	−1,218,062	−1,210,722
904764AH	UNILEVER CAPITAL CORP GLOBAL	−666,960	−940,050
06406HDA	BANK OF NEW YORK	−746,439	−759,829
	Total Sells		−9,146,100

		Buys	
Identifier	Description	Trade Position Amount	Market Value
298785DV	EUROPEAN INVESTMENT BANK GLOBAL	519,981	701,318
26442CAP	DUKE ENERGY CAROLINAS LLC	756,407	781,419
04010LAN	ARES CAPITAL CORP	783,805	843,738
06739FHV	BARCLAYS BANK PLC	886,885	949,169
FNA04015	FNMA Conventional Long T. 30yr	1,126,616	1,210,722
GNA06006	GNMA I Single Family 30yr	1,289,604	1,476,738
912810QE	US TREASURY BONDS	1,127,336	1,566,304
FGB04015	FHLM Gold Guar Single F. 30yr	1,506,907	1,616,690
	Total Buys		9,146,100

the government-related and corporate financial institutions categories. The total market value of the trades is $9,146,100. The tracking error declined from 7.48 basis points to 6.90 basis points. The decline in tracking error was aided by an increase in the total number of securities in the portfolio (seven securities were sold while eight were bought).

14.3 RISK DECOMPOSITION

As we mentioned in Chapter 12, an important part of the portfolio construction and management process is understanding the sources of risk in the portfolio. In this section, we provide an example of how a fixed income portfolio manager can use factor models to do that. We consider the 50-security portfolio from Section 14.2.2, and are concerned with decomposing the active risk relative to the benchmark (the composite index specified in Section 14.2.2).

As a first step, a portfolio manager would look at a summary report with basic information about the portfolio and the benchmark, which in this example is the composite index specified in the previous section. An example of such a report, generated with the POINT advanced portfolio analytics platform by Barclays Capital, is provided in Exhibit 14.5. The portfolio has

EXHIBIT 14.5 Summary report for the 50-security portfolio.

	Portfolio	Benchmark	Difference
Parameters			
Positions	50	6,780	
Issuers	29	946	
Currencies	1	1	
# positions processed	50	6,780	
# positions excluded	0	0	
% MV processed	100.0	100.0	
% MV excluded	0.0	0.0	
Analytics			
Market Value ($)	100,000,000	17,050,565,720	
Notional ($)	93,152,358	15,854,865,824	
Coupon (%)	3.90	3.35	0.55
Average Life (Yr)	7.99	7.68	0.31
Yield to Worst (%)	2.57	2.12	0.45
ISMA Yield (%)	2.59	2.02	0.57
OAS (bps)	98	47	51
OAD (Yr)	5.57	5.52	0.05
ISMA Duration (Yr)	5.97	6.38	−0.41
Duration to Maturity (Yr)	5.96	6.07	−0.12
Vega	−0.01	0.01	−0.02
OA Spread Duration (Yr)	5.64	5.84	−0.20
OA Convexity (Yr^2/100)	−0.11	−0.17	0.06
Volatility			
Total TE Volatility			7.48
Systematic Volatility	85.66	85.49	
Nonsystematic Volatility	6.46	2.40	
Default Volatility	0.47	1.20	
Total Volatility	85.90	85.53	
Portfolio Beta			**1.001**

50 positions and 29 issuers compared to 6,780 positions and 946 issuers in the benchmark. All holdings are dollar-denominated. (There is only one currency.) The portfolio duration is slightly lower than the benchmark duration, meaning that the portfolio has slightly less exposure to changes in the level of interest rates. The portfolio spread duration is also slightly lower than the benchmark spread duration, which means that the portfolio is slightly less sensitive to changes in spreads.[18]

The "Volatility" section of the table presents a breakdown of the standard deviation of the portfolio and the benchmark in terms of systematic and nonsystematic (idiosyncratic) risk. The portfolio has greater systematic and idiosyncratic risk than the benchmark. This is to be expected because the portfolio is not as broadly diversified as the benchmark: there are far fewer issuers in the portfolio than in the benchmark. In addition to systematic and idiosyncratic risk, the POINT portfolio analysis output includes an estimate of default volatility, which is based on proprietary credit risk analytics metrics of Corporate Default Probabilities (CDP), Conditional Recovery Rates (CRR), and default correlations.[19]

The three different sources of volatility—systematic, idiosyncratic, and default—are assumed to be independent. The total volatility (standard deviation) of the portfolio can be computed as[20]

$$85.90 = \sqrt{85.66^2 + 6.46^2 + 0.47^2}$$

which is slightly higher than the benchmark's total volatility of 85.53 bps per month.

As in the case of equities, one can compute a portfolio beta. In the report in Exhibit 14.5, the portfolio beta is 1.001, which is in line with an objective to track the benchmark closely. This means that when the return on the composite index that is the benchmark increases by a particular amount (e.g., 10%), the portfolio return will increase by 1.001 × 10%, or approximately 10.01%, on average.

In addition to looking at basic portfolio analytics, a fixed income portfolio manager would typically assess the portfolio allocation to market sectors relative to the benchmark. Exhibit 14.3 in Section 14.2.2 showed the sector

---

[18]Here the term "spreads" is used as a generic term—the spread may be not only due to exposure to credit risk but also other types of risks reflected in yields larger than Treasury yields.
[19]See Barclays (2012).
[20]See Chapter 2.7–2.8 for a definition of independent random variables and the calculation of standard deviations of sums of independent random variables.

allocations for the portfolio and the benchmark. Exhibit 14.6 summarizes the same information for the five sectors (Treasuries, Gov Agencies, Gov Nonagencies, Corporates, and MBS) in the "Net Market Weight" column, as well as the contribution of the different sector allocations to the portfolio tracking error. As we mentioned earlier, in this particular example the portfolio manager has overweighted the portfolio on the government-related and corporate (specifically, industrials and financials) sectors. The other sectors are underweighted relative to the benchmark.

The total contribution to tracking error from all the sector allocations is 7.48 bps per month, as we saw earlier in this chapter, and the individual contributions to tracking error from each sector are listed in column "Total Contribution to Tracking Error" in Exhibit 14.6. The total contributions are broken down into systematic, idiosyncratic, and default contributions. One can observe that the total idiosyncratic risk when measured in tracking error terms (5.49 bps) represents a large portion of the total portfolio risk (7.48 bps) compared to systematic risk. Again, this is because the portfolio has only 50 securities and is not as well diversified as the benchmark.

Corporates are a major contributor to idiosyncratic risk—they are over-weighted in the portfolio and also carry higher idiosyncratic risk at the individual security level. This highlights the significant "name" risk (that is, risk to individual issuers) to which the portfolio is exposed. At the same time, the Treasuries and Government Agencies sectors have negligible idiosyncratic risk contributions because a large proportion of the variation in the return of these securities can be explained by systematic yield curve factors.

Now let us look at the isolated tracking errors of the different sectors, which consider the volatilities of the sector returns (Exhibit 14.7). To understand why this should be of interest, consider the following example.

EXHIBIT 14.6 Systematic and idiosyncratic monthly tracking error for the 50-securities portfolio by asset class.

Sector	Net Market Weight (%)	Contribution to Tracking Error Systematic	Idiosyncratic	Default	Total Contribution to Tracking Error
Total	0.00	1.84	5.49	0.16	7.48
Treasuries	−3.00	−0.01	0.09	0.00	0.08
Gov Agencies	4.98	−0.05	0.04	0.00	0.00
Gov Non-Agencies	−0.51	0.04	0.32	0.00	0.36
Corporates	5.69	1.24	5.00	0.16	6.40
MBS	−7.17	0.60	0.04	0.00	0.64

EXHIBIT 14.7 Isolated monthly tracking error and liquidation effect for the 50-securities portfolio by sector.

Sector	Net Market Weight (%)	Isolated Tracking Error Value	Liquidation Effect on Tracking Error Value
Total	0.00	7.48	−7.48
Treasuries	−3.00	2.32	0.27
Gov Agencies	4.98	1.87	0.23
Gov Non-Agencies	−0.51	2.92	0.20
Corporates	5.69	7.50	−3.43
MBS	−7.17	6.67	2.05

Suppose a portfolio has more exposure to a sector than the benchmark does. This would mean that if the returns of the sector move, the portfolio returns will move to a greater extent than the return of the benchmark. But a good question to ask is also how volatile the returns of the sector are to begin with.

The isolated tracking error (risk) for Corporates in Exhibit 14.7, 7.50 bps per month, should be interpreted as follows. If the portfolio were to differ from the benchmark only with respect to its exposure to Corporates, then this mismatch relative to the benchmark would result in a monthly isolated tracking error of 7.50 bps. It is interesting to observe that the isolated tracking error for Corporates, 7.50 bps, is higher than the overall tracking error of the portfolio (7.48%). How is this possible? This is because exposures to some sectors act as hedges to exposures to other sectors. (For example, Corporates and Treasuries are hedging each other to a certain extent because one has positive active weight, the other has negative active weight, and some underlying factors such as yield curve risk affect both sectors.) This can be seen in the fourth column of Exhibit 14.7, in which the liquidation effect of Corporates on tracking error (the change in tracking error resulting from hedging away this source of risk, or in this case, making the active weight of this sector zero) is negative, while the liquidation effects of the other sectors are positive.

The sector analysis presented so far is useful as a starting point but does not provide a complete picture because it is not known how the portfolio exposures to the sectors are related to the exposures to underlying factors that drive the portfolio's return. For instance, consider an important factor: duration. Even though Treasuries are underweighted in the portfolio as shown in Exhibits 14.3, 14.6, and 14.7 (their active weight is −3.00%), their contribution to portfolio duration is positive (0.02, as shown in the last column in Exhibit 14.8).

EXHIBIT 14.8 Comparison of contributions to duration by asset class for the 50-securities portfolio and the benchmark.

	Portfolio	Benchmark	Difference
Duration	5.67	5.52	0.15
Treasury	1.93	1.91	0.02
Government-Related	0.46	0.46	0.00
Corporate	1.82	1.96	−0.14
MBS	1.45	1.19	0.26

The Barclays POINT system considers six groups of factors to represent sources of systematic risk:

1. Yield curve risk
2. Swap spread risk
3. Volatility risk
4. Government-related spread risk
5. Corporate spread risk
6. Securitized spread risk

The tracking errors for the six factors are shown in Exhibit 14.9. Let us provide some intuition on how to interpret the numbers in the exhibit. For example, the second column shows the isolated tracking error. The isolated tracking error for the volatility risk factor is 0.29 bps per month. The volatility risk factor is associated with changes in interest rate volatility, and is critical for quantifying the exposure of a portfolio to securities with embedded options such as callable bonds and agency MBS because they are impacted by changes in interest rate volatility. The value of 0.29 means that if the portfolio differs from the benchmark only with respect to its exposure to changes in interest rate volatility, then this mismatch relative to the benchmark would result in a monthly isolated tracking error of 0.29 bps per month.

The isolated tracking error for the securitized spread risk factor is 0.95 bps per month. The securitized spread risk factor incorporates the exposure to changes in the spreads in the agency MBS market. The value of 0.95 means that if the portfolio differs from the benchmark only with respect to its exposure to changes in the spread in the agency MBS sector, then this mismatch relative to the benchmark would result in a monthly isolated tracking error of 0.95 bps per month.

The contribution to tracking error for each factor is shown in the third column in Exhibit 14.9. The major risk exposures of the 50-security portfolio are swap spreads (0.15 bps), corporate spreads (1.52 bps), and idiosyncratic risk (5.49 bps).

EXHIBIT 14.9 Monthly tracking errors for risk factors.

	Isolated Tracking Error	Contribution to Tracking Error	Liquidation Effect on Tracking Error
Total	7.48	7.48	−7.48
Systematic	3.71	1.84	−0.98
1. Yield Curve	1.14	0.02	0.06
YC USD–Yield/Swap Curve	1.14	0.02	0.06
2. Swap Spreads	1.09	0.15	−0.07
3. Volatility	0.29	−0.01	0.02
Yield Curve	0.29	−0.01	0.02
4. Spread Gov-Related	0.65	0.06	−0.04
Treasury Spreads	0.64	0.06	−0.03
Other Gov Spreads	0.04	0.01	−0.01
5. Spread Credit and EMG	3.66	1.52	−0.66
Credit Investment Grade	3.78	1.51	−0.58
Emerging Markets	0.67	0.01	0.02
6. Spread Securitized	0.95	0.09	−0.03
US-MBS	0.95	0.09	−0.03
Idiosyncratic	6.41	5.49	−3.62
Credit Default	1.08	0.16	−0.08

The liquidation effect on tracking error is shown in the fourth column in Exhibit 14.9. For example, if the portfolio manager hedges the systematic risk, then the portfolio tracking error will decrease by 0.98 bps per month. Because the total portfolio tracking error is 7.48 bps per month, hedging the systematic risk would reduce the monthly tracking error for the portfolio to 6.50 bps per month.

Now let us analyze the exposure of the portfolio to a particular factor, yield curve risk. There are different interest rate benchmarks that can be used. The Treasury yield curve is a standard benchmark, as is the swap curve. During noncrisis periods, the Treasury and the swap curves tend to behave the same way; however, this is not usually the case during times of market turmoil such as the credit crisis of 2008. The Barclays POINT system decomposes the swap curve into Treasury curve and swap spreads, and gives portfolio managers the flexibility to analyze spread risk over the Treasury or the swap curve depending on their preferences.

There are also different measures for the exposure to changes in the shape of the yield curve. A common one is key rate duration. As explained earlier in this chapter, key rate duration is the approximate percentage change in the portfolio value for a 100 basis point change in the rate of a particular maturity holding all other rates constant. In terms of mismatch between the portfolio and a benchmark, it is the approximate differential

EXHIBIT 14.10 Treasury curve risk for the 50-securities portfolio.

Factor name	Portfolio exposure	Benchmark exposure	Net exposure	Factor volatility	Tracking error impact of an isolated 1 std. dev. up change	Tracking error impact of a correlated 1 std. dev. up change	Marginal contribution to tracking error
USD 6M key rate	0.096	0.122	−0.026	5.15	0.13	−0.26	0.182
USD 2Y key rate	0.880	0.673	0.207	10.78	−2.23	−0.75	1.081
USD 5Y key rate	1.205	1.402	−0.197	21.04	4.15	−0.61	1.703
USD 10Y key rate	1.416	1.286	0.130	21.67	−2.82	−0.58	1.692
USD 20Y key rate	1.016	1.029	−0.013	20.71	0.27	−0.52	1.449
USD 30Y key rate	0.972	0.995	−0.022	20.84	0.47	−0.48	1.335
USD 50Y key rate	0.000	0.034	−0.034	21.09	0.71	−0.45	1.267
USD Convexity	−0.105	−0.167	0.061	1.91	0.12	0.74	0.188

percentage change in the portfolio return relative to the benchmark return for a 100 basis point change in the rate for a particular maturity holding all other rates constant.

In the Barclays POINT system, the seven key rates are the 6-month, the 2-year, the 5-year, the 10-year, the 20-year, the 30-year, and the 50-year rate. The seven key rate durations with respect to the U.S. Treasury curve as well as the option-adjusted or effective convexity (in the last row) are shown in Exhibit 14.10.

The fourth column in Exhibit 14.10, "Net exposure," shows the mismatch between the key rate duration and the convexity between the portfolio and the benchmark. Consider, for example, the 10-year key rate duration mismatch of 0.130. The portfolio return change relative to the benchmark return change for a 100 basis point change in 10-year interest rates will be 0.130.

The fifth column Exhibit 14.10, "Factor volatility," shows the monthly factor volatility and helps estimate how likely a particular factor is to move. For example, the 10-year key rate has a factor volatility of 21.67 basis points per month, the largest of key rate volatilities. The factor volatility, being the standard deviation, represents the average movement for the factor (key rate). The isolated impact of that movement on the return of the 50-security portfolio (relative to the benchmark) holding other factors constant can be found to be

Return impact of an average movement = −(Net key duration)

× (Average rate movement)

The impact is summarized in column 6 ("Tracking error impact of an isolated 1 std dev up change") in Exhibit 14.10. For example, for the 10-year key rate, we have

$$\text{Return impact of an average movement} = -(0.130) \times (21.67)$$

$$= -2.82 \text{ basis points per month.}$$

For the six-month key rate, we have

$$\text{Return impact of an average movement} = -(-0.026) \times (5.15)$$

$$= 0.13 \text{ basis points per month.}$$

Note that the return impact is different if correlations between the factors are considered (column 7, "Tracking error impact of a correlated 1 std dev up change"). For example, the return impact of an average movement in the 10-year key rate is still negative (−0.58) but is reduced. The return impact of an average movement in the six-month key rate has turned from positive (0.13) to negative (−0.26).

The last column in Exhibit 14.10, "Marginal contribution to tracking error" shows the change to tracking error resulting from a one-unit increase in a particular key rate duration. This information is useful to a portfolio manager who tries to find an effective way to reduce the portfolio exposure to Treasury yield curve risk. For example, increasing the exposure to the 10-year key rate by 1 unit increases the portfolio tracking error by 1.692 basis points.

EXHIBIT 14.11   Swap spread risk for the 50-securities portfolio.

Factor name	Portfolio exposure	Benchmark exposure	Net exposure	Factor volatility	Tracking error impact of an isolated 1 std. dev. up change	Tracking error impact of a correlated 1 std. dev. up change	Marginal contribution to tracking error
USD 6M swap spread	0.096	0.096	0.000	5.25	0.00	0.18	−0.127
USD 2Y swap spread	0.480	0.416	0.064	4.06	−0.26	0.17	−0.089'
USD 5Y swap spread	0.829	0.886	−0.057	3.31	0.19	0.01	−0.002
USD 10Y swap spread	1.216	0.981	0.235	3.31	−0.78	−0.62	0.273
USD 20Y swap spread	0.770	0.765	0.005	4.03	−0.02	−0.06	0.034
USD 30Y swap spread	0.222	0.447	−0.224	4.08	0.91	0.62	−0.340
USD 50Y Swap Spread	0.000	0.032	−0.032	6.28	0.20	0.65	−0.549

Exhibit 14.11 summarizes the exposure of the portfolio to changes in the swap spread. (The swap spread is the difference between the swap curve and the Treasury yield curve.) Based on column 7 ("Tracking error impact of a correlated 1 std dev up change") in Exhibits 14.10 and 14.11, one can conclude that movements in swap spread factors have less impact on the portfolio than movements in Treasury yield curve factors.

Summary

- Important groups of factors in fixed income portfolio management include term structure factors, spread factors, currency factors, volatility factors, and prepayment factors.
- Structured fixed income portfolio selection methods include stratification and optimization.
- In the stratification approach, a portfolio manager considers "buckets" or "cells" for particular factors such as credit quality or industry. The portfolio manager can then select a few bonds for these buckets in such a way that the relative weight of all the bonds in a particular bucket in his portfolio is the same as the target weight of bonds with the corresponding characteristics.
- The procedure used in the stratification approach is helpful for visualizing mismatches between a portfolio and a benchmark but becomes cumbersome if multiple factors are considered.
- An optimization approach uses an optimizer to allocate (or rebalance) a portfolio in such a way as to pursue a particular goal and satisfy pre-specified constraints.
- Risk decomposition for fixed income portfolios allows portfolio managers to understand how changes in factors that drive market returns affect the portfolio and the benchmark.
- Analytical metrics of interest in decomposing the risk for a fixed income portfolio include high-level portfolio characteristics, the portfolio exposure to different sectors, and the portfolio exposure to factors representing important sources of sytematic risks.

CHAPTER 15

Constructing Liability-Driven Portfolios

The portfolio strategies discussion so far in this book has focused on managing funds relative to a benchmark that is a market index. That is, assets are managed against an index comprised of the same assets. In a liability-driven strategy, the goal is to manage funds to satisfy contractual liabilities.

Asset-liability management is a problem faced primarily by two major groups of institutional investors: life insurance companies and defined benefit pension plans. Life insurance products that include liabilities for the life insurance companies are annuities and guaranteed investment contracts. There are two types of pension plans: defined contribution plans and defined benefit plans. The former require that the plan sponsor contribute a specified amount to a plan participant's pension and once that contribution is made, it is the responsibility of the plan participant to invest the contribution to earn a sufficient return for retirement. That is, once a plan participant retires, no further payments are made by the plan sponsor, and there is no future obligation of the plan sponsor. In contrast, for a defined benefit plan, the plan sponsor agrees to make payments to plan participants when they retire. The annual payment is determined by a formula that is based on the number of years a plan participant was employed and an average of some specified number of years of income prior to retirement.

Although there is a long history of the use of liability-driven strategies by life insurance companies, that is not the case for defined benefit plans. In fact, the major reason cited by market commentators as to why there are major problems faced by defined benefit plans by corporations and municipalities is that plan sponsors and their advisors have failed to consider liabilities in formulating investment strategies, instead making investment decisions based on the expectations of future asset returns only. That is, plan sponsors have been making their asset allocation decision based on asset class performance as measured by market indexes for each asset class, not the liability structure. The passage of the Pension Protection Act of 2006 pushed more defined benefit plan sponsors to adopt liability-driven strategies.

In this chapter we discuss liability-driven strategies. We begin with a discussion of the risks faced by both life insurance companies and defined benefit plans seeking to satisfy liabilities. We then describe the two main types of strategies used to deal with the risks associated with strategies to satisfy liabilities—immunization and cash-flow matching—and give examples of how they are used in the case of life insurance products and defined benefit plans. The last section of this chapter reviews the use of techniques for optimization under uncertainty to address the asset-liability management problem.

15.1 RISKS ASSOCIATED WITH LIABILITIES

There are three risks associated with liabilities: (1) interest rate risk, (2) inflation risk, and (3) longevity risk.

15.1.1 Interest Rate Risk

In Chapter 13, we described how to calculate the duration of a bond. Duration is a measure of interest rate risk. The duration of a portfolio of bonds is the approximate percentage change in a portfolio's value for a 100 basis point change in interest rates assuming that interest rates change in a parallel fashion. Consequently, a portfolio duration of 5, for example, means that the portfolio value will change by approximately 5% for a 100 basis point change in interest rates. The concept of duration applies equally to liabilities as it does to a bond portfolio and is calculated in the same way. The interpretation of a liability duration is also the same. For example, a liability duration of 10 means that the approximate change in the value of the liabilities for a 100 basis point change in interest rates is approximately 10%.

The value of the liabilities is calculated by taking the present value of the liabilities discounted at suitable interest rates. While determining what the appropriate interest rates should be is critical, let us hold off on that issue for now. What is important to understand at this point is that the higher the interest rates at which liabilities are discounted, the lower the value of the liabilities, and vice versa.

The difference between the value of the assets and the liabilities is the *surplus*. That is,

$$\text{Surplus} = \text{Value of bond portfolio} - \text{Value of liabilities}$$

When interest rates change, the surplus will change based on the portfolio duration and liability duration as well as the current values of the portfolio and liabilities. For example, let us look at how the bond portfolio and liability values change when interest rates change by 100 basis points and the portfolio duration and liability duration are 5 and 10, respectively. We assume that the current value of the bond portfolio is $100 million and the value of the liabilities is $80 million. The surplus is then $20 million.

If interest rates change by 100 basis points, the bond portfolio will change by 5% or $5 million, whereas the liabilities will change by 10% or $8 million. Consequently, if interest rates increase by 100 basis points, the portfolio value will decline by $5 million but the liabilities will decline by more, $8 million. Hence, the surplus will increase by $3 million. If, instead, interest rates decline by 100 basis points, the surplus will decrease by $3 million.

From this simple illustration we can see why understanding the nature of the liability structure in terms of its interest rate risk cannot be ignored. Although it might seem in our illustration that a decline in interest rates would benefit an institutional investor, we can see that when an institutional investor must recognize liabilities, it is the relative duration of assets and liabilities and the current value of assets and liabilities that determines the impact on the surplus.

In a liability-driven strategy, the key is controlling the liability duration relative to the bond portfolio (in our illustration) or, in general, relative to the portfolio duration of the assets. For life insurance companies, the liability structure for some products may be such that assets available in the cash market can create a targeted portfolio duration needed to control interest rate risk. This may be difficult, however, for some insurance contracts, when the liabilities are long term and available durations for bonds in the cash market are shorter. In the case of the typical defined benefit plans, liability duration is typically much higher than available for bonds in the cash market. For example, the liability duration for a typical defined benefit plan will exceed 15 while the duration of long-term investment-grade bonds may be only 7. We discuss solutions later in this chapter when we focus on defined benefit pension plans (Section 15.3).

15.1.2 Inflation Risk

When the future payments of liabilities need to be adjusted for the rate of inflation, then just like assets, liabilities are subject to inflation risk. Some life insurance products have adjustments for inflation. Almost all defined benefit pension plans adjust plan participant payments for inflation. When projecting liabilities for pension plans, an assumed rate of inflation is made. Thus, the *inflation risk* for pension plans is that the projected inflation rate assumed will be less than the realized inflation rate. The sensitivity of the pension plan liabilities to inflation risk can be quantified by changing the inflation rate used in projecting liabilities and then revaluing the liabilities.

Dealing with inflation risk in a liability-driven strategy can be done by using inflation-protection securities. These securities, more popularly referred to as *linkers*, are issued by central governments and corporations. The linkers issued by the U.S. Department of the Treasury are called Treasury Inflation Protection Securities or TIPS.

15.1.3 Longevity Risk

The length of the liability of policyholders of a life insurance product such as an annuity and the postretirement payments to a plan participant for a defined benefit pension plan depend on an assumed life expectancy. *Longevity risk* is the risk that the actual life expectancy of life insurance policyholders and plan participants in a pension plan will exceed the life expectancy assumed in projecting the liabilities. Longevity risk means that there is the risk that the amount that will actually have to be paid to policyholders or plan participants will exceed the amount projected.

To appreciate the significance of longevity risk, consider the change in the U.S. life experience since 1950. The average life expectancy at birth for both sexes according to mortality tables was as follows: 1950, 68.2 years; 1960, 69.7 years; 1970, 70.8 years; 1980, 73.7 years; 1990, 75.8 years; 2000, 77 years; 2010, 78.7 years. It is projected to be 79.5 by 2020.

Consider the projected liabilities of a defined pension plan sponsor whose actuary used an expected life of 73.7 years in 1980 and an assumed retirement at age 65. In 1980, there would have been a projected payout of 8.7 (= 73.7 − 65) years after age 65. By 2010, the pension fund would have, on average, to make cash payments for five additional years (78.7 years minus 73.7 years).

As with inflation risk, the sensitivity to changes in the expected life used in the projection of liabilities and the new valuation for the liabilities based on that expected life can be used to assess the importance of longevity risk.

Liability-driven strategies to deal with longevity risk are complicated. They involve the use of over-the-counter derivative instruments whose payoff depends on life expectancy.

15.2 LIABILITY-DRIVEN STRATEGIES OF LIFE INSURANCE COMPANIES

Having reviewed the sources of liability risks, we discuss liability-driven strategies for life insurance companies in this section and defined benefit pension plans in the next section.

Liability-driven strategies of life insurance companies range from partial immunization (duration immunization) to complete immunization, or cash-flow matching. Financial derivatives can also be used to offset some of the risks embedded in the liability structure.[1] Finally, some aspects of the evaluation of liabilities are too complex to reassess on a regular basis. At the end of this section, we discuss advanced optimization-based and simulation-based approaches for modeling liability risk for life insurance companies.

15.2.1 Immunization

Immunization can be defined as the process by which a bond portfolio is created so that it has an assured return for a specific time horizon regardless of interest rate changes. That is, an immunization strategy deals solely with the interest-rate risk associated with liabilities and assets.

The spectrum of immunizations strategies is between two general categories:[2] *partial (duration) immunization*[3] and *complete (cash-flow matching) immunization*.[4] The former strategy is the one primarily used by life insurance companies in managing a guaranteed investment contract (GIC). A GIC issued by a life insurance company guarantees a fixed rate to a policyholder over a specified period of time, say five years. GICs are commonly purchased by sponsors of defined benefit pension plans as part of a fund's portfolio, and in general are popular investment vehicles. Insurance giant AIG notoriously used US$9 billion of the government bailout after the financial crisis in the 2007–2008 to pay out on guaranteed investment contracts it had sold to investors.

An extension of the duration-based immunization strategy as well as a complete immunization strategy with cash-flow matching are the two strategies used by life insurance companies for insurance products such as annuities where payments are made to policyholders over their lifetime starting at some future date.

We begin with the duration immunization strategy. The following are the important characteristics of this strategy:

1. A specified time horizon.
2. An assured rate of return during the holding period to a fixed horizon date.
3. Insulation from the effects of potential adverse interest rate changes on the portfolio value at the horizon date.

---

[1] The use of financial derivatives is discussed in more detail in Chapters 16–18.
[2] See also Stockton, Donaldson, and Shtekhman (2014).
[3] It is also sometimes referred to as *single-period immunization*.
[4] It is also sometimes referred to as *multiperiod immunization*.

The fundamental mechanism underlying immunization is a portfolio structure that balances the change in the value of the portfolio at the end of the investment horizon with the return from the reinvestment of portfolio cash flows (coupon payments and maturing securities). That is, immunization requires offsetting interest-rate risk and reinvestment risk. To accomplish this balancing act requires controlling duration and setting the present value of the cash flows from the bond portfolio to the present value of the liability. By setting the duration of the portfolio equal to the desired portfolio time horizon, the offsetting of positive and negative incremental return sources can under certain circumstances be assured. However, given the fact that duration is the tool that is used, the portfolio is only immunized if there is a parallel shift in the yield curve. If there is a change in interest rates that does not correspond to this shape-preserving shift, matching the duration to the investment horizon no longer assures immunization.

15.2.1.1 Partial Immunization Using Duration: An Example

We use an example to illustrate how duration immunization works. Suppose that a life insurance company has issued a GIC that is such that a liability of $1 million must be paid five years from now. We assume that the amount is fixed and is not adjusted for inflation over the time period. The life insurance company must invest enough money today to meet this future obligation. That is, ignoring any profit, the life insurance company must charge the policyholder a premium such that when that premium is invested at prevailing market interest rates for five years, the investment will generate $1 million that is then paid to satisfy the GIC liability.

To keep it simple, let us assume that the investment universe available to the life insurance company consists of two bonds, B_1 and B_2, with face values of $100, maturities of 12 years and 5 years, and coupon rates of 6% and 5%, respectively. For simplicity, we assume that the coupons are paid once per year rather than semiannually. How much should the life insurance company invest in the two bonds so that the overall portfolio (bonds and liability) is immunized against changes in interest rates?

Exhibit 15.1 contains the prevailing yield curve (column "Spot"), the discount factors computed from the yield curve (column "df"), the cash flows from bonds 1 and 2 (columns "B1" and "B2"), and the present values of the cash flows from the two bonds (columns "PV1" and "PV2"). The current prices of the bonds are determined by summing up the present values of the cash flows for each bond.[5] They are $89.66 and $120.10, respectively.

Now let us compute the durations of the bonds and the liabilities. As we explained in Chapter 13.4.1.1, duration can be interpreted as the

---

[5] See the equation for the value of a bond in Chapter 13.2.4.

EXHIBIT 15.1   Current yield curve, discount factors, cash flows from bonds 1 and 2, as well as present values of cash flows from the two bonds.

Year	Spot	df	B1	PV1	B2	PV2
1	3.64%	0.965	6	5.79	10	9.65
2	4.17%	0.922	6	5.53	10	9.22
3	4.70%	0.871	6	5.23	10	8.71
4	5.21%	0.816	6	4.90	10	8.16
5	5.45%	0.767	6	4.60	110	84.36
6	6.06%	0.703	6	4.22		
7	6.43%	0.646	6	3.88		
8	6.75%	0.593	6	3.56		
9	7.10%	0.539	6	3.24		
10	7.35%	0.492	6	2.95		
11	7.57%	0.448	6	2.69		
12	7.79%	0.406	106	43.09		
Price of bond today			B1	89.66	B2	120.10

approximate change in the value of the bond per unit change in interest rates, and the formula can be stated as

$$D = \frac{B_- - B_+}{2 \cdot B_0 \cdot \Delta y}$$

Exhibit 15.2 shows how the duration can be determined for bonds 1 and 2. We consider a shift in interest rates of $\Delta y = 25$ basis points[6] and compute the new yield curves, present values, and bond prices if interest rates shift up or down by this amount. The notation used is as follows: df− and df+ are the discount factors[7] under a negative shift and a positive shift of the yield curve, respectively, PV1− and PV1+ are the present values of the cash flows for bond 1 under a negative shift and a positive shift of interest rates, and PV2− and PV2+ are the present values of the cash flows for bond 2 under a negative shift and a positive shift in interest rates.

The bond prices are as follows: under a negative shift in interest rates, $B_{1-} = \$91.46$, and $B_{2-} = \$121.32$. Under a positive shift in interest rates, $B_{1+} = \$87.91$, and $B_{2+} = \$118.90$. This lets us compute the durations for the two bonds, D_1 and D_2. For example, for bond 1, we have

$$D_1 = \frac{91.46 - 87.91}{2 \cdot 89.66 \cdot 0.0025} = 7.91$$

---

[6]This means that we change the interest rate for each maturity in the table by the amount Δy.

[7]Calculated as $1/(1 + \text{Interest Rate})^{\text{Number of Years}}$ for each time period.

EXHIBIT 15.2 Effect of shift of $\Delta y = 25$ bp on bond prices.

df−	PV1−	PV2−	df+	PV1+	PV2+
0.967	5.80	9.67	0.963	5.78	9.63
0.926	5.56	9.26	0.917	5.50	9.17
0.878	5.27	8.78	0.865	5.19	8.65
0.824	4.94	8.24	0.808	4.85	8.08
0.776	4.66	85.37	0.758	4.55	83.37
0.713	5.28		0.693	4.16	
0.657	3.94		0.636	3.82	
0.604	3.63		0.582	3.49	
0.551	3.31		0.528	3.17	
0.504	3.02		0.481	2.88	
0.460	2.76		0.437	2.62	
0.418	44.31		0.395	41.91	
	91.46	121.32		87.91	118.90

Similarly, the duration for bond 2 can be computed to be 4.02.

To compute the duration of the liability of $1 million, we go through a similar procedure. The five-year spot rate is 5.45%, so the present value of the liability is

$$\frac{1,000,000}{(1+0.0545)^5} = \$766,950.05$$

Under a negative shift in interest rates of 25 bps, the value of the liability becomes

$$\frac{1,000,000}{(1+0.0545-0.0025)^5} = \$776,106.46$$

and under a positive shift in interest rates, it becomes $757,922.96. Therefore, the duration of the liability is 4.74.

Now let us control for interest rate risk. We construct a two-bond portfolio so as immunize against interest rate changes. To do so, we look for the number of units of bonds (x_1 and x_2) to invest so that the present value of the cash flows from the bonds equals the present value of the liability and the duration of the portfolio of bonds matches the duration of the liability. How do we compute the duration of the portfolio of bonds? Recall from Chapter 13.4.1 that the duration of a bond portfolio is the weighted average of the durations of the individual bonds, where the weights in the weighted average are the weights of the bonds in the portfolio. In this case, the weights can be expressed as $x_1/(x_1 + x_2)$ and $x_2/(x_1 + x_2)$.

We need to solve the following system of equations, in which the unknowns are the number of units x_1 and x_2 to invest in bond 1 and bond 2, respectively:

$$B_1 \cdot x_1 + B_2 \cdot x_2 = PV(\text{Liability})$$
$$D_1 \cdot x_1/(x_1 + x_2) + D_2 \cdot x_1/(x_1 + x_2) = D(\text{Liability})$$

In order to make this a linear system of equations, we multiply both sides of the second equation by $(x_1 + x_2)$. Hence, we want to find x_1 and x_2 that satisfy

$$B_1 \cdot x_1 + B_2 \cdot x_2 = PV(\text{Liability})$$
$$D_1 \cdot x_1 + D_2 \cdot x_1 = D(\text{Liability}) \cdot (x_1 + x_2)$$

This can be done with a simple linear optimization solver or a numerical procedure. (In the case of two bonds, it is easy to solve by hand, but in the case of larger portfolios it would require numerical implementation.) If we have an optimization solver, the decision variables will be the number of units to invest in bond 1 and bond 2, x_1 and x_2. We can maximize, for example, the expression on the left-hand side of the first equation, subject to constraints that are represented by the two equations. This will make sure that the two equations are satisfied. In our example, the optimal solution is to purchase 1,239.14 units of bond 1 and 5,460.68 units of bond 2.

15.2.1.2 Immunization Risk Let us now verify that this investment will indeed cover the liability if there are parallel shifts in the yield curve. Exhibit 15.3 summarizes the information on the price of the bonds, the value of the liability, and the total portfolio value under a positive and a negative shift of 1% (100 bps) in interest rates. We can see that the portfolio remains largely (although not perfectly) immunized against changes in interest rates.[8]

---

[8] You can play around with the number of units to invest in the two bonds to see that the change in the portfolio value for a different number of units invested in the bonds is worse. For example, a combination of 1,000 units of bond 1 and 5,639.21 units of bond 2 also results in a present value of $766,950.05, which offsets the present value of the liability. However, if interest rates shift by 100 bps, the value of the overall portfolio is −$1,952.73 (in the case of a negative shift) and $2,094.94 (in the case of a positive shift), which is a larger discrepancy than in the case of the immunized portfolio found in this section.

EXHIBIT 15.3 Immunization results.

	$\Delta y = 0$	$\Delta y = 100$ bp	$\Delta y = -100$ bp
Bond 1			
Units	1,239.14	1,239.14	1,239.14
Price	$89.66	$82.93	$97.15
Bond 2			
Units	5,460.68	5,460.68	5,460.68
Price	$120.10	$115.40	$125.07
Liability value	$766,950.05	$731,596.59	$804,373.54
Portfolio value (Bonds – Liability)	0	$1,324.19	–$1,048.30

A natural extension of the classical immunization strategy we described is a technique for modifying the assumption of parallel shifts in the yield curve, which is implicit in the use of duration for immunization. An approach that can handle any arbitrary interest rate change so that it is not necessary to specify an alternative duration measure was developed by Fong and Vasicek (1984). A measure of immunization risk is established against any arbitrary interest rate change, and the immunization risk measure is then minimized subject to the constraint that the duration of the portfolio is equal to the investment horizon, resulting in a portfolio with minimum exposure to any interest rate movements.

Let us explain immunization risk in more detail. Exhibit 15.4 contains information about two portfolios, A and B. The spikes in the two panels of the exhibit represent actual portfolio cash flows. The taller spikes depict the actual cash flows generated by matured securities while the smaller spikes represent coupon payments. Both portfolio A and portfolio B are composed of two bonds with duration equal to the investment horizon. Portfolio A is a *barbell portfolio*—a portfolio comprising short and long maturities and interim coupon payments. For portfolio B, the two bonds mature very close to the investment horizon and the coupon payments are nominal over the investment horizon. A portfolio with this characteristic is called *a bullet portfolio*. It is not difficult to see why the barbell portfolio should be riskier than the bullet portfolio. Assume that both portfolios have durations equal to the horizon length, so that both portfolios are immune to parallel rate changes. This immunity is attained as a consequence of balancing the effect of changes in reinvestment rates on payments received during the investment horizon against the effect of changes in market value of the portion of the portfolio still outstanding at the end of the investment horizon.

Portfolio A: High-risk immunized portfolio:

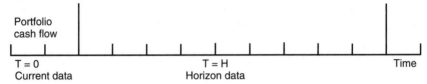

T = 0   T = H   Time
Current data   Horizon data

Note: Portfolio duration matches horizon length. Portfolio's cash flow dispersed.

Portfolio B: Low-risk immunized portfolio

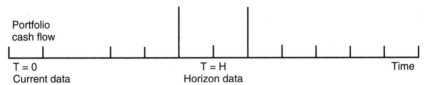

T = 0   T = H   Time
Current data   Horizon data

Note: Portfolio duration matches horizon length. Portfolio's cash flow concentrated around horizon dates.

Exhibit 15.4 Immunization risk.

When interest rates change in an arbitrary nonparallel way, however, the effect on the two portfolios is very different. Suppose, for instance, that short rates decline while long rates go up. Both portfolios would realize a decline of the portfolio value at the end of the investment horizon because they would experience a capital loss in addition to lower reinvestment rates. The decline, however, would be substantially higher for the barbell portfolio for two reasons. First, the lower reinvestment rates are experienced on the barbell portfolio for longer time intervals than on the bullet portfolio, so that the opportunity loss is much greater. Second, the portion of the barbell port-folio still outstanding at the end of the investment horizon is much longer than that of the bullet portfolio, which means that the same rate increase would result in a much greater capital loss. Thus the bullet portfolio has less exposure to whatever the change in the interest rate structure may be than the barbell portfolio.

It should be clear from this discussion that immunization risk is the risk of reinvestment. The portfolio that has the least reinvestment risk will have the least immunization risk. When there is a high dispersion of cash flows around the horizon date, as in the barbell portfolio, the portfolio is exposed to higher reinvestment risk. However, when the cash flows are concentrated around the horizon date, as in the bullet portfolio, the portfolio is subject to minimum reinvestment risk.

An extension to the standard immunization approach is key rate immunization, which explicitly recognizes that cash flows occurring at different times in the future demand different rates.[9]

15.2.1.3 Further Issues How often should the portfolio be rebalanced to adjust its duration? On the one hand, more frequent rebalancing increases transaction costs, thereby reducing the likelihood of achieving the target return. On the other hand, less frequent rebalancing results in the portfolio's duration wandering from the target duration, which will also reduce the likelihood of achieving the target return. Thus the portfolio manager of the life insurance company faces a trade-off: some transaction costs must be accepted to prevent the portfolio duration from wandering too far from its target, but some misalignment in the portfolio duration must be tolerated, or transaction costs will become prohibitively high.

In the actual process leading to the construction of an immunized portfolio, the selection of the investment universe is extremely important. Immunization theory assumes there will be no defaults and that securities will be responsive only to overall changes in interest rates. The lower the credit quality of the securities permitted in the portfolio, the greater the likelihood that these assumptions will not be met. Furthermore, securities with embedded options, such as call features or prepayments permitted in mortgage-backed securities, complicate and may even prevent the accurate estimation of cash flows and hence duration, which prevents immunization from achieving the desired effect. Finally, liquidity is a consideration for immunized portfolios because, as just noted, they must be rebalanced over time.

15.2.1.4 Complete Immunization Using Cash-Flow Matching An annuity policy is an example of an insurance product that obligates the insurer to make periodic payments to the insured for a specified period of time or until the death of the insured. Insurance companies facing multiperiod liabilities typically use one of two immunization strategies. The first is a duration-based multiperiod immunization strategy, an extension of the single-period duration-based immunization strategy discussed in Section 15.2.1.1, which involves the matching of duration of the assets and the liabilities, as well as satisfying other conditions. We will discuss this strategy in Section 15.3.1 when we discuss immunization for a defined benefit pension plan. The other multiperiod immunization strategy is cash-flow matching, which we discuss here.

---

[9] See Chapter 13.4.1.3.

Cash-flow matching is used to construct a portfolio that can fund a schedule of liabilities from portfolio return and asset value, with the portfolio's value diminishing to zero after payment of the last liability. A cash-flow matching strategy can be described intuitively as follows. A bond is selected with a maturity that matches the last liability. An amount of principal equal to the amount of the last liability is then invested in this bond. The remaining elements of the liability stream are then reduced by the coupon payments on this bond, and another bond is chosen for the next-to-last liability, adjusted for any coupon payments of the first bond selected. Going backward in time, this sequence is continued until all liabilities have been matched by payments on the securities selected for the portfolio.

Optimization techniques are more effective for constructing a least-cost cash-flow matching portfolio from an acceptable universe of bonds. Next, we show a simplified example to illustrate how the problem can be formulated and solved with optimization methods.

Consider an asset manager who is managing funds to satisfy the liabilities for a four-year annuity for policyholders. We will assume that the policy calls for semi-annual payments over the next four years based on an assumed expected life of four additional years. Hence, with these simplified assumptions the life insurance company is not addressing the issue of longevity risk if the policy actually calls for payments over the lifetime of the policyholders.

Let the cash obligations for the eight payment dates of the next four years be represented by a vector $\mathbf{m} = (m_1, \ldots, m_8)$. The life insurance company's asset manager is considering investing in five different high-investment-grade bonds. Over the next eight payment dates (i.e., semi-annually), bond i pays out coupons $\mathbf{c}_i = (c_{i1}, \ldots, c_{i8})$. If the bond matures at date t, the corresponding c_{it} equals the coupon rate plus the principal. Bonds 1–5 currently trade at ask prices $\mathbf{p} = (p_1, \ldots, p_5)$, where $p_1 = \$102.36$, $p_2 = \$110.83$, $p_3 = \$96.94$, $p_4 = \$114.65$, and $p_5 = \$96.63$. The relevant data are provided in Exhibit 15.5. The asset manager would like to ensure that the coupon payments from the bonds cover the annuity's obligations.[10]

To formulate this problem, the asset manager must be clear on what the objective of the fund is. Although it is not stated explicitly in the problem, it makes sense for the objective to be to minimize the cost of acquiring the bonds today while still meeting all expected future obligations.

The decision variables can be defined as the dollar amounts $\mathbf{x} = (x_1, x_2, x_3, x_4, x_5)$ to invest in each of the five bonds. The cost of acquiring

---

[10]Note that by making the assumption that these bonds are investment grade, we are assuming that the issuers of these bonds have a low probability of failing to meet their obligation to make the coupon payments.

EXHIBIT 15.5   Cash-flow matching example data.

Current bond price (p_i)	$102.36	$110.83	$96.94	$114.65	$96.63	
Cash flows (c_{it})						Obligations (m_t)
$t=1$	$ 2.50	$ 5.00	$ 3.00	$ 4.00	$ 3.50	$ 100,000.00
$t=2$	$ 2.50	$ 5.00	$ 3.00	$ 4.00	$ 3.50	$ 200,000.00
$t=3$	$ 2.50	$ 5.00	$ 3.00	$ 4.00	$ 3.50	$ 100,000.00
$t=4$	$ 2.50	$ 5.00	$ 3.00	$ 4.00	$ 3.50	$ 200,000.00
$t=5$	$ 102.50	$ 5.00	$ 3.00	$ 4.00	$ 3.50	$ 800,000.00
$t=6$		$ 105.00	$ 3.00	$ 4.00	$ 3.50	$ 1,200,000.00
$t=7$			$ 103.00	$ 4.00	$ 3.50	$ 400,000.00
$t=8$				$ 104.00	$ 103.50	$ 1,000,000.00

the bonds today is the sum of the amounts paid for the purchase of the five bonds:

$$\sum_{i=1}^{5} p_i \cdot x_i = \mathbf{p}' \mathbf{x}$$

The constraints are that at each payment date, the cash flows from the coupons of all the bonds are at least as large as the liabilities. Mathematically, the optimization problem can be stated as

$$\min_{x_1,\dots,x_5} \sum_{i=1}^{5} p_i \cdot x_i$$

$$\text{subject to} \quad \sum_{i=1}^{5} c_{it} \cdot x_i \geq m_t, \quad t = 1, \dots, 8$$

$$x_i \geq 0, \quad i = 1, \dots, 5$$

This formulation is a linear programming problem[11] because both the objective function and the constraints are linear functions of the decision variables x_1, x_2, x_3, x_4, x_5. We show its implementation with Excel Solver next.[12]

Exhibit 15.6 shows the spreadsheet set up for the cash-flow matching problem. Cells B4 through F4 are the decision variables. They can be left empty at the beginning. The input parameters, which are known in advance,

---

[11] See Chapter 6.2.2.
[12] See Chapter 6.6 for an introduction to optimization with Excel Solver.

	A	B	C	D	E	F	G	H	I
1	**Cash flow matching problem**								
2									
3	**Decision variables**	Bond 1	Bond 2	Bond 3	Bond 4	Bond 5			
4	amounts	6,000.00	28,103.61	3,555.18	-	9,661.84			
5									
6	**Objective function**								
7	minimize cost	$102.36	$110.83	$96.94	$114.65	$96.63	$ 5,007,293.41		
8									
9	**Constraints**						Total		Required
10	t=1	$ 2.50	$ 5.00	$ 3.00	$ 4.00	$ 3.50	$ 200,000.00	>=	$ 100,000.00
11	t=2	$ 2.50	$ 5.00	$ 3.00	$ 4.00	$ 3.50	$ 200,000.00	>=	$ 200,000.00
12	t=3	$ 2.50	$ 5.00	$ 3.00	$ 4.00	$ 3.50	$ 200,000.00	>=	$ 100,000.00
13	t=4	$ 2.50	$ 5.00	$ 3.00	$ 4.00	$ 3.50	$ 200,000.00	>=	$ 200,000.00
14	t=5	$ 102.50	$ 5.00	$ 3.00	$ 4.00	$ 3.50	$ 800,000.00	>=	$ 800,000.00
15	t=6	$ -	$ 105.00	$ 3.00	$ 4.00	$ 3.50	$ 2,995,360.68	>=	$ 1,200,000.00
16	t=7	$ -	$ -	$ 103.00	$ 4.00	$ 3.50	$ 400,000.00	>=	$ 400,000.00
17	t=8	$ -	$ -	$ -	$ 104.00	$ 103.50	$ 1,000,000.00	>=	$ 1,000,000.00

Exhibit 15.6 Excel spreadsheet set up for the cash-flow matching problem.

are the ask prices (cells B7:F7), the coupon payments for each bond at each time period (stored in the array B10:F17) and the liabilities at each time period (stored in cells I10:I17). Cells G7 and G10:G17 contain formula expressions for the objective function and the constraints of the problem, respectively. The formula for each cell is as follows:

G7:   =SUMPRODUCT(B7:F7,$B$4:$F$4)

G10: =SUMPRODUCT(B10:F10,$B$4:$F$4)

G11: =SUMPRODUCT(B11:F11,$B$4:$F$4)

G12: =SUMPRODUCT(B12:F12,$B$4:$F$4)

G13: =SUMPRODUCT(B13:F13,$B$4:$F$4)

G14: =SUMPRODUCT(B14:F14,$B$4:$F$4)

G15: =SUMPRODUCT(B15:F15,$B$4:$F$4)

G16: =SUMPRODUCT(B16:F16,$B$4:$F$4)

G17: =SUMPRODUCT(B17:F17,$B$4:$F$4)

The specifications for the Excel Solver dialog box are shown in Exhibit 15.7. The optimal strategy, shown in cells B4:F4 in Exhibit 15.6, is to purchase 6,000 units of Bond 1, 28,103.61 of Bond 2, 3,555.18 of Bond 3, none of Bond 4, and 9,661.84 of Bond 5. In practice, there will need to be rounding, and the bonds may need to be purchased in lots. These requirements can be imposed as additional constraints.

15.2.2 Advanced Optimization Approaches

So far, we have described how to hedge liability risk for insurance providers with a bond portfolio. In practice, once the premiums from the policyholders are pooled, insurance companies may invest them in a fixed income portfolio or in a portfolio with a substantial equity component. The latter strategy falls within the realm of return-driven strategies,[13] in which the focus is on generating return rather than hedging, and higher returns in the equity market are pursued to improve the portfolio return as a whole. There is

---

[13]van der Meer and Smink (1993).

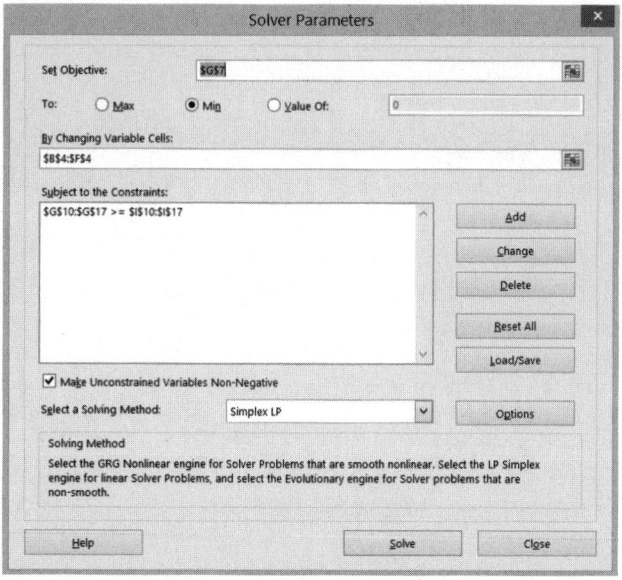

Exhibit 15.7 Excel Solver dialog box for the cash-flow matching problem.

some evidence that life insurers can substantially increase their profits and offer higher guarantees by investing a higher proportion of their assets in an optimally structured equity portfolio, although that may lead to higher variability in the mismatch between assets and liabilities. Advanced techniques for optimization under uncertainty[14] in combination with Monte Carlo simulation for the generation of future scenarios[15] have been applied in this context. For example, Consiglio, Saunders, and Zenios (2006) use stochastic programming[16] to find the optimal structure of the portfolio underlying an insurance company's fund. Gulpinar, Pachamanova, and Canakoglu (2015) study a formulation of the multi-period investment problem with equities using ideas from robust optimization,[17] finding that robust optimization strategies have good performance in terms of variability and relative return under unfavorable market regimes where the future realizations of equity returns follow probability distributions with lower means than expected.

---

[14]See Chapter 7.
[15]See Chapter 5.
[16]See Chapter 7.2.
[17]See Chapter 7.3.

15.2.3 Constructing Replicating Portfolios

As we mentioned earlier in this section, some aspects of the liabilities faced by insurance companies are difficult to model and hedge. In particular, there are complex actuarial calculations involved in the determination of the value of the liabilities, making it difficult to understand the behavior of life insurance liabilities under different economic scenarios. The creation of *replicating portfolios* has been suggested as an efficient way to recalculate liabilities, capital requirements, and embedded values so as to make actuarial calculations more accessible, quickly reassess liabilities as market conditions change, and project market-consistent balance sheets for insurance companies.[18] The idea of replicating portfolios, or *replios*, is to replace features of insurance contracts with capital market "equivalents," whose value can then be marked to market. As an example, guaranteed liabilities may be matched with zero-coupon bonds, maturity guarantees may be matched with put options, and longevity-related features may be matched with life table amortizing bonds or mortality swaps.

There are generally three ways to construct a replicating portfolio:[19]

1. *Balance sheet method:* Find a portfolio of assets whose current market value matches the fair value of liabilities under a range of sensitivities (i.e., small changes for model parameters).
2. *Aggregate cash flow method:* Find a portfolio of assets whose total future discounted (or rolled-up) cash flows match the total discounted (or rolled-up) liability cash flows closely in a range of scenarios.
3. *Annual cash flow method:* Find a portfolio of assets whose future cash flows by time match the liability cash flows closely in a range of scenarios for all years.

For all three approaches, stochastic optimization[20] can be used to build the replicating portfolio so that the difference between the cash flows of the assets in the replicating portfolio and the liability cash flows is minimized over a wide variety of scenarios generated from factor realizations.[21] The replicating portfolio is then validated by running a regression of its predicted value in multiple scenarios against the predicted values of liabilities in those

---

[18]Burmeister and Black (2007), Burmeister, Dorsel, and Matson (2010), and IBM Algo materials. IBM Algo's enterprise risk management (ERM) solutions are currently used by two thirds of the CRO forum, a group of professional risk managers focusing on developing best practices in risk management for the insurance industry. (www.thecroforum.org/).
[19]Burmeister, Dorsel, and Matson (2010).
[20]See Chapter 6.
[21]See Chapter 9 for an introduction to factor models.

scenarios. The goal is to obtain a replicating portfolio with high explanatory power for the value of the liabilities.

Significant use of replicating portfolios has been driven especially by large insurance companies. The main reasons for adoption of the idea include the fact that it is easier to run a large set of scenarios for asset portfolios than economic capital calculations for existing actuarial projection systems, the fact that custom-built liability models can be incorporated easily into the system, and the fact that multiple existing actuarial systems within a firm can be combined through a common cash flow and risk evaluation tool.[22]

Once the replicating portfolio has been created to match the liabilities portfolio, insurance companies can work with the replicating portfolio for the purposes of defining liability-driven strategies, evaluating compliance with solvency requirements, or measuring risk.

15.3 LIABILITY-DRIVEN STRATEGIES OF DEFINED BENEFIT PENSION FUNDS

In Section 15.1, we described the concept of surplus. For the typical defined benefit pension plan, the value of the liabilities exceeds the value of the assets. The economic health of a pension plan is measured by what is referred to as its *funding gap*, which is calculated as follows:

$$\text{Funding gap} = \text{Projected value of fund liabilities}$$
$$- \text{Market value of fund assets}$$

The funding gap is simply the amount of the pension plan's unfunded liability.

An alternative way of looking at the economic health of a pension plan is by looking at the plan's assets as a percentage of its projected liabilities. The ratio is called the *funding ratio*:

$$\text{Funding ratio} = \frac{\text{Market value of fund assets}}{\text{Projected value of the liabilities}}$$

The lower the funding ratio, the greater the funding gap is.

Pension fund rules are such that a funding gap does not have to be eliminated in a single year. That is, a plan sponsor does not have to make up the

---

[22]See Burmeister (2008).

unfunded liabilities by a lump-sum contribution with one payment. What a plan sponsor seeks to do is to utilize a liability-driven strategy to shrink the funding gap. In addition to performance in terms of the funding gap/funding ratio, there are annual contributions that a plan sponsor may have to make, referred to as the *annual required contribution*. That amount, determined by an actuary, has two components. The first is *normal cost*, which is the estimated cost of new benefits earned by plan participants during the year. The second is an amount that is based on the magnitude of the funding gap. Failure of the plan sponsor to provide the annual required contribution will result in an increase in the funding gap (decrease in the funding ratio). Plan sponsors seek to minimize the annual required contributions and the annual volatility of those contributions. For this reason, in designing a liability-driven strategy, pension plan sponsors seek to minimize annual contributions.

There are two main liability-driven strategies that are used by sponsors of defined benefit pension plans. We review them in detail next, and also include a discussion of advanced analytical techniques that have been used to solve the problem.

15.3.1   High-Grade Bond Portfolio Solution

One proposal advocated is to create a portfolio comprised of only high-grade bonds (corporates and U.S. Treasury securities) and interest rate derivatives.[23] This is an application of the duration-based immunization for multiperiod liabilities mentioned in Section 15.2.1.4. To understand what is done, ignore all risks other than interest rate risk. A first approximation for the funding gap's exposure to interest rate risk is the dollar duration[24] of the assets and liabilities. That is,

> Funding gap interest rate risk
>
> = Change in the funding gap due to interest rate risk
>
> = Dollar duration of projected liabilities
>
> − Dollar duration of fund assets

where the dollar duration of the projected liabilities is equal to the sensitivity of the dollar value of the projected liabilities to a 100 bp change in interest rates and the dollar duration of fund assets is equal to the sensitivity of the fund assets to a 100 bp change in interest rates. What we are doing here

---

[23]We discuss interest rate derivatives in detail in Chapter 18.
[24]See Chapter 13.4.1.1 for a definition of dollar duration.

is looking at dollar changes in projected liabilities and assets to changes in interest rates.

As interest rates change, the relative change in the market value of the assets and liabilities will depend on their respective dollar duration. In the typical case for a defined benefit pension plan, the dollar duration of the projected liabilities exceeds that of the dollar duration of the fund's assets. Then, a rise in interest rates will reduce the funding gap as the liabilities will decline by more than the assets. The interest rate risk is increased with a decline in interest rates. In that interest rate environment, the funding gap will increase.

For example, consider the following defined benefit pension plan:

Market value of fund assets = $500 million

Projected value of liabilities = $600 million

Portfolio duration (i.e., duration of fund assets) = 7

Liability duration (i.e., duration of projected liabilities) = 12

The funding gap and funding ratio for this hypothetical plan is $100 million (= $600 million − $500 million) and 83.33% (= $500 million/ $600 million), respectively.

Let us look at the dollar duration of the projected liabilities and fund assets assuming a 100 basis point parallel shift in interest rates:

Fund assets will change by about 7% for a 100 bp change in rates.

Projected liabilities will change by about 12% for a 100 bp change in rates.

The dollar duration (per 100 bp) change is then:

Portfolio dollar duration = 7% × $500 million = $35 million

Liability dollar duration = 12% × $600 million = $72 million

This means that the change in the funding gap for a 100 bp change in interest rates is roughly $37 million. More specifically, the risk is that interest rates will decline. In that case, the value of the liabilities will increase by $72 million but the value of the fund assets will increase by only $35 million, increasing the funding gap by $37 million.

To immunize (at least as a first approximation) against interest rate risk resulting in an adverse change in the funding gap using a bond-only portfolio, the fund's portfolio can be constructed and rebalanced so as to maintain the dollar duration match to prevent the funding gap from increasing.

Strategies for immunizing against interest rate risk so that the funding gap is kept low are those used in immunizing the interest rate risk for life insurance annuities: duration-based immunization strategy and cash-flow matching strategy.

Let us explain the situation faced by plan sponsors using a duration-based immunization strategy. Because the liability dollar duration cannot be changed, to immunize the interest rate risk, the portfolio dollar duration must be $72 million. The portfolio dollar duration for a 100 bp change in interest rates is

$$0.01 \times D_p \times \$500 \text{ million}$$

where D_p denotes the portfolio duration.

This amount must be equal to the dollar duration of the liabilities of $72 million. That is,

$$0.01 \times D_p \times \$500 \text{ million} = \$72 \text{ million}$$

Solving, we find D_p is equal to 12. That is, the portfolio duration must be the same as the liability duration to avoid a change in the funding gap as a result of a rise in interest rates.

This sounds simple but in practice there are two problems. First, as mentioned earlier, the duration of the liabilities may be more than 20. In contrast, the durations of Treasury bonds and high-grade corporate bonds are not close to 20, so it is difficult to obtain the necessary dollar duration to hedge interest rate risk. Even in our illustration, we may not be able to accomplish a portfolio duration of 12 with high-grade bonds. The solution is to use interest rate derivatives such as futures and swaps to "extend" dollar duration. Basically, derivatives allow for the leveraging of a portfolio so as to obtain a higher duration to match liabilities. Consequently, a pension plan sponsor seeking to duration-match all or part of the interest rate risk must be prepared to authorize the use of interest rate derivatives.

The second problem is that the matching of duration provides a hedge against interest rate risk only for a small change in interest rates. This can be dealt with by frequent portfolio rebalancing. If interest rates move substantially between rebalancing periods, duration matching is not sufficient as a condition for hedging. Instead, the convexity[25] of the assets and liabilities must be matched as closely as possible.

Although a liability-driven strategy that involves only a portfolio of high-grade bonds, Treasuries, and interest rate derivatives can hedge interest-rate risk, there are still other risks associated with bonds that may

---

[25] See Chapter 13.4.1.2 for a definition of convexity.

result in a strategy failing. High-grade bonds may have low credit risk but they do have some credit risk. In particular, there is default risk and for some issues there is call risk. There have been bonds that were initially rated as AAA by the credit rating agencies whose issuers have gone into bankruptcy. For high-grade callable bonds, there is call risk, which must be taken into consideration in computing the duration of the assets. Some bond-only strategies have used agency residential mortgage-backed securities because of the perceived low credit risk and higher promised yields compared to high-grade corporates. However, including such securities into the portfolio exposes the portfolio to call risk (in the case of mortgage-backed securities, referred to as prepayment risk).

In addition, there are risks that impact the market value of the bonds such as credit spread risk and liquidity risk that can result in a decline in the portfolio's market value and therefore an increase in the funding gap. The exposure to the other risks depends on the pension plan sponsor's risk tolerance, which in turn depends on the plan sponsor's ability to meet annual required contributions if the strategy results in an increase in the funding gap calling for additional contribution above normal cost.

15.3.2 Including Other Assets

The duration-based strategy described in Section 15.3.1 hedges only interest rate risk. To hedge against other risks associated with liabilities, such as inflation risk and longevity risk, other asset classes can be included. Asset classes that are highly correlated with these risks are selected so that a movement in the risk factors behind these risks that adversely impacts the funding gap on the liability side will be offset (in whole or in part) by a favorable impact on the assets. Inflation risk can be controlled by the use of inflation-protection fixed income instruments such as TIPS.

A more aggressive liability-driven strategy consists of creating two portfolios:

- A portfolio that pursues a strategy to manage risks.
- A portfolio that pursues a strategy to generate asset growth.

The second portfolio is referred to as the "performance-seeking portfolio"[26] or the "excess return portfolio."[27] Generating asset growth can be

---

[26]Badaoui, Deguest, Martellini, and Milhau (2014).
[27]Ross, Bernstein, Ferguson, and Dalio (2008). The authors provide an illustration of the strategy.

accomplished with asset classes such as equities, high-yield bonds, and alternative investments.

The total plan return can then be viewed as

Total plan return = Return on liability-immunizing portfolio

+ Return on performance-seeking portfolio

− Return on liabilities

Introducing cash market instruments that offer a greater risk premium than that offered by high-grade bonds results in exposure to other investment risks. Once again, the level of exposure that a plan sponsor is willing to accept depends on its risk tolerance, which in turn depends on the plan sponsor's ability to meet any additional contribution in excess of normal cost.

15.3.3 Advanced Modeling Strategies

As we mentioned in Section 15.3.2, additional asset classes can be used to improve the portfolio risk profile or generate extra return. Techniques for optimization under uncertainty have a long history of being used to construct optimal asset-liability management strategies with additional asset classes. Dynamic programming[28] approaches in which the state space is discretized and the optimal allocation strategy is found by backward induction were described in Barberis (2000) and Detemple and Rindisbacher (2008). Simulation-based approaches were suggested by Brandt, Goyal, Santa-Clara, and Stroud (2005) and Boender (1997). Stochastic programming[29] techniques have been the dominant advanced optimization approach used in practice.[30] They focus on finding optimal investment rules over a set of scenarios for the future returns on the assets and the liabilities of the pension fund. The application of robust optimization techniques for pension fund management over multiple time periods has also been studied.[31] It has been found to not have as much modeling flexibility as stochastic programming formulations of the problem but to result in strategies that have better worst-case performance under adverse market conditions.

---

[28] See Chapter 7.1.

[29] See Chapter 7.2.

[30] See Ferstl and Weissensteiner (2011), Consiglio, Saunders, and Zenios (2006), Boender, Dert, Heemskerk, and Hoek (2005), Kouwenberg (2001), Ziemba and Mulvey (1998), Gondzio and Kouwenberg (2001), Consigli and Dempster (1998), Consiglio, Cocco, and Zenios (2008), Escudero, Garín, Merino, and Pérez (2009), among others.

[31] See Gulpinar and Pachamanova (2013) and Pachamanova, Gulpinar, and Canakoglu (2014).

Summary

- In a liability-driven strategy, the goal is to manage funds (assets) to satisfy contractual liabilities.
- Asset-liability management is a problem faced primarily by two major groups of institutional investors: life insurance companies and defined benefit pension plans.
- Risks associated with liabilities include interest rate risk, inflation risk, and longevity risk.
- Interest rate risk has to do with the increase in the value of liabilities with adverse changes in interest rates.
- When projecting liabilities, an assumed rate for inflation is made. Inflation risk is the possibility that the projected inflation rate will be less than the realized inflation rate.
- Longevity risk is the risk that the actual life expectancy of life insurance policyholders or plan participants in a pension fund will exceed the life expectancy assumed in projecting the liabilities.
- Surplus is the difference between the value of the portfolio of assets and the value of the liabilities.
- Liability-driven strategies of life insurance companies include partial immunization (duration-based) strategies, complete immunization (cash-flow matching) strategies, and advanced modeling strategies.
- Immunization strategies select bonds in such a way that the duration of the bond portfolio matches the duration of the liabilities the insurance company faces.
- Cash-flow matching is the construction of a portfolio that generates cash flows that match the schedule of liabilities the insurance company faces.
- Advanced modeling strategies include the use of optimization under uncertainty techniques (stochastic programming and robust optimization) to find a portfolio allocation that maximizes the return to the insurance company while meeting all liabilities.
- Replicating portfolios of capital market equivalents to insurance policy features are sometimes constructed by insurance companies to simplify the risk management process.
- The funding gap is the difference between the projected value of fund liabilities and the market value of fund assets.
- The funding ratio is the ratio of the market value of fund assets to the projected value of the liabilities.
- Popular liability-driven strategies for pension funds seek to minimize the funding gap or maintain a particular level of the funding ratio.

- An all-high-grade bond portfolio strategy can be combined with interest rate derivatives to minimize the funding gap.
- In addition to bonds and interest rate derivatives, other asset classes can be included as part of a strategy to control for inflation risk and longevity risk potentially to increase return.
- A more aggressive liability-driven strategy is to create two port-folios: a portfolio that pursues a strategy to minimize risks and a portfolio that pursues a strategy to generate asset growth, called the performance-seeking portfolio.
- Advanced optimization techniques used for optimizing a portfolio while taking into consideration liabilities have included dynamic program-ing, simulation-based methods, stochastic programming, and robust optimization.

Derivatives and Their Application to Portfolio Management

Basics of Financial Derivatives

Derivative instruments, or simply *derivatives*, are contracts that derive their value from the behavior of cash market instruments such as stocks, stock indexes, bonds, currencies, and commodities that underlie the contract. There are three general categories of derivatives: (1) forwards and futures, (2) options, and (3) swaps. Derivatives are also classified based on the underlying asset or reference for the contract. *Commodity derivatives* have as their underlying traditional agricultural commodities (such as grain and livestock), imported foodstuffs (such as coffee, cocoa, and sugar), or industrial commodities. Derivatives based on a financial instrument or a financial index are classified as *financial derivatives* and include *equity derivatives*, *interest rate derivatives*, *credit derivatives*, and *currency derivatives*.

This chapter is the first of three chapters that cover the first three financial derivatives (equity derivatives, interest rate derivatives, and credit derivatives) and their applications to portfolio management. In this chapter we introduce the different types of financial derivatives, their risk-return characteristics, and the fundamentals of how they are priced. The next two chapters focus on the specific applications. Chapter 17 explains and illustrates the application of equity derivatives to equity portfolio management and Chapter 18 explains and illustrates the application of interest rate and credit default swaps to bond portfolio management.

16.1 OVERVIEW OF THE USE OF DERIVATIVES IN PORTFOLIO MANAGEMENT

Derivatives have several properties that make them excellent candidates for use in portfolio management. These properties are derived from the following three roles that derivatives serve in portfolio management:

1. To modify the risk characteristics of a portfolio (risk management).
2. To enhance the expected return of a portfolio (returns management).

3. To reduce transactions cost associated with managing a portfolio (cost management).

We can further reduce the role of derivatives to the single purpose of risk management and incorporate the other two roles into this one. Thus, we can easily argue that derivatives are used primarily to manage risk or to buy and sell risk at a favorable price.

Risk management is a dynamic process that allows portfolio managers to identify, measure, and assess the current risk attributes of a portfolio and to measure the potential benefits from taking the risk. Risk management also involves understanding and managing the factors that can have an adverse impact on the targeted rate of return. The objective is to attain a desired return for a given level of corresponding risk on an after-cost basis. This is consistent with the Markowitz efficient frontier described in Chapter 8. The role of derivatives in this process is to shift the efficient frontier in favor of the investor by implementing a strategy at a lower cost, lower risk and higher return, or to gain access to an investment that was not available due to some regulatory or other restrictions. We can, therefore, regard the management of portfolios as a sophisticated exercise in risk management.

The decision by a portfolio manager to use derivatives requires careful attention and must be explicitly incorporated into the investment process described in Chapter 1. Before derivatives are used as part of the investment process, investment managers must do their homework. Sanford and Borge (1995) recommend a process that portfolio managers interested in utilizing derivatives go through. Applying the process suggested by Sanford and Borge to the process of investment management, Collins and Fabozzi (1999) come up with the following set of guidelines for asset management firms on the use of derivatives:

- Define the investment process in terms of risk management.
- Establish clear investment objectives and acceptable risk tolerance level.
- Create a set of boundary conditions for the level of risk.
- Assess the full range of possible outcomes from using derivatives.
- Assess the impact of using derivatives on the portfolio's risk profile.
- Establish monitoring protocol to measure risk.
- Develop an adjustment response mechanism.

The process of using derivatives requires the portfolio manager to manage the investment process in terms of a risk management process. What this means is that the portfolio manager views the portfolio as a mechanism to capture the benefits of taking prudent risks. The reallocation of risk incorporates asset exposure, return enhancement, and cost management into a single theme of risk management. For portfolio managers, this means designing a portfolio that assumes a level of risk consistent with the investment objectives of the client. Derivatives provide portfolio managers with a quick and efficient method to realize the desired portfolio profile emanating from the manager's style. The combination of asset selection and establishing the optimal level of portfolio risks is the key to consistent portfolio performance. In order to accomplish this, however, portfolio managers must be clear about their objectives and tolerance for risk. Once the process is established, the portfolio manager can actively manage the portfolio in terms of risk and make the necessary adjustments when the benefits are no longer expected to accrue.

16.2 FORWARD AND FUTURES CONTRACTS

A *forward contract* is perhaps the simplest derivative. It is an agreement to buy or sell an asset at a specific time in the future for a specific price. Forward contracts are sold in the over-the-counter (OTC) market; that is, forward contracts are nonstandard and negotiated directly between a buyer and a seller. The buyer of a forward contract assumes a long position in the forward contract, and agrees to buy the underlying asset at the prespecified price and date in the future. The seller of a forward contract assumes a short position in the contract, and agrees to sell the underlying asset at the pre-specified price and date in the future. The prespecified price (or "delivery price") in the future is called the *forward price*. When the underlying is a rate such as an interest rate or a foreign exchange rate, the prespecified rate is referred to as a *forward rate*.

Futures are very similar to forwards, but they are standardized contracts traded on organized exchanges. Associated with every futures exchange is a clearinghouse, which performs several functions. One of these functions is to guarantee that the two parties to the transaction will perform. Because of the clearinghouse, the two parties need not worry about the financial strength and integrity of the party taking the opposite side of the contract. After initial execution of an order, the relationship between the two parties ends. The clearinghouse interposes itself as the buyer for every sale and as the seller for every purchase. The two parties are then free to liquidate their positions without involving the other party in the original contract, and without worry that the other party may default.

When a position is first taken in a futures contract, the investor must deposit a minimum dollar amount per contract as specified by the exchange. This amount, called *initial margin*, is required as a deposit for the contract. The initial margin may be in the form of an interest-bearing security such as a Treasury bill. The initial margin is placed in an account, and the amount in this account is referred to as the investor's equity. As the price of the futures contract fluctuates each trading day, the value of the investor's equity in the position changes.

At the end of each trading day, the exchange determines the settlement price for the futures contract. The settlement price is different from the *closing price*, which is the price of the security in the final trade of the day (whenever that trade occurred during the day). In contrast, the *settlement price* for a futures contract is that value that the exchange considers to be representative of trading at the end of the day. The exchange uses the settlement price to mark-to-market the investor's position, so that any gain or loss from the position is quickly reflected in the investor's equity account.

Maintenance margin is the minimum level by which an investor's equity position may fall as a result of unfavorable price movements before the investor is required to deposit additional margin. The maintenance margin requirement is a dollar amount that is less than the initial margin requirement. The additional margin deposited, called *variation margin*, is the amount necessary to bring the equity in the account back to its initial margin level. Unlike initial margin, variation margin must be in cash, not interest-bearing instruments. Any excess margin in the account may be withdrawn by the investor. If a party to a futures contract who is required to deposit variation margin fails to do so, the futures position is liquidated by the clearinghouse.[1]

Given that futures contracts are marked-to-market at the end of each trading day, they are subject to interim cash flows because additional margin may be required in the case of adverse price movements or because cash may be withdrawn in the case of favorable price movements. In contrast, a forward contract may or may not be marked-to-market. Thus, when a forward contract is marked-to-market, which is typically the case, there are interim cash flows just as with a futures contract. When a forward contract is not marked-to-market, then there are no interim cash flows. Because there is no clearinghouse that guarantees the performance of a counterparty in a forward contract, the parties to a forward contract are exposed to *counterparty risk*, the risk that the other party to the transaction will fail to perform. It is for this reason that forward contracts are typically marked-to-market. As we mentioned, this is not the case for futures contracts. Once a futures

---

[1]Although there are initial and maintenance margin requirements for buying securities on margin, the concept of margin differs for securities and futures. When securities are acquired on margin, the difference between the price of the security and the initial margin is borrowed from the broker. The security purchased serves as collateral for the loan, and the investor pays interest. For futures contracts, the initial margin, in effect, serves as "good-faith" money, an indication that the investor will satisfy the obligation of the contract. Normally, no money is borrowed by the investor.

contract is traded between two parties, the exchange itself (or the clearing-house associated with the exchange) becomes the counterparty to the trade. That is, neither party to the trade need be concerned with the other party to the original trade. Rather both parties are exposed to the counterparty risk of the exchange.

By virtue of being standardized contracts, futures contracts may not meet the precise needs of portfolio managers. Thus, if a portfolio manager needs to lock in the price for the underlying asset at dates that do not coincide with standardized settlement dates, the portfolio manager needs to find a futures contract with terms that are closest to the desired terms sought.

16.2.1 Risk and Return of Forward/Futures Position

Let's look at the risk and return relationship for the basic positions in forward and futures contracts. Without loss of generality, we discuss the relationship in terms of a futures contract.

Let T denote the time to delivery of the futures contract, K the futures price at which the underlying asset will be traded at time T, and S_T the cash market price (also called the *spot price*) of the underlying asset at T. The final payoff from a long position in a futures contract is the difference between the cash price of the underlying asset at the delivery date and the contract's futures price. That is, using our notation

Payoff of a long futures position at the delivery date $= S_T - K.$

This is because if the cash market price of the underlying asset S_T is higher than the futures price K, the holder of the long position will have made a profit by locking in the lower price through the contract. If, on the other hand, the cash market price of the underlying asset S_T is lower than the futures price K, the holder of the long position will realize a loss by locking in the higher price for the underlying asset.

By similar reasoning, the final payoff from a short position in a futures contract will depend on the cash market price at the delivery date and the contract's futures price. The final payoff can be expressed as

Payoff of a short futures position at the delivery date $= K - S_T.$

16.2.2 Leveraging Aspect of Futures

When taking a position in a futures contract, a party need not put up the entire amount of the investment. Instead, the exchange requires that only the initial margin be invested.

To see the implications, let us consider the following example. Suppose that an investor has \$100 and wants to invest in asset U, currently selling for

$100, because the investor anticipates that the asset's price will appreciate. The investor can use the initial funds of $100 to buy one unit of the asset in the cash market. The investor's payoff will then be based on the price action of one unit of asset U.

Suppose that the exchange where the futures contract for asset U is traded requires an initial margin of only 5%, which in this case would be $5 (5% × $100). Then the investor can purchase 20 contracts with a $100 investment, putting up an initial margin of $5 for each.[2] The investor's payoff will then depend on the price movement of 20 units of asset U. Thus, the investor can leverage[3] the $100 investment by buying futures. The degree of leverage equals 1/margin rate. In this case, the degree of leverage equals 1/0.05, or 20.

While the degree of leverage available in the futures market varies from contract to contract, as the initial margin requirement varies, the leverage attainable is considerably greater than in the cash market. At first, the leverage available in the futures market may suggest that the market benefits only those who want to speculate on price movements. This is not true. As we will see in the following two chapters, futures markets can be used to reduce price risk. Without the leverage possible in futures transactions, the cost of reducing price risk using futures would be too high for many market participants.

16.2.3 Pricing of Futures and Forward Contracts

When using derivatives, an investor should understand the basic principles of how they are valued. Although there are many models that have been proposed for valuing financial instruments that trade in the cash (spot) market, the valuation of all derivative models is based on arbitrage arguments. Basically, this involves developing a strategy or a trade wherein a package consists of a position in the underlying (that is, the underlying asset or instrument for the derivative contract) and borrowing or lending so as to generate the same cash flow profile of the derivative. The value of the package, also sometimes referred to as a *replicating portfolio*, is then equal to the theoretical price of the derivative. If the market price of the derivative deviates from the theoretical price, then the actions of arbitrageurs will drive the market price of the derivative toward its theoretical price until the arbitrage opportunity is eliminated.

---

[2]This example ignores the fact that the investor may need funds for the variation margin.
[3]*Leverage* basically means using borrowed capital to make an investment, hoping that the investment will increase in value and more than make up for the cost of borrowing.

In developing a strategy to capture any mispricing, certain assumptions are made. When these assumptions are not satisfied in the real world, the theoretical price can only be approximated. Moreover, a close examination of the underlying assumptions necessary to derive the theoretical price indicates how a pricing formula must be modified to value specific contracts.

Here we describe how futures and forward contracts are valued. The pricing of these contracts is similar. If the underlying asset for both contracts is the same, the difference in pricing is due to differences in features of the contract that must be dealt with by the pricing model.

We illustrate the basic model for pricing a futures contract. The issues associated with applying the basic pricing model to some of the more popular futures contracts are described in Chapter 17 (for stock index futures contracts) and in Chapter 18 (for Treasury futures). Moreover, although the model described here is said to be a model for pricing futures, technically it is a model for pricing forward contracts with no mark-to-market requirements.

We demonstrate the basic pricing model using an example. We make the following six assumptions for a futures contract that has no initial and variation margin and the underlying is asset U:

1. The price of asset U in the cash market is $100.
2. There is a known cash flow for asset U over the life of the futures contract.
3. The cash flow for asset U is $8 per year paid quarterly ($2 per quarter).
4. The next quarterly payment is exactly three months from now.
5. The futures contract requires delivery three months from now.
6. The current three-month interest rate at which funds can be lent or borrowed is 4% per year (approximately 1% per quarter).

Suppose that the futures price in the market is $105. Let's see if that can be the correct price. We can check this by implementing the following simple strategy:

- Sell the futures contract at $105.
- Borrow $100 for three months at 4% per year ($1 per quarter).
- Purchase asset U in the cash market for $100.

The purchase of asset U is accomplished with the borrowed funds. Hence, this strategy does not involve any initial cash outlay. At the end of three months, the following occurs:

- $2 is received from holding asset U (see assumption 3 above).
- Asset U is delivered to settle the futures contract.
- The loan (a total of $101) is repaid.

This strategy results in the following outcome:

From the settlement of the futures contract:

Proceeds from the sale of asset U to settle the futures contract = $105
Payment received from investing in asset U for three months =   2
Total proceeds   = $107

From the loan:

Repayment of the principal of the loan   = $100
Interest on loan (1% for three months)   =   1
Total outlay   = $101

The profit from this strategy is $6 ($107 − $101) and it is guaranteed regardless of what the cash price of asset U is three months from now. This is because the cash price of asset U three months from now never enters the analysis. There would be a profit even if zero cash flow was received from asset U (assumption 3 above). Moreover, this profit is generated with no investment outlay (ignoring any margin payments); the funds needed to acquire asset U are borrowed when the strategy is executed. In financial terms, the profit in the strategy we have just illustrated arises from a riskless arbitrage between the price of asset U in the cash market and the price of asset U in the futures market.

In a well-functioning market, arbitrageurs who could realize this riskless profit for a zero investment would implement the strategy described above. By selling the futures and buying asset U in order to implement the strategy, they would force the futures price down so that at some price for the futures contract, the arbitrage profit will be eliminated.

This strategy, which resulted in the capturing of the arbitrage profit, is referred to as a *cash-and-carry trade*. The reason for this name is that implementation of the strategy involves borrowing cash to purchase the underlying and "carrying" that underlying to the settlement date of the futures contract.

From the cash-and-carry trade we see that the futures price cannot be $105. Suppose instead that the futures price is $95 rather than $105. Let's try the following strategy to see if that price can be sustained in the market:

- Buy the futures contract at $95.
- Sell (short) asset U for $100.[4]
- Invest (lend) $100 for three months at 1% per year.

---

[4] As we explained earlier in the book, to sell a security short is to borrow it from a lender with the agreement to return it after a specified amount of time. The security

We assume once again that in this strategy there is no initial margin and variation margin for the futures contract. In addition, we assume that there is no cost to selling the asset short and no cost to lending the money. Given these assumptions, there is no initial cash outlay for the strategy just as with the cash-and-carry trade. Three months from now:

- Asset U is accepted for delivery to settle the long position in the futures contract.
- Asset U is used to cover the short position in the cash market.
- Payment is made of $2 to the lender of asset U as compensation for the quarterly payment.
- Payment is received from the borrower of the loan of $101 for principal and interest.

The strategy produces the following at the end of three months:

From the settlement of the futures contract:

Price paid for the purchase of asset U to settle the futures contract	= $95
Proceeds to the lender of asset U to borrow the asset	= 2
Total outlay	= $97

From the loan:

Principal from the loan	= $100
Interest earned on the loan ($1 for three months)	= 1
Total proceeds	= $101

The guaranteed profit from this strategy is $4 ($101 − $97) regardless of the price of asset U in the cash market at the delivery date. Thus, as with the cash-and-carry and trade, this strategy requires no initial cash outlay, but it will lock in a profit. In real-world markets, this opportunity would lead arbitrageurs to buy the futures contract and short asset U. The implementation of this strategy would raise the futures price until the arbitrage profit disappears.

This strategy is known as a *reverse cash-and-carry trade*. That is, with this strategy, the underlying is sold short and the proceeds received from the short sale are invested. We can see that the futures price cannot be

---

is sold in the cash market, and needs to be purchased in the future to close out the short position. This strategy is employed when the price of the security is expected to decline.

$95 or $105. What is the theoretical futures price given the assumptions in our illustration? It can be shown that if the futures price is $99, there is no opportunity for an arbitrage profit. That is, neither the cash-and-carry trade nor the reverse cash-and-carry trade will generate an arbitrage profit.

In general, the formula for determining the theoretical futures price given the assumptions of the model is

Theoretical futures price =

Cash market price + (Cash market price) × (Financing cost − Cash yield)

In the above equation, "Financing cost" is the interest rate to borrow funds and "Cash yield" is the payment received from investing in the asset as a percentage of the cash price.

Let's apply this equation to our illustration where the cash price of asset U is $100, the financing cost is 1%, and the cash yield is 2%. The theoretical futures price is

$$\$100 + [\$100 \times (1\% - 2\%)] = \$99$$

Note that the future price can be above or below the cash price of the asset depending on the difference between the financing cost and cash yield. The difference between these rates is referred to as the *net financing cost*. A more commonly used term for the net financing cost is the *cost of carry*, or simply, *carry*. Positive carry means that the cash yield exceeds the financing cost. (Note that while the difference between the financing cost and the cash yield is a negative value, carry is said to be positive.) Negative carry means that the financing cost exceeds the cash yield.

It is also important to note that at the settlement date of the futures contract, the futures price must equal the cash market price. The reason is that a futures contract with no time left until delivery is equivalent to a cash market transaction. Thus, as the delivery date approaches, the futures price will converge to the cash market price. This fact is evident from the formula for the theoretical futures price given above. The financing cost approaches zero as the delivery date approaches. Similarly, the yield that can be earned by holding the underlying approaches zero. Hence, the cost of carry approaches zero, and the futures price approaches the cash market price.

In deriving the theoretical futures price using the arbitrage argument, several assumptions had to be made. These assumptions, as well as the differences in contract specifications, will result in the futures price in the market deviating from the theoretical futures price as given by the equation above. We will see this in Chapter 17 when we discuss the pricing of stock index futures contracts.

16.3   OPTIONS

An *option* is a contract in which the option seller grants the option buyer the right but not the obligation to enter into a transaction with the seller to either buy or sell an underlying asset at a specified price on or before a specified date. The specified price is called the *strike price* or *exercise price*, and the specified date is called the *expiration date* or the *maturity date*. The option seller grants this right in exchange for a certain amount of money called the *option premium* or *option price*.

The option seller is also known as the *option writer*, while the option buyer is known as the *option holder*. The asset that is the subject of the option is called the *underlying*. The underlying can be an individual stock, a stock index, a bond, an interest rate, an exchange rate, or even another derivative instrument such as a futures contract. The option writer can grant the option holder one of two rights. If the right is to purchase the underlying, the option is referred to as a *call option*. If the right is to sell the underlying, the option is referred to as a *put option*.

An option can also be categorized according to when it may be exercised by the buyer, that is, by its exercise style. A *European option* can only be exercised at the option's expiration date. An *American option*, in contrast, can be exercised any time on or before the expiration date. An option that can be exercised before the expiration date but only on specified dates is called a *Bermudan option* or an *Atlantic option*.

Complex option contracts are referred to as *exotic options* or *exotics*. Examples of exotic options include *Asian options*, which pay the difference between the strike price and the average price of the underlying over a prespecified period, and *barrier options*, whose payoff is determined by whether the price of the underlying reaches a certain barrier over the life of the option. There is, however, virtually no limit to the possibilities for designing nonstandard derivatives.

Options, like other financial instruments, may be traded either on an organized exchange or in the OTC market. An option that is traded on an exchange is referred to as a *listed option* or an *exchange-traded option*. An option traded in the OTC market is called an *OTC option* or a *dealer option*. The advantages of a listed option are as follows. First, the exercise price and expiration date of the contract are standardized, making them more liquid (i.e., easier to trade prior to the expiration date). Second, as in the case of futures contracts, the direct link between buyer and seller is severed after the trade is executed because of the interchangeability of listed options. Finally, the transactions costs are lower for listed options than for OTC options.

The higher cost of an OTC option reflects the cost of customizing the option for an investor whose investment objectives are not satisfied by the standardized listed options. Although an OTC option is less liquid than a listed option, this is typically not of concern to the user of such an option. The explosive growth in OTC options suggests that portfolio managers find that these products serve an important investment purpose.

16.3.1   Risk and Return Characteristics of Options

There are four basic option positions:

1. Buying a call option (long a call option)
2. Selling a call option (short a call option)
3. Buying a put option (long a put option)
4. Selling a put option (short a put option)

Here we discuss the basic risk and return characteristics of the four basic option positions. In Chapters 17 and 18, we describe the risk and return characteristics of more complex strategies that utilize options.

We use asset U as the underlying in our example. The illustrations assume that each option position is held to the expiration date and not exercised early. Also, to simplify the illustrations, we assume that the underlying for each option is for 1 unit of asset U and we ignore transaction costs.

Buying call options: Assume that there is a call option on asset U that expires in one month and has a strike price of $100. The option price is $3. Suppose that the current (spot) price of asset U is $100. The profit from the long option position will depend on the price of asset U at the expiration date, and will be given by the expression

$$\max(S_T - K, \ 0) - \text{Call}$$

at expiration, where Call is the price of the option ($3 in this example). Exhibit 16.1 shows the profit and loss potential at the expiration date for buying a call option. The buyer of a call option benefits if the price rises above the strike price. If the price of asset U is equal to $103, the buyer of a call option breaks even. The maximum loss is the option price, and there is substantial upside potential if the asset price rises above $103.

It is worthwhile to compare the profit-and-loss profile of the call option buyer with that of an investor taking a long position in one unit of asset U. The payoff from the position depends on asset U's price at the expiration date (Exhibit 16.1). This comparison clearly demonstrates the way in which an option can alter the risk-return profile for investors. An investor who takes a long position in asset U realizes a profit of $1 for every $1 increase in asset U's price. As asset U's price falls, however, the investor loses dollar for dollar. If the price drops by more than $3, the long position in asset U

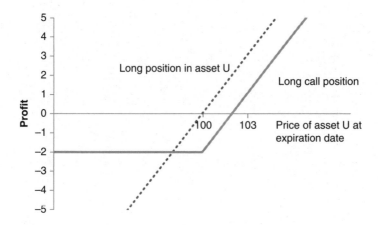

Exhibit 16.1 Profit/loss profile at expiration of a long call position and a long position in asset U.

results in a loss of more than $3. The long call position, in contrast, limits the loss to only the option price of $3 but retains the upside potential, which will be $3 less than for the long position in asset U. Which alternative is better, buying the call option or buying asset U? The answer depends on what the investor is attempting to achieve.

We can also use this hypothetical call option to demonstrate the speculative appeal of options. Suppose an investor has strong expectations that asset U's price will rise in one month. At an option price of $3, the speculator can purchase 33.33 call options for each $100 invested. If asset U's price rises, the investor realizes the price appreciation associated with 33.33 units of asset U. With the same $100, however, the investor can purchase only one unit of asset U selling at $100, thereby realizing the appreciation associated with one unit if asset U's price increases. Now, suppose that in one month the price of asset U rises to $120. The long call position will result in a profit of $566.67 (= $20 × 33.33 − $100), or a return of 566.67% on the $100 investment in the call option. The long position in asset U results in a profit of $20, only a 20% return on $100.

This greater leverage attracts investors to options when they wish to speculate on price movements. There are drawbacks to this leverage, however. Suppose that asset U's price is unchanged at $100 at the expiration date. The long call position results in this case in a loss of the entire investment of $100, while the long position in asset U produces neither a gain nor a loss.

Writing call options: To illustrate the option seller's, or writer's, position, we use the same call option we used to illustrate buying a call option. The profit/loss profile at expiration of the short call position (that is, the position of the call option writer) is the mirror image of the profit-and-loss profile of

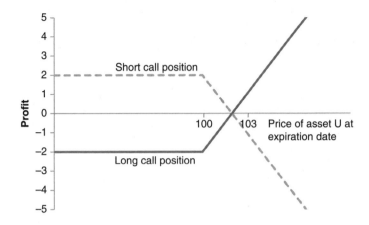

Exhibit 16.2   Profit/loss profile at expiration for a short call position and a long call position.

the long call position (the position of the call option buyer). That is, the profit of the short call position for any given price for asset U at the expiration date is the same as the loss of the long call position. Consequently, the maximum profit the short call position can produce is the option price. The maximum loss is not limited because it is the highest price reached by asset U on or before the expiration date less the option price; this price can be indefinitely high. This can be seen in Exhibit 16.2, which shows the profit/loss profile at expiration for a short call position, as well as for a long call position. More generally, the expression for calculating the profit from the short call position at expiration is

$$\text{Call} - \max(S_T - K, \, 0)$$

where Call is the price of the call.

Buying put options: To illustrate a long put option position, we assume a hypothetical put option on one unit of asset U with one month to maturity and a strike price of $100. Assume that the put option is selling for $2 and the price of asset U is $100. The profit for this position at the expiration date depends on the market price of asset U, and is more generally given by

$$\max(K - S_T, \, 0) - \text{Put}$$

where Put is the price of the put. The buyer of a put option benefits if the price falls.

The profit/loss profile at expiration of a long put position is shown in Exhibit 16.3. As with all long option positions, the loss is limited to the option price paid by the option buyer. The profit potential, however,

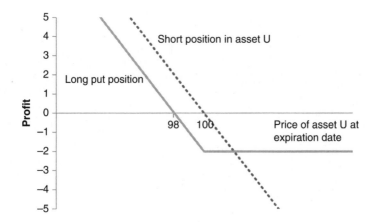

Exhibit 16.3 Profit/loss profile at expiration for a long put position and a short position in asset U.

is substantial: the theoretical maximum profit is generated if asset U's price falls to zero in the case of a put option. Contrast this profit potential with that of the buyer of a call option. The theoretical maximum profit for a call buyer cannot be determined beforehand because it depends on the highest price that can be reached by asset U before or at the option expiration date.

To see how an option alters the risk-return profile for an investor, we again compare it with a position in asset U. The long put position is compared with a short position in asset U because such a position would also benefit if the asset U's price falls. A comparison of the two positions is shown in Exhibit 16.3. The investor taking a short position in asset U faces all the downside risk as well as the upside potential, whereas an investor taking the long put position faces limited downside risk (equal to the option price) while still maintaining upside potential reduced by an amount equal to the option price.

Writing put options: The profit-and-loss profile for a short put option is the mirror image of the long put option. The maximum profit to be realized from this position is the option price. The theoretical maximum loss can be substantial should the price of the underlying fall; if the price were to fall all the way to zero, the loss would be as large as the strike price less the option price. Exhibit 16.4 depicts this profit/loss profile at expiration for both a short put position and a long put position. The expression for calculating the profit from the short put position at expiration is

$$\text{Put} - \max(K - S_T,\ 0)$$

where Put is the price of the put.

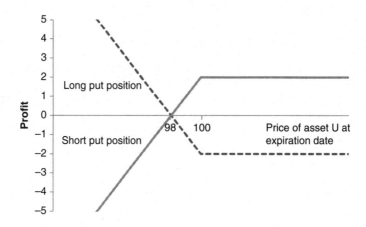

Exhibit 16.4 Profit/loss profile at expiration for a short put position and a long put position.

16.3.1.1 Summary of Option Risk and Return Positions To summarize, buying calls or selling puts allows the investor to gain if the price of the underlying rises. Buying calls gives the investor unlimited upside potential, but limits the loss to the option price. Selling puts limits the profit to the option price, but provides no protection if the price of the underlying falls, with the maximum loss occurring if the price of the underlying falls to zero. Buying puts and selling calls allows the investor to gain if the price of the underlying falls. Buying puts gives the investor upside potential, with the maximum profit realized if the price of the underlying declines to zero. However, the loss is limited to the option price. Selling calls limits the profit to the option price, but provides no protection if the asset's price rises, with the maximum loss being theoretically unlimited.

16.3.1.2 Risk and Return of Options versus Futures/Forwards Let's look at the difference between an option on the one hand and forward and futures contract on the other hand. First, unlike in a forward or a futures contract, one party to an option contract is not obligated to transact—specifically, the option buyer has the right but not the obligation to transact. The option writer does have the obligation to transact if requested to by the option buyer. In the case of a forward or futures contract, both parties are obligated to transact. Second, at the outset of the trade the counterparties in a forward or a futures buyer do not have to pay the other party to accept the obligation while an option buyer pays the seller the option price.

Because of the first difference between options and forward/futures, the risk-return characteristics of option contracts are different from those of futures and forwards. In the case of a forward or a futures contract, the buyer of the contract realizes a dollar-for-dollar gain when the price of the futures contract increases and suffers a dollar-for-dollar loss when the price of the futures contract decreases. The opposite occurs for the seller of a forward or futures contract. Because of this relationship, forward and futures contracts are said to have a linear payoff and referred to as *linear payoff derivatives*.

Options do not provide this symmetric risk-and-return relationship. The most that the buyer of an option can lose is the option price. While the buyer of an option retains all the potential benefits from a favorable price movement of the underlying, the gain is always reduced by the amount of the option price. The maximum profit that the writer may realize is the option price; however, the writer faces substantial downside risk. Because of this characteristic, options are said to have a *nonlinear payoff* and referred to as *nonlinear payoff derivatives*.

16.3.1.3 Risk Estimation for Portfolios Containing Options

As we explained in Chapters 8 and 10, standard deviation of portfolio return and tracking error are the most commonly used risk measures for portfolios. In portfolios whose return distributions can be assumed to be reasonably close to normal,[5] such risk measures are useful. For example, when factor models[6] are used to generate forecasts for future equity portfolio values in particular, the forecasts are often normally distributed because some factor models estimated with regression techniques have this property. However, real-world portfolio returns or value distributions are not normal. Exhibit 16.5 shows the returns on the S&P 500 Index—an example of a large portfolio—over a five-year period, with a normal distribution with the same mean and standard deviation superimposed on the histogram of S&P 500 Index returns for comparison. The S&P 500 Index returns distribution appears bell-shaped, so risk measures of distribution spread such as standard deviation are still relevant, but the returns are not normal—the tails of the distribution are fatter than the normal distribution's tails would be, and the peak of the distribution is higher.

Once options are introduced into a portfolio, their nonlinear payoff features make portfolio risk estimation even more complex. Tracking error and standard deviation no longer make sense. Simulation[7] is the only framework within which the risk profile of the portfolio can be analyzed with any degree of accuracy.

As an example, consider the distribution of a call option payoff at expiration and the distribution of the price of the underlying stock from which

---

[5] See Chapter 2.4 for a review of the normal distribution.
[6] See Chapter 9.
[7] See Chapter 5.

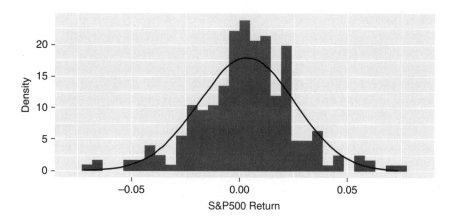

Exhibit 16.5 Weekly return distribution of the S&P 500 (March 2009 through March 2014) with a normal distribution with the same mean and standard deviation superimposed for comparison.

the call option payoffs were generated (Exhibit 16.6(b) and (a), respectively.) The skewness in the distribution of the call option payoffs is a lot more pronounced than the skewness in the distribution of the stock prices. When the payoffs of the financial instruments in the portfolio lead to nonsymmetric distributions of portfolio returns, standard-deviation-type risk measures can be very misleading. In this particular example, the loss in Exhibit 16.6(b) is limited, so a high standard deviation is related to more realizations of high payoffs. Thus, a high standard deviation for the return on the call position does not actually mean higher risk.[8]

To gain additional intuition, let us consider the example of a simple portfolio consisting of one share of Microsoft stock. The simulated Profit/Loss distribution over scenarios generated based on five years' worth of historical data assuming the current stock price is $47.29 is shown in Exhibit 16.7(a). A put with a strike price of $45 and a price of $1.07 is then added to the portfolio. The simulated Profit/Loss distribution for the portfolio with the put is shown in Exhibit 16.7(b).

It can be observed from Exhibit 16.7 that the portfolio with the put has very little downside risk. The effect of the put is that it has replaced the large losses on the left side of the graph in Exhibit 16.7(a) with more frequent losses but of much smaller magnitude. The maximum loss is limited and equal to the price of the put ($1.07) plus the difference between the

---

[8]See also the discussion in Chapter 5.2.3.

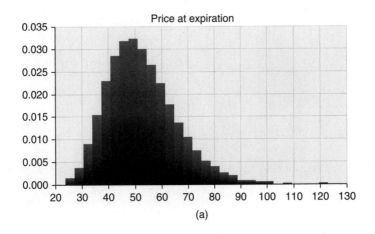

(a)

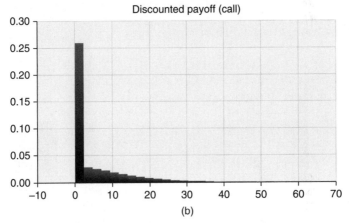

(b)

Exhibit 16.6 Probability distribution of (a) the price of a stock at expiration, and (b) the payoff of a call option on the stock at expiration.

current Microsoft stock price and the strike price of the option ($2.29 = $47.29 − $45).[9] This maximum loss happens with the highest frequency of all other values in the simulation, in about 11% of simulation trials (the value on the vertical axis) in the example in Exhibit 16.7(b).

---

[9] See FactSet (2008) for additional examples of the use of Monte Carlo simulation in portfolio risk estimation when various combinations of options are included in the portfolio.

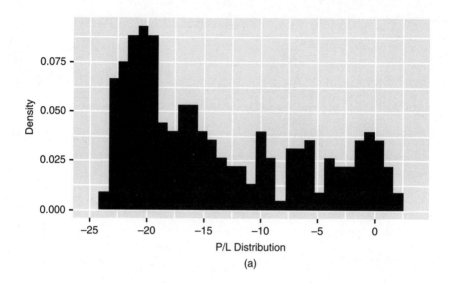

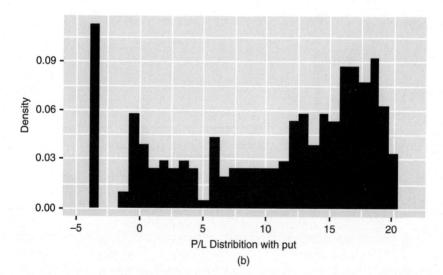

Exhibit 16.7 (a) Simulated profit/loss distribution for a portfolio containing one share of Microsoft stock assuming the current stock price is $47.29; (b) profit/loss distribution for a portfolio containing one share of Microsoft stock and one put with strike price of $45 and price of $1.07 assuming the current stock price is $47.29.

Estimating the risk of a portfolio by simulation is simple in concept. The following steps are followed:

1. Generate N realizations of the vector whose elements are the changes in value for the M securities in the portfolio.
2. For each of the N vectors (knowing the current portfolio weights), compute the resulting change in portfolio value.
3. Analyze different characteristics of the so-obtained future portfolio value probability distribution.

For example, if we would like to evaluate the 95% value-at-risk (95% VaR), we can record the change in portfolio value as the difference between the current portfolio value and the simulated portfolio value in each scenario, which represents the loss realized in each of the N scenarios. We can then estimate the 95th percentile of the loss distribution. Alternatively, if we would like to compute the probability that the loss will be greater than a certain value x, we can compute the loss probability as the percentage of all losses over the value x.

Theoretically, this algorithm for evaluating the probability distribution of portfolio changes is sound. The problem that arises in its actual implementation for large and complex portfolios, especially in Step 2, is the portfolio reevaluation step. Generating every scenario in Step 2 for a portfolio of thousands of securities requires running thousands of numerical algorithms, including additional simulations. This can be a very time consuming process. For example, suppose that we are trying to simulate N scenarios for each of M securities in the portfolio. The total number of scenarios for the portfolio value would be N^M. For a portfolio of 1,000 securities, each of which can be in one of 100 scenarios, we could have a total of $100^{1,000}$ scenarios—this is basically impossible to evaluate, even with today's advanced technology.

To reduce the number of scenarios, factors are identified that drive the changes in portfolio value, and the scenarios are simulated for those factors. Consider, for example, a bond portfolio of 100 bonds. To simulate the future value of the portfolio, we could use the current yield curve, the volatilities of the factors that drive the yield curve evolution process, and their correlation matrix. The yield curve, for instance, could be described by 11 risk factors representing the key rates, as we explained in Chapter 13.4.1.3. Further reduction in the number of factors is possible by using principal components analysis[10] and keeping only the first two to three components.

---

[10] See Chapter 4.4.

16.3.2 Option Pricing Models

Earlier in this chapter, it was explained how the theoretical price of a futures contract and forward contract can be determined on the basis of arbitrage arguments. An option pricing model uses a set of assumptions and arbitrage arguments to derive a theoretical price for an option. Deriving a theoretical option price is much more complicated than deriving a theoretical futures or forward price because the option price depends on the expected volatility of the underlying over the life of the option. Several models have been developed to determine the theoretical price of an option. Here we look at the general principles of pricing options.

The price of an option is made up of two components: the intrinsic value and the time premium over the intrinsic value. The *intrinsic value* of an option is the maximum of zero and the value the option would have if exercised immediately. The intrinsic value for an American call option at any point in time t before its expiration, for example, is $\max\{S_t - K, 0\}$, while the intrinsic value for an American put option at any point in time t before its expiration is $\max\{K - S_t, 0\}$. Here S_t is the underlying asset's price at time t, and K is the strike price. When the intrinsic value of an option is positive, we say that the option is *in-the-money*. When the intrinsic value is zero because the asset's price is less than the strike price (in the case of a call) or the asset's price is more than the strike price (in the case of a put), we say that the option is *out-of-the-money*. When the asset's price is equal to the strike price, the option is said to be *at-the-money*. An option that is at-the-money has an intrinsic value of zero.

The *time premium*, also called the *time value of an option*, is so named because of the possibility of future favorable movements in the underlying's price. It equals the amount by which the market price of the option exceeds its intrinsic value. For example, if the price of a call option with a strike price of $100 is $12 when the underlying's market price is $104, the time premium of this option is $8 ($12 minus its intrinsic value of $4). Had the underlying's market price been $95 instead of $104, then the time premium of this option would be the entire $12 because the option has no intrinsic value. All other things being equal, the time premium of an option will increase with the amount of time remaining to expiration. The time value of the option equals zero after the expiration date, or when it is optimal to exercise the option.

In addition to the type of option (call or put) and the exercise style (American or European), there are six factors that affect the price of an option. Exhibit 16.8 summarizes how each of the six factors affects the price of a European call and put option.

One can come up with bounds on the price of an option based on its intrinsic value and its time premium. It can be shown, for example, that the minimum price of an American call option at any point in time is its intrinsic

EXHIBIT 16.8 Summary of factors that affect the price of a European option.

Factor	Effect of an increase of factor on:	
	Call Price	Put Price
Market price of underlying	Increase	Decrease
Strike price	Decrease	Increase
Time to expiration of option	Increase	Increase
Expected return volatility	Increase	Increase
Short-term, risk-free interest	Increase	Decrease
Anticipated cash payments	Decrease	Increase

value. However, for most practical purposes this is not enough. Traders and investors need a way to calculate the exact price of an option.

For a long time, practitioners did not know how to approach pricing options. It was not until the Black and Scholes celebrated option pricing model was published[11] that the tools for tackling problems of pricing options of all kinds became available. Among those tools were:

- *No-arbitrage pricing:* The idea that the only kind of pricing that can be stable is one that does not give rise to arbitrage opportunities.
- *Perfect hedging:* The idea of creating a replicating portfolio that mimics payoffs of the option to be priced in all states of the world.
- *Ito's stochastic calculus:* A previously obscure tool for modeling random processes in physics that allowed for certain types of options to be priced exactly given assumptions about the random process followed by the price of underlying asset.

The idea behind deriving option pricing models is that if the payoff from owning, say, a call option can be replicated by (1) purchasing the underlying for the call option and (2) borrowing funds, then the price of the option will be (at most) the cost of creating the replicating strategy.

Next, we introduce the binomial method for pricing European and American options, as well as the Black-Scholes formula for European options. Chronologically, binomial pricing methods appeared after the Black-Scholes model—they were suggested by Sharpe (1978), Cox, Ross, and Rubinstein (1979), and Rendleman and Bartter (1979). However, the binomial methods provide an intuitive introduction to the main ideas of option pricing, so we discuss the binomial tree method first.

---

[11]Black and Scholes (1973).

16.3.2.1   Using Binomial Trees to Price European Options   Binomial trees are a very popular method for pricing both European and American options. Here we focus on European options. We begin with a simple one-period example and then generalize the example to multiple periods.

Simple one-period case: Suppose we would like to find the fair price of a European call option with strike price $K = \$52$ and time to maturity $T = 6$ months (0.5 years) on an asset whose current price is $50. Let us start simple. Suppose that at the end of $T = 0.5$ years the asset price can only be in one of two states: it can go up to $60, or it can go down to $42. The probability of the asset price going up is 60%. The probability of the asset price going down is 40%. The risk-free rate is 10%.

In what follows, we use the assumption that there is no arbitrage in the market to derive the option price. The main idea is the following. We set up a portfolio of the asset and the option in such a way that there will be no uncertainty about the value of the portfolio at the end of six months. We then argue that, because there is no risk, the return the portfolio will earn should equal the risk-free rate (otherwise, there will be an arbitrage opportunity). This enables us to work out the cost of setting up the portfolio, and therefore the price of the option. Because there are two financial instruments (the asset and the option) and only two possible outcomes (up or down), it is always possible to set up the riskless portfolio. Although this is a simple argument, it can be extended to a more general setting in which there are infinitely many possible states for the asset price. This is the idea behind the Black-Scholes formula, which we introduce in the next section.

Consider a portfolio that consists of a long position in Δ (pronounced "delta") units of an asset, and a short position in one call option. What is the value of Δ that makes the portfolio riskless?

- If the asset price goes up from $50 to $60, the value of the Δ units of the asset is $\$60\Delta$, and the value of the call option is $\max\{\$60 - 52, 0\} = \$8$. Therefore, the total value of the portfolio is ($\$60\Delta - \$8$).
- If the asset price goes down from $50 to $42, then the value of the Δ units of the asset is $\$42\Delta$, and the value of the call option is $\max\{\$42 - \$52, 0\} = \$0$. Therefore, the total value of the portfolio is $\$42\Delta$. This is illustrated in Exhibit 16.9.

In order for the portfolio to be riskless, its future value should be the same regardless of the state of the world in which the asset price ends up. Therefore, we have the condition

$$\$60\Delta - \$8 = \$42\Delta$$

Solving for Δ,

$$\Delta = \$8/\$18 \approx 0.4444$$

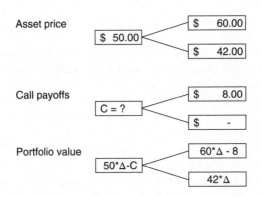

Exhibit 18.9 One-period binomial tree with values for an asset, payoffs for the call option, and the value of a portfolio consisting of a long position in Δ units of an asset and a short position in the option.

Therefore, a riskless portfolio would consist of

- A long position in 0.4444 units of the asset.
- A short position in 1 call option.

The value of the portfolio is $60 × 0.4444 −$8 (or 42 × 0.4444) = $18.67 in both states of the world.

Because the portfolio is riskless, it must earn the risk-free rate of interest, 10%. Given that the portfolio value is $18.67 half a year from the current date, the present value of the portfolio can be calculated by discounting its future value, $18.67, by the risk-free rate. Therefore, the value of the port-folio today is

$$\$18.67 \times e^{-0.10 \times 0.5} = \$17.76$$

We know the value of the asset components of the portfolio today—it is the current price of the asset ($50) times the number of shares (0.44). Therefore, we can find the value of the call option (C) today. Namely, we have

$50 × 0.4444 (the value of the shares today) – 1 × C$

$= \$17.76$ (the present value of the portfolio)

or C = $4.46

Notice that we never used the information about the probabilities of the asset price going up or down. In fact, all the information we needed about the asset was already incorporated into the values of the asset prices in the up and the down state. It turns out that there are different probabilities that are at play, and those are the probabilities that determine possible values for the asset price one period from now. We explain the intuition behind this fact next, as we generalize the method for pricing an option over multiple time periods and different types of options.

Denote the asset price today by S_0. Suppose that the asset price can go up to uS_0 or down to dS_0 over a given period (Δt). We would like to find the value f of an option written on the asset. Let the payoffs of the option in the up and the down state of the world be f_u and f_d, respectively.

We take a long position in Δ units of the asset and a short position in one call option. The portfolio values in the up and the down states are

$$(uS_0) \cdot \Delta - f_u \text{ and } (dS_0) \cdot \Delta - f_d$$

respectively. The two portfolio values are the same (that is, the portfolio is riskless) when

$$(uS_0) \cdot \Delta - f_u = (dS_0) \cdot \Delta - f_d$$

The equality is attained when

$$\Delta = \frac{f_u - f_d}{uS_0 - dS_0}$$

The above equation shows that Δ is actually the ratio of the change in the option price and the change in the asset price. It has an important role in risk management, as we will explain at the end of Section 16.3.2.2.

The present value of the portfolio is

$$((uS_0) \cdot \Delta - f_u) \cdot e^{-r \cdot (\Delta t)}$$

The value of the portfolio today is also ($S_0 \cdot \Delta - f$); therefore,

$$((uS_0) \cdot \Delta - f_u) \cdot e^{-r \cdot (\Delta t)} = (S_0 \cdot \Delta - f)$$

From here we deduce that the fair value of the option today is

$$f = S_0 \cdot \Delta - ((uS_0) \cdot \Delta - f_u) \cdot e^{-r \cdot (\Delta t)}$$

Substituting the value for Δ, we get

$$f = e^{-r \cdot (\Delta t)} \cdot (p \cdot f_u + (1 - p) \cdot f_d)$$

where

$$p = \frac{e^{r \cdot (\Delta t)} - d}{u - d}$$

The parameter p in the expression for the option price f can be viewed as a special probability. It is in fact called a *risk-neutral probability*. Note that if we use this new probability, the value of the option today equals the expected value of its future payoffs, f_u and f_d. In fact, this is the same probability that makes the value of the asset today equal to the expected value of its discounted future values when the discount rate is the risk-free rate. To see this, note that in our example we had

$$u = \$60/\$50 = 1.20$$
$$d = \$42/\$50 = 0.84$$
$$\Delta t = 0.5$$
$$f_u = \$8$$
$$f_d = \$0$$
$$p = \frac{e^{0.10 \cdot (0.5)} - 0.84}{1.20 - 0.84} = 0.5869;$$
$$1 - p = 0.4131$$

The value of the call option today was[12]

$$C = e^{-0.10 \cdot 0.5} \cdot (0.5869 \cdot \$8 + (1 - 0.5869) \cdot \$0) = \$4.47$$

The expected value of the asset under this probability distribution today, assuming that the asset's return is the risk-free rate, is

$$e^{-0.10 \cdot 0.5} \cdot (0.5869 \cdot \$60 + (1 - 0.5869) \cdot \$42) = \$50.00$$

which was indeed its current value.

Generalization to multiple periods: The formula for the price of the option as an expected value of its discounted payoffs under a risk-neutral probability measure can be derived for multiple time periods. For example, if we have two time periods, we get

$$f = e^{-2r \cdot (\Delta t)} \left[p^2 \cdot f_{uu} + 2 \cdot p \cdot (1 - p) \cdot f_{ud} + (1 - p)^2 \cdot f_{dd} \right]$$

---

[12]There is a one-cent difference with the previous estimate due to rounding error.

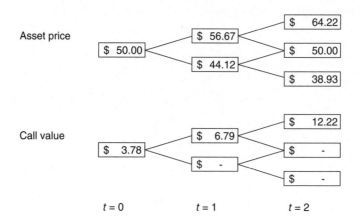

Exhibit 16.10 Pricing of a European call option using a two-period binomial tree.

Note that the coefficients in front of the terms containing the probabilities p count how many ways there are to get to the particular end node in the tree. For example, there are two ways to get a payoff of f_{ud}: the asset price can go up first and then down (probability $p \cdot (1 - p)$), or down first and then up (probability $(1 - p) \cdot p$). So, the probability of getting a payoff of f_{ud} is $2 \cdot p \cdot (1 - p)$. To get f, the expected value of the option today, we take the weighted average of all possible future payoffs (with weights that are products of the risk-neutral probabilities), and discount it to the present.

Exhibit 16.10 shows the example of pricing the same call option as in the previous section, but over two time periods rather than one. The parameters u, d, and p are slightly different—they are adjusted for the fact that each time period has a shorter length than the time period considered in the one-period example. Now $u = 1.13$, $d = 0.88$, $p = 56.99\%$. In practice, these parameters are estimated from observed price dynamics.[13]

At time 0, we start with an initial asset price of $50. At time 1, we have two possible prices: $50 \cdot 1.19 = \$56.67$ and $50 \cdot 0.88 = \$44.12$. At the option's expiration date, we have three (instead of two) possible values for the underlying asset price: $64.22, $50.00, and $38.93.[14] You can imagine that as one continues to divide the time to maturity into smaller and

---

[13] See Chapter 13 in Pachamanova and Fabozzi (2010).
[14] We have three final nodes because we built the binomial tree to be *recombining*. This keeps the dimension of the problem manageable. With a recombining tree, we have $t + 1$ nodes at time t. With a nonrecombining tree, we have 2^t nodes at time t. Thus, with a nonrecombining tree the number of nodes quickly becomes unmanageable.

smaller intervals, one will obtain a large number of possible prices for the asset at the expiration date, which will represent the possible states of the world better.

In Exhibit 16.10, we show the value of the option in the possible states of the world at time 0, 1, and 2. At time 2, we simply compute the payoffs of the option. For example, the top payoff at time 2 is $12.22 = \max\{\$64.22 - \$52.00, 0\}$. We fill out the remaining two nodes at time 2 similarly. If we use the formula for the value of the option at the beginning of this section, we get the following value for the European call price:

$$C = e^{-0.10 \cdot 0.5} \times (0.5699^2 \cdot \$12.22 + 2 \cdot 0.5699 \cdot (1 - 0.5699) \cdot \$0$$
$$+ (1 - 0.5699)^2 \cdot \$0) = \$3.78$$

Basically, we weighted all final payoffs at time 2 by the probabilities of obtaining them, and discounted the weighted average to time 0. For example, the payoff of $12.22 was weighted by 0.5699^2, because in order to obtain it, the asset price needs to go up at time period 1, and then up again at time period 2.

Let us show how one would compute the option value at each time period. Although we do not need to do it in the case of European options, it is instructive to do so.[15] The value of $6.79 obtained at time 1 in Exhibit 16.10 is the discounted expected payoff from the two nodes at time 2 that are reachable from the node at time 1:

$$\$6.79 = e^{-0.10 \cdot (0.5/2)} \cdot (0.5699 \cdot \$12.22 + (1 - 0.5699) \cdot \$0)$$

Note that the discount factor takes into consideration the fact that the time period is of length $T/2$. Similarly, we can compute the second possible value for the option at time 1. (It turns out that value is 0, since it is the expected value of two zero payoffs.)

At time 0, we compute the discounted expected value of the option values at time 1:

$$e^{-0.10 \cdot (0.5/2)} \cdot (0.5699 \cdot \$6.79 + (1 - 0.5699) \cdot \$0)$$

This gives the price of the option, $3.78.

---

[15]This intermediate calculation is useful for the pricing of non-European options for which early exercise is possible. The pricing of American and exotic options is beyond the scope of this book, as we focus on the role of derivatives for managing portfolio risk. The interested reader is referred to Hull (2014) for a more detailed introduction to option pricing, and to Pachamanova and Fabozzi (2010) for numerical examples of using simulation in option pricing.

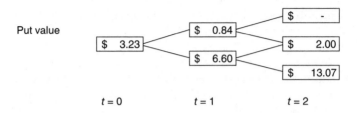

Put value

$t = 0$ $t = 1$ $t = 2$

Exhibit 16.11 Pricing a European put option with a two-period binomial tree.

We can similarly compute the price of a put option on the same underlying asset. The only thing we need to change is how we compute the option payoffs at time 2, which in turn changes the option values at time 0 and 1. (See Exhibit 16.11.)

What if there are more time periods? Suppose there are n time periods, each of length Δt (i.e., $\Delta t = T/n$, where T is the maturity of the option). Then,

$$
\begin{aligned}
f &= e^{-n \cdot r \cdot (\Delta t)} \left[p^n \cdot f_n + \binom{n}{n-1} \cdot p^{n-1} \cdot (1-p) \cdot f_{n-1} + \cdots \right. \\
&\quad \left. + \binom{n}{1} \cdot p \cdot (1-p)^{n-1} \cdot f_1 + (1-p)^n \cdot f_0 \right] \\
&= e^{-n \cdot r \cdot (\Delta t)} \left[\sum_{j=0}^{n} \binom{n}{j} \cdot p^j \cdot (1-p)^{n-j} \cdot f_j \right]
\end{aligned}
$$

In the above formula, $f_j = \max(u^j d^{n-j} S_0 - K, 0)$ for a European call option, and $f_j = \max(K - u^j d^{n-j} S_0, 0)$ for a European put option ($j = 0$, 1, ..., n).[16]

As we mentioned earlier, even though we assume that the asset price can only take a discrete set of values, if we divide the time to maturity of the

---

[16]The numbers $\binom{n}{k}$ (pronounced "n choose k") are the *binomial coefficients*. They count how many ways there are to choose k objects out of n. (In the particular context of option pricing, they count how many ways there are to get k "up" moves of the price of the asset out of n possible moves.) These coefficients appear in the formula for the binomial probability distribution. (See Chapter 2.3.) The binomial distribution associates a probability with k successes out of n trials, and the probability is computed exactly in the same way as in the option pricing formula above.

option T into many small time periods, there will be many possible values (end nodes) for the final asset price. This allows us to price the option quite accurately.

16.3.2.2 The Black-Scholes Formula for Pricing European Options

Instead of assuming that the future price for the asset can take only two values, uS_0 or dS_0, the Black-Scholes model assumes that the future asset price can take a continuous range of values with a specific probability distribution, the lognormal distribution.[17] The Black-Scholes formulas for a European call (C) and put (P) option are as follows:

$$C = S_0 \cdot e^{-qT} \cdot \Phi(d_1) - K \cdot e^{-rT} \cdot \Phi(d_2)$$

and

$$P = K \cdot e^{-rT} \cdot \Phi(-d_2) - S_0 \cdot e^{-qT} \cdot \Phi(-d_1)$$

where

$$d_1 = \frac{\ln(S_0/K) + (r - q + \sigma^2/2) \cdot T}{\sigma \cdot \sqrt{T}},$$

$$d_2 = d_1 - \sigma \cdot \sqrt{T}$$

K is the strike price,
T is the time to maturity,
q is the percentage of asset value paid annually as a cash distribution, and
Φ denotes the cumulative probability density function for the normal distribution.[18]

To illustrate the Black-Scholes option pricing formula, assume the following values:

- Current asset price (S_0) = $50
- Strike price (K) = $52
- Time remaining to expiration (T) = 183 days = 0.5 years (183 days/365, rounded)
- Asset return volatility (σ) = 0.25 (25%)
- Short-term risk-free interest rate = 0.10 (10%)

---

[17] See Chapter 3.1.4.
[18] The value for $\Phi(d)$ can be found with the formula =NORMDIST(d,0,1,1) in Excel.

EXHIBIT 16.12 Prices of European call and put options for different values of the time to maturity T and the volatility σ.

Time to expiration (years)			Volatility		
	Call	Put		Call	Put
	$ 3.78	$ 3.24		$ 3.78	$ 3.24
0.5	$ 3.78	$ 3.24	10%	$ 1.69	$ 1.15
1.0	$ 6.44	$ 3.49	20%	$ 3.08	$ 2.54
1.5	$ 8.76	$ 3.51	30%	$ 4.47	$ 3.94
2.0	$ 10.86	$ 3.43	40%	$ 5.87	$ 5.33
2.5	$ 12.81	$ 3.31	50%	$ 7.25	$ 6.71
3.0	$ 14.63	$ 3.15	60%	$ 8.63	$ 8.09
3.5	$ 16.35	$ 2.99	70%	$ 9.99	$ 9.46
4.0	$ 17.97	$ 2.82	80%	$ 11.35	$ 10.81

Plugging into the formula, we obtain

$$d_1 = \frac{\ln(50/52) + (0.10 - 0 + 0.25^2/2) \cdot 0.5}{0.25 \cdot \sqrt{0.5}} = 0.1502$$

$$d_2 = 0.1502 - 0.25 \cdot \sqrt{0.5} = -0.0268$$

$$\Phi(0.1502) = 0.5597$$

$$\Phi(-0.0268) = 0.4893$$

$$C = 50 \cdot 1 \cdot 0.5597 - 52 \cdot e^{-0.10 \cdot 0.5} \cdot 0.4893 = \$3.79$$

It is a good idea to check how sensitive the Black-Scholes price is to the values of different inputs. Prices of European call and put options calculated using the Black-Scholes formula for the input parameters above and different values of the time to maturity T and the volatility σ are shown in Exhibit 16.12.

It is easy to observe that both calls and puts become more valuable as the volatility of the process for the underlying price increases. Also, the call option becomes more valuable as the time to expiration increases. These calculations agree with the general summary in Exhibit 16.8.

Model assumptions: Although the Black-Scholes formula is still widely used in practice, it is important to realize that the formula only applies under very specific assumptions.

- *Assumption 1: The option to be priced is a European option.* The Black-Scholes model assumes that the call option is a European call option. It is not appropriate to use the Black-Scholes model (except as a part of approximation schemes) when options with American features are priced. The binomial option pricing model described earlier can easily handle American call options.

- *Assumption 2: The return volatility of the asset (σ) is constant and known.* The Black-Scholes model assumes that the expected asset return volatility is (1) constant over the life of the option and (2) known with certainty. If (1) does not hold, an option pricing model can be developed that allows the variance to change. The violation of (2), however, is more serious. Because the Black-Scholes model depends on the riskless hedge argument and in turn the return volatility of the asset must be known to construct the proper hedge, if the stock return volatility is uncertain, the hedge will not be riskless.

- *Assumption 3: The risk-free rate r is constant over the life of the option, and is the same for borrowing and lending.* The first assumption is unrealistic because interest rates change daily. The model can be made more realistic by using simulation.[19] The second assumption is unlikely to hold as well because in real-world financial markets borrowing rates are higher than lending rates. Realistically, the market price for a call option would be between the call prices derived from the Black-Scholes model using the two interest rates.

- *Assumption 4: The random process generating stock prices is a diffusion process.* To derive an exact option pricing model, an assumption is needed about the way asset prices move. The Black-Scholes model is based on the assumption that asset prices follow a diffusion process (geometric random walk).[20] In a diffusion process, the asset price can take on any positive value, but it does not jump from one price to another, skipping over interim prices. The Black-Scholes formula does not apply when asset prices follow a jump process; that is, when prices are not continuous and smooth, but exhibit jumps. Merton (1976) and Cox and Ross (1975) have developed alternative option-pricing models assuming a jump process for the price of the underlying.

- *Assumption 5: There are no transaction costs and taxes.* The Black-Scholes model ignores taxes and transaction costs. The model can be modified to account for taxes, but the problem is that there is not just one tax rate. Transaction costs include both commissions and the bid–ask

---

[19] See Chapter 5 in Pachamanova and Fabozzi (2010).

[20] In other words, the future asset price is assumed to be determined from the equation $S_T = S_0 e^{\left(r-q-\frac{1}{2}\sigma^2\right)\cdot T + \sigma \cdot \sqrt{T} \cdot \tilde{\epsilon}}$, where $\tilde{\epsilon}$ is a standard normal random variable. See Chapter 12 in Pachamanova and Fabozzi (2010).

spreads for the asset and the option, as well as other costs associated with trading options.

Estimating the parameters in the Black-Scholes formula: Most of the parameters in the Black-Scholes formula—the initial price for the asset, the time to maturity, the short-term risk-free interest rate—can be observed directly. The one parameter that needs to be estimated is the volatility of the return of the underlying asset. Market participants determine this input into the Black-Scholes option pricing model in one of two ways: (1) by calculating the implied volatility from current option prices or (2) by calculating the standard deviation using historical daily asset returns.

Calculation of the implied probability relies on the fact that an option pricing model relates a given volatility estimate to a unique price for the option. If the option price is known, the same option pricing model can be used to determine the corresponding volatility. Therefore, the volatility to use in the pricing model for an option we seek to value can be implied from observed market prices for other options on the same asset.

In addition to its use as input in an option pricing model, implied volatility has other applications in strategies employing options. The most straightforward application is a comparison of implied volatility with the estimate of volatility using historical return data, which we will describe shortly. If an investor believes that the estimated volatility using historical data is a better estimate than implied volatility, then the two volatility estimates can be compared to assess whether an option is cheap or expensive. Specifically, if the estimate of volatility using historical data is higher than implied volatility, then the option is cheap; if it is less than implied volatility, then the option is expensive.

A further use for implied volatility is to compare put and call options on the same asset and with the same time to expiration. Implied volatility can also be used to compare options on the same underlying asset and time to expiration but with different strike prices. For example, suppose that the implied volatility for a call option with a strike price of 90 is 8% when a call option with a strike of 100 has an implied volatility of 12%. Then, on a relative basis, the call option with a strike of 90 is cheaper than the call option with a strike of 100. One fact to keep in mind for the latter application, however, is that a phenomenon called *volatility smile* is often naturally observed in option markets where the underlying is an individual stock or a stock index. Namely, implied volatilities for options on the same stock or stock index but with different strike prices exhibit a pattern similar to the pattern in Exhibit 16.13. More specifically, options that are at-the-money tend to have a lower implied volatility than options that are out-of the-money or in-the-money. When trying to determine the "correct" volatility to use for

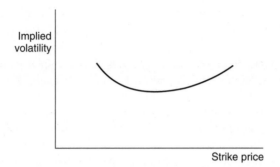

Exhibit 16.13   Volatility smile for in-the-money call options.

pricing a new option, practitioners often use a quick-and-dirty approach: they interpolate between volatility values on the smile.[21]

The second method used to estimate an asset's return volatility is to calculate the standard deviation of historical asset returns. In the case of individual assets and indexes, market practices with respect to the number of trading days that are used to calculate the daily standard deviation vary. The number of trading days can be as few as 10 or as many as 100. Since market participants are interested in annualized volatility, when daily returns are used as in the case of assets and indexes, the standard deviation is annualized as follows:

$$(\text{Daily standard deviation}) \cdot \sqrt{\text{Number of trading days in a year}}$$

Conventions about the number of trading days in a year to use vary as well. Typically, either 250, 260, or 365 trading days are used. The first two are used because they represent the number of actual trading days for certain options. Given the different conventions about the number of trading days of data to use for the estimation and the number of trading days in a year to use for annualizing the estimated historical daily volatility, estimates of historical volatility can vary significantly.

---

[21]If the Black-Scholes model truly applied to markets, the volatility smile phenomenon should not be observed. The fact that it exists implies that practitioners do not believe that the lognormal probability distribution for asset prices correctly represents extreme events. In the real world, extreme events (events that happen in the tails of the distribution) are more likely than the lognormal distribution would imply.

Whereas historical volatility estimates are backward-looking, implied volatility estimates are forward-looking, in the sense that the latter incorporate market participants' expectations about where the volatility will be. Generally, implied volatility estimates are preferred, but they are not always easy to produce. Sometimes, a combination of historical and implied volatilities is used.

Measuring sensitivities: In employing option strategies, a portfolio manager needs to know how sensitive the option price is to changes in any of the factors that determine it. Measures for the sensitivity of the option price with respect to the underlying factors are denoted by Greek letters, and are usually referred to as "the Greeks." The measures of the sensitivity of the option price with respect to the underlying asset, the time to expiration, and the volatility in the underlying asset return are as follows:

- *Delta*: We have seen the importance of understanding the relationship between the option price and the price of the underlying asset in developing the option pricing model. Employing options to control the price risk of a portfolio requires an understanding of how the option position will change as the price of the underlying asset changes. The ratio of the change in the option price and the change in the price of the underlying is referred to as *delta* (Δ). On an intuitive level, Δ is the number of units of the asset we should hold for each option shorted in order to create a riskless hedge.

- *Gamma*: Often, it is of interest to estimate the rate of change of the option delta as the asset price changes. The ratio of the change in delta and the change in the underlying asset price is commonly referred to as *gamma* (Γ).

- *Theta*: All other factors remaining constant, the longer the time to expiration, the greater the option price. Because each day the option moves closer to the expiration date, the time to expiration decreases. The theta (Θ) of an option measures the change in the option price relative to the decrease in the time to expiration, or, equivalently, it is a measure of *time decay*. Assuming that the price of the underlying asset does not change (which means that the intrinsic value of the option does not change), theta measures how quickly the time premium of the option changes as the option moves toward expiration. Theta is usually negative for an option (although there are exceptions), because as the time to maturity decreases, the option tends to become less valuable. Buyers of options prefer a low theta so that the option price does not decline quickly as it moves toward the expiration date. An option writer, on the other hand, benefits from an option that has a high theta.

- *Vega*: The option pricing models we considered so far assume that the volatility of the price of the underlying, σ, remains constant over time. In reality, this is not the case. The *vega* of a derivative is the rate of change of the option value with respect to the volatility of the underlying asset price.[22] If vega is high, the option value is very sensitive to small changes in the volatility of the underlying asset price.

16.4 SWAPS

Most generally, swaps are contractual agreements in which two counterparties agree to exchange returns on different assets over a prespecified period of time. There are numerous types of swaps, including equity swaps, interest rate swaps, and credit default swaps. We discuss equity swaps and how they are used in Chapter 17, and interest rate swaps and credit default swaps in Chapter 18. Here we provide only a brief description of these three common types of swaps and explain how equity swaps and interest rate swaps can be fundamentally viewed as a package of forward contracts, whereas a credit default swap is fundamentally a package of options.

We postpone the discussion of pricing of swaps until Chapter 18 where we explain how to price an interest rate swap. At this stage, we will only say that the main idea when pricing a swap is that its fair value should be the difference between the present values of the expected cash flows exchanged between the two parties in the swap.

16.4.1 Interest Rate Swaps

We begin with the most popular type of swap, an interest rate swap. In its most basic form, an *interest rate swap* is an agreement between two parties to exchange cash flows periodically. In a plain-vanilla swap, one party pays a fixed rate of interest based on a notional amount in return for the receipt of a floating rate of interest based on the same notional amount from the counterparty. These cash flows are exchanged periodically for the life of the swap.

Let's use a hypothetical interest rate swap to illustrate not only this type of swap but also its economic interpretation. We will refer to the two counterparties as party A and party B. The length of the swap is five years. The terms of the swap are as follows:

- Party A agrees to pay party B 5% per year.
- Party B agrees to pay party A the reference rate.

---

[22]Even though *vega* is the term used in the context of option "Greeks," there is no actual letter vega in the Greek alphabet.

The *reference rate* can be any market interest rate, the most common being LIBOR.[23] In our example, let's assume that the reference rate is one-year LIBOR.

The actual dollar amount of the payments swapped by the counterparties will be based on a pre-agreed *notional amount*. Let's assume that the notional amount for our hypothetical interest rate swap is $10 million. If one-year LIBOR at the time when an exchange of payments is to be made is 3%, the payments that would be swapped for our hypothetical interest rate swap are

- Party A pays party B $500,000 (= $10 million × 5%).
- Party B pays party A $300,000 (= $10 million × 3%).

Notice that there is no exchange of the notional amount ($10 million in our hypothetical swap). It is simply used as a benchmark for determining the dollar amount of the payments to be exchanged.

The economic interpretation of an interest rate swap is that the counterparties are entering into multiple forward contracts: party A is agreeing to deliver something at some time in the future (that something being the reference rate, one-year LIBOR), and party B is agreeing to accept delivery and make a payment of a fixed dollar amount (5% in our hypothetical swap). The reason we say that there are multiple forward contracts is that the agreement calls for making the exchange each year for the next five years.

16.4.2   Equity Swaps

An *equity swap* has the same interpretation as an interest rate swap. To see this, once again we use a hypothetical swap, this time one for which the counterparties are party C and party D. In our hypothetical equity swap the agreement is for one year with payments exchanged quarterly. The terms of the exchange are every quarter for one year as follows:

- Party C agrees to pay party D the total return earned on the S&P 500 Index.
- Party D agrees to pay party C each quarter the reference rate plus 100 basis points.

---

[23] As explained previously in the book, LIBOR is the London Interbank Offered Rate, the average estimated rate that a leading bank would pay when borrowing from other banks.

For example, let's assume that the reference rate is three-month LIBOR and the notional amount is $5 million. To illustrate the quarterly payments, assume that at the time a swap of payments is to be made, the total return on the S&P 500 for the quarter is 1% and three-month LIBOR is 3.2%. Then, the quarterly payments would be as follows:

- Party C pays party D $50,000 (= $5 million × 1%).
- Party D pays party C $40,000 (= $5 million × 3.2%/4).[24]

Note once again that there is no exchange of the notional amount ($5 million in our hypothetical swap).

The economic interpretation of an equity swap is that the counterparties are entering into multiple forward contracts: party C is agreeing to deliver something at some time in the future (that something being the total return on the S&P 500 Index), and party D is agreeing to accept delivery and make a payment of a floating-dollar amount based on a reference rate (three-month LIBOR in our hypothetical swap). In contrast to the interest rate swap, a floating-rate payment is exchanged for a floating-rate payment. This is not always the case—an equity swap could call for a fixed interest rate payment each quarter in exchange for the total return on the S&P 500 Index. What is important here is that the four payments to be swapped every quarter represent four forward agreements.

16.4.3 Credit Default Swaps

Now let's look at a *credit default swap*, the most common type of what is known as a *credit derivative*. A credit derivative is an instrument that a portfolio management can use to protect against credit risk. In a credit default swap, there are two counterparties. One counterparty is referred to as the *protection buyer* and the other is the *protection seller*. The protection buyer makes periodic payments to the protection seller in exchange for protection against a prespecified credit event. That is, a credit default swap has a payment by the protection seller to the protection buyer that is contingent upon the occurrence of a credit event. We describe credit events in Chapter 18. Unlike an interest rate swap and an equity swap where both parties are required to exchange payments as with a forward contract, in a credit default swap one party is required to make a payment only if a credit

---

[24]Notice that the payment by party D is divided by four. The reason is that three-month LIBOR is an annual rate as we quoted it here. The payment based on the total return of the S&P 500 Index is not divided by four because it is quoted in the example as a quarterly return.

event occurs. For this reason, one can view a credit default swap as a series of options where the credit protection buyer makes payments (which can be viewed as the option premium paid by an option buyer) in exchange for the right to receive a payout if a credit event occurs.

Summary

- In portfolio management, derivatives are used to (1) modify the risk characteristics of a portfolio (risk management), (2) enhance the expected return of a portfolio (returns management), and (3) reduce transactions costs associated with managing a portfolio (cost management).
- There are three general classes of derivatives: (1) forwards and futures, (2) options, and (3) swaps.
- A forward contract is the simplest derivative: an agreement to buy or sell an asset at a specific time in the future for a specific price.
- Forward contracts are sold in the over-the-counter market, that is, they are nonstandard and are negotiated directly between a buyer and a seller.
- A futures contract is very similar to a forward but it is a standardized contract traded on organized exchanges.
- An investor can leverage an investment by buying futures.
- A cash-and-carry trade involves borrowing cash to purchase the underlying of a futures contract and "carrying" that underlying to the settlement date of the futures contract in order to capture market mispricing resulting in an arbitrage profit.
- A reverse cash-and-carry trade involves buying a futures contract, selling short the underlying of a futures contract, and investing the proceeds of the short sale.
- An option is a contract in which the option seller grants the option buyer the right but not the obligation to enter into a transaction with the seller to either buy or sell an underlying asset at a specified price on or before a specified date.
- If the right granted by an option is to purchase the underlying, the option is referred to as a call option; if the right granted by an option is to sell the underlying, the option is referred to as a put option.
- An option can be categorized according to when it may be exercised by the buyer: a European option can only be exercised at the option's expiration date, whereas an American option can be exercised at any time on or before the expiration date.
- While forwards and futures have a linear payoff, options do not.
- The nonlinear payoff features of options lead to highly skewed portfolio return distributions when options are included in a portfolio.

- The return distribution and the risk of a portfolio that contains options cannot be understood properly without simulation.
- Two fundamental option pricing models used in practice are the Black-Scholes formula, which is only valid for European options, and binomial trees, which can be applied for both European and American options.
- Swaps are contractual agreements in which two counterparties agree to exchange returns on different assets over a prespecified period of time.
- An interest rate swap is an agreement between two parties to exchange cash flows related to reference rates periodically.
- In a plain-vanilla swap, one party pays a fixed rate of interest based on a notional amount in return for the receipt of a floating rate of interest based on the same notional amount from the counterparty.
- An equity swap has a similar structure to an interest rate swap but at least one of the rates involved in the swap is related to the realized return on a designated equity index. For example, one counterparty may agree to make periodic payments linked to the total return earned on the S&P 500 Index, while the other counterparty may agree make periodic payments linked to a reference rate such as LIBOR plus some spread.
- Interest rate swaps and equity swaps can be viewed as packages of forward contracts.
- In a credit default swap, one counterparty (the protection buyer) makes periodic payments to the other counterparty (the protection seller) in exchange for protection against a prespecified credit event.
- A credit default swap can be viewed as a series of options where the credit protection buyer makes payments (which can be viewed as the option premium paid by an option buyer) in exchange for the right to receive a payout if the credit event occurs.

CHAPTER 17

Using Derivatives in Equity Portfolio Management

In the previous chapter, the basics of financial derivatives were explained: types of financial derivatives (forwards, futures, options, and swaps), the principles of derivative pricing, and the potential applications in portfolio management. In this chapter and the one to follow, we discuss how derivatives can be used in equity and bond portfolio management. We provide more information about the contracts and their specifications and then show how they are actually used in practice. In doing so, we demonstrate some of the difficulties of implementing strategies involving derivatives.

17.1 STOCK INDEX FUTURES AND PORTFOLIO MANAGEMENT APPLICATIONS

In this section we look at how to use stock index futures contracts in portfolios. Before doing so, we discuss the basic features of stock index futures and the theoretical price of a stock index futures contract. In the previous chapter, the basic model for the theoretical price of a futures contract was explained. Our discussion of the pricing of stock index futures contracts in this chapter explains why their price would deviate from the price obtained from the basic model.

17.1.1 Basic Features of Stock Index Futures

The underlying for a stock index futures contract can be a broad-based stock market index or a narrow-based stock market index. Examples of broad-based U.S. stock market indexes that are the underlying for a futures contract are the S&P 500, Nasdaq Composite Index, and the Russell 2000 Index. Examples of non-U.S. broad-based stock market indexes that are the underlying for a stock index futures contract are Germany's DAX Index, the U.K.'s FTSE Index, Japan's Nikkei 225 Index, and Hong Kong's Hang

Seng Index. A narrow-based stock index futures contract is one based on a subsector or components of a broad-based stock index containing groups of stocks.

The dollar value of a stock index futures contract is the product of the futures price and a "multiple" that is specified for the futures contract. That is,

Dollar value of a stock index futures contract = Futures price × Multiple

For example, suppose that the futures price for the S&P 500 is 1410. The multiple for the S&P 500 futures contract is $250. Therefore, the dollar value of the S&P 500 futures contract would be $352,500 (= 1410 × $250). If an investor buys an S&P 500 futures contract at 1410 and sells it at 1430, the investor realizes a profit of 20 times $250, or $5,000. If the futures contract is sold instead for 1360, the investor will realize a loss of 50 times $250, or $12,500.

Stock index futures contracts are cash settlement contracts. This means that at the settlement date, cash will be exchanged to settle the contract. For example, if an investor buys an S&P 500 futures contract at 1410 and the futures settlement price is 1430, settlement would be as follows. The investor has agreed to buy the S&P 500 for 1410 times $250, or $352,500. The S&P 500 value at the settlement date is 1430 times $250, or $357,500. The seller of this futures contract must pay the investor $5,000 ($357,500 − $352,500). Had the futures price at the settlement date been 1360 instead of 1,430, the dollar value of the S&P 500 futures contract would have been $340,000. In this case, the investor must pay the seller of the contract $12,500 ($352,500 − $340,000). (In practice, the parties would be realizing any gains or losses at the end of each trading day as their positions are marked to market.)

Clearly, an investor who wants to short the entire market or a sector will use stock index futures contracts. The costs of a transaction are small relative to shorting the individuals stocks comprising the stock index or attempting to construct a portfolio that replicates the stock index with minimal tracking error.

17.1.2 Theoretical Price of a Stock Index Futures Contract

In Chapter 16, the following theoretical futures price was derived using an arbitrage argument:

Theoretical futures price = Cash market price + (Cash market price)

$$\times \text{(Financing cost} - \text{Cash yield)} \qquad (17.1)$$

In deriving the above theoretical futures price, six assumptions were made. If the general futures pricing model developed in Chapter 16 was applied to the pricing of stock index future contracts without recognizing that the contract specifications and market mechanics may be inconsistent with some of the six assumptions, one would find that the actual stock index futures price in the market would deviate from the theoretical futures price as given by equation (17.1). It may be possible to incorporate these institutional and contract specification differences into the formula for the theoretical futures price. In general, however, it is typically too difficult to allow for these differences in building a model for the theoretical futures price, so one develops a band or bounds for the theoretical futures price. As long as the futures price in the market remains within the band, no arbitrage opportunity is possible.

Here we look at some of the institutional and contract specification differences that cause stock index futures prices to deviate from the theoretical futures price as given by the basic pricing model.

17.1.2.1 Interim Cash Flows In deriving the basic pricing model in Chapter 16, it was assumed that no interim cash flows arise because of changes in futures prices (that is, there is no variation margin). For a stock index, there are interim cash flows. In fact, there are many cash flows that happen at the dividend dates of the companies comprising the index. To price a stock index future contract correctly, it is necessary to incorporate the interim dividend payments. However, the dividend rate and the pattern of dividend payments are not known with certainty. Consequently, they must be projected from the historical dividend payments of the companies in the index. Once the dividend payments are projected, they can be incorporated into the pricing model.

An additional consideration is that the value of the dividend payments at the settlement date will depend on the interest rate at which the dividend payments can be reinvested from the time they are projected to be received until the settlement date. The lower the dividend and the closer the dividend payments to the settlement date of the futures contract, the less important the reinvestment income is in determining the futures price.

17.1.2.2 Differences in Borrowing and Lending Rates In the derivation of the theoretical futures price in equation (17.1), it is assumed in the cash-and-carry trade and the reverse cash-and-carry trade that the borrowing rate and lending rate are equal. In real-world financial markets, however, the borrowing rate is higher than the lending rate. The impact of this inequality in rates is important and easy to quantify.

In the cash-and-carry trade, the theoretical futures price as given by equation (17.1) becomes

Theoretical futures price based on borrowing rate

= Cash market price + (Cash market price)

× (Borrowing rate − Cash yield)   (17.2)

For the reverse cash-and-carry trade, it becomes

Theoretical futures price based on lending rate

= Cash market price + (Cash market price)

× (Lending rate − Cash yield)   (17.3)

Equations (17.2) and (17.3) together provide a band within which the actual futures price can exist without allowing for an arbitrage profit. Equation (17.2) establishes the upper value for the band while equation (17.3) provides the lower value for the band. For example, assume that the borrowing rate is 6% per year, or 1.5% for three months, while the lending rate is 4% per year, or 1% for three months. Using equation (17.2), the upper value for the theoretical futures price is $99.50, and using equation (17.3), the lower value for the theoretical futures price is $99.

17.1.2.3 Transaction Costs The two strategies to exploit any price discrepancies between the cash market and theoretical futures price will involve the incurrence of transaction costs—the costs of entering into and closing the cash position as well as round-trip transaction costs for the futures contract. These transaction costs will cause a discrepancy between the theoretical futures price given by equation (17.1) and the actual futures price in the market. As in the case of differential borrowing and lending rates, transaction costs widen the band for the theoretical futures price.

17.1.2.4 Short-Selling Restrictions The reverse cash-and-strategy trade requires the short selling of the underlying. It is assumed in this strategy that the proceeds from the short sale are received and reinvested. In practice, for individual investors, the proceeds are not received, and in fact the individual investor is required to deposit margin (securities margin and not futures margin) to short sell. For institutional investors, the underlying may be borrowed, but there is a cost to borrowing. This cost of borrowing can be incorporated into the model by reducing the cash yield on the underlying. For strategies applied to stock index futures, a short sale of the stocks comprising the index means that all stocks in the index must be sold simultaneously. This may be difficult to do and therefore would widen the band for the theoretical futures price.

17.1.2.5 Deliverable Is a Basket of Securities The problem in arbitraging stock index futures contracts is that it may be too expensive to buy or sell every stock included in the stock index. Instead, a portfolio containing a smaller number of stocks may be constructed to track the index with the goal of having price movements that are very similar to changes in the stock index. Once the cash-and-carry and the reverse cash-and-carry strategies involve a tracking portfolio rather than a single asset for the underlying, however, the strategies are no longer riskless because of the risk that the tracking portfolio will not replicate the performance of the stock index exactly. For this reason, the market price of stock index futures contracts is likely to diverge from the theoretical futures price and have wider bounds (i.e., lower and upper theoretical futures prices) that cannot be exploited.

17.1.3 Portfolio Management Strategies with Stock Index Futures[1]

Prior to the development of stock index futures, an investor who wanted to speculate on the future course of stock prices had to buy or short individual stocks. Now, however, the stock index can be bought or sold in the futures market. But making speculation easier for investors is not the main function of stock index futures contracts. The other strategies discussed below show how institutional investors can effectively use stock index futures to meet various investment objectives.

17.1.3.1 Controlling the Risk of a Stock Portfolio As explained in Chapter 9, beta is a measure of the sensitivity of a portfolio to movements in the market. A portfolio manager who wishes to alter exposure to the stock market or a sector of the stock market can do so by rebalancing so that a portfolio's current beta will equal a targeted portfolio beta. In doing so, the portfolio manager will incur transaction costs. Because of the leverage inherent in futures contracts, portfolio managers can use stock index futures to obtain a target beta for the portfolio at a considerably lower cost. Buying stock index futures will increase a portfolio's beta, and selling them will reduce it.

---

[1]The illustrations in this section are adapted from Collins and Fabozzi (1999).

17.1.3.2 Hedging against Adverse Stock Price Movements *Hedging* involves the use of futures contracts as a substitute for a transaction to be made in the cash market. If the cash and futures markets move together, any loss realized by a portfolio manager seeking to a hedge on one position (whether cash or futures) will be offset by a profit on the other position. When the profit and loss are equal, the hedge is called a *perfect hedge*.

A *short hedge* is used to protect against a decline in the future cash price of the underlying. To execute a short hedge, the portfolio manager sells a futures contract. Consequently, a short hedge is also referred to as a *sell hedge*. By establishing a short hedge, the portfolio manager has fixed the future cash price and transferred the price risk of ownership to the party who has purchased the futures contract.

As an example of a portfolio manager who would use a short hedge, consider a pension fund manager who knows that the beneficiaries of the fund must be paid a total of $30 million four months from now. This will necessitate liquidating a portion of the fund's common stock portfolio. If the value of the shares that the portfolio manager intends to liquidate in order to satisfy the payments to be made decline in value four months from now, a larger portion of the portfolio will have to be liquidated. The easiest way to handle this situation is for the portfolio manager to sell the needed amount of stocks and invest the proceeds in a U.S. Treasury bill that matures in four months. However, suppose that for some reason, the portfolio manager is constrained from making the sale today. The portfolio manager can use a short hedge to lock in the value of the stocks that will be liquidated.

A *long hedge* is undertaken to protect against rising prices of future intended purchases. In a long hedge, the hedger buys a futures contract, so this hedge is also referred to as a *buy hedge*. As an example, consider once again a pension fund manager. This time, suppose that the portfolio manager is confident that there will be a substantial contribution from the plan sponsor four months from now, and that the contributions are targeted to be invested in common stock of various companies. The pension fund manager expects the market price of the stocks in which she will invest the contributions to be higher in four months and, therefore, takes the risk that she will have to pay a higher price for the stocks. The portfolio manager can use a long hedge to lock in effectively a future price for these stocks now.

Hedging is a special case of controlling a stock portfolio's exposure to adverse price changes. In a hedge, the objective is to alter a current or anticipated stock portfolio position so that its beta is zero. A portfolio with a beta of zero should generate a risk-free interest rate. This is consistent with asset pricing models. Thus, in a perfect hedge, the return will be equal to the risk-free interest rate. More specifically, it will be the risk-free interest rate corresponding to a maturity equal to the number of days until the settlement of the futures contract.

Therefore, a portfolio that is identical to the S&P 500 (i.e., an S&P 500 index fund) is fully hedged by selling an S&P 500 futures contract with 60 days to settlement that is priced at its theoretical futures price. The return on this hedged position will be the 60-day, risk-free return. Notice what has been done. If a portfolio manager wanted to eliminate temporarily all exposure to the S&P 500, the portfolio manager could sell all the stocks in the portfolio and, with the funds received, invest in a Treasury bill. By using a stock index futures contract, the portfolio manager can eliminate exposure to the S&P 500 by hedging, and the hedged position will earn the same return as that on a Treasury bill. The portfolio manager thereby saves on the transaction costs associated with selling a stock portfolio. Moreover, when the portfolio manager wants to get back into the stock market, rather than having to incur the transaction costs associated with buying stocks, she simply removes the hedge by buying an identical number of stock index futures contracts.

In practice, hedging is not a simple exercise. When hedging with stock index futures, a perfect hedge can be obtained only if the return on the portfolio being hedged is identical to the return on the futures contract. The effectiveness of a hedged stock portfolio is determined by (1) the relationship between the cash portfolio and the index underlying the futures contract and (2) the relationship between the cash price and futures price when a hedge is placed and when it is lifted (liquidated).

The difference between the cash price and the futures price is called the *basis*. It is only at the settlement that the basis is known with certainty. At the settlement date, the basis is zero. If a hedge is lifted at the settlement date, the basis is therefore known. However, if the hedge is lifted at any other time, the basis is not known in advance. The uncertainty about the basis at the time a hedge is to be lifted is called *basis risk*. Consequently, hedging involves the substitution of basis risk for price risk.

A stock index futures contract has a stock index as its underlying. Since a portfolio that a manager seeks to hedge will typically have different characteristics from the underlying stock index, there will be a difference in the return pattern of the portfolio being hedged and the futures contract. This practice—hedging with a futures contract that is different from the underlying being hedged—is called *cross hedging*. In hedging a stock portfolio, a manager must choose the stock index, or the combination of stock indexes, which best (but imperfectly) track the stock portfolio.

Consequently, cross-hedging adds another dimension to basis risk because the portfolio does not track the return on the stock index perfectly. Mispricing of a stock index futures contract is a major portion of basis risk and is largely random. The previous points about hedging can be made clearer with the following illustration, which also provides a blueprint for how hedging is implemented by a portfolio manager.

To implement a hedging strategy, it is necessary to determine not only which stock index futures contract to use, but also in how many of the contracts to take a position (i.e., how many to sell in a short hedge and buy in a long hedge). The number of contracts depends on the relative return volatility of the portfolio to be hedged and the return volatility of the futures contract. The *hedge ratio* is the ratio of volatility of the portfolio to be hedged and the return volatility of the futures contract.

It can be shown that the hedge ratio can be found by multiplying (1) the beta of the portfolio relative to the underlying stock index for the futures contract and (2) the beta of the stock index for the futures contract relative to the stock index futures contract.[2] The two betas are estimated using regression analysis, the statistical tool described in Chapter 4.2, using historical returns. Specifically, the first regression to be estimated to obtain the beta of the stock portfolio relative to the stock index is

$$r_P = \alpha_P + \beta_{PI} r_I + \epsilon_P \tag{17.4}$$

where

$\beta_{PI} =$ beta (sensitivity) of the stock portfolio relative to the stock index
$r_P \ =$ return on the stock portfolio to be hedged
$r_I \ =$ return on the stock index
$\alpha_P \ =$ intercept term
$\epsilon_P \ =$ error term

The second regression to be estimated to obtain the beta of the stock index relative to the stock index futures contract is

$$r_1 = \alpha_I + \beta_{IF} r_F + \epsilon_I \tag{17.5}$$

where

$\beta_{IF} =$ beta of the stock index relative to the stock index futures contract
$r_F \ =$ return on the stock index futures contract
$\alpha_I \ =$ intercept term
$\epsilon_I \ =$ error term

Given the estimated betas from (17.4) and (17.5), the hedge ratio is

$$\text{Hedge ratio} = \beta_{PI} \times \beta_{IF} \tag{17.6}$$

The coefficients of determination (the R^2 or R-squared) of the two regressions will indicate how good the estimated relationships are, allowing

---

[2] See Peters (1987).

the portfolio manager to assess the likelihood of success of the proposed hedge.[3]

Given the estimates for β_{PI} and β_{IF}, the number of futures contracts needed can be calculated by first determining the equivalent market index units of the market by dividing the market value of the portfolio to be hedged by the current index price of the futures contract:

$$\text{Equivalent market index units}$$
$$= \frac{\text{Market value of the portfolio to be hedged}}{\text{Current index value of the futures contract}} \tag{17.7}$$

Next, multiplying the equivalent market index units by the hedge ratio gives the beta-adjusted equivalent market index units. Since the hedge ratio is given by (17.6), we have

$$\text{Beta-adjusted equivalent market index units}$$
$$= \beta_{PI} \times \beta_{IF} \times \text{Equivalent market index units} \tag{17.8}$$

Finally, by dividing the beta-adjusted equivalent units by the multiple specified by the stock index futures contract, we get the number of contracts that should be used in the hedging strategy:

$$\text{Number of contracts} = \frac{\text{Beta-adjusted equivalent market index units}}{\text{Multiple of the contract}} \tag{17.9}$$

Let us illustrate cross-hedging using stock index futures. Suppose that a portfolio manager owned all 30 stocks in the Dow Jones Industrial Average (DJIA) on January 30, 2009. We are assuming that this is the portfolio to be hedged and its market value on that date was $100 million. Also assume that the portfolio manager wanted to hedge the position against a decline in stock prices from January 30, 2009, to February 27, 2009, using the March 2009 S&P 500 futures contract. On January 30, 2009, the March 2009 futures contract was selling for 822.5. Since the S&P 500 futures September contract is used here to hedge a portfolio of DJIA to February 27, 2009, this is a cross-hedge.

Using historical return data, the beta of the index relative to the futures contract (β_{IF}) was estimated to be 0.745. The DJIA in a regression analysis was found to have a beta relative to the S&P 500 (β_{PI}) of 1.05 (with an

---

[3]See Chapter 4.2.1.

R-squared of 93%). Given these estimates, the number of contracts needed to hedge the $100 million portfolio is computed as follows:

Equivalent market index units from equation (17.7)

$$= \frac{\$100,000,000}{822.5} = \$121,581$$

Beta-adjusted equivalent market index units using equation (17.8)

$$= 1.05 \times 0.745 \times \$121,581 = \$95,106$$

Finally, since the multiple for the S&P 500 contract is 250,

$$\text{Number of contracts to be sold} = \frac{\$95,106}{250} = 380$$

Now, what we have done is set up the hedge. It would be interesting to see what actually happened and why. During the period of the hedge, the DJIA declined on February 27, 2009, such that the portfolio lost $11,720,000. This meant a loss of 11.72% on the portfolio's $100 million. On February 29, 2009, the price of the S&P 500 futures contracts was 734.2. Because the contract was sold on January 30, 2009, for 822.5 and bought back on February 27, 2009, for 734.2, there was a gain of 88.3 index units per contract. Remember that the gain is due to the fact that the portfolio had a short position in the futures contract, which benefits from a decline in the price of the stock index futures contract. Since 380 S&P 500 futures contracts were sold and the gain per contract was 88.3 points, the gain from the futures position was $8,388,500 ($88.3 × 380 × 250). This means that the hedged position resulted in a loss of $3,331,500, or equivalently, a return of −3.31%. Remember that the unhedged position would have had a loss of 11.2%.

Let us see why this was not a perfect hedge. As explained earlier, in hedging, basis risk is substituted for price risk. Consider the basis risk in this hedge. At the time the hedge was placed, the cash index was at 825.88. The futures contract on February 27, 2009, was 822.5. The basis was equal to 3.38 index units (the cash index of 825.88 minus the futures price of 822.5). At the same time, it was calculated that, based on the cost of carry, the theoretical basis was 1.45 index units. That is, the theoretical futures price at the time the hedge was placed should have been 824.42. Thus, according to the pricing model the futures contract was mispriced by 1.92 index units. When the hedge was removed at the close of February 27, 2009, the cash index stood at 735.09, and the futures contract at 734.2. Thus, the basis changed from 3.38 index units at the time the hedge was initiated to 0.89 index units

(735.09 – 734.2) when the hedge was lifted. The basis had changed by 2.49 index units (3.38 – 0.89) alone, or $622.5 per contract (2.49 times the multiple of $250). This means that the basis alone cost $224,100 for the 360 contracts ($622.5 × 360). Thus, the futures position cost $224,100 due to the change in the basis risk.

Furthermore, the S&P 500 over this same period declined in value by 10.99%. With the beta of the portfolio relative to the S&P 500 index (1.05), the expected decline in the value of the portfolio based on the movement in the S&P 500 was 11.54% (1.05 × 10.99%). Had this actually occurred, the DJIA portfolio would have lost only $10,990,000 rather than $11,720,000, and the net loss from the hedge would have been $2,601,500, or −2.6%. Thus, there is a difference of a $730,000 loss due to the DJIA performing differently than predicted by beta.[4]

17.1.3.3 Constructing an Indexed Portfolio

As we explained in Chapter 10, some institutional equity funds are indexed to a broad-based stock market index. There are management fees and transaction costs associated with creating a portfolio to replicate a stock index that has been targeted to be matched. The higher these costs are, the greater the divergence between the performance of the indexed portfolio and the target index. Moreover, because an asset manager creating an indexed portfolio will not purchase all the stocks that make up a broad-based stock index, the indexed portfolio is exposed to tracking error risk. Instead of using the cash market to construct an indexed portfolio, the manager can use stock index futures.

Let us illustrate how and under what circumstances stock index futures can be used to create an indexed portfolio. If stock index futures are priced according to their theoretical price, a portfolio consisting of a long position in stock index futures and Treasury bills will produce the same portfolio return as that of the underlying cash index. To see this, suppose that an index fund manager wishes to index a $90 million portfolio using the S&P 500 as the target index. Also assume the following:

- The S&P 500 at the time was 1200.
- The S&P 500 futures index with six months to settlement is currently selling for 1212.
- The expected dividend yield for the S&P 500 for the next six months is 2%.
- Six-month Treasury bills are currently yielding 3%.

---

[4]Case 13.1 in the Practice section of Chapter 13 in Pachamanova and Fabozzi (2010) illustrates how simulation can be used to find a futures hedging strategy that takes into consideration the variability in the estimates.

The theoretical futures price found using equation (17.1) is:

Cash market price + Cash market price × (Financing cost − Dividend yield)

Because the financing cost is assumed to be 3% and the dividend yield is assumed to be 2%, the theoretical futures price is:

$$1200 + 1200 \times (0.03 - 0.02) = 1212$$

and, therefore, the futures price in the market is equal to the theoretical futures price.

Consider two strategies that the portfolio manager seeking to construct an indexed portfolio may choose to pursue:

Strategy 1. Purchase $90 million of stocks in such a way as to replicate the performance of the S&P 500.

Strategy 2. Buy 300 S&P 500 futures contracts with settlement six months from now at 1212, and invest $90 million in a six-month Treasury bill.[5]

Let's see how the two strategies perform under various scenarios for the S&P 500 value when the contract settles six months from now. We consider the following three scenarios:

Scenario 1. The S&P 500 increases to 1320 (an increase of 10%).

Scenario 2. The S&P 500 remains at 1200.

Scenario 3. The S&P 500 declines to 1080 (a decrease of 10%).

At settlement, the futures price converges to the value of the index. Exhibit 17.1 shows the value of the portfolio for both strategies for each of the three scenarios. As can be seen, for a given scenario, the performance of the two strategies is identical.

This result should not be surprising because a futures contract can be replicated by buying the instrument underlying the futures contract with borrowed funds. In the case of indexing, we are replicating the underlying instrument by buying the futures contract and investing in Treasury bills. Therefore, if stock index futures contracts are properly priced, a portfolio

---

[5]There are two points to note here. First, this illustration ignores margin requirements. The Treasury bills can be used for initial margin. Second, 600 contracts are selected in this strategy because with the current (assumed) market index at 1200 and a multiple of 250, the cash value of 300 contracts is $90 million.

EXHIBIT 17.1 Comparison of portfolio value from purchasing stocks to replicate an index and a futures/Treasury bill strategy when the futures contract is fairly priced. *Assumptions*: (1) amount to be invested = $90 million; (2) current value of S&P 500 = 1200; (3) current value of S&P futures contract = 1212; (4) expected dividend yield = 2%; (5) yield on Treasury bills = 3%; (6) number of S&P 500 contracts to be purchased = 300.

Strategy 1. Direct purchase of stocks

	Index value at settlement		
	1320	1200	1080
Change in index value	10%	0%	−10%
Market value of portfolio that mirrors the index	$99,000,000	$90,000,000	$81,000,000
Dividends (0.02 × $90,000,000)	$1,800,000	$1,800,000	$1,800,000
Value of portfolio	$100,800,000	$91,800,000	$82,800,000
Dollar return	$1,080,000	$180,000	$(720,000)

Strategy 2. Futures/T-Bill portfolio

	Index value at settlement*		
	1320	1200	1080
Gain/loss for 600 contracts (300 × $250 × gain/per contract)	$8,100,000	−$900,000	−$9,990,000
Value of Treasury bills ($90,000,000 × 1.03)	$92,700,000	$92,700,000	$92,700,000
Value of portfolio	$100,800,000	$91,800,000	$82,800,000
Dollar return	$1,080,000	$180,000	$(720,000)

*Because of convergence of cash and futures price, the S&P 500 cash index and stock index futures price will be the same.

manager seeking to construct an indexed portfolio can use stock index futures to create an index fund.

Several points should be noted. First, in strategy 1, the ability of the portfolio to replicate the S&P 500 depends on how well the portfolio is constructed to track the index. When the expected dividends are realized and the futures contract is fairly priced, the futures/Treasury bill portfolio (strategy 2) will mirror the performance of the S&P 500 exactly. Thus, the tracking error is reduced.

Second, the cost of transacting is less for strategy 2. For example, if the cost of one S&P 500 futures is $15, then the transaction costs for strategy 2 would be only $4,500 for a $90 million fund. This would be considerably less than the transaction costs associated with the acquisition and maintenance of a broadly diversified stock portfolio designed to replicate the S&P 500. In addition, for a large fund that wishes to index, the market impact cost is lessened by using stock index futures rather than using the cash market to create an index.

The third point is that custodial costs are obviously less for an index fund created using stock index futures.

The fourth point is that the performance of the synthetically created index fund will depend on the variation margin.

In creating an index fund synthetically, we assumed that the futures contract was fairly priced. Suppose, instead, that the stock index futures price is less than the theoretical futures price (i.e., the futures contracts are cheap). If that situation occurs, the portfolio manager can enhance the indexed portfolio's return by buying the futures and buying Treasury bills. That is, the return on the futures and Treasury bill portfolio will be greater than that on the underlying index when the position is held to the settlement date.

To see this, suppose that in our previous illustration, the current futures price is 1204 instead of 1212, so that the futures contract is cheap (undervalued). The futures position for the three scenarios in Exhibit 17.1 would be $150,000 greater (2 index units × $250 × 300 contracts). Therefore, the value of the portfolio and the dollar return for all three scenarios will be greater by $150,000 by buying the futures contract and Treasury bills rather than buying the stocks directly.

Alternatively, if the futures contract is expensive based on its theoretical price, a portfolio manager who owns stock index futures and Treasury bills will swap that portfolio for the stocks in the index. A portfolio fund manager who swaps between the futures and Treasury bills portfolio and a stock portfolio based on the value of the futures contract relative to the cash market index is attempting to enhance the portfolio's return. This strategy is referred to as a *stock replacement strategy*.

Transaction costs can be reduced measurably by using a return enhancement strategy. Whenever the difference between the actual basis and the theoretical basis exceeds the market impact of a transaction, an aggressive portfolio manager should consider replacing stocks with futures or vice versa.

Once the strategy has been put into effect, several subsequent scenarios may unfold. For example, consider an index manager who has a portfolio of stock index futures and Treasury bills. First, should the futures contract become sufficiently rich relative to stocks, the futures position is sold and the stocks repurchased, with program trading[6] used to execute the buy orders. Second, should the futures contract remain at fair value, the position is held

---

[6]Program trading could be any computerized trading. It is used for executing large orders.

until expiration, when the futures settle at the cash index value and stocks are repurchased at the market at close. Should the futures contract become cheap relative to stocks, the index manager who owns a portfolio of stocks will sell the stocks and buy the stock index futures contract.

17.2 EQUITY OPTIONS AND PORTFOLIO MANAGEMENT APPLICATIONS

In Chapter 16, we explained the difference between options and futures contracts. In contrast to futures, which have a linear payoff, options have nonlinear payoffs that will fundamentally alter the risk profile of an existing portfolio. Here we give an overview of various ways equity options can be used in portfolio management. Before doing so, we describe the different types of equity options.

17.2.1 Types of Equity Options

Equity options can be classified into four groups: (1) stock options, (2) index options, (3) Long-Term Equity Anticipation Securities™ (LEAPS), and (4) Flexible EXchange Options™ (FLEX options). All of the options are traded on an organized exchange.

Stock options are options on individual stocks. Typically, the underlying is 100 shares of the designated stock. All listed stock options in the United States may be exercised any time before the expiration date; that is, they are American-style options. Option contracts for a given stock are based on expiration dates that fit in a cycle, typically nine months for a stock.

Index options are options where the underlying is a stock index rather than an individual stock. An index call option gives the option buyer the right to buy the underlying stock index, while a put index option gives the option buyer the right to sell the underlying stock index. Unlike stock options where a stock can be delivered if the option is exercised by the option holder, it would be extremely complicated to settle an index option by delivering all the stocks included in the index. Instead, like stock index futures, index options are cash settlement contracts. This means that if the option is exercised by the option holder, the option writer pays cash to the option buyer. There is no delivery of any stocks.

Index options include industry options, sector options, and style options. The style options are based on the investment styles discussed in Chapter 12. The most liquid index options (with the corresponding ticker symbol shown in parentheses) are

- S&P 100 Index Option (OEX)
- S&P 500 Index Option (SPX)

- Nasdaq 100 Index Option (NDX)
- Dow Jones Industrial Average (DJX)
- Russell 2000 Index Options (RUT)

All of the above contracts are listed on the CBOE. Index options can have a European exercise style and are cash settled as we explained earlier. All stock index options have a multiple. The popular stock index options have a contract multiple equal to $100. The CBOE has created "mini" versions of some of the contracts wherein the underlying is one-tenth of the multiple used for the index. Since the multiple for the stock indexes listed above is $100, the mini-version's contract multiple is $10.

There are global stock indexes and country-specific stock market indexes on which options are traded. An example is the Euro STOXX 50 index option (ticker symbol OESX), which covers global and regional stock market indexes.

The dollar value of the stock index underlying an index option is equal to the current cash index value multiplied by the contract's multiple. That is,

Dollar value of the underlying index
= Cash index value × Contract multiple

For example, suppose the cash index value for the S&P 500 is 1800. Since the contract multiple is $100, the dollar value of the SPX is $180,000 (= 1800 × $100).

For a stock option, the price at which the buyer of the option can buy or sell the stock is the strike price. For an index option, the strike index is the index value at which the buyer of the option can buy or sell the underlying stock index. The strike index is converted into a dollar value by multiplying the strike index by the multiple for the contract. For example, if the strike index is 1600, the dollar value is $160,000 (= 1600 × $100). If an investor purchases a call option on the SPX with a strike index of 1600, and exercises the option when the index value is 1610, the investor has the right to purchase the index for $160,000 when the market value of the index is $161,000. The buyer of the call option would then receive $1,000 from the option writer.

Long-Term Equity Anticipation Securities™ (LEAPS) and FLexible EXchange Options™ (FLEX) are options that essentially modify an existing feature of either a stock option or an index option. For example, stock option and index option contracts have short expiration cycles. LEAPS are designed to offer options with longer maturities. These contracts are available on individual stocks and some indexes. Stock option LEAPS are comparable to standard stock options except the maturities can range up to 39 months from the origination date. Index options LEAPS differ in size compared with standard index options having a multiplier of 10 rather than 100.

FLEX options allow users to specify the terms of the option contract for either a stock option or an index option. The process for entering into a FLEX option agreement is well documented by the CBOE where these options trade. The value of FLEX options is the ability to customize the terms of the contract along four dimensions: underlying, strike price, expiration date, and settlement style. Moreover, the exchange provides a secondary market to offset or alter positions and an independent daily marking of prices.

17.2.2 Equity Portfolio Management Strategies with Options

Equity options can be used by portfolio managers to address a range of investment problems. Here we consider the use of calls, puts, and combinations in the context of the investment process, which could involve (1) risk management, (2) cost management, or (3) return enhancement.

17.2.2.1 Risk Management Strategies Risk management in the context of equity portfolio management focuses on price risk. Consequently, the strategies discussed here in some way address the risk of a price decline or a loss due to adverse price movement. Options can be used to create asymmetric risk exposures across all or part of the core equity portfolio. This allows the investor to hedge downside risk at a fixed cost with a specific limit to losses should the market turn down. The basic risk management objective is to create the optimal risk exposure and to achieve the target rate of return. Options can help accomplish this by reducing risk exposure. The various risk management strategies will also affect the expected rate of return on the position unless some form of inefficiency is involved. This may involve the current mix of risk and return or be the result of the use of options. Below we discuss two risk management strategies: protective put and collar.[7]

Protective put strategies: Protective put strategies are valuable to portfolio managers who currently hold a long position in the underlying security or investors who desire upside exposure and downside protection. The motivation is to hedge some or all of the total risk. Index put options hedge mostly market risk while equity put options hedge the total risk associated with a specific stock. This allows portfolio managers to use protective

---

[7]Other risk management strategies are discussed in Chapter 3 of Collins and Fabozzi (1999).

put strategies for separating tactical and strategic strategies. Consider, for example, a portfolio manager who is concerned about exogenous or nonfinancial events increasing the level of risk in the marketplace. Furthermore, assume the portfolio manager is satisfied with the core portfolio holdings and the strategic mix. Put options could be employed as a tactical risk reduction strategy designed to preserve capital and still maintain strategic targets for portfolio returns.

Protective put strategies may not be suitable for all portfolio managers. The value of protective put strategies, however, is that they provide the portfolio manager with the ability to invest in volatile stocks with a degree of desired insurance and unlimited profit potential over the life of the strategy.

The *protective put* involves the purchase of a put option combined with a long stock position (Exhibit 17.2). This is the equivalent of a position in a call option on the stock combined with the purchase of risk-free bond. In fact, the combined position yields the call option payout pattern described earlier. The put option is comparable to an insurance policy written against the long stock position. The option price is the cost of the insurance premium and the amount the option is out-of-the-money is the deductible. Just as in the case of insurance, the deductible is inversely related to the insurance premium. The deductible is reduced as the strike price increases, which makes the put option more in-the-money or less out-of-the-money. The higher strike price causes the put price to increase and makes the insurance policy more expensive.

The profitability of the strategy from inception to termination can be expressed as follows:

$$\text{Profit} = N_s(S_T - S_t) + N_p[\max(0, K - S_T) - \text{Put}] \qquad (17.10)$$

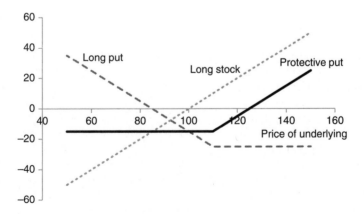

Exhibit 17.2 Payoff at expiration of a protective put strategy.

where

N_s = number of shares of the stock
N_p = number of put options
S_T = price of stock at termination date (time T)
S_t = price of stock at time t
K = strike price
Put   = put price

The profitability of the protective put strategy is the sum of the profit from the long stock position and the put option. If held to expiration, the minimum payout is the strike price (K) and the maximum is the stock price (S_T). If the stock price is below the strike price of the put option, the investor exercises the option and sells the stock to the option writer for K. If we assume that the number of shares N_s is equal to N_p, the number of put options, then the loss would amount to

$$\text{Profit} = S_T - S_t + K - S_T - \text{Put}$$
$$= K - S_t - \text{Put} \tag{17.11}$$

Notice that the price of the stock at the termination date does not enter into the profit equation.

For example, if the original stock price was \$100 (S_t), the strike price \$95 (K), the closing stock price \$80 (S_T), and the put premium (Put) \$4, then the profit would equal the following:

$$\text{Profit} = \$95 - \$100 - \$4 = -\$9$$

The portfolio manager would have realized a loss of \$20 without the hedge. If, on the other hand, the stock closed up \$20, then the profit would look like this:

$$\text{Profit} = S_T - S_t - \text{Put} = \$120 - \$100 - \$4 = \$16$$

The cost of the insurance is 4% in percentage terms and is manifested as a loss of upside potential. If we add transaction costs, the shortfall is increased slightly. The maximum loss, however, is the sum of the put premium and the difference between the strike price and the original stock price, which is the amount of the deductible. The problem arises when the portfolio manager is measured against a benchmark and the cost of what amounted to an unused insurance policy causes the portfolio to underperform the benchmark. Equity portfolio managers can use stock selection, market timing, and the prudent use of options to reduce the cost of insurance. The breakeven stock price is given by the sum of the original stock price and the put price. In this example, breakeven is $104, which is the stock price necessary to recover the put premium. The put premium is never really recovered because of the performance lag. This lag falls in significance as the return increases.

Collar strategies: An alternative to a protective put is a collar. A collar strategy consists of a long stock position, a long put, and a short call (Exhibit 17.3). By varying the strike prices, a range of trade-offs among downside protection, costs, and upside potential is possible. When the long put is completely financed by the short call position, the strategy is referred to as a *zero-cost collar*. Collars are designed for investors who currently hold a long equity position and want to achieve a level of risk reduction. The put strike price establishes a floor and the call strike price a ceiling.

The profit equation for a collar is simply the sum of a long stock position, a long put, and a short call. That is,

$$\text{Profit} = N_s(S_T - S_t) + N_p[\max(0, K_p - S_T) - \text{Put}]$$
$$- N_c[\max(0, S_T - K_c) + \text{Call}] \qquad (17.12)$$

where K_p and K_c are the strike price of the put and call, respectively, and Call is the price of the call option.

17.2.2.2 Cost Management Strategies Equity options can be used to manage the cost of maintaining an equity portfolio in a number of ways. Among the strategies are the use of short put and short call positions to serve as a substitute for a limit order in the cash market. Cash-secured put strategies

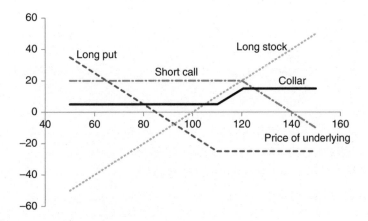

Exhibit 17.3 Payoff at expiration of a collar strategy.

can be used to purchase stocks at the target price, while covered calls or overwrites can be used to sell stocks at the target price. The target price is the one consistent with the portfolio manager's valuation or technical models and the price intended to produce the desired rate of return. Choices also exist for a variety of strategies derived from put/call parity relationships. There is always an alternative method of creating a position.[8]

17.2.2.3 Return Enhancement Strategies Equity options can be used for return enhancement. Here we describe the most popular return enhancement strategy: covered call strategy (Exhibit 17.4). Other return enhancement strategies include covered combination strategy and volatility valuation strategy.[9]

There are many variations of what is popularly referred to as a *covered call strategy*. If the portfolio manager owns the stock and writes a call on that stock, the strategy has been referred to as an *overwrite strategy*. If the strategy is implemented all at once (i.e., buy the stock and sell the call option), it is referred to as a *buy-write strategy*. The essence of the covered call is to trade price appreciation for income. The strategy is appropriate for slightly bullish investors who don't expect much out of the stock and want to produce additional income. These are investors who are willing either to limit upside appreciation for limited downside protection or to manage the costs

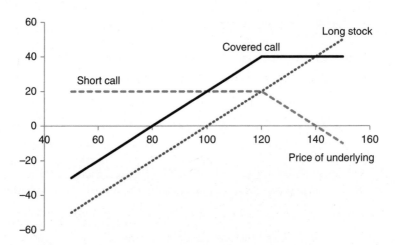

Exhibit 17.4 Payoff at expiration of a covered call strategy.

[8]Cost management strategies are discussed in Chapter 3 of Collins and Fabozzi (1999).

[9]These strategies are described in Collins and Fabozzi (1999).

of selling the underlying stock. The primary motive is to generate additional income from owning the stock.

Although the call premium provides some limited downside protection, this is not an insurance strategy because it has significant downside risk. Consequently, portfolio managers should proceed with caution when considering a covered call strategy. Although a covered call is less risky than buying the stock because the call premium lowers the breakeven recovery price, the strategy behaves like a long stock position when the stock price is below the strike price. On the other hand, the strategy is insensitive to stock prices above the strike price and is therefore capped on the upside. The maximum profit is given by the call premium and the out-the-money amount of the call option.

17.3   EQUITY SWAPS

As explained in Chapter 16.4, swaps are contractual agreements between two counterparties, which provide for the periodic exchange of a schedule of cash flows over a specified time period. In the exchange involving an equity swap, at least one of the two payments is linked to the performance of an equity index, a basket of stocks, or a single stock. In a standard or plain-vanilla equity swap, one counterparty agrees to pay the other the total return to an equity index in exchange for receiving either the total return of another asset or a fixed or floating interest rate. All payments are based on a notional amount and payments are made over a fixed time period.

Equity swap structures are very flexible, with maturities ranging from a few months to 10 years. The returns of virtually any equity asset can be swapped for another without incurring the costs associated with a transaction in the cash market. Payment schedules can be denominated in any currency irrespective of the equity asset and payments can be exchanged monthly, quarterly, annually, or at maturity. The equity asset can be any equity index or portfolio of stocks, and denominated in any currency, hedged or unhedged.

Equity swaps have a wide variety of applications including asset allocation, accessing international markets, enhancing equity returns, hedging equity exposure, and synthetically shorting stocks.

In Chapter 16.4.2, we gave the example of an equity swap that is a one-year agreement where the counterparty agrees to pay the investor the total return to the S&P 500 Index in exchange for dollar-denominated LIBOR on a quarterly basis. The investor would pay LIBOR plus a spread × 91/360 × notional amount.[10] This type of equity swap is the economic

---

[10]The multiplier 91/360 is used because the payments are quarterly.

equivalent of financing a long position in the S&P 500 Index at a spread to LIBOR. The advantages of using the swap are no transaction costs, no sales or dividend withholding tax, and no tracking error or basis risk versus the index.

The basic mechanics of equity swaps are the same regardless of the structure. However, the rules governing the exchange of payments may differ. For example, a U.S. investor wanting to diversify internationally can enter into a swap and, depending on the investment objective, exchange payments on a currency-hedged basis. If the investment objective is to reduce U.S. equity exposure and increase Japanese equity exposure, for example, a swap could be structured to exchange the total returns to the S&P 500 Index for the total returns to the Nikkei 225 Index. If, however, the investment objective is to gain access to the Japanese equity market, a swap can be structured to exchange LIBOR plus a spread for the total returns to the Nikkei 225 Index. The cash flows can be denominated in either yen or dollars. The advantages of entering into an equity swap to obtain international diversification are that the investor exposure is devoid of tracking error, and the investor incurs no transaction taxes, custodial fees, withholding fees, or market impact associated with entering and exiting a market. This swap is the economic equivalent of being long the Nikkei 225 financed at a spread to LIBOR at a fixed exchange rate.

There are numerous applications of equity swaps, but all assume the basic structure outlined above. Investors can virtually swap any financial asset for the total returns to an equity index, a portfolio of stocks, or a single stock. There are dealers prepared to create structures that allow an investor to exchange the returns of any two assets. The schedule of cash flows exchanged is a function of the assets. For example, an investor wanting to outperform an equity benchmark may be able to accomplish this by purchasing a particular bond and swapping the cash flows for the S&P 500 total return minus a spread.

Summary

- The underlying for a stock index futures contract can be a broad-based stock market index or a narrow-based stock market index.
- Stock index futures are cash settlement contracts.
- The actual price of a stock index futures contract may deviate from the theoretical price because of interim cash flows, differences in borrowing and lending rates, transaction costs, short-selling restrictions, and the fact that stock index futures contracts on a broad market index cannot

be arbitraged precisely because the underlying index is only tracked with a limited number of stocks for cost reasons.

- An investor who wants to short the entire market or a sector will use stock index futures contracts. The costs of a transaction are small relative to shorting the individual stocks.
- Stock index futures can be used to obtain a target beta for the portfolio at a relatively low cost, to hedge adverse stock price movements, or to construct an index fund synthetically.
- A portfolio manager looking to protect against the decline in the future cash price of an underlying may use a short hedge by selling a futures contract.
- The effectiveness of a hedged stock portfolio is determined by (1) the relationship between the cash portfolio and the index underlying the futures contract and (2) the relationship between the cash price and the futures price when a hedge is placed and when it is lifted (liquidated).
- The basis is the difference between the cash price and the futures price.
- Basis risk is the uncertainty about what the basis will be when the hedge is lifted.
- Cross-hedging is a strategy of hedging a portfolio using a futures contract with a different underlying than the portfolio being hedged.
- The hedge ratio is the ratio of volatility of the portfolio to be hedged and the return volatility of the futures contract.
- To estimate the inputs to the hedge ratio, one can use regression analysis.
- The hedge ratio can be found by multiplying (1) the beta of the portfolio relative to the underlying stock index for the futures contract and (2) the beta of the stock index for the futures contract relative to the stock index futures contract.
- Exchange-traded equity options include (1) stock options, (2) index options, (3) Long-Term Equity Anticipation Securities, and (4) FLexible EXchange Options. The underlying for stock options and index options are individual stocks and stock indexes, respectively.
- Long-Term Equity Anticipation Securities (LEAPS) and Flexible EXchange Options (FLEX) are options that modify an existing feature of either a stock option or an index option.
- Equity options can be used by portfolio managers for (1) risk management, (2) cost management, and (3) return enhancement.
- Protective put strategies, which involve the purchase of a put option combined with a long stock position, are used by portfolio managers to limit downside risk while preserving capital and maintaining strategic targets for portfolio returns.

- Collar strategies consist of a long position in a stock, a long put, and a short call. The put exercise price establishes a floor and the call exercise price a ceiling on the downside and the upside, respectively.
- Covered call strategies involve a long position in a stock and a short position in a call on that stock. The primary motive to use them is to generate additional income from owning the stock.
- Equity swaps have a wide variety of applications, including asset allocation, accessing international markets, enhancing equity returns, hedging equity exposure, and synthetically shorting stocks.

CHAPTER 18

Using Derivatives in Fixed Income Portfolio Management

In the previous chapter our focus was on the application of derivatives to the management of an equity portfolio. In this chapter, we look at how fixed income portfolio managers can use interest rate derivatives (Treasury futures, Treasury futures options, and interest rate swaps) to control interest rate risk and how credit derivatives (in particular credit default swaps) can be used to control credit risk.

18.1 CONTROLLING INTEREST RATE RISK USING TREASURY FUTURES

There are several interest rate futures contracts that are available to portfolio managers. The contracts commonly used to control the interest rate risk of bond portfolios are Treasury bond and note futures contracts. We describe these contracts here, their pricing in terms of deviations from the basic futures pricing model in Chapter 16, and how they are used.

The Treasury bond and note futures contracts are traded on the Chicago Mercantile Exchange (CME). The underlying instrument for the bond futures contract is $100,000 par value of a hypothetical 20-year, 6% coupon bond. This hypothetical bond's coupon rate is called the *notional coupon*. There is also an ultra-Treasury-bond futures contract. An acceptable deliverable for the ultra-Treasury-bond futures contract is a bond with a maturity of at least 25 years, allowing bond portfolio managers to better manage the longer end of the yield curve. The Treasury bond futures contract is effectively a short maturity bond futures contract and the ultra-Treasury-bond futures contract is effectively a long maturity bond futures contract with a duration that is better suited for managing duration for portfolios of long-term bonds. There are three Treasury note futures contracts: 10-year, 5-year, and 2-year. All three contracts are modeled after the Treasury bond futures contract and are traded on the CME.

The underlying instrument for the 10-year Treasury note contract is $100,000 par value of a hypothetical 10-year, 6% Treasury note. Treasury futures contracts trade with March, June, September, and December settlement months. The futures price is quoted in terms of par being 100. Because the bond and notes futures contracts are similar, for the remainder of our discussion we focus on the bond futures contract.

We have been referring to the underlying instrument as a hypothetical Treasury bond. Whereas some interest rate futures contracts can only be settled in cash, the sellers of Treasury bond futures contracts must deliver some Treasury bond at settlement, unless they choose to liquidate their position prior to the settlement date by buying back the contract. This begs the question "which Treasury bond?" The CME allows the seller to deliver one of several Treasury bonds that the CME specifies are acceptable for delivery. Traders who are short a particular bond are always concerned about the risk of being unable to obtain sufficient securities to cover their position.

The bond issues that meet the delivery requirements for a particular contract are referred to as *deliverable issues*. The CME selects the Treasury issues that are acceptable for delivery from all outstanding Treasury issues that have at least 15 years to maturity from the first day of the delivery month. For settlement purposes, the CME specifies that a given issue's term to maturity is calculated in complete three-month increments (that is, complete quarters). For example, if the actual maturity of an issue is 15 years and 5 months, it would be rounded down to a maturity of 15 years and 1 quarter (three months). Moreover, all bonds delivered by the seller must be of the same issue.

Keep in mind that, while the underlying Treasury bond for this contract is a hypothetical issue and therefore cannot itself be delivered into the futures contract, the bond futures contract is not a cash settlement contract. The only way to close out a Treasury bond futures contract is either to initiate an offsetting futures position or to deliver one of the deliverable issues.

The delivery is as follows. On the settlement date, the seller of the futures contract (the *short*) is required to deliver to the buyer (the *long*) $100,000 par value of a 6%, 20-year Treasury bond. As noted, no such bond exists, so the short must choose one of the deliverable issues to deliver to the long. Suppose the seller selects a 5% coupon, 20-year Treasury bond to settle the futures contract. Because the coupon of this bond is less than the notional coupon of 6%, this would be unacceptable to the buyer who contracted to receive a 6% coupon, 20-year bond with a par value of $100,000. Alternatively, suppose the seller is compelled to deliver a 7% coupon, 20-year bond. Since the coupon of this bond is greater than the notional coupon of 6%, the seller would find this unacceptable. How does the exchange adjust for the fact that deliverable issues have coupons and maturities that differ from the notional coupon of 6%?

To make delivery equitable to both parties, the CME publishes conversion factors for adjusting the price of each deliverable issue for a given contract. Given the conversion factor for a deliverable issue and the futures price, the adjusted price is found by multiplying the conversion factor by the futures price. The adjusted price is called the *converted price*. That is,

$$\text{Converted price} = \text{Contract size} \times \text{Futures settlement price} \times \text{Conversion factor}$$

For example, suppose the settlement price of a Treasury bond futures contract is 110 and the deliverable issue selected by the short has a conversion factor of 1.25. Given the contract size is $100,000, the converted price for the deliverable issue is $100,000 × 1.10 × 1.25 = $137,500.

The price that the buyer must pay the seller when the deliverable issue is delivered is called the *invoice price*. The invoice price is the converted price plus the deliverable issue's accrued interest. That is, the invoice price is:

$$\text{Invoice price} = \text{Contract size} \times \text{Futures settlement price} \times \text{Conversion factor} + \text{Accrued interest}$$

In selecting the issue to be delivered, the short will select from all the deliverable issues the one that will give the largest rate of return from a cash-and-carry strategy. We explained this strategy in Chapter 16 where we derived the theoretical futures price. In the case of Treasury bond futures, a cash-and-carry strategy is one in which a cash bond that is acceptable for delivery is purchased with borrowed funds and simultaneously the Treasury bond futures contract is sold. The bond purchased can be delivered to satisfy the short futures position. Thus, by buying the Treasury issue that is acceptable for delivery and selling the futures, an investor has effectively sold the bond at the delivery price (that is, the converted price).

A rate of return can be calculated for this strategy. This rate of return is referred to as the *implied repo rate*. Once the implied repo rate is calculated for each deliverable issue, the issue selected for delivery will be the one that has the highest implied repo rate (that is, the issue that gives the maximum return in a cash-and-carry strategy). The issue with the highest return is referred to as the *cheapest-to-deliver issue* (CTD issue). This issue plays a key role in the pricing of a Treasury futures contract.[1]

---

[1] While a particular Treasury bond may be the CTD issue today, changes in interest rates, for example, may cause some other issue to be the CTD issue at a future date.

In addition to the choice of which acceptable Treasury issue to deliver—sometimes referred to as the *quality option* or the *swap option*—the short has at least two more options granted under CME delivery guidelines. The short is permitted to decide when in the delivery month, delivery actually will take place. This is called the *timing option*. The other option is the right of the short to give notice of intent to deliver up to 8:00 P.M. Chicago time after the closing of the exchange (3:15 P.M. Chicago time) on the date when the futures settlement price has been fixed. This option is referred to as the *wildcard option*. The quality option, the timing option, and the wildcard option—in sum referred to as the *delivery options*—mean that the long can never be sure which Treasury bond issue will be delivered or when it will be delivered.

18.1.1 Strategies for Controlling Interest Rate Risk with Treasury Futures

Portfolio managers can use interest rate futures to alter the interest rate sensitivity, or duration, of a portfolio. Those with strong expectations about the direction of the future course of interest rates will adjust the duration of their portfolios so as to capitalize on their expectations. Specifically, a portfolio manager who expects rates to increase will shorten duration; a portfolio manager who expects interest rates to decrease will lengthen duration. While portfolio managers can use cash market instruments to alter the duration of their portfolios, using futures contracts provides a quicker and less expensive means for doing so (on either a temporary or permanent basis).

A formula to approximate the number of futures contracts necessary to adjust the portfolio duration to some target duration is[2]

$$\frac{\text{(Target portfolio duration} - \text{Current portfolio duration)} \times \text{Portfolio market value}}{\text{Dollar duration of the futures contract}} \qquad (18.1)$$

The dollar duration of the futures contract is the dollar price sensitivity of the futures contract to a change in interest rates.

Notice that if the portfolio manager wishes to increase the portfolio's current duration, the numerator of the formula is positive. This means that futures contracts will be purchased. That is, buying futures increases the duration of the portfolio. The opposite is true if the objective is to shorten the portfolio's current duration: the numerator of the formula is negative

---

[2]Simulation can be used to determine a better estimate for the number of futures contracts necessary but this formula is a good rule of thumb used in industry.

and this means that futures must be sold. Hence, selling futures contracts reduces the portfolio's duration.

Hedging is a special case of risk control where the target duration sought is zero. If cash and futures prices move together, any loss realized by the hedger from one position (whether cash or futures) will be offset by a profit on the other position. As we explained in Chapter 17.1.3.2, when the net profit or loss from the positions is exactly as anticipated, the hedge is referred to as a perfect hedge. Hedging in bond portfolio management is more complicated than the examples with stock index futures we gave in Chapter 17.1.3.2. In bond portfolio management, typically the bond to be hedged is not identical to the bond underlying the futures contract and therefore there is cross-hedging. This may result in substantial basis risk.

Conceptually, cross-hedging is more complicated than hedging deliverable securities because it involves two relationships. In the case of Treasury bond futures contracts, the first relationship is between the CTD issue and the futures contract. The second is the relationship between the security to be hedged and the CTD issue.

The key to minimizing risk in a cross-hedge is to choose the right hedge ratio. The hedge ratio depends on volatility weighting, or weighting by relative changes in value. The purpose of a hedge is to use gains or losses from a futures position to offset any difference between the target sale price and the actual sale price of the security.

Accordingly, the hedge ratio is chosen with the intention of matching the volatility (that is, the dollar change) of the Treasury bond futures contract to the volatility of the bond to be hedged. Consequently, the hedge ratio for a bond is given by

$$\text{Hedge ratio} = \frac{\text{Volatility of bond to be hedged}}{\text{Volatility of Treasury bond futures contract}} \qquad (18.2)$$

For hedging purposes, we are concerned with volatility in absolute dollar terms. To calculate the dollar volatility of a bond, one must know the precise time that volatility is to be calculated (because volatility generally declines as a bond moves toward its maturity date), as well as the price or yield at which to calculate volatility (because higher yields generally reduce dollar volatility for a given yield change). The relevant point in the life of the bond for calculating volatility is the point at which the hedge will be lifted. Volatility at any other point is essentially irrelevant because the goal is to lock in a price or rate only on that particular day. Similarly, the relevant yield at which to calculate volatility initially is the target yield. Consequently, the "volatility of bond to be hedged" referred to in equation (18.3) for the hedge ratio is the price value of a basis point for the bond on the date the hedge is expected to be delivered. The *price value of a basis point* (PVBP) for a bond is computed by changing the yield of a bond by one basis point and determining the change in the bond's price. It is a measure of bond price volatility to interest rate changes and is related to duration.

To calculate the hedge ratio given by equation (18.3), the portfolio manager needs to know the volatility of the Treasury futures contract. Fortunately, knowing the volatility of the bond to be hedged relative to the CTD issue and the volatility of the CTD bond relative to the futures contract, we can modify the hedge ratio given by equation (18.2) as follows:

$$
\text{Hedge ratio} = \frac{\text{Volatility of bond to be hedged}}{\text{Volatility of CTD issue}}
$$

$$
\times \frac{\text{Volatility of CTD issue}}{\text{Volatility of Treasury futures contract}} \tag{18.3}
$$

The second ratio above can be shown to equal the conversion factor for the CTD issue. Assuming a fixed yield spread between the bond to be hedged and the CTD issue, equation (18.3) can be rewritten as

$$
\text{Hedge ratio} = \frac{\text{PVBP of bond to be hedged}}{\text{PVBP of CTD issue}}
$$

$$
\times \text{Conversion factor for CTD issue} \tag{18.4}
$$

where PVBP is equal to the price value of a basis point.

Given the hedge ratio, the number of contracts that must be short is determined as follows:

$$
\text{Number of contracts} = \text{Hedge ratio} \times \frac{\text{Par value to be hedged}}{\text{Par value of the futures contract}} \tag{18.5}
$$

For example, suppose that the amount to be hedged is $20 million and a Treasury bond futures contract is used for hedging. The par value for a Treasury bond futures contract is $100,000. The ratio in the above equation is then 200 (= $20,000,000/$100,000), which means that the number of futures contracts that must be sold for a bond to be hedged is 200 contracts.

18.1.2 Pricing of Treasury Futures

In Chapter 16.2.3, we explained the basic pricing model for a generic futures contract. We also explained how the model must be modified for stock index futures in Chapter 17.1.2. Let's look at how the specifics of the Treasury futures contract necessitate the refinement of the theoretical futures pricing model. The assumptions that require a refinement of the model are the assumptions that (1) there are no interim cash flows and (2) the deliverable asset and the settlement date are known.

With respect to interim cash flows, for a Treasury futures contract the underlying is a Treasury note or a Treasury bond. Unlike a stock index futures contract, the timing of the interest payments that will be made by the U.S. Department of the Treasury for every issue that is acceptable as deliverable for a contract is known with certainty and can be incorporated into the pricing model. However, the reinvestment interest that can be earned from the coupon payment from the payment dates to the settlement date of the contract is unknown and depends on prevailing interest rates at each payment date.

Now let's look at the implications of the assumption that there are a known deliverable and a known settlement date. Neither assumption is consistent with the delivery rules for some futures contracts. For U.S. Treasury note and bond futures contracts, for example, the contract specifies deliverable issues that can be delivered to satisfy the contract. Although the party that is long the contract (that is, the buyer of the contract) does not know the specific Treasury issue that will be delivered, the long can determine the CTD issue from among the deliverable issues. It is this issue that is used in obtaining the theoretical futures price. The net effect of the short's option to select the issue to deliver to satisfy the contract is that it reduces the theoretical future price by an amount equal to the value of the delivery option granted to the short.

Moreover, unlike other futures contracts, the Treasury bond and note contracts do not have a delivery date. Instead, there is a delivery month. The short has the right to select when in the delivery month to make delivery. The effect of this option granted to the short is once again to reduce the theoretical futures price. More specifically,

Theoretical futures price adjusted for delivery options

= Cash market price + (Cash market price)

× (Financing cost − Cash yield)

− Value of the delivery options granted to the short   (18.6)

18.2 CONTROLLING INTEREST RATE RISK USING TREASURY FUTURES OPTIONS

Interest rate options can be written on a fixed income security or an interest rate futures contract. The former options are called *options on physicals* and the latter are called *futures options*. The most liquid exchange-traded option on a fixed income security is an option on Treasury futures traded on the CME. Goodman (1985) gives three reasons why futures options on Treasuries are preferred to options on physicals as the options vehicle of choice for institutional investors:

1. Unlike options on Treasury securities, options on Treasury futures do not require payments for accrued interest to be made. Consequently, when a futures option is exercised, the call buyer and the put writer need not compensate the other party for accrued interest.
2. Futures options are believed to be "cleaner" instruments because of the reduced likelihood of delivery squeezes. Market participants who must deliver a Treasury security are concerned that at the time of delivery, the Treasury to be delivered will be in short supply, resulting in a higher price to acquire the security. Because the deliverable supply of futures contracts is more than adequate for futures options currently traded, there is no concern about a delivery squeeze.
3. In order to price any option, it is imperative to know at all times the price of the underlying instrument. In the bond market, current prices are not as easily available as price information on the futures contract. The reason is that Treasury securities trade in the OTC market and, consequently, there is less price information compared to Treasury futures which are traded on an exchange.

However, portfolio managers do make use of over-the-counter (OTC) options. Typically they are purchased by institutional investors who want to hedge the risk associated with a specific security or index. Besides options on fixed income securities, there are OTC options on the shape of the yield curve or the yield spread between two securities. A discussion of these OTC options is beyond the scope of this chapter. Because the most common option used in bond portfolio management is the exchange-traded futures option on Treasury securities, we limit our discussion to this derivative.

A futures option gives the buyer the right to buy from or sell to the writer a designated futures contract at the strike price. If the futures option is a call option, the buyer has the right to purchase one designated futures contract at the strike price. That is, the buyer has the right to acquire a long futures position in the designated futures contract. If the buyer exercises the call option, the writer acquires a corresponding short position in the futures contract.

A put option on a futures contract grants the buyer the right to sell one designated futures contract to the writer at the strike price. That is, the option buyer has the right to acquire a short position in the designated futures contract. If the put option is exercised, the writer acquires a corresponding long position in the designated futures contract. There are futures options on all the Treasury bond and note futures contracts. A summary of the rights of the buyer and the obligation of the seller and what the payoff is if the buyer exercises follows:

- Call buyer has the right to purchase one futures contract at the strike price.
    - If exercised, the seller has a short futures position.
    - If exercised, the seller pays the buyer (current futures price – strike price).
- Put buyer has the right to sell one futures contract at the strike price.
    - If exercised, the seller has a long futures position.
    - If exercised, the seller pays the buyer (strike price – current futures price).

The CME's Treasury bond futures contracts have delivery months of March, June, September, and December. As with stock index futures contracts, there are flexible Treasury futures options. These futures options allow counterparties to customize options within certain limits. Specifically, the strike price, expiration date, and type of exercise (American or European) can be customized subject to CME constraints.

Because the parties to the futures option will realize a position in a futures contract when the option is exercised, the question is, what will the futures price be? That is, at what price will the long be required to pay for the instrument underlying the futures contract, and at what price will the short be required to sell the instrument underlying the futures contract?

Upon exercise, the futures price for the futures contract will be set equal to the strike price. The position of the two parties is then immediately marked to market in terms of the then-current futures price. Thus, the futures position of the two parties will be at the prevailing futures price. At the same time, the option buyer will receive from the option seller the economic benefit from exercising. In the case of a call futures option, the option writer must pay to the buyer of the option the difference between the current futures price and the strike price. In the case of a put futures option, the option writer must pay the option buyer the difference between the strike price and the current futures price.

For example, suppose an investor buys a call option on some futures contract in which the strike price is $140. Assume also that the futures price is $150 and that the buyer exercises the call option. Upon exercise, the call buyer is given a long position in the futures contract at $140, and the call writer is assigned the corresponding short position in the futures contract at $140. The futures positions of the buyer and the writer are immediately marked to market by the exchange. Because the prevailing futures price is

$150 and the strike price is $140, the long futures position (the position of the call buyer) realizes a gain of $10, while the short futures position (the position of the call writer) realizes a loss of $10. The call writer pays the exchange $10, and the call buyer receives $10 from the exchange. The call buyer, who now has a long futures position at $150, can either liquidate the futures position at $150 or maintain a long futures position. If the former course of action is taken, the call buyer sells a futures contract at the prevailing futures price of $150. There is no gain or loss from liquidating the position. Overall, the call buyer realizes a gain of $10. The call buyer who elects to hold the long futures position will face the same risk and reward of holding such a position, but still realizes a gain of $10 from the exercise of the call option.

Suppose, instead, that the futures option is a put rather than a call, and the current futures price is $125 rather than $150. If the buyer of this put option exercises it, the buyer would have a short position in the futures contract at $140; the option writer would have a long position in the futures contract at $140. The exchange then marks the position to market at the then-current futures price of $125, resulting in a gain to the put buyer of $15, and a loss to the put writer of the same amount. The put buyer, who now has a short futures position at $125, can either liquidate the short futures position by buying a futures contract at the prevailing futures price of $15 or maintain the short futures position. In either case, the put buyer realizes a gain of $15 from exercising the put option.

18.2.1 Strategies for Controlling Interest Rate Risk Using Treasury Futures Options

In our review of the use of options in equity portfolio management in Chapter 17.2.2, we explained how they can be used for risk management, return enhancement, and cost management. We do not repeat the explanation of the applications here. Instead, we explain how futures options can be used for hedging and return enhancement. More specifically, we illustrate a protective put strategy (a risk management application) and a covered call writing strategy (a return enhancement application). As will be seen, the applications are complicated by the fact that the option is not an option on a physical but a futures option.

Buying puts on Treasury futures is one of the easiest ways to purchase protection against rising rates. As explained in Chapter 17, this strategy is called a *protective put strategy*. We also explained the technical aspects of implementing this strategy for stock index futures. Here we explain the complexities associated with implementing this strategy where what is to be protected is an individual bond issue.

In our explanation of the process, we assume that the bond issue to be protected is an investment grade non-Treasury security. The reason for the credit quality being investment grade is that we are protecting against an adverse movement in interest rates. The lower the investment-grade rating of a bond, the more of its price depends on its equity component.

This protective put strategy is a cross-hedge because the bond to be hedged and the underlying for the Treasury options futures contract are not the same. There are many candidate Treasury options futures contracts that can be employed as the hedging instrument. In the explanation of the process, we see how we need to use the CTD issue to implement the strategy.

Given the bond issue to be hedged and the particular Treasury options futures contracts that are used, the process involves the following steps:

Step 1: Determine the minimum price for the bond to be hedged. If there was a put option on the bond to be hedged, then this would be its strike price.

Step 2: Given the minimum price for the bond to be hedged, the yield for that bond can be computed. This is simple. It involves computing the yield given the minimum price determined in Step 1. This gives us the minimum yield for the bond to be hedged. Now we need to link this minimum yield to get the strike price for the Treasury options futures contract.

Step 3: Given the minimum yield for the bond to be hedged, the minimum yield on the CTD issue can be determined. Remember that the bond to be hedged is a non-Treasury security and it will trade in the market at a higher yield than the CTD issue, which is a Treasury security. To determine the minimum yield on the CTD issue, a credit spread must be assumed. This credit spread is typically found by using a simple linear regression.[3] What is important to bear in mind is that the strategy is dependent on this assumed relationship (i.e., the assumed credit spread). Once this step is completed, the resulting credit spread added to the minimum yield for the bond to be hedged gives the minimum yield for the CTD issue.

Step 4: Given the minimum yield for the CTD issue found in Step 3 and the coupon rate and maturity of the CTD issue, the target price for the futures option can be determined using the basic yield-price calculation; that is, given a bond's coupon, principal (which is assumed

---

[3] See Chapter 4.2.1.

to be 100), and maturity, the price can be determined.[4] This price for the CTD issue corresponds to the minimum price for the bond to be hedged found in Step 1.

Step 5: Given the minimum price for the CTD issue, the strike price for the futures option is calculated. Remember there are several candidate futures contracts for a given expiration date over which the hedge is sought. For each one, the corresponding strike price is found by multiplying the minimum price for the CTD issue by the conversion factor for the associated futures option.

The five steps described above are always necessary to identify the appropriate strike price on a put futures option. The process involves estimating

- The relationship between price and yield.
- The assumed relationship between the yield spread between the bonds to be hedged and the CTD issue.
- The conversion factor for the CTD issue.

As with hedging with futures, explained earlier in this chapter, the success of the hedging strategy will depend on (1) whether the CTD issue changes and (2) the yield spread between the bonds to be hedged and the CTD issue.

The hedge ratio is determined using equation (18.5) because we will assume a constant yield spread between the bond to be hedged and CTD issue. To compute the hedge ratio, the portfolio manager must calculate the price value of a basis point for the CTD issue and the bond to be hedged at the option expiration date and at the yields corresponding to the futures' strike price of the yield. To obtain the number of put futures options that should be purchased for the put protective strategy, equation (18.6) uses "par value of the futures options contract" instead of "par value of the futures contract."

18.2.2 Pricing Models for Treasury Futures Options

In Chapter 16.3.2.2, we discussed the Black-Scholes option pricing model. In this section, we provide an overview of pricing models for options on Treasury futures options. In general, these options are much more complex than options on stocks or stock indexes because of the need to take into consideration the term structure of interest rates.

The most commonly used model for pricing futures options is the one developed by Black (1976). The Black model was initially developed for valuing European options on forward contracts. There are two problems

---

[4]See Chapter 13.2.4.

with this model. The first is the assumptions about the underlying asset for the futures contract. Specifically, there are three unrealistic assumptions:

1. The probability distribution for the prices assumed permits some probability—no matter how small—that the price can take on any positive value. But, unlike stock prices, Treasury futures prices (the underlying in the case of a Treasury futures contract) have a maximum value. So any probability distribution for the Treasury futures prices assumed by an option pricing model that permits prices to be higher than the maximum value could generate nonsensical option prices.

2. In the pricing model for futures options it is assumed that the short-term interest rate is constant over the life of the option. Yet the price of a Treasury futures contract will change as interest rates change. A change in the short-term interest rate changes the rates along the yield curve. Therefore, to assume that the short-term rate will be constant is inappropriate for pricing Treasury futures options.

3. The volatility (standard deviation) of futures prices is constant over the life of the option. However, as a bond moves closer to maturity, its price volatility declines. Therefore, the assumption that price volatility is constant over the life of a Treasury futures option is inappropriate.

The second problem is that the Black model was developed for pricing European options on forward contracts. Treasury futures options, however, are American options. This problem can be overcome. The Black model was extended by Barone-Adesi and Whaley (1987) to American options on futures contracts. This is the model used by the CME to settle the flexible Treasury futures options. However, this model was also developed for equities and is subject to the first problem noted above. Despite its limitations, the Black model is the most popular option pricing model for options on Treasury futures.

18.3 CONTROLLING INTEREST RATE RISK USING INTEREST RATE SWAPS

In its most basic form, an interest rate swap is an agreement between two parties to exchange cash flows periodically. In a plain-vanilla swap, over the life of the contract one party pays a fixed rate of interest based on a notional amount in exchange for a floating rate of interest based on the same notional amount from the counterparty. Typically, no principal is exchanged at the beginning or end of a swap.

The fixed rate on a swap is ordinarily set at a rate such that the net present value of the swap's cash flows is zero at the start of the swap contract. This fixed rate is called the *swap rate*. The difference between the swap rate and the yield on an equivalent-maturity Treasury is called the *swap spread*.[5] The floating rate on a swap is typically benchmarked off the London Interbank Offered Rate (LIBOR) or constant maturity Treasury (CMT) rate. In a plain-vanilla swap, the floating rate is three-month LIBOR, which resets and pays quarterly in arrears. Although different types of interest rate swaps exist, including vanilla swaps, basis swaps, indexed-amortizing swaps, and callable swaps, to name a few, here our focus is on generic interest rate swaps as hedge instruments.

The party to a swap that pays the swap spread is referred to as the *fixed-rate payer* or, equivalently, the *floating-rate receiver*. The party that receives the fixed-rate is referred to as the *fixed-rate receiver* or, equivalently, *the floating-rate payer*. Here we simply refer to the two parties as the fixed-rate payer and fixed-rate receiver.

In Chapter 16, we explained why an interest rate swap can be interpreted as a package of forwards or futures contracts. Another way of thinking about an interest rate swap from the prospective of the fixed-rate receiver is that it is equivalent to a position that is long a fixed-rate bond position (i.e., owning a fixed-rate bond), which is completely financed at the short-term interest rate that is the reference rate for the swap. In a completely financed long bond position, fixed-rate interest payments are received and floating rate financing costs are paid periodically, with the final principal payment from the bond used to repay the initial financing of the bond purchase. On a net basis, a completely financed bond position has zero cost, like a swap, and the periodic cash flows replicate the cash flows on a swap. In fact, a swap from the perspective of the fixed-rate receiver is a fully leveraged bond position where the financing rate is equivalent to the swap's reference rate. Hence, this alternative view of an interest rate swap from the perspective of the fixed-rate receiver is appealing because it implies that a swap can be used as an alternative hedging vehicle to Treasury futures contracts to manage interest rate risk. The position of a fixed-rate receiver is equivalent to shorting a fixed-rate bond and investing the proceeds in a floating-rate bond. Once again, this is appealing because it suggests that swaps can be used as an alternative instrument to manage interest rate risk.

18.3.1 Strategies for Controlling Interest Rate Risk Using Interest Rate Swaps

To control a portfolio's interest rate risk using an interest rate swap, it is necessary to understand how the value of a swap changes as market interest rates change. As explained in Chapter 13.4.1.1, the measure used to quantify

---

[5] We saw these concepts in Chapter 14.1.1 in the context of term structure factors used for bond portfolio risk management.

the change in the dollar value of a fixed-income instrument to changes in interest rate is dollar duration. Therefore, it is necessary to determine the dollar duration of an interest rate swap in order to implement effectively a risk control strategy with this derivative.

As explained above, from the perspective of a fixed-rate receiver, the interest-rate swap position can be viewed as long a fixed-rate bond plus short a floating-rate bond. The dollar duration of an interest-rate swap from the perspective of a fixed-rate receiver is simply the difference between the dollar duration of the two bond positions that make up the swap; that is,

Dollar duration of an interest rate swap

= Dollar duration of a fixed-rate bond

– Dollar duration of a floating-rate bond (18.7)

Let's look at the relative magnitude of the two components in equation (18.7). Consider first the dollar duration of a floating-rate bond. The dollar duration will depend on what the length of time to the reset date is. The shorter this length of time, the smaller the dollar duration of a floating-rate bond is. Since in a typical interest-rate swap the time to the next reset date is very short, the dollar duration of a floating-rate bond will be small. In contrast, the dollar duration of a fixed-rate bond will be considerably greater. Thus, a good approximation of the dollar duration of an interest-rate swap is the dollar duration of a fixed-rate bond.

The implication here is that if a portfolio manager wants to increase the dollar duration of a portfolio using an interest-rate swap, the portfolio manager should take a position as a fixed-rate receiver. This is economically equivalent to leveraging a portfolio's interest-rate exposure by adding dollar duration. By entering into an interest-rate swap as the fixed-rate payer, instead, the portfolio manager reduces the portfolio's dollar duration.

Suppose that a portfolio manager has a target duration for the portfolio. That target duration can be used to obtain the target dollar duration for the portfolio. The target portfolio dollar duration is the sum of the current dollar duration of the bond portfolio and the dollar duration of the interest-rate swap. That is,

Target dollar duration of portfolio = Current dollar duration of portfolio

+ Dollar duration of swap (18.8)

Solving for the dollar duration of the swap,

Dollar duration of swap = Target dollar duration of portfolio

– Current dollar duration of portfolio (18.9)

For example, consider a $100 million bond portfolio that has a current duration of 5 and the portfolio manager wants to increase the portfolio duration to 6 (i.e., 6 is the target duration). We know that for a 100 basis point change in interest rates, the current portfolio value will change by 5%. Therefore, the dollar duration is $5 million (=5% × $100,000,000). Similarly, the change in the portfolio value that the portfolio manager seeks for a target duration of 6 is 6% and the dollar duration is $6 million. Therefore, from equation (18.9), using interest-rate swaps the portfolio manager must add to the portfolio $1 million in dollar duration. The dollar duration of a swap contract can be determined by changing interest rates by 100 basis points and computing the average change in the value of the swap.

In our example, to increase the portfolio dollar duration using an interest-rate swap, the portfolio must be the counterparty that is a fixed-rate receiver. Suppose instead that the portfolio manager seeks to reduce the target duration to 4.5. In this case, the target dollar duration is $4.5 million and from equation (18.9), the dollar duration of a swap to achieve the target duration is to reduce the dollar duration by $500,000. The portfolio manager should then enter into a swap as the fixed-rate payer.

18.3.2   Pricing of Interest Rate Swaps

Although there is a wide variety of interest rate swaps available to a portfolio manager to control interest rate risk, the main idea when pricing all of them is that the fair value of a swap should be the difference between the present values of the expected cash flows exchanged between the two parties in the swap. Again, we focus on the generic interest rate swap.

In a generic interest rate swap, the cash flows on the fixed component (i.e., the fixed-rate payments) are known at the inception of the swap. However, the future cash flows on the floating component are unknown because they depend on the future value of the reference rate. The future floating rates for purposes of valuing a swap are derived from forward rates that are embedded in the current yield curve.[6] By utilizing forward rates, a swap net cash flow can be derived throughout the life of a swap. The sum of these cash flows discounted at the corresponding forward rate for each time

---

[6]Forward rates are the rates that can be locked in between two dates in the future under terms agreed upon today. Forward rates are extrapolated from the current Treasury yield curve. Examples include the six-month forward rate three years from now, the one-year forward rate two years from now, etc.

period is the current value of the swap. Mathematically, the value of a swap position is:

$$\text{Swap value} = \sum_{t=1}^{T} PV \ (\text{Fixed cash flow}_t - \text{Floating cash flow}_t) \quad (18.10)$$

where $PV(x)$ denotes the present value of x and $t = 1, \ldots, T$ are the dates at which payments are made. The *fair swap rate* is the fixed rate that makes the swap value zero.

An alternative approach to pricing a generic interest rate swap is to view it as two simultaneous bond payments made by the two parties. Namely, think of the fixed-rate payer as paying the notional amount to the fixed-rate receiver at the termination date, and of the fixed-rate receiver as paying the notional amount to the fixed-rate payer at the termination date. This slight modification does not change the actual cash flows and value of the swap, because the payments of the notional amounts cancel out at the termination date. However, it does help us imagine the stream of payments from the fixed-rate payer as the value of a fixed-coupon bond, and the stream of payments from the fixed-rate receiver as the value of a floating-rate bond.

Let the notional amounts be 100, and let v denote the premium (per annum) paid by the fixed-rate payer. Assume that the payments happen at dates 1, 2, $\ldots$, T, and that the time interval between payments is Δt. (This time interval is typically a quarter.)

At time 0, the value of the fixed-rate bond is

$$100 \times v \times (\Delta t) \times \sum_{t=1}^{T} B(0, t) + 100 \times B(0, T) \quad (18.11)$$

where $B(0,t)$ denotes the value (at time 0) of a zero-coupon bond with a face value of 1 and maturity t. (This is because the collection of payments during the life of the swap can be thought of as a portfolio of zero-coupon bonds of face value 1 with maturities equal to the times of the swap payments.)

The value of the floating-rate bond at time 0 is 100. To see this, note that the fixed-rate receiver can replicate the value of the bond by investing 100 today at the current interest rate, and earning just enough interest to pay the first coupon on the floating-rate bond to the fixed-rate payer. Then, the fixed-rate receiver can invest 100 again at the prevailing interest rates after the first swap payment, and earn enough interest to pay the second floating-rate coupon, with 100 left over. Continuing in the same way, the fixed-rate receiver can reinvest the 100 until the last time period, when he or she pays the 100 to the fixed-rate payer. Therefore, the present value of the investment from the perspective of the fixed-rate receiver is 100. From the perspective of the fixed-rate receiver, the value of the swap today is the difference between the fixed-rate payer's payments and the payments that must be made. That is,

$$100 \times v \times (\Delta t) \times \sum_{t=1}^{T} B(0,t) + 100 \times B(0,T) - 100 \qquad (18.12)$$

The fixed rate v that makes the value of the swap equal to zero at time 0 is the fair price of the swap at time 0 and is the swap rate. It is easy to see that the value of v (the swap rate) should be

$$v = \frac{1 - B(0,T)}{(\Delta t) \times \sum_{t=1}^{T} B(0,t)} \qquad (18.13)$$

The values of $B(0,t)$ can be determined from today's yield curve.[7] They are in fact the discount factors that apply to different maturities.

18.4 CONTROLLING CREDIT RISK WITH CREDIT DEFAULT SWAPS

Thus far, we have discussed derivatives that can be used to control interest rate risk. Now we look at a derivative that can be used to control credit risk. The general category of derivatives to control credit risk is referred to as *credit derivatives*. The most commonly used type of credit derivative is the *credit default swap* (CDS) and for that reason we focus only on credit default swaps in this section.

There are two parties to a CDS: a *credit protection buyer* and a *credit protection seller*. The credit protection seller provides protection against some "credit event" for a periodic fee paid by the credit protection buyer. The CDS *swap premium* payment is the periodic payment made by the credit protection buyer to the credit protection seller.

The documentation of a CDS sets forth (1) the underlying for which the protection is being provided and (2) the specific credit event(s) for which protection is being provided. The underlying for which credit protection is being provided is a reference entity or a reference obligation. The *reference*

---

[7]In practice, they are determined from the swap rate curve, which, as explained earlier in the book, is a plot of swap rates against maturities in much the same manner as the bond yield curve.

entity is the issuer of the debt instrument for which credit protection is being sought. The *reference obligation* is the particular debt issue for which the credit protection is being sought. For example, a reference entity could be Exxon Mobile. The reference obligation would be a specific Exxon Mobile bond issue.

There are two types of CDS: *single-name CDS* and *index CDS*. As the name suggests, in a single-name CDS, there is only one reference entity or one reference obligation. In an index CDS, denoted by CDX, there is a standardized basket of reference entities. The two most actively traded CDXs on corporate bonds for reference entities in North America are the North America Investment Grade Index (CDX.NA.IG), which has 125 corporate reference entities that have an investment-grade rating and the North America High Yield Index (CDX.NA.HY) with 100 corporate entities that have a noninvestment-grade rating. For European corporate bonds, the most active CDX is the iTraxx Europe, which has 125 corporate reference entities. All three CDX use equal weighting of the reference entities. So for the CDX.NA.IG and the iTraxx Europe each reference entity is 0.8% of the index while for the CDX.NA.HY each reference entity is 1% of the index. The three index CDXs above are available in maturities from 1 to 10 years, with the greatest liquidity at 5-, 10-, and 7-year maturities.

The periodic swap premium payment made by the credit protection buyer to the credit protection seller is based on the swap rate and the notional amount. Consider first the swap premium payment for a single-name CDS (i.e., where the underlying is only one reference entity or reference obligation). Because typically the swap premium payments are quarterly, the payment is[8]

Quarterly swap premium payment = (Notional amount × Swap rate)/4

For example, assume that the swap rate is 2.8% and the notional amount is $10 million. Then the quarterly swap premium payment is

Quarterly swap premium payment = ($10,000,000 × 0.028)/4 = $70,000

The quarterly swap premium payment over the life of a single-name CDS is the same each quarter.[9] For an index CDS, however, the quarterly

---

[8]The calculation has been simplified here. The division by four assumes all quarters have the same number of days. In practice, the product of the notional amount and swap rate is multiplied by the ratio of the actual number of days in the quarter/360. This is the daycount convention used in the swap market.

[9]The dollar amount actually changes because of the different number of days in the quarter; however, the notional amount and the swap rate are constant.

swap premium may decline because the notional amount each quarter may change. This is because an index CDS is written on a standardized basket of reference entities. If a credit event occurs for any of the reference entities in the index, then the notional amount is reduced accordingly as a result of the removal of those reference entities from the index.

18.4.1 Strategies for Controlling Credit Risk with Credit Default Swaps

As with other derivatives we have already discussed, to appreciate the potential application of a single-named CDS and an index CDS to control a portfolio's credit risk, it is helpful to look at the economic interpretation of these derivative products from the perspective of the counterparties. In our explanation we assume a single-name CDS where the reference obligation is bond XYZ issued by some corporation.

Consider an investor who purchases bond XYZ. The investor would make a cash outlay equal to bond XYZ's price, which we denote by P_0. Assuming that the issuer of bond XYZ does not default, the investor will receive semiannual cash inflows equal to one half of bond XYZ's annual coupon rate. The semiannual coupon payments will be received by the investor as long as the issuer of bond XYZ does not default. If the investor sells bond XYZ at time T, then there will be a cash inflow equal to bond XYZ's sale price. We denote this price by P_T. Suppose that at time T a credit event occurs that causes bond XYZ's price to fall below the purchase price paid by the investor (i.e., $P_T < P_0$). The investor then realizes a loss equal to the $P_0 - P_T$.

Let's look at the cash flow for the credit protection seller in a single-name CDS where the reference obligation is bond XYZ. This party to the CDS receives a quarterly payment based on the CDS swap spread. That is, there is a cash inflow equal to the quarterly swap premium payment. However, the swap premium payments are made only if the issuer of bond XYZ does not trigger a credit event. Thus, as with an investor who buys bond XYX, there are periodic cash inflows as long as there is no adverse credit event that stops the payments (default in the case of owning the cash bond and credit event in the case of a CDS). It seems like this cash flow characteristic of the credit protection seller's position is similar to that of an investor who buys a cash bond.

Let's now suppose that a credit event occurs. The credit protection seller must make a payment to the credit protection buyer. This payment represents a cash outlay or loss for the credit protection seller. Yet, an investor in bond XYZ would also realize a loss if an adverse event occurs. Once again, this cash flow attribute is similar for both the credit protection seller and an investor in a bond.

Consequently, the credit protection seller has an economic position that is analogous to an investor in a cash bond. This is reasonable because both the credit protection seller and the investor who is long a cash bond are buyers of the bond issuer's credit risk. This interpretation is the same for an index CDS. Using the same cash flow analysis, it can be shown that the credit protection buyer is analogous to an investor who is short a bond in the cash market.

Now that we have the economic interpretation of a single-name CDS and an index CDS, we can appreciate how portfolio managers can use this derivative. CDS like many of the other derivatives described in this and the previous chapter is a more transactionally efficient vehicle for executing portfolios strategies and portfolio rebalancing. CDSs on corporate entities or specific obligations are generally more liquid than the underlying bonds. This makes it more efficient for portfolio managers to alter the exposure to one or more corporate bonds or a corporate bond index using CDS than transacting in the cash market.

Suppose that a bond portfolio manager wants to change credit exposure to either an individual corporate bond or a corporate bond index. To do so, the portfolio manager would sell protection (i.e., be the credit protection seller in a CDS) because as explained earlier this is analogous to a long position. Creating a long position in individual corporate names or a corporate bond index is often easier and less costly in the CDS market given its liquidity. A portfolio manager can reduce the exposure to a particular corporate issuer held in a portfolio by buying protection using a single-name CDS or reduce the exposure to a corporate bond index by using an index CDS. This is done by being the credit protection buyer.

18.4.2 General Principles for Valuing a Single-Name Credit Default Swap

In this section, we describe the general principles for valuing single-name CDSs on a corporate bond issuer.[10] By valuing we mean determining the fair value of the CDS swap spread. As in valuing other derivatives, the general principle is that there is a relationship between the cash and the derivatives market.

As a reference obligation of the CDS, we consider a floating-rate debt obligation outstanding that has a maturity of T, is trading at par value, and offers a coupon rate of LIBOR plus a spread denoted by F. The coupon reset formula for this floating-rate debt obligation is equal to LIBOR $+ F$.[11]

---

[10]For a more detailed discussion, see Chen, Fabozzi, and O'Kane (2003).

[11]That is, at each coupon payment date for the floating-rate date obligation, the coupon is determined to be the current value of the LIBOR rate plus the spread F.

We assume that the CDS written on this floating-rate debt obligation requires physical delivery. To simplify further, we assume that the coupon payment dates for the floating-rate debt obligation are the same as the dates on which payments must be made to the credit protection seller of the single-name CDS.

Suppose that an investor has purchased the floating-rate debt obligation of the reference entity by using borrowed funds. The investor can do this by using a *repurchase agreement* (repo) and paying the *repo rate*.[12] The repo rate is available for a time period equal to the maturity of the floating-rate debt obligation, which is T years. The borrowing rate for the repo (i.e., the repo rate) is LIBOR + B, where B is the spread over LIBOR, which is assumed to be constant over the repo's life.

In addition to the above, we make the following assumptions:

- There is no counterparty risk with respect to the counterparty in the CDS and the counterparty in the repurchase agreement.
- There are no transaction costs.
- There is no difficulty in shorting bonds in the market.
- Should a credit event occur, it does so one day following a coupon payment date.

The objective is to analyze how the premium for a single-name CDS with a maturity of T for some reference entity is determined. We denote this CDS premium by s. To do so, consider the following strategy:

- The investor purchases the floating-rate debt obligation with maturity T issued by the reference entity.
- The investor obtains the funds needed to purchase the floating-rate debt obligation by borrowing for the life of that debt obligation (which is also the term of the CDS), T, in the repo market.
- The investor becomes a credit protection buyer, and hedges the credit risk associated with the floating-rate debt obligation by entering into a CDS with a maturity of T where the reference entity is the issuer of the floating-rate debt.

---

[12]A repurchase agreement is the sale of a security with a commitment by the seller to buy the same security back from the purchaser at a specified price at a designated future date. The difference between the repurchase price and the sale price is the dollar interest cost of the loan. The implied interest rate from the dollar interest cost of the loan is the repo rate.

Let's look at the payoff for the two possible scenarios: no credit event occurs and a credit event occurs.

- *No-credit-event scenario:* If no credit event occurs, then the floating-rate debt obligation matures. Over the life of the debt obligation, the interest earned is equal to LIBOR + F each period. The cost of borrowing (i.e., the repo rate) for each period is LIBOR + B. Hence, LIBOR + F is received from ownership of the floating-rate debt obligation and LIBOR + B is paid out to borrow funds. The net cash flow is therefore what is earned: $F - B$. Consequently, given the assumptions made above, the strategy will have a payoff of $F - B$ in the no-credit-event scenario.
- *Credit-event scenario:* If a credit event occurs, there is physical delivery of the floating-rate debt obligation by the credit protection buyer to the credit protection seller. The credit protection seller then pays the full value of the floating-rate obligation to the credit protection buyer. By assumption, the credit event is assumed to occur right after the floating-rate debt obligation's coupon payment is made. Because the credit event's occurrence means that the CDS agreement is terminated, there are no further coupon payments and no accrued CDS payments. The proceeds obtained from the credit protection seller are used to repay the amount borrowed to purchase that security. As a result, the repo loan is repaid and the same payoff for the strategy as in the scenario where no credit event is realized (i.e., $F - B$).

Like the pricing arguments we presented in Chapter 16, a no-arbitrage requirement in this context means that the CDS spread, s, must be equal to the payoff under both scenarios, $F - B$. Thus, as a first approximation (because of the simplifying assumptions), the CDS spread is the difference between the spread over LIBOR at which the reference entity could issue a par floating-rate debt obligation (F) and the spread over LIBOR to borrow funds in order to purchase that floating-rate debt obligation (B).

As we said, this calculation is only an approximation. For example, one of the assumptions that should be noted is that the repo rate is constant over the repo's life, which is typically not the case. That is, one cannot borrow in the repo market at a fixed rate for several years. However, by entering into a CDS, one is effectively locking in a borrowing rate for the term of the CDS. This is the appeal of using a CDS rather than creating the same financing position with a repo. Another questionable assumption is that for corporate issuers that are reference entities for a single-name CDS, there is not likely to be a floating-rate debt obligation trading at par. More sophisticated CDS pricing models are available but they are beyond the scope of this book.[13]

Summary

- Interest rate derivatives can be used to manage the interest rate exposure (duration) of a fixed income portfolio.
- Treasury bond and note futures contracts are exchange-traded contracts that at the settlement date grant the seller (the short) the right to deliver one of several Treasury bonds that are acceptable. The bond among the acceptable issues that has the highest implied repo rate is the cheapest-to-deliver issue.
- A portfolio manager who expects interest rates to increase will shorten the portfolio duration; a portfolio manager who expects interest rates to decrease will lengthen duration.
- Treasury futures contracts can be used to change a portfolio's interest rate sensitivity, or duration. To increase the duration of the portfolio, futures contracts should be purchased. To shorten the duration of the portfolio, futures contracts should be sold.
- Because of complicated quality, timing, and wildcard delivery options for Treasury futures, the exact value of such futures is difficult to determine, and can deviate from the theoretical value of a futures contract substantially.
- The underlying for Treasury futures options are Treasury futures.
- Buying puts on Treasury futures is one of the easiest ways to purchase protection against rising interest rates.
- The protective put strategy with Treasury futures options is usually a cross-hedge because the bonds to be hedged and the underlying for the Treasury options futures are not the same.
- Treasury futures options are typically priced using the Black model; however, one should be wary of a number of assumptions in the model that do not hold true for Treasury futures options.
- Interest rate swaps are used to control a portfolio's interest rate risk.
- The position of the fixed-rate receiver in an interest rate swap is equivalent to shorting a fixed-rate bond and investing the proceeds in a floating-rate bond.
- If a portfolio manager wants to increase the dollar duration of a portfolio using an interest rate swap, the portfolio manager should take a

---

[13]See, for example, White (2014) for a summary of pricing of and risk management applications with CDSs.

position as a fixed-rate receiver. Conversely, to reduce the portfolio's dollar duration, the portfolio manager should enter into an interest rate swap as the fixed-rate payer.

- The fixed rate on a swap is ordinarily set at a rate such that the net present value of the swap's cash flows is zero at the start of the swap contract. At any point in time, the fair value of a swap is the fixed rate that makes the net present value of all outstanding cash flows zero.
- The credit risk of a portfolio can be managed with credit default swaps.
- In a credit default swap, the credit protection seller has an economic position that is analogous to an investor in a cash bond. The credit protection buyer is analogous to an investor who is short a bond in the cash market.
- A credit protection seller can increase exposure to a bond issuer or a bond index; credit exposure can be reduced by entering into a credit default swap as a credit protection buyer. A credit default swap is a more transactionally efficient vehicle for altering credit exposure and portfolio rebalancing because it is generally more liquid than the underlying corporate bonds.

Basic Linear Algebra Concepts

This appendix provides a very basic introduction to linear algebra concepts. Some of these concepts are intentionally presented here in a somewhat simplified (not as general as it could be) form. Our goal is not to teach all intricacies of this very important field in mathematics, but to enable readers to understand the linear algebra notation and applications described in this book.

A.1 SYSTEMS OF EQUATIONS

Consider a very simple equation:

$$a \cdot x = b$$

In this equation, x is a variable, and a and b are input data. To find the value of the variable x, we would simply write

$$x = b/a$$

Equivalently, we could have written

$$x = a^{-1} \cdot b$$

Consider now a simple system of two linear equations:

$$3 \cdot x_1 + 8 \cdot x_2 = 46$$
$$10 \cdot x_1 - 7 \cdot x_2 = -15$$

The variables in this system are x_1 and x_2, and the input data consist of the coefficients 3, 8, 10, -7 and the constants to the right of the equal sign, 46 and -15. The way we would normally solve this system of equations is to express one of the variables through the other from one of the equations and plug into the other equation:

$$x_2 = \frac{46 - 3 \cdot x_1}{8}$$

$$10 \cdot x_1 - 7 \cdot \frac{46 - 3 \cdot x_1}{8} = -15$$

Therefore, $x_1 = 2$ and $x_2 = 5$.

It is convenient to introduce new array notation that allows us to treat systems of equations similarly to a single equation. Suppose we put together the coefficients in front of the variables x_1 and x_2 into a 2×2 array $\mathbf{A}$, the constants to the right-hand side of the two equations into a 2×1 array $\mathbf{b}$, and the variables themselves into a 2×1 array $\mathbf{x}$.[1] We have

$$\mathbf{A} = \begin{bmatrix} 3 & 8 \\ 10 & -7 \end{bmatrix}, \mathbf{b} = \begin{bmatrix} 46 \\ -15 \end{bmatrix}, \text{and } \mathbf{x} = \begin{bmatrix} x_1 \\ x_2 \end{bmatrix}$$

We would need to be careful in defining rules for array algebra so that, similarly to the case of solving a single equation, we can express an array of variables through the arrays for the inputs to the system of equations. Namely, we want to be able to write the system of equations as

$$\mathbf{A} \cdot \mathbf{x} = \mathbf{b}$$

and express the solution to the system of equations as

$$\mathbf{x} = \mathbf{A}^{-1} \cdot \mathbf{b}$$

This would substantially simplify the notation when dealing with arrays of data.

A.2 VECTORS AND MATRICES

Vectors and *matrices* are the terms used to describe arrays of data like the arrays $\mathbf{A}$, $\mathbf{b}$, and $\mathbf{x}$ in the previous section. Matrices can be arrays of any dimensions, for example, $N \times M$. The array $\mathbf{A}$ in the previous section was a matrix array. Vectors are matrices that have only one row or column, and are typically written as column arrays of dimensions $N \times 1$. You can imagine them as a listing of coordinates of a point in N-dimensional space. The $\mathbf{b}$ and the $\mathbf{x}$ arrays in the previous section were vector arrays. When an array

---

[1]Note that the first index counts the number of rows in the array, and the second index counts the number of columns in the array.

consists of a single number, that is, it is of dimension 1×1, it is referred to as a *scalar*.

Typically, vectors and matrices are denoted by bold letters in order to differentiate arrays from single elements. Vectors are usually denoted by bold small letters, while matrices are denoted by bold capital letters. An individual element of a vector or a matrix array is represented by a small nonbold letter that corresponds to the letter used to denote the array, followed by its row-and-column index in the array. The element in the ith row and the jth column of the matrix array **A**, for example, is denoted a_{ij}. For the matrix **A** in Section A.1, the element in the first row and second column is $a_{12} = 8$.

Some important matrix arrays include the *null matrix*, **0**, whose elements are all zeros, and the *identity matrix*, usually denoted **I**, which contains 1s in its left-to-right diagonal, and zeros everywhere else. It is referred to as the identify matrix because every other matrix multiplied by a matrix **I** of the appropriate dimensions equals itself. We will introduce matrix multiplication in the next section.

Geometrically, vectors are represented as directed line segments or arrows. For example, the vector [2 5] can be thought of as the directed line segment connecting the origin (point (0,0) in space) to the point with coordinates (2,5). Vectors with more than two entries are directed line segments in more than two dimensions. The length of a vector (also referred to as the *norm* or the *magnitude* of a vector) can be calculated simply by calculating the Euclidean distance between its initial and end points. In this example, the length of the vector [2 5] would be

$$\sqrt{2^2 + 5^2} = 5.39$$

A matrix can be thought of as an operator—it allows operations such as rescaling and rotations to be performed on a vector.

A.3 MATRIX ALGEBRA

Matrix algebra works differently from classical algebra, but after a little bit of getting used to, the definitions of array operations are logical. We list some common operations below.

Matrix equality. Two matrices are equal only if their dimensions are the same and they have the same elements. Thus, for example,

$$\begin{bmatrix} 0 & 0 & 0 \\ 0 & 0 & 0 \\ 0 & 0 & 0 \end{bmatrix} \neq \begin{bmatrix} 0 & 0 \\ 0 & 0 \end{bmatrix}$$

Transpose. The transpose of an $N \times M$ matrix with elements that are real numbers is an $M \times N$ matrix whose elements are the same as the elements of the original matrix, but are "swapped" around the left-to-right diagonal. The transpose of a matrix $\mathbf{A}$ is denoted $\mathbf{A}^T$ or $\mathbf{A}'$. For example, the transpose of the matrix $\mathbf{A}$ in Section A.1 is

$$\mathbf{A}' = \begin{bmatrix} 3 & 10 \\ 8 & -7 \end{bmatrix}$$

The transpose of a vector makes a column array a row array, and vice versa. For example,

$$\mathbf{b}' = \begin{bmatrix} 46 \\ -15 \end{bmatrix}' = [46 \quad -15]$$

Multiplication by a scalar. When a matrix is multiplied by a scalar (a single number), the resulting matrix is simply a matrix whose elements are all multiplied by that number. For example,

$$5 \cdot \mathbf{A} = 5 \cdot \begin{bmatrix} 3 & 8 \\ 10 & -7 \end{bmatrix} = \begin{bmatrix} 15 & 40 \\ 50 & -35 \end{bmatrix}$$

The notation $-\mathbf{A}$ means $(-1) \cdot \mathbf{A}$, that is, a matrix whose elements are the negatives of the elements of the matrix $\mathbf{A}$.

Sum of matrix arrays. When two matrices are added, we simply add the corresponding elements. Note that this implies that the matrix arrays that are added have the same row and column dimensions. For example, the sum of two 2×3 matrices will be a 2×3 matrix as well:

$$\begin{bmatrix} 1 & 2 & 3 \\ 4 & 5 & 6 \end{bmatrix} + \begin{bmatrix} 7 & 8 & 9 \\ 10 & 11 & 12 \end{bmatrix} = \begin{bmatrix} 8 & 10 & 12 \\ 14 & 16 & 18 \end{bmatrix}$$

Multiplication of matrix arrays. Matrix multiplication is perhaps the most confusing array operation to those who do not have a background in linear algebra. Let us consider again the example in Section A.1. We found that the values for the variables x_1 and x_2 that satisfy the system of equations are $x_1 = 2$ and $x_2 = 5$. Therefore, the vector of values for the variables is

$$\mathbf{x} = \begin{bmatrix} 2 \\ 5 \end{bmatrix}$$

Recall also that

$$\mathbf{A} = \begin{bmatrix} 3 & 8 \\ 10 & -7 \end{bmatrix}, \mathbf{b} = \begin{bmatrix} 46 \\ -15 \end{bmatrix}$$

and that we need $\mathbf{A} \cdot \mathbf{x} = \mathbf{b}$ to be true for the system of equations if our matrix algebra is to work in a useful way.

Let us compute the array product $\mathbf{A} \cdot \mathbf{x}$. Note that we cannot simply multiply $\mathbf{A}$ and $\mathbf{x}$ element-by-element, because A is of dimension 2×2 and $\mathbf{x}$ is of dimension 2×1. It is not clear which elements in the two arrays "correspond" to each other. The correct way to perform the multiplication is to multiply and add together the corresponding elements in the first row of $\mathbf{A}$ by the elements of $\mathbf{x}$, and the corresponding elements in the second row of $\mathbf{A}$ by the elements of $\mathbf{x}$:

$$\mathbf{A} \cdot \mathbf{x} = \begin{bmatrix} 3 & 8 \\ 10 & -7 \end{bmatrix} \cdot \begin{bmatrix} 2 \\ 5 \end{bmatrix} = \begin{bmatrix} 3 \cdot 2 + 8 \cdot 5 \\ 10 \cdot 2 - 7 \cdot 5 \end{bmatrix} = \begin{bmatrix} 46 \\ -15 \end{bmatrix} = \mathbf{b}$$

In general, suppose that we want to multiply two matrices, $\mathbf{P}$ of dimensions $N \times M$ and $\mathbf{Q}$ of dimensions $M \times T$. We have

$$\mathbf{P} \cdot \mathbf{Q} = \underbrace{\begin{bmatrix} p_{11} & \cdots & p_{1M} \\ \vdots & \ddots & \vdots \\ p_{N1} & \cdots & p_{NM} \end{bmatrix}}_{N \times M} \cdot \underbrace{\begin{bmatrix} q_{11} & \cdots & q_{1T} \\ \vdots & \ddots & \vdots \\ q_{M1} & \cdots & q_{MT} \end{bmatrix}}_{M \times T}$$

$$= \underbrace{\begin{bmatrix} \sum_{i=1}^{M} p_{1i}q_{i1} & \cdots & \sum_{i=1}^{M} p_{1i}q_{iT} \\ \vdots & \ddots & \vdots \\ \sum_{i=1}^{M} p_{Ni}q_{i1} & \cdots & \sum_{i=1}^{M} p_{Ni}q_{iT} \end{bmatrix}}_{N \times T}$$

In other words, the (i,j)th element of the product matrix $\mathbf{P} \cdot \mathbf{Q}$ is obtained by multiplying element-wise and then adding the elements of the ith row of the first matrix ($\mathbf{P}$) and the jth column of the second matrix ($\mathbf{Q}$). Multiplications of more than two matrices can be carried out similarly, by performing a sequence of pairwise multiplications of matrices; however, note that the dimensions of the matrices in the multiplication need to agree. For example, it is not possible to multiply a matrix of dimensions $N \times M$ and a matrix of dimensions $T \times M$. The number of columns in the first matrix must equal the number of rows in the second matrix. Similarly, in order to multiply more than two matrices, the number of columns in the second matrix must equal the number of rows in the third matrix, and so on. A product of an $N \times M$, an $M \times T$, and a $T \times S$ matrix will result in a matrix of dimensions

$N \times S$. Thus, matrix multiplication is not equivalent to scalar multiplication in more ways than one. For example, it is not guaranteed to be commutative, that is, $P \cdot Q \neq Q \cdot P$.

It is possible to perform matrix multiplication in a way that is closer to standard arithmetic operations, that is, to multiply two matrices of the same dimensions so that each element in one matrix is multiplied by its corresponding element in the second matrix. However, using direct element-wise matrix multiplication is the special case rather than the default. Element-wise matrix multiplication is referred to as the *Hadamard product*, and is typically denoted by "$\bullet$" rather than "$\cdot$."

Matrix inverse. We would like to be able to find the vector **x** from the system of equations in Section A.1 in a way similar to the calculation of the value of the unknown variable from a single calculation. In other words, we would like to be able to compute **x** as

$$x = A^{-1} \cdot b$$

This necessitates defining what A^{-1} (pronounced "**A** inverse") is. The inverse of a matrix **A** is simply the matrix that, when multiplied by the original matrix, produces an identity matrix. In other words,

$$A \cdot A^{-1} = I$$

How to find A^{-1} is not as straightforward. Software packages such as MATLAB have special commands for these operations. Intuitively, the way to find the inverse is to solve a system of equations, where the elements of the inverse matrix are the variables, and the elements of **A** and **I** are the input data.

It is important to note that not all matrices have inverses. However, some kinds of matrices, such as symmetric positive definite matrices, which are typically used in financial applications, always do. (See the definition of symmetric positive definite matrices in the next section.) A square matrix that has an inverse is called a *nonsingular* matrix.

A.4 IMPORTANT DEFINITIONS

Some special matrices are widely used in financial applications. Most often, practitioners are concerned with covariance and correlation matrices. Such matrices are special in that they are symmetric and, theoretically, need to be positive definite.

Additionally, when building statistical models, one often uses data transformations and decomposition techniques that are easier to understand when presented in terms of vectors or matrices. The concepts of orthogonality, eigenvalues, and eigenvectors appear in many of the modeling techniques referenced in the book. We explain what these terms mean below.

Symmetric matrix. A matrix **A** is symmetric if the elements below its left-to-right diagonal are mirror images of the elements above its left-to-right diagonal. A symmetric matrix is the same as its transpose, that is, $\mathbf{A} = \mathbf{A}'$. Covariance and correlation matrices are always symmetric.

Positive definite and positive semi-definite matrices. The main idea behind defining a positive definite matrix is to create a definition of an array that shares some of the main properties of a positive real number. Namely, the idea is that if you multiply the equivalent of a square of a vector by it, you will obtain a positive quantity. If a matrix **A** is positive definite, then

$$\mathbf{z}'\mathbf{A}\mathbf{z} > 0$$

for any vector **z** of appropriate dimensions.

Similarly, a positive *semi*-definite matrix shares some properties of a *nonnegative* real number. Namely, if a matrix **A** is positive semi-definite,

$$\mathbf{z}'\mathbf{A}\mathbf{z} \geq 0$$

for any vector **z** of appropriate dimensions.

Scalar (dot, inner) product. The scalar (dot or inner) product of two vectors **u** and **v** is the expression

$$\|\mathbf{u}\| \cdot \|\mathbf{v}\| \cdot \cos\theta$$

where θ is the angle between the two vectors and $\|\mathbf{u}\|$, $\|\mathbf{v}\|$ are their magnitudes (lengths), $\|\mathbf{u}\| = \sqrt{\mathbf{u} \cdot \mathbf{u}}$ and $\|\mathbf{v}\| = \sqrt{\mathbf{v} \cdot \mathbf{v}}$.

Orthogonal and orthonormal vectors. Two vectors **u** and **v** are orthogonal if the angle between them is 90°; that is, they are perpendicular to each other. Another way to state it is by saying that their scalar (dot) product is 0 (because $\cos 90° = 0$). The vectors are orthonormal if they are orthogonal and their lengths are each 1. Orthogonality is important in situations in which we try to show that two variables are uncorrelated or independent.

Orthogonal matrix. An orthogonal matrix **A** has orthonormal row and column vectors. In other words,

$$\mathbf{A}\mathbf{A}' = \mathbf{A}'\mathbf{A} = \mathbf{I}$$

An orthogonal matrix always has an inverse, which is its transpose. (Because by definition if $\mathbf{A}'\mathbf{A} = \mathbf{I}$, then $\mathbf{A}'$ must be the same as **A**'s inverse $\mathbf{A}^{-1}$.)

Eigenvectors and eigenvalues. An *eigenvector* **v** of a square matrix **A** is a vector that satisfies the following equality:

$$\mathbf{Av} = \lambda \, \mathbf{v}$$

Multiplying a vector by a matrix is a linear transformation of that vector ("stretching," "rotation," "shrinking," etc.). An eigenvector is a vector that does not rotate under the transformation applied by **A**. It may only change its magnitude or point in the opposite direction. The value λ, called an *eigenvalue*, determines how much the magnitude of **v** changes. If $\lambda > 1$, the vector **v** is "stretched"; if $0 < \lambda < 1$, the vector **v** is "shrunk"; if $\lambda = 1$, the vector **v** remains unchanged, and if $\lambda < 0$, the vector **v** reverses direction.

If a square matrix **A** of dimension $N \times N$ has N distinct eigenvectors (but not necessarily distinct eigenvalues), then it can be represented as

$$\mathbf{A} = \mathbf{VDV}^{-1}$$

where **D** is a diagonal matrix formed from the eigenvalues of **A**, and the columns of **V** are the corresponding eigenvectors of **A**. This is called *spectral decomposition* or *eigendecomposition*. Spectral decomposition can always be performed for square symmetric matrices such as covariance and correlation matrices most used in portfolio applications.

References

Adcock, C., and N. Meade. 1994. "A Simple Algorithm to Incorporate Transaction Costs in Quadratic Optimization." *European Journal of Operational Research* 79 (1): 85–94.

Almgren, R., and N. Chriss. 2000. "Optimal Execution of Portfolio Transactions." *Journal of Risk* 3:5–39.

Almgren, R., C. Thum, E. Hauptmann, and H. Li. 2005. "Equity Market Impact." *Risk* 18:57–62.

Amenc, N., F. Goltz, L. Martellini, and P. Retkowsky. 2011. "Efficient Indexation: An Alternative to Cap-Weighted Indices." *Journal of Investment Management* 9 (4): 1–23.

Amenc, N., F. Goltz, and A. Lodh. 2012. "Choose Your Betas: Benchmarking Alternative Equity Index Strategies." *Journal of Portfolio Management* 39 (1): 88–111.

Amenc, N., F. Goltz, A. Lodh, and L. Martellini. 2012. "Diversifying the Diversifiers and Tracking the Tracking Error: Outperforming Cap-Weighted Indices with Limited Risk of Underperformance." *Journal of Portfolio Management* 38 (3): 72–88.

American Statistical Association. 1999. "Ethical Guidelines for Statistical Practice." www.amstat.org/committees/ethics/index.html.

Apelfeld, R., G. B. Fowler, and J. P. Gordon. 1996. "Tax-Aware Equity Investing." *Journal of Portfolio Management* 22 (2): 18–28.

Arnott, R. D., J. Hsu, and P. Moore. 2005. "Fundamental Indexation." *Financial Analyst Journal* 61 (2): 83-99.

Asness, C., Frazzini, A., and L. H. Pedersen. 2012. "Leverage Aversion and Risk Parity." *Financial Analysts Journal* 68:47–59.

Authers, J. 2014. "Is 'Smart Beta' Smart Enough to Last?" *Financial Times*, June 11.

Axioma. 2007. "Transaction Cost Models and Market Impact." *Axioma ClienTip*. 27 (April). www.updatefrom.com/axioma/070427_eflier/images/axioma_client ips070427.pdf.

Badaoui, S., R. Deguest, L. Martellini, and V. Milhau. 2014. "Dynamic Liability-Driven Investing Strategies: The Emergence of a New Investment Paradigm for Pension Funds? A Survey of the LDI Practices for Pension Funds." *EDHEC-Risk Institute Publication* (July). www.edhec-risk.com/features/RISK Article.2014–07–02.5714.

Bai, J. 2003. "Inferential Theory for Factor Models of Large Dimensions." *Econometrica* 71:135–171.

Bailey, D., and M. Lopez de Prado. 2014. "The Deflated Sharpe Ratio: Correcting for Selection Bias, Backtest Overfitting, and Nonnormality." *Journal of Portfolio Management* 40 (5): 84–107.

Balkema, A., and L. de Haan. 1974. "Residual Life Time at Great Age." *Annals of Probability* 2:792–804.

Barberis, N.C. 2000. "Investing for the Long Run when Returns Are Predictable." *Journal of Finance* 55:225–264.

Barclays. 2012. "POINT® Innovative Multi-Asset Portfolio Analysis: The Difference Is Clear." https://ecommerce.barcap.com/indices/download?IPRS-Point-Brochure.

Barone-Adesi, G., and R. E. Whaley. 1987. "Efficient Analytic Approximation of American Option Values." *Journal of Finance*, 301–320.

Barra. 1998. *Risk Model Handbook United States Equity: Version 3*. Berkeley, CA: Barra. Barra is now MSCI Barra.

Barra on Campus. 2003. Handbook.

Baygun, B., and R. Tzucker. 2005. "Portfolio Strategies for Outperforming a Benchmark." In *Advanced Bond Portfolio Management*, edited by F. J. Fabozzi, L. Martellini, and P. Priaulet. Hobken, NJ: John Wiley & Sons.

Bazaraa, M., H. Sharali, and C. Shetty. 1993. *Nonlinear Programming: Theory and Algorithms*. New York: John Wiley & Sons.

Bellman, R. 1957. *Dynamic Programming*. Princeton, NJ: Princeton University Press.

Bensalah, Y. 2000. "Steps in Applying Extreme Value Theory to Finance: A Review." *Bank of Canada Working Paper*, 2000–2020.

Ben-Tal, A., T. Margalit, and A. Nemirovski. 2000. "Robust Modeling of Multi-Stage Portfolio Problems." In *High-Performance Optimization*, edited by H. Frenk, K. Roos, T. Terlaky, S. Zhang, 303–328. Dordrecht: Kluwer.

Bertsekas, D. 2005. *Dynamic Programming and Optimal Control*, vol. I, 3rd ed. Belmont, MA: Athena Scientific.

———. 2012. *Dynamic Programming and Optimal Control, vol. II (Approximate Dynamic Programming)*, 4th ed. Belmont, MA: Athena Scientific.

Bertsimas, D., C. Darnell, and R. Soucy. 1999. "Portfolio Construction through Mixed-Integer Programming at Grantham, Mayo, Van Otterloo and Company." *Interfaces* 29 (1): 49–66.

Bertsimas, D., and D. Pachamanova. 2008. "Robust Multiperiod Portfolio Management with Transaction Costs." *Computers and Operations Research*. Special issue on *Applications of Operations Research in Finance* 35 (1): 3–17.

Bertsimas, D., and J. Tsitsiklis. 1997. *Introduction to Linear Optimization*. Belmont, MA: Athena Scientific.

Birge, J. 1985. "Decomposition and Partitioning Methods for Multistage Stochastic Linear Programs." *Operations Research* (33): 989–1007.

Black, F. 1972. "Capital Market Equilibrium with Restricted Borrowings." *Journal of Business* 45(3): 444–455.

———. 1976. "The Pricing of Commodity Contracts." *Journal of Financial Economics*, 161–179.

Black, F., and R. Litterman. 1992. "Global Portfolio Optimization." *Financial Analysts Journal* 48 (5): 28–43.

Black, F., and M. Scholes. 1973. "The Pricing of Options and Corporate Liabilities." *Journal of Political Economy* 81 (3): 637–654.

Blattberg, R., and N. Gonedes. 1974. "A Comparison of the Stable and Student Distributions as Statistical Methods for Stock Prices." *Journal of Business* 47:244–280.

Boender, G. C. E. 1997. "A Hybrid Simulation/Optimization Scenario Model for Asset/Liability Management." *European Journal of Operational Research* 99 (1): 126–135.

Boender, G., C. Dert, F. Heemskerk, and H. Hoek. 2005. "A Scenario Approach of ALM." In *Handbook of Asset and Liability Management*, vol. 2, edited by S.A. Zenios and W.T. Ziemba. Amsterdam: North-Holland.

Bogentoft, E., H. E. Romeijn, and S. Uryasev. 2001. "Asset/Liability Management for Pension Funds Using CVaR Constraints." *Journal of Risk Finance* (Fall): 57–71.

Bollerslev, T. 1986. "Generalized Autoregressive Conditional Heteroskedasticity." *Journal of Econometrics* 31 (June): 307–327.

———. 1987. "A Conditionally Heteroscedastic Time-Series Model for Speculative Prices and Rates of Return." *Review of Econometrics and Statistics* 69 (3): 542–547.

Bouchard, J.-P., M. Potters, and J.-P. Aguilar. 1997. "Missing Information and Asset Allocation." In *Science and Finance: Capital Fund Management*.

Boudt, K., P. Carl, and B. G. Peterson. 2010. "Asset Allocation with Conditional Value-at-Risk Budgets." *Journal of Risk* 15 (3): 39–68.

Boudt, K., B. G. Peterson, and C. Croux. 2008. "Estimation and Decomposition of Downside Risk for Portfolios with Non-Normal Returns." *Journal of Risk* 11 (2): 79–103.

Boyd, S., and L. Vandenberghe. 2004. *Convex Optimization*. Cambridge: Cambridge University Press.

Brandt, M. W., A. Goyal, P. Santa-Clara, and J. R. Stroud. 2005. "A Simulation Approach to Dynamic Portfolio Choice with an Application to Learning about Return Predictability." *Review of Financial Studies* 18:831–873.

Breger, L., and O. Cheyette. 2005. "Fixed Income Risk Modeling." Chapter 8 in *Advanced Bond Portfolio Management*, edited by F.J. Fabozzi, L. Martellini, and P. Priaulet. Hoboken, NJ: John Wiley & Sons.

Burmeister, C. 2008. "Portfolio Replication–Variable Annuity Case Study." ERM symposium presentation. www.ermsymposium.org/2008/pdf/handouts/Q/Q5_burmeister.pdf.

Burmeister, C., and R. Black. 2007. "Replicating Portfolios in Algo Risk." IBM Algorithmics white paper. ww1.prweb.com/prfiles/2009/11/25/3262544/0_AlgoWP0907ReplicatePortfolios.pdf.

Burmeister, C., M. Dorsel, and P. Matson. 2010. "Replicating Portfolios in the Insurance Industry." Society of Actuaries Investment Symposium, March. https://www.soa.org/uploadedFiles/Files/Pd/2010-ny-dorsel.pdf.

Campbell, J. Y., M. L. Lettau, B. G. Malkiel, and Y. Xu. 2001. "Have Individual Stocks Become More Volatile? An Empirical Exploration of Idiosyncratic Risk." *Journal of Finance* 56 (1): 1–43.

Campbell, J., A. Lo, and A. MacKinlay. 1997. *The Econometrics of Financial Markets*. Princeton, NJ: Princeton University Press.

Carino, D., and W. Ziemba. 1998. Formulation of the Russell-Yasuda Kasai Financial Planning Model. *Operations Research* 46 (4): 433–449.

Cattell, R. B. 1988. "The Meaning and Strategic Use of Factor Analysis." In *Handbook of Multivariate Experimental Psychology*, edited by J.R. Nesselroade and R. B. Catell. New York: Springer.

Ceria, S., A. Saxena, and R. Stubbs. 2012. "Factor Alignment Problems and Quantitative Portfolio Management." *Journal of Portfolio Management*, 38 (2): 29–43.

Ceria, S., and R. Stubbs. 2006. "Incorporating Estimation Errors into Portfolio Selection: Robust Portfolio Construction." *Journal of Asset Management* 7 (2): 109–127.

Chalabi, Y., D. Scott, and D. Würtz. 2010. "The Generalized Lambda Distribution as an Alternative to Model Financial Returns." Working paper. https://www.rmetrics.org/sites/default/files/glambda_0.pdf.

Chaves, D., J. Hsu., F. Li., and O. Shakernia. 2011. "Risk Parity Portfolio vs. Other Asset Allocation Heuristic Portfolios." *The Journal of Investing* 20 (1): 108–118.

Chen, N.-F., R. Roll, and S. Ross. 1986. "Economic Forces and the Stock Market." *Journal of Business* 59 (July): 383–403.

Chen, R., F. J. Fabozzi, and D. O'Kane. 2003. "The Valuation of Credit Default Swaps." In *Professional Perspectives on Fixed Income Portfolio Management*, vol. 4, edited by Frank J. Fabozzi. Hoboken, NJ: John Wiley & Sons.

Chen, X., M. Sim, and P. Sun. 2007. A Robust Optimization Perspective on Stochastic Programming. *Operations Research* 55 (6): 1058–1107.

Chincarini, L., and D. Kim. 2006. *Quantitative Equity Portfolio Management: An Active Approach to Portfolio Construction and Management*. New York: McGraw-Hill.

Choueifaty, Y., and Y. Coignard. 2008. "Toward Maximum Diversification." *Journal of Portfolio Management* 34 (4): 40–51.

Choueifaty, Y., T. Froidure, and J. Reynier. 2011. "Properties of the Most Diversified Portfolio." Working paper, TOBAM.

Christoffersen, P., V. Errunza, K. Jacobs, and J. Xisong. 2012. "Is the Potential for International Diversification Disappearing? A Dynamic Copula Approach." *Review of Financial Studies* 25 (12): 3711–3751.

Collins, B., and F. J. Fabozzi. 1999. *Derivatives and Equity Portfolio Management*. New York: John Wiley & Sons.

Consigli, G., and M.A.H. Dempster. 1998. "Dynamic Stochastic Programming for Asset-Liability Management." *Annals of Operations Research* 81:131–162.

Consiglio, A., F. Cocco, and S.A. Zenios. 2008. Asset and Liability Modeling for Participating Policies with Guarantees. *European Journal of Operational Research* 186 (1): 380–404.

Consiglio, A., D. Saunders, and S. A. Zenios. 2006. "Asset and Liability Management for Insurance Products with Minimum Guarantees: The UK Case." *Journal of Banking & Finance* 30:645–667.

Constantinides, G. 1983. "Capital Market Equilibrium with Personal Taxes." *Econometrica* 51:611–636.

Cox, J. C., and S. A. Ross. 1975. "The Pricing of Options for Jump Processes." Rodney L White Center working paper, no. 2–75. (University of Pennsylvania, Philadelphia, PA).

Cox, J. C., S. A. Ross, and M. Rubinstein. 1979. "Option Pricing: A Simplified Approach." *Journal of Financial Economics* 7 (3): 229–263.

Cremers, J. H., M. Kritzman, and S. Page. 2003. "Portfolio Formation with Higher Moments and Plausible Utility." 272–12 Revere Street working papers, November 22.

_____. 2005. "Optimal Hedge Fund Allocations: Do Higher Moments Matter?" *Journal of Portfolio Management* 31 (3): 70–81.

Dammon, R. M., and C. S. Spatt. 1996. "The Optimal Trading and Pricing of Securities with Asymmetric Capital Gains Taxes and Transaction Costs." *Review of Financial Studies* 9 (3): 921–952.

Dammon, R. M., C. S. Spatt, and H. H. Zhang. 2001. "Optimal Consumption and Investment with Capital Gains Taxes." *Review of Financial Studies* 14 (3): 583–617.

_____. 2004. "Optimal Asset Location and Allocation with Taxable and Tax-Deferred Investing." *Journal of Finance* 59 (3): 999–1037.

DeMiguel, V., L. Garlappi, F. Nogales, and R. Uppal. 2009 "A Generalized Approach to Portfolio Optimization: Improving Performance by Constraining Portfolio Norms." *Management Science* 55 (5): 798–812.

DeMiguel, V., L. Garlappi, and R. Uppal. 2009. "Optimal versus Naive Diversification: How Inefficient Is the 1/N Portfolio Strategy?" *Review of Financial Studies* 22 (5): 1915–1953.

Detemple, J., and M. Rindisbacher. 2008. Dynamic Asset Liability Management with Tolerance for Limited Shortfalls." *Insurance: Mathematics and Economics* 43 (3): 281–294.

DiBartolomeo, D. (2000). "Recent Advances in Management of Taxable Portfolios." *Manuscript*, Northfield Information Services. www.northinfo.com/documents/69.pdf.

Disatnik, D., and S. Benninga. 2007. "Shrinking the Covariance Matrix—Simpler Is Better." *Journal of Portfolio Management* 33 (4): 56–63.

Effinger, A., and E. Balchunas. 2015. "Funds Run by Robots Now Account for $400 Billion." *Bloomberg Markets*, March 16.

Ellis, K., R. Michaely, and M. O'Hara. 2000. "The Accuracy of Trade Classification Rules: Evidence from Nasdaq." *Journal of Financial and Quantitative Analysis* 35:529–551.

Embrechts, P., C. Klüppelberg, and T. Mikosch. 1997. *Modelling Extremal Events for Insurance and Finance*. Berlin: Springer-Verlag.

Embrechts, P., F. Lindskog, and A. McNeil. 2003. "Modelling Dependence with Copulas and Applications to Risk Management." In *Handbook of Heavy Tailed Distribution in Finance*, edited by S. Rachev. Amsterdam: Elsevier.

Embrechts, P., S. Resnick, and G. Samorodnitsky. 1999. "Extreme Value Theory as a Risk Management Tool." *North American Actuarial Journal* 3 (2): 30–41.

Engle, R.F. 1982. "Autoregressive Conditional Heteroscedasticity with Estimates of the Variance of U.K. Inflation." *Econometrica* 50:987–1008.

Engle, R., S.M. Focardi, and F.J. Fabozzi. 2008. "ARCH/GARCH Models in Applied Financial Econometrics." In *Handbook of Finance*, vol. 3, edited by Frank Fabozzi. Hoboken, NJ: John Wiley & Sons.

Engle, R. F., V. Ng, and M. Rothschild. 1990. "Asset Pricing with a Factor-ARCH Covariance Structure: Empirical Estimates for Treasury Bills." *Journal of Econometrics* 45:213–238.

Escudero, L. F., A. Garín, M. Merino, and G. Pérez. 2009. "On Multistage Stochastic Integer Programming for Incorporating Logical Constraints in Asset and Liability Management under Uncertainty." *Computational Management Science* 6:307–327.

Evans, J. L., and S. H. Archer. 1968. "Diversification and the Reduction of Dispersion: An Empirical Analysis." *Journal of Finance* 23 (5): 761–767.

Fabozzi, F. J. 2009. *Institutional Investment Management*. Hoboken, NJ: John Wiley & Sons.

Fabozzi, F. J., S. Focardi, and P. Kolm. 2006. *Financial Modeling of the Equity Market*. Hoboken, NJ: John Wiley & Sons.

Fabozzi, F. J., S. Focardi, and P. Kolm. 2010. *Quantitative Equity Investing: Techniques and Strategies*. Hoboken, NJ: John Wiley & Sons.

Fabozzi, F. J., S. M. Focardi, S. T. Rachev, and B. Arshanapalli. 2014. *Basics of Financial Econometrics*. Hoboken, NJ: John Wiley & Sons.

Fabozzi, F. J., P. Kolm, D. Pachamanova, and S. Focardi. 2007. *Robust Portfolio Optimization and Management*. Hoboken, NJ: John Wiley & Sons.

Fabozzi, F. J., L. Martellini, and P. Priaulet. 2005. *Advanced Bond Portfolio Management*. Hoboken, NJ: John Wiley & Sons.

FactSet. 2008. "Obtaining Non-Normal Portfolio Return Distributions for Derivative-Containing Portfolios from a Variance-Covariance Based Risk Model." White paper.

Falk, M., Hüsler, J., and Reiss, R. 1994. *Laws of Small Numbers: Extremes and Rare Events*. Basel: Birkhäuser.

Fama, E. F. 1963. "Mandelbrot and the Stable Paretian Hypothesis." *Journal of Business* 36 (4): 420–429

_____. 1965. "The behavior of stock prices." *Journal of Business*, XXXVIII, 1 (January): 34–105.

_____. 1970. "Efficient Capital Markets: A Review of Theory and Empirical Work." *Journal of Finance* 25 (2): 383–417.

Fama, E., and K. French. 1992. "The Cross-Section of Expected Stock Returns." *Journal of Finance* 47 (2): 427–465.

_____. 1993. "Common Risk Factors in the Returns on Stocks and Bonds." *Journal of Financial Economics* 33:3–56.

_____. 1995. "Size and Book-to-Market Factors in Earnings and Returns." *Journal of Finance* 50:131–155.

_____. 1996. "Multifactor Explanations of Asset Pricing Anomalies." *Journal of Finance* 51:55–84.

_____. 1998. "Value versus Growth: The International Evidence." *Journal of Finance* 53:1975–1999.

_____. 2004. "The Capital Asset Pricing Model: Theory and Evidence." *Journal of Economic Perspectives* 18 (3): 25–46.

Fama, E., and J. D. MacBeth. 1976. "Risk, Return and Equilibrium: Empirical Tests." *Journal of Political Economy* 81 (3): 607–636.

Fama, E., and R. Roll. 1968. "Some Properties of Symmetric Stable Distributions." *Journal of the American Statistical Association* 63 (323): 817–837.

Ferguson, R. B. 2014. "Big Idea: Data & Analytics Interview with J.R. Lowry (SSGX)." *MIT Sloan Management Review*, May 27.

Ferstl, R., and A. Weissensteiner. 2011. Asset-Liability Management under Time-Varying Investment Opportunities. *Journal of Banking and Finance* 35 (1): 182–192.

Focardi, S., and F. J. Fabozzi. 2004. *The Mathematics of Financial Modeling and Investment Management*. Hoboken, NJ: John Wiley & Sons.

Fong, H. G., and O. A. Vasicek. 1984. "A Risk Minimizing Strategy for Portfolio Immunization." *Journal of Finance* 30:1541–1546.

Forbes, C., M. Evans, N. Hastings, and B. Peacock. 2011. *Statistical Distributions*, 4th ed. Hoboken, NJ: Wiley-Interscience.

Fragniere, E., and J. Gondzio. 2005. "Stochastic Programming from Modeling Languages." Chapter 7 in *Applications of Stochastic Programming*, edited by S. Wallace and W. Ziemba. Philadelphia, PA: Society for Industrial and Applied Mathematics.

Freund, R. 2004. Lecture Notes in Nonlinear Optimization. Unpublished manuscript, available online from the MIT Open CourseWare site, http://ocw .mit.edu/OcwWeb/Sloan-School-of-Management/15–084JSpring2004/Lecture Notes/index.htm.

Glasserman, P. 2004. *Monte Carlo Methods in Financial Engineering*. New York: Springer-Verlag.

Gnedenko, B. 1943. "Sur la distribution limite du terme maximum d'une série aléatoire." *Annals of Mathematics* 44:423–453.

Goldfarb, D., and G. Iyengar. 2003. "Robust Portfolio Selection Problems." *Mathematics of Operations Research* 28 (1): 1–38.

Gondzio, J., and R. Kouwenberg. 2001. "High-Performance Computing for Asset-Liability Management." *Operations Research* 49 (6): 879–891.

Goodman, L. 1985. "Introduction to Debt Options." In *Winning the Interest Rate Game: A Guide to Debt Options*, edited by F.J. Fabozzi, 13–14. Chicago: Probus Publishing.

Gulpinar, N., and D. Pachamanova. 2013. "A Robust Optimization Approach to Asset Liability Management under Time-Varying Investment Opportunities." *Journal of Banking and Finance* 37 (6): 2031–2041.

Gulpinar, N., D. Pachamanova, and E. Canakoglu. 2015. "A Robust Asset-Liability Management Framework for Investment Products with Guarantees." *OR Spectrum*, to appear.

Gulpinar, N., B. Rustem, and R. Settergren. 2004. "Simulation and Optimization Approaches to Scenario Tree Generation." *Journal of Economic Dynamics and Control* 28:1291–1315.

Harvey, C., Y. Liu, and H. Zhu. 2014. " ... and the Cross-Section of Expected Returns." Working paper, Duke University. http://papers.ssrn.com/sol3/papers .cfm?abstract_id=2249314.

Hasbrouck, J. 1991. "Measuring the Information Content of Stock Trades." *Journal of Finance* 46:179–207.

Hillier, R.S., and J. Eckstein. 1993. "Stochastic Dedication: Designing Fixed Income Portfolios Using Massively Parallel Benders Decomposition." *Management Science* 39 (11): 1422–1438.

Ho, T. 1992. "Key Rate Durations: Measures of Interest Rate Risk." *Journal of Fixed Income* 2 (September): 29–44.

Ho, Thomas S. Y. 1999. "Key Rate Duration: A Measure of Interest Rate Risk Exposure." In *Interest Rate Risk Measurement and Management*, edited by S. Nawalkha and D. R. Chambers. New York: Institutional Investors.

Hogan, K., P. Hodges, M. Potts, and D. Ransenberg. 2015. "Rewarding Risk: How the Science of 'Rewarded Risk' Is Redefining Diversification." BlackRock white paper, January.

Huang, C., and R. Litzenberger. 1988. *Foundations for Financial Economics*. Englewood Cliffs, NJ: Prentice Hall.

Hull, J. 2014. *Options, Futures and Other Derivatives*, 9th ed. Upper Saddle River, NJ: Prentice Hall.

Ingersoll, J 1987. *Theory of Financial Decision Making*. Savage, MD: Rowman and Littlefield.

Jean, W. H. 1971. "The Extension of Portfolio Analysis to Three or More Parameters." *Journal of Financial and Quantitative Analysis* 6 (1): 505–515.

Jorion, P. 1986. "Bayes-Stein Estimator for Portfolio Analysis." *Journal of Financial and Quantitative Analysis* 21 (3): 279–292.

_____. 1992. "Portfolio Optimization in Practice." *Financial Analysts Journal* 48 (1): 68–74.

J. P. Morgan & Co. 1997. *CreditMetrics*. Technical document.

Kaiser, H. F. 1960. "The Application of Electronic Computers to Factor Analysis." *Educational and Psychological Measurement* 20:141–151.

Kahn, R., and M. Lemmon. 2015. "Smart Beta: The Owner's Manual." *Journal of Portfolio Management* 41 (2): 76–83.

Kahneman, D., and A. Tversky. 1979. "Prospect Theory: An Analysis of Decision under Risk." *Econometrica* 47 (2): 263–290.

Khodadadi, A., R. Tutuncu, and P. Zangari. 2006. "Optimization and Quantitative Investment Management." *Journal of Asset Management* 7 (2): 83–92.

Kim, W.C., J.H. Kim and F.J. Fabozzi. 2016. *Robust Equity Portfolio Management*. Hoboken, NJ: J. Wiley & Sons.

Kolm, P., R. Tutuncu, and F. Fabozzi. 2014. "60 Years of Portfolio Optimization: Practical Challenges and Current Trends." *European Journal of Operational Research* 234:356–371.

Kopman, L., and S. Liu. 2011. "Treatment of Fixed Transaction Costs in Barra Optimizer." *MSCI Barra Research Paper No. 2011–10.* http://papers.ssrn.com/sol3/papers.cfm?abstract_id=1915219.

Kouwenberg, R. 2001. "Scenario Generation and Stochastic Programming Models for Asset Liability Management." In *European Journal of Operational Research* 134 (2): 279–292.

Kritzman, M. 1993. "What Practitioners Need to Know... About Factor Methods." *Financial Analysts Journal* (January–February): 12–15.

Ledoit, O., and M. Wolf. 2003. "Improved Estimation of the Covariance Matrix of Stock Returns with an Application to Portfolio Selection." In *Journal of Empirical Finance* 10 (5): 603–621.

Lee, C.M.C., and M. J. Ready. 1991. "Inferring Trade Direction from Intraday Data." *Journal of Finance* 46:733–746.

Lee, J-H., and D. Stefek. 2008. "Do Risk Factors Eat Alphas?" *Journal of Portfolio Management* 34 (4): 12–25.

Lee, J-H., D. Stefek, and A. Zhelenyak. 2006. "Robust Portfolio Optimization–A Closer Look." *MSCI Barra Research Insights report*, June.

Lee, W. 2011. "Risk Based Asset Allocation: A New Answer to an Old Question?" *Journal of Portfolio Management* 37 (4): 11–12.

Lévy, P. (1924). "Théorie des erreurs. La Loi de Gauss et les Lois Exceptionelles." *Bulletin de la Société Mathématique de France* 52:49–85.

Levy, H., and H. M. Markowitz. 1979. "Approximating Expected Utility by a Function of Mean and Variance." *American Economic Review* 69 (3): 308–317.

Lintner, J. 1965. "The Valuation of Risk Assets and the Selection of Risky Investments in Stock Portfolio and Capital Budgets." *Review of Economics and Statistics* 47 (1): 13–37.

Lloyd, W., B. Manium, and M. Gustavsson. 2002. "Tracking Error." In *Professional Perspectives on Fixed Income Management*, edited by F.J. Fabozzi. New York: John Wiley & Sons.

Lobo, M. S., M. Fazel, and S. Boyd. 2007. "Portfolio Optimization with Linear and Fixed Transaction Costs and Bounds on Risk." *Annals of Operations Research* 152 (1): 341–365.

Loucks, M., J. A. Penicook, and U. Schillhorn. 2008. "Emerging Markets Debt." In *The Handbook of Finance*, vol. 1, edited by F. J. Fabozzi, 339–346. Hoboken, NJ: John Wiley & Sons.

Maginn, J. L., and D. L. Tuttle (eds.). 1990. *Managing Investment Portfolios: A Dynamic Process.* New York: Warren, Gorham & Lamont, sponsored by the Institute of Chartered Financial Analysts, second edition.

Maillard, S., T. Roncalli, and J. Teiletche. 2010. "The Properties of Equally Weighted Risk Contributions Portfolios." *Journal of Portfolio Management* 36 (4): 60–70.

Malkiel, B. G. 2002. "How Much Diversification Is Enough?" *Proceedings of the AIMR Seminar, "The Future of the Equity Portfolio Construction."* (March): 26–27.

Mandelbrot, B. 1963. "The Variation of Certain Speculative Prices." *Journal of Businessxye* 36 (4), 394-419,

Markowitz, H. 1952. "Portfolio Selection." *Journal of Finance* 7:77–91.

_____. 1959. *Portfolio Selection: Efficient Diversification of Investments*. New York: John Wiley & Sons.

McNeil, A. 1997. "Estimating the Tails of Loss Severity Distributions Using Extreme Value Theory." *ASTIN Bulletin*, 27 (1): 117–137.

McNeil, A., R. Frey, and P. Embrechts. 2005. *Quantitative Risk Management: Concepts, Techniques and Tools*. Princeton, NJ: Princeton University Press.

McNeil, A. J., and T. Saladin. 1997. "The Peaks over Thresholds Method for Estimating High Quantiles of Loss Distributions." *Proceedings of the XXVIIIth International ASTIN Colloquium*, 23–43.

Merton, R. C. 1974. "On the Pricing of Corporate Debt: the Risk Structure of Interest Rates." *Journal of Finance* 29 (2): 449–470.

_____. 1976. "Option Pricing When Underlying Stock Returns Are Discontinuous." *Journal of Financial Economics* 3:125–144.

_____. 1995. *Continuous-Time Finance*. Cambridge, MA: Blackwell, revised edition.

Michaud, R. O. 1998. *Efficient Asset Management: A Practical Guide to Stock Portfolio Optimization and Asset Allocation*. Oxford: Oxford University Press.

Mitchell, J. E., and S. Braun. 2013. "Rebalancing an Investment Portfolio in the Presence of Convex Transaction Costs, Including Market Impact Costs." *Optimization Methods and Software* 28 (3): 523–542.

Mossin, J. 1966. "Equilibrium in a Capital Asset Market." *Econometrica* 34 (4): 768–783.

MSCI Barra. 2003. *Barra On Campus Handbook*.

Mulvey, J., R. Vanderbei, and S. Zenios. 1995. "Robust Optimization of Large-Scale Systems." *Operations Research* 43 (2).

Mulvey, J., R. Rush, J. Mitchell, and T. Willemain. 2000. "Stratified Filtered Sampling in Stochastic Optimization." *Journal of Applied Mathematics and Decision Sciences* 4 (1): 17–38.

Natarajan, K., D. Pachamanova, and M. Sim. 2008. "Incorporating Asymmetric Distributional Information in Robust Value-at-Risk Optimization." *Management Science* 54 (3): 573–585.

Nemhauser, G., and L. Wolsey. 1999. *Integer and Combinatorial Optimization*. New York: Wiley.

Northfield Information Services. 2009. "Linking Equity and Credit Risk." Presentation at Asia Research Seminar. www.northinfo.com/documents/365.pdf.

Northfield Information Services. 2015. "Northfield Transaction Cost Model." www.northinfo.com/documents/354.pdf.

O'Cinneide, C., B. Scherer, and X. Xu. 2006. "Pooling Trades in a Quantitative Investment Process." *Journal of Portfolio Management* 32 (4): 33–43.

Oxford University and the IBM Institute for Business Value. 2012. "Analytics: The Real-World Use of Big Data." (October).

Pachamanova, D. A., and F. J. Fabozzi. 2010. *Simulation and Optimization in Finance: Modeling with MATLAB, @RISK, or VBA*. Hoboken, NJ: John Wiley & Sons.

Pachamanova, D. A. and F. J. Fabozzi. 2014. "Recent Trends in Equity Portfolio Construction Analytics. *Journal of Portfolio Management* 40 (3): 137–151

Pachamanova, D., N. Gulpinar, and E. Canakoglu. 2014. "Robust Data-Driven Approaches to Pension Fund Asset-Liability Management under Uncertainty." In *Optimization Paradigms and Decision Making under Uncertainty for Financial Applications*, edited by P. Brandimarte, G. Consigli, and D. Kuhn. Springer's International Series in Operations Research and Management Science, to appear.

Parets, J. C. 2013. "Relative Rotation Graphs Explained." (January 11). www .allstarcharts.com/relative-rotation-graph-explained/.

Peters, E. E. 1987. "Hedged Equity Portfolios: Components of Risk and Return." *Advances in Futures and Options Research* 1 (B): 75–92.

Pfaff, B. 2013. *Financial Risk Modeling and Portfolio Optimization with R*. Chichester, UK: John Wiley & Sons.

Pickands, J. 1975. "Statistical Inference Using Extreme Order Statistics." *Annals of Statistics* 3:119–131.

Pogue, G. 1970. "An Extension of the Markowitz Portfolio Selection Model to Include Variable Transactions Costs, Short Sales, Leverage Policies, and Taxes." *Journal of Finance* 25 (5): 1005–1027.

Qian, E. 2005. "Risk Parity Portfolios." *Research Paper*, PanAgora Asset Management.

_____. 2006. "On the Financial Interpretation of Risk Contribution: Risk Budgets Do Add Up." *Journal of Investment Management* 4 (4): 1–11.

Rachev, S. and S. Mittnik. 2000. *Stable Paretian Models in Finance*. Hoboken, NJ: John Wiley & Sons.

Rachev, S., S. Mittnik, F. Fabozzi, S. Focardi, and T. Jašić. 2007. *Financial Econometrics: From Basics to Advanced Modeling Techniques*. Hoboken, NJ: John Wiley & Sons.

Ramberg, J. S., and B. W. Schmeiser. 1972. "An Approximate Method for Generating Symmetric Random Variables." *Communications of the ACM* 15:987–990.

_____. 1974. "An Approximate Method for Generating Asymmetric Random Variables." *Communications of the ACM*, 17 (2), 78–82.

Ramberg, J. S., P. R. Tadikamalla, E. J. Dudewicz, and E. F. Mykytka. 1979. "A Probability Distribution and Its Uses in Fitting Data." *Technometrics*, 21 (2): 201–214.

Rachev, S., and S. Mittnik. 2000. *Stable Paretian Models in Finance*. New York: John Wiley & Sons.

Rachev, S. T., S. Mittnik, F. J. Fabozzi, S. M. Focardi, and T. Jašić. 2007. *Financial Econometrics: From Basics to Advanced Modeling Techniques*. Hoboken, NJ: John Wiley & Sons.

Rendleman, R., and B. Bartter 1979. "Two-State Option Pricing." *Journal of Finance* 34:1093–1110.

Rockafellar, R. T., and S. Uryasev. 2002. "Conditional Value-at-Risk for General Loss Distributions." *Journal of Banking and Finance* 26:1443–1471.

Ross, P., D. Bernstein, N. Ferguson, and R. Dalio. 2008. "Creating an Optimal Portfolio to Fund Pension Liabilities." Chapter 47 in *Handbook of Finance*, vol. 2, edited by Frank J. Fabozzi. Hoboken, NJ: John Wiley & Sons.

Ross, S. A. 1976. "The Arbitrage Theory of Capital Asset Pricing." *Journal of Economic Theory* 16 (December): 343–362.

Russell Investments. 2014. "Russell-Axioma Factor Indexes (Long-Only): Construction and Methodology." White paper. www.russell.com.

Ruszczynski, A., and A. Shapiro. 2003. *Stochastic Programming, Handbook in Operations Research and Management Science*. Amsterdam: Elsevier Science.

Sanford, C. S., and D. Borge. 1995. "The Risk Management Revolution." www.trry .uga.edu/about/history/sanford/risk-management-revolution.

Saxena, A., C. Martin, and R. Stubbs. 2012. "Aligning Alpha and Risk Factors, a Panacea to Factor Alignment Problems?" *Axioma research paper*. www.axioma .com/downloads/Axioma-AAF-Constraints.pdf.

Scherer, B. 2002. "Portfolio Resampling: Review and Critique." *Financial Analysts Journal* 58 (6): 98–109.

Sharpe, W. F. 1963. "A Simplified Model for Portfolio Analysis." *Management Science* 9 (January): 277–293.

_____. 1964. "Capital Asset Prices." *Journal of Finance* 19 (3): 425–442

_____. 1978. *Investments*. Englewood Cliffs, NJ: Prentice-Hall.

_____. 1994. "The Sharpe Ratio." *Journal of Portfolio Management*, 21 (1): 49–58.

Shepherd, S. 2014. "Smart Beta for Corporate Bonds." ETF.com.

Sklar, A. 1959. "Fonctions de répartition à n dimensions et leurs marges." *Publications de l'Institut de statistique de l'Université de Paris*, 8:229–231.

Stein, D. M. 1998. "Measuring and Evaluating Portfolio Performance After Taxes." *Journal of Portfolio Management* 24 (2): 117–124.

Stockton, K., S. J. Donaldson, and A. Shtekhman. 2014. "Liability-Driven Investing: A Tool for Managing Pension Plan Funding Volatility." Vanguard Investment Counseling and Research. https://institutional.vanguard.com/iam/pdf/ICRLDI .pdf.

Stubbs, R. 2013. "Consistent Portfolio Management: Alpha Construction." Axioma Research Paper No. 044. www.axioma.com/downloads/AxiomaResearch-ConsistentPortfolioConstruction.pdf.

Stubbs, R., and P. Vance. 2005. "Computing Return Estimation Error Matrices for Robust Optimization." *Report*, Axioma.

Thomas, R. 2014. "Innovations in Smart Beta." Plenary talk (State Street Global Advisors), BSAS Asset Allocation Conference, January 14, 2014, Boston, MA.

Tobin, J. 1958. "Liquidity Preference as Behavior Towards Risk." *Review of Economic Studies* 25 (2): 65-86.

Tukey, J.W. 1962. "The Future of Data Analysis." *Annals of Mathematical Statistics* 33 (1): 1–67.

Um, S. 2014. "How to Capture Alpha through Beta." Headlines, *Chief Investment Officer* (August 6).

van der Meer, R., and M. Smink. 1993. "Strategies and Techniques for Asset-Liability Management: An Overview." *Geneva Papers on Risk and Insurance* 18 (67): 144–157.

Vardharaj, R., F. J. Fabozzi, and F. J. Jones. 2004. "Determinants of Tracking Error for Equity Portfolios." *Journal of Investing* 13 (2): 37–47.

Volpert, K. E. 1997. "Managing Indexed and Enhanced Indexed Bond Portfolios." In *Managing Fixed Income Portfolios*, edited by Frank J. Fabozzi, 191–211. New York: John Wiley & Sons.

White, R. 2014. "The Pricing and Risk Management of Credit Default Swaps, with a Focus on the ISDA Model." OpenGamma Quantitative Research white paper. www.opengamma.com/sites/default/files/pricing-and-risk-management-credit-default-swaps-opengamma.pdf.

Würtz, D., Y. Chalabi, W. Chen, and A. Ellis. 2009. *Portfolio Optimization with R/Rmetrics, Rmetrics eBook*. Rmetrics Association and Finance online, Zurich. https://www.rmetrics.org/files/freepdf/PortfolioOptimizationSample.pdf.

Yu, L., X. Ji, and S. Wang. (2003). *Stochastic Programming Models in Financial Optimization: A Survey*. http://citeseerx.ist.psu.edu/viewdoc/summary?doi=10.1.1.202.8459.

Zenios, S., and P. Kang. 1993. "Mean-Absolute Deviation Portfolio Optimization for Mortgage-Backed Securities." *Annals of Operations Research* 45:433–450.

Ziemba, W., and J. Mulvey, eds. 1998. *Worldwide Asset and Liability Modeling*. Cambridge: Cambridge University Press.

Ziemba, W. T. 2003. *The Stochastic Programming Approach to Asset, Liability, and Wealth Management*. Charlottesville, VA: CFA.

Index

A

ABSs. *See* Asset-backed securities
Active management, 387, 389–390
  full-blown active, 390
Active/passive strategy, 264
Active portfolio strategy, 6–7
Active return, 261
Active risk decomposition. *See* Portfolio
Actual tracking error, 264
A-D. *See* Anderson-Darling
Adaptive decision variables, 185
Ad hoc methods, 16
Ad hoc portfolio selection, 331
A-D tests, 136
Adverse stock price movements,
  hedging (usage), 495–500
After-cost basis, 450
Agency residential mortgage-backed
  securities market, 362
Aggregate cash flow method, 437
Aguilar, J.-P., 226
AIG, bailout, 424
Algorithmic trading, 14
Alpha, 6, 232
  calculation/interpretation,
    261–264
  construction, factor models (usage),
    243–244
  models, 243
  strategies, 6–7
  tracking error, contrast, 261–264
Altera, acquisition, 14–15
Alternative asset classes, 3
Amenc, N., 271, 273–275
American option, 459
Amortizing securities, 369
AMPL language, 169

Analytics, 10–11
Anderson-Darling (A-D) test, 136
Annual cash flow method, 437
Annualized tracking error, 262–263
Annual required contribution, 439
Anticipative decision variables, 185
APT. *See* Arbitrage Pricing Theory
AR. *See* Autoregressive
Arbitrage
  arguments, 454
  opportunities, identification, 159
Arbitrage Pricing Theory (APT), 236,
  240
ARCH. *See* Autoregressive conditional
  heteroscedasticity
Archimedean copula family, 65
ARMA. *See* AutoRegressive Moving
  Average
Arnott, R.D., 271
Arrow-Pratt risk aversion coefficient,
  216
Arshanapalli, B., 106
Asian options, 459
Asness, C., 228
Asset, 442–443
  liability, management, 11
  management firms, guidelines, 450
  manager, funds management, 432
  pools, 364
  purchase, 455
  selection, 115
Asset allocation, 219
  decision, 1–3
  models, 11, 16–17
  optimization problem, 16–17
Asset-backed securities (ABSs), 362,
  364

Asset-backed securities (ABSs),
(*Continued*)
market, 362
prepayment options, 370
Asset classes, 1–3
alternative asset classes, 3
duration, contributions (comparison),
415e
50-securities portfolio, 413e
nontraditional asset classes, 3
returns, co-movements (correlations),
258e
risk factor breakdown, example, 241e
traditional asset classes, 3
Asset diversification, 203
capital market line, 216–220
case, 204–208
classical mean-variance optimization
framework, 208–212
efficient frontiers, 212–215
expected utility theory, 220–226
exponential utility function, 224
linear utility function, 223–224
logarithmic utility function, 224–226
power utility function, 224
quadratic utility function, 221–223
Asset price
denotation, 474
probabilities, 473–474
Asset returns
correlations, 242
co-variation, 108
volatility, 481
Atlantic option, 459
At-the-money options, 482–483
Authers, J., 273
Automated trading, 14
Autoregressive conditional
heteroscedasticity (ARCH) models,
23, 125–129
usage, 78
Autoregressive (AR) model, 108
AutoRegressive Moving Average
(ARMA), 108
Average active exposure, 350

Average daily volume (ADV) measures,
284
AVERAGE formulas, 261
Average life, 370
calculation, 370
Average movement, return impact,
417–418
Axioma, 21, 170, 242, 334
Axioma U.S. Equity Medium Horizon
Fundamental Factor Risk Model,
output, 274

B
Backfilling, 253
Backtest overfitting, 18
Backward-looking tracking error,
forward-looking tracking error
(contrast), 264–265
Badaoui, S., 442
Bai, J., 117
Bailey, D., 18
Balance sheet method, 437
Balchunas, E., 276
Balkema, A., 99
Bank for International Settlements
(BIS), 51
Barbell portfolio, 429–430
Barbell strategies, 392
Barclays 2012, 412
Barclays Capital U.S. Aggregate Bond
Index, 17, 269
Barclays Capital U.S. Credit Index, 405
Barclays Capital U.S. MBS Index, 405
Barclays Capital U.S. Treasury Index,
405
Barclays POINT system, 399, 415–417
Barone-Adesi, G., 527
Barra on Campus, 326, 330, 398, 399,
401
Barrett, Rick, 334
Barrier methods, 167
Barrier options, 459
Bartter, B., 471
Basel Committee on Banking
Supervision, 51

Basis, 496
  risk, 496
Bazaraa, M., 228
Benchmark
  selection, 260
Benchmarks, 260, 268–272
  curve, selection, 400
  sector allocation, 408e
Benders decomposition, 188
Ben-Tal, A., 198, 322
Bermuda option, 459
Bernoulli distribution (p=0.3), 33e
Bernoulli probability distribution,
  32–33
Bernoulli random variable, 32
Bernstein, D., 442
Bertsekas, D., 181, 183
Bertsimas, D., 167, 198, 322
Beta, 6, 232
  beta-adjusted equivalent market
    index units, 498–499
  coefficients, 246
  distribution PDF, 91
  estimated betas, 497
  function, 80
  investing, 272–276
  portfolio beta, 494
  smart beta, 273
  strategies, 390–391
  sum, 333
Beta distribution, 79, 90–91
  probability density functions,
    examples, 91e
Bid-ask spreads, 481–482
Bimodal distributions, 46
Binary optimization problem, 161
Binary variables, introduction,
  406
Binomial coefficients, 478
Binomial distribution, 35
  PMF, 37
  shape, 37e, 38e
  success probability (p=0.30), 36e
  usage, 35
Binomial probability distribution,
  34–37

formula, coefficients (appearance),
  478
Binomial trees
  method, 471
  one-period binomial tree, 473
  recombining, 476
  two-period binomial tree, usage,
    476e, 478e
  usage, 472–479
Birge, J., 188
BIS. *See* Bank for International
  Settlements
Bivariate elliptic distribution, example,
  93e
Bivariate normal distribution, values
  (simulation), 93e
Black, F., 216, 471
Black, R., 437
BlackRock, 257, 273
Black-Scholes formula, 472
  model assumptions, 480–481
  parameters, estimation, 482–484
  usage, 479–485
Black-Scholes model, 471
Black-Scholes model, application, 483
Black-Scholes option pricing formula,
  illustration, 479–480
Blattberg, R., 82, 96
Bloomberg L.P., 20
Boender, G.C.E., 181, 443
Bogentoft, E., 181, 189
Bondholder option provisions,
  370–371
Bond market
  fixed income instruments, 361–365
  sectors, 361–365
Bond portfolio
  duration, 378–379
  high-grade bond portfolio solution,
    439–442
  management strategies, 387e
  VaR/CVaR, estimation, 385
Bonds
  callable bonds, 369
  cash flows, 426e
  convertible bond, 371

Bonds (*Continued*)
  convexity, 380
    measure, 380
  dollar price change, 377
  embedded options, presence, 375
  exchangeable bond, 371
  high-yield bonds, 373–374
  indexing strategy, 402
  investment-grade bonds, 373, 432
  investment risks, 371–375
  issue, hedging, 525
  junk bonds, 373–374
  maturity, 365
  minimum price, determination, 525
  minimum yield, 525
  noninvestment-grade bonds,
    373–374
  payoff, provisions, 368–370
  prices, 426–427
    interest rate, relationship, 372e
    interest rates, relationship, 245
    shift, effect, 427e
  putable bond, 371
  refunding, prohibition, 369
  valuation, 367–368
  volatility, 519–520
  yields, 368
Bootstrapping, 72–73
  historical data, 188
Borge, D., 450
Borrowing
  cost, 537
    incorporation, 493–494
  rates, lending rates (differences),
    492–493
Bottom-up investment strategy, 251
Bouchard, J.-P., 226
Box uncertainty set, three dimensions,
  196e
Boyd, S., 229
Breger, L., 398, 399
Broad-based stock market index, usage,
  500
Buckets, 403
Bullet maturity, 369
Bullet portfolio, 429–430

Bullet strategies, 392
Burmeister, C., 437, 438
Butterfly (factor), 399–400
Buy hedge, 495
Buy-write strategy, 510–511

C
Callable bonds, 369, 402
Call and refunding provisions, 369–370
Call buyer, rights, 523
Call features, 431
Call futures options, 523
Call option, 459
  buyer, profit and loss profile,
    460–461
  payoff, 467e, 473e
    distribution, 465–466
  purchase/sale, 460
  writing, 461–462
Call premium, provision, 511
Call risk, 371, 372–373
Calmar ratio, 20
Canakoglu, E., 198, 436, 443
Capital
  difference, histogram/summary
    statistics, 146e
  histogram/summary statistics, 144e
  loss, increase, 430
  output distribution, 143e
Capital Asset Pricing Model (CAPM),
  235, 270
  beta, 19, 245
Capital IQ, 254
Capital market equivalents, 437
Capital Market Line (CML), 216–220
Cardinality constraints, 161, 286–287
Carino, D., 181
Carry, 458
  positive carry, 458
Carrying, 456
Cash-and-carry strategy, 517
Cash-and-carry trade, 456
  assumption, 492
  reverse cash-and-carry trade,
    457–458

theoretical futures price, 493
Cash-flow matching (complete
   matching)
  data, example, 433e
  immunization, 424
  problem
    Excel Solver dialog box, 436e
    Excel spreadsheet setup, 434e
  usage, 431–435
Cash market, theoretical futures price
  (price discrepancies), 493
Cash obligations, 432
Cash-secured put strategies, 509–510
Cash settlement contracts, 491
Cash yield, 458
Cattell, R.B., 120
Cauchy distribution PDF, 94
CDF. *See* Cumulative distribution
  function
CDP. *See* Conditional Default
  Probabilities
CDSs. *See* Credit default swaps
Cell-based approach, 403
Cells, 403
Center for Research in Security Prices
  (CRSP), 252
Central limit theorem (CLT), 69–71
Central moments, 225
Central tendency
  basis, 48e
  measures, 44–47
Ceria, S., 291, 322
Chance-constrained models, 191–193
Chance-constrained stochastic
  programming problem, 192
Changing variable cells, 171–172
Chaves, D., 228
Cheapest-to-deliver (CTD) issue,
  517–519
  conversion factor, 526
  minimum yield, 525–526
  usage, 525
Chen, N.-F., 193, 240
Cheyette, O., 398, 399
Chicago Mercantile Exchange (CME)
  contracts trades, 515–516

conversion factors publication, 517
Treasury bond futures contracts,
  delivery months, 523
Treasury futures, trading, 522
Chincarini, L., 18, 240, 326, 327, 330
Chi-square distribution, 79, 88–89
  PDF, 89
  probability density function, 89e
Chi-square goodness-of-fit tests, 89
Chi-square hypothesis, 136
Chi-square test statistic, critical value,
  89
Choueifaty, Y., 226, 227
Christoffersen, P., 275
Chryssikou, 183
CI. *See* Confidence interval
Classical mean-variance optimization
  framework, 208–212
  problem, formulations (alternative),
    215–216
Clayton copula, 65
  examples, 66e, 67e, 68e
Closing price, 452
CLT. *See* Central limit theorem
CML. *See* Capital Market Line
CMOs. *See* Collateralized mortgage
  obligations
CMT. *See* Constant maturity Treasury
Cocco, F., 181, 443
Coefficient of variation (CV), 49–50
COIN-OR. *See* Computational
  Infrastructure for Operations
  Research
Collar strategies, 509
  expiration payoff, 509e
Collateralized mortgage obligations
  (CMOs), 365
Collinearity, 113
Collins, B., 450, 510
Combinatorics, 36
Commercial mortgage-backed securities
  (CMBS), 364–365
  market, 362
Commodity derivatives, 449
Complete (cash-flow matching)
  immunization, 424

Compounding distributions, usage,
141–142
Computational Infrastructure for
Operations Research (COIN-OR)
project, 169
Concave function, 157
example, 158e
Conditional Default Probabilities
(CDP), 412
Conditional expectation, 62
Conditional PDF, 62
Conditional probability, 61–63
Conditional Recovery Rates (CRRs),
412
Conditional value-at-risk (CVaR), 19,
53–54
calculation, 127
estimation, 385
measure, 385
metrics, 353
normal CVaR, 54
optimization, 294–297
Confidence degree, 71
Confidence interval (CI), 71–72, 194
CONOPT, 168
Consigli, G., 181, 436, 443
Constant maturity Treasury (CMT)
rate, 528
Constraints, 152, 405
impact, 291
set, writing, 186–187
Continuous distributions, 38–39
Continuous probability distributions
description, notation (usage), 79–80
return, realization, 135
Continuous random variable, CDF
example, 42e
Continuous uniform distribution, 79,
80–82
probability distribution function,
examples, 82e
Continuum, display, 38–39
Contracts, number, 498, 520
Controlled turnover, 275
Conversion factors, 526
CME publication, 517

Converted price, equation, 517
Convertible bond, 371
Convex function, 157, 211
example, 158e
Convexity, 379–382
adjustment, 380–381
effective convexity, 381–382
measure, 379–380
scaling, 381
quadratic approximation, 380
standard convexity, 381–382
Convex programming, 157–158
Convolution, 60
Copulas, 64–66
density function, 65
functions, types, 66e, 67e
Corporate bonds, 363
index, usage, 535
market, 362
Corporate debt, LIBOR/swap curve
(usage), 400
Corporate spread risk, 415
Correlation
coefficient, 56, 205
Pearson correlation coefficient, 69
incorporation, 142–144
matrix, 57
maximum de-correlation weighting,
275
random variable dependence, 55–57
sample, 69
Spearman correlation, 69
Cost function, 181–182
Cost management strategies, 509–510
Cost of carry, 458
Counterparty risk, 452–453
Country-specific stock market indexes,
505
Coupons
coupon-bearing security, 367
payments, 426
periodic coupon payments,
366–367
rate, 365, 366–367
reset dates, 367
reset formula, 367

Covariance
  random variable dependence, 55–57
  sample, 69
Covariance matrix, 57
  decomposing, 248
Covered call strategy, 510–511
  expiration payoff, 510e
Cox, J.C., 471
CPLEX, 17
  optimization package, 171
cplexAPI[33] package, 171
Credit default swaps (CDSs), 487–488
  documentation, 532–533
  index CDS, 533
  single-name CDS, 533
  swap premium, 532
  usage, 532–538
Credit derivatives, 449, 487, 532
Credit enhancement agreements,
    complication, 386
Credit event, occurrence (absence), 537
Credit event risk, 400
  factors, 401
Credit-event scenario, 537
CreditMetrics, 228
Credit protection buyer, 532
Credit protection seller, 532
  cash flow, 534
Credit quality, 404e
  buckets/cells, 403
Credit risk, 371, 373–374
  control, credit default swaps (usage),
    532–538
  measurement, 384
  representation, 406
Credit spread
  change, 393
  factors, 400–401
  risk, 374
Cremers, J.H., 226, 292
Cross hedging, 496
Cross-sectional data, 11
  collection, 245
Cross-sectional regression, 247
CRRs. *See* Conditional Recovery Rates
CRSP. *See* Center for Research in
    Security Prices

Crystal Ball, usage, 137
CTD. *See* Cheapest-to-deliver
Cumulative distribution function
    (CDF), 41–42
  example, 42e
Cumulative probability
  concept, 41–44
  difference, 43e
Currency derivatives, 449
Currency risk factors, 401
Current yield curve, 426e
CUSIPs, 252
Custodial costs, 503
CV. *See* Coefficient of variation
CVaR. *See* Conditional value-at-risk

D
Dalio, R., 442
Dantzig, George, 166
Data, 11–12
  alignment, 252–253
  frame, usage, 261
  in-sample (test) data, 18
  linear transformation, 119
  out-of-sample (validation) data, 18
  set, average/standard deviation,
    261
  snooping, 254
Database Management Systems
    (DMBS), 14
Data management
  issues, 251–254
Dealer option, 459
Debentures, 363
Decision variables, 152, 163, 405
  copy, 187
  definition, 186
  linear functions, 211
  usage, 16, 158, 290
Default correlations, 412
Default-free cash flow, 367
Default process, 385
Default risk, 373–374
  market risk, dependence, 385–386
Defined benefit pension plans,
    liability-driven strategies, 438–443

Defined benefit plans, 420
Defined contribution plans, 420
Degrees of freedom, number (increase),
    148
Deguest, L., 442
de Haan, L., 99
Deliverable
  availability, 521
  securities basket, 494
Deliverable issues, 516
Delivery
  date, 457
  options, 518
  squeezes, 522
Delta, 472–473, 484
DeMiguel, V.L., 275
Dempster, M.A.H., 181, 443
Density generator, 93
Dependent variables, 109
Derivatives, 449
  commodity derivatives, 449
  credit derivatives, 449
  currency derivatives, 449
  equity derivatives, 449
  financial derivatives, 449
  interest rate derivatives, 449
  linear payoff derivatives, 465
  role, 477
    reduction, 450
  usage, 449–451, 490, 515
    process, 450–451
  values, infinite sum, 225
Dert, C., 181, 443
Descriptive statistics, 68
  usage, 138
Dickey-Fuller test, 113
Dimensionality reduction, 119–120,
    249
Discount factors, 426e
  considerations, 477–478
Discrete distributions, 34–37, 80–82
  generation, 188
Discrete probability distribution, 38
  variance, 190
Discrete random variable, CDF
  example, 42e

Discrete uniform distribution, 80
  probability mass function, 81e
Dispersion, 47
Distressed debt, 374
Distributions
  characteristic, measure (kurtosis), 44
  description, 44–55
  loss/profit (L/P) distribution, 51
  parameters, 135–136
  profit/loss (P/L) distribution, 51
  stable family, differentiating property,
    95–96
  superclass/family, 91
Diversification, 204–208
  effect, 206–207
  preference, 203–204
  proliferation, 60
  redefining, 226–230
Diversification ratio (DR), 226–227
Dividend payments, 362
  value, consideration, 492
Dividend yield, 246
DJIA. See Dow Jones Industrial Average
DJX. See Dow Jones Industrial Average
DMBS. See Database Management
  Systems
Dollar duration, 376–377
  calculation, 377
Dollar loss, 50
Donaldson, S.J., 424
Dorsel, M., 437
Dow Jones Industrial Average (DJIA)
  (DJX), 269, 498–499
Downgrade risk, 374, 400
DR. See Diversification ratio
Duration, 375–379
  bets, absence, 389
  calculation/equation, 376
  contributions, comparison, 415e
  determination, 426
  dollar duration, 376–377
  duration-based immunization
    strategy, plan sponsor usage, 441
  duration-based multiperiod
    immunization strategy, 431
  effective duration, 377–378

immunization, 423–424
inclusion, 403
key rate duration, 382–383
Macaulay duration, 377–378
modified duration, 377–378
option-adjusted duration, 378
rate duration, 382
strategies, 392
usage, example, 425–428
Durbin-Watson statistic, 113
Dynamic programming, 181–183
field, treatment, 181

E

Earnings variability, 246
Earnings yield (E/P), 243
EBITDA/EV, 252
Eckstein, J., 181
Economic forecasts, usage, 393
EDHEC-Risk Institute, 273
Effective convexity, 381–382
Effective duration, 377–378
example, 4043e
effFrontier, usage, 214
Efficient frontiers, 212–215
construction, 214
plotting, Excel Solver (usage), 214
Efficient Market Theory, 13–14
Effinger, A., 276
Eigendecomposition, 248, 548
Eigenvalues, 248, 548
Eigenvectors, 248, 548
Elbow, 120–121
Element-wise matrix multiplication,
546
Ellipsoidal uncertainty set, 196e
Elliptical distributions, 92–94, 221
Embedded options, presence, 375
Embrechts, P., 64, 127
Emerging market debt, impact, 401
Emerging market risk factors, 401
Empirical probability distribution, 66,
68
Employee Retirement Income Security
Act (ERISA), 282–283

End-of-year capital, 138
End-of-year distribution,
histogram/summary statistics,
138e
Engle, R.F., 108, 129
Enhanced indexing, 386, 388–389
strategy, 263–264, 409
Enterprise risk management (ERM),
437
Epsilon (terms), 234
Equally weighted portfolios, returns
(mean/standard deviation), 207e
Equations
linear system, 428
systems, 541–542
Equity derivatives, 449
Equity factors, usage, 325–327
Equity options
types, 504–506
Equity options, portfolio management
applications, 504–511
Equity portfolio management
cost management strategies, 509–510
strategies, options (usage), 506–511
Equity portfolio management,
derivatives (usage), 490
Equity swaps, 486–487, 511–512
Equivalent market index units
beta-adjusted equivalent market
index units, 498
calculations, 498–499
Error, 107
Errunza, V., 275
Escudero, L.F., 443
Estimate, variability, 71
Estimation error, notion, 319
Euclidean norm, 197
European call option
prices, time to maturity/volatility
values, 480e
pricing, two-period binomial tree
(usage), 476e, 478e
European option, 459
price, factors (summary), 471e
pricing
binomial trees, usage, 472–479

European option, (*Continued*)
  Black-Scholes formula, usage,
    479–485
  valuation, 526–527
European put option prices, time to
    maturity/volatility values, 480e
Euro STOXX 50 index option (OESX),
    505
Eurozone, 400
EV. *See* Extreme value
Evaluation period, 8–9
EVT. *See* Extreme Value Theory
Ex ante tracking error, 264
Excel regression output, example, 111e
Excel Solver, 23
  constraint dialog box, 173e
  dialog box, 172e, 435e, 436e
  Options dialog box, 174e
  portfolio allocation
    model, example, 176e
    problem inputs, 177e
  usage, 171–175
Excel spreadsheet, setup, 434e
Excess kurtosis, 94
  report, 55
Excess portfolio return, writing, 238
Excess, probability distribution, 98
Excess return portfolio, 442–443
Exchangeable bond, 371
Exchange-provided market indexes, 269
Exchange-traded fund, returns (usage),
    109
Exchange-traded option, 459
Exercise price, 459
Exotic options, 459
Expected return
  enhancement, 449
  estimation, 319
  formulation, 215
  maximization formulation, 215
Expected utility framework, 220–221
Expected utility theory, 220–226
Expiration
  date, 459
  payoff, 507e, 509e, 510e
Explanatory variables, 109

Exponential distribution, 79, 87–88
  memoryless property, 88
  probability distribution function,
    example, 88e
Exponential generalized beta
    distribution, 92
Exponential moving average, 126
Exponential utility function, 224
Ex post tracking error, 264
Exposures, vector, 266
External (macroeconomic) factors, 240
Extracted (statistical) factors, 240
Extreme events, 44
Extremes, asymptotic probability
    distribution, 98
Extreme value (EV) distributions,
    standard forms (PDFs), 100e
Extreme value (EV) models, 101–104
Extreme Value Theory (EVT), 79, 98,
    102
Exxon Mobile bond issue, reference
    obligation, 533

F
Fabozzi, F.J., 53, 106, 109, 129, 149,
    152, 167, 188, 197, 198, 214, 218,
    228, 249, 253, 295, 322, 450, 476,
    477, 481, 500, 510
Face value, 366
Factor, 232
  analysis, 107, 116–118
  attribution
    growth, 351e
    style factors, 349e
  currency risk factors, 401
  emerging market risk factors, 401
  equity factors, usage, 325–327
  exposure
    limits, 275
    targeting, 333–334
  factor-based fixed income portfolio
    construction/evaluation, 398
  factor-based investing, 256
  factor-based portfolio optimization,
    204

fundamental factor models, 246–247
growth potential/growth factors, 326
hybrid factor models, 250
K-dimensional vector, 117
liquidity factors, 327
loadings, 116–117, 236, 267
macroeconomic factors, 240, 327
   models, 245–246
models, 232
   building/updating, 251
   long-horizon factor models, 350, 353
   usage, 15, 117, 233–239, 243–244
neutrality, 275
numbers, reduction (goal), 118
operating efficiency factors, 326
operating profitability factors, 327
prepayment risk factors, 402
returns, 267
   historical performances, 352e
selection, usage, 239–243
solvency factors, 326–327
statistical factor models, 248–250
style factors, exposure analysis, 338e
technical factors, 327
term structure factors, 399–400
valuation/value factors, 326
volatility, 417
volatility risk factors, 402
Factor-based equity portfolio
equity factors, usage, 325–327
performance evaluation, 325
portfolio
   construction, 325
   performance evaluation, 346–350
risk decomposition, 334–342
selection, 331–334
stock screens, 328–331
stress testing, 343–346
Factor-mimicking portfolio (FMP), 243
FactSet, 250, 467
FactSet Research Systems, 20, 21
Fair swap rate, 531
Fama, E., 96, 217
Families, 91

Farm Credit Financial Assistance Corporation, 363
Fat-tailed distribution, 78
Fat tails, 23, 77, 94
Feasible portfolios, 214e
Federal agency securities, 363
   market, 362
Ferguson, N., 442
Ferstl, R., 181, 443
Finance, return models (usage), 106
Financial analytics, 11
Financial derivatives
   basics, 449
   usage, 423–424
Financial economics literature, factor models (usage), 233–236
Financial leverage, 246
Financial returns
   amplitude, variation, 125
   distributions
      modeling, 91–97
      tails, modeling, 98–104
   empirical distributions, 77
Financials, 363
Financial screening, 11, 15
Financial security, performance, 400
Financing cost, 458
Firm characteristics (fundamental factors), 240
Firm-wide security exposure, 344e
First moment, 45
Fisher-Tippett-Gnedenko Theorem, 98
Fitch Ratings, 373
Fixed-coupon bond, value, 531
Fixed horizon data, holding period, 424
Fixed income analytics, 375–386
Fixed income instruments, 361–365
Fixed income portfolio
   beta strategies, 390–391
   factor-based fixed income portfolio construction/evaluation, 398
   management, 361
      derivatives, usage, 515
   risk (estimation), simulation (usage), 384–386
   strategies, spectrum, 386–391

Fixed income risk factors, usage, 398–402
Fixed income securities, 3, 362
features, 365–371
Fixed-rate payer, 528
Fixed-rate receiver, 528
interest rate swap perspective, 529
notional amount, payment, 531
Flexible EXchange Options (FLEX options), 504
Floating-rate bond, value, 531–532
Floating-rate debt obligation, coupon payment dates, 536
Floating-rate payer, 528
Floating-rate receiver, 528
Floating-rate securities, 367
FMP. *See* Factor-mimicking portfolio
Focardi, S.M., 106, 109, 129, 152, 167, 188, 198, 218, 249, 253, 322
Fong, H.G., 429
Forward contracts, 451–458
pricing, 454–458
Forward/futures position, risk/return, 453
Forward-looking tracking error, backward-looking tracking error (contrast), 264–265
Forward price, 451
Forward rate, 451
current market consensus, 530
Forwards
futures, comparison, 451
options, risk/return (contrast), 464–465
fportfolio, 214
Fragniere, E., 187
Frank copula, 65, 66e, 67e
Frazzini, A., 228
Froidure, T., 227
Fundamental factors, 326–327
models, 250
Fundamental factors (firm characteristics), 240
models, 246–248
Fundamental investing, 256
Fund assets, market value, 438

Funding gap, 438, 440
interest rate risk, calculation, 439
Funding ratio, 438, 440
Future portfolio risk/return, forecasts, 353
Futures
forwards, comparison, 451
leveraging aspects, 453–454
options, 521–522
impact, 522
risk/return, contrast, 464–465
price
convergence, 501
volatility (standard deviation), 527
Futures contracts, 451–458
delivery, 453
initial/variation margin, absence, 457
number, formula, 518
pricing, 454–458
model, 455
put option, impact, 522–523
settlement, 456, 457
Futures options
models, 526–527
pricing model, 527

G
GAAP. *See* Generally Accepted Accounting Principles
Gamma, 484
distribution, 79, 90
probability density function, example, 90e
function, 82
GAMS language, 169
GARCH. *See* Generalized Autoregressive Conditional Heteroscedasticity
Garin, A., 443
Garlappi, L., 275
Gaussian (normal) copula, 65
examples, 66e, 67e, 68e
GDP. *See* Gross domestic product
Geer, Andrew, 334

Generalized Autoregressive Conditional
Heteroscedasticity (GARCH), 23
  models, 125–126
  usage, 78
Generalized beta distribution, 92
Generalized extreme value (GEV)
  distribution, 98–99
Generalized lambda distribution (GLD),
  96–97
  family, 92
Generalized Pareto distribution (GPD),
  99–101
  probability density function
  equation, 100
  example, 101e
Generally Accepted Accounting
  Principles (GAAP), 243
General obligation debt, 364
Genetic algorithms, 168
GEV. *See* Generalized extreme value
GIC. *See* Guaranteed investment
  contract
Glasserman, P., 148
GLD. *See* Generalized lambda
  distribution
Global minimum variance (GMV)
  portfolio, 215
Global optima, local optima (contrast),
  155–156
Global stock indexes, 505
GMV. *See* Global minimum variance
GNU Linear Programming Kit, 171
Goldfarb, D., 322
Goltz, F., 271, 273–275
Gondzio, J., 187, 443
Gonedes, N., 82
Good-faith money, 452
Goodness-of-fit test, rule (absence), 136
Gossett, W.S., 82
Government National Mortgage
  Association (GNMA), 365
Government-related spread risk, 415
Government-sponsored enterprises
  (GSEs), 363
GPD. *See* Generalized Pareto
  distribution

GPM. *See* Gross profit margin
Greeks, The, 484
Gross domestic product (GDP), 327
Gross profit margin (GPM), 327
Growth at a Reasonable Price (GARP),
  328
Growth factors, 326
  portfolio, relationship, 350
  time series analysis, 350
Growth potential factors, 326
Growth strategies, 264
GSEs. *See* Government-sponsored
  enterprises
Guaranteed investment contract (GIC)
  account, presence, 5
  issue, 425
  management, 424
Guaranteed investment contract (GIC)0
  liability, 425
Guaranteed liabilities, zero-coupon
  bonds (matching), 437
Gulpinar, N., 188, 198, 436, 443
Gumbel copula, 65, 66e, 67e

H
Hadamard product, 546
Harvey, C., 239
Heavy tails, presence, 125
Hedges
  buy hedge, 495
  long hedge, 495
  perfect hedge, 495
    examination, 499–500
  ratio, 497
    calculation/determination, 519,
    520, 526
  sell hedge, 495
  short hedge, 495
Hedging, 519
  controlling, 495–496
  cross hedging, 496
  perfect hedging, 471
  strategy, implementation, 497
  usage, 495–500
Heemskerk, F., 181, 443

Heteroscedasticity, 125
Heuristic, 167
Higher-frequency asset returns data,
   heavy tails (presence), 125
High-grade bonds, 441
   portfolio solution, 439–442
High minus low book-to-price ratio
   (HML), 244
High-yield bonds, 373–374
Hillier, R.S., 181
Histograms
   marginal distributions, example, 63e
   usage, 353
Historical volatility estimates, 484
Hodges, P., 2
Hoek, H., 181, 443
Hofert, Marius, 65
Hogan, K., 2
Holding constraints, 283
Homoscedasticity, 125
   assumption, 113
Hsu, J., 228, 271
Huang, C., 223
Hull, J., 477
Hybrid factor models, 250
Hypothesis testing, 73–75

I
IBES. *See* Institutional Broker Estimates
   System
IBM Algo
   enterprise risk management (ERM),
     437.
   portfolio risk management, 22
IBM Algorithmics, 20
IBM Cognos, 14
IBM ILOG CPLEX, 17, 168–169, 198
IBM SmartCloud, 22
IBM SPSS Modeler, 14
Identity matrix, 543
Idiosyncratic monthly tracking error,
   413e
Idiosyncratic (nonsystematic) risk, 412
   corporates, contribution, 413
IID, 70

I_i-dimensional vectors, 160
Immunization, 424–438
   categories, 424
   mechanism, 425
   multiperiod immunization, 424
   results, 429e
   risk, 428–431
     example, 430e
   single-period immunization, 424
   strategy, extension, 429
Immunized portfolio, construction, 431
Implied probability, calculation, 482
Implied repo rate, 517
Importance sampling, 188
Independent variables, 109
Index CDS, 533
Index, dollar value (calculation), 505
Indexed portfolio, construction,
   500–504
Indexes, 268–272
   market indexes, 268–270
   noncapitalization weighted indexes,
     270–272
Index funds, 133–134
   creation, 503
   custodial costs, 503
Indexing, 260
   criticism, 388
   strategy, 389
     pursuit, 388
Index options, 504
   types, 504–505
Individual security selection strategies,
   394–396
Industrials sector, 363
Infinite variance, 78
Inflation risk, 422–423
Information ratio (IR), 19
   tracking error, relationship, 265
Ingersoll, J., 181, 216
Initial margin, 451–452, 455
   Treasury bills, usage, 501
Input variables
   impact, visualization, 143
   usage, 141–142
In-sample (test) data, 18

Institutional Broker Estimates System
(IBES) database, 252
Institutional investors
account types, 5
investment objectives, 4
options vehicle, 522
Insurance cost, 508
Integer programming (IP), 161,
167–168
Integration, concept, 39
Intercept term, concern (absence), 115
Interest rate risk, 371–372, 421–422
control, 427
interest rate swaps, usage, 527–532
strategies, Treasury futures (usage),
518–520
Treasury futures options, usage,
521–527
Treasury futures, usage, 515–521
immunization, 440–441
measurement, 375–383
Interest rates
bond price, relationship, 372e
changes, portfolio return attribution,
399, 430
derivatives, 449
expectations strategies, 391–392
level, decrease, 394
shift, 426
swaps, 485–486
rates, relationship, 400
term structure, 363, 368
Interest rate swaps
dollar duration, calculation, 529
position, fixed-rate receiver
perspective, 529
pricing, 530–532
usage, 527–532
Interim cash flows, 492
absence, 452
Interior point methods, 166
Intersector allocation strategies, 391,
393–394
In-the-money call options, volatility
smile, 483e
In-the-money option, 470, 482–483

Intrasector allocation strategies, 391,
393–394
Intrinsic value, 470
Inverted yield curve, 368
Investing, single-period view, 282
Investments
horizon, 429
investment-grade bonds, 373
market, 365
management process, regression
applications, 114–115
manager, requirements/limitations
(constraints), 17
objectives, setting, 4–5
policy, setting, 114
risk/return, leverage (effect), 276e
strategy, type (selection), 6–7
Invoice price, equation, 517
IP. *See* Integer programming
IR. *See* Information ratio
iShares Exchange-Traded Funds, 257
Isolated tracking error, 414
ITG, 170
Ito's stochastic calculus, 471
iTraxx Europe, 533
Iyengar, G., 322

J
Jacobs, K., 275
Jasic, Teo, 109, 249
J-dimensional vector, 160
JdK RS-Ratio, 13
Jensen's alpha, 19
Ji, X., 188
Joint (scatterplot) distributions,
example, 63e
Joint probability, 61–62
Joint probability distributions, 61–63
Jorion, P., 315
Junior notes, 364
Junk bonds, 373–374

K
Kahneman, D., 226
Kahn, R., 256, 257

Kaiser, H.F., 121
Kaiser's criterion, 121
Kang, P., 181
Karmakar, Narendra, 166
Karush-Kuhn-Tucker (KKT) conditions, 166–167
Key rate duration, 382–383, 416
K factors, 236, 249
Kim, D., 18, 240, 326, 327, 330
KKT. *See* Karush-Kuhn-Tucker
Kojadinovic, Ivan, 65
Kolmogorov-Smirnov (K-S) test, 136
Kolm, P., 152, 167, 188, 198, 218, 228, 253, 322
Kouwenberg, R., 181, 443
Kritzman, M., 116, 226, 292
Kurtosis, 44, 55, 142
  excess kurtosis, report, 55
k values, 73, 82

L
Ladder strategies, 392
Lagged values, 107
Lazanas, Anthony, 405
LEAPS. *See* Long-Term Equity Anticipation Securities
Lee, J-H., 291, 321
Lee, W., 228
Left-skewed distribution, 54, 77
Lemmon, M., 256, 257
Lending rates, borrowing rates (differences), 492–493
Leptokurtic distributions, 77
Leverage, 453–454
  effect, 276e
  meaning, 454
  usage, 494
Levy distribution PDF, 94–95
Levy, P., 94, 226
Liabilities
  dollar duration, 440
  liability-driven objectives, 5
  liability-driven portfolios modeling strategies, 443
  liability-driven portfolios, construction, 420

liability-driven strategy, 441–442
  risks, 421–423
Liability-driven strategies
  types, 439
  usage, 420, 422–438
LIBOR. *See* London Interbank Offered Rate
Li, F., 228
Life insurance companies, liability-driven strategies, 423–438
Lindskog, F., 64
Linear algebra
  concepts, 541
  definitions, 546–548
  equations, systems, 541–542
  matrices, 542–543
  matrix algebra, 543–546
  vectors, 542–543
Linear expressions, 107
  sums/differences, involvement, 158
Linear optimization
  formulations, 158
  problems, 159, 296
  solver, usage, 428
Linear payoff derivatives, 465
Linear programming (LP), 157–158
Linear regression model, 233
Linear relationship, determination, 110e
Linear transformation, 119
Linear utility function, 223
Lintner, J., 216
Liquidation effect, 414e
Liquidity
  factors, 327
  risk, 371, 374–375
Listed option, 459
Litzenberger, R., 223
Liu, Y., 239
Local optima, global optima (contrast), 155–156
Location parameter, 94
Lodh, A., 274, 2731
Logarithmic utility function, 224–226
Lognormal distribution, 79, 83–85
  probability distribution function, 84e

Log returns, 85
London Interbank Offered Rate
    (LIBOR), 367, 486–487
  benchmarking, 528
  borrowing cost, 537
  coupon rate, 535–536
  LIBOR/swap curve, usage, 400
  spread, 512, 537
Long call position, expiration
    (profit/loss profile), 461e, 462e
Longevity risk, 423
Long hedge, 495
Long-horizon factor models,
    350, 353
Longitudinal data, collection, 245
Long-only (no-short-selling)
    constraints, 283
Long position, expiration (profit/loss
    profile), 461e
Long put option, expiration (profit/loss
    profile), 462–463, 463e, 464e
Long stock position, sum, 509
Long-Term Equity Anticipation
    Securities (LEAPS), 504, 505–506
Look-ahead bias, 253–254
Lopez de Prado, M., 18
Loss/profit (L/P) data, usage, 52e
Loss/profit (L/P) distribution, 51
Low discrepancy, 150
LP. *See* Linear programming
L/P. *See* Loss/profit
Lynch screen, description, 328

M
Macaulary duration, 377–378
Macaulay, Frederick, 378
Macroeconomic (external) factors, 240,
    327
  models, 245–246
Maechler, Martin, 65
Maginn, J.L., 4
Maillard, S., 228, 271, 274
Maintenance margin, 452
Malkiel, B.G., 207–208
Mandelbrot, B., 92, 94, 208

Margalit, T., 198, 322
Marginal distributions, computation,
    63
Marginal (histograms) distributions,
    example, 63e
Marginal probability distribution, 63
Marginals, 66e
  example, 67e
Marked-to-market futures contracts,
    452–453
Market analytics, 10, 12–15
Market capitalization
  market indexes, 270
  usage, 271
Market conditions, simulated
    value-at-risk, 355e
Market indexes, 268–270
  groups, classification, 268
  returns, linear relationship
    (determination), 110e
Market interest rate, 486
Marketplace price efficiency, 7
Market portfolio, 217–218
Market research reports, 10
Market risk, default risk (dependence),
    385–386
Market sectors, 403
Market-wide credit spread
  factors, 401
  risk, 400
Markowitz efficient frontier, 450
Markowitz framework, consistency,
    221
Markowitz, Harry, 49, 60, 203, 226,
    281, 292
  framework, 208–209
Markowitz mean-variance formulation,
    214–215
Martellini, L., 271, 273, 275, 442
Martin, C., 242, 291
MATLAB, 168–169
Matrices, 542–543
  identity matrix, 543
  null matrix, 543
  positive definite/semi-definite
    matrices, 547

Matrix
  algebra, 543–544
  arrays, 152
    multiplication, 208, 544–545
    sum, 544
  equality, 543
  inverse, 546
  matrix-vector notation, 152
  nonsingular matrix, 546
  notation, 208
  orthogonal matrix, 547
  symmetric matrix, 547
  transpose, 208, 544
Matson, P., 437
Maturity, 365–366, 403
  date, 459
  guarantees, 437
  swap rates, 532
  value, 366
Max $f(x)$, optimal objective function
  values, 155e
Maxima, 98
Maximization, minimization (contrast),
  154–155
Maximum de-correlation weighting,
  275
Maximum drawdown, 20
Maximum Sharpe ratio weighting, 275
maxSharpe, usage, 214
MBSs. *See* Mortgage-backed securities
McCoy, Bill, 334
McNeil, A., 64, 127
MDP, 227
Mean
  central tendency measure, 44, 45–46
  sample, 68
Mean-risk stochastic models, 189–191
Mean-variance efficient portfolios,
  214e
Mean-variance framework, application
  (limitation), 281
Mean-variance optimization
  factor models, usage, 236–239
  framework, 208–212
  problem, formulations (alternative),
    215–216

Mean-variance portfolio optimization,
  203
Median, central tendency measure, 44,
  46
Memoryless property, 88
Merino, M., 443
Merton, R.C., 181
MGF. *See* Moment-generating function
Michaud, R., 315
Milhau, V., 442
Min -$f(x)$, optimal objective function
  values, 155e
Minima, 98
Minimization
  maximization, contrast, 154–155
  problem, 319
Minimum holding constraints,
  287–288
Minimum variance portfolio, 215
Minimum volatility weighting, norm
  constraints (usage), 275
Minor risk factor mismatches, 386, 389
MINOS, 168, 197
MIP. *See* Mixed integer programming
Misalignment, constraints (impact), 291
Mitchell, J.E., 189
Mittnik, S., 94, 109, 249
Mixed integer programming (MIP),
  161, 168
Mode, central tendency measure, 44,
  46–47
Modeling, enabling, 12
Modeling language, problem
  (formulation), 187
Modern Portfolio Theory (MPT), 22,
  78, 203
  usage, 77
Modified duration, 377–378
  calculation, 378
Moment-generating function (MGF), 45
Moments, concept, 45
Momentum, 246
Monte Carlo simulation, 133, 189, 436
  capital
    difference, histogram/summary
      statistics, 146e

output distribution, 143e
correlations, incorporation, 142–144
decisions, evaluation, 144–147
example, 133–140
inputs, probability distributions
(selection), 135–136
input variables/compounding
distributions, 141–142
output, interpretation, 137–140
random number generation, 149–150
scenarios, number, 147–149
strategies, comparison, 145e
system, example, 134e
usage, 467
reason, 140–147
Monthly tracking errors, 416e
Moody's Investors Service, 373
Moore, P., 271
Mortgage-backed securities (MBSs),
362, 402
market, 415
prepayments, 431
options, 370
Mortgage-passthrough securities, 365
MOSEK, 168
solver interface, 171
Moving average, 108
defining, 126
MSCI Barra, 21, 170, 242, 334, 402
market/fundamental data, 251
MSCI Factor Indexes, 271
Multiaccount optimization, 304–308
Multicollinearity, 113, 245
Multifactor risk model, usage, 266–268
Multinomial distributions, 46, 62
Multiperiod immunization, 424
Multi-period investment problem,
formulation, 436
Multiperiod modeling, value (question),
282
Multiperiod portfolio optimization
models, 282
Multi-period settings, 180–181
Multiple periods, generalization,
475–476
Multiple testing problem, 18

Multistage stochastic programming
models, 184
Multivariate normal distributions, 62
Multivariate probability distributions
contours, 67e
probability density functions, 66e
Mulvey, J.R., 181, 183, 189, 443
Municipal bonds, 364
market, 362
Municipal security structures, types,
364
Mutual fund, proceeds (usage), 162

N
NASDAQ 100 Index Option (NDX),
505
Natarajan, K., 193, 198, 322
NAV. *See* Net asset value
N-dimensional vector, 160
NDX. *See* NASDAQ 100 Index Option
Neighborhood (solutions), 155
Nemirovski, A., 198, 322
Net asset value (NAV), 162
Net exposure, 417
Net financing cost, 458
Net Market Weight, 413
Net profit margin (NPM), 327
Ng, V., 108
Nikkei 225 Index, total returns, 512
No-arbitrage pricing, 471
No-credit-event scenario, 537
Nogales, F., 275
Nominal spread, 383
Nonagency residential mortgage
securities market, 362
Nonanticipativity conditions, writing,
187
Noncapitalization weighted indexes,
270–272
Nondeterministic parameters, 180
Non-European options, pricing, 477
Nonfinancial index, 367
Noninvestment-grade bonds, 373–374
Nonliability-driver objectives, 5
Nonlinear payoff, 465

Nonnegativity constraints, 164–165
Nonrecombining tree, 476
Nonsingular matrix, 546
Nonsystematic (idiosyncratic) risk, 232, 412
Nontraditional asset classes, 3
Non-Treasury bond market, 395
Non-Treasury securities, holding, 393
Non-U.S. bond market, 362
Nonweighted market capitalization indexes, 272
Normal (Gaussian) copula, 65
    examples, 66e, 67e, 68e
Normal CVaR, 54
Normal distribution, 38–41
    standard normal distribution, 40e
Normalization, 247
Normalized portfolio, 118
Normal random variable, realizations, 63e
Normal VaR, 52
Norm constraints, usage, 275
NORMDIST command, 54
NORMINV (RAND()), usage, 137
North America High Yield Index, 533
North America Investment Grade Index, 533
Northfield, 334
Northfield Financial Services, 21
Northfield Information Services, 21, 170, 242, 401
No-short-selling (long-only) constraints, 283
Notional, 366
Notional amount, 486
    payment, 531
Notional coupon, 515–516
NPM. *See* Net profit margin
Null hypothesis, 73
Null matrix, 543

O

OAS. *See* Option-adjusted spread
Objective cell, 171
Objective function, 152, 405

usage, 16
weighted average, maximization, 183
writing, 186
OESX. *See* Euro STOXX 50 index option
OEX. *See* Standard & Poor's 100 Index Option
OLS. *See* Ordinary least squares
One-period binomial tree, 473e
One-sample hypothesis tests, 74
Open-end investment company, proceeds (usage), 162
Operating efficiency factors, 326
Operating profitability factors, 327
Operating profit margin (OPM), 327
OPM. *See* Operating profit margin
Optimal objective function values, example, 155e
Optimal solution, 153, 166
Optimization, 403
    advanced approaches, 435–436
    algorithms, 166–168
    approach, 405–408
    Excel Solver, usage, 171–175
    formulations, 152–157
    integer programming, 161
    linear programming, 158–159
    local optima, global optima (contrast), 155–156
    minimization, maximization (contrast), 154–155
    mixed integer programming, 161
    modeling, 151
        context, 107
        languages, 168–169
    multiple objectives, 156–157
    portfolio allocation example, solution, 175–178
    problem
        formulation, 229
        relaxation, 167
        solution, 406
        statement, 433
    quadratic programming, 159–160
    randomized search algorithms, 168
    robust optimization, 154, 194–198

second-order cone programming
(SOCP), 160–161
software, 168–170
implementation, example, 170–178
solver, 195
unconstrained optimization, 152–153
Optimization problem
convex programming, 157–158
decision variables, 163
formulation, 211
example, portfolio allocation,
161–166
modification, 153
portfolio manager problem, data,
162e
types, 157–161
Optimization under uncertainty, 180
chance-constrained models, 191–193
dynamic programming, 181–183
mean-risk stochastic models,
189–191
multistage models, 184–189
robust optimization, 194–198
stochastic programming, 183–193
Optimizer, usage, 409
Option-adjusted duration, 378
Option-adjusted spread (OAS), 384
zero-volatility OAS, 384
Option-free bonds, convexity measure,
382
Options, 459
delivery options, 518
equity options, portfolio management
applications, 504–511
holder, 459
intrinsic value, 470
life, risk-free rate, 481
premium, 459
price, 459
components, 470
pricing model, 470–485
quality option, 518
risk/return
characteristics, 460–469
contrast, 464–465
positions, summary, 464

swap option, 518
time value, 470
timing option, 518
types, 459
vehicles, 522
wildcard option, 518
Options on physicals, 521–522
Ordinary least squares (OLS), 109
Orthogonal matrix, 248, 547
Orthogonal vectors, 547
Orthonormal vectors, 547
OSL/SE (IBM), 189
Out-of-sample (validation) data, 18
Out-of-the-money option, 470,
482–483
Over-the-counter (OTC) market, 451,
459
Treasury securities trade, 522
Over-the-counter (OTC) option, 459
cost, increase, 459–460
Overwrite strategy, 510–511

P
Pachamanova, D.A., 53, 149, 152, 167,
193, 197, 198, 214, 218, 295, 322,
436, 443, 476, 477, 481, 500
Page, S., 226, 292
Parameters, 68
Parametric models, usage, 188
Paretian distributions, 92, 94, 96, 208
Pareto-Levy distributions, 94
Parsimony, 114
Partial immunization (duration
immunization), 423–424
duration, usage (example), 425–428
Par value, 365, 366
Passive investment strategy, 260
Passive portfolio strategy, 6–7
PCA. *See* Principal components analysis
PDFs. *See* Probability density functions
Peaks-over-threshold (POT) approach,
102–103
Pearson correlation coefficient, 69
Pedersen, L.H., 228
Pension plans, types, 420

Pension Protection Act (2006), 420
Percentage price change
  convexity adjustment, 380–381
  total estimated percentage price
    change, 380–381
Percentiles, 50
Perez, G., 443
Perfect hedge, 495
  examination, 499–500
Perfect hedging, 471
Performance
  attribution, 20, 254–256
    analysis, 115
  evaluation, 11, 18–20, 115
  measurement, 8–9, 115
  performance-seeking portfolio,
    442–443
Periodic coupon payments, 366–367
P&G
  example, Excel regression output,
    111e
P&G stock (returns), linear relationship
  (determination), 110e
Pickands-Balkema-deHaan theorem,
  102
Pickands, J., 99
P/L. *See* Profit/loss
Plan sponsor, impact (failure), 439
PMF. *See* Probability mass function
POINT advance portfolio analytics,
  411–412
Poisson distribution, 79, 85–87
  probability mass function, example,
    86e
Poisson PMF, 86
Pool of assets, 364
Portfolio
  active return, 261
  active risk decomposition, 336e
  ad hoc portfolio selection, 331
  adjustment, 9
  analytics, 1
    overview, 10–22
    systems, 20–22
  asset components, value, 473
  beta, 494

change, issues, 409
conditional value-at-risk (CVaR)
  optimization, 294–297
constraints, usage, 282–291
construction, 395, 437–438
  cash-flow matching, usage, 432
  tracking error, usage, 260
diversification, 257
dollar duration, 440
  change, 441
duration, 378–379
  contribution, 379
efficient frontier, 213e
end-of-year return, 19
equally weighted portfolios, returns
  (mean/standard deviation), 207e
equity portfolio management,
  derivatives (usage), 490
example, 407e–408e
expected return, 153
  change, 206e
  enhancement, 449
  standard deviation, pairings, 213e
factor-based equity portfolio, 325
factor-based fixed income portfolio
  construction/evaluation, 398
feasible portfolios, 214
50-securities portfolio, 414e
funds, addition/withdrawal, 409
growth factor, relationship, 350
indexed portfolio, construction,
  500–504
liability-driven portfolios,
  construction, 420
maturity, key rate duration, 382–383
mean, computation, 207e
mean-variance efficient portfolios,
  214
monitoring, 8
optimization, tail risk measures
  (usage), 291–297
options (presence), risk estimation
  (usage), 465–469
performance
  evaluation, 346–350
  metrics, 353

strategy testing/evaluation, 17–20
present value, 474–475
profit/loss (P/L) distribution, 51
quantitative equity portfolio
   management, advances, 281
rebalancing, 9, 408–410
   optimizer, usage, 409
   trades, optimal set, 410e
resampling, 314–317
returns
   attribution, 399
   variability, 19
risk
   characteristics, modification, 449
   estimation, 469
   management, derivatives (role), 477
sector allocation, 408e
selection, 331–334, 402–410
simulated profit/loss distribution,
   468e
simulated value-at-risk
   current/extreme market conditions,
     355e
   example, 354e
standard deviation
   change, 206e
   computation, 207e
stocks, number (limits), 275
strategy
   development/implementation, 6–8
   selection, 114–115
summary report, 411e
target dollar duration, calculation,
   529–530
tracking error, 405
value, 428, 473e
   comparison, 474, 502e
value-at-risk (VaR) optimization, 192,
   292–294
variance
   computation, 209–210
   minimization, 212
volatility, ratio, 497
Portfolio allocation
   ad hoc methods, 16
   example, solution, 175–178

Excel Solver example, 176e
   problem, Excel Solver inputs, 177e
   stratification approach, usage,
     404–405
   tracking error, 408
Portfolio construction, 7–8
   inputs, formulation, 7
Portfolio management, 1
   applications, 490–511
   derivatives, usage, 449–451
   fixed income portfolio management,
     361
   process, 4–9
   process, stratification (usage), 332
   strategies, stock index futures (usage),
     494–504
Portfolio manager
   economic forecasts, usage, 393
   example, 395
   indexing strategy, pursuit, 388
   loss, 508
   problem, data, 162e
   pursuit, 388
   stratification approach, application,
     409
   views, changes, 409
Positive carry, 458
Positive definite matrices, 547
Positive semi-definite matrices, 547
Positive semi-definite matrix, 159
POT. *See* Peaks-over-threshold
Potters, M., 226
Potts, M., 2
Power utility function, 224
Pre-agreed notional amount, 486
Predicted tracking error, 264
   calculation, 265–268
Predictor variables, 109
Preferred stock, 361–362
Prepayments, 370
   options, 370
   provisions, 369, 370
   rate, assumption, 370
   risk, 371, 372–373
     factors, 402
Present value, example, 428

Price-to-earnings (P/E) ratio, 246
Price value of a basis point (PVBP),
 519–520
Price-weighing method, 16
Price, yield (relationship), 526
Primal-dual interior point methods, 167
Primary risk factor matching, 386,
 388–389
Principal, 366
Principal components
 example, 122e
 standard deviations, 123e
 stocks data, representation (example),
  124e
Principal components analysis (PCA),
 107, 118–125, 248
Private Export Funding Corporation,
 363
Private-label RMBS, 365
Probabilistic parameters, 180
Probabilities, assignation, 31–32
Probability density functions (PDFs),
 38–43
 examples, 68e, 82e
Probability distributions, 31, 66–76,
 77, 527
 Bernoulli probability distribution,
  32–33
 binomial probability distribution,
  34–37
 comparison, risk/central tendency
  basis, 48e
 definition, 31–32
 evaluation, algorithm, 469
 examples, 79–91, 467e
 first moment, 45
 fourth moment, 55
 joint probability distributions, 61–63
 selection, 135–136
 third moment, 54
Probability mass function (PMF),
 32–33, 37, 78
Probability theory, 66–76
Profit/loss (P/L) distribution, 51
Profit/loss (P/L) profile, 461e
Program trading, 14

ProShares Large Cap Core Plus, 276
Protection buyer, 487
Protection seller, 487
Protective put
 put option, purchase/involvement,
  507
 strategies, 506–507, 524
  expiration payoff, 507e
Pure bond index
 matching, 386
 strategy, 387–388
Pure bond index matching strategy,
 387–388
Putable bond, 371
Put buyer, rights, 523
Put options, 459
 impact, 522–523
 purchase, 460, 462–463
 sale, 460
 usage, 437
 writing, 463
Put price, 371
p-value, 111–112
 examination, 115
PVBP. *See* Price value of a basis point
Python (open source alternative), 169

Q
Qian, E., 228
Quadratic optimization programming,
 159
Quadratic programming (QP), 157,
 159–160
Quadratic utility function, 221–223
Qualitative asset managers, impact, 11
Quality issues, 251–254
Quality option, 518
Quantile-quantile (Q-Q) plots, 102, 112
Quantitative asset management,
 traditional asset management
 (contrast), 9–10
Quantitative asset managers, impact, 11
Quantitative equity portfolio
 management
 advances, 281

multiaccount optimization, 304–308
portfolio
  constraints, 282–291
  resampling, 314–317
portfolio optimization, tail risk
  measures (usage), 291–297
robust parameter estimation,
  312–314
robust portfolio optimization,
  317–323
taxes, usage, 308–312
transaction costs, usage, 297–304
Quantitative investment management
  system, 12e
Quantitative modeling, 11
Quantitative portfolio management, 10
Quarterly swap premium payment,
  533–534

R
R^{23} (open source alternative), 169
Rachev, S., 94, 106, 109, 249
Randomized search algorithms, 168
Random noise (white noise), 107
Random number generation,
  149–150
Random shock, 106
Random variables, 31, 32
  addition, 142
  Bernoulli random variable, 32
  central moments, 225
  conditional expectation, 62
  constant, addition, 142
  dependence, 55–57
  distribution, observations, 34e
  marginal distributions, 93e
  multiplication, 142
  name, 34
  range, 50
  sum, 57–61
    convolution, 61e
    standard deviation, 59
    variances, 193
  tilde, denotation, 134
  value, probability calculation, 43e

Range (random variables), 50
Rank correlation, 69
Ransenberg, D., 2
RapidMiner, 14
Rate duration, 382
Rating agencies, 373
Rcplex^{34} package, 171
Realizations
  connected graph, 58e
  pairs, plotting, 57
Real-time market data, analysis, 10
Recombining, 476
Recovery rate, 385
Redemption value, 366
Reference entity, 532–533
Reference obligation, 533
Reference rate, 486
  future value, 530–531
Regression
  analysis, 108–115
  applications, 114–116
  error, 240
  example, 109–114
  residuals, 112
  usage, 497
Reinvestment rates, 430
Reis, Ed, 334
Relative Rotation Graphs (RRGs), 13
Relative strength, 12
Relative value strategies, 391
Rendleman, R., 471
Replicating portfolios (replios), 454
  construction, 437–438
  usage, 438
Research Affiliates, 273
Residential mortgage-backed securities
  (RMBS), 364–365
  private-label RMBS, 365
Residual risk matrix, 242
Response variables, 109
Retkowsky, P., 271, 275
Return attribution analysis, 115
Return on total capital (ROTC), 327
Return on total equity (ROTE), 327
Returns
  attribution analysis, 8–9

Returns (*Continued*)
distributions
characteristics, modeling
(categories), 78
fat-tailed/skewed characteristics, 78
stability, assumption, 78
empirical distribution, 77
enhancement, 506
strategies, 510–511
enhancing strategies, 391
estimation models, usage, 106–108
expected return formulation, 215
extreme returns, cluster occurrences,
78
factor returns, historical performance,
352e
impact, 417
leverage, effect. *See* Investment.
normal distributions, assumption, 78
scenarios, 191e
Revenue bonds, 364
Reverse cash-and-carry trade,
457–458
assumption, 492
theoretical futures price, 493
Reward function, 181–182
Reynier, J., 227
Right-skewed distributions, 54
Risk
attribution, 254–256
aversion, formulation, 215–216
basis, 48e
budget, representation, 406
characteristics, modification, 449
control, 494, 519
counterparty risk, 452–453
credit spread risk, 374
downgrade risk, 374
elimination, diversification (impact),
207–208
equilibrium market price, 220
estimation, 465–469
forecasts, 350–356
indifference, 223
inflation risk, 422–423
leverage, effect. *See* Investment.

longevity risk, 423
management, dynamic process, 450
measurement, 11
measures, 47–54
minimization, 519
neutrality, 223
parity, 228
portfolios, 229
premium, 220
profile, 216
risk-based allocation strategies, 204
risk-based performance attribution,
347e
risk-factor investing, 256–258
strategies, 256
risk-parity-based investment
strategies, 274
simulation, 350–356
Risk decomposition, 254–256,
334–343, 410–419
asset detail, 341e
industry detail, 340e
sector by market cap, 339e
style factors, 337e
Risk factor
constraints, 284–286
correlations, 258e
example, 241e
exposures, 342e
mismatches, 387, 389–390
model, 242
estimation, 245
selection, 250–251
monthly tracking errors, 416e
tracking errors, 415
volatility risk factors, 402
Risk-free rate, 481
Risk-neutral investors, 223
Risk-neutral probability, 475
products, 476
Risk-return profile (alteration), option
(usage), 463
@RISK, usage, 137
Risky assets, short-selling restrictions,
216
Risky portfolio construction, 219

RMBS. *See* Residential
mortgage-backed securities
RMetrics financial modeling tools suite,
214
Rmosek[35], 171
RMSE. *See* Root-mean-squared-error
Robust optimization, 154, 193–198
formulations, usage, 198
Robust parameter estimation, 312–314
Robust portfolio optimization,
317–323
Roll, R., 96, 240
Romeijn, H.E., 181, 189
Roncalli, T., 228, 271, 274
Root-mean-squared-error (RMSE)
measures, 136
Ross, P., 442
Ross, S.A., 240, 327, 471
ROTC. *See* Return on total capital
ROTE. *See* Return on total equity
Rothschild, M., 108
Round lot
constraints, 288–290
definition, 161
Round-trip transaction costs, 493
R package copula, 65
RRGs. *See* Relative Rotation Graphs
R Square, 112
R-Squared, 242
R-squared (hybrid model), 334, 499
Rubinstein, M., 471
Rules-based trading, 14
Rush, R., 189
Russell 1000 Low Beta Factor Index,
274
Russell 2000 Index Options (RUT), 505
Rustem, B., 188
Ruszczynski, A., 183, 189
R value, computation, 72

S
Sampling, 66–76
distribution, 73
stratified sampling, 332
Sanford, C.S., 450

SAS Predictive Analysis, 14
Saunders, D., 436, 443
Saxena, A., 242, 291
Scalar multiplication, 544
Scalar number, 543
Scalar product, 547
Scale parameter, 80
Scatterplot, 109
Scatterplot (joint) distributions,
example, 63e
Scenarios, 183
generation, 189
number, 147–149
reduction, 469
tree
creation, methods, 188
example, simplification, 185e
Scherer, B., 315
Scholes, M., 471
Scores, 120
Scree plot, 120, 124e
SDP. *See* Semidefinite programming
SDP3, 198
Second-order approximation, 379
Second-order cone programming
(SOCP), 157, 160–161, 193
Sector analysis, 414
Securities
basket, 494
individual security selection
strategies, 394–396
short position, 163
Securities portfolio
summary report, 411e
swap spread risk, 418e
Treasury curve risk, 417e
Securitization, 362
Securitized spread risk, 415
SeDuMi, 198
Seed, impact, 147, 149
Selection bias, 18
Sell hedge, 495
Semidefinite programming (SDP), 152,
158
Semi-deviation, 292
Senior notes, 364

Sensitivities, measurement, 484–485
Separate Trading of Registered Interest and Principal of Securities (STRIPS), 363
Separation, 219
Sequential quadratic programming methods, 167
Settergren, R., 188
Settlement date, 521
Settlement price, 451–452
Shakernia, O., 228
Shapiro, A., 183, 189
Sharali, H., 228
Sharpe-like (reward/risk) ratios, impact, 20
Sharpe-Lintner-Mossin model, 235
Sharpe ratio, 20, 275
    maximum Sharpe ratio weighting, 275
    usage, 218–219
Sharpe, William F., 50, 216, 218, 233, 273, 471
Shepherd, S., 390
Shetty, C., 228
Shift (factors), 399–400
Short (futures contract), 516
Short call position, expiration (profit/loss profile), 462e
Short futures position, payoff, 453
Short hedge, 495
Short position, 163
    expiration, profit/loss profile, 463e
Short put position, expiration (profit/loss profile), 464e
Short selling, 162
Short-selling restrictions, 493–494
Short-term factor models, 251
Short-term forecasts, 350, 353
Short-term returns, behavior (differences), 78
Shtekhman, A., 424
Sim, M., 193, 198, 322
Simple one-period case (European options), 472
Simplex algorithm, 166
Simulated annealing, 168

Simulated VaR, 53
    current/extreme market conditions, 355e
    example, 354e
Simulation
    modeling, 133
    usage, 140–147, 384–386
Single-index market model, 233
Single-index model, 233
    usage, 234–235
Single-name CDS, 533
    credit protection seller, 536
    economic interpretation, 535
    premium, 536
    reference obligation, 534
    valuation principles, 535–538
Single-period immunization, 424
Single-period settings, 180–181
Sinking fund bonds, 403
Skew, 54
Skewed distribution, 78
Skewness, 142
Sklar, A., 64
Small cap minus big cap (SMB), 244
Smart beta, 273
Smart order trading, 14
SNOPT, 168
SOCP. *See* Second-order cone programming
Soft constraints, 291
Solvency factors, 326–327
SPDR S&P500 ETF, returns (usage), 109
Spearman correlation, 69
Special purpose entity (SPE), 364
Specific risk, 232
Spectral decomposition, 548
Speculative elements, 373
SPInE (CHARISMA), 189
Spot price, 453
Spread, 47
    duration, 383
    nominal spread, 383
    products, 400
    risk, government-related spread risk, 415

static spread, 383
zero-volatility spread, 383
SPX. *See* Standard & Poor's 500 Index
Option
Stable Paretian distributions, 92,
94–96, 208
Standard Cauchy distribution,
probability density function
(comparison), 95e
Standard convexity, 381–382
Standard deviation, 47–49
change, 206e
equation, 483
sample, 69
Standard error, 112
Standard forms, probability density
functions (example), 100e
Standard normal distributions, 93e
probability density function,
comparison, 95e
Standard & Poor's 100 Index Option
(OEX), 504
Standard & Poor's 500 (S&P500), 269
excess return, 110
Index, 271, 465, 487
investment, capital
(histogram/summary statistics),
144e
replication, portfolio ability, 502
stocks, equally weighted portfolio
returns (mean/standard
deviation), 207e
value, scenarios, 501
weekly return distribution, 466e
Standard & Poor's 500 Index Option
(SPX), 504, 505
Standard & Poor's Corporation, 269,
373
Static spread, 383
Statistical estimation models,
106, 245
Statistical factor models, 248–250,
334
Statistical (extracted) factors, 240
Statistical hypothesis testing, 317
Statistically significant values, 74
Statistical shrinkage, 320

Statistics
concepts, 31
course, usage, 23
measurement, 66–76
STDEV formulas, 261
Stefek, D., 291, 321
Step function, 42
Stochastic control, 181–182
Stochastic parameters, 180
Stochastic programming, 154,
183–193
Stock index futures, 490–504
contracts
cash settlement contracts, 491
theoretical price, 491–494
features, 490–491
Stocks
broad-based stock market index,
usage, 500
index futures
contracts, 497
usage, 494–504
Microsoft stock, portfolio (simulated
profit/loss distribution), 468e
number, limits, 275
options, 504
portfolio, risk control, 494
preferred stock, 361–362
price at expiration, probability
distribution, 467e
price movements, hedging (usage),
495–500
prices (generation), random process
(usage), 481
purchase, portfolio value
(comparison), 502e
replacement strategy, 503
return processes, example, 121e
screens, 328–331
stratification, 332–333
value, movement, 34e
Stockton, K., 424
STOXX, 273
Strategic strategies, 391
Strategy testing, 17–18
portfolio performance, 17–20
Stratification, 332–333

Stratification, (*Continued*)
  approach, 403–405
    application, 409
    example, 333e, 404e
Stratified sampling, 332
Stress testing, 343–346
  returns, display, 345e
Strike price, 459
  increase, 507
Stripped mortgage-backed securities,
  365
STRIPS. *See* Separate Trading of
  Registered Interest and Principal of
  Securities
Structured products, 364–365
  sector, 362
Structure trades, 394
Stubbs, R., 242, 291, 322
Student's *t* distribution, 71, 79,
  82–83
Style factors
  exposure analysis, 338e
  factor attribution, 349e
Subordinate notes, 364
Substitution swap, 395
  assessment, importance, 395
Success, probability, 37e, 38e
SUMPRODUCT function, 175
SunGard APT, 334
Sun, P., 193
Superclasses, 78, 91
Supermetrics Data Grabber, 14
Surplus, 421–422
  equation, 421
Survival bias, 253
Swaps, 485–485
  equity swaps, 486–487
  options, 518
  rates, 527–528
  spread risk, 415
  value, 531
  yield curve, interest rate swap rates
    (relationship), 400
Symmetric matrix, 547
Synthetically created index fund,
  performance, 503

Systematic monthly tracking error, 413e
Systematic risk, 232, 412

T
Tabu search, 168
Tactical strategies, 391
Tail risk measures, usage, 291–297
Tails
  fatness, measurement, 55
  modeling, 98–104
Tangency portfolio, 217–218
Target duration, 518
Tax-backed debt, 364
Taxes
  absence, 481–482
  usage, 308–312
Taylor series, 225
t distribution, 72
  PDFs, examples, 83e
  spreading, decrease, 148
Technical factors, 327
Teiletche, J., 228, 271, 274
Tennessee Valley Authority, 363
Term structure factors, 399–400
Term to maturity, 365–366
Theoretical futures price
  derivation, 458, 492
  equation, 491, 501
Theta, 484
Thomson Reuters, 20
Tilde, usage, 134
Time decay, measure, 484
Time horizon, 424
Time periods, impact, 478
Time premium, 470
Time series analysis, usage, 350
Time series data, 11
Time-series data, 245
Timing option, 518
Tobin, J., 216
Tolerance, 166
Top-down investment strategy, 251
Top-down value-added strategies, 391
Top down yield curve strategies, 392

Total plan return, 443
Tracking error, 19, 260, 408
   actual tracking error, 264
   alpha, contrast, 261–264
   annualized tracking error, 262–263
   calculation, 261–264
      example, 262e
      factor model basis, 275
      multifactor risk model, basis,
         266–268
      variance-covariance method, 266
   constraints, 290
   contribution, 415
   data, example, 262e
   ex ante tracking error, 264
   ex post tracking error, 264
   forward-looking tracking error,
      backward-looking tracking error
      (contrast), 264–265
   impact, 418
   information ratio, relationship, 265
   interpretation, 261–264
   isolation, 414e
   marginal contribution, 418
   minimization, 406
   monthly tracking error, 416e
   predicted calculation, 265–268
   predicted tracking error, 264–266
   total contribution, 413
   usage, 260
Trade duration, 88
Trade universe, 10
Trading models, 11
Trading turnover (TT), 327
Traditional asset classes, 3
Traditional asset management,
   quantitative asset management
   (contrast), 9–10
Transaction costs, 493
   absence, 481–482
   reduction, 450, 502–503
   usage, 297–304
Transaction size constraints, 287–288
Treasury bills
   usage, 501
   yield, 502e

Treasury bonds
   futures contracts, 516
      delivery months, 523
   investment, capital
      (histogram/summary statistics),
      144e
Treasury curve risk, 417e
Treasury futures
   contract, volatility (knowledge), 520
   options, pricing models, 526–527
   pricing, 520–521
   puts, purchase, 524
   trading, 522
   usage, 515–521
Treasury securities, 362–363
   options, 522
   trades, 522
Trials, 133
Tsitsiklis, J., 167
t-statistic, 74
TT. *See* Trading turnover
Tukey, J.W., 96
Turnover
   constraints, 284
   control, 275
Tuttle, D.L., 4
Tutuncu, R., 228
t value, computation, 72
Tversky, A., 226
Twist (factor), 399–400
Two-period binomial tree, usage, 476e,
   478e
Two-sample hypothesis tests, 74

U
Um, S., 256
Uncertainty sets, 194
   shape, 198
Uncertain variable, realizations, 184
Unconstrained optimization, 152–153
Underlying, 459
Unimodal distributions, 46
Upgrade, 374
Uppal, R., 275
Upward-sloping yield curve, 368e

Ural, Cenk, 405
Uryasev, S., 181, 189
Utilities, 363
Utility functions, 220
  approximation, 225
  examples, 222e
Utility theory, 203

V

Valuation factors, 326
Value-added fixed income strategies, 391–396
Value-added strategies, 391
Value-at-Risk (VaR), 19, 50–53
  calculation, 127
  conditional value-at-risk, 53–54
  estimation, 385
  measure, 385
  metrics, usage, 353
  95% VaR, computation, 52e
  normal VaR, 52
  optimization, 292–294
  simulated VaR, 53
Value factors, 326
Value Line Composite Index, 269
Values, sampling, 139
Value strategies, 264
Value weighting, 16
Vance, P., 322
Vandenberghe, L., 229
Vanderbei, R., 183
Variable annuity account, 5
Variables, contrast, 156e
Variance, 47–49
  infinite variance, 78
  sample, 69
Variance-covariance method, 266
Variance inflation factor (VIF), 113–114
Variation margin, 455
  absence, 492
Vasicek, O.A., 429

Vector autoregressive models, construction, 188
Vectors, 542–543
  norm/magnitude, 543
  orthogonal vectors/orthonormal vectors, 547
Vega, 484–485
VIF. *See* Variance inflation factor
Volatility
  clustering, 78, 125
  fluctuations, incorporation, 78
  historical volatility estimates, 484
  risk, 415
    factors, 402
  smile, 482–483
    example, 483e

W

Wang, S., 188
Weatherstone, Dennis, 51
Weighted average life, 370
Weighted moving average, 126
Weights, total magnitude (restriction), 118
Weight sum, squares, 118
Weissensteiner, A., 181, 443
Whaley, R.E., 527
White noise (random noise), 107
Wildcard option, 518
Willemain, T., 189
Wilshire 5000, 269

X

Xignate, 20
Xignite, 21
Xisong, J., 275

Y

Yan, Jun, 65
Yield, 365, 367–368
  inverted yield curve, 368

spread
  CTD issue, relationship, 526
  widening, 394
  upward-sloping yield curve, 368e
Yield curve, 368
  management, 515–516
  observation, 385
  parallel shift, 375
  risk, 415
    usage, 399
  scenario analysis, 383
  strategies, 391, 392–393
  top down yield curve strategies, 392
  trading strategies, 391
Yield to call, 369–370
Yield to first call, 370
Yield to first par call, 370
Yield to maturity (YTM), 368
Yield to worst, 370
Yu, L., 188

Z
Zenios, S., 181, 183, 436, 443
Zero-coupon bonds, 367
  guaranteed liabilities, matching,
    437
  issuance, absence, 362–363
  value, denotation, 531
Zero-coupon instruments, demand,
    362–363
Zero-coupon notes, issuance (absence),
    362–363
Zero-volatility OAS, 384
Zero-volatility spread (z-spread),
    383
Zhelenyak, A., 321
Zhu, H., 239
Ziemba, W.T., 181, 443
z-scores, 41
z-scores
  defining, 119